Reading Heidegger's *Black Notebooks 1931–1941*

Reading Heidegger's *Black Notebooks 1931–1941*

edited by Ingo Farin and Jeff Malpas

The MIT Press
Cambridge, Massachusetts
London, England

This book was set in Syntax and Times New Roman by the MIT Press. Printed and bound in the United States of America.

Library of Congress Cataloging-in-Publication Data is available.

ISBN: 978-0-262-03401-2

10 9 8 7 6 5 4 3 2 1

Contents

Acknowledgments

Brought together relatively quickly in direct response to the controversy that emerged with the publication of the first volumes of Heidegger's so-called *Black Notebooks* (*Schwarze Hefte*) in 2014, this has been a demanding volume to organize and produce. We are extremely grateful to all of our authors not only for agreeing to participate, but also for accommodating themselves so well to the tight schedule the project required. At the MIT Press, we would like to thank Philip Laughlin for seeing the worth of the volume and giving such strong support to its publication, and Judith Feldmann and Elizabeth Judd for their work in preparing the typescript for publication (thanks all the more deserved given the complexity of the material and the range of authors). We also would like to thank Adrian Staples for proofreading the volume and putting together the index. In addition, Ingo Farin would like to thank the Deutsche Literaturarchiv at Marbach for permission to see and read Heidegger's *Schwarze Hefte* in the original. Finally, we are also grateful to the *Los Angeles Review of Books* and the *Journal for Cultural and Religious Theory* for allowing Gregory Fried and Michael Fagenblat to make use of previously published material from those journals in their contributions here.

Introduction

Ingo Farin and Jeff Malpas

The first series of Heidegger's so-called *Black Notebooks*, spanning the years from 1931 to 1941, were released in three volumes (94, 95, and 96) of the *Gesamtausgabe* in the spring of 2014.[1] These three book volumes contain the transcripts of fourteen individual volumes of notebooks, numbered II–XV by Heidegger himself. The first volume of the notebooks is missing and may have been destroyed by him. Heidegger gave titles to the individual notebooks, using the simple title *Überlegungen* or *Considerations* for the notebooks from the third to the fifteenth, the more cumbersome title *Winke X und Überlegungen II und Anweisungen*, or *Hints X and Considerations II and Instructions*, for the second notebook, and *Überlegungen und Winke III, or Considerations and Hints III*, for the third notebook.

Heidegger continued the practice of writing notebooks after 1941, and so there are many more extant notebooks than just those that make up the *Überlegungen*. It is believed that he wrote thirty-four or thirty-six notebooks in all, of which the last were composed in the early 1970s. All of the additional notebooks are currently held (as are the original notebooks that make up the *Überlegungen*) in the Heidegger Archives at the Deutsche Literaturarchiv in Marbach, Germany, and all are scheduled for publication in forthcoming volumes of the *Gesamtausgabe* in the near future. The first of these, containing the notebooks *Anmerkungen I–V (Schwarze Hefte 1942–1948)*, has already appeared, in March 2015, as volume 97 in the *Gesamtausgabe*.[2] This volume also contains an individual notebook that was found only after the publication of the first three volumes in 2014.

It has become customary to refer to these notebooks in general as the *Black Notebooks* after the black oilcloth booklets into which Heidegger originally transcribed his thoughts. But while this generic title has some practical advantages, it must not be forgotten that Heidegger put great care into distinguishing them from one another—something reflected in his practice of titling each notebook individually. Moreover, because the *Black Notebooks* encompass some thirty-four notebooks written over a period of forty years, it is prudent to refer to individual notebooks or sets of notebooks whenever possible. For this reason, we refer to the first of the now published sets of notebooks, those that span the years 1931 to 1941 (the years that appear in the title of this volume), by using the title Heidegger chose for them—*Überlegungen* or *Considerations*—while we use the common name *Black*

Notebooks only when talking about the entire collection of extant notebooks. Although not all of our authors consistently follow this practice, the fact that, for the most part, the only published volumes available at the time they were writing, and the volumes that have provoked the initial controversy surrounding the *Black Notebooks*, were the *Überlegungen* means that most references to the *Notebooks* in the contributions here can be taken as being to the *Überlegungen* unless otherwise noted.

The publication of the *Überlegungen*, and the material the volumes contain, has provoked an enormous controversy that extends well beyond the confines of academic philosophy. That Heidegger was an enthusiastic supporter of the Nazi Party during the early 1930s is well known. However, the *Notebooks* not only provide further evidence of the extent of that enthusiasm, as well as demonstrating Heidegger's increasing estrangement from National Socialism (however one interprets this) after 1934, but they contain a number of anti-Semitic passages. Moreover, those passages come almost entirely from the later volumes of the *Überlegungen,* at a time when Heidegger had become deeply critical of Nazism, a point that itself raises questions about the relation between Heidegger's Nazism and his anti-Semitism.

Since Heidegger is undoubtedly one of the most influential thinkers of the twentieth century, and a thinker who continues to be a major influence on contemporary thought, the material the *Notebooks* contain has led to much controversy over their relevance to our understanding and assessment of Heidegger's philosophy. The editor of the *Notebooks*, Peter Trawny, has argued that the *Notebooks* show anti-Semitism as contaminating Heidegger's philosophical thought.[3] Friedrich-Wilhelm von Herrmann's attempt to disarm Trawny's criticism has drawn the ire of Jean-Luc Nancy, who reaffirms the charge that there is a "systematic" connection between Heidegger's philosophy and his anti-Semitism.[4] Richard Wolin writes that "what has now become indubitably clear is that racial prejudice against non-Germanic peoples—the English, the Russians, the French, the Americans, and, especially, the Jews—lies at the very center of Heidegger's philosophical project," and Wolin goes on to claim that, on the basis of what is given in the *Notebooks*, "any discussion of Heidegger's legacy that downplays or diminishes the extent of his political folly stands guilty, by extension, of perpetuating the philosophical betrayal initiated by the Master himself."[5] Although there have been controversies over Heidegger's political beliefs and commitments in the past, the publication of the *Notebooks* has thus taken matters to a new level. Some have claimed that they put Heidegger beyond the pale so far as contemporary philosophy is concerned, and that there can no longer be any possibility of treating Heidegger as a serious and worthwhile thinker. Somewhat less dramatically, but perhaps no less radically, Thomas Sheehan has said that the controversy over the *Notebooks* should be seen as an opportunity to "rethink, from scratch, what [Heidegger's] work was about."[6] François Fédier, in contrast, has defended the *Black Notebooks*, arguing that understood properly they will not distract but will contribute to the significance of Heidegger's overall work.[7]

The discussion that has swirled around the *Notebooks* so far has been further complicated by several other developments. The resignation of Günter Figal from the presidency
of the *Heidegger-Gesellschaft* on the grounds, as he put it, that after the new revelations in
the *Black Notebooks*, especially the anti-Semitic passages, he could no longer function as a
"representative" of Heidegger's thought, added to the level of controversy.[8] Shortly afterward, the University of Freiburg announced that the chair occupied by Figal—the chair
that Heidegger and Husserl had occupied previously—would not be filled with Figal's
retirement, but instead a junior position would be established in the area of logic and analytic philosophy of language.[9] Although the University of Freiburg insisted that the decision was made for internal university reasons, and was entirely unrelated to any issues
arising out of the *Black Notebooks*, the timing was unfortunate to say the least, and the
development simply added to the sense of escalating controversy, with over 3,000 academics around the world signing a letter of protest at the announcement. The turmoil around
Heidegger's name was further increased when, in March 2015, the publishing house of
Heidegger's *Gesamtausgabe*, Klostermann, took the extraordinary step of writing a letter
to the editors of the volumes dealing with Heidegger's writings during the 1930s and 1940s
asking them to check whether any incriminating passages in the volumes they had edited
had been deleted or changed, or alternative variants omitted. The letter was triggered by
the discovery that on at least one occasion an egregious reading error (the misreading of an
abbreviation in Heidegger's manuscript to mean "natural science" when it referred instead
to "National Socialism") had been reproduced in the published volume.[10] Whatever one
may think of Klostermann's unparalleled reaction to the discovery of the error, Heidegger
researchers are now also faced with the problem of potentially corrupt texts in the *Gesamtausgabe*. It is thus understandable that more and more researchers are demanding that the
Heidegger Archives be opened to unrestricted scholarly scrutiny.

The controversy aroused by the publication of the *Überlegungen* and the subsequent
developments has been so heated, and has provoked such a level of interest both inside and
outside philosophy, that it seemed important to try to bring together some of the scholarly
discussion surrounding the *Notebooks* into a single volume that would also try to address
the issues at stake in a comprehensive fashion, and in a way that also focused, as far as possible, on the issues themselves rather than on any personal animosities. It may be argued
that it is too early to attempt a genuine appraisal of the meaning and significance of the
Notebooks' contents—that more time is needed to gain proper critical distance. Yet there
is also an advantage in reacting in a timely manner, and in providing a forum in which the
current controversy can be played out as well as documented. Our aim in this book has
been to draw together a range of responses to the *Überlegungen* and to the *Notebooks* more
generally—to include responses from authors who have not so far voiced their opinions
as well as from those who have already made contributions. No single viewpoint prevails;
there is considerable divergence in the way different authors assess the material in the
Black Notebooks. Even similar passages are read in different ways by different authors

(and sometimes *translated* differently, as is evident in the discussions below), and it can be argued that this divergence underscores the enormous difficulty in interpreting Heidegger, as well as the vanity of supposing that the matter can be definitively resolved.[11]

The book contains nineteen contributions, arranged in four parts. Part I, "The Reading of Heidegger's *Black Notebooks*," is the most general, addressing some of the broad interpretive issues raised by the *Notebooks*, their role in connection with the understanding and evaluation of Heidegger's thinking as a whole (including certain key themes, of which the most notable is the critique of technological modernity), and issues related to their literary style. Part II, "The *Black Notebooks* and Other Works," looks at the relationship between the *Notebooks* and other works by Heidegger—most notably *Being and Time,* but also the *Contributions* and other contemporaneous works. Part III, "Metaphysics, Anti-Semitism, and Christianity," deals specifically with the issue that has provoked the most controversy, namely, the anti-Semitic content of the *Notebooks*, as well as Heidegger's relationship to Judaism, but also encompassing, in Holger Zaborowski's contribution (chapter 13), Heidegger's antagonistic relation to Christianity—something the *Notebooks* clearly bring out. Finally, part IV, "Philosophy, Politics, and Technology," returns to a somewhat broader perspective, but with a particular eye to the political and historical dimensions of the *Notebooks*. Here Heidegger's involvement with Nazism is a central focus, as is the historical background in the 1930s and early 1940s against which the *Notebooks* (or at least the *Überlegungen*) were written. Heidegger's critical approach to technology, science, and modernity—already touched on in part I—reappears as an important topic of discussion, and inevitably so, since it is so closely connected with the political as well as historical background. The divisions between the parts and chapters at work here are not, however, clear-cut, and the issues at stake clearly overlap and intersect to such an extent that many topics recur in chapters across all four parts.

All the contributions were commissioned especially for this book, although two, those by Gregory Fried (chapter 4) and Michael Fagenblat (chapter 10), draw on material originally published in review form elsewhere. The contributions by Peter Trawny (chapter 11) and Friedrich-Wilhelm von Herrmann (chapter 6) were translated from German into English by Ingo Farin. The contributors range across a broad swath of contemporary Heidegger scholarship, including some who have not normally made Heidegger a key figure in their research. Some authors who have contributed to the debate elsewhere are not represented here, perhaps most notably Richard Wolin,[12] but also Richard Polt,[13] and this is partly a function of availability, but also reflects a deliberate editorial intention to broaden the range of participating voices. One especially notable omission is Thomas Sheehan, who was included in the original list of authors, but who was, in the end, unable to participate. Sheehan has contributed to the debate elsewhere,[14] arguing against the claim, advanced particularly by Emmanuel Faye (and to some extent Richard Wolin), that Heidegger's Nazi and anti-Semitic views, as reflected in the *Überlegungen,* also affect his early work, not only the work of the 1930s or later. Sheehan thus argues that the Nazism and anti-Semitism of the *Überlegungen* are not present in any philosophically significant way in the work from the 1920s, and in particular, are not present in *Being and Time*. Sheehan's argument against Faye on this point is developed in a paper that Sheehan intends to make public soon.

Although it omits some well-known voices, this book does contain contributions from the two key figures who might be considered to represent opposing sides of the debate, Peter Trawny and Friedrich-Wilhelm von Herrmann, each of whom adopts a very different approach to the issues at stake. Within the spectrum that these two figures may be thought to mark out, a wide range of views are included here. As editors, it is neither our role nor our intention to try to adjudicate between those views (hence the relative brevity of this introduction), although as contributors ourselves, we have to a greater or lesser extent taken a stand on many of the relevant issues.[15] We hope that our readers think through these issues themselves on the basis of the evidence and views we have been able to bring together in this volume. Undoubtedly, new evidence and other views will emerge with the passage of time, but we hope this book provides a useful and important foundation for further research and debate.

Notes

1. Martin Heidegger, *Überlegungen II–VI (Schwarze Hefte 1931–1938)*, Gesamtausgabe 94, ed. Peter Trawny (Frankfurt: Klostermann, 2014); *Überlegungen VII–XI (Schwarze Hefte 1938/39)*, Gesamtausgabe 95, ed. Peter Trawny (Frankfurt: Klostermann, 2014); *Überlegungen XII–XV (Schwarze Hefte 1939–1941)*, Gesamtausgabe 96, ed. Peter Trawny (Frankfurt: Klostermann, Frankfurt, 2014).

2. *Anmerkungen I–V (Schwarze Hefte 1942–1948)*, Gesamtausgabe 97, ed. Peter Trawny (Frankfurt: Klostermann, 2015).

3. See Peter Trawny, *Heidegger und der Mythos der jüdischen Weltverschwörung* (Frankfurt: Klostermann, 2014).

4. See Jean-Luc Nancy, "Tatsachen aus Heften," http://faustkultur.de/2148-0-Nancy-Tatsachen-aus-Heften.html#.VSd1yNymg1.

5. Richard Wolin, "National Socialism, World Jewry, and the History of Being: Heidegger's *Black Notebooks*," *Jewish Review of Books*, Summer 2014, http://jewishreviewofbooks.com/articles/993/national-socialism-world -jewry-and-the-history-of-being-heideggers-black-notebooks/.

6. Quoted in Jennifer Schuessler, "Heidegger's Notebooks Renew Focus on Anti-Semitism," *New York Times*, March 30, 2014, http://www.nytimes.com/2014/03/31/books/heideggers-notebooks-renew-focus-on-anti-semi tism.html.

7. In a 2014 interview with the German newspaper *Die Zeit*, www.zeit.de/2014/03/francois-fedier-ueber-martin -heidegger.

8. See Günter Figal's interview with Eggert Blum, available at http://www.swr.de/swr2/kultur-info/philosoph -guenter-figal-tritt-als-vorsitzender-der-martin-heidegger-gesellschaft-zurueck/-/id=9597116/did=14891960/ nid=9597116/t9lvuo/index.html.

9. See http://www.zeit.de/2015/14/uni-freiburg-philosophie-lehrstuhl-professur.

10. See http://www.zeit.de/2015/13/antisemitismus-martin-heidegger-philosoph-schwarze-hefte.

11. Just as we have not attempted to resolve the differences between contributors in relation to the *Black Note-books*, so we have also allowed other differences in approach to remain. So, for instance, some authors write of "Being" whereas others refer to "being," and we have allowed both usages to remain. In this respect, our aim has been to avoid the imposition of too uniform a style that might obscure differences in approach or interpretation.

12. See Wolin, "National Socialism, World Jewry, and the History of Being: Heidegger's *Black Notebooks*."

13. Richard Polt's "Inception, Downfall, and the Broken World: Heidegger above the Sea of Fog" is referred to by several of the contributors below. It was presented at a conference at Emory University (September 5–6, 2014) on "Heidegger's *Black Notebooks*: Philosophy, Politics, Anti-Semitism"; the spoken presentation can be heard on YouTube, https://www.youtube.com/watch?v=_ZpWnYGqBPw&index=3&list=PLgEhVQ4kQGSpaE84Ha2Zec5t7b8c_8CKP.

14. Sheehan was a participant in the two-day conference on the *Black Notebooks* (held on September 11–12, 2014) organized by Richard Wolin at CUNY, a small part of which is available on YouTube, https://www.youtube.com/watch?v=hMizd8GplEA.

15. It is partly because of a desire to give the book an impartial framing that we have restricted our analyses of the debate to our individual chapters. However, in those chapters that begin and end the volume, we have tried to bring a set of fairly comprehensive, though not entirely neutral, perspectives to the issues at hand. Thus we introduce readers to the issues surrounding the *Black Notebooks* and offer some critical commentary on the way those issues might be viewed.

I THE READING OF HEIDEGGER'S *BLACK NOTEBOOKS*

1

On the Philosophical Reading of Heidegger: Situating the *Black Notebooks*

Jeff Malpas

> What provokes one to look at all philosophers half suspiciously, half mockingly, is not that one discovers again and again how innocent they are—how often and how easily they make mistakes and go astray; in short, their childishness and childlikeness—but that they are not honest enough in their work ...
> —Nietzsche[1]

1 Introduction: The *Black Notebooks* and the "Heidegger Affair"

The publication of Heidegger's *Überlegungen* or *Considerations* from the years 1931–1941 (part of the so-called *Schwarze Hefte* or *Black Notebooks*),[2] along with the appearance of Peter Trawny's own critical monograph,[3] is only the latest act in the ongoing "Heidegger affair" that began almost immediately after the war, in 1946–1947, with discussions in the French journal *Les temps modernes*.[4] It was taken up again in the 1960s in several books and articles, including those by Paul Hühnerfeld and Guido Schneeberger,[5] but gained real intensity in the late 1980s with critical works by Victor Farias,[6] Hugo Ott[7], and more recently, in the 2000s, Emmanuel Faye.[8]

From a European perspective, the affair is inextricably bound to the larger issue concerning the thinking through, and the coming to terms with, the horrendous events of the 1930s and 1940s—the emergence of the German dictatorship of Hitler, the unfolding of the Second World War, and the Holocaust—events in which European thought and culture (which need not be taken to be restricted to Europe alone) were themselves implicated and from which they cannot be entirely disentangled. In its current instantiation, in the midst of resurgent right-wing politics across Europe and rising anti-Semitism, the affair also plays into a volatile contemporary situation in which memories of those earlier events are still very much alive. From an English-speaking perspective, the affair has other elements too, since many of the reactions to it draw on and feed back into a long-standing suspicion of European thought that takes the horrors of Europe's modern past to be rooted in the claimed failings of such thought, and in what are seen to be the illiberal prejudices and dispositions, as well as the supposed philosophical incompetence, of thinkers such as Heidegger, but also Hegel and Nietzsche.[9]

In this latter respect, the Heidegger affair has provided a stage for the playing out of the antagonism of English-speaking philosophy toward so-called continental thought, and has often been seen as providing a demonstration of the assumed moral and political superiority of the sort of thinking that "analytic" thought supposedly exemplifies—thinking typically presented as sober and clear in contrast to the intoxication and obscurity of the continental (such "analytic" thinking remains closely associated with an English-speaking milieu in spite of the European origins on which it also draws or, indeed, its contemporary European instantiations). If from a European perspective the Heidegger affair is sometimes taken to show a failure *of philosophy*, then from across the Channel and over the Atlantic (and down in the Southern Hemisphere, too), it is often seen to demonstrate a more specific failure of *European* or *continental* philosophy as such.

Although the latter reading has been less explicit in many reactions to the *Considerations* than previously (but is certainly not absent), there remains a tendency for the *Considerations* to be read so as to confirm a set of preexisting suspicions concerning the failings of the German philosopher, the inadequacy of his philosophy, and the flawed character of the style or tradition of thinking he is taken to represent. The reading of the *Considerations* so far has thus frequently been *polemical* rather than strictly *philosophical*—it has also often been strongly *personal* in its orientation: it is the figure of Heidegger himself, and not merely his philosophy, that is in question, and his personal actions and character are taken as directly indicating the character of his philosophical thinking. The *Considerations* have thus been taken by many to provide the "smoking gun" that definitively demonstrates the fact of Heidegger's Nazism and anti-Semitism, and on this basis, also establishes once and for all the unacceptability of Heidegger's work within the canon of respectable thinking.

In addition to any political issues they raise, and interpretively prior to them, the reading of the *Considerations* brings into view some important questions concerning the nature of philosophical engagement—and especially concerning the role of the personal in philosophical thought and engagement. Here the personal encompasses the person of the *philosophical author,* so that the question arises as to the relation between the author and the philosophy, but also (if less frequently addressed) the person of the *philosophical reader*, so that the question arises as to the relation between the reader and the philosophy read. In each case, part of what is at issue is the way the personal life, dispositions, affections, and prejudices—whether political or otherwise—of the person are relevant, or should be relevant, to an understanding of and engagement with the philosophical work. Some of these questions are quite general in nature—they can be said to relate to philosophical authorship and readership as such—but some also take on a more specific character that pertains to the fraught historical context in which Heidegger's work and the reading of it are embedded.

Both these sets of questions are essentially *hermeneutical* in character, but their hermeneutical character, even the questions themselves, are seldom directly taken up in the discussion of the issues at stake. Indeed, the discussion of those issues is frequently conducted in a way strangely divorced from any attention to hermeneutic questions—in a way that can even appear hermeneutically naive. One might argue that this is not surprising—after all, is not the very term *hermeneutics*, in its contemporary philosophical usage, inextricably associated with Heidegger's name, and so might not a suspicion of hermeneutics itself be in play here? That may be so in some cases, but not in general, and what actually seems to be at work is more to do with a narrowing of focus onto the question of moral judgment—Heidegger's own failures in judgment and the judgment of Heidegger himself. In some cases, indeed, the very attempt to turn the matter back to broader interpretive considerations is seen as evidence of a failure to appreciate the moral questions at issue. The oddity of such a reaction, of course, is that the moral does not itself stand apart from the interpretive nor from the hermeneutical, and to suppose that moral judgment can be exercised independently of such considerations may itself be viewed as a particular form of moral blindness.

Part of my aim here is briefly to take up some of these hermeneutical questions, and so to explore some of the interpretive assumptions and approaches that seem to shape so much of the reading of the *Considerations*. In addition, I want to consider how that reading connects with broader ways of reading Heidegger's thought, and the issues that it draws to our attention. This means, however, that my focus is not on trying to untangle the details of the *Considerations*, or on engaging in a forensic investigation as to Heidegger's culpability as a Nazi or an anti-Semite. My aim is not to attack Heidegger, but nor is it to defend him. Indeed, the widespread tendency to construe the debate in just these terms is part of what is philosophically problematic about it (one might well wonder as to the genuine philosophical productivity of much of that debate when it remains framed in such terms).[10] Instead my concern is to direct attention back to the question of the philosophical ideas at issue in Heidegger's work. I aim to do this, first, by looking to the complexities of reading itself, and especially the reading of a thinker such as Heidegger—it is this that occupies the largest part of my discussion below, and, second, to look more specifically at the *Considerations* as they stand in relation to the broader development of Heidegger's thinking, and especially as they might relate to what I have elsewhere termed the "topological" character of that thinking.

2   The Complexities of Reading

(i)   Questions of Interpretive Evidence

That Heidegger was a Nazi and that he also held anti-Semitic views are simple facts[11]— but they are just that, and as facts they are all *too* simple. The real question concerns the significance to be attached to these facts and how they should be interpreted. Indeed, despite a widespread tendency to assume the contrary, neither of the central terms in play here—neither Nazism nor anti-Semitism—is a term that carries a single, straightforward, and unequivocal meaning (even if much of the discussion in which these terms figure would suggest otherwise). Apart from anything else, exactly how such terms should be understood is historically dependent—one cannot make sense of what is at issue merely by assuming that what Nazism or anti-Semitism means now is identical with what it meant in 1931, 1933, or 1941, or that the connotations and significance that attach to the terms now, and that attached to them then, are the same.

Heidegger's anti-Semitism, however crude it may appear from the entries in the *Considerations*, seems fundamentally to have been based in a form of cultural anti-Semitism of a sort that was widespread in Germany and Europe before the Second World War and did not disappear afterward (not even from German academic circles).[12] That it was so widespread, and that it indeed continued after the war, even after the Holocaust, is partly a function of the fact that it was indeed based in ideas of *cultural* rather than *natural* difference—which is not to say that such cultural anti-Semitism might not have been assimilated to or transformed into more naturalized forms.[13] None of this makes such anti-Semitism any more acceptable (especially since it is often unclear whether anti-Semitism, in any particular case, is indeed focused on "culture" or "nature"—to say nothing of the uncertainties surrounding the distinction between the very concepts of nature and culture themselves), but it can make for potential differences in how one understands it as an idea and an attitude—can make for differences, in other words, in how it is understood *philosophically*.

In the case of Nazism, it is widely recognized that Heidegger's own adherence to "the movement" (which is itself an equivocal term in this context) was based on his idiosyncratic version of National Socialism. For a time, but only for a time, Heidegger appears to have seen the possibility of a convergence between a National Socialism derived from his own thinking and the National Socialism embodied in the person of Adolf Hitler.[14] Understanding how Heidegger might have considered such a convergence possible is crucial to understanding his involvement with the Nazis in 1930–1934, but it is also crucial to understanding his break from Nazism. That break cannot be set aside as merely an expression of pique or sour grapes on Heidegger's part (even if something of this was part of the personal context of that break)—certainly not if the original involvement is itself seen as philosophically grounded, and that it was philosophically grounded is surely what makes it of genuine interest and significance. Recognizing the equivocal character of "Nazism" in the Heideggerian context is thus crucial to understanding how Heidegger was implicated with Nazism, but it also renders suspect the straightforward identification of Heidegger and Nazism.

As soon as one recognizes the need to clarify what is at issue in talk of Heidegger's Nazism and anti-Semitism, the fact that Heidegger was indeed a Nazi and an anti-Semite starts to appear rather more complicated and much less straightforward. Moreover, that Heidegger was a Nazi and an anti-Semite are facts that pertain, in the first instance, to Heidegger's *biography*, but whether and to what extent they are to be taken as relevant to Heidegger's *philosophy* is not something that can simply be assumed. Even given the way in which a body of philosophical thinking can be seen to emerge out of personal life of the philosopher, still one cannot move from the life to the philosophy without a degree of interpretive effort—the life is no less in need of interpretation than is the philosophy, and the philosophy can shed light on the life just as the life can shed light on the philosophy. Interpretation does not move in one direction alone.

Moreover, in trying to establish the interconnection of life and thought, what must be done is to show how the life entails certain claims or commitments (expressed in actions and decisions as well as in what is written and said), and then to show that those claims and commitments are also present within the philosophy or vice versa, and how those claims and commitments entail other claims and commitments within that philosophy or within that life. The exploration of the interconnection between life and thought is thus an exploration of sets of entailments and implications—entailments and implications that need to be concretely identified—and cannot take the form merely of assuming that the general character of a life is reflected in the thought, or of the thought (or aspects of the thought) in the life.

Of course, the claims and commitments that may be taken to describe the content of a life or of a body of thought will almost always exhibit a degree of inconsistency. Neither a single life nor a single body of thought ever presents itself as a completely integrated whole—the fact that both develop over time implies as much—and both life and thought will also be characterized by indeterminacy and ambiguity. People are as prone to misunderstanding themselves—at least when they consciously try to make sense of their life and thought—as they are to misunderstanding others. Even the philosopher—even Heidegger himself—has no more authority in telling us how his or her thought is to be interpreted than do we as interpreters of that same body of thought. A thinker's own self-explanations and self-interpretations thus merely add to the body of what is to be interpreted, providing more evidence that interpretation must address, rather than providing a definitive determination of or direction for that interpretation.

The interpretive injunction that one cannot, in interpreting a body of thinking, prioritize the facts of the life over the content of that thinking—so that the reading derived from the life also needs to be supported by evidence that supports that reading in the thinking itself[15]—is essentially an injunction that requires that one look to the whole body of evidence in the attempt to understand a thinker, and not merely to any one part of that evidence. This is especially important in the case of the material from the *Considerations,* and from the *Notebooks* more generally. This material is not interpretively more authoritative simply because it includes Heidegger's personal reflections. In fact, it might well be argued that the private character of the reflections that the *Considerations* contain (even if later intended for publication) means that they ought to be read in light of the other published work, rather than the other way around. Even if one insisted that greater authority had to be attached to the *Considerations,* and that the direction of interpretation did not run from the other works to the *Considerations*, still the *Considerations* cannot be interpreted as if they stood alone, and their interpretation has to be undertaken in conjunction with the wider task of interpreting Heidegger's work as a whole—a matter on which I shall have more to say below.

Unfortunately, for much of the discussion as it has unfolded so far, not only is there a tendency for the *Considerations* to be read and interpreted apart from their location within the larger body of Heidegger's work, but most readings have tended to focus only on certain passages in the *Considerations*—especially the same anti-Semitic passages—that then become the key for more general interpretive claims. As a result, much of the debate so far concerning the *Considerations* has tended to remain fixated on a relatively small number of passages, often apart from their wider context even within the *Considerations* themselves.

Although hermeneutically problematic, this tendency toward what amounts to a form of selectively focused reading is partly a result of the nature of the *Considerations*, and of the *Notebooks*, as a disparate collection of reflections on a wide range of topics, and so as lacking the sort of overarching thematic or organizational unity that would normally be associated with a single work. Individual passages thus lack the sort of contextual embedding that one finds elsewhere. The selectivity evident here has also been encouraged by the way the material from the *Notebooks* has been made public. Almost all of the passages that have drawn most attention appeared in piecemeal form prior to the publication of the *Considerations* in their entirety (the material thus originally appeared in papers and presentations on the *Considerations* that drew on specific passages—and always, of course, passages that have, at least on first reading, a highly provocative content). In similar fashion, specific anti-Semitic passages from *Anmerkungen I–V*, *Gesamatausgabe* 97 (*Anmerkungen* can be taken in English as *Remarks* or *Observations*), also appeared prior to the actual publication of the volume as a whole. Such selectivity runs the obvious risk of already implying a particular interpretive stance, without supplying the argument for it, purely on the basis of the salience it gives to the passages selected.

(ii)   Questions of Philosophical Understanding

Although the discussion of Heidegger's Nazism and anti-Semitism is often presented as a relatively simple matter—as if it were just a matter of showing that he really was both—such a presentation is not only simple, but also a simplification. Indeed, that it is a simplification is part of what gives the issue such a sensationalist character and that enables the headline hyperbole that seems often to dominate its public discussion.

To some extent, the simplification that appears here can be seen as an expression of the often direct and immediate personal reaction that many readers of Heidegger have in the face of the seeming discrepancy between the seeming power and insight of so many of Heidegger's major philosophical works, and the bald facts of his Nazism and anti-Semitism. Michael Dummett reports his own shock at first encountering the virulent racism and anti-Semitism expressed in Gottlob Frege's diaries.[16] Many readers of Heidegger have undoubtedly experienced a similar shock, perhaps disappointment,[17] and even a sense of betrayal at what they have encountered in the *Considerations* or elsewhere, or on first learning, having perhaps already come to admire Heidegger as a philosopher, of some of the details of his biography (perhaps not only his Nazi entanglement, or his anti-Semitism, but his duplicity, his tendency toward self-aggrandizement, his exploitative relationships with women). That one might find some of Heidegger's writings and actions so personally offensive as to be impossible to overcome, and an insurmountable barrier to any philosophical engagement, is an understandable reaction that requires neither explanation nor justification. If we wish, however, to go beyond such a personal reaction, and indeed to engage philosophically, then we have no choice but to engage with the philosophical and interpretive complexities that Heidegger presents to us.

Engaging with the complexities of Heidegger's thought is all the more important given the very fact of Heidegger's Nazism and anti-Semitism. Whatever we may think of Heidegger before or after the emergence of the material in the *Considerations*, his work is an inextricable and central element in the European thought of the twentieth century. That it is so is partly because it stands in such an important relation to previous thinking—especially to the work of Kant and Nietzsche. Moreover, just as English-language philosophy cannot be entirely disentangled from European thought, so the influence and relevance of Heidegger's thinking also goes beyond the horizons of Europe alone, and may even be said to have filtered into aspects of analytic thinking. Engaging with Heidegger's philosophy requires that we try to think through his work and through the tradition of which it is a part—which means thinking Heidegger in relation to Kant and Husserl, to Arendt and Gadamer, to Foucault and Derrida—as well as the traditions that run alongside and even that stand opposed to it. It also means thinking and reading his work with a sense of the historical context to which it belongs.

In this latter respect, part of what the *Considerations* surely bring home is the extent to which every philosophy is indeed "of its time," subject to the blindnesses and prejudices of that time, just as every philosophy is also subject to the blindnesses and prejudices of the thinker herself. The real measure of the significance of a philosopher is determined by the extent to which their thinking is able to transcend the blindnesses and prejudices their work will inevitably contain, and to continue to speak to us in our own time in a way relevant to it. Clearly there are some thinkers whose work does not do this, and who we therefore cannot read—and certainly cannot read with any sense of having learned something.

Heidegger is surely not an example of a thinker who falls into the latter category. Instead his work has a significance and relevance that transcends its evident biases —in spite of assertions by some commentators to the contrary—and the very extent of his influence, and his embeddedness in twentieth- and twenty-first-century thought, would seem to confirm this. One of the ironies, moreover, is that the very embeddedness at issue here is an embeddedness that connects Heidegger's thought to the tradition of twentieth- and twenty-first century *Jewish* thinking—and not only to the work of thinkers such as Arendt, Jonas, Levinas, as well as Husserl, but also to figures like Rosenzweig and Bubner. The close proximity of Heidegger to Jewish thinking is not only important for our understanding of those Jewish thinkers, but, perhaps even more significantly, for how we understand

Heidegger's own thought. In spite of his anti-Semitism, then, it turns out that Heidegger cannot properly be read other than in a way that takes account of what might even be said to be the "pro-Semitic" character of key elements within that thinking (and one cannot be sure what Heidegger might have thought of this "inner connection" between his own and Judaic thought).[18] Again, the simple fact of Heidegger's Nazism and anti-Semitism turns out to be less illuminating than we might have supposed, and the real picture rather more complex than is so often assumed.

Engaging with the complexities that are indeed at issue in the reading of Heidegger, and refusing the tendency to simplification, not only requires reading the Heidegger of the 1930s and 1940s in relation to the rest of Heidegger's thought, and in a way that retains its integral connection with the larger tradition, but it also requires resisting the language of "contamination," "infection," and "taint" that is so common in discussions of Heidegger's relation to Nazism and anti-Semitism. The effectiveness of such language depends more on the sheer emotional charge it carries than on any argumentation it advances.

"Contamination," "infection," and "taint" can arise, after all, out of mere proximity, and when present, leave little or no room for compromise—that which is contaminated, if it cannot be "purified," tends to be reviled and rejected. Not only does the language of contamination, infection, and taint provide a way of advancing the case against Heidegger himself without the need to engage in the complexities of what is at issue (and by covering over the fact of their simplification), but it also serves to promote the case against any genuine engagement with Heidegger's thought—such engagement risks the same contamination, the same infection, the same taint. It is strange to find such language—a language so characteristically employed by Nazis and anti-Semites themselves—at work in a context in which the dangers of irrationality are at the same time so frequently warned against.

The way the language of contamination, infection, and taint is employed here, and the desire for some sort of purification of thinking that it seems to imply, seem tied to a tendency that not only characterizes a certain type of response to Heidegger's Nazism and anti-Semitism, but also to Nazism and the Holocaust and even to the Second World War more generally. It is a response that involves setting these phenomena and events apart from us, absolving ourselves of any responsibility for those phenomena and events, focusing guilt and responsibility for those phenomena and events on the moral corruption of "others." It is precisely this tendency that underpins the idea, so often invoked in English-speaking philosophical circles, that it was indeed *European* thought, in particular, that prepared the way for, and was complicit in, the horrors of Nazism and the Holocaust.

What is in question here is not whether one can or should pass moral judgment on certain actions or decisions—there can be no question, for instance, that Heidegger's decision to commit himself to the National Socialist "Revolution" was not merely a "mistake" but a horrendous failure of moral as well as political judgment. Yet such judgment should not to preclude the attempt to understand, it certainly need not rule out the possibility of engagement, and it must also imply recognition of the need for humility. There is surely nothing of which humans are capable that is not also a possibility to which we are ourselves connected just by virtue of our being human. Evil is not something *outside* or *beyond* the human, but a failure *of* the human. This is partly why the Holocaust is so horrific—it is a horror that proceeds, not from something that is *other* than human, nor from some *single person* (Hitler) or *exclusive group of persons* (the Nazis, the Germans, the Europeans) such that they could be set apart, excluded, or quarantined from the rest of us, but from a possibility that belongs to human being itself, even though it is also a possibility that consists essentially in the denial and destruction of human being.[19] One might add that true judgment never sets the one judged apart from the one who judges, but rather proceeds from recognition of the human character of evil as well as good—which is why all judgment ought properly to contain an element of sorrow or compassion, even if it may be hard to recognize or feel.[20]

The language of contamination, infection, and taint, and with it the tendency toward exclusionary forms of judgment, becomes especially problematic inasmuch as it readily serves to conceal our own areas of blindness, our own failings, and even our own complicity in some of the phenomena that we rightly condemn—our own *partial* complicity, though it may be said to be distant or contentious, in an event such as the Holocaust.[21] I write this piece in Tasmania, a place that may be thought to be far from Auschwitz or Dachau. Yet Tasmania, or Van Diemen's Land, as it was known, has its own racism, its own history of genocide, its own history of human degradation and denial, some of whose roots are those out of which the Holocaust also grew. In Tasmania, one is not at all far from the camps, and all too close to the horrors that humanity is capable of enacting. Even though it may vary in extremity, and may even be seen as taking on a unique form in the Holocaust itself, inhumanity is something in which everyone and everyplace seems to have some share that is their own. No exclusive judgment then, no judgment that simply removes those we judge from us or us from them, no judgment that does not also allow of understanding and even engagement—our engagement with Heidegger requires this as does every such case.

One cannot remove Heidegger from the tradition of twentieth-century philosophy, but nor can one remove Heidegger's thinking of the 1930s and 1940s from the larger body of his thought. If one wishes genuinely to engage with Heidegger's thinking, whether his very early or his late thought, then one cannot do so in some selective fashion, setting aside his thinking from the troublesome years prior to and during the Second World War, since to do so means to rule out an understanding of the way Heidegger's thinking might have retained continuity in spite of the uncertain paths—the *Holzwege* if not *Irrwege*—on which he loses himself in that time, and rules out an understanding of how the new orientation of the postwar period emerges.[22] Heidegger's thinking during the 1930s and early 1940s is thus important precisely because of the way it can be seen as *transitional*—as standing between the early thinking that culminates in *Being and Time* and the later thinking of the postwar essays. Heidegger's own talk of "another beginning" (in the *Contributions* and elsewhere) can be read, in this regard, as referring not only to the other beginning of philosophy itself, but also to the other beginning that belongs to Heidegger's own thinking. These two beginnings are necessarily connected (what Heidegger calls the *Kehre*, "the turning," is itself the turn from the one beginning to the other), and both are perhaps more significant in the direction they give to thinking than in the possibility of their attainment.[23]

Part of what surely led Heidegger into Nazism, apart from any personal *political* tendencies, is the fact that the political crisis in which Germany found itself in the late 1920s and early 1930s—a crisis to which many saw the Nazis as offering a direct response—coincided for Heidegger with his own philosophical crisis, a crisis that had arisen out of what can only be described as the failure of *Being and Time* and the particular philosophical direction it embodied. Part of what occurs, as a result, is a different focus on the issue of human being that is no longer so attentive to individual *Dasein* (hence the abandonment of many of the existential themes of *Being and Time*), along with a different method and style of approach (one much less geared to the sort of Kantian "analysis" of the earlier work), along with a reconceptualization of time and temporality now undertaken from within a more encompassing political-cultural and historical frame—although always interpreted philosophically. In this respect, Heidegger's attempt to rearticulate the philosophical vision that is unsuccessfully and incompletely worked out in *Being and Time* partially converges with the political project that he initially identifies (in the early 1930s) with Hitler and National Socialism. It is a vision that in its rearticulated form comes to focus on the idea of a people (*Volk*), the historical destiny of a people, and the way that destiny is played out within the history of being.[24] Here the history of being (*Seinsgeschichte*) is inseparable, so it would seem, from this idea of such a collective destiny.

The rethinking of time and temporality, in particular, that occurs here brings with it a rethinking of space and spatiality, and so also brings a more direct explication of a set of topological notions into view (notions already evident even earlier in the very idea of the clearing—*die Lichtung*). In the very early 1930s, however, the move toward a more topological orientation is still relatively unclear. Moreover, as Heidegger's lectures on "Nature, History, State" in 1933–1934 also show,[25] his thinking about spatiality at this time is both still inadequately worked out and apparently constrained by his focus on the idea of a "people." Consequently, the idea of spatiality that appears here—in the sense other than that associated with mere quantitative extension—is in terms of the *space of a people* (*Raum des Volkes*).[26] Much of what creates problems in the 1930s and 1940s is precisely this overshadowing of Heidegger's thinking by the idea of a people, and the understanding of the history of being associated with this—something that remains even after the entanglement with Nazism.

The rethinking of spatiality, and the move toward a more explicitly articulated notion of place, seems to emerge in Heidegger's thinking primarily through the engagement with Hölderlin,[27] even if it also occurs rather slowly, and still retains problematic elements even up until the early 1940s (it is not until the lectures, seminars, and essays of the late 1940s and after that the topological character of Heidegger's thinking becomes an explicit element in that thinking). It is particularly important to see this move toward a more evident topological orientation as occurring in, and developing partly out of, Heidegger's philosophical engagements in the 1930s and early 1940s. This is made especially clear by the entries in the *Notebooks* themselves, specifically in the *Anmerkungen*, or *Remarks*, from 1946. It is here that notions of place take on an overt significance that is directly connected with Heidegger's understanding of his own project—Heidegger thus talks of both the "place of being" (*Ortschaft des Seyns*) and of the "topology of being" (*Topologie des Seyns*)[28]—and in a way that presages key themes in the work of the late 1940s, 1950s, and 1960s. Moreover, what is also clear from these entries is the way in which this explicitly topological turn in the mid-1940s comes out of Heidegger's reflection on the previous two decades (the very presence of such reflection marking out these postwar entries from the almost entirely unreflective entries that make up the earlier *Considerations*).

It is commonplace to treat any thinking that gives priority to place and space as already predisposed to the sort of exclusionary and repressive politics associated with Nazism as well as with conservative politics more generally. What we see in Heidegger in the 1930s, however, is the beginning of a move toward a mode of topological thinking that develops as part of a move away from Nazism, and that culminates in the explicit topology of the mid-1940s onward. Even though they have little to offer in terms of illuminating the development of a topological perspective in Heidegger's thinking—for that one must look, so far as the material from the 1930s is concerned, to his lectures on Hölderlin, especially the river poems,[29] as well as to a careful reading of the *Contributions*[30]—the *Considerations* nevertheless provide significant confirmation of Heidegger's own critical distancing of himself from Nazism in the period from 1935 onward. Moreover, the move away from Nazism is itself connected, as the *Considerations* also make clear, to Heidegger's developing critique of technological modernity—a critique that, as the works of the postwar period indicate, is closely tied to Heidegger's thinking of place.

The great paradox of modernity is that at the same time as it offers more and more potential for improvement in the material quality of human lives, it also threatens the character of those lives in fundamental ways. Like the bargain Mephistopheles makes with Faust, the price modernity seems to demand for the material improvement it offers for human life is the loss of what is genuinely human about that life. This is not only the view we find in Heidegger (although Heidegger's own version of this critique is little appreciated and poorly understood in much English-speaking writing on technology), but is rather part of a deeper and more pessimistic tradition within Western thought.

Elements of this tradition can be found in Adorno and Arendt as much as in Heidegger; they are present in Nietzsche, to some extent in Weber, as well as in Foucault; they are evident in the work of Camus and René Char; they can be discerned too in the work of more recent writers such as Richard Sennett and Zygmunt Bauman (to take but two examples), and even, from within the analytic tradition itself, in the work of Georg Henrik von Wright.[31] One might argue that adherents of this tradition are less commonly found in English-language thought, although Bauman and Sennett, as well as von Wright, all write in English, and Thoreau and Emerson, as well as Blake and Wordsworth, can be seen as belonging to this tradition also. The critique of modernity need not be antidemocratic nor antiliberal (much depends, in any case, on what these terms are taken to mean—once again, the assumption of their univocity is a common if dangerous mistake), although it does sometimes manifest itself, in the twentieth century especially, as a rejection of a certain form of "Americanism"—where the latter has to be understood as a term for the global culture of modernity that has, over the last hundred years or so, often been identified with the United States, and continues to be so identified throughout much of the world outside of North America.

The critique of technological modernity at issue here is most definitely not the same as the antimodernism often taken to be an element in Nazism—Nazism has no critique of technological modernity, and at times, as Jeffrey Herf has shown, actually appears to embrace modernity and the technological.[32] The relation between modernity and Nazism—and between modernity and fascism—is complex. Nazism seems to be an essentially modern phenomenon, and yet it encompasses both modernist and antimodernist elements. Heidegger seems to have viewed Nazism, initially, as providing the basis for a challenge to certain problematic aspects of modernity (there is a fundamental ambiguity in his comment about Nazism as the site for "the confrontation between global technology and modern humanity"[33]), and, later, as itself embodying many of those same aspects—as embodying what he refers to in the *Considerations*, and elsewhere, as *Machenschaft*, machination, and *Rechnung,* calculation.[34] In this way, Nazism comes to be an expression of the essence of technological modernity, an expression, in other words, of what Heidegger later names as *das Gestell*. In the *Considerations*, it becomes apparent that Heidegger views the Jews as an embodiment of technological modernity also—seeming thereby to accept uncritically the common stereotype of the Jew as the "rootless cosmopolitan" obsessed with money. Yet neither the Jews nor the Nazis have any unique status in this regard—in the 1930s and early 1940s, as far as the comments in the *Considerations* are concerned, Heidegger seems to find *Machenschaft* and *Rechnung* reigning almost everywhere.

The critique of technological modernity that appears in the *Considerations* is clearly, however, only a precursor to the later thinking as expressed in essays such as "The Question Concerning Technology"—it is not identical with it, and so has to be distinguished from it. Indeed, part of what marks out the earlier from the later critique is the way the former presents technological modernity as operating in and through the power of certain groups, whether they be Nazis or Jews, to take but two examples, and also as a form of humanly oriented instrumentalism. It is thus that Heidegger's anti-Semitism is not touched by his separation from Nazism—not only was his anti-Semitism of a different character from the anti-Semitism at the forefront of Nazi ideology, but Heidegger's still-developing critique of modernity draws, somewhat opportunistically and uncritically, on the stereotype of the Jew as symbolic of the same technological modernity that is also supposed to be at work in Nazism.

Significantly, the critique of technological modernity that Heidegger develops after the war sloughs off many of the crudities that characterize it in the 1930s and 1940s, and it is by that later stage also more closely and directly connected to Heidegger's more carefully worked out understanding of space and place, and their relation to being and human being. The shift can thus be connected with philosophical shifts within the structure of the thinking at issue, and cannot, at least not without argument, be treated as merely a consequence of the change in political circumstances (which is not to say that they do not also have an impact). The discussion of technology in "The Thing," from 1949, thus begins with an analysis of the way the apparent removal of distance accomplished by modern radio and television nevertheless fails to brings things near to us, since what it does is actually to obliterate the sense of both the near and the far, and in so doing also to obliterate the appearance of the thing *as* thing. This is not peculiar just to television and radio. A more fundamental claim is at work here: that the real changes brought about by technological modernity are brought about through changes in place and space or in the way they themselves appear.[35] This is not something evident in the attacks on technological modernity that appear in the *Considerations*, and unsurprisingly so, since in the earlier period Heidegger had still not arrived at a developed articulation of the topology with which the later critique is so closely connected.

Like those other critiques of technological modernity that can be found in the work of Weber, Adorno, Camus, and von Wright, Heidegger does not focus merely on any technological device or set of such devices, but rather on technological modernity as a mode of *ordering* of the world—a mode of ordering that he identifies as present in the system that turns the Rhine both into a source of hydroelectric power and a destination for the tourist industry. All ordering, one might say, is spatial, but the ordering of technological modernity also involves a particular form of the spatial—a form that ties the spatial to the measurable, the extended, the quantifiable, and the boundless, and that also treats the temporal as implicated within this same spatial structure. Time is convertible into space on this account, and space is convertible into time, and both are capable of conversion into the measurable and the numerical. What results, and what underpins technological modernity, is thus a form of ordering that has nothing *but ordering* as its goal, and that reduces everything to the pure orderability of quantity, measure, and number. It is this ordering or orderability, and the drive toward it, that Heidegger calls *das Gestell*. Within it, everything appears in terms always of that plethora of other elements with which it is connected, that it uses and by which it can be used, that can be transformed into it and into which it can be transformed.[36]

Though the connection is seldom made, Heidegger's account of *Gestell*, and the way it takes up everything that is as part of a globalized network of connections that constantly produces more connections, is almost identical to the contemporary vision of the connected, networked world that is part of the rhetoric of globalized capital and bureaucratized governance—a rhetoric that has also permeated academic discourse in the humanities and social sciences.[37] Spatial flows, unbounded connections, global networks—these are the concepts that rule contemporary thinking as they are also supposed to rule the contemporary world. Everything within that world is reducible, in principle if not always in practice, to what can be measured and quantified. The emphasis on measure, number, and quantity, and the manner in which that emphasis is expressed and developed, brings technological modernity into close proximity with modern capitalism. One might argue that technological modernity, as Heidegger understands it, is thus identical with the form taken by modern corporatized, globalized capitalism, although this would also require a rethinking of what capitalism itself might be. In this respect, the complaint that Heidegger's critique of technological modernity is disconnected from any account of modern economic structures may be said to miss the extent to which the underlying structure of technological modernity as articulated by Heidegger cuts across the usual distinctions between social, political, and economic structures. Thus, even though capitalism is not given much attention anywhere in Heidegger's writings (nor is communism), this does not mean that his work has no relevance to the understanding of contemporary capitalism or that it is disconnected from all or any of the issues to which capitalism gives rise.

It is a striking feature of many contemporary discussions of technology, and even of many contemporary discussions of Heidegger, that the Heideggerian critique of technological modernity is often dismissed as deeply flawed or inadequate.[38] The fact that it leaves much implicit is one possible reason, but such a dismissal also appears rather shortsighted, given the clear affinities of the Heideggerian critique for that larger tradition of European "pessimism" and technological critique that, as I noted above, extends from Weber to Sennett and Thoreau to Camus. Moreover, very few of the critics of Heidegger on technological modernity attempt any sustained engagement with the details of the Heideggerian position—at least there seems little attempt to understand that critique in its own terms. It seems that it is enough merely to claim that Heidegger's account is too general and encompassing, too concerned with the question of "essence," too preoccupied with metaphysics, too focused on the technologies of the past. Almost never is there any sense of the larger context into which the critique of technological modernity fits, and certainly not of its topological character.

There is no doubt that Heidegger's critique of technological modernity during the 1930s—developed through his analysis of the ideas of *Rechnung* and *Machenschaft*, and evident in works such as the *Considerations*—is underdeveloped and flawed in many respects. It often remains within a fairly conventional structure, is expressed in ways that draw on contemporary prejudices (including anti-Semitic prejudices[39]), and is not developed as part of any more ramified or integrated set of concepts. It is only as it comes to separate itself from contemporary conventionalities and biases, and from the contingencies of circumstance, and as it is better connected with an understanding of the topology of being (thereby also connecting the calculative and quantitative with a certain mode of spatialization and temporalization, and, perhaps most importantly, with the refusal of bound or limit), that Heidegger's criticism of technological modernity takes on the form of a more significant critique. Yet although this development does not occur until later, it nevertheless arises out of the earlier account—and so out of the thinking evident in the *Considerations*, among other works. Moreover, what the *Considerations* themselves show is the way that developing critique is central to Heidegger's thinking even in the 1930s, and is itself tied to Heidegger's engagement with as well as disengagement from Nazism. The problem of thinking through Heidegger's involvement with Nazism is not separable from the problem of thinking through the development of his critique of technology, and that also includes thinking through the way the later critique differs from the earlier even as it arises out of it. The material now evident in the *Considerations* thus ought to make clear the importance of a closer engagement with Heidegger's critique of technology as it develops across his thinking—an engagement that has, however, been all too rare up until now.

That such engagement has indeed been rare, and the dismissal of Heidegger's critique all too quick, may indicate something about the very context in which the debate over the Heidegger affair has been positioned. Much of that debate has been concerned, not merely to demonstrate the fact of Heidegger's political and moral culpability during the 1930s, but more importantly, to show that his culpability extends to all of his thinking, or, if not to *Being and Time* and before (Heidegger's magnum opus often seems to be accorded a degree of quarantine), then certainly to the later thinking. Some of this is explained by concern over Heidegger's failure to show remorse or properly to address the horror of the Holocaust, but it also seems connected with the aversion to the later thinking that is common among many, especially English-language, readers. The later Heidegger is often viewed as the real enemy of sober rationality, of clear thinking, and so also, of the modern, progressivist project typically associated with contemporary "Western" societies.[40] Moreover, any genuine engagement with the complexities in Heidegger's work, especially those surrounding his entanglement with Nazism and anti-Semitism, is difficult without also recognizing the complexities present in our own situation—without recognizing the failures and moral ambiguities to which we ourselves are prone—and such recognition is itself rare. Heidegger's Nazi sympathies and anti-Semitic attitudes thus become the focus for the attempt to remove Heidegger from academic discourse, not merely because of his sometime failure as a human being or as a thinker, but more importantly perhaps, because of the way his work offends against the belief in modernity, in "reason," in technology, in capitalism, in "the West"—because it offends, perhaps, against our belief in ourselves. Heidegger's Nazism and anti-Semitism allow us to put Heidegger to one side, or apparently so, and also to put to one side his criticism and his pessimism—to put to one side the uncertainties his work raises about our own thinking, and even, perhaps, to quiet the political questions (on both the left *and* the right—if these terms any longer have meaning) to which that thinking also gives rise.

3   Conclusion: The Failures of Thinking

To reiterate the point: none of what has been said above mitigates or diminishes Heidegger's moral and personal failings, nor is it intended to do so, but it ought to make us more careful in the manner of our own judgments—and this must include the judgments we make, not only about Heidegger, but also about his philosophy, and about philosophy more broadly. It is sometimes said that what is at issue in the question of Heidegger's Nazism, and one might extend this to his anti-Semitism also, is not his failings as a person or thinker, but rather a failing of philosophy itself. In this fashion, Heidegger's failings come to be seen as philosophy's failings, and we may, as a result, find ourselves inclined to abandon philosophy, rather just the philosopher. Here is one significant area, however, where we should indeed be careful in our judgment—the seeming failure of philosophy, if it is failure in this case, cannot be taken as a reason for philosophy's abandonment.

If philosophy is understood merely as a certain institutionalized discipline, then the failure of philosophy supposedly exemplified in Heidegger's case may be taken to indicate something of the failure of a certain institutionalized and professionalized form of philosophy—but in that case, it is more a failure of such institutionalization and professionalization than of philosophy as such. It is a failure that surely threatens today in a way different in kind, but not necessarily in degree, from the way it threatened, and was also realized, across many disciplines in the 1930s. Contemporary forms of academic institutionalization and professionalization seem increasingly to be moving toward decreased capacity for independent action and decision within institutions and on the part of academics, and so also toward a diminished sense of moral agency or the capacity to resist and to dissent (tendencies evident across many societies, including those of North America, the United Kingdom, and Australasia).

Yet if the heart of philosophy is just the attempt to think, then the failure of philosophy would also be the failure of thinking, and no matter how disastrous, such a failure cannot lead to the abandonment of thinking. That thinking fails, may even be inevitably given over to failure (thinking offers no guarantees), reflects the incompleteness of thinking—reflects the fact that thinking is a task that cannot be refused, but only continued. Even to countenance the abandonment of thinking is to threaten to lapse into senselessness. The underlying mistake is to suppose that we can think *without failing*—what should be surprising is not when our thinking fails us, but rather when it is, in some sense, successful. It is precisely because thinking is incomplete and failing—itself a function of the radicality of our finitude—that questioning and listening, as the later Heidegger so often insists, are so central to thinking. One of Heidegger's own failings in the 1930s and 1940s is that he does not seem to pay sufficient heed to this, but rather places the emphasis on answer and decision (something present in the very style of his writing in that period).

The emphasis on questioning here is relevant to our attitude toward the challenge presented by technological modernity (it is partly why there can be no single or simple response here), but it is especially relevant to philosophy's relation to politics. One of Heidegger's mistakes was surely to think, like Plato, that philosophy offered a surer basis for political engagement than is available to others—that the philosopher in politics is less prone to failure than the mere politician (which is perhaps why Heidegger could imagine that he was capable of guiding even Hitler—*Den Führer führen*). This is surely one of the vanities of philosophy—that philosophy can guide politics, that it can provide the ground for political decision. If, however, we take the recognition of the failing character of thinking as lying at the heart of philosophy, as perhaps it should, then perhaps the proper and only role for philosophy in relation to politics can be one, not of decision, but precisely of constant questioning—of a constant reiterating of the failing and incomplete character of political thinking no less than of any other thinking.

Such questioning is not only relevant to philosophy in its relation to politics, however; but as it derives from what philosophy itself is, from what thinking might itself be, so such questioning is also central to philosophy's relation to itself. This relation is part of what is at issue in the attempt to think through the issues surrounding Heidegger's *Black Notebooks*—it is at issue in terms of the hermeneutical problems that surround the engagement with those works, in Heidegger's own relation to them, in their place and the place of the ideas they contain in contemporary philosophy, and in our own engagement with the *Notebooks*, with the questions they raise, and with ourselves.

Notes

1. "On the Prejudices of Philosophers," *Beyond Good and Evil,* trans. Walter Kaufmann (New York: Random House, 1989), §5, p. 12.

2. Edited by Peter Trawny and published in Frankfurt by Klostermann, the separate volumes include *Überlegungen II–VI (Schwarze Hefte 1931–1938), Gesamtausgabe* 94 (2014); *Überlegungen VII–XI (Schwarze Hefte 1938/39), Gesamtausgabe* 95 (2014); *Überlegungen XII–XV (Schwarze Hefte 1939–1941), Gesamtausgabe* 96 (2014); *Anmerkungen I–V (Schwarze Hefte 1942–1948, Gesamtausgabe* 97 (2015); *Gesamtausgabe* 98 (not yet published).

3. Peter Trawny, *Heidegger und der Mythos der jüdischen Weltverschwörung* (Frankfurt: Klostermann, 2014).

4. Including Karl Löwith, "Les implications politiques de la philosophie de l'existence chez Heidegger," *Les temps modernes* 2 (1946): 343–360.

5. See Paul Hühnerfeld, *In Sachen Heidegger* (Hamburg: Hoffmann and Campe, 1959), and Guido Schneeberger, *Nachlese zu Heidegger: Dokumente zu seinem Leben und Denken* (Bern: Suhr, 1962).

6. Victor Farías, *Heidegger et le nazisme*, trans. Mynain Bernarroch and Jean-Baptiste Grasset (Paris: Verdier, 1987).

7. Hugo Ott's *Martin Heidegger: Unterwegs zu seiner Biographie* (Frankfurt: Campus Verlag, 1988). Michael E. Zimmermann lists much of the relevant literature from the postwar discussion, up to and including the work of Ott, in Zimmermann, *Heidegger's Confrontation with Modernity: Technology, Politics, and Art* (Bloomington: Indiana University Press, 1990), 179–281.

8. Emmanuel Faye, *Heidegger: L'introduction du nazisme dans la philosophie: Autour des séminaires inédits de 1933–1935* (Paris: Albin Michel, 2005).

9. An attitude exemplified in Bertrand Russell's work, and in the treatment he accords German philosophy in his *History of Western Philosophy* (London: Allen and Unwin, 1946) and elsewhere. See Thomas Akehurst, "Bertrand Russell Stalks the Nazis," *Philosophy Now* 97 (2013): 20–22.

10. I have little doubt that, in some quarters, all of this will be taken to confirm my own supposed failure to grasp the real issues at stake here and the limitations of my philosophical approach. That this is so is itself an

indication of the difficulty of trying to engage with the issues while not giving in to the simplification common on both sides (simplification of fact and interpretation as well as of judgment). It also reveals the preference of many readers for avoiding any serious attempt to think through the complications and ambiguities involved (and it indicates the extent to which the contemporary debate tends often to descend into personal attack, not only with respect to Heidegger himself, and to become embroiled in personal animosities). My own engagement with Heidegger has not focused on his Nazism and anti-Semitism, partly because my aim has not been to reconstruct Heidegger's thought in a way that somehow recaptures his own "inner" intentions and aims (something I think is in any case hermeneutically suspect), nor has it been simply to work within the conventional framework of contemporary Heidegger studies. Indeed, one might even go so far as to say that Heidegger himself is of only peripheral interest to the work in which I am engaged and in which his name figures. My interest in Heidegger is and has always been determined by the extent to which his work can be drawn on with respect to a set of key philosophical issues centering on place, truth, presence, and human being. Judging Heidegger's culpability as a Nazi or anti-Semite has little relevance to that project, since the project is driven, not by Heidegger's thinking as such, but by the issues themselves. Indeed, my own claim is that if we think through those issues, even drawing on many of the insights Heidegger's own work affords, then we arrive at exactly the contrary position to that associated with Nazism and anti-Semitism. One might even say that my project, far from being one that simply assumes or minimizes Heidegger's Nazism and anti-Semitism, can instead be read as setting Heidegger *against* Heidegger, aiming to show how the orientation implicit in the underlying philosophical issues leads (and partly, as I argue below, leads Heidegger himself) in a direction exactly contrary to that of Nazism and anti-Semitism, as well as of other forms of oppressive and discriminatory politics. Where it leads, in fact, is toward a much more human and humane conception—a conception according to which human finitude is understood as tied to human placedness; in which the fact of human finitude is tied to recognition of human suffering; in which the ontological is seen as inextricably tied to the ethical; in which acknowledgment of limit and failure, as well as the possibility of beginning anew, is fundamental to the possibility of a genuinely human life.

11. If the fact of Heidegger's Nazism has always been publicly evident, his anti-Semitism has been less so prior to the publication of *Considerations* (although it could be taken as implicit in his support for Nazism in the early 1930s)—yet it was certainly evident privately to many of his friends and colleagues, including Jaspers and Arendt (as is revealed by some of the correspondence between them).

12. If I use the word *seems* here, as I elsewhere also use the term *appears*, it is not because I intend the term ironically (so that *seems* means "not really"), but simply to allow for the possibility of the interpretive complications that might arise and that, if they were to be addressed, might require further discussion and argument.

13. I have avoided putting this in terms of the cultural as against the *racial*, since there seems to me an enormous ambiguity surrounding the latter term. Race is often taken to be a naturally, or *biologically*, based notion, and yet given that the concept of race has no real natural or biological basis, it seems one cannot assign it any significant content, if one is to assign it any content at all, other than cultural.

14. As Ingo Farin shows in chapter 19, part of what the *Considerations* demonstrate is the extent to which Heidegger does indeed move away from his early commitment to National Socialism. That does not mean, of course, that his views therefore became politically anodyne—but it does, once again, complicate the picture of Heidegger's relation to Nazism.

15. So, for instance, the claim that Heidegger's thinking is anti-Semitic at its core cannot be supported merely by showing that Heidegger expressed or held anti-Semitic views—and this would remain the case even if it were Heidegger himself who made that claim (which is only to say that Heidegger might misunderstand the actual implications of his thinking). What needs to be shown is that anti-Semitism is indeed at work in the thinking, and that means showing where and how anti-Semitic attitudes are actually present in, and operative on, that thinking.

16. See Michael Dummett, *Frege: Philosophy of Language* (New York: Harper & Row, 1973), xii: "There is some irony for me in the fact that the man about whose philosophical views I have devoted, over years, a great deal of time to thinking, was, at least at the end of his life, a virulent racist, specifically an anti-semite. This fact is revealed by a fragment of a diary which survives among Frege's Nachlass, but which was not published with the rest by Professor Hans Hermes in *Freges nachgelassene Schriften*. the diary shows Frege to have been a man of extreme right-wing political opinions, bitterly opposed to the parliamentary system, democrats, liberals, Catholics, the French and, above all, Jews, who he thought ought to be deprived of political rights and, preferably, expelled from Germany. When I first read that diary, many years ago, I was deeply shocked, because I had revered Frege as an absolutely rational man, if, perhaps, not a very likeable one. I regret that the editors of Frege's Nachlass chose to suppress that particular item. From it I learned something about human beings which I should be sorry not to know; perhaps something about Europe, also."

17. In *The Reckless Mind: Intellectuals in Politics* (New York: NYREV, 2001), xii–xiii, Mark Lilla talks of his "sense of disappointment," not only in relation to Heidegger, but apparently with regard to all the thinkers he discusses—Heidegger, Arendt, Jaspers, Schmitt, Benjamin, Foucault, Derrida, and also, of course, Plato. Lilla also stresses, however, that he has no wish to dismiss these thinkers on the grounds of their seeming political inadequacies.

18. Two works that explore this connection are Màrlene Zarader, *The Unthought Debt: Heidegger and the Hebraic Heritage*, trans. Bettina Bergo (Stanford, CA: Stanford University Press, 2006), and Peter Eli Gordon, *Rosenzweig and Heidegger: Between Judaism and German Philosophy* (Berkeley: University of California Press, 2003). Although neither of these works takes up the point directly, I would also argue that one of the key points of connection here is precisely in relation to the role of place and the topological. The connection between Heidegger and Judaic thinking is also discussed by Michael Fagenblat in chapter 10 of the present book.

19. Hannah Arendt makes a similar point in her 1945 essay "Organized Guilt and Universal Responsibility," in *Essays in Understanding* 1930–1954, ed. Jerome Kohn, 121–132 (New York: Harcourt, Brace, 1994). She writes "For many years now we have met Germans who declare that they are ashamed of being German. I have often felt tempted to answer that I am ashamed of being human" (p.130).

20. If this aspect of judgment is evoked by the humanity of the one judged, then can a figure such as Hitler be said to have lost so much of their humanity that they can no longer be judged in this way—can no longer be judged with any recognition of their being as human? Were this to be so, however, then the evil that Hitler presents would again have been removed from the human, would become something outside of the human, and we would lose sight of it as a possibility we possess. Perhaps the right response is not to say that we cannot judge a figure such as Hitler in light of their being human (on the contrary, it is surely on that basis and that basis alone that we are able to judge them at all), but rather that it becomes *humanly difficult* to judge a figure like Hitler and to retain a sense of his humanity, and certainly to have any sense of compassion or sorrow that is directed toward him in that judgment.

21. Apart from the way German anti-Semitism and German fascism have their origins in a cultural heritage broadly shared across both Anglo-Saxon and European societies, one can also look, more specifically, to British and American support for Hitler in the 1920s and 1930s (including support from British and American industrialists in particular); to the widespread anti-Semitism present in Britain and France, as well as the United States, prior to the Second World War; and to issues concerning the Allied response to the Holocaust itself. On the latter see David S. Wyman, *The Abandonment of the Jews: America and the Holocaust* (New York: Pantheon Books, 1984), and Henry L. Feingold, *Bearing Witness: How America and Its Jews Responded to the Holocaust* (Syracuse, NY: Syracuse University Press, 1995), especially chapter 13, "Who Shall Bear Guilt for the Holocaust?," 255–278.

22. That it is a new orientation, even though one that also remains within the framework of the topology that I have argued characterized all of Heidegger's thought (see especially my *Heidegger's Topology: Being, Place, World* [Cambridge, MA: MIT Press, 2006]), seems to me incontrovertible—and remains so no matter how we are disposed to rethink the shift in Heidegger's thinking that occurs in the 1930s and 1940s.

23. See my discussion of the two beginnings in "Re-Orienting Thinking: Philosophy in the Midst of the World," *Commonplace Commitments: Thinking through the Legacy of Joseph P. Fell*, ed. Peter S. Fosl, Michael J. McGandy, and Mark Moorman (Lewisburg, PA: Bucknell University Press, 2015).

24. See James Phillips, *Heidegger's Volk: Between National Socialism and Poetry* (Stanford, CA: Stanford University Press, 2005); see also Laurence Hemming, *Heidegger and Marx: A Productive Dialogue over the Language of Humanism* (Evanston, IL: Northwestern University Press, 2013), especially 160–184.

25. Available in English translation in Martin Heidegger, *Nature, History, State: 1933–1934*, ed. and trans. Gregory Fried and Richard Polt (London: Bloomsbury, 2013).

26. See Heidegger, *Nature, History, State: 1933–1934*.

27. See Stuart Elden, *Mapping the Present: Heidegger, Foucault, and the Project of a Spatial History* (London: Continuum, 2001), 33–42.

28. See especially *Anmerkungen I–V, Gesamtausgabe* 97, 201–202.

29. On Hölderlin's *The Rhine* and *Germania* in 1934–1935, in English as Martin Heidegger, *Hölderlin's Hymns "Germania" and "The Rhine,"* trans. William McNeill and Julia Ireland (Bloomington: Indiana University Press, 2014), and on Hölderlin's *The Ister* in 1941–1942, appearing in English as Martin Heidegger, *Hölderlin's Hymn "The Ister,"* trans. William McNeill and Julia Davis (Bloomington: Indiana University Press, 1996).

30. One of the shortcoming of my *Heidegger's Topology* is that it gives too little attention to the *Contributions*—a work imbued with a thoroughly topological sensibility in its constant invocation, for instance, of notions of "the between," "timespace," "clearing," "open," "leap," "encounter" and "approach," and even "event." It is important not to ignore the topological resonances in these terms; to do so is to fail to heed the character of Heidegger's own language. To gloss over the topological character of that language is to refuse the real challenge of thinking that Heidegger presents to us.

31. See, for instance, Georg Henrik von Wright, "Dante between Ulysses and Faust," in *Knowledge and the Sciences in Medieval Philosophy* (*Acta Philosophica Fennica* 48), ed. Monika Asztalos, John E. Murdoch, and Ilkka Niiniluoto, 1–9 (Helsinki: Yliopistopaino 1990). Among this latter group of thinkers, Von Wright's work is the least known though no less interesting.

32. See Jeffrey Herf, *Reactionary Modernism: Technology, Culture, and Politics in Weimar and the Third Reich* (New York: Cambridge University Press, 1986).

33. Martin Heidegger, *Introduction to Metaphysics,* trans. Gregory Fried and Richard Polt (New Haven, CT: Yale University Press, 2000), 213.

34. See, for instance, *Überlegungen XII–XV, Gesamtausgabe* 96, 195; *Besinnung, Gesamtausgabe* 66, ed. Friedrich-Wilhelm von Herrmann (Frankfurt: Klostermann, 1997), 16ff.; *Die Geschichte des Seyns, Gesamtausgabe* 69, ed. Peter Trawny (Frankfurt: Klostermann, 1998), 225ff.

35. For more on this see my *Heidegger's Topology*, 278–303.

36. See my *Heidegger's Topology.*

37. See my "Putting Space in Place: Relational Geography and Philosophical Topography," *Planning and Environment D: Space and Society* 30 (2012): 226–242.

38. See, for instance, Don Idhe, *Heidegger's Technologies: Postphenomenological Perspectives* (New York: Fordham University Press, 2010), as well as Don Idhe, "Can Continental Philosophy Deal with the New Technologies?," *Journal of Speculative Philosophy* 26 (2012): 321–332.

39. It is the Jews who supposedly possess a "marked talent for calculation," *Überlegungen XII–XV, Gesamtausgabe* 96, p. 56.

40. The later thinking stands in sharp contrast to the philosophically more conventional thinking evident in *Being and Time*, eschewing the usual forms of philosophical discourse, and also lapsing, as many would have it, into mysticism and poetry (a lapse that may be viewed as originating in the intoxicated years of the 1930s). However one reads the later thinking, and whether one does indeed take it as a "lapse" into mysticism, it nevertheless remains true that the later thinking represents a direct challenge to conventional philosophical thinking in a way the early thinking does not. One might argue that one of the limitations of the later thinking is indeed Heidegger's seeming inability to respond adequately to the Holocaust. Yet one might also argue, as I have here, that part of what marks out the late from the early thinking is that the former develops out of the problematic engagement with Nazism, and partly in response to it. The early thinking, including the thinking of *Being and Time*, lacks access to the lessons of that engagement, even while it also contains elements that feed into it. The later thinking is thus especially important if we are to think through the philosophical issues Heidegger's engagement with Nazism brings to the fore.

2

Heidegger's *Notebooks*: A Smoking Gun?

Fred Dallmayr

In this fast-paced age, Martin Heidegger—alone among recent philosophers—seems to be exempt from the rapid change of fashions and the quick obsolescence of ideas. Now, some forty years after his death, a new publication keeps the intellectual world on edge: I refer to the so-called *Schwarze Hefte* or *Black Notebooks* covering the period from 1931 to 1941, recently published in three volumes by Klostermann.[1] With the announcement of this publication, the air instantly bristled with intellectual tension. One is reminded of the atmosphere prevailing at the time of the Hühnerfeld study and after the publication of the Farías book.[2] But this time the tension is further heightened because the term *Notebooks* seems to promise an abundance of personal disclosures previously kept from view.

Even when the text was still in page proofs, the verdict of some leading experts was clear and firm: here was the proof one had always been looking for; this was the "smoking gun" one had always suspected! In the eyes of some readers, the *Notebooks* were about to put an end to the entire Heidegger "business," robbing it of intellectual legitimacy. Anyone who afterward still was preoccupied with Heidegger's work was ipso facto excommunicated from the intellectual community if not banished from the human race. The term *excommunicate* does not seem ill-chosen because, in many respects, the "Heidegger affair" has acquired religious-theological overtones, with anathemas hurled quickly at apostates.

For me, the affair is not theological in that sense. In my view, Heidegger is still mainly a philosopher, and philosophy is basically an enterprise of questioning that leaves no room for anathemas of any kind.[3] It is precisely on this point that, on reading the *Notebooks*, I felt occasionally put off or somewhat disoriented or disappointed. The collected notes are sometimes written in an assertive or declamatory style—where I would have wanted to add some question marks. In a way, the entries—and their numbers are huge—can be compared to what we now call blogs or op-eds. Anybody who uses the Internet nowadays is quickly overwhelmed by an avalanche of such blogs. However, the Internet offers a remedy: we can always hit the "delete" button. Perhaps it would have been desirable if Heidegger had more frequently hit that button or else had used Occam's razor.

As I see it, the problem is that entries sometimes seem to have been written quickly or in haste, and without sufficient circumspection. This impression applies especially to the entries on "Jews" and "World Jewry," which are likely to give offense. Some readers have detected about five or six entries in this category in the books. In many ways, the comments on "World Jewry"[4] strike me as excessively abstract speculations, not adequately supported by concrete details. Likewise, the characterization of "the Jews" as being wholly addicted to "calculating rationality"[5] seems inadmissibly summary and misleading. Although some Jews—like some members of other groups—may have this particular calculating penchant, there are too many counterexamples (e.g., Theodor Adorno, Walter Benjamin) to undermine the thesis. One of the merits of modern social science—from comparative politics to cultural anthropology—is to render untenable the assertion of a fixed national identity or an "essential" ethnic character.

Given my own background, the latter point is particularly relevant to me. Having been trained both in philosophy and in one of the social sciences, I have always tried to navigate between the two shores. This means that I have always placed myself at the border of a "pure" or self-contained philosophy, while also staying aloof from a myopic positivism. In Heideggerian terms, I have tried to keep the "ontological" and the "ontic" shores close together or at least in communication. This inclination has also inspired my attempt—ill-fated or ill-conceived according to some—to build a bridge between Freiburg and Frankfurt, or between hermeneutical ontology and critical social inquiry.[6] None of these observations, I should add, render invalid Heidegger's critique of a one-sided or hegemonic calculating rationality, which unhappily is on the rise today. The danger of this hegemony is clearly evident in today's academy—where the humanities and the "soft" social sciences are increasingly under siege and sometimes simply abolished.

I have to correct or qualify my previous description of the *Notebooks* as a collection of "blogs": they are also, of course, much more than that. From another, more sympathetic angle, the *Notebooks* can be seen as the logbook of a journey: an intellectual and spiritual journey undertaken by Heidegger during extremely turbulent and perplexing years. In a way, the books bear witness to his (sometimes desperate) effort to find a path in the social-political and intellectual wilderness of the time. Small wonder that the chosen path often seems like a *Holzweg*, a dead end, a *chemin qui ne mène nulle part*. The path was clearly hazardous, full of risks, and devoid of reliable signposts. Heidegger did not believe that one could simply sink back into traditional intellectual, cultural, or religious routines, no matter how time-tested and comforting they may be. At the same time, he did not claim that one can willfully fabricate a path, proclaim marching orders, projects, panaceas. So, the only way to find one's way was by going—"*caminante, se hace camino al andar*" (Antonio Machado).

One of the recurrent leitmotifs of Heidegger's logbook is the notion of "transition" or "going beyond" (*Übergang*). To this extent, the notes challenge us to move forward beyond actuality to potentiality, from the reality of prevailing decay into the horizons of a promising or promised future. As we read at one point, "*An age of transition*—that does not seem to be anything worthwhile [*nichts Rechtes*]. Yet such ages are alone historically decisive;

in them one needs to overcome what dominates [*herrscht*]." One needs to be "*in*" them and yet "*beyond*" them, shunning both what is "merely new" and what is "only old."[7] Overcoming what dominates means above all overcoming the dominant *idola fori*, including all the modern and contemporary ideologies, from liberalism (or liberal capitalism) to communism to nationalism—including National Socialism. What is defunct in (capitalist) liberalism is the reliance on acquisitive anthropocentrism, while communism and nationalism are vitiated by fostering a collectivist or "herd" mentality (on a class or ethnic level). What is common to all the dominant ideologies is their dogmatic self-assurance and resort to relentless media indoctrination. What is absent in all of them is a space for innovative thinking and for that basic questioning that—for Heidegger (as I understand him)—is the lifeblood of philosophy and also the sine qua non of genuine humanity.

Given its prominence in the public eye, some comments on National Socialism deserve to be lifted up. Here is a stark and startling sentence: "National Socialism is a *barbaric principle*"—at least when it is taken (as it commonly is) as a purely "ontic" or power-political doctrine devoid of genuine reflection.[8] The term *barbaric* is elucidated in another passage that presents the rejection or renunciation of philosophical thinking as the "*road into barbarism*."[9] The intellectual deficiency, and hence nullity, of National Socialist ideology is underscored in another entry that insists that philosophy proper can never be politically instrumentalized—with the consequence that a "National Socialist philosophy" is a contradiction in terms resembling the idea of a "courageous or else cowardly triangle."[10] Accordingly, the description of the majority of National Socialist leaders at the time is unflattering, if not devastating: "elementary school teachers gone berserk, unemployed technicians, and displaced petty bourgeois people."[11]

Some key terms of National Socialist ideology were *Rasse* ("race") and *Volk* (lit. "folk"; "people, nation"). The *Notebooks* acknowledge, of course, the "ontic" existence of racial or ethnic differences—but only as sociological background that must not be elevated into the meaning or purpose of social existence. Repeatedly, the notes denounce a "sordid biologism" that sees social life rooted "plantlike" in ethnic soil.[12] The critical dissection and deconstruction of folk ideology are the topic of numerous entries. "The *Volk*," one entry states, "Okay, but to what *end*, and *why Volk*? … And *where* is the *Volk*?"[13] Another passage fulminates against the "idolatry of *Volk*," the latter taken as "something 'ready-at-hand' (*Vorhandenes*) that embraces everything and is 'organically' grown"—adding that this "animalization and mechanization of *Volk*" neglects how the latter only emerges on the basis of *Dasein* (which raises the question of Being).[14] At another point, Heidegger stresses the danger of *Volk* seen as a "totalizing agency" that, sidestepping the Being question, gets caught up in its own "totality."[15] From here on, there is a crescendo in the *Notebooks*' language—as when *Volk* is called "the monstrosity of a life instinct declaring itself eternal."[16] A bit later, *Volk* is presented as "the name for something that is mere unity, denying differences," as a subjectivity writ large (read: collective selfishness) whose character is further hardened by "the primacy accorded to the biological construal of the term."[17]

According to some experts, Heidegger had little or no sympathy for other nationalities or ethnic groups. I find little or no evidence for this claim in the *Notebooks*. But there is ample evidence that he had little sympathy for some Germans at the time. The *Notebooks* often display a deep sense of frustration and disappointment. One passage refers mockingly to the epithet often used for Germans, "the *Volk* of poets and thinkers." "One hears," we read, "that the Germans have now mutated from a '*Volk* of poets and thinkers' into a 'nation of poets and soldiers.'"[18] Another passage refers to a popular or idiomatic expression whereby people bereft of hope are said to be "forsaken [*verlassen*] by all the gods": "It seems as if contemporary Germans should now be credited with the distinction of having been forsaken by all the gods."[19] And here, for good measure, is another passage reflecting utter frustration: "What is the reason for this preponderance of good-natured and well-mannered [*anständig*] intellectual depravity of the Germans? ... What is the cause of this aberration from one's task? Is it that we no longer want any mindfulness [*Besinnung*]? But where does this not-wanting or unwillingness come from?"[20]

In conclusion, I will of course be accused of having read and interpreted the *Notebooks* selectively. But given the large number of entries, this is inevitable; no one can hope to cover all of them in a limited space. So the discussion and debate will continue. I only hope that they will be constructive and illuminating and not descend into the free-for-all that some academics unfortunately value. I find it advisable at my age to concentrate on texts that offer the chance of a *paideia*—that is, of a learning experience. From that standpoint, I can say that I have learned a great deal by reading the *Notebooks* (selectively). More importantly, I have been the beneficiary of the wealth of insights offered in Heidegger's writings over the years, though I am not an expert and cannot claim that I understand everything in the *Notebooks* and other writings. Let me close with a few passages from the *Notebooks* that do make sense to me: "All over the world, why is there today no willingness to acknowledge that we do *not* possess the truth and need to start asking questions again?" Or: "When will come the guides on the silent paths of early dawn? (For now we only have the incessant noisemakers, the trumpeters of the long-outdated.)" And finally: "Human being—a steep path in a growing wind!"[21]

Notes

1. See Martin Heidegger, *Überlegungen II–VI* (*Schwarze Hefte 1931–1938*); *Überlegungen VII–XI* (*Schwarze Hefte 1938/39*); *Überlegungen XII–XV* (*Schwarze Hefte 1939–1941*); *Gesamtausgabe* 94–96, ed. Peter Trawny (Frankfurt: Klostermann, 2014). All translations from the German are my own.

2. See Paul Hühnerfeld, *In Sachen Heidegger* (Hamburg: Hoffmann and Campe, 1959); Victor Farías, *Heidegger et le Nazism*, trans. Mynain Bernarroch and Jean-Baptiste Grasset (Paris: Verdier, 1987); Victor Farías, *Heidegger and Nazism*, ed. Joseph Margolis and Tom Rockmore (Philadelphia: Temple University Press, 1989).

3. One recalls here the curses with which Spinoza was expelled from his community in 1656. Half a century earlier Galileo had been charged with heresy by the Church. With regard to the "smoking gun" of the *Notebooks*, one is sometimes reminded of the fabled "weapons of mass distraction" supposedly in Iraq.

4. Especially *Überlegungen XII–XV, Gesamtausgabe* 96, pp. 46, 262).

5. *Überlegungen XII–XV, Gesamtausgabe* 96, p. 56.

6. See, for example, Fred Dallmayr, *Between Freiburg and Frankfurt: Toward a Critical Ontology* (Amherst: University of Massachusetts Press, 1991).

7. *Überlegungen II–VI, Gesamtausgabe* 94, p. 194.

8. *Überlegungen II–VI, Gesamtausgabe* 94, p. 194.

9. *Überlegungen II–VI, Gesamtausgabe* 94, p. 226.

10. *Überlegungen II–VI, Gesamtausgabe* 94, p. 348.

11. *Überlegungen II–VI, Gesamtausgabe* 94, p. 187. As one should note, the *Notebooks* also offer a series of critical and partly self-critical observations on the period when Heidegger served as rector in Freiburg (April 1933 to April 1934) (see *Überlegungen II–VI, Gesamtausgabe* 94, pp. 111–116, 154–155, 162). At one point, Heidegger describes a key text of the period—"The Self-Assertion of the German University"—as "the small interlude of a big mistake" (see *Überlegungen II–VI, Gesamtausgabe* 94, p. 198; also Heidegger, "Die Selbstbehauptung der deutschen Universität," in *Das Rektorat 1933/34: Tatsachen und Gedanken* (Frankfurt: Klostermann, 1983)). I certainly wish his observations on this period had been more self-critical. I also wish his critique had translated more often into practical conduct. (I realize, of course, how easy it is to make this recommendation in normal times—while, in a totalitarian context, one's life and that of one's family are at stake. For this reason, it is of the utmost importance not to allow politics to deteriorate to the point where decent action becomes equivalent to suicide.)

12. For example, *Überlegungen II–VI, Gesamtausgabe* 94, p. 143.

13. *Überlegungen II–VI, Gesamtausgabe* 94, p. 195.

14. *Überlegungen II–VI, Gesamtausgabe* 94, p. 223.

15. *Überlegungen II–VI, Gesamtausgabe* 94, pp. 446–447.

16. *Überlegungen II–VI, Gesamtausgabe* 94, p. 497.

17. *Überlegungen II–VI, Gesamtausgabe* 94, p. 521.

18. *Überlegungen II–VI, Gesamtausgabe* 94, p. 514.

19. *Überlegungen II–VI, Gesamtausgabe* 94, p. 519.

20. *Überlegungen II–VI, Gesamtausgabe* 94, p. 510.

21. *Überlegungen II–VI, Gesamtausgabe* 94, pp. 41, 319, 369.

3

Reading Heidegger's *Black Notebooks*

Steven Crowell

What would it be like to take philosophy with absolute seriousness, to make it the alpha and omega of one's life? Is it possible to do so within the university today, or is it perhaps incompatible with being a professor of philosophy? It might be thought that Heidegger's life provides a cautionary answer to these questions. Richard Rorty, for one, believed that Heidegger had many good ideas but that his thought and life were undermined by the conviction that philosophy was of singular importance.[1] No one who thinks as Rorty does will gain much pleasure from reading Heidegger's *Black Notebooks*, and even some who *do* think that philosophy matters deeply, as I do, will be troubled by what one finds there. But not, perhaps, for the reasons you might think.

1 Confessions and Impressions

Much has been made of the anti-Semitism that is supposed to be found in the *Black Notebooks*. I will have nothing to say about that. In September 2013 I was on a bus in Bogotá with the editor of the *Black Notebooks*, Peter Trawny, who told me, with a certain resignation, that their contents would once again explode the complacency of the community of Heidegger scholars. It was not long before he was proved correct. Even before their official publication, the journalists, bloggists, and other self-appointed public intellectuals had all weighed in, drawing equally quick responses from the academic "faithful" (as Heideggerians are routinely and dismissively called). My own reaction was somewhat different: "Shit! Three more massive volumes of Heideggeriana to plow through. Didn't I just finish skimming thousands of pages of Heidegger's *Seminare* on Hegel, Kant, and Leibniz? How do my colleagues manage to get to the bottom of such publications so quickly?" I still have no answer to that question.

As a result, my title is in various senses misleading. The following reflections can be construed as "Reading Heidegger's *Black Notebooks*" only in the sense that reading part of a book is reading a book. Specifically, the title should be "Reading *Überlegungen II–VI (Schwarze Hefte 1931–1938)*"—hereafter referred to as "volume 94."[2] More importantly, I don't really know *how* one should read these texts, what they ask of us, and what our response to that invitation ought to be. My first thought was that we stand toward them much as the early readers of Nietzsche's notebooks from the 1880s stood toward his project for a book titled *The Will to Power.* I still think that this idea has merit, despite Heidegger's caution, dating from some time in the 1970s, that the "recordings" (*Aufzeichnungen*) in the *Black Notebooks* do not contain "notes for a planned system."[3] True as that is, it will be as tempting for readers of the *Black Notebooks* to find in them the key to the "real" Heidegger as it was for those early readers of Nietzsche's notebooks to find in them the key to his "real" doctrine—one of those readers being Heidegger himself. Richard Wolin, for instance, writes that "what the *Black Notebooks* now provide, in contrast to the lectures and theoretical treatises that have already been published, is access to Heidegger's *innermost philosophical thoughts.*"[4] I doubt that, but despite Heidegger's caveat, one of the most interesting things about volume 94 is the way it models itself in relation to the mistaken way that *Nietzsche's* notebooks have been read as "notes for a planned system." Beyond Heidegger's familiar claim that Nietzsche remains a captive of metaphysics, the language of volume 94, if I read it correctly, suggests that it has been guided by Nietzsche's notebooks in roughly the way that Dante was guided by Virgil: "In the middle of the journey of [his] life," having "come to himself in a dark wood where the straight way was lost,"[5] Heidegger, seeking the Paradiso of an "other beginning," would find writerly guidance in one who himself had to remain in Purgatorio.

Beyond the obvious Nietzscheanism of Heidegger's numbered entries—many of them introduced by pithy, italicized words or phrases—and apart from the many overt and covert references to Nietzschean themes in the entries themselves, it is Nietzsche as an exemplar of how thinking demands to be written that most shapes the discursive structure of volume 94. And, as Heidegger was supposed to have said, "Nietzsche hat mich kaputt gemacht." Whatever may be found in the first volume of the *Black Notebooks*, which we do not possess, or in the later volumes, which as of this writing I have not read, the contents of volume 94 seem to tell us something about what this means.

Every reading implicates a reader—in this case, me. Given Heidegger's situation during the period covered by volume 94, the most salient thing about me is that I am a professor of philosophy at a university—"ein bestallter Lehrer der Philosophie," as Heidegger puts it, writing about himself with deep ambivalence[6]—and I have written extensively about Heidegger. Since I pursue philosophical questions phenomenologically, however, I engage with Heidegger's writings not so much as a historian but as someone who holds that Heidegger, like Husserl and others, is a source of indispensable phenomenological insights. I confess, then, that I am not a great fan of the "middle" Heidegger, preoccupied with *Seinsgeschichte*, who comes into his own during the period spanned by volume 94. For this is Heidegger at his least phenomenological.

Beginning in 1912 and concluding around 1931 (perhaps the missing first *Notebook* could help us be more precise here), Heidegger is a phenomenologist, and again in the early 1950s he returns to a recognizably phenomenological idiom and practice, emblematized by his claim, in 1962, that "our task is to cease all overcoming, and leave metaphysics to itself."[7] But I have never been able to make much philosophical sense of this middle period—one that not coincidentally includes Heidegger's ill-fated entry into university politics, and so also the politics of the National Socialist regime. There seems little in it that can be redeemed on the basis of phenomenological evidence, and so I have taken the massive historical armature developed in these works to be a more or less provocative *Irrweg*—a view embraced within the *Black Notebooks* by Heidegger himself, at least as a question: "Perhaps only my *errors* still have the power to provoke in an age that is over-burdened by truths from which the truth has long been missing."[8]

The idea that *Irre* is inseparable from truth is a theme from this period that incensed Heidegger's critics, prompting Habermas to suggest that the narrative of *Seinsgeschichte* should be read as a mythological self-indemnification following upon Heidegger's disastrous political engagement. Much of it looked like that to me. Certainly, nothing is easier than to cherry-pick passages from volume 94 that strongly suggest that Heidegger is talking nonsense. Richard Wolin offers this example, hardly the worst offender: "Yet Being—what is Being? It is It itself. The thinking that is to come must learn to experience that and to say it."[9] Still, one of the surprising effects, for me, of reading the *Black Notebooks* has been the growing conviction that Heidegger's obsessions during this period are anything but subterfuge. What we seem to find there is the emergence of an authentic project, which might be phrased: *Wozu Philosophen in dürftiger Zeit?* What are philosophers for in a time of need? It is in light of *this* question that these texts ask to be understood, and since they were clearly meant for publication, they seek to *communicate*. Thus it is hardly surprising to find Heidegger returning repeatedly to matters of authorship and audience here, since the nature and possibility of communication lie within the scope of questioning, in *print*, the vocation of philosophy. The *Black Notebooks* ask us to consider what it might mean, now, to think philosophically by calling what we think we know about philosophy into question.

Do we really know that doing so does not entail a return to the "first beginning" so as to "preserve its *Anfänglichkeit*"?[10] What if it were true that philosophical scholarship (which Heidegger calls *Historie*) is far less important than the "futural" *Geschichtlichkeit* of "essential decision"? Isn't it possible that science, *Geltung,* is a large part of the problem, not the solution? What would it mean to take seriously the idea that we now occupy an "age of passage"[11] in which thinking's task is to attend to the "signs" of the "passing god"—or perhaps even the idea that "only a god can save us"? Is there any easy way to decide these questions, at least if they are understood as serious ones arising neither from a philosophy professor seeking "verification" through phenomenological evidence nor from a self-indemnifying failed politician, but instead from one who is trying to be nothing but a thinker? Might not the answers challenge our current ideals of individual autonomy and equality? These ideals are not things that we should easily give up, but that does not mean that they, or anything else, can serve as philosophical bedrock. What if all philosophy could offer, now, were the demand that we be open to some new questions?

2   Questions

Doesn't volume 94 bear out Heidegger's own long-familiar account of what led to his involvement in university politics and the peculiar sort of resistance to the regime that followed his disillusionment with (or rejection by) actually existing National Socialism? Why shouldn't we expect such resistance to be focused in the only arena where Heidegger mattered, the arena of thought? When in a 1935 lecture course Heidegger spoke of the "inner truth and greatness of this movement"—that is, of National Socialism—he apparently did not deliver the parenthetical remark that showed up both in the version he published in 1953 as *Einführung in die Metaphysik* and in the *Gesamtausgabe* version, published in 1983: "namely, the encounter between global technology and modern man." When the addition was made cannot be determined, since the relevant page in the manuscript is missing, but the idea, advanced by Habermas among others, that the addition represents "a later self-understanding falsely projected back to 1935," seems undercut by the "considerations" we find in volume 94.[12]

What in 1933 others noted as Heidegger's *Privat-Nationalsozialismus* is extensively treated in volume 94 under the heading of "spiritual National Socialism." This is no mere "'theoretical' foundation" for the political movement but a "constructing in advance" in which "what is decisive" is the "attuning and vision-generating [*bildschaffende*] power of the projection." Such a spiritual National Socialism is "just as necessary" as the political and social movement, but it is not what the movement calls the "brain workers" that are supposed to complement its "manual workers."[13] Spiritual National Socialism guards against such "bourgeois-ification [*Verbürgerlichung*] of the movement" by "destroying" the "spirit of the bourgeoisie" together with the "bourgeois-managed 'spirit' (culture)."[14]

No doubt Heidegger had political hopes for "the movement" in 1933, but his tone soon changes. In an entry from 1934, introduced as an "*Abschiedsrede*," Heidegger takes leave of the hopes expressed in his *Rektoratsrede* by imaginatively addressing his younger "comrades" who are "poised to leap into a new beginning," while he himself "stands at the end of a failed year." The year has not been "lost," however, since "failure is the highest form of human experience."[15] Heidegger acknowledges a "great error,"[16] but it is not the error of backing the regime. In his mind, he never did belong to it, and the *Black Notebooks* are replete with mockery of its platitudes. Rather, the error lay in believing that the student body had a yearning for radical "questioning" and could be led to recognize its destiny therein.[17] The fault was not in spiritual National Socialism as such but in Heidegger's Nietzschean "prematurity"—"the moment of my engagement [*Einsatz*] was too early"[18]— and in the belief that thinking could have immediate "effects."[19] That very thinking, in turn, had "risked too little what would alienate" and had "rushed too soon into what would be intelligible."[20] In any case, by 1935 Heidegger had indeed begun, as Christian E. Lewalter claimed with Heidegger's concurrence, to see actually existing National Socialism as a "further symptom of decline" in the *Verfallsgeschichte der Metaphysik*,[21] while retaining a belief in the "inner truth and greatness" of spiritual National Socialism. However dubious it is as an editorial practice, the parenthetical remark pretty accurately represents what National Socialism had always meant to Heidegger, and certainly by 1935.

Was Heidegger wrong or self-serving to see his "error" in these terms, rather than in the terms imposed on his project by right-thinking people, then and now? Heidegger's use of militaristic—and even "fascist" (Habermas)—language can be appalling, but are we so sure we understand it? If we see actually existing National Socialism as Heidegger himself saw it—as the naive response to a crisis whose roots lie in philosophy—might it not be that Heidegger was both politically naive (or indeed, vicious) and *correct* in his diagnosis?

In any case, this is the picture that seems to emerge from the "recordings" Heidegger made at the time in his *Black Notebooks*. But *did* he make them at the time? As Peter Trawny writes in his editor's afterword, "The manuscripts," now housed in Marbach, "have been revised and corrected. They show very few slips of the pen. The earlier drafts are not extant."[22] Further, internal evidence shows that in some cases Heidegger has organized them in ways that may not reflect their original composition. For instance, it is likely that the heading "Aus der Zeit des Rektorats"[23] was a later addition, and possibly also the order of the writings that fall under it. So again our question: How do we read what is recorded here?

Trawny claims that their closest generic relative would be the "philosophical diary [*Denktagebuch*],"[24] and that seems right, but the emphasis must be placed on *Denken* if we hope to read the *Tagebuch* correctly. What then does Heidegger's diary tell us about his engagement in university politics and his subsequent withdrawal?

At the outset we find a series of purely philosophical complaints. The early pages are full of reflections on the reception of *Being and Time*, a text whose point has been missed entirely. Instead of renewing the question of being, academic "gossip and chatter"[25] has assimilated it to Jaspers's existentialism or to ontology in the manner of Nicolai Hartmann.[26] The emphasis on individual existence was not the main thing; it served only to get beyond the "philosophy of consciousness."[27] Even if everyone missed the point, however, by 1931 Heidegger recognizes that he himself is partly to blame. The writings from the period have all become "alien" to him.[28] There will be no second edition of *Being and Time*, since this would amount to a complete rethinking and rewriting.[29] The "great enemy"[30] or opponent who could "refute" *Being and Time* by succeeding in doing what it failed adequately to do—namely, to motivate a certain kind of philosophical *Verantwortlichkeit*[31]— has not appeared, so Heidegger must become his own "great enemy."[32] The response to *Being and Time* demonstrates the need to overcome the question of being as it is posed there, since this question limits itself to being as grounded in *Dasein*'s understanding of being.[33] Now, in contrast, there must be "no philosophy for its own sake"; rather, its role is to "maintain the severity of the clarity of the concept" in thinking the truth of being itself.[34]

However, overcoming the standpoint of *Being and Time* seemed to require a venture into metaphysics, the traditional locus of the bond between the truth of being and the "human being" (*der Mensch*). In the works of the late 1920s and early 1930s—Heidegger's "meta-physical decade"[35]—Heidegger experiments with a "free world-projection" of the human being's place in "beings as such and as a whole" based on the ontology of *Dasein* as care. Given many different names—metontology, metaphysical ontic, metapolitics—it is this project, prefigured in *Being and Time*,[36] that leads Heidegger into the arms of the National Socialists and underwrites his belief, soon recognized as erroneous, that philosophy can take the lead in reforming the university. The metaphysics of *Dasein* rejects the tradi-tional definition of human being in terms of "life" (*animale rationale*) and instead locates that essence in *Dasein*'s character as *Welt-bildend* (world-forming, world-imagining). As forming and imagining, the human being stands under a "historical mandate" since it *is* the "happening" of the "world event [*Weltereignis*]" (p. 96).[37] For Heidegger, this means that metaphysics shows the human being's destiny to lie in the "empowering of being [*Ermächtigung des Seins*]."[38]

But such empowering cannot *now* be accomplished without undoing the "disempower-ing of essence [*Entmächtigung des Wesens*]"[39] that took place in the "first beginning," when being came to be understood as *idea*. The "history" of metaphysics—that is, the pos-sibility-generating power of the first beginning in the form of such disempowering—thus calls for a "second" or "new" or "other" beginning. The identification of being with *idea* leads to nihilism: the *"Sinnlosigkeit des Sinnes."*[40] Why, however, does this metaphysical picture bring Heidegger into alliance with National Socialism, or rather, to the idea of a spiritual National Socialism that allows him to personalize being itself as "our"—that is, Germans'—being?[41] Why is it that "the German alone can poetize Being anew and renew the essence of *theoria* and create logic"?[42] How does it happen that Heidegger's late and systematically rather vestigial mention of a "people" (*Volk*) in *Being and Time*[43] metasta-sizes, some five years later, into a full-blown *völkisch* metaphysics?

This too is a function of the ambiguously metaphysical character of Heidegger's think-ing at this time. The human being finds itself thrown into the world, which, as *Weltereignis,* is historical (i.e., *futural*). To speak of the futural here is to emphasize that what things mean is not a function of their history as *historia rerum gestarum*; rather, such meaning is always at issue, a matter of what is possible. If, therefore, the human being cannot be adequately characterized in terms of the "ontic" notions of natural, cultural, or historical situatedness, it nevertheless involves an aspect of "contingency" that appears to be insepa-rable from a certain sort of particularity. Hence Heidegger can write that "the *metaphysics of Dasein* must, according to its innermost constitution, deepen and extend itself into the *metapolitics of 'the' historical people.*"[44]

What this means is by no means clear, particularly in light of the quotes around *the*, but in the first discussion of politics in the *Black Notebooks*, Heidegger links metaphysics, in Nietzschean fashion, to the idea of "assuming [control over] what is [*das Seiende*] in and through breeding [*Zucht*] the empowering of being" in "the young"—whom Heidegger pointedly distinguishes from "the youth [*die Jugend*]."[45] If now the "world is being transformed" and "the human being stands in the breach,"[46] the moment is ripe for a metaphysical turn, for eradicating, through breeding, that which stands in the way of the empowering of being. Heidegger sees both the old *Bildungs* ideal (with its disempowering of being through the *idea*) and the new National Socialist educational program in which philosophy provides "support and justification for some political program"[47] as parts of the problem. "Breeding," then, is another name for metapolitics, the struggle with the ancients over the *Anfänglichkeit* of the first beginning.[48] In contrast to prior ages of "freeing through enlightenment," such struggle today requires binding ourselves to the "originary powers" to be found in the tradition.[49] Compared to that struggle, the work of *Being and Time* was mere "play."[50]

Spiritual National Socialism is the name for this struggle, but its essence is not of today.[51] With that admission, however, the whole of Heidegger's "ontic" vocabulary is thrust into ambiguity. In the German *Volk*, ordinary "ontic" Germans, Heidegger senses "a glorious awakening of *volkliche* will" and an opportunity "to reconnect the most secret *volkliche* mandate [*Auftrag*] of the Germans with the great beginning."[52] But these very same ontic Germans of today "lack patience,"[53] and they are *a-tolmos*.[54] What "German" means, metaphysically, is just the "historical mandate" itself, an aptitude for which must be prepared by a breeding that "incites the clarity of questioning and shelters the severity of the concept."[55] Thus the "German" is, at best, something futural, and the decision that confronts it comes not from geopolitical threats but from the "first beginning." It is the decision in the face of this mandate that transforms Germans from a mass into a *Volk*, not any concern with "Germanness [*Deutschheit*]."[56]

Thus, it is hardly surprising that Heidegger's view of metaphysics as metapolitics would lead him, however reluctantly,[57] to engage in university reform. If the sole effect of philosophy is to confront a person with the decision of whether to risk another beginning, must it not look as though the traditional university structure, its technological conception of science, and its antiquarian view of history and culture were part of the problem? If it were indeed true that the global crisis had its roots in an ancient and overlooked way of seeing things—that is, in the first beginning's disempowering of being through the *idea*—how *could* one in good conscience maintain the university's status quo? Heidegger's proposals for restructuring the university may seem naive and opportunistic,[58] but beyond all facile Plato-in-Syracuse analogies and all scoffing at *den Führer führen*, if one believes that philosophy is at the root of the crisis, will one not also reasonably think that a philosophical struggle is also at the root of its overcoming? It may be a strange nationalism that finds the referent of its term solely in the future, but Heidegger cannot be blamed for playing the hand he was dealt. Heidegger soon recognized that his hopes for metapolitics were doomed by the imperatives of ontic politics. *Überlegungen IV* makes continual note of the Rektorat's "abject failure," and indeed its *necessary* failure. But where does that leave us? Today, once again, there is everywhere a call for university reform, and philosophy, reduced to platitudes about "critical thinking," is hardly at the forefront. Instead, we have "best practices" drawn from the corporate world, students-as-consumers, and the hegemony of what Heidegger calls *Machenschaft*, in which humanistic learning has no place—indeed, is no longer understood at all. And the wider political landscape? Given the global sclerosis in domestic and international politics, war without end, the polarization of wealth and opinion, environmental degradation, and other grim realities, does one really sound like a total crank, beyond the pale of reasonableness, to say, as Heidegger said, that while National Socialism was indeed a failure, "I am not convinced that democracy is the answer"?[59] What would it mean for us, now, to take philosophy seriously?

The obvious reply is that politically we have no choice but to muddle through; working piecemeal, with the help of experts, is always better than entrusting ourselves to apocalyptic visions. But what if this gamble, this belief that we know how things are, is wrong? What if our situation is such that this attitude is both a symptom of the problem and a contributing factor? For a philosopher—who, as Richard Rorty knew, is not the same thing as a pragmatist—this complacent stance will not suffice. It is a failure of nerve and an admission of defeat. It may well be that philosophy should not have a seat at this table, but such is the question forced on us by the metaphysical interpretation—Heidegger's own interpretation—of his time as rector.

Heidegger, in any case, did not abandon philosophy. If he once believed that university politics was a philosophical way out of the "stall" in which a philosophy professor of his time flourished,[60] what was he to do when his bet on actually existing Germans fell through?

One thing he might have done is to spend the rest of his life developing a vast mythology that would relieve him of responsibility for his actions and decisions. Another might be to reflect on the task of philosophy to see what could have gone wrong with the "metaphysical" view of things, in which a peculiar sort of futural nationalism was to have "effects" on good old ontic nationalism. The latter path seems suggested by the *Black Notebooks*, as Heidegger increasingly realizes that being in a "time of passage" requires "those in passage" to "step back" from direct engagement.[61] This step back is grounded in the fundamental commitment of Heidegger's postrectoral thinking: "that we *don't have* the truth."[62] Under such circumstances, thinking can have only a "preparatory" role. What does such thinking look and sound like?

3   Heidegger's Esoteric Philosophy

Is Heidegger's commitment to the idea that we don't have the truth anything more than an excuse for philosophical mystification? To say that we don't have the truth is not to say that we cannot be correct much of the time; rather, it is to challenge the dominance of the correct as the measure of what is.[63] But what other measure of thinking could there be, and what form would thinking in light of such a measure take?[64] These questions are pursued in *Überlegungen IV–VI* (1934–1938), and they are nothing if not questions of reading, writing, and communicating. To answer them Heidegger adopts Nietzsche as his Virgil, a guide who helps him imagine those to whom he is speaking and how he must speak to them.

To approach Heidegger's new commitment as a literary question, a question of how to write and read, we first note how Heidegger's characterization of his situation changes after the Rektorat. Recall that his own analysis of the failure rests, in part, on his belief that his engagement was "premature."[65] After the Rektorat, Heidegger confronts the communicative implications of the futurality that had already played a major role in his attempted metaphysics of *Dasein*, implications reinforced by Heidegger's dawning recognition that the time of passage is not from one metaphysical beginning to another, but from metaphysics to what it "forgets" and conceals. Nietzsche stands at the threshold here.

It is of course not hard to see those Heidegger calls "*die Übergänglichen,*" among whom he counts himself, as heirs of Zarathustra—a bridge to the overman that Nietzsche himself would not cross. Through his "turn away" (*Wendung*) from metaphysics, Nietzsche cannot escape its Platonistic pull. Nietzsche's thinking has "the power to provoke" us toward the other beginning, but not in its own terms. This is because "our" task—and here Heidegger speaks of himself alone, though in anticipation of readers—is different. As persevering in the passage from "a concern with beings … to the question of being itself," we no longer, like Nietzsche, "turn away" from something. Indeed, this is "at bottom no longer a turning at all, but the passage into a wholly other beginning that, *as* the other, returns the first and only One—the *aletheia tes phuseos*—to itself and precisely does *not* disavow it."[66]

But to anticipate readers in this way is to confess that one does not have them. The thinking of the other beginning is thus addressed to "the few."[67] After the Rektorat Heidegger's thinking can rightly be called—following the title of Trawny's book—an "esoteric philosophy."[68] Heidegger's previous *Lehrtätigkeit*, his supposedly "historical" (*historisch*) lecture courses, were "masks," not to be understood as "historical examinations of what is past" but as "*geschichtliche Besinnungen,*" which would enable their hearers to "authentically experience the happening—namely, in its originary futurality."[69] Though they fell on deaf ears, these *Vorspiele einer Philosophie der Zukunft* remain necessary. Placing his hopes in "those few who will come later and will grasp what *geschichtliche Besinnung* means for those of us in passage," Heidegger sees the lectures as a necessary prerequisite for what he calls "true nonstudents."[70] The few must pass through these exoteric presentations in order to learn to recognize the difference between a "historically [*historisch*] false" interpretation and the teacher's genuinely *geschichtlich*, futural, message. "But such [nonstudents] are rare. Hence a philosophy can be creatively understood, at the earliest, 100 years *after* its appearance."[71]

Nietzsche had grasped this point, but the earlier Heidegger had not: what a philosophy in passage must *say* "stands opposed, in its essentiality, to becoming known by the many."[72] Heidegger sees his own failure now as a "failure of self-confidence," a failure to draw the ultimate literary and communicative conclusions "from what I already knew"[73]—that is, a failure "to leap far enough ahead," instead "risking too little what is alienating and counting too early on intelligibility."[74] In volume 94, Heidegger often adopts the first-person singular—not because he is giving us access his "innermost philosophical thoughts" in a diary, but because thinking is *einsam* and demands it.[75] Heidegger can embrace this grammatical mode thanks to the courage he has gained through his failure, but "the form of this philosophy will necessarily be very ramified and peculiar."[76]

The form of volume 94, the literary quality of the text, is determined by Heidegger's newfound willingness to "risk what is alienating," but that also means "it is time to disappear from the public."[77] The esoteric doctrine of *Denken* and *Besinnung* is for the few, "who will be defenseless in the public sphere."[78] The whole literary-metaphysical complex of science, correctness, meaning, and *Geltung* will make it impossible for such thinking to be heard as anything but self-indulgent mythmaking. Heidegger knows he is defenseless. There was no need to wait for Internet memes to link *Dasein* with Dada; Heidegger did it for us. Thinking perhaps of Carnap, he writes: "From the side of the 'disciplinarians' ['*massgebender*'], philosophy has now been declared 'dadaism.'" But these schoomarms "are more correct than they know." The characterization "does in fact pertain to philosophy—from the point of view of those excluded from it." Defenseless, Heidegger continues: If "bringing being to word" is equated with "dadaism," we must ask "Where are we, when such an idea becomes possible and this 'way of conceiving' philosophy takes the lead in the construction of 'German culture'"?[79]

How to bring being to word? Early on, before taking courage, Heidegger had seen the problem: The point is the "empowering of being"—but "by means of treatises? Certainly not—rather, solely through *that* happening that ripens and clears in the thrown understanding that [such treatises] require."[80] The treatises themselves are secondary.[81] Still, Heidegger asks, "must there not be communication?" Yes of course, he answers, but "not the kind that makes appeal to the masses [*massenhafte*]."[82] Instead, "there is a hidden communication through the *essence*"—which, because of its hiddenness, is not properly called "communication."[83] The "aloneness of the individual arising from the essential ground of things cannot be forced into the 'singleness' of community, however zealous the latter might be for the '*thou* relation' and however seemingly eager for 'authority.'"[84] Instead, it is a matter of conviction or "belief," "reliance on the ground" (*Vertrautsein im Grund*):

Knowing and believing—I cannot ever know that I know—if I know—but can only believe that I know. This *believing*, then, the originarily attuned reliance on the ground—the grounding swing in the *Grundstimmung*. Hence nonsense: to set as a measure for being and the question of being absolute certainty as self-knowing knowledge (evidence). Out of this conviction [*Glauben*] (grounding of the ground) the poetizing thinking in inquiring into being.[85]

Das dichtende Denken. Here Heidegger names the literary form of the *Black Notebooks*. But his thoughts about it are in flux.

In 1931 he sounds like a Deleuzian, illustrating the point by means of the concept of thinking itself: To say "thinking is ..."—that is, to characterize thinking in some way—is

already a kind of poetizing: "Such circumscribing poetizes from itself; for what thinking is is nowhere simply found and gathered up—but reveals itself only to a prescribing-
forming [*vorschreibend-bildenden*] projection," a projection that is "the reaching-out to the
concept."[86] So conceptual thought is already poetizing. The human being is *Welt-bildend*.
"People are always taking issue with my '*Bildersprache*,'" Heidegger remarks, "as though
language were ever spoken in any other way."[87] But he soon comes to see poetizing thinking otherwise. If at first he considers it a mark of Selbst*be*hauptung, after the Rektorat, in
the time of passage where thinking can only be preparatory, he abjures the idea that such
thinking can "build." Radical questioning is "Selbst*ent*hauptung."[88]

For Heidegger, this Selbst*ent*hauptung changes the meaning of poetizing thinking. After
the Rektorat, "the thinker's thinking is pondering: he meditates on what the poet"—here,
Hölderlin—"has already poetized." Such pondering is not, however, "the bringing-to-con-
cepts of what was previously presented in poetic form—as thinking-after it must follow
along on the indicated path."[89] Poetizing thinking must find its own form.[90] In volume 94
Heidegger calls this form "naming" (*Nennen*) and asks, "Why is the word, especially the
simple naming-saying-questioning [word], so impotent today"?[91] How can we "arrive, and
arrive once more, at the simplicity of the grounding word"?[92] But Heidegger's understanding of naming is not what it would become in the later writings on language. Here, it is
inserted precisely in the "historical" reflection of one who thinks and writes in a time of
passage. What does naming look like in such times?

Perhaps the most important literary lesson Heidegger draws from his Virgilian Nietzsche
is that a form of writing is possible that is neither a finished work nor a fragment. In
volume 94 Heidegger understands *Werk* as he did in *The Origin of the Work of Art*: it is
the site where the essential is "put up for decision" by installing the strife between earth
and world "in a being."[93] In the Artwork essay Heidegger admits that it remains a question
whether art can still "work" in this way today, and the situation is no less questionable in
the case of thinking. "The thinking of the beginning must abandon the idea of coming to
rest in a well-rounded 'work.'"[94] Instead, the challenge is precisely to see whether, "from
the fact that the secret of history left us only with fragments, we can finally learn something about the *manner* in which we have to bring before us a *denkerisches Werk* and pass
it on to those who come after."[95] What Heidegger learns, then, is that neither Hölderlin's
poetry[96] nor Nietzsche's writings are properly understood as "fragments," elements of a
work whose conditions were already in place but that was never completed. Rather, he
finds in them a distinctly futural kind of writing that, in the case of Nietzsche—"the most
futural thinker"[97]—becomes Heidegger's own exemplar.

Against the interpretation of *Wille zur Macht* as a fragment of a planned system—a
reading that mirrors the general tendency of *das Heutige* (including the National Socialists, and including even Heidegger's early self) "to collapse back into 'metaphysics' as
usual"[98]—Heidegger recognizes that what looks fragmentary is a new literary form that
"*sets the end* of Western philosophy first of all in motion."[99] Thus "all efforts—including

Nietzsche's own—in the direction of an ordinary forming of a work [*Werkgestaltung*] are off the mark: for as little as the beginning can be something finished, neither can the essential end."[100] Instead, Heidegger discerns in Nietzsche a response to the claim of a "hidden work form [*verborgene Werkgestalt*]," a way of writing for a time of passage. That Nietzsche combined such a response with an "explicit effort toward a finished work [*ausgesprochene Werkbemühung*]" is because he "still followed a path through Plato that denied him the leap into the free"[101]—that is, he thought "*against* metaphysics but still with its property, employing its distinctions and concepts."[102]

Here Heidegger condemns his own metaphysical decade as well, and with the distinction between "hidden work form" and "explicit effort toward a finished work," he indicates the point at which Nietzsche the writer must remain in Purgatorio. Heidegger understands better than Nietzsche himself did that writing the "passage" has its own form. From the Dantescan perspective of one who has recognized the healing distinction between the *Leitfrage* and the *Grundfrage*,[103] Heidegger can recognize that Nietzsche's entire corpus (not just the *Nachlass*) must be read as feeling its way toward the "hidden work form."[104] But it will be for Heidegger to write in such a way that we are brought before "Greek thinking" (i.e., the first and only beginning) not "to renew it" but "to free ourselves from what is outmoded (i.e., what has become stale and common), in order that we may allow that which measures [*das Maßstäbliche*] to dawn on us."[105] Thus Nietzsche is a literary exemplar for a kind of writing akin to silence.

After the war Jaspers argued against reinstating Heidegger's right to teach, terming the latter's thinking "dictatorial." But the *Black Notebooks* suggest someone who has recognized that there is no place in the public sphere for the kind of thinking called for today. Thus they make great demands on us as readers. Commenting on the difficulty of placing oneself in the appropriate relation to Nietzsche's writings, Heidegger noted twin dangers: taking them as "finished works" allows for "simple-minded refutation," while treating them as "unfinished"—as fragments—leads to "the arbitrary combination of apparently random pieces."[106] I cannot say that this chapter, now nearing its conclusion, has altogether avoided the latter danger. To avoid it requires that one be up to the task of thinking in the form appropriate to a time of passage.

Was Rorty then right that Heidegger's late work only has a private significance and that Heidegger was wrong to expect his readers to take from it any more than an aesthetic pleasure—or to shrink from it in aesthetic horror? Elsewhere I have argued that Heidegger's ontology in *Being and Time*, which I defend on phenomenological grounds, entails something like an ethics of discourse drawn from authentic *Dasein*'s accountability for reasons.[107] From this point of view, I read Heidegger's complaint that "Nietzsche hat mich kaputt gemacht" as an admission that his own supposedly historically mandated esoteric form of thinking was a dead end. And I have already confessed my suspicions about the phenomenological legitimacy of Heidegger's middle-period fascination with *Seinsgeschichte*. But for all that, I cannot see that Heidegger's *Kampf um die Maßstäbe* is any less pressing for us than it was for him.

Notes

An earlier version of this chapter was delivered at a conference on Heidegger's *Black Notebooks* held on September 11–12, 2014, at the CUNY Graduate Center. My thanks go to Richard Wolin, the conference organizer, and other participants for discussions that have materially improved the chapter.

1. See, for instance, Rorty's claim that Heidegger "was never able to see politics or art as more than epiphenomenal—never able to shake off the philosophy professor's conviction that everything else stands to philosophy as superstructure to base" (Richard Rorty, "Heidegger, Contingency, and Pragmatism," in Richard Rorty, *Philosophical Papers*, vol. 2: *Essays on Heidegger and Others* [Cambridge: Cambridge University Press, 1991], 49).

2. Martin Heidegger, *Überlegungen II–VI (Schwarze Hefte 1931–1938), Gesamtausgabe* 94, ed. Peter Trawny (Frankfurt: Klostermann, 2014). All translations from volume 94 are my own.

3. *Überlegungen II–VI, Gesamtausgabe* 94, p. 1.

4. Richard Wolin, "National Socialism, World Jewry, and the History of Being: Heidegger's *Black Notebooks*," *Jewish Review of Books*, summer 2014, 40.

5. Dante, *Dante's Inferno*, trans. John D. Sinclair (New York: Oxford University Press, 1970), 23.

6. *Überlegungen II–VI, Gesamtausgabe* 94, p. 83.

7. Martin Heidegger, "Time and Being," in *On Time and Being*, trans. Joan Stambaugh (New York: Harper & Row, 1972), 24. See also Tobias Keiling, *Seinsgeschichte und phänomenologischer Realismus: Eine Interpretation und Kritik der Spätphilosophie Heideggers* (Tübingen: Mohr Siebeck, 2015).

8. *Überlegungen II–VI, Gesamtausgabe* 94, p. 404.

9. Wolin, "National Socialism, World Jewry, and the History of Being," 41.

10. *Überlegungen II–VI, Gesamtausgabe* 94, p. 100.

11. *Überlegungen II–VI, Gesamtausgabe* 94, p. 100.

12. See Martin Heidegger, *An Introduction to Metaphysics*, trans. Ralph Mannheim (New Haven, CT: Yale University Press, 1959), 199; Martin Heidegger, *Einführung in die Metaphysik, Gesamtausgabe* 40, ed. Petra Jaeger (Frankfurt: Klostermann, 1983), 208; Jürgen Habermas, "Martin Heidegger—Werk und Weltanschauung," in Jürgen Habermas, *Texte und Kontexte* (Frankfurt: Suhrkamp, 1991), 74f.

13. *Überlegungen II–VI, Gesamtausgabe* 94, pp. 134–135.

14. *Überlegungen II–VI, Gesamtausgabe* 94, p. 136.

15. *Überlegungen II–VI, Gesamtausgabe* 94, pp. 160–161.

16. *Überlegungen II–VI, Gesamtausgabe* 94, p. 278.

17. *Überlegungen II–VI, Gesamtausgabe* 94, p. 286.

18. *Überlegungen II–VI, Gesamtausgabe* 94, p. 155.

19. *Überlegungen II–VI, Gesamtausgabe* 94, p. 378.

20. *Überlegungen II–VI, Gesamtausgabe* 94, p. 448.

21. Lewalter, quoted in Habermas, "Martin Heidegger—Werk und Weltanschauung," 74.

22. *Überlegungen II–VI, Gesamtausgabe* 94, p. 534.

23. *Überlegungen II–VI, Gesamtausgabe* 94, p. 111.

24. *Überlegungen II–VI, Gesamtausgabe* 94, p. 531.

25. *Überlegungen II–VI, Gesamtausgabe* 94, p. 9.

26. *Überlegungen II–VI, Gesamtausgabe* 94, p. 10.

27. *Überlegungen II–VI, Gesamtausgabe* 94, p. 21.

28. *Überlegungen II–VI, Gesamtausgabe* 94, p. 19.

29. *Überlegungen II–VI, Gesamtausgabe* 94, p. 22.

30. *Überlegungen II–VI, Gesamtausgabe* 94, p. 9.

31. *Überlegungen II–VI, Gesamtausgabe* 94, p. 16. Ingo Farin has suggested that the indecipherable symbol that shows up on this page as well as on a few other pages might stand for *Verantwortlichkeit*, since it appears to be

a combination of V and A.

32. *Überlegungen II–VI, Gesamtausgabe* 94, p. 37.

33. *Überlegungen II–VI, Gesamtausgabe* 94, pp. 67–69, 75–76.

34. *Überlegungen II–VI, Gesamtausgabe* 94, p. 92.

35. On this designation, see Steven Crowell, *Husserl, Heidegger, and the Space of Meaning: Paths Toward Transcendental Phenomenology* (Evanston, IL: Northwestern University Press, 2001), chap. 12.

36. For instance, Heidegger there mentions "a 'metaphysic of death'" that would include questions "of how and when death 'came into the world,'" and "what 'meaning' it can have and is to have as an evil and affliction in the aggregate of entities" (Martin Heidegger, *Being and Time*, trans. John Maquarrie and Edward Robinson (New York: Harper & Row, 1962), 292).

37. *Überlegungen II–VI, Gesamtausgabe* 94, p. 96. Heidegger later (*Überlegungen II–VI, Gesamtausgabe* 94, p. 407) rejects the language of "happening," in part because of its popularity.

38. *Überlegungen II–VI, Gesamtausgabe* 94, p. 62.

39. *Überlegungen II–VI, Gesamtausgabe* 94, p. 89.

40. *Überlegungen II–VI, Gesamtausgabe* 94, p. 424.

41. *Überlegungen II–VI, Gesamtausgabe* 94, p. 73.

42. *Überlegungen II–VI, Gesamtausgabe* 94, p. 27.

43. Heidegger, *Being and Time*, 436: "Destiny" is "how we designate the historizing of the community, of a people [*Volk*]."

44. *Überlegungen II–VI, Gesamtausgabe* 94, p. 124.

45. *Überlegungen II–VI, Gesamtausgabe* 94, pp. 61–62, 124.

46. *Überlegungen II–VI, Gesamtausgabe* 94, p. 63.

47. *Überlegungen II–VI, Gesamtausgabe* 94, p. 61.

48. *Überlegungen II–VI, Gesamtausgabe* 94, p. 63. The German terms *Zucht, zuchten*, and their derivatives— like the English terms "breeding," "to breed," and so on—have quite a wide semantic field. On the one hand, they are used in connection with what might be called "animal husbandry" and, more ominously, eugenics. On the other hand, they can refer to the instilling of humanistic qualities, "manners," in human agents. It is quite impossible, on the basis of volume 94 alone, to determine precisely where Heidegger's usage falls within this semantic range. On the one hand, there is no evidence that he is thinking about literal eugenics; on the other, his critique of the *Bildungs* ideal suggests that his notion of *Zucht und Zuchtung*, like Nietzsche's, is not synonymous with the equally available notions of *Erziehung* (education; *educere*). What *can* be said is that *Zucht* is bound up with Heidegger's notion of metapolitics, in which the educator plays a role very different from that of a Socratic interlocutor.

49. *Überlegungen II–VI, Gesamtausgabe* 94, p. 126.

50. *Überlegungen II–VI, Gesamtausgabe* 94, p. 68.

51. *Überlegungen II–VI, Gesamtausgabe* 94, p. 114.

52. *Überlegungen II–VI, Gesamtausgabe* 94, p. 109.

53. *Überlegungen II–VI, Gesamtausgabe* 94, p. 28.

54. *Überlegungen II–VI, Gesamtausgabe* 94, p. 95.

55. *Überlegungen II–VI, Gesamtausgabe* 94, p. 82. Later, Heidegger explicitly rejects the idea that such things can be bred. Referring to "the future human being" he asks, "Can we 'breed' them? No. The guardians [*Wächter*] must be able to watch/waken [*wachen können*] and for that must themselves be the most alert [*wachste*] and thereby the most inspired [*erweckteste*]." And such "metamorphosis of human being" is a matter of the "onset [*Anfall*] of Beying itself" (*Überlegungen II–VI, Gesamtausgabe* 94, pp. 334–335).

56. *Überlegungen II–VI, Gesamtausgabe* 94, pp. 92, 101. Nevertheless, race does play a part in it: "Race [*Rasse*]" is "only a condition on being a *Volk* but never what is unconditional and essential" (*Überlegungen II–VI, Gesamtausgabe* 94, p. 351; see also p. 189).

57. *Überlegungen II–VI, Gesamtausgabe* 94, p. 110.

58. For instance, he mentions the idea of separating the *Fachschulen,* like medicine and law, from the *Führerschulen,* where radical questioning and conceptual severity in the struggle for *Anfänglichkeit* would be bred (*Überlegungen II–VI, Gesamtausgabe* 94, p. 113).

59. Martin Heidegger, "'Only a God Can Save Us': *Der Spiegel*'s Interview with Martin Heidegger," in *The Heidegger Controversy: A Critical Reader*, ed. Richard Wolin (Cambridge, MA: MIT Press, 1993), 104.

60. *Überlegungen II–VI, Gesamtausgabe* 94, p. 83.

61. *Überlegungen II–VI, Gesamtausgabe* 94, p. 396.

62. *Überlegungen II–VI, Gesamtausgabe* 94, p. 332.

63. *Überlegungen II–VI, Gesamtausgabe* 94, p. 447.

64. Rorty ("Heidegger, Contingency, and Pragmatism," 36–37) rejects the very idea that what Heidegger was after had anything to do with "measures" of thinking; instead, he is supposed to want us to cultivate a poetic sensibility for contingency. But this is certainly not how Heidegger saw the matter, for whom "questioning [is] the *Kampf um die Maßstäbe*" (p. 278).

65. *Überlegungen II–VI, Gesamtausgabe* 94, p. 155.

66. *Überlegungen II–VI, Gesamtausgabe* 94, p. 322.

67. *Überlegungen II–VI, Gesamtausgabe* 94, p. 326.

68. Peter Trawny, *Adyton: Heideggers esoterische Philosophie* (Berlin: Matthes & Seitz, 2010).

69. *Überlegungen II–VI, Gesamtausgabe* 94, p. 358.

70. *Überlegungen II–VI, Gesamtausgabe* 94, p. 359.

71. *Überlegungen II–VI, Gesamtausgabe* 94, p. 359.

72. *Überlegungen II–VI, Gesamtausgabe* 94, p. 448.

73. *Überlegungen II–VI, Gesamtausgabe* 94, p. 303.

74. *Überlegungen II–VI, Gesamtausgabe* 94, p. 448.

75. *Überlegungen II–VI, Gesamtausgabe* 94, p. 304. See the remarks concerning the "groveling in the biographical" of which Heidegger accuses contemporary Nietzscheans, and his own explanation for Nietzsche's use of the first-person singular (*Überlegungen II–VI, Gesamtausgabe* 94, p. 374).

76. *Überlegungen II–VI, Gesamtausgabe* 94, p. 354.

77. *Überlegungen II–VI, Gesamtausgabe* 94, p. 98.

78. *Überlegungen II–VI, Gesamtausgabe* 94, p. 410.

79. *Überlegungen II–VI, Gesamtausgabe* 94, pp. 247–248.

80. *Überlegungen II–VI, Gesamtausgabe* 94, p. 39.

81. In denying that what is necessary can be accomplished by "writing the thickest books possible" (*Überlegungen II–VI, Gesamtausgabe* 94, p. 54), Heidegger is thinking of the failed enterprise of *Being and Time*. It is not inconceivable that he is also thinking of Jaspers, of whom he writes that "the sharpest objection to his 'thinking' is the extensiveness of his scribblings [*Schriftstellerei*], in which *not a single essential-thinking question* is to be found" (*Überlegungen II–VI, Gesamtausgabe* 94, p. 399).

82. *Überlegungen II–VI, Gesamtausgabe* 94, p. 54.

83. *Überlegungen II–VI, Gesamtausgabe* 94, p. 40.

84. *Überlegungen II–VI, Gesamtausgabe* 94, p. 40.

85. *Überlegungen II–VI, Gesamtausgabe* 94, p. 35.

86. *Überlegungen II–VI, Gesamtausgabe* 94, p. 65.

87. *Überlegungen II–VI, Gesamtausgabe* 94, p. 100.

88. *Überlegungen II–VI, Gesamtausgabe* 94, p. 65.

89. *Überlegungen II–VI, Gesamtausgabe* 94, p. 299.

90. *Überlegungen II–VI, Gesamtausgabe* 94, p. 354.

91. *Überlegungen II–VI, Gesamtausgabe* 94, p. 390.

92. *Überlegungen II–VI, Gesamtausgabe* 94, p. 391.

93. The "creators know beings from out of Beying, in that they set the truth of Beying into the 'work' and place it among beings, so that beings become more in being" (*Überlegungen II–VI, Gesamtausgabe* 94, p. 398).

94. *Überlegungen II–VI, Gesamtausgabe* 94, p. 354.

95. *Überlegungen II–VI, Gesamtausgabe* 94, p. 390.

96. *Überlegungen II–VI, Gesamtausgabe* 94, pp. 346, 403.

97. *Überlegungen II–VI, Gesamtausgabe* 94, p. 369.

98. *Überlegungen II–VI, Gesamtausgabe* 94, p. 370.

99. *Überlegungen II–VI, Gesamtausgabe* 94, p. 374.

100. *Überlegungen II–VI, Gesamtausgabe* 94, p. 374.

101. *Überlegungen II–VI, Gesamtausgabe* 94, p. 367.

102. *Überlegungen II–VI, Gesamtausgabe* 94, p. 377.

103. *Überlegungen II–VI, Gesamtausgabe* 94, p. 437.

104. *Überlegungen II–VI, Gesamtausgabe* 94, p. 376.

105. *Überlegungen II–VI, Gesamtausgabe* 94, p. 357.

106. *Überlegungen II–VI, Gesamtausgabe* 94, p. 453.

107. Steven Crowell, *Normativity and Phenomenology in Husserl and Heidegger* (Cambridge: Cambridge University Press, 2013), especially chap. 10.

4

The King Is Dead: Martin Heidegger after the *Black Notebooks*

Gregory Fried

As a human being, Martin Heidegger is dead; that much is certain. But there is another Heidegger, one who has remained very much alive through his writings, because his more than sixty years of philosophical contributions will amount to a collected works of over 100 volumes. Few thinkers of the past 100 years can rival his impact on twentieth- and now twenty-first-century philosophy. His work has influenced figures ranging from Jean-Paul Sartre and the existentialist Left in France; to Jacques Derrida and deconstructionism; to Jan Patočka, a founder of the Charta 77 movement in Czechoslovakia that launched a civic-intellectual resistance movement against the communist government; to Hans-Georg Gadamer and Jürgen Habermas in Germany—to mention only some of the best-known European figures who owe an intellectual debt to Heidegger. Then there are the German expatriates who came to the United States: Herbert Marcuse, an inspiration to the New Left; Leo Strauss, credited with providing the intellectual foundation for the neoconservatives; Paul Tillich, who channeled Heideggerian thought into theology; and Hannah Arendt, who probably did more than anyone else to secure Heidegger's reputation in the English-speaking world after World War II.[1] For decades, Heidegger's reach has also extended beyond Europe and North America: he is read seriously in Japan and China, in Latin America, even in Iran. Heidegger's reach is global.

But Heidegger's legacy also bears a dark stain, one that his influence has never quite managed to wash out. Why would Heidegger, one of the most celebrated philosophers of the last century, embrace National Socialism, one of the most infamous regimes of any century? That question underlies the uproar that has greeted the publication of the *Schwarze Hefte* (*Black Notebooks*), the collective name Heidegger gave to the black-covered journals in which he assembled his thoughts from the early 1930s to the early 1970s.[2] It is all the more striking that this uproar has occurred even before the more than 1,200 pages of these first three volumes of a planned twelve have been translated into English.[3]

Of course, Heidegger could not hide the fact that he had joined the Nazi Party in the spring of 1933 with great fanfare, that he had assumed the role of rector of Freiburg University as a representative of the regime, and that he had given impassioned speeches in support of the party, in particular for the decisive plebiscites of November 1933 that rallied support for Hitler's policies, both domestic and foreign.[4] There have also been clear indications of anti-Semitism, such as a 1929 letter of recommendation, discovered in 1989, in which Heidegger warned that "we stand before the choice of again providing forces and educators genuinely rooted in the soil for our German spiritual life or finally surrendering that life to a growing Jewification [*Verjudung*] in the wider and narrower sense."[5]

Nevertheless, Heidegger managed to emerge from World War II with his reputation mostly intact. The Allies' denazification program, which aimed to rid German society of Nazi ideology, targeted regime supporters like him. Freiburg came under French control, and the new authorities there forced Heidegger into retirement and forbade him to teach. But in 1950, the now independent university revoked the ban. This resulted in large part from Heidegger's outreach campaign to French intellectuals with anti-Nazi credentials, including Sartre and the resistance fighter Jean Beaufret. In short order, he won a wide following in France. Once Heidegger's international reputation was secure, the university gave him emeritus status and allowed him to resume teaching.[6] Despite Heidegger's well-known contempt for publicity and the media, he proved himself to be a master of public relations.[7]

Heidegger's Impact

When he began teaching after the First World War, Heidegger was just another obscure junior lecturer without a secure university position. He had published nothing of note. Nevertheless, in that early period, a strange kind of subterranean fame preceded him. Late in her life, Hannah Arendt described what it was like to be Martin Heidegger's student when he was a young teacher in Marburg, Germany. Heidegger's peculiar fame, she explained, was based entirely on the extraordinary effect of his lectures on the old works of the great figures in philosophy—Plato, Aristotle, Kant, and others—which opened up philosophical questions in ways that astonished the students: "These lectures dealt with texts that were generally familiar; they contained no doctrine that could have been learned, reproduced, and handed on. There was hardly more than a name, but the name traveled all over Germany like the rumor of the hidden king."[8] When Heidegger finally did publish *Being and Time*, the groundbreaking work that secured his fame and career nearly overnight in 1927, its triumphant reception stemmed in part from the eight years of adulation by students who expected no less of him than coronation as king in philosophy.

Those students included many who would go on to become influential thinkers in their own right. Ironically, many of them were Jews. Whatever Heidegger's anti-Semitism was then, he must have kept it private. He was clearly adept at wearing a mask for years, even decades. Heidegger's kingdom extended well beyond Jewish students. There was Gadamer, of course, and Habermas, an avid reader of Heidegger who was one of the few to criticize him openly after the war.[9] Most such students and admirers were shocked when he came out in support of the Nazis, and he managed to convince most of his followers after the war that this episode was merely a brief, clumsy attempt to protect the university until his resignation as its head in 1934.

What is particularly remarkable about Heidegger's legacy is its political diversity, from Leo Strauss on the Right, considered the founding inspiration for the neoconservative movement in the United States, to those on the Left such as Sartre and Derrida, who combined Heideggerian ideas with Marxism or forged new intellectual movements, such as deconstructionism. Even Marcuse's work, which played a key role in the emergence of the New Left and the counterculture of the 1960s through its critique of the dehumanizing effects of mass society, consumerism, and technology run amok, derived in part from Heidegger's analysis of human beings' everyday inauthenticity and his critique of modern hyperrationalism. Heidegger's diverse influence is all the more striking because, though his overt involvement with National Socialism in 1933 and 1934 has been widely known, his publications have had, until recently, virtually nothing to say about political philosophy or ethics as conventionally understood. That has changed in the last decade or so, with the posthumous publication of works long locked away, such as the *Notebooks*, where the link is unmistakable: "Thinking purely 'metaphysically' (that is, with the history of Be-ing [*Seyn*]), in the years 1930–1934 I took National Socialism as offering the possibility of a crossing-over to an other inception and gave it this meaning."[10] Note that this period dates from *1930*. This was three years before Hitler came to power, demonstrating that Heidegger took the movement seriously longer than most had suspected. Now the time has come for a reckoning.

The Core Question

The first three translated volumes comprise the *Black Notebooks* from 1931 to 1941. They contain writings in a variety of styles, from schematic notes to pithy observations and occasional translations from the Greek, but the great majority are entries ranging from a few paragraphs to essays of several pages. These are not off-the-cuff jottings; Heidegger clearly labored over them carefully, intending them "not as 'aphorisms' or 'clever adages' but as discreet signposts"[11] on the path to a revolutionary way of thinking he was formulating that would overturn over two millennia of Western thought. The period covered by the first three volumes includes the years during which the National Socialists rose to power and the outbreak of the Second World War. Heidegger's involvement in these world-historical events is well known: in April 1933, he accepted the leadership of Freiburg University under the new Nazi regime, joined the party in an elaborate public ceremony in May, helped enforce anti-Jewish laws against faculty and students, gave speeches in favor of Hitler's decisive plebiscite in November—and then abruptly resigned his position as head, or rector, of the university in April 1934.[12]

But what is it, specifically, about Heidegger's thought that has proved so gripping to so many? His writings are notoriously difficult because of the peculiar terminology he develops to express his ideas, but once one gets a feel for the core question he is asking, one can see that in seeking to overturn 2,500 years of Western thought he assumes he needs a new conceptual language for a new approach. That question is announced by the title of the work that made him famous in 1927: *Being and Time*. In the *Notebooks*, Heidegger returns often to that book, regretting some of its shortcomings but always reaffirming what remained essential to him: the question of the meaning of Being as the most fundamental question of all philosophy.[13] In English, the question of Being might best be expressed by asking what it means for anything, any being at all, to be. Being, as what it means "to be," is not itself a being or a thing, however exalted.[14] The sheer audacity of Heidegger's task, to construe anew what thinking is and what it is about, has clearly proved powerfully attractive, and for several generations, there was no obvious link between this audacity and his political beliefs or conduct.

Heidegger himself makes audacity the guiding spirit of the *Notebooks*. His epigraph for the first volume is *panta gar tolmêteon*, a quote from Plato's *Theaetetus* (196d2): "One must risk [or dare] everything."[15] *Tolma*, which he translates with the German *Wagnis*, a daring risk, is a word Heidegger also picks up from Sophocles's "Ode to Man" in *Antigone*,[16] and it permeates the *Notebooks*, because he sees a spirit of reckless daring as essential to the risk of crossing over to a new inception of history.[17] According to Heidegger, for 2,500 years, the West has answered the Being question in ways indebted to Plato. Plato asked how it is possible for any being—be it chair, dog, mountain, triangle, law—to be meaningful to us in the first place, as what it is or even seems to be. His explanation is perhaps the most famous in philosophy: because of the Ideas, a word we have in English thanks largely to Plato. In ordinary Greek, an *idea* is a thing seen with the eye, a distinct form that distinguishes this being (a chair, say, or a dog, or a square) from that one (a table, or a cat, or a circle), thereby giving the visible world a navigable meaning. Plato's Ideas, however, are seen with the mind's eye, not the body's: when we ask what a tangible object truly is, be it chair or dog, or mathematical things like triangles and numbers, or even abstractions like law or courage, the answer is not this dog or that triangle or this law or that courageous act, for these are all just transient exemplars; it is the Idea of the dog, triangle, law, or courage. The Ideas, as what each thing truly is, transcend the transitory. Being for Plato exists in a realm beyond time, beyond change, beyond the senses; the world of chairs and dogs and triangles on a blackboard, even historical concepts like law, are simply dimmer or brighter reflections of what truly is.

Throughout the *Notebooks*, Heidegger reaffirms his view that this Platonic misconception of Being as the eternal and unchanging basis of all reality has driven Western thought ever since, even if it no longer uses Plato's language of Ideas. Following Nietzsche, Heidegger holds that both Judaism and Christianity became carriers of Platonism for the people, with God taking the place of the Ideas as the source of all that is real. Modernity set in with Descartes, who made the self-conscious human subject displace God as the touchstone of reality: the methodologies of the sciences decide what really is, and the technologies that the sciences set loose serve the human subject as the presumptive new master of the objective universe (even if a master still in swaddling clothes). Despite how far the sciences may think themselves advanced beyond Platonism, Heidegger's argument is that they still hold that the meaning of what is must be expressed in the form of timeless laws and formulas, accessible only to the mind, that transcend the seemingly given world around us.[18]

Heidegger comes to call everything that has happened since Plato *metaphysics*, his word for all thinking that attempts to explain what it means to be by reference to some thing, some other being, whether that be the Ideas, God, the human subject, or the laws of modern mathematical physics. Metaphysics, he claims, has utterly forgotten the simplicity and corresponding difficulty of the question of what it means to be. Being is not the eternal; it is the radically finite: the meaning of Being is bound up with how we interpret what any thing is and all beings are as a whole, but that meaning is always bounded by time for Heidegger. He is the most radical historicist: truth as meaning is not the securing of a subject's representation as corresponding to an eternal, objective reality; truth is the time-bound unfolding of how the world simply is meaningful to us as historical human beings, embedded in a given time, place, and tradition. The "event" of that unfolding truth is not our subjective possession to control; it both needs us and happens to us in the opening up of a meaningful historical world for us.[19]

In the *Notebooks*, Heidegger sharpens a critique of modernity and the West familiar from his other works. He gives the forgetting of the question of Being and the ascent of metaphysics the name *nihilism* because metaphysics treats that question as if it were nothing. By elevating the human subject to the center of what is, modernity has brought on the fullest expression of metaphysics, which Heidegger calls *machination* throughout the *Notebooks*.[20] Machination aims at the total domination of nature, both as material stuff and as forms of energy, and acknowledges as a "being" only what can be subjected to this domination. The human subject, once so proudly presuming to wield science and technology as the crown and scepter of its own deification, finds itself instead subject to machination as just another resource: "human resources," as we are now pleased to call ourselves. What remains is what Heidegger follows Ernst Jünger in calling the "total mobilization" of all such resources for all domains of activity: industry, war, education, culture, even entertainment, all in service to a titanic will to power. The only standard left is "the gigantic": that which makes sheer quantity into quality. We bow before the idol of quantity, in stuff and in power, as the only quality that matters.

Heidegger the National Socialist

Throughout the *Notebooks*, Heidegger describes the trajectory of Platonism that culminates in this titanic nihilism as the fulfillment of "the first inception" of Western history. For Heidegger, an inception is more than a beginning, which can be factually dated on a timeline; an inception is an event that establishes and sustains the meaning of a historical world for human beings across generations, even millennia. The first inception began when the Greeks first asked the question of Being, but they fumbled it when Plato allowed philosophy to lapse into metaphysics. The *Notebooks* demonstrate how ardently, even desperately, Heidegger hoped for "an other inception," especially during those early years of the 1930s, when he had thought that National Socialism might be the catalyst for a "crossing-over" to a new history. "What will come, no one knows";[21] no one knows, because it will not be "the" other inception, or even "another" inception, as if it were a definite cyclical occurrence, but rather an entirely "other" inception that cannot be predicted or measured by the standards of the first one. All *Heidegger* knows is that it will require the complete transformation of what it means to be human, away from the self-deifying subjectivism of modernity: "Where and how will modern humanity arrive at a transformation of its essence, one that rips humanity away from its dehumanization and makes it ripe for the abysses of Be-ing," a transformation that depends on "an originary decision between the grounding of a truth of Be-ing and the establishment of the machination of beings in their ultimate supremacy"—a decision Heidegger thinks humanity may "no longer will or be able to will."[22]

In the entries from the early 1930s, Heidegger indicates he believes the German people have a special role to play in this decision to overturn history, not because of race, as in conventional Nazi doctrine, but because Germans have the potential to name anew what is at issue in thinking: "Only the German can give new poetic voice to Being."[23] Through their philosophers, their language, their poets, Germans alone represent the decisive counterpoint to the Greeks at the first inception of history; only they, Heidegger believes at this moment of revolution, might see metaphysics through to its bitter end and find a way to express a new mode of thinking, but only "if we—if precisely the Germans—are strong enough to take on this highest and most reticent care, the care for the truth of Be-ing."[24] This would only happen, though, if the German people, the *Volk,* actually grasp this as their decisive historical task.[25] While Heidegger does accept that race "is *one* necessary condition of historical *Dasein* (thrownness) that expresses itself indirectly," he rejects its apotheosis in conventional Nazi ideology: "*One* condition gets elevated to the unconditional,"[26] and by 1940, he says, "All race-thinking is modernist; it moves along the path of conceiving man as subject."[27] The *Volk* is not to be *defined* racially-biologically (which is only one feature of historical thrownness, according to Heidegger) but rather by its ability to take on *Dasein*'s fateful burden and make itself question-worthy, not as a "what" as in the racial conception of human being, but rather as a "who" for whom the epochal questions of the age remain powerfully open by asking, "Who are we?"—and not answering right away with crude biological racism or unsophisticated folk history.[28]

This also explains why Heidegger took on the role of head of his university: to lead a new generation along this path of ending one era and starting another. In the entries from 1933, we feel his excitement: "The university is dead; long live the future school of higher learning for the education of the Germans to knowledge"; "The great experience and joy—that the Führer has awakened a new reality that sets our thinking on the right path and gives it the forcefulness to have an impact."[29] But there is also doubt: "National Socialism is not a complete and eternal Truth fallen from heaven—taken as such it will become an aberration and buffoonery."[30] Heidegger wants to rebuild the university from the ground up, to take nothing for granted, to unite the faculty and students across the disciplines in a spirit of questioning that prepares the ground for that other inception of history. He sees this task as requiring a boldness and an appetite for radical change, but everywhere he finds resistance from *Spießbürgerei*, a word almost impossible to translate: it expresses such a depth of virulent contempt for the cowardice, lack of imagination, and conformism of the many who pretend to be Nazi revolutionaries that "bourgeoisie" or "yuppiedom" would not even scratch the surface of Heidegger's loathing. "Is it any wonder," he asks in 1933, "how *Spießbürgerei* rises up all around, conceited half-culture, petit bourgeois phony education—how the inner requirements of German socialism are not even recognized and therefore also not desired?"[31]

The *Notebooks* demonstrate the intensity of Heidegger's ambitions for the Nazi revolution in a way that also makes clear his own hubris, even megalomania: the revolution will succeed only if the German *Volk*, the youth, the university, even the Nazi Party itself, understand what is at stake on *his* terms, as a decision about the crossing-over from the first to an other inception of Western history as an ongoing question about what it means to be. Even the word *revolution* is not strong enough for what Heidegger wanted: "*Revolutions*—these are overturnings of what is already familiar but never transformations into the entirely Other. They can prepare such transformations, but they can also undermine them."[32] However dramatic, *revolution* suggests a merely cyclical reversal masquerading as radical change, where the metaphysical understanding of Being entrenched in Western history is just reintroduced in a different form. Heidegger sought a radical overturning that would not simply shake things up but plow them under. He wanted a transformation of history and humanity so profound that nothing in the last two millennia could have prepared the West for it, precisely because the horizons of meaning for history had been determined by metaphysics since the collapse of the first inception into the metaphysics inaugurated by Plato.

By the late 1930s, the *Notebooks* demonstrate the inevitable consequences of such extraordinary hubris and risk-taking on a grand scale: a Heidegger lost to bitter despair. Of his tenure as head of his university and the speech he gave to inaugurate it, he says: "The great error of this speech consists in this, that it still assumed that there would be a hidden generation of those ready to question in the context of the German university, that it still hoped to bring them to dedicating themselves to the work of inner transformation."[33] Heidegger had not failed; Germans, the university, the revolution itself had failed to shoulder the task set for them by history. Virtually nothing and no one escapes his withering criticism and scorn. The university is incapable of genuine, creative questioning; the German people fail to find the strength for the essential tasks of thinking; National Socialism caves in to its petit bourgeois careerists; America represents the full-fledged outbreak of gigantism on the world stage; racial doctrine emerges as just another manifestation of a modern thinking that reduces what it means to be human to some biological feature that can be adapted to meta-physics' machination programs. The only consistent exception to Heidegger's sweeping condemnations is his beloved German poet, Friedrich Hölderlin, whom he grants the honor of prefiguring the overturning needed by Western history in the confrontation between the Greek inception and what should have been its German rejoinder.[34]

Even if we grant Heidegger's longing for a radical departure in history, why would he embrace the Nazi revolution at its dawn, especially given the Nazis' grotesque and virulent anti-Semitism? Didn't the communists also promise a transformative break with history? For one thing, the *Notebooks* show that the Nazi revolution was only an *opportunity* for Heidegger, a moment when the overturning might be possible, not guaranteed. He was proud enough to think he could become the leader in spirit of this movement, as Marx was to communism, but the movement failed him and the historical rupture it should have served, not the other way around. Furthermore, communism itself was, for Heidegger, just another form of Platonism: "Marxism cannot be defeated once and for all unless we first confront [Plato's] doctrine of Ideas and its two-millennia-long history," he proclaimed in a lecture course in 1933–1934.[35] Much like the Christian end-times and apocalypse, com-munism promises an end to history, a complete fulfillment of human destiny. Platonism in all its forms, according to Heidegger, explains what it means to be human as something grounded in a timeless realm beyond history that applies universally to all human beings, whether as created in God's image, or as bearers of human rights that apply to "all men"—as the American Declaration of Independence would have it—or as participants in commu-nism's world revolution that would put an end to the question of what humanity has been and will become. To all such movements Heidegger applies the name "liberalism," not in the parochial, contemporary sense of modern welfare liberalism, but rather in a sense that reaches back to Plato and that defines human "liberty" on the basis of an appeal to timeless and universal truths. In the Nazis, Heidegger thought he had found a movement that would reject universalistic liberalism in all its forms—Christianity, the secular Enlightenment, communism—in favor of a politics that would ground human history in the communal belonging of a finite historical people.[36]

By the end, though, the *Notebooks* show Heidegger accusing Nazism itself of falling prey to liberalism through its metaphysical reduction of all human differences to race, its treating the *Volk* as kind of super-subject akin to conventional liberalism's subjective individual, and its capitulation to the idols of machination and gigantism. For example: "All well-meaning excavation of earlier *Volk*-lore, all conventional cultivation of custom, all extolling of landscape and soil, all glorification of the 'blood' is just foreground and smokescreen—and necessary in order to obscure what truly and solely *is*: the uncondi-tional dominion of the machination of destruction."[37] Or, in describing various types of

Nazi "science" and propaganda about the *Volk*: "The disaster here does not lie in one specific doctrine [about the German *Volk*] *but rather in the manner* of 'thinking,' which is nothing other than the *cogito ergo sum* [I think, therefore I am] of Descartes applied to the gigantism of the body of the *Volk* in the following form: *ego* non *cogito ergo sum* [I do *not* think, therefore I am]."[38]

The promise of the Nazi revolution had devolved, for Heidegger, into a kitschy mishmash of blood-and-soil mythmaking, its followers qualified only by their willingness *not* to think or to question the meaning of modernity. Heidegger even entertains the view that a complete tragedy, in the sense of a catastrophic downfall, might be the only way past this dead end: "If a truth lies in the power of the 'race' (the innate), will and should the Germans then lose—give up—organize away their historical essence, or will they be forced to bring it to the most tragic outcome?"[39] Heidegger's *tolma* has brought him to the verge of unhinged apocalypticism for his nation: only by precipitating a *Götterdämmerung* will the crossing-over from metaphysics now be possible.

Is Heidegger's Philosophy Tainted?

In connection with this apocalyptic recklessness, we must mention Heidegger's anti-Semitism, because surely the Holocaust was part of Germany's descent into self-destruction. While I have treated this topic in the *Notebooks* elsewhere,[40] it may suffice to cite a profoundly shocking passage from a lecture course in the fall of 1933. Here, Heidegger is not writing private notes for publication seventy-five years later; he is speaking to a lecture hall full of students in an introductory course, in his capacity as Nazi rector of the university:

An enemy is each and every person who poses an essential threat to the *Dasein* of the people and its individual members. The enemy does not have to be external, and the external enemy is not even always the more dangerous one. And it can seem as if there were no enemy. Then it is a fundamental requirement to find the enemy, to expose the enemy to the light, or even first to make the enemy, so that this standing against the enemy may happen and so that *Dasein* may not lose its edge. The enemy can have attached itself to the innermost roots of the *Dasein* of a people and can set itself against this people's own essence and act against it. The struggle is all the fiercer and harder and tougher, for the least of it consists in coming to blows with one another; it is often far more difficult and wearisome to catch sight of the enemy as such, to bring the enemy into the open, to harbor no illusions about the enemy, to keep oneself ready for attack, to cultivate and intensify a constant readiness and to prepare the attack, looking far ahead with the goal of total annihilation.[41]

Heidegger's cynicism is breathtaking: he is willing to allow the *manufacture* of an enemy ("even first to make the enemy"), "so that *Dasein* may not lose its edge." At some level, then, Heidegger must have recognized the propagandistic fabrications of Nazi anti-Semitism. True, Heidegger does not mention the Jews, but even so, a mature thinker bears a responsibility for using such language to an audience of young people about a hidden enemy among them, at the dawn of a revolution soaked in vitriolic, eliminationist anti-Semitism.

As early as April 1933, in a prefiguration of the Nuremberg Laws, the Nazis had passed laws to expel Jews from civil service, which included teachers and university professors, so this was very much a live issue on Heidegger's campus, and as rector, he himself would have had the responsibility to implement those laws. Who else, given Nazi propaganda, would young students have imagined infesting the "*Dasein* of a people" in this way? Communists? Perhaps. But no one more than the Jews—and as *internationalist* socialists, the communists were an open, not a hidden enemy, of a *National* Socialism. Heidegger shared with more conventional Nazis the belief that communism was merely an epiphenomenon of a deeper worldwide Jewish threat. This is why the Nazi Party could accept former communists into its ranks, but there could be no such thing as a *former Jew*—except in "total annihilation."

I have spoken often with fellow Heidegger scholars about this appalling passage. Many resist its implications, not because they are anti-Semites, but because it is so horrific, with its paean to the "goal of total annihilation"—and in 1933, not 1941!—that connects Heidegger in spirit if not in deed to one of the greatest crimes in history. For many who have taken Heidegger seriously as a thinker, it can be hard to know what to do with a philosophy that would dare such pronouncements. Nevertheless, the community of Heidegger scholars must get over their shock at this horror and confront what is at issue, for it transcends the man Heidegger himself.

Heidegger: Dead or Alive?

There is more than one way for philosophers to die. As human beings, they all die, just like the rest of us. As the name for a body of work, they can also die through neglect, refutation, or scorn. Heidegger is dead, and to be frank, he is better off that way. It might mean the end of Heidegger the man as the object of an intellectual cult. It might mean the end of treating his works as the object of endless reverential exegesis. That leaves only his genuine questions, which were never his to begin with. Now those still interested in his thinking will have to make those questions their own, in their own idiom, if those questions are to live at all as philosophy. At his best, Heidegger might want to be dead in this way, if it would mean that the philosophical questions could live.

However we might judge Heidegger, and however much of his philosophy is, to use Peter Trawny's apt word, *contaminated* by his anti-Semitism,[42] it is worth taking stock of how much in crisis we remain. Twenty-five years after Francis Fukuyama proclaimed "The End of History?" (as a question!) in the triumph of liberalism at the close of the Cold War, the liberal West has failed again and again to live up to the universalistic promise of that supposed triumph: it failed in Sarajevo and Srebrenica, in Rwanda, in the Congo; it has fumbled its "War on Terror." Today, the far Right is ascending across Europe, with xenophobia and anti-Semitism on the rise. The massacre of the *Charlie Hebdo* journalists has left not just France but all Europe reeling, without a clear way forward in balancing the liberal notion of absolute freedom of inquiry and expression with the sensibilities of populations long alienated from the body politic. Europe and the United States stand paralyzed in the face of a Russian irredentism grounded in nationalist mythology and contempt for the rule of law—not that the United States has much of a leg to stand on after a war of choice in Iraq and a program of torture justified as "enhanced interrogation." Neoliberal policies have left the global economy in a shambles, and worse, our only operational measure for economic success is growth for growth's sake and binge-purge consumption as the model for happiness. Liberalism in its wider modern sense, as the Baconian quest for the relief of the human estate through the technological conquest of nature, by reducing all matter and energy to a resource, has brought us to the point that the United Nations' Intergovernmental Panel on Climate Change now tells us we have fifteen years to halt global warming or the results will be catastrophic and irreversible.[43]

"To be or not to be"—that truly is the question we face in the twenty-first century, and not just as a matter of human survival. It is also the question of Being itself, and what it means to be human. We may rightly despise Heidegger for his anti-Semitism and Nazism, and his entire body of thought must be reconsidered in light of increasingly decisive evidence of how deeply he adhered to these convictions. But who *we* are, and who *we* are going to be as human beings in a newly global world, is very much the question, and we seem allergic even to asking it seriously. As a genuine adversary, Heidegger brings what is at issue into focus; if we don't raise the question at all and think it through, we will lurch blindly to our fate. As we persist in fouling our own nest in the relentless quest for power upon power, resource upon resource, as we ramp up the apocalyptic lethality of our weaponry, as the march of technology continues to transform even human nature itself, in the coming century we will have to confront the question of "to be or not to be"—and what it means to be human on this earth. If we cannot feel the force of that question, we cannot even begin to answer it.

Notes

This chapter reworks a review published in the *Los Angeles Review of Books*. I am grateful to the LARB and to my editors there, Martin Woessner and Arne DeBoever, for permission to revise and reprint. See Gregory Fried, "The King Is Dead: Heidegger's 'Black Notebooks,' *Los Angeles Review of Books*, September 13, 2014, http://lareviewofbooks.org/review/king-dead-heideggers-black-notebooks. I am also grateful to Lauren McGillicuddy for editorial assistance.

1. See Martin Woessner, *Heidegger in America* (Cambridge: Cambridge University Press, 2011).

2. Martin Heidegger, *Überlegungen II–VI (Schwarze Hefte 1931–1938)*, *Gesamtausgabe* 94, ed. Peter Trawny (Frankfurt: Klostermann, 2014); *Überlegungen VII–XI (Schwarze Hefte 1938/39)*, *Gesamtausgabe* 95, ed. Peter Trawny (Frankfurt: Klostermann, 2014); *Überlegungen XII–XV (Schwarze Hefte 1939–1941)*, *Gesamtausgabe* 96, ed. Peter Trawny (Frankfurt: Klostermann, 2014).

3. All translations of excerpts from the *Notebooks* here are my own; I am grateful to Richard Polt for his translations of some passages, which I have consulted in collaboration with him, but the ultimate responsibility for the renderings is my own.

4. See the materials collected in *The Heidegger Controversy: A Critical Reader,* ed. Richard Wolin (Cambridge, MA: MIT Press, 1993).

5. Ulrich Sieg, "'Die Verjudung des deutschen Geistes': Ein unbekannter Brief Heideggers," *Die Zeit*, December 22, 1989, 40.

6. See Hugo Ott, *Martin Heidegger: A Political Life*, trans. Allan Blunden (New York: Basic Books, 1993), 329, 348–350, 359–367.

7. For example, there is the case of his manipulation of the famous interview with *Der Spiegel* in 1966, "Only a God Can Save Us." See Lutz Hachmeister, *Heideggers Testament: Der Philosoph, der Spiegel und die SS* (Berlin: Propyläen, 2014).

8. Hannah Arendt, "Martin Heidegger at Eighty," trans. Albert Hofstadter, *New York Review of Books*, October 21, 1971, http://www.nybooks.com/articles/archives/1971/oct/21/martin-heidegger-at-eighty/.

9. See Jürgen Habermas, "Martin Heidegger: On the Publication of the Lectures of 1935," in *The Heidegger Controversy: A Critical Reader*, ed. Richard Wolin (Cambridge, MA: MIT Press, 1993).

10. *Überlegungen VII–XI, Gesamtausgabe* 95, p. 408.

11. *Überlegungen VII–XI, Gesamtausgabe* 95, p. 274.

12. See Ott, *Martin Heidegger: A Political Life*, 133–260.

13. For example, see *Überlegungen II–VI, Gesamtausgabe* 94, pp. 22, 512–513; *Überlegungen VII–XI, Gesamtausgabe* 95, p. 256; *Überlegungen XII–XV, Gesamtausgabe* 96, pp. 215–216.

14. Thomas Sheehan puts this very well: "At least since Homo sapiens came on the scene some 200,000 years ago, 'to be' has meant 'to be meaningful'"; see his *Making Sense of Heidegger: A Paradigm Shift* (Lanham, MD: Rowman & Littlefield, 2015), 111.

15. *Überlegungen II–VI, Gesamtausgabe* 94, p. 3.

16. See Martin Heidegger, *Einführung in die Metaphysik, Gesamtausgabe* 40, ed. Petra Jaeger (Frankfurt: Klostermann, 1983), 121, 157, 170, 181.

17. For some striking passages, see *Überlegungen II–VI, Gesamtausgabe* 94, pp. 315, 323; *Gesamtausgabe* 95, pp. 95, 133, 186; *Überlegungen XII–XV, Gesamtausgabe* 96, p. 51.

18. See, for example, *Überlegungen II–VI, Gesamtausgabe* 94, p. 424; *Überlegungen VII–XI, Gesamtausgabe* 95, pp. 244, 248, 254–258, 310–313, 322.

19. See *Überlegungen II–VI, Gesamtausgabe* 94, pp. 344, 520; *Überlegungen XII–XV, Gesamtausgabe* 96, pp. 108–109.

20. For representative passages, see *Überlegungen II–VI, Gesamtausgabe* 94, pp. 364–366, 425, 472; *Überlegungen VII–XI, Gesamtausgabe* 95, pp. 392–399, 403–404; *Überlegungen XII–XV, Gesamtausgabe* 96, pp. 52–57, 105–107, 238, 260–261.

21. *Überlegungen II–VI, Gesamtausgabe* 94, p. 441.

22. *Überlegungen VII–XI, Gesamtausgabe* 95, pp. 300, 278.

23. *Überlegungen II–VI, Gesamtausgabe* 94, p. 27.

24. *Überlegungen VII–XI, Gesamtausgabe* 95, p. 186.

25. See *Überlegungen II–VI, Gesamtausgabe* 94, p. 109: "to link back the most secret task of the German *Volk* to the great inception."

26. *Überlegungen II–VI, Gesamtausgabe* 94, p. 189; see also *Überlegungen II–VI, Gesamtausgabe* 94, p. 351; *Überlegungen VII–XI, Gesamtausgabe* 95, pp. 41, 298–301, 381–382, 414–415.

27. *Überlegungen XII–XV, Gesamtausgabe* 96, p. 48.

28. See *Überlegungen II–VI, Gesamtausgabe* 94, pp. 350, 443–445; *Überlegungen VII–XI, Gesamtausgabe* 95, pp. 298–299.

29. *Überlegungen II–VI, Gesamtausgabe* 94, pp. 125, 111.

30. *Überlegungen II–VI, Gesamtausgabe* 94, pp. 114–115.

31. *Überlegungen II–VI, Gesamtausgabe* 94, p. 135.

32. *Überlegungen VII–XI, Gesamtausgabe* 95, p. 48.

33. *Überlegungen VII–XI, Gesamtausgabe* 95, p. 286.

34. For example, see *Überlegungen VII–XI, Gesamtausgabe* 95, p. 66; *Überlegungen XII–XV, Gesamtausgabe*

96, p. 60.

35. Martin Heidegger, *Sein und Wahrheit*, *Gesamtausgabe* 36/37, ed. Hartmut Tietjen (Frankfurt: Klostermann, 2001), 151.

36. See *Sein und Wahrheit*, *Gesamtausgabe* 36/37, p. 166.

37. *Überlegungen VII–XI, Gesamtausgabe* 95, pp. 381–382.

38. *Überlegungen VII–XI, Gesamtausgabe* 95, pp. 299–300.

39. *Überlegungen II–VI, Gesamtausgabe* 94, p. 168.

40. See Gregory Fried, "What Heidegger Was Hiding: Unearthing the Philosopher's Anti-Semitism," *Foreign Affairs* 93 (November–December 2014): 159–166; also Gregory Fried, "A Letter to Emmanuel Faye," *Philosophy Today* 55 (2011): 219–252, at 227–230. For clearly anti-Semitic passages in the *Notebooks*, see *Überlegungen VII–XI, Gesamtausgabe* 95, pp. 97, 326; *Gesamtausgabe* 96, pp. 46, 56, 243, 262.

41. Heidegger, *Sein und Wahrheit*, *Gesamtausgabe* 36/37, pp. 90–91.

42. Peter Trawny, *Heidegger und der Mythos der jüdischen Weltverschwörung* (Frankfurt: Klostermann, 2014), 12, 16, 65, 93, 99–100.

43. See Justin Gillis, "Climate Efforts Falling Short, U.N. Panel Says," *New York Times*, April 13, 2014, http://www.nytimes.com/2014/04/14/science/earth/un-climate-panel-warns-speedier-action-is-needed-to-avert-disaster.html. See also the Intergovernmental Panel on Climate Change's findings in *Climate Change 2014: Synthesis Report*, ed. The Core Writing Team, Rajendra K. Pachauri, and Leo Meyer (Geneva: World Meteorological Association, 2014), http://www.ipcc.ch/report/ar5/syr/.

5

Heidegger's Black Night: The *Nachlass* and Its *Wirkungsgeschichte*

Babette Babich

Digital Philosophy and the "New" "Heidegger Scandal"

In a world of Heidegger studies so becalmed that the Heidegger Circle in the United States, the same Circle to which Heidegger addressed one of his last letters on science and technology,[1] spends its time on the Internet debating Tom Sheehan's claim to reduce Being (*Sein* and *Seyn*) to "meaning" along with more recondite worries, grieved as it were to the smallest nib, the tiniest point, and thus into that inaudibly humming world of occasional e-missives posted with either no response or only to small circles of back-and-forthings that flare and die, into all of this that is the life of digital or online philosophy burst the so-called *Schwarze Hefte*, the so-called *Black Notebooks*.

This "*Ereignis*" quickly became Heidegger's own "black night" where former distinctions could no longer be made and where everything to be addressed turned on a single theme. What is of central importance is that this event did not transpire in the usual way of the academic bombshell—that is, by way of a journal article (from one perspective, the *original* form of publication of Heidegger's *Being and Time*),[2] nor did it hit the bookstores like Richard Rorty's *Mirror of Nature* or Alasdair MacIntyre's *After Virtue* or Alexander Nehamas's *Life as Literature* or indeed, for a clearly continental contender, Gilles Deleuze's *Nietzsche and Philosophy*.[3] Neither was this a 'performance event' like one of Jacques Derrida's famously long lectures before an audience of hundreds of eager comparative literature and language students (rather than philosophy-minded listeners).

By way of digital postings, now in book form to be sure, we have word-positive, explicit proof of Heidegger's anti-Semitism, views contained in secret notebooks, which, we are informed, he kept "hidden" until now. But, and of course, it transpires that there is no "secret" to the secret notebooks (understood as covert or concealed texts), and saying so seems to be a cover term for expressing difficulties in commandeering open "access" to archives that are not archives at all but family papers held by a philosopher's sons.[4]

Hence this same "secret" has been disseminated by various journalists as well as politically minded historians of philosophy and of course political theorists for some time. In addition to the indications given in the prepublication history of the *Beiträge*, Silvio Vieta[5] was also known to possess one of the unavailable notebooks, which has in the interim duly been sold off for publication. To this extent, Heidegger did not "hide" the *Black Notebooks*. Rather, his plan was to locate them as "omega" to his work—in no nefarious sense but simply because anything placed at the end of an edition of a thinker's works cannot help but punctuate it.

Yet to note that Heidegger chose the position of these notebooks in organizing his collected works also reveals the seeming calculation of the arrangement. And this seems ironic given Heidegger's own critique of "calculation."[6] What cannot be disputed is that the arrangement is a publisher's dream. Klostermann couldn't be happier with the business advantages of Heidegger's programmatic schedule for publishing his works, nor indeed (because it helps sell books) are they dismayed by the scandal guaranteed by that schedule (the latter should be taken with a grain of salt because since the *Beiträge*, Heidegger's "scheduled" *Nachlass* publication plan has been as ignored as many other deceased author's wishes have tended to be). But there is much more at stake for Klostermann in this regard and also for the editor, Peter Trawny himself, for whereas academic books on Heidegger are more than likely to languish dead-born into the dustbin, Trawny's editor's commentary is in its *third edition* now, less than a year after initial publication.

With respect to the *Beiträge*, I have elsewhere observed that Heidegger found Nietzsche's style compelling for his own work: I argue further that Heidegger took Nietzsche's fate at the hands of his editors as a cautionary tale with respect to his own philosophical destiny.[7] In Nietzsche's case that would be the editors of his *Nachlass*, those who produced the *Will to Power*, and that would include those editors who take it upon themselves to produce "critical" editions. Thus Heidegger had been elected to that editorial board that was to produce a Nazi edition of Nietzsche's works and from which, given what he saw as the projected official plan for publication, he quickly resigned. Offending Nietzscheans at the time of his first Nietzsche lectures and still today, Heidegger was to foreground Nietzsche's unpublished work qua unpublished and designated *The Will to Power* Nietzsche's "major work."[8] Dissonant and absurd on the face of it, the declaration disquieted both philosophers and philologists for seemingly good reasons. Nietzsche's *Will to Power* is an *editorial* product, we say, and we blame Nietzsche's sister as we blame her for most things, including, as has recently been argued, any taint of anti-Semitism, so absolving Nietzsche of the same. For his own part, unlike the average Nietzsche scholar (again: then and now), Heidegger's response to the editorial compilation that was Nietzsche's *Will to Power* failed to decry the consequences for understanding Nietzsche's thought but affirmed the value of Nietzsche's *Nachlass*, characterizing the published works as "vestibule" to the main edifice of the unpublished work.

And Heidegger goes on, as I argue, to parallel Nietzsche himself.[9] This is not Heidegger's "*ressentiment*" or personal preoccupation with his reception (almost all philosophers worry about their reception) or his worries that he wasn't adequately or rightly understood (similarly a common affair) or (and this habit was shared with Husserl and Nietzsche) his own reading and rereading of his own work. What Heidegger does in the *"Black" Notebook* entitled *Reflections XIV* is offer a reflection on the hermeneutic *working effect* or outcome of the reading of philosophical and poetic texts—that is, read phenomenologico-historically, by discussing a parallel with the transformed reception of Hölderlin's poetry by way of the edition so crucial for World War I (Hölderlin was issued to German soldiers in a wartime edition, the slim Insel edition, meant to be carried in their backpacks, just as Nietzsche's *Zarathustra* would be issued in a special *"Kriegsausgabe"* during World War II). If Nietzsche scholars remain anxious about the association of Nietzsche and National Socialism, by contrast, the association with Hölderlin's editor Norbert Von Hellingrath who fell in World War I but not less with the special wartime edition of his works, would transform the reception of the poet, arguably making Hölderlin who he is today.[10] Heidegger contends that what holds for the Hölderlin of the late hymns likewise holds for the Nietzsche *Nachlass* we know as the *Will to Power.*[11]

A *Black Notebook* included in *Gesamtausgabe* 96 thus features a quote from Hölderlin as its first epigraph, including the same reference to the "little things" that recurs in Heidegger's reflections on technology as he reprises these in his lectures for the Munich Academy of Fine Arts in 1950, lectures he will publish in 1954 as *The Question Concerning Technology*. The poetic lines are quite literally "nothing technological":

Von Wegen geringer Dinge
Verstimmt wie vom Schnee war
Die Gloke, womit
Man läutet
Zum Abendessen.

By ways of little things
Distuned as from snow was
The bell, wherewith
is rung
to supper.[12]

Describing this as a prose poem (the above translation retains this "distuning" or disvoicing all the way to "supper" where other versions do not), Heidegger underscores its poetic force. Borrowing his esotericism from Hölderlin and Nietzsche, complete with biblical echoes in each case,[13] Heidegger repeats the same lines in *Über den Anfang, Gesamtausgabe* 70, in a section on explication: "Those, who can hear, are few. No one knows their number. Even the number is indifferent. And they themselves do not know each other."[14] The lines are set in the context of an earlier aphorism directed, to echo the parallel, at the heart of hermeneutics: "All interpretation moves in the circle."[15]

The epigraph on the opposite page explicates the concluding themes of Heidegger's later lecture on technology, as the epigraph has it: "What *poetry* is becomes manifest here: that no longer needs to be 'art' and that is *techne* and that is 'poesie' (*poiesis*)."[16] In the text to follow, we are asked to consider the *unpublished Hymns* of Hölderlin together with, very specifically, the *unpublished* Nietzsche of the *Will to Power*, and here Heidegger adds a further parallel with the *unpublished* Hegel, namely his *Lectures on Aesthetics*, the publication of which unpublished material is in each case to be read as backward-working, thereby yielding nothing less than an effectively dynamic hermeneutics and in the process transforming the work of a published lifetime.

Time turns around: possibilities are reviewed and reworked; a poet is reconceived, a thinker is differently understood.

Each dialectical instantiation corresponds to a written work: authored by Hölderlin, Nietzsche, Hegel. In each case Heidegger cites not the authorial but much rather an editorial project including in each case, sine qua non, an authoritative editor. While we may (we do) blame Nietzsche's sister for the sheer fact of or existence of the *Will to Power*, we are grateful to Norbert von Hellingrath for bringing the hymns of Hölderlin's benightedness (or madness) to light and we acknowledge Heinrich Gustav Hotho for Hegel's *Lectures on Aesthetics* and it will do to be mindful of its role for our understanding of Hegel.

In all publications, all lectures, all conference programs, all university appointments, who is published, invited to speak, or called to a chair—and who not—reflect constellations having nothing to do with the author, nothing in this case to do with Hölderlin, Nietzsche, Hegel. The *Nachlass* by contrast has the potential to be read beyond the academic environment, not to mention editorial power politics. That Heidegger's point is made in the context of the reception of his own work (here from 1927 to 1941), and thus in the context of an array of sets of power politics, does not gainsay the history of the reception of the three nineteenth-century authors cited or the stakes of the political game always in play.

Like all his points, Heidegger's point here is about time, illustrating the "fate" or destining of a text. As we recall Aristotle arguing in tragic Greek fashion,[17] it is said that a man's children may, by their ill deeds, alter a man's felicity even after death. And a book, Nietzsche tells us, is a child.

The publication of unpublished texts changes published texts, inviting us to reflect on the reception of those same texts. Heidegger is at pains to indicate this in his reading of Nietzsche, but in the *Schwarze Hefte* he points to Hölderlin and Hegel too.[18] The controversies surrounding the notebooks themselves illustrate Heidegger's thesis on the backward-working effects of the *Nachlass*.

Here, in the instructions Heidegger gave for his own collected works—the so-called *Ausgabe letzter Hand*—what may merit attention from scholars has to do with another kind of calculation, apart from the calculative direction initiated by Heidegger or that of his editors (or indeed because that too is another story: his publisher). This is the calculation of the modern media industry as such. For this reason I began by noting the relevance of social media—that is, what we call "digital" media—in tandem with reception effects.[19] This also happens to correspond to Heidegger's concern in his own reflections on technology from the start, especially his *The Age of World Picture*, indicating a concern with print and broadcast media as such. For his part, Heidegger's publication strategy attests to a controlling technology, thematizing media as *Ge-Stell*. Indeed, print media and mediation qua 'crystallization' of opinion/worldviews constitute *Gestell* for Heidegger, beginning with the forester walking the forest path, as we may recall from *The Question Concerning Technology*. Nor do radio and film fail to make an appearance at the end of the *Turning*, "But we do not yet hear, we whose hearing and seeing are perishing through radio and film under the rule of technology" (again and precisely qua *Ge-Stell*).[20]

To raise questions of publication strategies and media technologies is also to ask the question of the particular technology that is the book as such: the book qua book. An author's *Nachlass* includes course outlines and correspondence as well as, in the broadest application of the term or the most literally in the ontic sense of *Nachlass*, the author's library as such, sometimes including lists of library borrowings, but above all drafts, and, as these are other than drafts, notebooks like the ones we are discussing, and so on.[21] Here the question concerns the texts of the *Nachlass*, be they more intellectually oriented like Heidegger's *Beiträge* (published as *Contributions to Philosophy*) or *Besinnung* (published as *Mindfulness*) or indeed the current *Schwarze Hefte* (including as yet unpublished volumes).[22]

Are the *Schwarze Hefte* books? Do the multiple parts of the *Beiträge* constitute a book? Does the order Heidegger created for these multiple sections or parts in the case of the *Beiträge* matter? (I have argued that it does.) Is the *Beiträge*, as I contend, a text Heidegger compiled and designed to be read on the model of Nietzsche's *Will to Power* in order to be counted as a posthumous *Hauptwerk*? Or is the *Beiträge*, as Otto Pöggeler has emphasized, Heidegger's second major work after *Being and Time*?[23] Is it just Heidegger's "symphony," as William J. Richardson has suggested?[24] Or is it simply so much word jazz, as Simon Blackburn seems to have concluded in his review of the English translation, repeating the translator's choice of words: "enquivering"?[25]

Where Heidegger's *Beiträge* caused a stir because of its opacity[26] (in contrast to the more sedate reception of his *Besinnung*),[27] Peter Trawny was able to capture the attention of journalists in France (where the scandal would begin) by arguing in a press release that the forthcoming work under his editorship featured "final"—and finalizing—proof *not* of Heidegger's enduring party membership as a card-carrying Nazi, but much more grievously (underlining Trawny's main concern as editor), "proof" certain of his anti-Semitism.[28]

Trawny reads Heidegger's anti-Semitism in good editorial fashion, by way of Heidegger's deployment of a specific set of words: a *Stichwortverzeichnis*, a glossary. In this specifically damning case, keywords include *Judentum*, all talk of race, any invocation of "calculation" in this context, and so on, and above all Heidegger's very explicit use of the term, *Weltjudentum*.[29] The result, thanks to word-frequency analysis and automated text searches, substitutes for the tiresome obligation to read Heidegger's German in these notebooks. We no longer have the Nazi Heidegger of yesteryear but now and henceforth (and this would also be Heidegger's own point regarding the impact of the *Nachlass*, albeit turned against its author but no less supportive of Heidegger's point regarding the *Nachlass* as such), the anti-Semitic Heidegger, Heidegger the Jew hater.

Translating *Weltjudentum* is problematic because "World Jewry" does not seem quite right. Thus English-language scholars had some initial trouble agreeing on a translation of the term[30] because, as many commentators have noted, the very constellation gives us pause. For Trawny too: simply by speaking of *Weltjudentum* Heidegger invokes a long-standing propaganda campaign contra the Jews drawn from Heidegger's putative reading of the *Protocols of the Elders of Zion*—which, as Trawny has subsequently acknowledged, need not presuppose that Heidegger himself actually *read* the *Protocols*. Yet Trawny's report of the reference to the *Protocols of the Elders of Zion* is cited last in in an entire chapter of numbered types or kinds of "world-historial anti-Semitism [*seinsgeschichtlichen Antisemitismus*]" in Heidegger in Trawny's book length commentary on Heidegger's *Schwarze Hefte*. The reference to the title of *The Protocols of the Elders of Zion* is not to be sure Heidegger's but Jaspers's, who reports that he had in conversation with Heidegger disparaged those who allude to the *Protocols*, only to hear Heidegger's unsettling response: "But there is a dangerous international association [*internationale Verbindung*] of Jews."[31] How are we to interpret this response? For Jaspers it is a sign of Heidegger's blindness; for Trawny, it is the "smoking gun"[32] that tells us how to read Heidegger's references to *Weltjudentum* precisely in fateful terms—that is, as instances of "*seinsgeschichtliche-Antisemitismus*."

Further debate urges us to read Heidegger's reflections in a world-historical context not merely regarding Jews but Catholics.[33] We may note, as other commentators have also noted, his slurs against Russians, against Slavs in general, against the Chinese, and as Trawny points out, against the "Jesuits," to which company Heidegger himself once belonged, as against the "English," and then, too, the "Americans" and especially against "Americanism."[34]

Scholarship is now, as it seems, henceforth to be about proscription, so that it has been suggested that the study of Heidegger be banned in philosophy, as Emmanuel Faye has recommended for the past decade and in political theory going back even further, as Richard Wolin has argued; and in theology and other fields still further yet, as Tom Sheehan and other participants in the debate have pointed out: a proscription that began one might say with the suspension of Heidegger's right to teach philosophy in the wake of his failed de-Nazification. Most recently, to add to the disciplinary fields of proscription, Christian Fuchs has urged the elimination of all references to Heidegger from media studies and theoretical discussions of technology, digital and otherwise.[35] Citing Faye's contention that Heidegger, "who has espoused the foundations of Nazism [and so] cannot be considered a philosopher,"[36] Fuchs's solution is shunning, exclusion from theory, noncitation.[37]

What does it mean for scholars to call for a "ban"? Still more insidiously, what does it mean when scholars announce that other thinkers shouldn't be "considered philosophers"? Why the rush to tell others what to read—and what to think about what they read?

Indeed, are all these scholarly authority figures right? *Should* we read the *Schwarze Hefte*? What does Heidegger's reference to *Weltjudentum* mean, apart from Trawny's argument that it inevitably channels the *Protocols of the Elders of Zion* and the terrible legacy of that fake "book"? And what is a "fake" book? Are we really asking this question? Are we asking about the technical definition of or about the historical force of the book as such? What, once again, is a book?

Never mind asking about books, we say. Doesn't this line of questioning obscure the point? Doesn't Heidegger's use of the term *Weltjudentum* alone betray a fanatical encounter with a fanatical forgery, namely, the *Protocols of the Elders of Zion*? That is, isn't Heidegger replicating the same anti-Semitism that produced such a dangerous forgery? I think that is a fair question, and I find the responses of Emmanuel Faye, of Peter Trawny, and to the extent that I have had access to them, of Donatella di Cesare and many others enlightening. But isn't it fair in a hermeneutically minded, historicist spirit to ask whether it makes a difference that when Heidegger writes of *Weltjudentum* there was (already) a well-known, quite active, movement associated with the same terminology led by Theodor Herzl and thus dating back to the late nineteenth century? Hence if we bracket his derogatory modifier, "dangerous" (and if we also bracket the question of the danger posed for whom?), we nevertheless find an "international association," Zionism, and one that sought via this same world collectivity (Herzl speaks of a "Jewish Company") through which a Jewish state might be established as Herzl writes in *The Jewish State*.[38]

May we, *can* we, *should* we, *ought* we (I need every modal verb), undertake to understand this formula in the context of what Michael Berkowitz calls, if not "world Jewry" as such, at least beyond German borders: "West European Jewry" as Berkowitz traces the very specifically nationalist growth of the Zionist movement from 1897 to 1914?[39] Berkowitz's *Zionist Culture and West European Jewry before the First World War* features Theodor Herzl on its cover, and thus one might think of "world Jewry," in the quite specific sense of Herzl's *Welt*, the name of the periodical Herzl founded in 1897 (and which exists, with transformations, to this day)[40] and which was in Herzl's own time, particularly since 1903, an organ of what Herzl himself named "world"—meaning *universal*—"Zionism," in addition to the still more significant relevance of the term under its transformation as horrifically deployed by the Nazis.

Herzl is cited as saying: "As long as the Jews are forced to live together with other peoples, anti-Semitism will continue to exist. The peace longed for by all peoples will come to be fact when World Jewry also participates in a national homeland."[41] Summarizing Herzl's thinking on the needful founding of such a "national homeland" as including three factors, Howard Caygill details: "The political principle that the Jews are a nation without a homeland; the affirmation of technology as a means for realizing a Jewish polity; and the 'driving force' of the 'Jewish tragedy' in Europe for which the Dreyfus affair had provided a chilling presentiment."[42] Caygill adds, and this is in my view, a key political theological insight, that "Herzl's response to the Dreyfus Affair was a sombre rethinking of the modern revolutionary principles and the realization that confessional fraternity would always threaten the principles of equality and fraternity."[43] As Herzl writes, "Anti-Semites will become our surest friends, anti-Semitic countries our allies."[44]

Geopolitically, the "smoking gun" can also be used to describe the "scrap of paper," written by Leon Simon in a London hotel on the seventh month of the year in question, dated July 17, 1917 (7/17/17), and subsequently officially issued by the British government on November 2, 1917. The Balfour Declaration is celebrated as linking Lord Rothschild with the eventual founding of the state of Israel.[45] In the period between the autumn declaration of 1917 and the spring founding of Israel on May 14, 1948, Herzl's *Welt* effort to establish a state for the stateless Jews of the world would come to be mired in a flood of murderously "dangerous" associations far beyond any possible "appropriation."

Henceforth in that terrible interim, the term *Weltjudentum* itself will be converted along with a host of other "world"-style appellations, like *world Bolshevism, world banking*, and so on, such that World Jewry, the very idea, ends as murderous propaganda in the Nazi arsenal.[46] To the extent that Heidegger invokes the "world" language in this historical context, how could he not be contaminated by this legacy, even without any reference to or even any knowledge of the *Protocols*? Trawny, author of a study on the phenomenology of *world* in Heidegger can also tell us what world means for Heidegger.[47]

Can we say, then, that the term and the claims on its behalf are unsupportable in Heidegger yet unremarkable in Herzl and the Zionist magazine, *Welt*? Should we have a game of dueling notebooks, Heidegger versus Herzl? And besides, isn't this more a topic for historians specializing in world history, German history, or the history of Israel and Zionism than for philosophy?

But as philosophers, I think, we are not permitted simply to ignore Heidegger's intentions in favor of historians' interpretation of those intentions, as Miguel de Beistegui suggested in a powerful question posed not to me but to Tracy B. Strong, who presented an earlier version of his contribution to this book at a conference in Johannesburg.[48] Nor, I would say, should we leave these issues to political theorists, cultural anthropologists, or other social scientists, not to mention to the many journalists (including Wolin and Sheehan) who have from the start set the public terms of the debate on the *Black Notebooks*.

Nor could we, even if we wanted to. The Zeitgeist, like the Nietzschean "dog" of the spirit that it is, follows us and turns on us as it turns on itself.

This chapter could have been even more detailed (like the bass beat, the scandal goes on), but the preliminary point regarding digital and social media that is this turn of events—advance notices and press releases, editions and new editions of an editor's afterword, fights between current and past editors, all of which is exceptional even in the always scandal-ridden context of Heidegger studies, never mind ordinary scholarly work—has already taken place largely on the Internet (with the exception of the enduring influence of what we may call "Sheehan I"),[49] with its own stratified archaeologies. Only recently disseminated via blogs, hence the need for the language of "digital archaeology," today's

Heidegger scandal transpires on Facebook, via video, via shared online articles and posts: instant announcement with instant commentary on no less than three dedicated Facebook group pages, if we do not count the Heidegger Circle email list.

But the question that must be asked here concerns this digitalization. What is the effect of the medium of dissemination and expression on reflection? What has happened to scholars? What has happened to scholarship? I am not attempting to ask Heidegger's question regarding what he called thinking, but a perfectly ontic question: What are we doing? And the answer is patent as it the opposite of Nietzsche's ideal for philology, what he called his friendship for the *lento*, "slow reading."[50] By contrast, we are reading very quickly, over quickly, reading immensely complicated, on balance fairly diverse texts, taking multiple volumes at a time, all of them texts unpublished by the author,[51] all in the absence of any consideration of genre or style, all *as if* the context were immediately clear, all *as if* the tone were in every case unproblematic, and in each case accompanied by authoritative, that is, editorial commentary. Is this the new scholasticism?

All of these points bear on Heidegger's concerns, both with respect to the themes of his *Being and Time* (*Sein*) and the later reflections (*Seyn*), in addition to his views on technology, science, calculation, machination (*Machenschaft*), the relation between thinking and theology, between Heidegger's reading of *Existenz* and Jaspers's *Existenzphilosophie* (Heidegger yields the term to Jaspers without reserve), and Heidegger's discussions of Nietzsche versus Krieck, and of Baeumler. Also relevant are Heidegger's views on Kierkegaard via a celebration of anthropologism, which Heidegger surmises may work for the theologian, specifically in this case, Otto Bollnow (Heidegger reflects, with no little sarcasm, that when a student claims to interpret the intentions of the master, the master is often a victim of seemingly well-meaning but not necessarily well-founded intentions meant to advance the student more than anything else),[52] and so on and so on.

Other issues should be considered with respect to Heidegger's style in the context of the orchestrated media impact of the books themselves, which have produced the inevitable clashes between editors' and commentators' voices. Here and for the sake of what I have already indicated is the urgent need for a dedicated "Heidegger philology," we can note Heidegger's characteristic didacticism as this tends to manifest itself in his writings.[53] If Nietzsche is esoteric and writes for those related to him, directing what he says at those who are yet to be born (and may never be born), Heidegger is not for nothing the teacher of Leo Strauss.[54] Thus we may note Heidegger's "cadence,"[55] as I have elsewhere described the specific didactic, instructional tactic he employs: with a "letting fall" of a statement, with all the assumptions and convictions associated with it, routinely enough also including a certain anticipatory dissonance with the reader's presumptions or what Gadamer names prejudices. In his 1925 Warburg lectures, Erwin Panofsky had articulated the architectural elements of this scholarly tradition, referring to Aristotle and spatial infinity in his discussion of perspective transformations in art and architecture,[56] and we profit from Panofsky's recapitulation in 1948 of the same scholastic lineage that can be traced in every cathedral element (down to the architectural tracery itself), as in "the customary apparatus of parts, distinctions, questions and articles,"[57] the core inceptive tactic of scholasticism: it seems that, the *videtur quod*.[58]

For his part, Heidegger tends to intensify this seeming truth or apparent claim, drawing on what Manfred Riedel names the "acroamatic" element,[59] an element that may (at its best) involve what I call "concinnity" but that always intensifies the contention as such (e.g., the provocative nature of the claim *We are not thinking* in the lecture course *What Is Called Thinking?*, Heidegger's first course after his postwar return to teaching). In this way, Thomist scholastics similarly counterbalance their own argumentative form, *sed contra* (i.e., here we read in 1951, *Science does not think*), only then to recapture the original point together with the counterpoint, thereby articulating a summary synthesis, for the Thomists: *respondeo dicendum*, familiar to Heideggerians as "retrieval."

Explicating the *Nachlass*, Heidegger emphasizes the need for a phenomenological-hermeneutic, including the *epoché*: bracketing the background prejudice that is the usual scholarly reception of a received author. Here the interpretive epoché amounts in effect to a bracketing of the brackets: Hölderlin as limited to the published poems, or as is still in force to this day: the scholar's tactic of limiting the reading of Nietzsche to the published works (as opposed to *The Will to Power*) or the Hegel of the *Phenomenology* apart from the Hegel of the lecture courses. Here the work of Ernst Podach on Nietzsche's supposedly "suppressed manuscripts" is relevant to Heidegger's own methodological remonstrations: to read these unpublished texts as if they were just as Podach presents them, so many literary remainders or leftover drafts or discards from the writer's workshop.[60] Although there is more to say on Heidegger and Podach, what is clear is that for the philologist Heidegger, as for the philologist Nietzsche, there is and can be no such thing. We reify the text and to this extent we suppose that there is a core text and that repetition is thus a kind of plagiarism: authorly or self-plagiarism but plagiarism nonetheless. We make such judgments because we do not know how to read, or more accurately, because we are not reading, we are "searching" keywords.

By contrast, Heidegger offers us a methodical meditation on the phenomenology of hermeneutic time—that is, the literally, explicitly philologically, *interpretive* time of a text and its constellation in time and for an author over time. Writing in his own context of the claim, the "An-Spruch" of *Seyn*, Heidegger reflects with respect to "Hölderlin":

When we take the hymns unpublished by the poet as "*Nachlass*" we have already misapprehended the whole of it, even if we had yet to begin any endeavor regarding these poetic compositions. We take them as the left behind, the not-as-yet-rendered-complete; whereupon one believes one knows, based upon what has become familiar, what would have been made of the "unfinished"; in this way we elide the actual task, to understand this seemingly unfinished precisely as the actually decisive, the other beginning in another ordinance which compels us to abandon only that which is familiar. Thus the "*Nachlass*" is revealed as what is already well advanced ahead of us, which leaves us today together with those yet to come even further behind.[61]

As Heidegger argues with regard to the key to his own phenomenological hermeneutic of published/unpublished texts, as we scholars distinguish between these:

"*Nachlass*" is here an erroneous title, one that quite inverts the true relation of time and prevents us from ourselves recognizing that in the supposed incompleteness which as such conceals what is to come, from which we remain excluded as long as we zealously and apparently advanced only regret and—consider what is present as the basis for a false estimation of that which (according to our—utterly inadequate—opinion) could have and should have been. Even here, literary-historical titles (i.e., standard opinions) propagate their damage [*Unwesen*] and bar the preparation for real decisions.[62]

The damage or wastage is interesting here in the array of observations Heidegger makes regarding the *Nachlass*. Thus, and in more ways than his none-too-successful appropriation of Nietzsche's aphoristic style, Heidegger is indebted to Nietzsche. A classicist is by definition concerned with nothing but posthumous texts and Heidegger's inclusion of himself among this company only means that Nietzsche takes a historical-philological perspective on writing, reading, and being read. It is not for nothing that Nietzsche begins his scholarly career with an inaugural lecture challenging the conventions of the historical Homer, no matter whether it be the Homer of the people's mouth (*Volksmund*) or Homer, the putative literary figure himself.[63] Regarding what we may here now characterize as such posthumous or zombie texts, especially appropriate in the case of the *Schwarze Hefte*, Heidegger is both lamenting but also echoing Nietzsche's promise of being a posthumous writer whose time is yet to come. Nor is Nietzsche the only one to yield to the allure of such a claim: Kant worries about the temptations of "the shadowy gift of posthumous fame [*Shattenwerke von Nachruhm*],"[64] later reflecting that it might take a century or more before his own works could *begin* to be read. In this tradition of writerly self-pity, Heidegger counts off more than a century, setting the date that people will *begin* to be able to read *Being and Time* four centuries hence: "Perhaps in the year 2327?"[65] Seemingly catching himself, Heidegger adds: "Or is that, too, an error, nourished by history and its arithmetic?"[66]

To this extent, Kant and Hume but Nietzsche as well, and as underscored in both the *Beiträge* and the *Schwarze Hefte*, Heidegger too, all exemplify the typical sentiment of feeling misunderstood while longing for recognition in a later age. And if we may mock Heidegger for this compensatory hope (even as we pardon Nietzsche and Hume—and we may not have known that Kant shared the same anxiety), all of these authors without exception would have been familiar with Marcus Aurelius on the vanity of seeking posthumous fame. Marcus Aurelius repeats this sentiment (in a later meditation on the caliber of those who esteem others—echoing Aristotle's elimination of fame as an ultimate good—and hence the foolishness of valuing *supposedly* famous men). This supposition and associated presumptions is a key theme in Diogenes Laertius and, more satirically, in Lucian, because this last is the point of the so-called *hyperanthropos*, the decidedly non-Nazi-like source for Nietzsche's *Übermensch*. For his own part, Marcus Aurelius writing "to himself," Tὰ εἰς ἑαυτόν (*ta eis heauton*), the title of what we call his *Meditations*, returns to the theme of fame and underscores its emptiness, echoing Heraclitus (favored by both Nietzsche and Heidegger), as Marcus Aurelius writes: "Life is a war and the dwelling place of a sojourner, posthumous fame is oblivion."[67]

Heidegger cites Heraclitus on war but somehow we, classicists and philosophers alike, manage to miss the Stoic echoes surrounding Heraclitus's "dark" or obscure aphorism on war. But if it is one thing to name oneself posthumous, it is another to micromanage or plan for it. Hence even if Heidegger might be said to have conceived his own *Nachlass* in a fashion parallel to Nietzsche (or, as in the *Schwarze Hefte* passages cited above: paralleling Hölderlin or Hegel), Heidegger's *Nachlass* could not be the same as any of the exemplars he invokes. Whether Heidegger did this semideliberately, through the accident of *chairos*, or by giving publishing directives affecting his own posterity, publishing the *Beiträge* along with *Besinnungen* together with the lecture courses and so on, the publication of these notebooks, no matter whether this works for or against him, offers an object lesson and a current illustration of Heidegger's thesis on the retroactive influence of the *Nachlass*.

Reading the *Black Notebooks* and the Question Concerning Technology

If the *Nachlass* is now to be seen as inverting "the true relation of time,"[68] the question of *whether* we should read the *Black Notebooks* becomes (or may become) the question of *how* we should read them. Let's take a sentence, by no means a neutral one (how could we find such a thing, given the backward-working force of the texts we are discussing?), but just a "sentence."

102. The "last man" races through Europe. [*Der "letzte Mensch" rast durch Europa.*][69]

Who, as Heidegger famously reminds us to ask, are we talking about? The editor's footnote cites Nietzsche's *Thus Spoke Zarathustra* for the definition of the "last man" as the "most contemptible," the "most despicable." Is this a racial reference? Is Nietzsche himself invoking the Jews? Is Heidegger? Anti-Semitic as we now take Heidegger to have been in many and some will say in all respects, this reading still seems unlikely. Thus it would be incoherent to simply substitute the Jews in place of the "last man" (with or without Heidegger's criticisms of the rootlessness of the Jews or their talent for calculation). The "last man" has a broader claim and one that overpowers, indeed and at breakneck speed, the Europe of Heidegger's day. Thus the term is not, in context, a term referring literally to the Americans (ditto the above parenthetical reflection), or the French or the Russians or even the English. To whom then does it refer?

Maybe we can be more literal; maybe Heidegger is secretly criticizing National Socialist ambitions with respect to Europe, and thus the "last man" could denote the Germans themselves, trying as they were to race through Europe. The war was meant to flash by like lightning, important for a people who still remembered the pain of the first, Great War.

In the same vein, and later in the same volume, we read two aphorisms, seemingly perfectly emblematic of the so-called later Heidegger, patterned straight out of the schematism of the *Beiträge* itself:

215. In philosophy, truth is not first grounded by evidence but rather the essence of truth is grounded. But what is this grounding? Until now it has remained hidden and emerged only displaced and misinterpreted by "science" into appearance. The grounding as Da-sein; in which however, the in-sistence in (event) [*(Ereignis)*].[70]
216. The efforts of thinking concerning such at their beginning: dark, intricate, yet unhewn diurnal passages; still not the simple way through the field into the dawn of the early year.[71]

Reading these subsequent entries we may wish to revisit Heidegger's invocation of Nietzsche's concept of the "last man." But we lack context unless we project it as we are inclined to, which we do when we hunt for evidence of anti-Semitism, and ingenious scholars could probably make a case for the anti-Semitism of this quote. But in fact for the most part, there is little contextualization (even the background reference to the publication and reception of *Sein und Zeit* must be added: it is not as explicit in the text as one would like). In the case of the above texts there is, if at all, only the most elliptical reference to the then-current world circumstance of war or even to Heidegger's political views. At the same time, one *can* read both texts as referring to Germany and war.

The passage through the scholar's "Long March" (as one may regard the scandal-assigned reading of the *Black Notebooks*) is by turns illuminating and challenging, because like Nietzsche's notebooks from his own *Nachlass*, we are reading without a particular context apart from the context of any given paragraph or section, or indeed in some cases, any single sentence. And that only means that, as Nietzsche says, "we scholars" are at liberty to impose whatever frame of reference we like.

We can do this because we are reading *sentences*, as in the case of aphorism 102 or the pair matched above, 215 and 216. Note in particular that we are reading sentences apart from the scholastic achievement and contextualization that is the monograph, the book qua book. Heidegger makes the distinction even more complicated with his reference to *ways not works*. The "work," as Heidegger speaks of his own contributions to thought, as he speaks of Nietzsche's *Will to Power* as a "masterwork," a work of mastery can indeed be followed were we to track a course through it, much as Heidegger in the aphorism quoted above speaks of the obscure and "still unhewn passages" of the new day of the early year.

Now if Heidegger is not (or not only) a scholastic thinker, despite Caputo and Sheehan, who read him as such (we may call this the Fordham mafia), but also contra (or despite) those who read him as a mystic, sometimes insightfully so as in the different cases of Reiner Schürmann and even Joan Stambaugh among others, or indeed as a poet, the "ways" Heidegger leaves open for phenomenology will be opposed to the monumental cathedra of "works" as these are usually known: treatises, masterpieces.[72]

Reading the *Beiträge* parallels a reading of *The Will to Power* and if the theme here does not concern the issue of the level of the text (Nietzsche's aphorism turns out to be a more difficult form than many imagine, not excluding Heidegger),[73] what does matter for us is just, even without reference to the scholarly book, that we are reading mere sentences and sheer paragraphs of the same sentences, and even less than that, given the terms of the present scandal and the digital mediation of today's philosophizing, we are on the lookout for keywords, specific terminology. In this case, a hermeneutic suited to the paragraphs and sentences of the *Schwarze Hefte* will not need to consider context. This is not because context is irrelevant (that is never true) but just because we happen to be reading Heidegger's *Schwarze Hefte* as classics scholars might comb through (the sadly "to-be-stretched," i.e., drawn-and-quartered Saint) Hippolytus not to learn about the details I have just parenthetically added about Hippolytus or indeed about anything he might have to say but just, let us suppose, in order to parse Heidegger's favorite quotation "But lightning governs the world [*ta de panta oiakizei keraunos*]" (reading Hippolytus, qua attributed to Heraclitus). Or else, as we read Clement or Diogenes Laertius (Nietzsche's special expertise)[74] assuming that we might be on the hunt for a not-yet-attributed "fragment" from someone more important than the doxographer in question (and the doxographer in question is *never* important).[75] "We scholars," as Nietzsche liked to say as he constantly sought to teach us our history—that is, our historiography—simply skip the doxographer's text, as Plato's frogs hug the shores, reading, as scholars do, no more than the likely citations (inevitably and unavoidably to pernicious effect, as Charles Kahn reminds us at the outset of his 1960 book on Anaximander,[76] a point so forgotten that Catherine Osborne needed more recently to contextualize it further, not that her own work has attracted sufficient attention among philosophers). Thus, we read the *Schwarze Hefte* in just this erratic fashion, ignoring everything else Heidegger seems to be addressing, all in order to look not for hitherto-unattributed pre-Socratic fragments but rather and only for his comments on Jews, on calculation, on machination.

Reading in an age no longer solely oriented toward the "world picture" but toward a new style of (non)reading: gathering nothing, selecting less, we need only search for words, keywords; none of the irrelevant details of what Heidegger is writing need concern us. The digital nonbookish prowess of today's (non)scholar far surpasses the peripatetic conference-going scholar Heidegger denounced as needing no library at all. This well-known passage from Heidegger's "The Age of World Picture" has a retrospective poignancy: "The research man no longer needs a library at home. Moreover, he is constantly on the move. He negotiates at meetings and collects information at congresses. He contracts for commissions with publishers. The latter now determine along with him which books must be written."[77] So much Heidegger hermeneutic, so little time. But, one more time, how should we read the one, solitary sentence cited above: "The 'last man' races through Europe"?[78] Can we count by numbers: Is code involved, as musicologists argued for years with respect to Plato's numbers in the *Republic*,[79] now recently reprised more mechanically via computer-based text searches?[80]

I will leave the numbering strategy to others more arithmetically or stichometrically or even kabbalistically inclined, but for now we might take a step backward, numberwise, to the longer "aphorism" in the same *Überlegungen IV*, gathered under the title *Was es gilt* (What counts) (including the parenthetical directive to compare it with the commentary to *Die Kehre der Umkehrung*), which begins: "98. It counts, to spring into there-*being* as historical."[81] Here the subsection heading, the opening sentence, acting as if it is a continuation of, or as responding to, the section heading, permits us to ask if the delimited section 102 should be read as standing alone or (and this is a separate issue, inasmuch as reading is a tissue of separate issues, folded and crossed) should be juxtaposed to aphorisms 101 and 103 or (now arbitrarily) to, say, the two aphorisms discussed above?

Once again, is this last man Nietzsche's or are we talking about somebody else? How many last men are there in philosophy—and who was Nietzsche speaking of, anyway?

We read further now in the last 'Black Notebook' volume of GA 96, in *Überlegungen XV*, prefaced by an epigraph on an unnumbered recto page, concluding with an important reference to the coordination between "planetarism" (today we would say "global" and mean it approvingly) and "its idiotism,"[82] where Heidegger leaves off numbering his aphorisms altogether with the still-Nietzschean tone of the single line (no number): "The 'modern' [*neuzeitliche*] human being has it in mind to make himself the servant of desertification [*Verwüstung*]."[83]

The theme of the desert and its increase stays with Heidegger: it is more significant than the mantra of "not thinking," the charge that we are not thinking, more significant than the claim that even "science does not think," and so on. The desert sentence is followed by another sentence reflecting on historicity and essence, succeeded by a meditation on "power politics [*Machtpolitik*]."[84] Then there is the reflection that one had just "discovered," albeit "late enough, and only by half again" "'Americanism,'" set off in scare quotes—as "political enmity."[85] Given the period in which he was writing, the sentence is and can only be a deeply Heideggerian irony and one that does not seem to depict a perfect card-carrying adherent of the Nazi regime. But we can now address the point because the breakneck language recurs, not racing across Europe but around the earth itself:

Something races around the globe, of which nobody anywhere has a grip, *assuming* it was *ever* the case that anyone steered who believed he was steering. The essence of power uncoils its mischief and it thereby becomes the devastation of the overpowering. The mood of the human being has become so fickle that *he* thinks to gain information regarding himself by making the human being the basic theme of "knowledge," i.e., concerning historico-technico-biological explanation and planability. The "flood" of American anthropologism, which scholars already as of 1912 had resisted, inundating the last embankments that might here and there have been able to stand. The "certified psychologist" not only replaces the "professor of philosophy" (in a trivial result of university renewal). The "certified psychologist" becomes the model for the only possible "thinker."[86]

Heidegger is talking about one political people as opposed to another—we catch the reference to "Americanism" again, this time in the form of a specifically American "anthropologism" (note that this is the term of rebuke Husserl raises contra Heidegger's own *Being and Time*)—and yet he is not speaking of adversaries, Russian, English contra Germans, and so on. To this extent Americans are indeed intended but only in the sense that what is meant has to do with what then becomes in the following passage the discussion of the rootlessness of World Jewry, in the same ecliptic force of the reference to the English that as it happens is nothing "English" in essence, any more than it is anything American. For Heidegger and to be sure, as we already know from the 1935 lecture, given in three versions, on "The Origin of the Work of Art," the rootlessness in question begins with those masters, to use Nietzsche's name for them, who effectuate the most decisive of all translations in the history of the West, as the history of Western metaphysics, and that is the translation, the re-rendering of the Greek on (and in) Roman terms—that is, "the transposition [*Übersetzung*] of Greek experience into another kind of thinking [*Denkungsart*]."[87] For Heidegger, this was literally fatal for thinking as he explains this in terms of the transformation of philosophic reflection by means of nothing less seemingly harmless than translation: "*Roman thought* takes over the Greek words without a corresponding, equally authentic experience of what they say, without the Greek word."[88] And both Athens and Jerusalem were indeed helpless before the most calculating movement the world has ever known: the measure and breadth of Rome itself—that is, the Roman Empire—but now one might well end by speaking of the ambitions of the Reich.

What is central, as Heidegger insists on pointing out in the *Schwarze Hefte*, as endemic to Nietzsche's reading of noble-versus-slave morality is that it is applicable not to Greece, as might be supposed of Nietzsche, but only to Rome. The point Heidegger makes is not as he claims anti-Nietzsche, because it is in fact Nietzsche's point from the inception of *The Genealogy of Morals* as an exactly philological methodology ultimately needing a reflection on nothing but translation and what things are called (including his reflections on Christians and Jews, which are of course not Greek references),[89] all the while emphasizing as Nietzsche very ambiguously, precisely, emphatically emphasizes (and this is also a question of translation, the *exchangeability* of words as such: "What do words matter [*Was liegt an Worten*]!"[90]

To return to Heidegger, the key seems to be this same manifestly irresistible "American anthropologism."[91] And once again, we note that *anthropologism* was the term of rebuke posed contra Heidegger's first book by Husserl, the only man apart from Max Scheler whose judgment mattered to him; it was a sore point between Heidegger and Jaspers that Jaspers was not that man., And we may now add that this is nothing but "psychologism" (another Husserlian reproach). Here we recall that "the 'certified psychologist' not only replaces the 'professor of philosophy' (as the trivial result of university reform). The 'certified psychologist' becomes the typification of the only 'possible' 'thinker.'"[92]

What accelerates across and hence spans the globe is an Americanism "in essence" (the standard Heideggerian motif) "nothing" fundamentally American. Keeping the racing metaphor, Heidegger concretizes the "pacemaker" of "globalism and idiotism" by speaking of this "Americanism" as "by far the dreariest form of the 'historical' lack of historicity [*Geschichtslosigkeit*] precisely in its ownmost heritage ahistorical."[93]

I am not seeking to use the above gloss to play on Heidegger's teasing gestures regarding the essence of this or that as having in essence "nothing to do" with this or that. What is at stake is the focus, as Heidegger contextualizes the frame, with his own emphasis, "*Planetarism* corresponds to *idiotism*."[94] Heidegger is concerned with globalism and with the root of the colloquially abusive term *idiot*, then not only in Germany but the world over, a diagnostic rubric for a level of cognitive disability. This standard meaning is not what he is invoking: "This word does not here mean the psychiatric definition of stupidity of intellect and spirit."[95] Thus Heidegger explicates the term "idiotism" as he uses it here:.

It is thought in the history of being and thinks the *idion*—one's own, in which today's human being finds itself within the order of the masses. This ownness is the same, in which the other and everyone in whom "one" finds oneself and is reciprocally affirmed. Idiotism entails: that one shifts what is one's own to what belongs to everyone; for example, the correlatedness of "Illustrated Magazines"; the liability of the wholly generic claim of radio broadcasting, where "no one" speaks, which nevertheless entails that for every howsoever insignificant a "concert," each and every violinist and trumpeter is to be called out by first and last name. One finds oneself everywhere in one's ownmostness, which however belongs exactly to everyone. Idiotism is the essential reduction to the cosmopolitan—that is, the planetary. This reductionism includes dispensing with all reflectivity, to the extent that such dispensation is not acknowledged *as* a dispensing with, as little indeed as the possibility of reflection. Idiotism is thus by no means a prerogative of "idiots" (i.e., of limitedly gifted persons).[96]

This passage contributes not only to political reflections on the public and the private, already in force in Werner Jaeger's *Paideia* (1938), from which Heidegger takes the contrast. Speaking of the *bios politicos* to distinguish between *idion* and *koinon,* Jaeger writes, "Man is not only 'idiotic,' he is also 'politic.'"[97] But such classical political reflections, in terms to be reprised by Arendt in *The Human Condition*,[98] are not merely "existential" reflections on the authentic and the inauthentic but are, I would argue, to be put in context with then-current studies of radio and media (Arnheim, Brecht, Anders, and Adorno).[99] Thus Heidegger warns us that "the idiotistic essence of radio broadcasting is, for example, still for the most part insufficiently applied."[100] The same criticisms can be made today of the Internet and its "shallows," as Nicholas Carr observes,[101] paralleling my characterization of Facebook in *The Hallelujah Effect* as a preternaturally autistic medium, a self-referentiality in full force even for tweeting or texting.[102] Heidegger finds this (and more) in radio. Thus in a spirit more commonly associated with Horkheimer and Adorno (and perhaps above all Heidegger's student, Günther Anders), Heidegger writes:[103]

It isn't enough that a [radio] device is up and running in every home, on every floor. Each and every "family" member, the servants, the children must have their *own* set up [*Gerät*] so to be *everyone*—to quickly and easily know and hear and "be" what every other person is as well. The radio apparatus [*Rundfunkgerät*] is the symbol of the togetherness of planetarism and idiotism.[104]

The concern is ontological. Again, especially given the resonance with Hannah Arendt, a resonance that begins with her allusion to what Heidegger above names "planetarism" in her own discussion of Sputnik,[105] Heidegger turns out to have more to say on topics on which his previously published references (film, radio, "world picture," etc.) may have been too sparse. Thus scholars of technology not only increasingly fail to read Heidegger but even go to the extreme of suggesting that Heidegger's analyses may have been just fine for analyzing one's grandfather's tools or tractors in the American Midwest or what have you, but with little to offer our brave, new digital humanities sourced and outsourced, connected and hacked. What would happen, if we were to read the *Schwarze Hefte* for hints regarding his understanding of technology? We know that several commentators have already taken the notebooks as an opportunity to endorse our never-once-threatened faith in technology as the ultimate "saving power" , far from Heidegger's Hölderlinian "danger" or Heidegger's later claim that "only a god" can save us.

Let us return to the first sentence of a paragraph quoted above, now in a slightly different rendering: "Something races around the globe, of which nobody anywhere has a grip, *given* that it was *ever once* the case that something ruled that meant to be ruling."[106] The 'ruling' theme—despite its "Heideggerism"—corresponds to a central thematic in the (received or mainstream) politics of technology known as the "technics-as-out-of-control" debate.[107] To be sure, Heidegger has never been particularly welcome in the political philosophy of technology to the extent that he does not advocate getting the out-of-control under control. What matters here is not only that Heidegger wasn't simply failing to read his Nietzsche the way Nazi authorities would have had him read Nietzsche for their purposes but more significantly (as a reading of the *Überlegungen* makes clear) that Heidegger may also have had an unacceptable view of nothing less than *Geschichte*, nothing less than *Geschick*, because for him what is at stake is always an aletheic affair. As Heidegger says in his lecture "The Origin of the Work of Art," "Wherever those decisions of our history that relate to our very being are made, are taken up and are abandoned by us, go unrecognized and are rediscovered via new inquiry, there the world worlds."[108]

In this sense, Heidegger's allusion to the ever-constant novelty of the new world is not only an obvious reference to America but (in a European context) also entails reference to propaganda not qua political propaganda alone: "The new becomes ever newer, ever more up to the minute, cheaper, faster, more arbitrary, and hence necessarily more shrill and more penetrating. It has, and along with it everything actual, surrendered the force of decision to groundless intrusiveness. The essence of that which one proximally names 'Americanism' is ready made."[109] I think we need to read the Heidegger of the *Schwarze Hefte* on radio and film (and extend his reflections to Twitter and YouTube) if only for the sake of modern media technology, and I have argued that these reflections may even help us read his passages on world Jewry and the Jews. But saying this does not mean mistaking the aspiration for the doing. The task is not thereby resolved; the task, as Heidegger put it in his "Epilogue" to his reflections on the work of art, is to "see the question."[110]

Can we include in this hermeneutic effort to "see the question," Heidegger's cautionary word contra hermeneutics at the conclusion of *Gesamtausgabe* 96 ("Everyone interprets. No one thinks [*Alle Welt interpretiert. Niemand denkt*]")?[111] The text resonates with several points cited above and with the Heidegger who brings hermeneutics into phenomenology: he calls us to go beyond interpretation.

If only because there cannot be hermeneutics (as we know it) apart from Heidegger, we are called to reflect on the hermeneutical nature of critical thinking, critical *theory*, critical *reading*.[112] For Gadamer, as also for Nietzsche too, to read will always be to read "otherwise" simply because, just as with understanding, there is nothing to be done for it: "*We understand in a different way*," Gadamer reminds us, "*if we understand at all.*"[113] Here, from a Nietzschean perspective, interpretation or hermeneutic critique always includes the questioners themselves. For Gadamer and in a deeply Heideggerian sense, "The real power of hermeneutical consciousness is our ability to see what is questionable."[114]

The Jews, Heidegger contends, live in accord with "the principle of race [*dem Rasseprinzip*]."[115] This is beyond commentary but many writers have already had a great deal to say about it. The paragraph is numbered 38,[116] and reading the last sentence in the paragraph (in Richard Polt's translation), we read "The Jews, *with their marked gift for calculation*, have already been 'living' for the longest time according to the principle of race, which is why they also defend themselves as vigorously as they can against its unrestricted application."[117] The sentence is *logically* impossible, the constellation offensive, with or without the promise of still more offensive bits yet to come, as Donatella Di Cesare says of the fourth volume now appearing in print and as Trawny has also hinted. For here Heidegger blames the victim, and this, as Adorno has made unavoidably clear: is simply unsupportable.

What may escape our notice, however, is Heidegger's focus on machination, and that is why we should return to Heidegger's questioning with respect to machination and technology: "That in the age of machination, race is elevated to the explicit and specifically arranged 'principle' of history (or historiology) is not the arbitrary invention of the 'doctrinaire' but a *resultant* of the power of machination, which must reduce beings in all spheres into scheduled [*planhafte*] calculation."[118]

There is no conclusion and every answer, to quote Adorno once again, is false.[119] To list a few of the myriad questions that still stand, just to begin with the inflammatory, the dangerous, the painful ones quoted above as they repeat and repeat, as they must be underscored: What is the race principle? Can we find it in use? The Nazis, all too factually, used it as did those who lived by the principle of apartheid in South Africa, but also inconveniently enough Israel and Gaza follow it today, like other nations, explicitly and tacitly. Heidegger says that the inasmuch as the Jews "have already been living"[120] by means of this principle, they count on, rely on, depend on being able to live according to the same principle.[121] Is this—*can we even ask*—true? No, it is not true, not at all. Jews in general, as such, do not, as such, "live" by the principle of race distinction (Jews vs. non-Jews) and if and a distinction of this kind may be found it is *not always* the case. By no philosophical, logical, or critical criteria may it be said that "the" Jews "live" by this principle—in however "gifted" a fashion one cares to dress such bigotry.

But to return to the point of the earlier context, because this is where we began—what, again, about Herzl? What is the principle according to which the state of Israel was founded: Why should such a homeland for a long homeless "state" have been founded, as indeed it was? World Jewry would refer then, *in potentia*, to the state to be of a stateless nation.

But if we now ask whether the Jews live by the principle of race, we can answer the question in the same way in which we can ask: Was Adorno Jewish. Well, in the eyes of the Nazis, yes, but in the eyes of Israel, no. Do Jews now live by the principle of race? Ask the Semitic residents of Gaza who happen to be Palestinian Semites as well as being non-Jews. Do the Jews live by the principle of race? Ask the 700 or so surviving Samaritans, non-Jews in the eyes of the state of Israel, but who call themselves Hebrews and Israelites, and have done so for millennia, with the same religious traditions and even what is in effect the *same* Pentateuch or Torah, older if anything,[122] preserving (this is the meaning of the word "Samaritan": *Samerim*) the same Torah, the same tradition in all respects apart from the crucial exception of the position of the Temple Mount in their reception of that shared biblical tradition (they say Mt. Gerizim vs. Mt. Moriah, the temple Mount of Jerusalem).[123] Do Jews live by the principle of race? Hard to say, but now, most recently, ask the Ethiopian Jews given contraceptive injections without their knowledge and against their will,[124] but also ask those Jews who seek to carry out *aliyah* or "return" to Israel but who trace their Jewish blood inconveniently on the side of their father's mother rather than their own mother: the last being a complicated calculation, a matter of generational numbers. But what is in each case to be determined is whether one may name oneself as belonging to a people. Is this calculation, this calculus, racial? Of course I cannot answer any of these questions, and just asking them is upsetting in itself. And asking them is not, as some may claim, to effectively answer them. For such questions need to be posed and may perhaps shed light on Heidegger's last word (it can hardly be a conclusion) to the third volume of the *Schwarze Hefte*.

For Heidegger makes a similar argument with respect to Russians and Germans, invoking the German ignorance of Russia as reprehensible, and in precise contrast to "the Russians who have for a century known a great deal and very precisely," as Heidegger writes, "concerning the Germans," namely with respect to "their metaphysics and their poetry. Yet the Germans have no comprehension of Russia."[125] For Heidegger and precisely with respect to the most "practical-political questions" that might be considered, the one thing, the only thing that would really make a difference would be to have made the question of the Russians themselves a question for the Germans themselves and thus to have some idea "who the Russians actually [*eigentlich*] are."[126] Yet lacking any idea of their adversary entails that Germany is victimized by *itself* just "to the extent that technology and communism storm against the West out of the East [*gegen den Westen aus dem Osten*], what storms in truth is the West against the West in a monstrous self-destruction of its own forces and tendencies."[127]

The Germans are to blame: *selber Schuld!*—they are themselves guilty. For Heidegger this guilt is not merely a failure of education and interest in the Other (though it is also that) but it is part of the fateful character of history, inasmuch as "history has, in addition to its public face, a hidden one."[128] Here Heidegger's conclusion to the third volume of the *Notebooks* is uncomfortably inconclusive. Like a potboiler, one can hardly wait for the next installment. Perhaps this will yield yet another meaning of the *Kehre*, and given Heidegger's *Nachlass* hermeneutics, this too will only be about time and the impact of the text: whereby the next set of revelations may be expected to reverse everything again.

There is more in the "Reflections" and "Indications," as Heidegger himself titles the *Notebooks*, and there will be much to question concerning our disappointment in Heidegger, but if we do not fail to consider the texts themselves, there is also much of value for philosophical thinking and scholarship. And we remain in fairly desperate need of a "Heidegger philology," as Heidegger himself argued from the start in constructing/deconstructing his *Nachlass* hermeneutics, beginning with his Dilthey reflections, in order to do justice to the published/unpublished materials that may help us understand a poetic work of art, a philosopher's thought.

Notes

1. Martin Heidegger, *Reden und andere Zeugnisse eines Lebensweges*, Gesamtausgabe 16, ed. Hermann Heidegger (Frankfurt: Klostermann, 2000), 747–748. In 2001, the current author organized one effort on the part of the Heidegger Circle to respond to Heidegger's letter to the tenth meeting of the Heidegger Circle in Chicago, April 11, 1976. The letter was republished in full in the conference proceedings and an English translation was made available at the conference itself (Babette Babich, convenor/editor, *Proceedings of the 35th Annual Meeting of the North American Heidegger Conference: Heidegger on Science and Technology*. New York, Fordham University, May 2001).

2. As William J. Richardson's invaluably scholarly bibliographical listing tells us, in the entry for 1927 and in addition to publishing a "history of the philosophical chair" at Marburg on the occasion of the university's 400th anniversary (*Die Philipps-Universität zu Marburg 1527–1927*), Heidegger also published "*Sein und Zeit*. Erste Hälfte," in *Jahrbuch für Philosophie und Phenomenologische Forschung* (Halle), VII, 1–438 (William J. Richardson, *Heidegger: Through Phenomenology to Thought* [New York: Fordham University Press, (1963) 2003], 676).

3. See, for instance, Richard Rorty, *Philosophy and the Mirror of Nature* (Princeton: Princeton University Press, 1979), Alasdair MacIntyre, *After Virtue* (Notre Dame: University of Notre Dame Press, 1981), Alexander Nehamas, *Life as Literature* (Cambridge, MA: Harvard University, 1985), or Gilles Deleuze, *Nietzsche and Philosophy*, trans. Hugh Tomlinson (London: Athlone Press, 1983). I refer here just to the titles of contemporary books that made a marked difference in academic philosophy in the Anglophone world and thus books that could be said to have had game-changing impact. These are not necessarily the most important or even the most influential hence I leave out Rawls and Dennett and Williams, not to mention the sort of popular salvo issued by Straussians such as Allan Bloom.

4. This is a separate issue and one that will inevitably, organically, be solved as many things are and at the most intimate level because death—the death of the sons in this case—resolves all such worries.

5. Silvio Vietta, whose mother had an affair with Heidegger, as Vietta told the author in Heidelberg in May 2013, was given the notebook by Heidegger himself. Author of a study of Heidegger, Nazism, and technology, *Heideggers Kritik am Nationalsozialismus und an der Technik* (Tübingen: Niemeyer, 1989), Vietta's book

produced little scholarly engagement. In the interim, however, Vietta has published a new book: *"Etwas rast um den Erdball…" Martin Heidegger: Ambivalente Existenz und Globalisierungskritik* (Munich: Fink, 2015).

6. This is a complex affair as scholars such as Alfred Denker and Holger Zaborowski have observed. What is the relevance of family interests (and family interests are typically part of the interests attending publication) in Heidegger's lifetime or in our own?

7. See Babette Babich, "Heidegger against the Editors: Nietzsche, Science, and the *Beiträge* as *Will to Power*," *Philosophy Today*, 47 (2003): 327–359. Later I discuss this in a specifically French context: "Le sort du *Nachlass*: Le problème de l'œuvre posthume," in *Mélivres/Misbooks: Études sur l'envers et les travers du livre*, ed. Pascale Hummel (Paris: Philogicum, 2009), 123–140. I examine it specifically with reference to politics in German as "Heideggers 'Beiträge' zwischen politische Kritik und die Frage nach der Technik," in *Eugenik und die Zukunft*, ed. Stefan Sorgner, H. James Birx, and Nikolaus Knoepffler (Freiburg: Karl Alber, 2006), 43–69.

8. See Babette Babich, "Heidegger's Will to Power," *Journal of the British Society for Phenomenology* 38 (2007): 37–60.

9. To this extent my earlier arguments over the years cannot but underscore Trawny's suggestion that Heidegger is all about setting up a kind of "philosophical legacy [*Vermächtnis*]" (Peter Trawny, *Heidegger und der Mythos der jüdischen Weltverschwörung* [Frankfurt: Klostermann, 2014], 14).

10. "150,000 copies of a specially durable wartime *Zarathustra* were distributed to the troops" (Steven Aschheim, *The Nietzsche Legacy in Germany, 1890–1990* [Berkeley: University of California Press, 1994], 135). I thank Nicholas Martin for discussing the legacy of *Zarathustra* and war at a conference he co-organized at the University of Birmingham in 2014.

11. Heidegger, "Überlegungen XIV," *Überlegungen XII–XV (Schwarze Hefte 1939–1941), Gesamtausgabe* 96, ed. Peter Trawny (Frankfurt: Klostermann, 2014), 207. Unless otherwise indicated, translations are my own.

12. Hölderlin, "Entwurf zu Kolomb" IV2, p. 595 (Columbus Draft); Heidegger, "Überlegungen XIV," *Überlegungen XII–XV, Gesamtausgabe* 96, p. 168; Heidegger's lecture on Hölderlin's Homecoming, June 21, 1943, in *Erläuterungen zu Hölderlins Dichtung* (1936–68)*, Gesamtausgabe* 4, ed. Friedrich-Wilhelm von Herrmann (Frankfurt: Klostermann, 1996). Keith Hoeller translates: Put out of tune / By humble things, / as by snow / Was the bell, with which / The hour is rung For the evening meal" (*Elucidations of Hölderlin's Poetry* [Amherst, NY: Humanity Books, 2000], 222). This is included in *Erläuterungen* elsewhere, but for a discussion of Heidegger's "agenda," see Adrian del Caro, "The Columbus Poems of Hölderlin and Nietzsche," *Colloquia Germanica* 21 (1988): 144–158. Interestingly enough, as one of Del Caro's notes points out, the Columbus motif in Hölderlin seems to bridge the early and the late Hölderlin.

13. This is to be sure a more complicated tradition, one that is not limited to Heidegger and that has grown up around the reception of Norbert von Hellingrath. See Stefan Zweig, *The Struggle with the Daemon: Hölderlin, Kleist, Nietzsche*, trans. Eden Paul and Cedar Paul (London: Pushkin Press, [1925] 2012); Bernhard Böschenstein, *Leuchttürme: Von Hölderlin zu Celan, Wirkung und Vergleich* (Frankfurt: Insel, [1977] 1982); and Bernhard Böschenstein, "Frucht des Gewitters," in *Zu Hölderlins Dionysos als Gott der Revolution* (Frankfurt: Insel, 1989) and Böschenstein and Heino Schmull, eds., *Paul Celan: Der Meridian; Endfassung—Entwürfe— Materialien* (Frankfurt: Suhrkamp, 1999). More recently, just to limit further references to English-language discussions, see Lucas Murrey, *Hölderlin's Dionysiac Poetry: The Terrifying-Exciting Mysteries* (Frankfurt: Springer, 2014).

14. Martin Heidegger, *Über den Anfang, Gesamtausgabe* 70, ed. Paola-Ludovico Coriando (Frankfurt: Klostermann, 2005), 168.

15. Heidegger, *Über den Anfang, Gesamtausgabe* 70, p. 167.

16. Heidegger, "Überlegungen XIV," *Überlegungen XII–XV, Gesamtausgabe* 96, p. 168.

17. Where else but from the Greeks—specifically, Aristotle (always Nietzsche's antipode)—do we get our notion of destiny? This is Athens, not Jerusalem.

18. I discuss this in German in two publications, "Dichtung, Eros, und Denken in Nietzsche und Heidegger: Heideggers Nietzsche Interpretation und die heutigen Nietzsche-Lektüre," in *Heidegger und Nietzsche, Heidegger-Jahrbuch 2*, ed. Alfred Denker, Marion Heinz, John Sallis, Ben Vedder, and Holger Zaborowski (Freiburg: Karl Alber, 2005), 239–264, and "Heideggers *Wille zur Macht*: Nietzsche—Technik—Machenschaft," in *Heidegger und Nietzsche*, ed. Babette Babich, Alfred Denker, and Holger Zaborowski, trans. Heidi Byrnes, Harald Seubert, and Holger Schmid (Amsterdam: Rodopi, 2012), 279–316. Also see the other informative essays in these two edited collections.

19. One can hardly imagine that scandal was what Heidegger had in mind, but authorial intention is the least of it.

20. Heidegger, "The Turning," in *The Question Concerning Technology*, trans. William Lovitt (San Francisco: Harper & Row, 1977), 48. I discuss the question of *Ge-Stell* with reference to media and communications in "Constellating Technology: Heidegger's *Die Gefahr* / The Danger," in *The Multidimensionality of Hermeneutic Phenomenology*, ed. Babette Babich and Dimitri Ginev (Frankfurt: Springer, 2014), 153–182 (see especially 162ff.). With explicit reference to Heidegger's student Günter Anders, see Babette Babich, "*O, Superman!* or Being towards Transhumanism: Martin Heidegger, Günther Anders, and Media Aesthetics," *Divinatio* 37 (2013): 83–99.

21. Thus in response to a student who wrote to ask about the nature of the *Nachlass* as such (the question had more to do, of course, with why one would make such surviving personal papers public), I replied by citing an email inquiry I had recently received. It was from Thomas Lannon, head of the Archives and Manuscripts Division of the New York Public Library, asking if I could help him "locate anyone who had access to the papers of the late Professor Joan Stambaugh. She left no heirs, so the chances are slim … but there is no doubt that any material that was preserved would have interest for scholars now and above all in the future." Referencing this query, I suggested that when a scholar or public figure dies, their notes, postcards, and cocktail-napkin scribblings—even their recipes (e.g., just confining ourselves to phenomenology and to texts as such: Malwida Husserl's recipe for her Christmas cookies)—may be important to preserve. In the future, I added, an author's email correspondence, perhaps even a record of texts and tweets sent and received, would also be fair game for conservation efforts and thus eventually for publication. The point of the student's question remains the question not of conservation but of publication, though of course withholding material would not, as I wrote, solve the problem, for if Heidegger had expurgated any part of the text or had attempted to destroy these texts, we would fault him for that. Think of the (now) halcyon days of the textual debates concerning the "inner truth and greatness" of National Socialism in Heidegger's *An Introduction to Metaphysics*, trans. Ralph Manheim (New Haven, CT: Yale University Press, 1959), 199.

22. The reason I refer to these notebooks using a collective rubric replicating part of the German title for the published volumes has to do with this undecided question of translation. The range of notebooks is still incomplete; there are said to be five more (depending on the time period, they may be of less interest to journalists than to Heidegger scholars), and it remains to be seen whether the title of the Fourth Division will ultimately be translated by notebook title, *Reflections* (sometimes in advance or afterward, affixing *Hints*), or as the collective rubric: *The Black Notebooks*.

23. See, in addition to his other discussions, Otto Pöggeler, *Neue Wege mit Heidegger* (Freiburg: Karl Alber, 1992).

24. See William J. Richardson, "Dasein and the Ground of Negativity: A Note on the Fourth Movement in the Beiträge-Symphony," *Heidegger Studies* 9 (1993): 35–52.

25. Simon Blackburn, "Enquivering," *New Republic*, October 30, 2000, 43–48. I discuss all this and more in an essay on Heidegger's *Parmenides* and the matter of translation, "Truth Untrembling Heart," in *Being Shaken: Ontology and the Event*, ed. Michael Marder and Santiago Zabala (London: Palgrave Macmillan, 2014), 154–176.

26. The same stir, in another example of the backward-working, future-transforming effect of the unpublished papers on the lineage of previously published works, is now revealed as having been nothing more than a kind of tempest in a teapot.

27. Martin Heidegger, *Besinnung, Gesamtausgabe* 66, ed. Friedrich-Wilhelm von Herrmann (Frankfurt: Klostermann, 1997); translated into English by Parvis Emad and Thomas Kalary as *Mindfulness (Besinnung)* (London: Continuum, 2006).

28. Trawny makes this distinction to separate his approach from those previously taken by others contra Heidegger, like Faye and Farías. In his book on the *Black Notebooks*, Trawny notes Holger Zaborowski's discussion of the same theme, without taking up the complexities Zaborowski details in his own 2010 book (which somehow did not merit media attention five years ago) on Heidegger *and* errancy *and* guilt. See note 12 in Trawny's *Heidegger und der Mythos der jüdischen Weltverschwörung*, citing Holger Zaborowski, "*Eine Frage von Irre und Schuld?*": *Martin Heidegger und der Nationalsozialismus* (Frankfurt: Fischer, 2010).

29. Heidegger, "Überlegungen XV," *Überlegungen XII–XV, Gesamtausgabe* 96, p. 262. As a German commentator writing in the *Frankfurter Allgemeine Zeitung* expresses it: "War Martin Heidegger ein Nationalsozialist? Die Antwort lautet schon lange: ja. … War Martin Heidegger Antisemit? Die Antwort lautet spätestens von

heute an: ja" (Jürgen Knaube, "Die Endschlacht der planetarischen Verbrecherbanden," *Frankfurter Allgemeine Zeitung*, December 3, 2014). Trawny argues that there is an execrable problem here even as he argues that one can be, as Richard Wolin quotes him as saying in his own review in the *Jewish Review of Books*, "constructive," and even as he argues for the value of continued Heidegger studies, for Trawny it remains the case, in a striking parallel with Habermas's language with respect to the danger that once was attributed to the influence of Nietzsche: "The being-historical construction can lead to a contamination of Heidegger's thinking" (Trawny, *Heidegger und der Mythos der jüdischen Weltverschwörung*, 93).

30. This was the subject of some discussion for the mailing list of the Heidegger Circle in the United States, and it also provoked heated discussion over the course of four days at the Paris meeting, *Heidegger et les Juifs*, in January 2015. See the contributions, including the author's own "Heidegger et ses '*Juifs*,'" in *Heidegger et les "Juifs,"* ed. Joseph Cohen and Raphael Zagury-Orly (Paris: Grassett, 2015), 411–453.

31. Heidegger, cited by Jaspers as cited in Trawny, *Heidegger und der Mythos der jüdischen Weltverschwörung*, 45.

32. See Fred Dallmayr, chapter 2, this volume.

33. Heidegger remained a Catholic according to many of his readers or commentators, even after his conversion to the state religion in Weimar and Nazi Germany and today's German Evangelical Protestantism (i.e., Lutheranism) and despite certain hints of animism, polytheism, and atheism, all concentrated in the particular iconography of the star on his gravestone in his hometown of Messkirch. Note that the star is not to be resolved in two-dimensional form, as some have sought to do, by counting points, as it were. The star is a specifically three dimensional one and its interpretation must accord with other local instantiations of the same figure and form.

34. Trawny, *Heidegger und der Mythos der jüdischen Weltverschwörung*, 26–27.

35. Christian Fuchs, "Martin Heidegger's Anti-Semitism: Philosophy of Technology and the Media in the Light of the *Black Notebooks*; Implications for the Reception of Heidegger in Media and Communication Studies," *Triple C: Communication, Capitalism & Critique* 13 (2015): 55–78.

36. Fuchs, "Martin Heidegger's Anti-Semitism."

37. Fuchs, "Martin Heidegger's Anti-Semitism."

38. See specifically Theodor Herzl, *Der Judenstaat: Versuch einer modernen Lösung der Judenfrage* (Vienna: M. Breitenstein, 1896).

39. Michael Berkowitz, *Zionist Culture and West European Jewry before the First World War* (Cambridge: Cambridge University Press, 1993). For a recent discussion of Herzl and "world Jewry," see Hermann Levin Goldschmidt, *The Legacy of German Jewry* (New York: Fordham University Press, 2007), as well as, yet more broadly, Schlomo Sand, *The Invention of the Jewish People*, trans. Yael Lotan (London: Verso, 2009).

40. For a broad overview, see Joanna Nittenberg, ed., *Wandlungen und Brüche: Von Herzls "Welt" zur Illustrierten Neuen Welt, 1897–1997* (Vienna: INW, 1997).

41. Cited under the rubric "Weltjudentum" in Cornelia Schmitz-Berning, *Vokabular des Nationalsozialismus* (Berlin: de Gruyter, 2007), 689. This topic exceeds the current essay, but see for a beginning, Baruch Kimmerling, *The Invention and Decline of Israeliness: State, Society, and the Military* (Berkeley: University of California Press, 2005) and see further Sand's historical reflection, *The Invention of the Land of Israel: From Holy Land to Homeland*, trans. Geremy Forman (London: Verso, 2012).

42. Howard Caygill, *Levinas and the Political* (London: Routledge, 2002), 14.

43. Caygill, *Levinas and the Political*, 14.

44. Theodor Herzl, *The Complete Diaries of Theodor Herzl*, ed. Raphael Patai, trans. Harry Zohn (New York: Herzl Press and Thomas Yoseloff, 1960), 19.

45. It hardly needs to be noted that this is a hugely complicated theme. The "scrap" reads: "H[is] M[ajesty's] G[overnment] accepts the principle that Palestine should be reconstituted as the Nat[iona]l Home of the J[ewish] P[eople]. HMG will use its best efforts to secure the achievement of this object, and will discuss the necessary methods and means with the Z[ionist] O[rganization]." For the language of the "scrap of paper" "scrawled" by Leon Simon and recently auctioned off (as it turned out, above the higher end of the auction range set between $500,000 and $800,000, at $884,000), see Donald MacIntyre's article, "The Birth of Modern Israel: A Scrap of Paper That Changed History," *Independent,* May 26, 2005. See also Malcolm Yapp, *The Making of the Modern Near East, 1792–1923* (London: Routledge, 1988).

46. Jeffrey Herf, *The Jewish Enemy: Nazi Propaganda during World War II and the Holocaust* (Cambridge, MA: Harvard University Press, 2009).

47. Peter Trawny, *Martin Heideggers Phänomenologie der Welt* (Freiburg: Karl Alber, 1997).

48. See Tracy B. Strong's chapter in this volume.

49. For what we may call "Sheehan I" on Heidegger, see Sheehan, *"Caveat Lector:* The New Heidegger," *New York Review of Books* 28, no. 19 (December 4, 1980): 39–41, as well Sheehan's review of Farías, "Heidegger and the Nazis," *New York Review of Books* 35, no. 10 (June 16, 1988): 38–47.

50. Nietzsche, *Morgenröte*, Vorwort 5, in *Samtliche Werke: Kritische Studienausgabe*, ed. Giorgio Colli and Mazzino Montinari, 15 vols., vol. 3 (Munich: De Gruyter, 1999), 17.

51. See not only my own essay (cited above), "Le sort du *Nachlass*: Le problème de l'œuvre posthume," but also the range of other essays on the genre of "misbooks" in Hummel's edited collection, *Mélivres/Misbooks: Études sur l'envers et les travers du livre.*

52. "Ein gewisser Bollnow, ein Vielschreiber, der sich sogar zu meinen 'Schülern' zählt und *'es'* daher wissen muß, veröffentlicht jetzt eine Schrift über das *Wesen* der Stimmungen. Schreiben und Meinen kann man über Alles; warum auch nicht einmal 'über' die Stimmungen. 'Psychiater' und andere *Leute* haben davon vielleicht einen Nutzen. Und sie sollen ihn reichlich haben" (Heidegger, "Überlegungen XIV," *Überlegungen XII–XV, Gesamtausgabe* 96, p. 216). The sarcasm is patent: Bollnow appropriates a concept he attributes to Heidegger. The issue is not a matter of possessiveness but relevance. For Heidegger as he goes on to ask, "what has any of that to do with *Being and Time*?—what has this scribbling to do with philosophy"? (*Überlegungen XII–XV, Gesamtausgabe* 96, p. 217). At stake is not today's now frequently touted *"ressentiment"* as having to be the driving motor whenever Heidegger criticizes anyone but Heidegger's understanding of his own work and his long-standing conviction that this work was not understood.

53. See Babette Babich, "A Musical Retrieve of Heidegger, Nietzsche, and Technology: Cadence, Concinnity, and Playing Brass," *Man and World* 26 (1993): 239–260.

54. See, for example, Catherine H. Zuckert and Michael Zuckert, "Strauss: Hermeneutics or Esotericism," in *The Routledge Companion to Hermeneutics*, ed. Jeff Malpas and Hans-Helmuth Gander (London: Routledge, 2014), 127–136.

55. See Babich, "A Musical Retrieve of Heidegger, Nietzsche, and Technology." Trawny uses a rhetorically otherwise freighted term here by speaking of "Aroma" (Trawny, *Heidegger und der Mythos der jüdischen Weltverschwörung*, 14).

56. See Erwin Panofsky, "Die Perspektive als 'symbolische Form,'" in *Vorträge der Bibliothek Warburg 1924–1925* (Nendeln, Liechtenstein: Kraus Reprint, [1927] 1967).

57. Erwin Panofsky, *Gothic Architecture and Scholasticism* (Latrobe: Archabbey, [1951] 1957), 59.

58. Panofsky, *Gothic Architecture and Scholasticism*, 68.

59. Manfred Riedel, *Hören auf die Sprache: Die akroamatische Dimension der Hermeneutik* (Frankfurt: Suhrkamp, 1989).

60. See Erich F. Podach's *Nietzsches Zusammenbruch* (Heidelberg: N. Kampmann, 1930).

61. Heidegger, "Überlegungen XIV," *Überlegungen XII–XV, Gesamtausgabe* 96, p. 207.

62. Heidegger, "Überlegungen XIV," *Überlegungen XII–XV, Gesamtausgabe* 96, p. 207.

63. For a discussion, see the section titled "Hermeneutics and the *Leavings of the Past*" of Babette Babich, "Nietzsche and the Ubiquity of Hermeneutics," in *The Routledge Companion to Hermeneutics*, ed. Jeff Malpas and Hans-Helmuth Gander (London: Routledge, 2014), 85–97 (especially 90–93).

64. Kant, *Kritik der reinen Vernunft*, B426.

65. Heidegger, "Überlegungen XIV," p. 196.

66. Heidegger, "Überlegungen XIV," p. 196.

67. Marcus Aurelius, *Meditations* II.17. Cf. the more conventionally and protractedly sophistic argument on vanity beyond death: "He who has a powerful desire for posthumous fame does not consider that every one of those who remember him will himself also die very soon; then again also they who have succeeded them, until the whole remembrance shall have been extinguished as it is transmitted through men who foolishly admire and then perish" (Marcus Aurelius, *Meditations* IV).

68. Heidegger, "Überlegungen XIV," *Überlegungen XII–XV, Gesamtausgabe* 96, p. 207.

69. Heidegger, "Überlegungen IV," *Überlegungen II–VI, Gesamtausgabe* 94, p. 239.

70. "In der Philosophie wird nicht das Wahre durch Beweise erst begründet, sondern das Wesen der Wahrheit wird gegründet. Was aber ist diese Gründung? Bisher blieb sie verborgen und kam nur verstellt und durch 'Wissenschaft' mißdeutet zum Vorschein. Die Gründung als Da-sein; dieses aber die Inständigkeit im (Ereignis)" (Heidegger, "Überlegungen IV," *Überlegungen II–VI, Gesamtausgabe* 94, p. 271).

71. "Die denkerische Bemühung um den an deren Anfang: Dunkle, verwickelte, unausgehauene Gänge unter Tag; noch nicht der einfache Weg durchs Feld im Frühjahrsmorgen" (Heidegger, "Überlegungen IV," *Überlegungen II–VI, Gesamtausgabe* 94, p. 271).

72. Thus, and no matter whether we are scholastically minded or not, the ideal of the medieval *summa* remains with us whenever we read anything. Erwin Panofsky reflects that we when cite chapter and verse, or refer to any text, we are "unsuspecting heirs to Scholasticism" (Panofsky, *Gothic Architecture and Scholasticism*, 33). As scholars, we use the technology of the book, and our citation practice thus refers to a technically specific *Ge-Stell*. When we provide "an exact quotation, we must either refer to the pages of a printed edition conventionally accepted as authoritative (as we do with Plato and Aristotle), or to a scheme introduced by some humanist of the Renaissance." As Panofsky explains: "We take it for granted that major works of scholarship, especially systems of philosophy and doctoral theses, are organized according to a scheme of division and subdivision, condensable into a table of contents or synopsis, where all parts denoted by numbers or letters of the same class are on the same logical level; so that the same relation of subordination obtains between, say, sub-section (a), section (i), chapter (I) and book (A) as does between, say, sub-section (b), section (ii), chapter (IV) and book (C)" (Panofsky, *Gothic Architecture and Scholasticism*, 32).

73. The aphorism is a particularly challenging notion for Nietzsche and thus, if I am correct, for Heidegger. On Nietzsche's aphorism, including further literature on the theme, see Babette Babich, "The Genealogy of Morals and Right Reading: On the Nietzschean Aphorism and the Art of the Polemic," in *Nietzsche's On the Genealogy of Morals*, ed. Christa Davis Acampora (Lanham, MD: Rowman & Littlefield, 2006), 171–190.

74. See Friedrich Nietzsche, *Frühe Schriften*, vol. 5 (Munich: Beck, 1994), 125ff. Few people today read, as Nietzsche did read, Diogenes Laertius but see Jonathan Barnes, "Nietzsche and Diogenes Laertius," *Nietzsche-Studien* 15 (1986): 16–40. I discuss this problem in Babette Babich, "Nietzsche and the Ubiquity of Hermeneutics"; see also Thomas H. Brobjer, *Nietzsche's Philosophical Context: An Intellectual Biography* (Champaign: University of Illinois Press, 2008), as well a bit elliptically, David Lachterman, "*Die ewige Wiederkehr des Griechen*: Nietzsche and the Homeric Tradition," in *Nietzsche und die antike Philosophie*, ed. Daniel Conway and Rudolf Rehn (Trier: Wissenschaftlicher Verlag, 1992).

75. For more, see Catherine Osborne, *Rethinking Early Greek Philosophy: Hippolytus of Rome and the Presocratics* (London: Duckworth, 1987).

76. See Charles Kahn, *Anaximander and the Origins of Greek Cosmology* (New York: Columbia University Press, 1960).

77. Martin Heidegger, "The Age of the World Picture," in Martin Heidegger, *The Question Concerning Technology and Other Essays*, trans. William Lovitt (New York: Harper & Row, 1977), 115–154 (quote on 122).

78. Heidegger, "Überlegungen IV," *Überlegungen II–VI, Gesamtausgabe* 94, p. 239.

79. This is a serious note because a serious tradition reads Plato and the Bible in this fashion. On those who did their mathematical calculations the old-fashioned way by reading and counting, see Ernest McClain, *The Pythagorean Plato: Prelude to the Song Itself* (York Beach, ME: Nicolas Hays, 1978), and John Bremer, "Some Arithmetical Patterns in Plato's 'Republic,'" *Hermathena* 169 (2000): 69–97.

80. For an example of someone who happens to do his philosophical research via digital means, see Jay Kennedy, "Plato's Forms, Pythagorean Mathematics, and Stichometry," *Apeiron: A Journal for Ancient Philosophy and Science* 43 (2010): 1–32.

81. Heidegger, *Überlegungen II–VI, Gesamtausgabe* 94, p. 237.

82. Heidegger, "Überlegungen XV," *Überlegungen XII–XV, Gesamtausgabe* 96, p. 250.

83. Heidegger, "Überlegungen XV," *Überlegungen XII–XV, Gesamtausgabe* 96, p. 259.

84. Heidegger, "Überlegungen XV," *Überlegungen XII–XV, Gesamtausgabe* 96, p. 260.

85. Heidegger, "Überlegungen XV," *Überlegungen XII–XV, Gesamtausgabe* 96, p. 260.

86. Heidegger, "Überlegungen XV," *Überlegungen XII–XV, Gesamtausgabe* 96, p. 267.

87. Martin Heidegger, *Holzwege, Gesamtausgabe* 5, ed. Friedrich-Wilhelm von Herrmann (Frankfurt am Main: Klostermann, [1950] 2003), 7; the text cited is translated into English in *Poetry, Language, Thought*, trans. Albert Hofstadter (New York: Harper & Row, 1971), 23.

88. Heidegger, *Holzwege*, 7; in English in *Poetry, Language, Thought*, 23.

89. The fourth section of the first book of Nietzsche's *Zur Genealogie der Moral: Eine Streitschrift* invokes the "pointer" (*Fingerzeig*) of translation and the roots of the same via etymology as the means of resolving conflict, whether regarding the question of what values are revalued (renamed) or in terms of the rendering of one position into another. Thus the section begins with reflecting on the different meanings of terms in ancient Greek and ends—after a stylistically derailing interlude invoking the Aryan and the Celt—with the Roman, whereby Nietzsche translates the Latin *bonus* as "the warrior [*den Krieger*]" and finishes by invoking "our German 'gut' itself [*Unser deutsches 'Gut' selbst*]" as the godlike, with an allusion to a no less "noble" name than that of Goethe (Friedrich Nietzsche, *Kritische Studienausgabe* [Berlin: De Gruyter, 1980], vol. 5, 264).

90. Nietzsche, *Kritische Studienausgabe*, vol. 5, 264.

91. Heidegger, *Holzwege*, 7; in English in *Poetry, Language, Thought*, 23.

92. Heidegger, "Überlegungen XV," *Überlegungen XII–XV, Gesamtausgabe* 96, p. 267.

93. The quote glossed here reads as whole: "Der eigentliche Schrittmacher der Einheit von Planetarismus und Idiotismus, aber auch ihr eigentlich gemäßer Erbe, ist der Amerikanismus, die wohl ödeste Gestalt der 'historischen' Geschichtslosigkeit" (Heidegger, *Überlegungen XV*, *Überlegungen XII–XV, Gesamtausgabe* 96, p. 266).

94. Heidegger, *Überlegungen XV*, *Überlegungen XII–XV, Gesamtausgabe* 96, p. 265.

95. Heidegger, *Überlegungen XV*, *Überlegungen XII–XV, Gesamtausgabe* 96, p. 265.

96. Heidegger, *Überlegungen XV*, *Überlegungen XII–XV, Gesamtausgabe* 96, p. 265.

97. Werner Jaeger, *Paideia: The Ideals of Greek Culture,* vol. 1: *Archaic Greece: The Mind of Athens*, trans. Gilbert Highet, 2nd ed. (Oxford: Oxford University Press, 1945), 111. The edition on which the translation was based first appeared in 1933 and the second edition in 1935.

98. Hannah Arendt, *The Human Condition*, 2nd ed. (Chicago: University of Chicago Press, [1958] 1998), 35.

99. I discuss these authors in the context of a reading of media technology and specifically with reference to radio; see Babette Babich, "Adorno's Radio Phenomenology: Technical Reproduction, Physiognomy, and Music," *Philosophy and Social Criticism* 40, no. 10 (October 2014): 957–996.

100. Heidegger, "Überlegungen XV," *Überlegungen XII–XV, Gesamtausgabe* 96, p. 265.

101. Nicholas Carr, *The Shallows: What the Internet Is Doing to Our Brains* (New York: Norton, 2011).

102. See the first three chapters of Babette Babich, *The Hallelujah Effect: Philosophical Reflections on Music, Performance Practice and Technology* (Surrey: Ashgate, 2013).

103. See the following editorial compendium (i.e., and in the fashion of Nietzsche's *Will to Power*, a collection of published and unpublished works and excerpts, edited, in Anders's name, by Gerhard Oberschlick): Günther Anders, *Über Heidegger* (Munich: Beck, 2001). For a very informative contrast between Anders in his own epoch and Peter Sloterdijk at the time, also see Ludger Lütkehaus, "In der Mitte sitzt das Dasein: Die Philosophen Günther Anders und Peter Sloterdijk lesen zweierlei Heidegger," *Die Zeit*, May 2002, 42. For a discussion of Heidegger and Anders, see my "*O, Superman!* or Being towards Transhumanism: Martin Heidegger, Günther Anders, and Media Aesthetics."

104. Heidegger, "Überlegungen XV," *Überlegungen XII–XV, Gesamtausgabe* 96, p. 265.

105. For a discussion of this reference, see Roger Berkowitz, "Being Human in an Inhuman Age," *HA: The Journal of the Hannah Arendt Center for Politics and the Humanities at Bard College* 2 (2012): 112–121.

106. Heidegger, "Überlegungen XV," *Überlegungen XII–XV, Gesamtausgabe* 96, p. 265.

107. See classically enough in English, and clearly drawing on Heidegger with reference to the politics of technology, the work of Langdon Winner but also George Kateb and John Street.

108. Heidegger, "The Origin of the Work of Art," in *Poetry, Language, Thought*, 43.

109. Heidegger, "Überlegungen XV," *Überlegungen XII–XV, Gesamtausgabe* 96, p. 272.

110. Heidegger, "The Origin of the Work of Art," 77.

111. Heidegger, "Überlegungen XV," *Überlegungen XII–XV, Gesamtausgabe* 96, p. 276.

112. See the interview with Donatella di Cesare: "Selbstvernichtung der Juden: Exklusiv-Interview mit Donatella Di Cesare," *Hohe Luft: Philosophie-Zeitschrift*, February 10, 2015.

113. Hans-Georg Gadamer, *Truth and Method*, trans. Garrett Barden (New York: Continuum, 1975), 264; my emphasis.

114. Hans-Georg Gadamer, "The Universality of the Hermeneutic Problem (1966)," in Hans-Georg Gadamer, *Philosophical Hermeneutics*, trans. David E. Linge (Berkeley: University of California Press, 1976), 3–17 (quote on 13).

115. Heidegger, "Überlegungen XII," §38, *Überlegungen XII–XV, Gesamtausgabe* 96, p. 56.

116. Heidegger, "Überlegungen XII," §38, *Überlegungen XII–XV, Gesamtausgabe* 96, p. 56.

117. Heidegger, "Überlegungen XII," §38, *Überlegungen XII–XV, Gesamtausgabe* 96, p. 56. Thanks to Richard Polt, who shared this translation via email with the members of the Heidegger Circle.

118. Heidegger, "Überlegungen XII," §38, *Überlegungen XII–XV, Gesamtausgabe* 96, p. 56.

119. For references and discussion, see my forthcoming essay, "'The Answer Is False': Archaeologies of Genocide," in *Adorno and the Concept of Genocide*, ed. Ryan Crawford and Erik M. Vogt (Amsterdam: Brill/Rodopi, 2015).

120. Heidegger, "Überlegungen XII," §38, *Überlegungen XII–XV, Gesamtausgabe* 96, p. 56. Thanks again to Richard Polt.

121. Heidegger, "Überlegungen" XII, §38, *Überlegungen XII–XV, Gesamtausgabe* 96, p. 56. I again thank Richard Polt.

122. *The Israelite Samaritan Version of the Torah: First English Translation Compared with the Masoretic Version*, trans. Benyamim Tsedaka and Sharon Sullivan (London: Eerdmans, 2013).

123. Reinhard Pummer, *The Samaritans* (Leiden: E. J. Brill, 1987). See also John Bowman, *The Samaritan Problem* (New York: Pickwick Press, 1975). For extensive further references, see Yitzakh Magen, "The Dating of the First Phase of the Samaritan Temple on Mt Gerizim in Light of Archaeological Evidence," in *Judah and the Judeans in the Fourth Century B.C.E.*, ed. Oded Lipschitz et al. (Winona Lake, IN: Eisenbrauns, 2007), 157–211.

124. Alistair Dawber, "Israel Gave Birth Control to Ethiopian Jews without Their Consent," *The Independent*, January 27, 2013; Phoebe Greenwood, "Ethiopian Women in Israel 'Given Contraceptive without Consent,'" *Guardian*, February 28, 2013.

125. Heidegger, "Überlegungen XV," *Überlegungen XII–XV, Gesamtausgabe* 96, p. 276.

126. Heidegger, "Überlegungen XV," *Überlegungen XII–XV, Gesamtausgabe* 96, p. 276.

127. Heidegger, "Überlegungen XV," *Überlegungen XII–XV, Gesamtausgabe* 96, p. 276.

128. Heidegger, "Überlegungen XV," *Überlegungen XII–XV, Gesamtausgabe* 96, p. 276.

II   THE *BLACK NOTEBOOKS* AND OTHER WORKS

6

The Role of Martin Heidegger's *Notebooks* within the Context of His Oeuvre

Friedrich-Wilhelm von Herrmann

I. The Philosophical Dimension of the *Notebooks*

Martin Heidegger's book *Besinnung* (*Mindfulness*) contains an "Appendix" titled "Looking Back on My Career." It includes a text "Supplement to Wish and Will (Concerning the Preservation of Works Endeavored)."[1] Among these "Works Endeavored" belong Heidegger's unpublished manuscripts from 1937–1938. Heidegger enumerates seven different sorts of manuscripts under the heading, "I. What Is On Hand":

(1.) The Lecture Courses; (2.) The Lectures; (3.) Notes for the Seminars; (4.) Sketches for the Work (including my criticism of *Being and Time*); (5.) Considerations and Hints, Notebooks II-IV-V; (6.) Lecture Course on Hölderlin and Sketches for "Empedocles"; (7.) *Of the Event (Contributions to Philosophy)*, see also (# 4).[2]

Under the heading "Regarding Each of These Points," Heidegger then adds important explanations concerning the seven sorts of manuscripts. Of special significance for us are the comments concerning points (5), (7), and (4). Regarding (5), Heidegger writes:

What is recorded in these notebooks, particularly in notebooks II, IV, V, reveals also, at least in part, the basic attunements [*Grundstimmungen*] of my questioning into and my indications of the most advanced horizons for my endeavors in thought. While these notebooks seem to be the product of circumstance, they display the unceasing endeavor concerning the one and only question.[3]

Heidegger wrote the text "Concerning the Preservation of Works Endeavored" in 1938, after completing the manuscript for the book *Contributions to Philosophy (Of the Event)*.[4] Thus Heidegger only mentions the *Notebooks* II–V of the *Überlegungen* (*Considerations*), which have been published now in volume 94 of the *Gesamtausgabe*.[5] *Notebook* I is nowhere to be found and not mentioned anywhere by Heidegger. It seems likely that he himself put it aside. The reason for this we can only guess. Maybe it contained notes for the planned revision of *Being and Time* for the third edition in 1931, based on the 1930 Lecture Course "The Essence of Freedom,"[6] where the subject matter of *Being and Time* is embedded in "Being and Freedom." Notebook II of the *Überlegungen* (*Considerations*)

begins in October 1931. It is the time when Heidegger embarks on his ontohistorical thinking. Thus the *Black Notebooks* belong to the long period of ontohistorical thinking, lasting
from 1930–1931 to the first half of the 1970s. The *Überlegungen* (*Considerations*) from
1931 through 1941 (now published as volumes 94–96 in the *Gesamtausgabe*) belong to
Heidegger's project of ontohistorical thinking, which took shape in the "Sketches for the
Work" and the big treatises, *Contributions to Philosophy (Of the Event) (1937/38)*[7] and *The
Event (1941/42)*.[8]

Three things stand out in the explications to "(5) Considerations and Hints": *1. the basic
attunement of questioning; 2. the indications toward the most advanced horizon of the
endeavors of thinking; and 3. the character of the unceasing effort concerning the one
and only question.* The "basic attunements" that accompany the ontohistorical questioning are shock (*Erschrecken*), restraint (*Verhaltenheit*), and diffidence (*Scheu*). Heidegger
specifies the "most advanced horizons for the endeavors of thinking" in "(4) Sketches for
the Work": "The difference between beings and being, Da-sein and truth, time-space, the
modalities, attunement, language, the method and the essence of the question." The "one
and only question" of these endeavors of thought along the axis of ontohistorical thinking
is "the question concerning the truth of being [*Seyn*]," as staked out within the mentioned
"horizons of thinking."[9] Heidegger sees the "Sketches for the Work" as "attempts" to grasp
the entire problematic of *Being and Time* more originally and to understand this from
within the mentioned horizons of thinking. Within these horizons belong the *Überlegungen*
(*Considerations*) as well, insofar as they, like the "Sketches for the Work," serve the one
and only question concerning the truth of being (*Seyn*).

Under section (4) Heidegger also says important things about the *Contributions to Philosophy (Of the Event)*: "Since the spring of 1932 the main features of the plan have been
in place, at first taking shape in the draft *Of the Event*."[10] All of the subsequent treatises—
Besinnung (*Mindfulness*) (1938–1939), "Die Überwindung der Metaphysik" ("The Overcoming of Metaphysics") (1938–1939),[11] *Die Geschichte des Seyns* (*The History of Being*)
(1938–1940),[12] *Über den Anfang* (*On the Beginning*) (1941),[13] *Das Ereignis* (*The Event*)[14]
(1941–1942), and *Die Stege des Anfangs* (*Pathways of the Beginning*)[15] (1944)—are new
variants of the original plan for the edifice of ontohistorical thinking as established in the
spring of 1932.

Whereas the ontohistorical treatises clear the way for the decisive main path of ontohistorical thinking, insofar as they gather and think through the thoughts for the edifice of this
thinking, the *Überlegungen* (*Considerations*) are companions on this main path, and they
supplement it. As such, they are subordinated to and coordinated with the great trailblaz-
ing works and, consequently, not placed before or over them. Therefore, the entries in the
Black Notebooks, short or long, are only accessible and comprehensible by way of the big
treatises. This fact is the sole reason why, following Martin Heidegger's wish, the *Black
Notebooks* constitute the conclusion to the *Gesamtausgabe* and are to be published after all
other volumes have been released.

The *Notebooks*, titled *Überlegungen* (*Considerations*), are often ontohistorical, critical commentaries about contemporary affairs. Additionally, they are supplements to earlier works, because they again tackle previously stated views and occasionally subject them to a critical review. For instance, we find such a reference to previous positions in entries 201, 202, and 204 of volume 94. These entries revisit and supplement the theme of "man and animal," following the comparative studies into world-poor animals and world-forming man from the Lecture Course 1929–1930, *The Basic Concepts of Metaphysics: World-Finitude-Solitude*.[16]

Since 1931 Heidegger would jot down in his *Notebooks* occasional thoughts that did not belong in a manuscript in progress or could not be incorporated into one or the other existing manuscripts under some key concept. Heidegger kept pencil and notepad on his bedside table, in order to jot down occasional thoughts that came to him during a sleepless hour, which he would carefully write up in his *Black Notebooks* the next day.

II.   How to Do Justice to the *Black Notebooks*

In two of the three volumes of the *Überlegungen* (*Considerations*), volumes 95 and 96,[17] readers will find thirteen passages of one, two, or four sentences, and in one case even five sentences, where Heidegger offers comments, from an ontohistorical, critical perspective, about "international Jewry" and "World Jewry." Based on these passages, which amount to hardly more than two and a half of the 1,250 pages of the three volumes, the editor of these volumes has taken it on himself to denounce not just these thirteen passages as "anti-Semitic," but the whole body of ontohistorical thought as such.

According to a transcript made by an American professor who in September 2014 participated at a conference at Emory University, the editor claimed that Heidegger's anti-Semitic references with regard to Judaism were "part of a systematic configuration." However, in his critical comments concerning "international Jewry," Heidegger makes use of concepts such as groundlessness; absence of history; mere calculation with what exists; the gigantic; absence of world; empty rationality and capacity for calculation; the forgetfulness of being; machination of beings; absence of bounds as such; and the uprootedness of all beings from being. Everyone who has carefully worked through the ontohistorical treatises—that is, the main texts of ontohistorical thinking—sees at once that the concepts listed are just ontohistorical concepts by means of which Heidegger characterizes the spirit of the *newest new age* and thus the *present age*, insofar as this age principally understands itself from out of the spirit of the mathematical natural science and modern technology. And this means that these concepts are not anti-Semitic as such (i.e., they do not refer to the Jewish spirit only but reflect the spirit of the present time). In other words, when Heidegger characterizes the spirit of "international Jewry" he includes it within the modern spirit of the present age. It must be understood as a reflex of the then-dominant Zeitgeist that Heidegger specifically mentions and critically questions "World Jewry," even though the operative characteristic used is also that of the general modern spirit of the present age. The ontohistorical approach has its own conceptuality; it is not anti-Semitic in its essence and not the result of an anti-Semitic outlook. Instead, the ontohistorical approach arises from a phenomenological perspective that experiences the phenomena in their own historicity, making them visible and intelligible.

The scandal is not to be found in these thirteen passages from the *Überlegungen* (*Considerations*); rather, the only scandal is the distorted and disparaging, deeply corrupt reading of these passages. The book by the editor, which, as Ingeborg Schüßler correctly judged, is not a philosophical work at all, is not a book of adequate and serious interpretation. *His thesis of an anti-Semitism in the thought of Martin Heidegger is not a seriously sustainable interpretation, but a mere assertion without any accompanying proof.*

In my capacity as the philosophical "senior advisor" of the *Gesamtausgabe*, as Martin Heidegger referred to me in writing, and as his private assistant in the last four years of his life, I recommended the current editor of the *Black Notebooks* to the literary estate to merely serve as text *editor*, not as text *interpreter*.

A proper companion book to the *Überlegungen* (*Considerations*) by the editor would have had to have a totally different conception and content. If such a book were to contain an explanation of the thirteen offending passages by the author, the explanation would have to work out and present the *philosophical dimension* of the "*Überlegungen*" (*Considerations*) and the sundry critical statements in this context—just as I did in the first section of this chapter. Only this would have done justice to the three volumes of the *Black Notebooks*. Instead, the editor leaves out the philosophical dimension of the *Black Notebooks* entirely, and pursues his purely ideological-political agenda by completely ignoring the philosophical content of the *Überlegungen* (*Considerations*) and their relation to other manuscripts featuring Heidegger's ontohistorical thinking. In this way he misleads readers of his entirely unphilosophical book and the audience of his entirely unphilosophical lectures by conjuring up the deceptive view that the *Black Notebooks* in their entirety present an anti-Semitic outlook. His approach to the *Black Notebooks* is, therefore, through and through distorting and thus deeply untrue.

There is a passage in the *Contributions (Of the Event)* that fully confirms my view. This passage reads as follows: "Sheer idiocy to say that experimental research is Nordic-Germanic, and that, by contrast, rational research is *foreign*! In that case we would have to resolve to count Newton and Leibniz among the 'Jews.' It is precisely the projection of nature in the mathematical sense that constitutes the presupposition for the necessity and possibility of '*experimentation*.'"[18] Heidegger is directing his acerbic criticism *against* the proposition of the then-current National Socialist understanding of the natural sciences, according to which experimental research was Nordic-Germanic and rational research "foreign" (i.e., Jewish). Heidegger explicitly declares that the National Socialist attribution of experimental research to the Nordic-Germanic spirit and rational research to the Jewish spirit is "sheer idiocy," because experimental research in the natural sciences requires rational grounding through the mathematical projection of nature, which was mainly instituted by Newton and Leibniz. If the division of experimental and rational research corresponded to a Germanic-Jewish divide, the National Socialists would have to count the great rationalists Newton and Leibniz as "Jews," which they obviously were not. Heidegger puts quotation marks around "Jews," because he refers to Jews using the National Socialist jargon. This quote from the *Contributions to Philosophy* is clear proof that Heidegger, unlike the National Socialists, does not understand rational research and thought as specifically Jewish, and that Heidegger, therefore, does not identify the rational as such with a particular people. Therefore, this quotation is not an example that supports the attribution of an anti-Semitic tendency to Heidegger's thought, but is rather a counter-example—it shows that in discussing the positive sciences and philosophy Heidegger does not follow an anti-Semitic line of thinking.

My outline of the philosophical dimension of the three volumes of the *"Überlegungen"* (*Considerations*) and my analysis of the conceptuality of these thirteen brief passages make it clear that these passages are not systematic "building blocks"—that is, not constitutive arguments within the edifice of ontohistorical thinking. Of course, to understand this assertion in its full meaning one must have a clear understanding of what is meant by the inner systematics and structure of a philosophy. In other words, one must be able to think systematically and to distinguish between a systematic and a merely incidental thought (Hegel: *nebenher gesagt*). In the *Contributions to Philosophy* and, particularly, in his first Lecture Course on Schelling given at the same time, Heidegger himself emphasizes: "Every philosophy is systematic, but not every philosophy is a system."[19] Every philosophy and hence also ontohistorical thought is intrinsically systematic—that is, structured and conjoined. Heidegger expresses the systematic character of ontohistorical thinking by the word *structure* (*Gefüge*), which indicates the inner juncture and order of the questioning. The *Black Notebooks* of the *Überlegungen* (*Considerations*) with their enumerated entries are shaped by the incessant endeavor regarding the one and only question concerning the truth of being (*Wahrheit des Seyns*), which is systematically developed within a firm structure of questioning (*Fragen*) vis-à-vis that which is questioned about (*des Gefragten*). To see this, to elaborate on this, and to grasp this is what alone does justice to these writings. For this one must distinguish between the systematic thought of the structure and the incidental thought that does not belong to the systematic structure of the philosophy in question. Accordingly, we can say that the thirteen passages at issue in volumes 95 and 96 of the *Gesamtausgabe* contain merely incidental thoughts, the elimination of which would not affect the structure of the question concerning the truth of being (*Seyn*). In full and strict accord with this fact we must emphasize that these thirteen passages are "philosophically without import," as my colleague István Fehér from Budapest acutely and aptly put it. In his distinguished Jewish disciples such as Hannah Arendt, Hans Jonas, and Karl Löwith, Martin Heidegger found a great gift for creative thinking instead of a predilection for rational thought alone. In fact, in the *Festschrift* for Heidegger's eightieth birthday, Jonas published a text that particularly pleased Heidegger.[20]

Notes

1. Martin Heidegger, *Besinnung*, *Gesamtausgabe* 66, ed. Friedrich-Wilhelm von Herrmann (Frankfurt: Klostermann, 1997), 419–428.

2. Heidegger, *Besinnung*, *Gesamtausgabe* 66, p. 419.

3. Heidegger, *Besinnung*, *Gesamtausgabe* 66, p. 426.

4. Martin Heidegger, *Beiträge zur Philosophie (Vom Ereignis)*, *Gesamtausgabe* 65, ed. Friedrich-Wilhelm von Herrmann (Frankfurt: Klostermann, 1989).

5. Martin Heidegger, *Überlegungen II–VI (Schwarze Hefte 1931–1938)*, *Gesamtausgabe* 94, ed. Peter Trawny (Frankfurt: Klostermann, 2014).

6. Martin Heidegger, *Vom Wesen der menschlichen Freiheit: Einleitung in die Philosophie*, *Gesamtausgabe* 31, ed. Hartmut Tietjen (Frankfurt: Klostermann, 1982).

7. Heidegger, *Beiträge zur Philosophie (Vom Ereignis)*, *Gesamtausgabe* 65, p. 65.

8. Martin Heidegger, *Das Ereignis*, *Gesamtausgabe* 71, ed. Friedrich-Wilhelm von Herrmann (Frankfurt: Klostermann, 2009).

9. Heidegger, *Besinnung, Gesamtausgabe* 66, p. 424.

10. Heidegger, *Besinnung*, *Gesamtausgabe* 66, p. 424.

11. In Martin Heidegger, *Metaphysik und Nihilismus*, *Gesamtausgabe* 67, ed. Hans-Joachim Friedrich (Frankfurt: Klostermann, 1999), 4–174.

12. Martin Heidegger, *Die Geschichte des Seyns*, *Gesamtausgabe* 69, ed. Peter Trawny (Frankfurt: Klostermann, 1998).

13. Martin Heidegger, *Über den Anfang*, *Gesamtausgabe* 70, ed. Paola-Ludovika Coriando (Frankfurt: Klostermann, 2005).

14. Heidegger, *Das Ereignis*, *Gesamtausgabe* 71.

15. Martin Heidegger, *Die Stege des Anfangs (1944)*, *Gesamtausgabe* 72, ed. Friedrich-Wilhelm von Herrmann (Frankfurt: Klostermann, forthcoming).

16. Martin Heidegger, *Die Grundbegriffe der Metaphysik: Welt-Endlichkeit-Einsamkeit*, *Gesamtausgabe* 29/30, ed. Friedrich-Wilhelm von Herrmann (Frankfurt: Klostermann, 1992).

17. Martin Heidegger, *Überlegungen VII–XI (Schwarze Hefte 1938/39)*, *Gesamtausgabe* 95, ed. Peter Trawny (Frankfurt: Klostermann, 2014); Martin Heidegger, *Überlegungen XII–XV (Schwarze Hefte 1939–1941)*, *Gesamtausgabe* 96, ed. Peter Trawny (Frankfurt: Klostermann, 2014).

18. Heidegger, *Beiträge zur Philosophie (Vom Ereignis)*, *Gesamtausgabe* 65, p. 163.

19. Martin Heidegger, *Schelling: Vom Wesen der menschlichen Freiheit (1809)*, *Gesamtausgabe* 42, ed. Ingrid Schüßler (Frankfurt: Klostermann, 1988), 51.

20. Hans Jonas, "Wandlungen und Bestand: Vom Grunde der Verstehbarkeit des Geschichtlichen," in *Durchblicke: Martin Heidegger zum 80. Geburtstag*, ed. Vittorio Klostermann, 1–26 (Frankfurt: Klostermann, 1970).

7

The Critique and Rethinking of *Being and Time* in the First
Black Notebooks

Jean Grondin

I. A Preliminary Remark on the Anti-Semitism of the *Black Notebooks*: Who Can Cast the First Stone?

> Wait and see what's going to happen when the curious mob storms the posthumous work! [*Wie, wenn sich einmal die Meute der Neugierigen auf den "Nachlass" stürzt!*]
> —Heidegger, *Gesamtausgabe* 66, p. 427

There are two types of readers of the *Black Notebooks*: those who have read them (patiently, painstakingly at times, because they are voluminous—well over 1,300 pages have been published so far—and don't have the argumentative structure and captivating character of a completed work) and those who haven't, yet gleefully talk about them and their "blatant" anti-Semitism. Those who haven't read them but chatter about them can remind one of the famous section 35 of *Being and Time* on *Gerede* (chatter, gossip, rumor, Twitter), where Heidegger says that *Gerede* is "the chance to understand everything without prior effort to approach the thing itself."[1] Nonetheless, "the thing is as it is because one says it is so."[2] So it is often with the comments one encounters on the anti-Semitism of the *Black Notebooks*; hell, even the editor of the volumes in question claims that they attest to Heidegger's fundamental and philosophical anti-Semitism! So it must be so. Case closed, the *Öffentlichkeit* or public sphere has spoken: Heidegger was not only a Nazi (which everybody already knew), he was a rabid anti-Semite, hence a philosopher who should be dismissed from the canon, and, perhaps more importantly, the same would hold for his wide following in the ipso facto compromised tradition of continental philosophy. The motives and glee of those who dismiss Heidegger on those grounds are understandable. The *Gerede* is particularly powerful in the field of philosophy, all the more so perhaps because it depends, sadly, more than other disciplines on chatter. But as a matter of intellectual honesty, one should only take seriously those who have read the *Notebooks*.

For those who have read them and who view Heidegger as an important thinker, these anti-Semitic passages are troubling. They are not, however, surprising. No one doubts that Heidegger passionately endorsed National Socialism during the period of his embarrassing rectorate and for some years thereafter. This latest chronological characterization remains vague and has to remain so because Heidegger himself, as we learn in the *Notebooks*, maintained in 1938–1939 his "affirmation" (*Bejahung*) of the "movement" of National Socialism, and for "philosophical reasons" (*aus denkerischen Gründen*) to boot, well after he broke with its "contemporary figure" and its "visible forms."[3] He eerily seemed to renew this affirmation in 1953 (!) when he published—without any explanatory footnote, much to the understandable dismay of Jürgen Habermas at the time—his lecture course of 1935, *Introduction to Metaphysics*, where he obdurately praised the "inner truth and greatness" of the *movement* of National Socialism.[4]

In *Überlegungen XI*, written in 1938–1939, he confesses that he supported National Socialism from 1930 (hence much earlier than many thought) to 1934 because he saw in it the philosophical possibility of a transition to a new beginning,[5] in the spirit of his thinking of the history of Being, which had concluded that the "first beginning" of philosophy had led to a dead end, evident in Heidegger's eyes in the technological worldview. Its devastating rationalization of the world would be the direct consequence of the understanding of Being out of its *eidos* in Greek philosophy, which would itself testify to the forgetfulness of Being and, worse still, the forgetfulness of this forgetfulness. Only a new beginning could save us. From 1930 to 1934, if we are to believe his own chronology, he perceived and welcomed glimpses of this new beginning in, of all things, the "movement" of National Socialism. In his *Notebooks*, he clearly recognizes that he then misunderstood (*verkannt*) and underestimated (*unterschätzt*) the "real forces" at work within this movement. This, he allows, was an illusion (*Täuschung*). Nonetheless, "out of the recognition of this illusion" resulted precisely, following his twisted logic, the necessity of an affirmation of the "movement" of National Socialism "on philosophical grounds."[6] His agreement with the "actual" Nazis was never total, but he fashioned his own, "spiritual" view of National Socialism, a view about which the *Notebooks* are quite instructive.[7] Convinced that the "movement" heralded "the possibility of a transition to a new beginning" that his philosophy was after, he also highlighted aspects of Hitler's "revolution" that appealed to him—most notably, it seems, the "coming to itself" of the German people[8]—and downplayed other aspects of the regime. He was never fond of its biological rhetoric[9] and its penchant for the gigantic, but Heidegger said precious little about the suppression of democracy, its institutions, and the dismissal of his Jewish colleagues and very close students, like Karl Löwith and Hannah Arendt, to say nothing of Edmund Husserl and many others.[10] In his *Notebooks*, he routinely rants about the tyranny of technology (*Tyrannei der Technik*)[11] or that of the "mediocre,"[12] but does not complain about the actual political tyranny the Nazis had imposed on Germany.

In his relative "defense" ("damage control" is a prosperous industry in Heidegger studies), it must be said that, unfortunately, not many Germans openly protested against the antidemocratic and anti-Semitic measures of the Nazis at the time. In the eyes of many, if not most, the democracy of the Weimar Republic had produced a chaotic, ungovernable state with high unemployment, which was constantly "humiliated" by the triumphant Allies. One should not forget that what one could call the *democratic consensus*—that is, the widespread conviction that liberal democracy is the best, or "least worst," form of government—only emerged *in the aftermath of* the Second World War, as a consequence of the failure of fascism (which had remained attractive to many in Italy, Spain, Japan, and elsewhere) and, during the Cold War, as an answer to Soviet-style communism.

Until recently, some believed or wanted to believe that anti-Semitism was a part of the Nazi program Heidegger never agreed with. He never seemed to mention it in his many pronouncements as rector or in his lecture courses. Hence the dismay of the editor of the *Notebooks*, Peter Trawny, when he came across a host of anti-Semitic passages. He spoke in the first chapter of his influential book about the need to revise the thesis[13] of Heidegger's hostility to anti-Semitism. It is understandable that a German Heidegger scholar who had been close to Heidegger's thinking and his circle would feel that way. However, anti-Semitism was so prominent in the Nazi ideology from the outset that it would have been naïve to believe that Heidegger did not sympathize with some aspects of anti-Semitism. This vague sympathy (we have to use this prudent expression because Heidegger was certainly not a very vocal or vociferous advocate of anti-Semitism, say, someone who wrote pamphlets against the Jews) should not surprise us. We have known for some time—from her granddaughter, no less—that Heidegger's wife had strong anti-Semitic feelings and maintained them, incredibly, to the end of her life[14]. In light of this and the obvious anti-Semitic disposition of the regime, what is startling is perhaps how little Heidegger spoke of anti-Semitism, in his public pronouncements and his *Black Notebooks*. If it had been a major part of his philosophical outlook, as Trawny seems to suggest when he speaks of an anti-Semitism grounded in Heidegger's view of the history of Being, he surely would have said more about it and could have written public essays on the subject, which would have endeared him to the authorities. As some scholars have noted, the thirteen or so passages that have anti-Semitic content amount to less than three pages[15] in the three volumes of the *Hefte* published so far, and there are none in the first volume (*Gesamtausgabe* 94), penned prior to the start of the war. I would not say, however, that these passages are irrelevant. On the contrary, they are distressing and should be analyzed carefully and within their context—that is, the triple context in which they stand in the *Hefte*, more generally in the philosophy of Heidegger, and in the context of their times. On this, I will only say two things:

1. What Heidegger writes about the Jews is related to his view of modernity, indeed of the history of Western civilization since the Greeks, as an epoch characterized by the emergence of a calculating rationality, which he understands as a forgetfulness of Being. We can follow this understanding of history in the first volume of the *Hefte* and Heidegger's *Contributions to Philosophy*. In them, the Jews play no part whatsoever (unfortunately, one must add, because Heidegger only seems attentive to the origins

of our civilization in Athens, not those in Jerusalem). Nor do real historical players or events, for that matter, downgraded to mere facts of *"Historie"* (i.e., the history written by historians), which would have nothing to do with *Geschichte*, the profound undercurrent of what is really happening in the history of Being. Its main "event" would be, strangely, the forgetfulness of Being, attributable to the focus on graspable entities (*das Seiende*) and the urge to "explain" them rationally, which would have led to the hegemony of the technological age. Was this the most pressing danger facing humanity and the Germans in the late 1930s? Heidegger thought so and fit everything, even what he thought he knew about the Jews, into this grand and at the same time incredibly restrictive and monomaniacal perspective on the history of humankind.

2. What the passages concerning the Jews in the *Notebooks* reveal very clearly is that Heidegger did not escape the influence of the prejudices of his time and the propaganda of the Nazis in spite of his claim to have broken with the "actual form" of the Nazi movement. This does not honor him, but Heidegger lived in an extremely totalitarian society where the press and all means of communication were severely controlled. He believed there was such a thing as a Jewish conspiracy and that the *Protocols of Zion* were real. He didn't know, as we do, that they were a "myth" and himself fell victim to the "prevailing" *Gerede*. Subjugated by Nazi propaganda in wartime (those who denounce Heidegger from the comfort of their computer screens, where they have access to multiple sources of information, should ask themselves if they have ever lived in such an environment), he, like many Germans, viewed "World Jewry" as supporting the "enemy." The anti-Semitic passages in the *Hefte* are despicable, replete with paranoid clichés about "calculating" and scheming Jews, and a thinker of Heidegger's stature should have known better, but he was a son of the prejudices of his times, his terribly dark times in which it was difficult to see clearly.

This is why, looking beyond the recurrent discussion of Heidegger's own and very abstruse National Socialism, one can view the debate about the anti-Semitism of the *Black Notebooks* as directing a question *to us*: What is the anti-Semitism *of our time*? I ask this because I think no honest intellectual today will adhere to any form of anti-Semitism. For us, this has thankfully become impossible. But does this mean that anti-Semitism hasn't been replaced? More directly: who among us is really free from subtle forms of mistrust or stigmatization of those who don't think, speak, vote, or dress like we do? In contemporary Western societies, many other groups have taken the place of the Jews (and there still are circles in the West where Jews or the "powerful Jewish Lobby" are thoroughly despised). After 9/11, it will often be Arabs or "Muslims" who will bear the brunt of such hatred when Islamophobes identify them with terrorists. Academia is certainly not free of these biases. What do natural scientists really think of the representatives of the "soft" sciences? Even within philosophy, there are similar forms of stigmatization. What do analytic philosophers really think, and say among themselves, about continental philosophers and vice versa?

Husserlians about Heideggerians and vice versa? He or she who is without prejudice of this sort should cast the first stone at the harrowing anti-Semitism of the *Black Notebooks*.

II. The *Notebooks* in Their Relation to *Being and Time*

There is no other choice but to *always* write this book *anew*, and only this. At the risk of remaining the man of only one book. Beyond this one there is no other. [*Es gibt gar keine andere Wahl, als dieses Buch*immer wieder*zu schreiben, und nur dieses. Auf die Gefahr hin, ein homo unius libri zu bleiben. Über dieses unum gibt es kein aliud.*]
—*Gesamtausgabe* 94, p. 22

The reading of the *Black Notebooks* has just begun. We should thus be weary of the hasty readings they have elicited so far. It takes time for the true value of philosophical works to be assessed. At this stage, any reading can only be presented as a hypothesis, a mere angle on a work with many layers. The hypothesis I would like to pursue in the present context is that the *Notebooks* cast a helpful light on what happened to the project of *Being and Time* in the early 1930s and how it is that Heidegger was led to his relatively new perspective on the history of Being. The *Notebooks* indeed help us see how Heidegger, very early on, became critical of his own fundamental ontology and, more specifically, of what he wanted to undertake in the third section of *Being and Time*, titled "Time and Being." In this section he wished to explore the temporality of Being itself. Following the ambitious project set forth in 1927, Heidegger first wanted to unfold the temporality (or *Zeitlichkeit*) of our *Dasein* and did so in the second section of *Being and Time*. There, Heidegger presented the complex structure of our "ecstatic" temporality and his main conviction was straightforward enough: the original temporality of our Being lies in the courage and resoluteness to confront its mortality. To this finite character of our temporality he opposed the endless and infinite temporality of our "vulgar" understanding of time as derivative. This thesis was clear. However, the last two sentences of the extant book asked pointed questions leading into what was yet to come: "Is there a way from the original *time* [of *Dasein*, which had just been presented over 206 pages] to the sense of *Being*? Does *time* manifest itself as the horizon of *Being*?" The second section thus ended with open questions, a cliffhanger as it were, which could be viewed at the time as a way of entertaining the suspense regarding the third section, indeed the entire second part of *Being and Time*.

It is only in the foreword to the seventh edition of *Being and Time* in 1953, the only one he ever added to new editions, that Heidegger decided to delete the qualification of "First Part" to the existing work, which, he assured, was "appropriate" in the earlier editions. However, after a quarter of a century, he stated, the second part could no longer be added without presenting the first one in a new way. At the same time, he called attention to the publication of his 1935 lecture course *Introduction to Metaphysics*, mentioned earlier. It would explain, one could surmise, why a second part of *Being and Time* could no longer be added to the first one without rewriting it completely. Since this lecture course, the first one Heidegger published, presented metaphysics as a history of the forgetfulness of Being, one could garner from this self-reference that it was the "language of metaphysics," as he would put it in his "Letter on 'Humanism'"[16] of 1947, that was responsible for the interruption, or as some like Theodore Kisiel have called it,[17] the demise of *Being and Time*. Why and when Heidegger distanced himself from the two-part project of *Being and Time* has always been a thorny question to assess. The main reason for this was that there were very few publications by Heidegger immediately after 1929, the year in which he published *Kant and the Problem of Metaphysics*, *What Is Metaphysics?*, and *On the Essence of Ground*. After that prolific year followed a sudden silence on Heidegger's part: the 1930 lecture "On the Essence of Truth" was only published in 1942, and in 1933 came his rectoral address, where, to say the least, the philosophical project of *Being and Time* did not seem to be his priority. In 1935 and 1936, he gave lectures on Hölderlin and on the origin of the work of art, which were only published in 1950 and 1951 in the *Holzwege* and *Interpretations of Hölderlin's Poetry*. In these short pieces, which were circulated among his students and the curious, he seemed to espouse a new kind of philosophy, very much influenced by Hölderlin, of whom one would be hard-pressed to find any traces in *Being and Time*. What had happened to fundamental ontology? Wasn't Heidegger supposed to be working on the missing sections of the work of which he proudly presented the outline in 1927, all the more so since it was in those sections that he promised to directly address what he heralded as the central question of philosophy and his thinking in the introduction to the work of 1927, that of Being? The "Letter on 'Humanism'" made popular the notion that Heidegger's philosophy had undergone a turn (*Kehre*) of some kind, which enabled the readers in that period to distinguish between a Heidegger 1 (that of *Being and Time*) and a Heidegger 2. We now know that this issue is far more complicated. First of all, *Being and Time* was by no means "Heidegger 1," since the early lectures have taught us that there was an even earlier Heidegger that was quite different from what *Being and Time* offered. Second, it was very hard to tell when "Heidegger 2" began: Was it in the late thirties, perhaps in the aftermath of his political involvement, as Habermas suggested in *The Philosophical Discourse of Modernity* (1985), or earlier?

One of the illuminating aspects of the *Notebooks* is that they afford us a glimpse of the intellectual itinerary of Heidegger in the early 1930s that led him to his relatively new departure in the *Contributions to Philosophy* of 1936–1938, which can thus be seen as an attempt to "rewrite," as it were, the third section of *Being and Time* and its second part. The *Notebooks* supplement the lack of published texts from this decisive period. Until now we only had the many lecture courses from this period, but they too remained relatively silent about Heidegger's own philosophical development. We now learn from the *Notebooks* that Heidegger viewed the historical interpretations of his lecture courses as a "mask"[18] of some sort. One can challenge this self-reading, naturally, but in the *Notebooks* the mask is off—for better or worse, since they also reveal that Heidegger was not immune to the rampant anti-Semitism of his time.

The *Notebooks* certainly allow us to better follow Heidegger's inner musings in the early 1930s and his attitude toward his own work. Regarding *Being and Time*, one is struck by the critical tone of most of his remarks on the work that had made him famous, and by the fact that we encounter them only a few years after its publication. Instead of basking in the glory of this opus, in which many such as Löwith saw the most impressive book in philosophy since Hegel's *Phenomenology of the Spirit*, Heidegger seemed intent on "deconstructing" it and pointing out its fallacies. The *Notebooks* are to a large extent—at least from the perspective I would like to explore here—a journal detailing the reasons why the *Being and Time* project could not be carried out as planned. Franco Volpi famously said of the *Contributions to Philosophy* of 1936–1938 that they were not Heidegger's second major work, but the diary of a shipwreck,[19] that of Heidegger's *Being and Time*, if not his entire philosophy. One could contend that this is even truer of the *Notebooks*, since they do have the allure of a diary, which is not the case with the *Beiträge*, whose outlook is more systematic.

In this regard, it is regrettable that the earliest volume of the *Notebooks* has not been preserved. We don't know why. Friedrich-Wilhelm von Herrmann suspects that they contained notes regarding the planned reworking of *Being and Time*.[20] They would have been priceless for the reading I am privileging here. However, all hope is not lost: it is known that very early on Heidegger wrote a self-critique of *Being and Time*, which will eventually be published in volume 82 of his *Gesamtausgabe*.[21] In the meantime, we can rely on the *Notebooks*, which have the added advantage of building a bridge to the rethinking of the question of Being in the *Beiträge*.

The first extant text of the *Notebooks* dates from October 1931. Early on, we encounter this self-criticism:

Being and Time did not on its way—*not however in its goal and task*—overcome three "temptations" of the environment:

1. The "*foundational*" attitude that comes from Neo-Kantianism (see p. 113)
2. The "existentiell"aspect—Kierkegaard—Dilthey
3. The"scientificity"—Phenomenology (see p. 128f.)

It is from here that the"idea of *Destruktion*" is determined (see p. 128f.) [...]

   One would have to show to what extent these three conditions all stem from one inner decline of philosophy: a forgetfulness of the basic question; and that they, *for this very reason*, and not because they represent trends of today, are totally inappropriate, to precisely open the way for the *fundamental* question.[22]

Heidegger underlines the "not however in its goal and task" at the outset of this precious confession. This is important because it stresses that Heidegger did indeed want to remain faithful to the goal and task of *Being and Time* as a whole, that of reawakening the question of Being and understanding it out of its own temporality. What impeded this task, we now discover, were the temptations of the environment: the foundational hubris, the "existentiell" pathos, and the obsession with scientificity. Heidegger clearly pinpoints who is responsible for what: his early Neo-Kantian upbringing probably imparted to him the desire for a "foundation" (in this regard, one has only to think of the idea of a fundamental ontology, which according to section 3 of *Being and Time* would ground the other sciences and the ontologies on which they rest),[23] Kierkegaard and Dilthey (this last name is a little surprising) made him sound as if he wanted to offer a philosophy of existence, and the phenomenological heritage wedded him to the idea of scientificity. It is interesting to note that Heidegger clearly recognized and let go of all three temptations as early as 1931.[24] On these grounds, it is safe to say that the project of *Being and Time* was doomed. It was so tied to these ambitions that it could no longer be carried out as planned. How could however Heidegger maintain "the goal and task" of *Being and Time*?

The first thing to do was to hold back the pivotal third section, "Time and Being": "Obviously the first, insufficient version of the third section of the first part had to be destroyed [*vernichtet*]. Its critical-historical reflection can be found in the lecture course of the summer of 1927."[25] Heidegger alludes here to the reworking of this section that can be found in his course on "The Main Problems of Phenomenology," which, not coincidentally, was the first volume to appear in the *Gesamtausgabe* in 1975. Heidegger already remarked at the beginning of this *Vorlesung*[26] that it contained a new version of the third section. The course indeed gives us an idea of what "Time and Being" wanted to say but also, and perhaps more significantly, of why it failed in Heidegger's eyes.[27] Its stated aim was to unfold the "temporality [*Temporalität*] of Being" as somehow distinct from the temporality (*Zeitlichkeit*) of *Dasein*. To do so, Heidegger refers to the three "ecstasies" of the temporality of *Dasein* he had distinguished in section 69 of *Being and Time*, related to the future, the past, and the present. He tells us in *Gesamtausgabe* 24 that these ecstasies possess their own specific "horizontal schema":[28] the idea is that Being itself, in its *own* temporality (*Temporalität*), is to be understood out of the original ecstasies (*Entrückungen*) of *Dasein*'s *Zeitlichkeit*.[29] We get the transition from the temporality of *Dasein* to that of Being, but at the same time its problematic character: how can it be called the temporality *of Being* if it stills depends on the way *Dasein* lives its temporality? Heidegger even asserts that this "*Temporalität* [hence of Being] is the most original unfolding of temporality itself" (*die ursprünglichste Zeitigung der Zeitlichkeit als solcher*).[30] The difficulty is obvious: we come to this *Temporalität* of Being through the temporality of *Dasein*, yet this temporality of Being would in turn ground the temporality of *Dasein*? This doesn't sound very convincing, and Heidegger himself was obviously not satisfied with his own analysis. It struck him as too schematic, too dependent on Kantian terminology.[31] Even at the moment he was presenting it (!), he went as far as to point out that it contained a "fundamental untruth" in that it proposed an "objectification" (*Vergegenständlichung*) of Being, "that is, the projection of Being in the horizon of its intelligibility" (*Verstehbarkeit*). In this way, "the projection of Being would turn it into something ontic."[32] This was a major flaw, which certainly jeopardized the project of a fundamental ontology that wanted to move from the temporality of *Dasein* to that of Being.

Did Heidegger abandon this project? He certainly relinquished the idea of presenting the temporality of Being by focusing solely on the projection of Being by *Dasein*, which seemed to make Being (1) something ontic and (2) something that would depend on the understanding of *Dasein*. However, Heidegger did not renounce the idea of presenting the temporality of Being out of itself, as it were. For this, though, a new departure was needed. It was perhaps first realized in the *Beiträge*, which Heidegger did not publish either, when he set forth the idea that it was urgent to jump or "leap" directly into Being—that is, in the way Being itself unfolds, what Heidegger then called the truth of Beyng or the *Wahrheit des Seyns*, in order to show how *Da-sein* itself "sprang out" of this truth of Being (or the essence of truth).[33] *Da-sein* had to be grounded in Being, not the other way around.

It cannot be my aim here to propose an interpretation of the *Beiträge*. I only want to suggest that they can be viewed, with the help of the *Notebooks*, as the (provisional) arrival point of Heidegger's thinking process in reworking the project of *Being and Time* and especially its unpublished, unpublishable section on the enigmatic temporality of Being.

In March 1932, Heidegger writes:

Today (March 1932) I am clearly at the point where the entire literary work until now (*Being and Time*, *What Is Metaphysics?*, the Kant book, and *On the Essence of Ground* I and II) has become strange to me. Strange like a path that has been abandoned, over which some grass and bushes have grown. It is nonetheless a path of which it can be said that it leads into *Da-sein* as temporality. A path on whose fringes there are a lot of contemporary falsehoods, so much so that these "markers" were taken to be more important than the path itself. But to this day nobody understood it, nobody walked it through and back, i.e. nobody tried to refute it. For that it would be necessary to understand its "goal" or, more prudently said, the space [*da*] in that it wanted to lead and transport. But that is not the case, even though everyone is shouting about "ontology" as something well known. […] But why note this, when the question itself has become always more problematic for me.[34]

Heidegger again alludes to the fact that he held fast to the goal or, as he more carefully writes, the "space" in which he wanted to lead, the "*da*" of Being in *Da-sein*. Time and again, he bemoans the existentiell misunderstanding of *Being and Time*, blaming for that his contemporaries—the repetitive whining about the contemporaries is one of the painful aspects of the *Notebooks*—or himself for not having stated more clearly that the existentiell was just a means to get to this "*da*" of Being:

Being and Time […]: what was *means and way* in order to raise the question of Being to begin with, all who read it as a philosophy of existence turned it into the goal and result. It is so easy and satisfying, and thus tranquilizing, to single out all that was borrowed from Kierkegaard; proud of this "detective" work one settles down, puts on airs and leaves the real problem, yes, to whom? To nobody because one doesn't see the problem because of too much philosophy of existence. But why blame the contemporaries—if this is the case—when the author had the stupidity to hold back [*zurückhalten*] the main thing. Or perhaps there was an "unconscious" prudence in this thanks to which this main thing was prevented from being hacked to pieces in the big mush of "situation," "existence," and "decision."[35]

Zurückhalten—to hold back, to leave aside—is the term Heidegger always uses to describe the fact that he did not publish the third section of *Being and Time*. It is the expression he uses in the "Letter on 'Humanism'" and elsewhere.[36] It was "stupid" not to publish what he had written in that section because it could have given a better idea of his intentions regarding the temporality of Being. Yet it was also wise since it too would have been misunderstood. Heidegger seems to allude here to something very dear to him that is at the same time difficult to convey. In a most precious annotation of the *Notebooks*, he alludes to what he calls his fundamental insight:

My fundamental experience: the essential occurring of Being [*die Wesung des Seins*]—which was first approached as the *understanding* of Being; hence the danger of an "idealism"; but at all times [what was leading was] the opposition to understanding—as a thrown projection; and this as *Dasein*. But this finally turns out to be a wrong way [*Abweg*]; nonetheless it makes it possible to carry out in a more original and purer way the originally obscure fundamental experience—better still: it makes it possible to start asking the question of Being by radically leaping into the overbearing restraint of the endurance within the essential occurring of Being.[37]

This is indeed Heidegger's basic experience: the *Wesung des Seins* (not yet written, as in the *Beiträge*, with a *y*), the sheer occurring and unfolding of Being or, the way the lecture on *What Is Metaphysics?* puts it, the marvel of all marvels that there is Being and not nothing and that we are breathtakingly part of it. It is this event of Being as emergence, which the first Greeks balbutiatingly called *phúsis*, that Heidegger wishes to reawaken against the privilege bestowed on the beings (*das Seiende*) that come to the fore in this emergence and capture all the attention of our calculating minds.

Is it a stretch to believe that the reawakening of this experience of the emergence and *thus* of the temporality of Being itself is what Heidegger aimed at in *Being and Time*, and especially in its third section devoted to the *temporality of Being*, which he thought through anew in the *Beiträge*? *Being and Time*, the *Notebooks* say, is not "a philosophy about time, even less a doctrine about the 'temporality' of man, but surely and clearly *a* way toward the foundation of the truth of Being, of Being itself."[38]

One has to understand this, or try to, without the horizontal, foundational, scientific and existentiell framework it was couched in in *Being and Time*.[39] Heidegger's fundamental insight, we recall, is that of the *Wesung des Seyns*, the occurring of Being. It is obvious that *Wesung* must be understood here in a temporal way, as the unfolding out of itself of Being. This is in all likelihood the idea that *Being and Time* wanted to express when it alluded to the temporality (= *Wesung*, unfolding) of Being. But Heidegger was unsatisfied with the transcendental framework of *Being and Time* and its objectification of Being, as he clearly states in the *Beiträge*:

Therefore it was necessary to overcome, at the decisive moment, the crisis of the question of Being in the way that that question necessarily had to be expounded at first [in *Being and Time*], especially in order to avoid an objectification of Beyng [*Vergegenständlichung des Seyns*]. This happened, on the one hand, by *withholding* the "temporal" interpretation [*die "temporale" Auslegung*] of Beyng, and, at the same time, by attempting to make the truth of Being "visible" independently of that interpretation. ... The crisis could not be mastered merely by thinking further in the already established direction of questioning.[40]

The *Notebooks* published thus far help us to see how Heidegger tried to remain true to his original plan, which was to unfold the temporality of Being out of which our own *Dasein* springs. Despite its best intentions, the transcendental framework of *Being and Time* would have made that impossible in that it objectified Being and made it dependent on the *understanding* of Being. In his *Notebooks* and the *Beiträge*, Heidegger attempts to leap into Being and its own temporality (Beyng as *Ereignis*). It remains to be seen whether Heidegger, in so doing, really overcomes the transcendental and foundational ambition of philosophy and metaphysics.[41] It is not certain either that this thinking has the salvific benefit Heidegger attaches to it. However that may be, the reading of the *Notebooks* has just begun, and at the same time perhaps that of *Being and Time* as well.

Notes

1. *Being and Time*, original German pagination, p. 169.

2. *Being and Time*, p. 168.

3. "Out of the full recognition of the earlier illusion about the essence and the historical essential force of National Socialism results directly the necessity of its affirmation and precisely for philosophical reasons. With that it is said that this 'movement' remains independent from its actual contemporary figure and the duration of these now visible forms" (*Überlegungen VII–XI (Schwarze Hefte 1938/39), Gesamtausgabe* 95, ed. Peter Trawny (Frankfurt: Klostermann, 2014), 408).

4. *Einführung in die Metaphysik, Gesamtausgabe* 40, ed. Petra Jaeger (Frankfurt: Klostermann, 1983), 208.

5. *Überlegungen VII–XI, Gesamtausgabe* 95, p. 408.

6. *Überlegungen VII–XI, Gesamtausgabe* 95, p. 408.

7. On this "spiritual National Socialism," see Martin Heidegger, "Überlegungen und Winke III," *Überlegungen II–VI, Gesamtausgabe* 94, pp. 135f.

8. "The *first goal* is the *coming to itself* of the people out of its roots and the overtaking of its mission through the state. The next goal is the provisional creation of the community of the people as the Self of the people" (*Überlegungen II–VI (Schwarze Hefte 1931–1938), Gesamtausgabe* 94, ed. Peter Trawny (Frankfurt: Klostermann, 2014), 136). I must confess I have always found Heidegger's political pronouncements extraordinarily vacuous.

9. See for instance *Überlegungen II–VI, Gesamtausgabe* 94, pp. 143, 157, 233, 521, etc.

10. On Heidegger's many Jewish students see the collection by M.-A. Lescourret, ed., *La dette et la distance: De quelques élèves et lecteurs juifs de Heidegger* (Paris: Éditions de l'Éclat, 2014). The book is highly critical of Heidegger, yet the editor rightly notes (p. 16) that despite their differences and bitter disappointment, the many Jewish pupils of Heidegger who became productive thinkers in their own right, like Hannah Arendt, Karl Löwith, Leo Strauss, Günther Anders, Hans Jonas, Helmut Kuhn, and even Emmanuel Levinas, never denied their debt to their teacher.

11. *Überlegungen II–VI, Gesamtausgabe* 94, p. 363.

12. *Überlegungen II–VI, Gesamtausgabe* 94, p. 497 (*Tyrannei des Kleinen*).

13. Peter Trawny, *Heidegger und der Mythos der jüdischen Weltverschwörung* (Frankfurt: Klostermann, 2014), 9 (indeed it is the first line of the book one reads): "Introduction: The necessity of revising a thesis."

14. See Gertrud Heidegger's foreword to her edition of the correspondence of her grandparents: *"Mein liebes Seelchen!" Briefe Martin Heideggers an seine Frau Elfriede 1915–1970* (Munich: Deutsche Verlags-Anstalt, 2005), 12.

15. See Friedrich-Wilhelm von Herrmann, chapter 6, this volume. Trawny ("Heidegger et les *Cahiers noirs*," *Esprit* 407 (August–September 2014): 133–148 (especially 134)) would reply that quantity is not philosophically important. This is a valid point, but the scarcity of Heidegger's anti-Semitic pronouncements does seem to confirm that the issue wasn't an obsession for him, let alone an essential part of his history of Being. He probably felt it was part of the "visible form" of National Socialism and not essential to its "movement" as he imagined it (in that, he was quite naive). Trawny is well aware that Heidegger also wrote in his *Notebooks* that anti-Semitism was "stupid and reprehensible" (*töricht und verwerflich*) since he quotes this utterance (*Heidegger und der Mythos der jüdischen Weltverschwörung*, 93). Heidegger probably doesn't say it often enough, but he does say it, and we are told by Trawny that how often something is said is not paramount. The "quantity-is-not-important" argument cuts both ways.

16. *Wegmarken, Gesamtausgabe* 9, ed. Friedrich-Wilhelm von Herrmann (Frankfurt: Klostermann, 2004), 325 (Martin Heidegger, "Letter on 'Humanism,'" in Martin Heidegger, *Basic Writings* [San Francisco: Harper, 1977], 207).

17. Theodore Kisiel, "The Demise of *Being and Time*: 1927–1930," in *Heidegger's Being and Time: Critical Essays*, ed. Richard Polt, 189–214 (Lanham, MD: Rowman & Littlefield, 2005).

18. *Überlegungen II–VI, Gesamtausgabe* 94, pp. 243, 257.

19. Franco Volpi, *Aportes a la filosofía de Martin Heidegger* (Madrid: Maia ediciones, 2010), 15. The title of the first piece in this unfortunately posthumous book—intended as an afterword to Volpi's translation of the *Beiträge* into Italian—is "Contributions to Philosophy?" (note the question mark, which is from Franco Volpi), "The Diary of a Shipwreck," the Italian version of which can be found in Franco Volpi, *La selvaggia chiarezza* (Milan: Adelphi, 2011).

20. See von Friedrich-Wilhelm von Herrmann, chapter 6, this volume.

21. See Friedrich-Wilhelm von Herrmann, "Die 'Beiträge zur Philosophie (Vom Ereignis)' als Grundlegung des seinsgeschichtlichen Denkens," *Heideggers Beiträge zur Philosophie/Les Apports à la philosophie de Heidegger*, ed. E. Mejía and I. Schüssler (Frankfurt: Klostermann, 2009), 26.

22. *Überlegungen II–VI, Gesamtausgabe* 94, p. 75.

23. *Überlegungen II–VI, Gesamtausgabe* 94, p. 77, explains that this thirst for foundation and "conditions of possibility" orients the understanding of Being toward the idea of production and producibility (*Herstellbarkeit*), thus failing to grasp the temporality of Being itself. See also *Überlegungen II–VI, Gesamtausgabe* 94, p. 81: "The intention of 'foundation' only gives the illusion of a radical questioning, but remains on the surface of *what* needs to be founded."

24. In this respect, the *Notebooks* do tend to confirm Gadamer's reading of *Being and Time* (see Hans-Georg Gadamer, *Heidegger's Ways* [Albany: SUNY Press, 1994]) as a failed and very temporary attempt on Heidegger's part to espouse the transcendental vocabulary of Neo-Kantianism and Husserlian phenomenology.

25. *Überlegungen II–VI, Gesamtausgabe* 94, p. 272.

26. *Die Grundprobleme der Phänomenologie, Gesamtausgabe* 24, ed. Friedrich-Wilhelm von Herrmann (Frankfurt: Klostermann, 1997), 1.

27. On the intent of this third section as it is reworked in *Die Grundprobleme der Phänomenologie, Gesamtausgabe* 24, see my early book *Le tournant dans la pensée de Martin Heidegger*, 2nd ed. (Paris: PUF, [1989] 2011), especially chap. 4, 71–80: "L'intention de 'Temps et être' à l'époque de *Sein und Zeit*."

28. *Die Grundprobleme der Phänomenologie, Gesamtausgabe* 24, p. 429.

29. *Die Grundprobleme der Phänomenologie, Gesamtausgabe* 24, p. 428.

30. *Die Grundprobleme der Phänomenologie, Gesamtausgabe* 24, p. 429.

31. Heidegger acknowledges as much in *Die Grundprobleme der Phänomenologie, Gesamtausgabe* 24, pp. 445f. See also Heidegger's "Aufzeichnungen zur Temporalität: Aus den Jahren 1925 bis 1927," *Heidegger Studies* 14 (1998): 11–23.

32. *Die Grundprobleme der Phänomenologie, Gesamtausgabe* 24, p. 459.

33. See for example *Beiträge zur Philosophie (Vom Ereignis), Gesamtausgabe* 65, ed. Friedrich-Wilhelm von Herrmann (Frankfurt: Klostermann, 1989; 2nd ed., 1994), 8; Martin Heidegger, *Contributions to Philosophy*, trans. Richard Rojcewicz and Daniela Vallega-Neu (Bloomington: Indiana University Press, 2012), 9: "No one understands what 'I' am here thinking: to let *Da-sein* arise out of the truth of Beyng (i.e., out of the essential oc-

currence of truth) in order to ground therein beings as a whole and as such and, in the midst of them, to ground the human being."

34. *Überlegungen II–VI, Gesamtausgabe* 94, p. 19.

35. *Überlegungen II–VI, Gesamtausgabe* 94, p. 74. Compare *Überlegungen II–VI, Gesamtausgabe* 94, p. 503.

36. *Wegmarken, Gesamtausgabe* 9, p. 325; 65, p. 451; 66, p. 414, and passim.

37. *Überlegungen II–VI, Gesamtausgabe* 94, p. 248. Compare *Überlegungen II–VI, Gesamtausgabe* 94, p. 362: "The ground experience of my thinking: the predominance of Beyng over all beings [*die Übermacht des Seyns vor allem Seienden*]."

38. *Überlegungen II–VI, Gesamtausgabe* 94, p. 272. Compare *Überlegungen II–VI, Gesamtausgabe* 94, pp. 367, 375.

39. "It means nothing else but to *correspond* to the essence of Being. That's the meaning of authentic existence, but which in BT is presented in a much too existentiell way and from the exterior. And I say this because the question of being remains too much caught in the scholarly and its dross" (*Überlegungen II–VI, Gesamtausgabe* 94, p. 56).

40. *Beiträge zur Philosophie (Vom Ereignis), Gesamtausgabe* 65, p. 451; *Contributions to Philosophy*, (modified) translation by Richard Rojcewicz and Daniela Vallega-Neu, 355.

41. On the metaphysical character of Heidegger's thinking and its *aporiae*, see my *Du sens des choses: L'idée de la métaphysique* (Paris: PUF, 2013).

8

The Existence of the *Black Notebooks* in the Background

Laurence Paul Hemming

Almost at the beginning of the first of Heidegger's *Black Notebooks* we find Heidegger asserting that *Being and Time* is, however imperfectly, really the only attempt since Parmenides to inquire anew into the question of being.[1] How are we to understand the publication of Heidegger's *Black Notebooks*? How do they relate to what we know of Heidegger's other work, especially *Being and Time*, and the other material published in his lifetime? To what place in his vast, but as-yet-incomplete, *Collected Works* (or *Gesamtausgabe*), should the notebooks be assigned? By far the larger part of the *Collected Works*—especially his Marburg and Freiburg lecture courses, seminars, and exercises—is material that Heidegger had specified be prepared for publication only after his death. Heidegger wanted no historical-critical edition of his works, but asked that the *Collected Works* should appear (as *the Klostermann* prospectus for it tells us) as "an edition straight from the hand" (*eine Ausgabe letzter Hand*), without philological apparatus or indices. This phrase, likely Heidegger's own, perhaps should better be translated "edition of the most recent hand." Heidegger reworked much of his material not once but repeatedly, rarely dating or documenting the emendations (indeed, some of the material itself has been difficult, sometimes impossible, to date precisely). All of this begs a question to which Heidegger himself was extremely sensitive: When we study "Heidegger," and any text of Heidegger's, what, or who, is our subject? Is it "Heidegger, the man and his times," or in attending to Heidegger's writing can we bring to lie open before us what Heidegger himself struggled to open up: which for him concerned the occurring of being itself, which he persistently named as only coming to light through the *question*—namely the "question of being"?

For all the volumes in his *Collected Works*, Heidegger wrote really only one book, published in German in 1927 as *Sein und Zeit*, in English in two translations as *Being and Time*, the first in 1962, and the second in 1996 (although subsequently revised). The final section of the introduction to *Being and Time* makes clear that what was actually published comprised only the first two of the three projected sections of the first part, and none of the second part. In the *Black Notebooks* Heidegger goes so far as to remark that he is in danger of being a man of one book, a book that he had no choice but to write and that he would always be writing.[2] This book concerns the relation of *Dasein* to the *Seinsfrage*, or question of being, *das Sein*. This question is constituted both by the history of being (*Seinsgeschichte*), and the forgetfulness of being (*Seinsvergessenheit*). A peculiarity of this phrase, from the very beginning, was Heidegger's approach to interpreting the *of* in "of being." Here the genitive *of* can be interpreted as both subjective ("being itself forgets") and "objective" ("being gets forgotten"). The subjective genitive in no way ascribes some kind of "agency" to being: "being" has no psychological faculty of memory (and "being" is not a masked name for an "absolute subject" or any kind of god). Rather the character of being as such is to withdraw, which manifests itself as its own forgetfulness. We could, if we were determined to speak of agency in relation to "forgetting," say that "being, in a sense, causes, and so results in, a forgetfulness toward it." The "question" always concerns how we find ourselves already in a manifest relation to being as a whole—and so in what way that manifest relation occurs, how it takes place. In other words, being is always related to the concrete, actual, and factical relations of our own existing—of existence itself.

A habit of Anglophone commentary on Heidegger was set in stone by the first English translation of *Being and Time*, of leaving the word *Dasein* untranslated almost throughout the text, on the grounds that it had a very precise and technical meaning for Heidegger. Too many commentators, who maybe knew a bit of German but didn't necessarily know much German philosophy, took this to mean that Heidegger had "invented" the word. *Dasein* is a very ordinary German term: it means "existence," existence in its actuality. It has in German all the ambiguities that the English word *existence* has—which Heidegger was well aware of and exploited to the full. While we can understand *a* "*Dasein*" as *an* "existence," there can at the same be "*Dasein* in general," but to speak of it with the word untranslated does not help us come close to hearing "existence" in general as a way of inquiring into being as a whole. Yet to German ears, it is immediately obvious that *Dasein* and *das Sein* belong together and are different ways of speaking of the same. The other way of considering human existence, as "subjectivity" or "the subjectivity of the subject" as an "essence" of being human that every human "generally has within herself" comes to predominate, even when we believe ourselves to be discussing *Dasein* in general. An essence of this kind has always to be expressed as an ideal: Heidegger is uninterested in the ideal form of anything, let alone existence or being. To be preoccupied with ideal forms is to be drawn away from inquiring into the actual, factical, concrete forms of existence as we find ourselves already within them, already "in midst" of all there "is." When Heidegger speaks of "essence" (*das Wesen, die Wesung*) he speaks only of this "in midst," this occurring that we are already within and inextricably *of* (in both the "objective" and "subjective" genitive senses above). Heidegger's thought was, from the very outset, and explicitly, opposed to any understanding of subjectivity, or the subjectivity of the subject: he is apt to remark that in the proposition "I think, inasmuch as I am" the only unexamined part of that sentence is the "I am" that is always taken as a given, and never as the wherein that I have to inquire into, and so as a *question*.

Kant, as Heidegger himself points out, was one of the first German philosophers to give the entirely ordinary German term, *Dasein* ("existence"), a technical meaning: in this he was followed by Fichte, Hegel, Schelling, Feuerbach, Marx, and a host of others. Nevertheless the untranslated word *Dasein* quickly became, in translations of Heidegger's texts and the commentary on them, a proper noun in English, standing as a name for the human being—"Mr. or Ms. Anthrōpos," we might almost say. The ambiguity in German that Heidegger had sought to exploit in pursuing the question of being has disappeared from view—that, therefore, there can be "existence in general," or kinds of existence in particular (my existence in modern London), or *an existence* (you, me, her over there), and then even stones and hillsides can be said to be "in existence," or to exist. The second English translation of *Being and Time* attempted to solve the problem by uniformly hyphenating the word, *Da-sein*. Heidegger had done the same, but not in 1927, when the book was written, only later, from about 1935 or 1936, and again for very technical reasons. *Being and Time* was written with the intention of opening up and clarifying the relation of what Heidegger then called the "structures" of existence (*Dasein*) to the question of being, and yet it is possible to see at once how confusions and anachronisms appear that were not of Heidegger's making.

The other "books" Heidegger wrote—the book on Kant, the Nietzsche books, the *Introduction to Metaphysics*, even the *Contributions to Philosophy* (now almost universally referred to among Heidegger scholars as the *Beiträge*)—although often heavily edited by Heidegger himself, nevertheless began life either as lecture material or personal notebooks. Other collections of texts, like *Wegmarken* (known in English now through its translated name as *Pathmarks*) or *Holzwege* (*Off the Beaten Track*), are—like the chapters in the as-yet-untranslated *Vorträge und Aufsätze*, precisely "Lectures and Essays"—often, but not always, reworked from earlier versions or unpublished sources.

The *Black Notebooks* are not books even of this kind. They stand in an entirely different relation to Heidegger's *Collected Works* when compared to his book *Being and Time*, let alone to the collections of edited materials he produced in his own lifetime. How are we to understand that relation? As a genre the *Black Notebooks* belong to a now immense body of Heidegger's secondary material, much of which has come to light only very recently, consisting of what at the time were private notes and sketches of varying degrees of clarity and completion. Comparisons have been made to Nietzsche's *Nachlaß*, the huge body of material in short, aphoristic form that contained, among other things, sketches for an unwritten masterwork to have been titled *The Will to Power*, and from which Nietzsche's sister Elisabeth and the guest editor she appointed, Heinrich Köselitz (Peter Gast), put together several versions of a work in that name.

The bulk of this secondary Heidegger material stems from 1936 to 1948, part of which the editor of Heidegger's *Collected Works*, Friedrich-Wilhelm von Herrmann, has grouped together under the title *Das Ereignis* ("The Event"). He has referred to these volumes as "seven major treatises of the history of being."[3] They begin with the volume now known as *Contributions to Philosophy* or *Beiträge*,[4] but extend through six more volumes (one unpublished at the time of writing) covering a multitude of notebooks.[5] In this material Heidegger works out an understanding of the meaning and history of being and existence, often in a style startlingly different from what he said or published in his lifetime. These volumes also function as a kind of political commentary on aspects of the upheavals of the years leading up to, during, and immediately following the Second World War. Like the *Black Notebooks* the comments are at times scathingly critical of the political style and language of the Nazis, and can speak sharply of Heidegger's view of the criminality that marked these years. Added to these volumes are others, containing looser notes, often even more difficult to decipher or place. Two vast volumes of material of this kind, *Zum Ereignis Denken* ("*Toward Ereignis Thinking*"), appeared in 2013, also edited by Peter Trawny, the editor of the *Black Notebooks*. Appearing to date from the beginning of the 1930s, and stretching up into the 1940s, and so in many ways coextensive with the *Black Notebooks*, they also correspond to the years of the *Das Ereignis* notebooks, and form a further level of commentary and amplification of the *Das Ereignis* themes. What they contain is often, however, even less polished: at times repetitive, sometimes cryptic in its brevity, sometimes even unfinished. Finally, there is a handful of other volumes, one of which contains sketches for unfinished works and dialogues over the poetry of Hölderlin (*Zu Hölderlin / Griechenlandreisen*—"Concerning Hölderlin / Journeys in Greece"),[6] and another a volume of notes—in one case simply from a bundle of papers that may possibly date from 1940—on technology, and the background sketches and plans for Heidegger's *Bremen Lectures*.[7]

The *Black Notebooks* partly predate, partly overlap, and certainly prepare the ground for this vast and unruly body of material, which is as yet little explored and far from fully understood. Except that the *Black Notebooks* in large part extend over the period of the Nazi rule of Germany, and cover the period of Heidegger's year as Rector of Freiburg University and the time of his decision to join the Nazi Party, it is difficult to see why the *Black Notebooks* have excited so much more general interest (including in national newspapers) than these other bodies of material, which at times say things no less contentious. On what are these different, but interlocked, volumes of notes and sketches commenting, and what are they amplifying? Each other—or something else?

The years of chaos in Germany before 1933, and then the Nazi era itself, seem to have brought Heidegger time, in abundant quantity, during which he was able to write prolifically in private, if not so easily in public. His publications during these years are sparse, and he hints at difficulty, implicitly from the authorities, in getting material into print.[8] Moreover, the content of what he wrote was, for the times, dangerous. His increasingly critical attitude toward the regime after 1934 could easily have earned him imprisonment at the very least. Even now, in fact, perhaps now more than ever, much of what he wrote is difficult to interpret or place in context. In what are essentially private reactions, sometimes to public events, it is hard to discriminate what is being reacted to and the degree to which

Heidegger himself is able to place events in their wider or widest context. Moreover, the interpretative keys, which (because they are written privately) are familiar to Heidegger, demand considerable effort to acquire even for a reader very familiar with Heidegger's better-known works. Who now is familiar with the critique of "Americanism," common to a number of thinkers (Ernst Jünger, among others) in the Germany of the period between the two world wars? How well prepared is a modern thinker for Heidegger's 1934–1935 suggestion that "Carl Schmitt thinks as a liberal," or the impeccable suggestion, borne out by Heidegger's notes and notebooks, but that were unavailable to Lacoue-Labarthe when this latter thinker made the claim, that Heidegger had interpreted Nazism as a form of humanism?[9]

The *Black Notebooks* reveal Heidegger to be profoundly concerned with the political situation of the years immediately prior to the Second World War. At the organizational level (as the *Black Notebooks* and others of his own admissions show), Heidegger was an ill-prepared and, at best, naive, participant in the cut and thrust of actual political life, especially the factional, tribal jostling that marked the Nazis' style. This is of less significance than Heidegger's almost brooding need to interpret what made particular political situations possible, and on what sense of destiny—human or otherwise—they were founded. Heidegger was attempting to think through the movements of liberalism, communism (including Marxism), and fascism from within his own understanding of philosophy, which means, within the understanding of what he had started to call "beyng" (*das Seyn*). Much has been made of the one place in *Being and Time* where the word *Volk* appears.[10] In reality, almost nothing is said of any significance with Heidegger's use of this term in *Being and Time*; as much as it refers to a "people," it can also mean "nation"—indeed, Marx uses it in this sense. Use of the word *Volk* was not unique to the Nazis; historically, reference to *das Volk* can be found in every German political thinker. In *Being and Time* Heidegger speaks only of the occurrence equally of the community or nation: only later did Heidegger (also like Marx) come to ponder deeply how a nation becomes aware of its destiny—Marx at one time speaks of the proletariat as a class with no natural "land" or country of its own, but that has the need to emerge as a nation in order to carry out certain fundamental, historical, tasks (including its own self-negation). In the *Black Notebooks*, after the rectorate, Heidegger defines the "political" not in the narrow terms of parties and movements, but broadly, as how "the nation brings itself back to itself," and adds that "the nation only 'is' on the foundation of existence (*Da-sein*)."[11] If Heidegger had avoided the question of the historical occurrence of a people as a nation in *Being and Time*, the actual historical questions thrown up by the German situation, especially after 1933, and then again in the wake of his disillusionment with the Nazis after 1934, drew him into how and in what way a nation is founded, in effect forcing him to give a historical and political context to the structures of existence he had identified in whatever preliminary ways in *Being and Time*. We presume all too easily that Heidegger's disillusionment with the Nazis will bring him back into proximity with our own instinctive and educated (because this is what we have been taught) flinching away from what and who the Nazis were: but if Nazism really is a form of humanism, and if it is really humanism, or an understanding of it, that Heidegger came to reject, then there is no reason at all why this should be the case. Heidegger's disillusionment with Nazism in some senses makes it all the harder to see in which direction, progressively after December 1934, he was headed: it can be very difficult to understand why that direction might bring us no easy comfort. Nevertheless, the *Black Notebooks* reveal the extent to which Heidegger returned to the question that *Being and Time* had either to some extent sidestepped or only raised in a preliminary way.

All of these volumes of notes and notebooks appear for us at a time when the deliberative capacity to evaluate the work of important thinkers becomes ever more difficult. If Heidegger had time to write and reflect, how much less time is there now for that degree of reflection. Without time, an unreflective outlook—stampeded by the requirement to form opinions and justify them through the organs of not only conventional mass, but also "social," media—conditions so much of what can be said and heard in the public sphere. What we bring in advance to texts—the views that are formed and opinions that take hold with lightning speed, (and against which we have to measure our own capacity for judgment), all this has the capacity to blind us to what we actually find. This process is intensified in an age of digitization, where because we know in advance what we are looking for in a text, we do not examine or read fully the text, but can merely search its contents for the precise locations of what we already believe it to contain. Everything else can be set aside.[12]

Heidegger himself had spoken about how, through what he called a technical-calculating style of communication, language (and so writing as well) comes to be understood only as information.[13] The recent publication of a vast "Heidegger Concordance," based on digitized resources, is only part of this trend. The editors of the *Concordance* note in their introduction that "a list of concepts will never be a substitute for a real philosophical reading of Heidegger's texts,"[14] but, impressive as this mighty enterprise is, precisely because it itself is not based on a philosophical reading but an electronic one, its capacity to assist in a philosophical reading is to a large extent conditioned by the means employed to generate it.[15]

Much of what has been written about Heidegger concerns only what he himself wrote, as if philosophy and thinking were nothing other than a conversation, often written, about and between texts, and so as if there really were nothing beyond the text. And yet what does it mean to attain to the authentic text? Is there ever mere information? Does not every text appear through an irony, the irony of the conditions under which it was written, and for whom; of what it takes for granted and what it leaves out or, by its silence in *not* admitting, it denies? What of the irony we have to afford the text in order to understand how far away from where *I* stand now is the world the text before me brings into view and lets live all over again? This irony need not be constituted by the presumption that the text, or its author, actively sought from the outset to hide something from us; but rather, faced with the naked text and our bare reading of it, much continues to elude our grasp. The irony here is of a certain forgetfulness, the forgetfulness of being itself, and our incapacity, through the sheer facticity of existence, to overcome what time covers over and withdraws from our capacity to read.

Especially every text that concerns the political shape of an era requires this ironic reading. It is one thing to find in a text terms that shock us to our very core—terms such as *World Jewry* that are almost impossible to utter without extreme qualification in the present age. It is quite another to remember that only eighty years ago every German newspaper and radio program, as well as all political and much daily public discourse, was dominated by what to us is now unutterable. This does not exculpate in the least Heidegger's (or the wider) taking up of unutterable terms, nor does it diminish his apparently at times shocking willingness to venture what we ourselves could never espouse, but it does mean that he took up and deliberated these terms in a context that itself is difficult for us to understand, and that it was not possible for him in 1935 to understand these terms and their effects and (then future) history as we do now. We live the other side not only of the most hideous crimes that these terms were employed to legitimate and mask from view, but also the other side of a very definite history of the reception of those crimes, which we cannot ignore or overlook.

The reception of Heidegger's work also has a very definite history of its own, which has profoundly influenced the interpretation of his work. Before bringing ourselves into a more direct relation to the *Black Notebooks*, is it perhaps necessary to recapitulate that history and its effects? The interpretation of Heidegger's thought has been driven, not only by what Heidegger published, and what of him has been published posthumously, but even more importantly, by the order in which his work came to appear. Things have for a long time remained hidden or their significance has been difficult to see. For a long time the 1946 essay known in English as *The Anaximander Fragment* appeared as an intriguing and curious example of what seemed to be Heidegger's passing interest in pre-Socratic Greece. Published in German in 1950, it first appeared in English in 1975, in a translation by David Farrell Krell. It is only since 2010 that we have had the full-length lecture course (some 350 pages of text), prepared for delivery for the fall of 1942 but never actually given, on which the shorter (52-page) essay was based: the material of the lecture course substantially alters our understanding of the essay. Furthermore, only since 2012 have we had the text of the 1932 lecture course that represented Heidegger's first real attempt to handle the Anaximander fragment, material that again throws considerable light on how over a ten-year period Heidegger's analysis matured and developed. These three pieces, together with other references to Anaximander (whose significance we now see more clearly) and lectures on Heraclitus and Parmenides, allow us to see not only how Heidegger interpreted the whole Greek experience of the pair presence/presencing as the way in which the Greeks experienced being itself, but also why Heidegger begins to speak not only of being as *das Sein*, but also with the archaic form, *das Seyn* (translators have begun to use the old English form *beyng* to render the German archaism, as seen above). Heidegger had found in these fragments, and in Homer and Pindar (to whom he makes frequent reference, especially in these texts), a more archaic Greek form of speaking of being. In the Attic Greek of Plato and Aristotle "being," "to be," appears as *on, einai*. In Anaximander, in Parmenides and Heraclitus, and in Homer and Pindar, being appears in a more archaic, poetic, form as *eon, emmenai*. This same word, *emmenai* if accented differently, means not "to be," but "to dwell": something the Greek ear might easily have heard.

The difference between *das Sein* and *das Seyn* was, for Heidegger, not merely terminological, by which we might mean it does not simply refer to a "to what" that *das Seyn* might refer to and *das Sein* not (and the other way about), and so a question of "reference" and "meaning" (*Bedeutung und Sinn*). For Heidegger the difference is historical: bringing this difference to the fore by drawing attention to its older names provides for us a passageway through to the understanding of the *originary* experience of being from the one (far more familiar to us) that begins to identify being as a theme (Aristotle's "being insofar as it is being"). Every reference to *das Seyn*, *to eon*, and its cognates names this passageway, rather than naming a difference in some "whatness" or quiddity. In Heidegger's view this originary experience lay unthematized, but was actively present, in the earlier (pre-Socratic) texts of antiquity. An originary experience of being, therefore, that these just post-Homeric Greeks knew and knew of, is allowed to press in and become present: we might understand this as an overcoming of a forgetting. This originary experience stands over against the transformation of that experience *over time* (and so as it becomes a history) such that the originary pressing-in and letting-become-present (even while it still occurs) comes to be named *otherwise* (by Plato, by Aristotle, and by what comes after them) and yet names "the same": the being, the beyng, of beings.

The essay *The Anaximander Fragment*, which seemed in 1950 and 1975 to be an essay about interpretation, a tour de force of how to read and interpret an obscure line of Greek, turns out in fact to be only a fraction of the foundational body of thinking through which Heidegger came to understand the whole of the history of how being is spoken of—the history of being itself, and its forgetting. Of the two lecture courses on Anaximander published in 2010 and 2012, together with a volume of two fundamentally important courses on Heraclitus from 1943 and 1944, only a single part has found its way into English.[16] Until they can all be read in English, this development in understanding how foundational the Anaximander Fragment is for Heidegger's thought is unlikely to come about.

Why would the future of the interpretation of Heidegger's work depend on what of his appears in English? A further complication in the reception of Heidegger has been how the fundamentally different environment in which he is now read itself stands over against the period in which he wrote. A major stumbling block to the reading of Heidegger has been the paucity, even among very skilled philosophers, of those who have the knowledge of the Greek and Latin languages and texts that were an ordinary part of Heidegger's own technical training. Heidegger had a classical German *Gymnasium* education that predated both the First World War and the substantial dismantling of that tradition by the Nazis (who distrusted it). Consequently Heidegger had at his disposal a facility with texts from antiquity that few today have been equipped to read. Many of Heidegger's supposed neologisms are no more than his own skilled attempts to render into German important Greek terms. Just for one example, the word *Mitsein*, unlike *Dasein* a coinage apparently unique to Heidegger, renders the Greek terms *sunousia, suneimi, suneinai*—"being-present-with": sometimes Heidegger speaks of *Miteinandersein*, "being-with-another." Heidegger speaks of this in German and in Greek in a 1929 *Festschrift* essay in honor of Edmund Husserl when quoting the seventh of Plato's *Letters*;[17] he uses the same translation in a lecture course of 1928–1929.[18] Of greater significance is that the Greek term can be found almost at the beginning of Plato's *Sophist*, in a passage Heidegger knew well and commented on. He interprets it explicitly as delineating "*Logos* as method of the investigation,"[19] because *Mitsein, Miteinandersein* is what is required as that continuity in speaking that indicates the way we are held together "as a whole" or in a unity (elsewhere he says *koinōnia*) and continuity with each other that constitutes the possibility of our being able to speak, and so of our being, at all. Without access to references like these it is near impossible to see how, from the very outset, Heidegger understood himself to be bringing into the present questions that had first raised themselves in antiquity, at the beginning of Greek philosophy. If he only later came to thematize it specifically, he set out from the position of the "first beginning" of thought among the Greeks.

The reception of Heidegger's work, both in his native land and in the United States and Britain, has been resisted in many university departments of philosophy. Studying Heidegger has often been relegated to departments of English, European Languages, and even Geography and History. This has meant that even when there is no shortage of people reading Heidegger, there has often been an acute shortage of people who are technically trained in reading what Heidegger himself had read and was familiar with, and who can rely on a systematic philosophical training to assist them.

The order in which the material of Heidegger's writing has appeared, itself very far from the order in which it was written, has been frequently further disturbed and confused by the order in which it has been translated. This means that interpretative keys to Heidegger's work, developed from texts written at one time in his life, have been established and brought to bear on (often earlier) texts where these keys are not yet fully developed, or do not even exist.

Even here there have been complicating factors: the early translators of Heidegger struggled to bring his sometimes difficult, even surprising, German into not only English, French, and the other European languages, but also Japanese, Turkish, and many others besides. Heidegger himself attacked some of the results. He despised Sartre's rendering of *Dasein* as *être-là*, which corresponds very closely to an English rendering, "being-there," and yet it recurs not infrequently in the work of multitudes of English commentators. It can be found all the way through the textbooks and companions used to introduce especially undergraduates to Heidegger's thought.

It is worth pausing to ask what is at issue, for Heidegger and for us, in the question of the possibilities for translating *Dasein*. It is worth noting that the *Black Notebooks* return, not just once, but repeatedly, to the question of the meaning and interpretation of the term *Da-sein*: Heidegger was acutely aware both of the misinterpretations of his work and the need to clarify, for himself and others, how his most central terms were to be understood. If *Being and Time* was a systematic attempt to make impossible the thought of the subjectivity of the subject, at the same time it needed to show how concepts like "the subject" and "consciousness" had become possible, and on what basis they had arisen. In a seminar of 1967 Heidegger spelled out that with the translation of *Dasein* as "being-there," "all that was gained as a new position in *Being and Time* came to be forsaken."[20] This is because consciousness, which is grounded in representative thinking, posits the human being as an object to itself, on which consciousness "reflects." Heidegger asks "is the human being here, in the manner of a chair?" On the contrary, he argues *Being and Time* shows how the understanding of *Dasein* lets the openness of the "here" come to light, in which beings encounter one another, and do not "think about" objects but "see" what is "here." At the same time, *Being and Time* shows that consciousness itself, the ability to represent objects in consciousness, "is only possible on the basis of the *Da*, as a mode derivative of it."

If Heidegger never completed *Being and Time*, nevertheless it remained the work of his that he most expected those who engaged with him to read. In the *Black Notebooks* he remarks "one cannot get beyond *Being and Time*. Indeed, and fortunately so."[21] In this same passage, however, Heidegger speaks of how the thinking and speaking of beyng (a term unknown in *Being and Time*) is the more originary place from where the authentic thought and speech of *Being and Time* alone can spring. Thought like this, the *Black Notebooks*—or at least this note within it—remains within the province of thinking that was attempted in *Being and Time*, even as it begins to employ a language that has already to some extent moved beyond it.

If Heidegger never broke himself away—deliberately so—from the interpretation of *Being and Time*, two scholars in particular exemplify the attempt to break the work *Being and Time* away from the rest of its author's writings. Karl Löwith and Emmanuel Levinas both argued that the Heidegger of *Being and Time* was a fundamentally different thinker from the man of his later work. Both, in differing ways, were students of Heidegger. Both later counted themselves among his sharpest critics. One, first a Marxist, then a Lutheran, was uprooted from his native Germany variously to Italy, Japan, and the United States because under the terms of the Nazi racial laws he was classified a Jew. The other, a Jewish scholar, fought the Nazis as a French soldier and suffered at the hands of the Nazis under the terms of the Geneva Convention, as a prisoner of war. Neither could justify or forgive Heidegger for throwing in his lot with Hitler in 1933: both found a hermeneutical means to rescue the work from its author, and set apart (an earlier) "Heidegger the philosopher and author of *Being and Time*" from a later Heidegger, the Nazi. Along with thinkers like Adorno and Marcuse, neither believed that the Heidegger who emerged from the war ever left behind or parted from his Nazi sympathies.[22]

Löwith's assertion, in his 1946 denunciation of Heidegger's Nazi commitments in France, that there was a "turn" in Heidegger's work ushered in a preoccupation among Heidegger scholars—supporters and critics alike—with the periodization of Heidegger's thought. Immediately the question with any new material of Heidegger's is "to what period does it belong?" If, therefore, we wish to assert that the *Black Notebooks* represent a Heidegger other than that of *Being and Time*, we have to confront the reality that Heidegger thought otherwise: the *Black Notebooks*, along with so much else, represent Heidegger's continued engagement with and return to the central question of *Being and Time*, and the meaning of existence, *Da-sein*.

Heidegger, on the contrary, understood his entire later work as a way of amplifying and explaining the fundamental insights of *Being and Time*. In this respect it could be said that he never ceased to rewrite his earlier work. A remark in the 1946 "Letter on 'Humanism'" spoke about the missing third division of the first part of *Being and Time*. The third division of the first part was to have been titled *Time and Being*, where, from being and time "here everything turns itself about."[23] Heidegger added: "The division in question was held back, because thinking failed in the adequate saying of this turn, and so did not succeed with the help of the language of metaphysics."[24] But this remark, which has often been read to imply that *Being and Time* was somehow still a work of "metaphysics," is misleading: a marginal note to Heidegger's own copy of the "Letter on 'Humanism,'" later reproduced in the version published in his collected works, suggests that it is the "Letter on 'Humanism'" that is written "with the language of metaphysics, and that knowingly."[25] The question of audience was always paramount for Heidegger; the "Letter on 'Humanism'" had been addressed to Jean Beaufret and to the French philosophers—Sartre especially (there is more than a little evidence to suggest that the "Letter" was a response to Sartre's 1945 lecture *Existentialism Is a Humanism*[26]).

In a letter to William Richardson, published at the beginning of Richardson's masterful *Heidegger: Through Phenomenology to Thought*, published in 1963, Heidegger appeared to confirm Löwith's claim that there was a "turn" in his thought that resulted in a "Heidegger I" and "Heidegger II." On closer inspection, however, Heidegger had not said that his thought had changed, but that he sought to describe a fundamental transformation in thought itself, a change that arose "because I have remained within the matter to be thought through *Being and Time*."[27]

Richardson's assertion of a Heidegger I and Heidegger II had the effect of separating the periodization of Heidegger's work from the question of Heidegger's complicity with Nazism. The schema to which Richardson gave birth in the wake of Löwith's "turn" does not hold up. If it is true that much of the language of *Being and Time* appears to change or even disappear after about 1929, it reappears at important moments. In the *Zollikon* seminars, held with Medard Boss and his students over a period of several years between 1959 and 1969, Heidegger repeatedly resorts to the language of *Being and Time* to illustrate the issues at hand, as if the ink on the pages of the first edition of 1927 was barely dry.

At the same time there is evidence that Heidegger suppressed in public language that he felt led to misunderstandings. In public, for instance, he held back further discussion of the language of *Dasein*. The editor of a lecture course of 1937–1938, exactly contemporary with the *Black Notebooks*, added an appendix under the title *The Question of Truth* from Heidegger's hand that, he noted, contained the instruction "not to be delivered." It begins with Heidegger saying "there can not be even one mention of *Da-sein*, because it would immediately be interpreted as an object and the determination of the essence of truth would be degraded merely as a 'new' theory."[28] Later in the same text Heidegger amplifies what he believes is being misunderstood, and what the lecture course, he must at least have hoped, had paved the way for: that the human being, the *anthrōpos* (as the Greeks named it) or "man," is that one who comes to be "not simply merely any man," but "that one and that one," him or her who is capable of preparing for truth its ground and proper place, "which *is* the here (*Da*)."[29] The "here" in question is the "here" of "here-being" (existence, *Dasein*).

A careful reading of both Richardson and the "Letter on 'Humanism'" shows that Heidegger's claim to have "remained within the matter to be thought through *Being and Time*" contains a great deal of substance. It is because *Dasein*, incorrectly propagated as "being-there," had the effect of perpetuating the language of metaphysics, and this language was perpetuated by those who were taking up Heidegger's terms, that we can understand what Heidegger actually meant when he had said in the "Letter" that what was attempted in *Being and Time* "did not succeed with the help of the language of metaphysics." The erroneous help at hand had come from others—not least, from figures like Sartre—who could not abandon the thinking of subjectivity. At the same, Heidegger's essay on *Plato's Doctrine of Truth*, written in 1940 and published in 1942, ends with a systematic description of the history of Western thought since Plato (and so with the entire "history of metaphysics") as a significant part of the "history of being" as a humanism—a humanism, moreover, that it is clear Heidegger rejects. Given Heidegger's private rejection of Nazism and the language of National Socialism, it is impossible now to read this rejection—written and published in the crucible of the Second World War itself—as anything other than the claim that Nazism is itself part of the history of that humanism. Indeed, Heidegger's claim that he had difficulty publishing this text under the conditions of wartime Germany is tantamount to saying that this identification did not go unnoticed. Why else would the publication of an essay on "Plato's Doctrine of Truth" have been so problematic? If humanism is another name for the history of metaphysics, and if Nazism is a humanism, then Nazism *itself* belongs to the history of metaphysics, a history that remains unconsummated with Nazism's eclipse. If this was at least dimly visible in the Germany of 1942, how visible was this in the France of 1946? It is difficult to say.

Is Richardson's schema of a Heidegger I and a Heidegger II incorrect? Within the terms of his own interpretation, it would seem so. However, there is indeed a second Heidegger lying behind the first—a Heidegger who withholds from view the thinking that made the Heidegger of his own lifetime possible. *This* Heidegger begins—perhaps with the *Black*

Notebooks themselves—to unfold a thinking that (in the words of the title of §5 of the *Beiträge*) is for "the few and the rare."

It is here that we gain an important insight into the meaning of the *Black Notebooks*, which explains perhaps why Heidegger believed that the material in them needed to be published. The *Black Notebooks*, and the other sketches and material that remained private during his lifetime, contained his own commentary on the unfolding of the province of thought to which *Being and Time* preeminently belongs and from which it springs, the thought made possible by an understanding of the meaning of the term *beyng*. For Heidegger, if the history of metaphysics *and its effects* remains uneclipsed even after the demise of Nazism, then the political future of Europe, the West, and indeed the globe remains as standing within that history, and remains part of the forgetfulness of being, and so is not able fully to comprehend its own destiny.

If this really is Heidegger's understanding, there is no reason why we have to concur with it: at the same there is every reason, given that it remains part of what Heidegger had understood by the very phrase "history of metaphysics," that we should seek out how Heidegger understood what he himself was attempting to bring to light. In other words, there is every reason why we should engage with Heidegger's actual explanation of what he understood. We must ask, is it for the sake of understanding the current situation of the West that Heidegger sought to put the *Black Notebooks*, these private and at times shocking thoughts, into the public domain?

There is important confirmation of this from the note appended to the *Collected Works* edition of the "Letter on 'Humanism'" that I have already drawn attention to. Here Heidegger added that, if the "Letter on 'Humanism'" still spoke in the language of metaphysics, "the other language remains in the background."[30] The background in question took shape in the form of his private notebooks.

In his lifetime this background language almost never came to the fore, and even when it did in the spoken word, it seems this language was excised from the written record. Heidegger began to speak of being as *das Seyn* in the pages of the *Black Notebooks*, at the end of the section that records some of his thoughts about the collapse of his rectorate, and so, we may presume, around the end of 1934 or the beginning of 1935.[31] If *das Seyn* is an archaic form of *das Sein*, it was also the way "being" continued to be written in Schwabian dialect at least until the nineteenth century. Heidegger was himself Schwabian, but, perhaps as important for him, so too was Hölderlin, and *das Seyn* was the way Hölderlin, as well as Hegel and indeed Schelling, wrote and referred to "being." Unfortunately the English archaism *beyng* does not have the poetic associations that *das Seyn* has in its relation to Hölderlin's German. While there are earlier references to *das Seyn* in what appear to be reworked passages or marginal notes, apart from the *Black Notebooks*, the other place where Heidegger begins for the first time to write of *das Seyn* with frequency and with the significance this term came to hold for a language that "remains in the background" occurs in the first of his full lecture courses on Hölderlin, in the winter semester of 1934–1935, in a course that runs parallel to the period of some of the *Black Notebooks*.[32] Here, in these lectures, Heidegger distinguishes between "everyday" and "poetic" "beyng."

Exactly contemporaneous with these lectures is a letter to Elisabeth Blochmann of December 1934, where Heidegger also makes use of the archaic form *beyng* with direct reference to Hölderlin. He says "the poet is that one who founds beyng in going-ahead— grounds through manifesting in going ahead and through first naming and saying raises the beyng in its beyng."[33] In the *Black Notebooks* Heidegger refers to "Hölderlin as the 'transition.'"[34] Transition to where or what? To ask this question is to focus on the *object* Hölderlin, on the "man." The German word *Übergang* also means "passageway," even "bridge." Hölderlin—Hölderlin's poetry—lets the passageway *itself* be seen: the transiting between being and beings. Hölderlin founds the most originary experience of beyng and lets it speak and be spoken. This is the "grounding of its place (*Da-Sein*)."[35]

Heidegger sees the poet as *that* one who is capable of preparing for being its ground and proper place, and who sets out in advance of all others the "here" of beyng, *das Seyn* itself, and so through whom existence (*Da-sein*) *itself* occurs as the founding of beyng. As so often with Heidegger, his interpretations are not abstract or conjectural: "that one" has already come to pass, is one who can be found in history—preeminently it is Hölderlin. This understanding of the poet as the founding of beyng quickly established itself as the ground of "the language that held itself back."

In 2007 Günter Figal published an earlier, "first," version of Heidegger's very well-known essay and lecture "On the Origin of the Work of Art," a version that had existed from some point in 1935 (it was discovered in a drawer by Heidegger's son, Hermann), and so predates the version of 1936 that Heidegger himself had edited and first published in 1950. This "first" version contains a sentence that reproduces the thought in the letter to Blochmann almost exactly—"poetry—the essence of art—is *founding of beyng*. Thus not the production of beings."[36] It is impossible not to hear in this Heidegger's critique of Hegel's, and by the standards of the time in which he was writing, Marx's understanding of humanity as "the productive," the species that takes over the whole of nature and from out of it produces, and so literally by means of manufacture and economic advance, creates and forges, its own destiny. In other words, the political commentary that is also present in the *Black Notebooks* manifestly speaks here. From this early appearance of "beyng," the "language that remains in the background," Heidegger immediately proceeds to discuss the relation of "beyng" to the "here" (*Da*), as the way in which "man" takes over the "here," "not as individual, also not as community" (thus with all the indications of what was not said of *das Volk* in *Being and Time* in 1927). Only through an adequate taking over of the "here" of "here-being" (*Dasein*, existence) does humanity stand among beings as among beings and nonbeings, and so stand toward beyng as such: "This character, being this 'here,' we name history. Insofar as humanity is this 'here,' that means is historical, it becomes a nation."[37] Here, then, is the fulfillment of what was not said in *Being and Time*, where community and nation were merely equated. Yet what is said here is entirely consistent with what is said in *Being and Time*, even if it is an amplification.

Amplifying yet further, in the *Black Notebooks* Heidegger repeatedly explains that man is "inständlich," even "inständlicher"—literally, stood-within, stood-more-firmly (one commentator has "steadfast") in existence (*Da-sein*): we could almost say, "more rooted." Here it becomes clear the extent to which *Dasein*, existence, names the *place* wherein being "exists," rather than the "object" that somehow just, and already, "is."

This passage from the "first" version of "On the Origin of the Work of Art," in the precise form it takes of relating the "here" to the formation of a historical "people," is hinted at by the version of this essay published in 1950 during Heidegger's lifetime, but actually is absent—or rather, it has been excised from public view. Yet without it we are far less clear what Heidegger means when he speaks in the later version of "the historical existence of a nation."[38] In other words, in this small passage from an earlier version of an essay with which many Heidegger scholars are otherwise very familiar, we can see that the language that held itself back was a language held back by Heidegger himself—a language that belongs to the *Black Notebooks* but that, it would seem, was kept away from the scholarly community. To add to all the difficulties of interpreting Heidegger that I have attempted to bring to the fore—all the complex plaits and knotted interlacing of what has furrowed the corpus of Heidegger's work from the one at whose hand it was delivered—we must therefore add a final strand, namely, Heidegger's own withholding.

Only really once did the "language that was held back" make anything like a fuller public appearance in Heidegger's lifetime—in 1949 in the so-called *Bremen* lectures. Organized by a former student (Heinrich Wiegand Petzet) after Heidegger had failed the denazification process overseen by Constantin von Dietze in the French zone of occupied Germany, and after which the Allies banned him from teaching in the university, these four lectures (only three of which, it seems, were actually delivered, although the undelivered lecture, *Die Gefahr* ("The Danger"), appears to have circulated in some form or other) were given to an audience of wealthy, educated, but not academic, Germans. The language was quite unlike anything of Heidegger's previously heard. Published in full only in 1994 as volume 79 of the *Collected Works*, parts of the lectures formed the basis for the essays "Das Ding" ("The Thing"), "Die Kehre" ("The Turning"), and later "The Question Concerning Technology." Until they appeared, together with The Danger, in 1994, it was almost impossible to gain a sense of them as a unity. They speak to the heart of the effort to reconstruct post-Nazi Germany, in a city where the ships that would reopen trade with the rest of the globe were being launched and fitted out. The *danger* in question refers, without question, to a line from Hölderlin's ode, "Patmos." Only slowly has the Heidegger that was held back (often by Heidegger himself), the Heidegger of the *Black Notebooks* and later, come into public view. We are perhaps still unready for him, even now. The suspicion remains—and not without foundation—that it is only the Heidegger yet emerging from out of the shrouded shadows of which the *Black Notebooks* are but a part, who can unlock more fully the secrets of Heidegger's more public works, especially those published in his lifetime. However, these secrets do not concern Heidegger, or his work, but what it is his work was about: the question, the historical and even the political question, within the meaning of existence (and so here, in the "now" of our present lives), of being, of beyng itself.

Notes

1. Martin Heidegger, *Überlegungen II–VI (Schwarze Hefte 1931–1938)*, *Gesamtausgabe* 94, ed. Peter Trawny (Frankfurt: Klostermann, 2014), 9. Heidegger refers here (in 1931) to the first part of *Being and Time*.

2. Martin Heidegger, *Überlegungen VII–XI (Schwarze Hefte 1938/39)*, *Gesamtausgabe* 94, ed. Peter Trawny (Frankfurt: Klostermann, 2014), 22.

3. Friedrich-Wilhelm von Herrmann, "Editor's Afterword," in Martin Heidegger, *Das Ereignis*, *Gesamtausgabe* 71, ed. Friedrich-Wilhelm von Herrmann (Frankfurt: Klostermann, 2009), 343.

4. Martin Heidegger, *Beiträge zur Philosophie (Vom Ereignis)*, *Gesamtausgabe* 65, ed. Friedrich-Wilhelm von Herrmann (Frankfurt: Klostermann, 1989).

5. The other six volumes are: *Besinnung*, *Gesamtausgabe* 66, ed. Friedrich-Wilhelm von Herrmann (Frankfurt: Klostermann, 1997); *Metaphysik und Nihilismus. 1. Die Überwindung der Metaphysik (1938/39), 2. Das Wesen des Nihilismus (1946–1948)*, *Gesamtausgabe* 67, ed. Hans-Joachim Friedrich (Frankfurt: Klostermann, 1999); *Die Geschichte des Seyns. 1. Die Geschichte des Seyns (1938/40). 2. Κοινόν: Aus der Geschichte des Seyns (1939)*, *Gesamtausgabe* 69, ed. Peter Trawny (Frankfurt: Klostermann, 1998); *Über den Anfang (1941)*, *Gesamtausgabe* 70, ed. Paola-Ludovika Coriando (Frankfurt: Klostermann, 2005); *Das Ereignis*, *Gesamtausgabe* 71, ed. Friedrich-Wilhelm von Herrmann (Frankfurt: Klostermann, 2009); and *Die Stege des Anfangs (1944)*, *Gesamtausgabe* 72, ed. Paola-Ludovika Coriando (Frankfurt: Klostermann, forthcoming).

6. Martin Heidegger, *Zu Hölderlin/Griechenlandreisen*, *Gesamtausgabe* 75, ed. Curd Ochwadt (Frankfurt: Klostermann, 2000).

7. Martin Heidegger, *Metaphysik, Wissenschaft, Technik*, *Gesamtausgabe* 76, ed. Claudius Strube (Frankfurt: Klostermann, 2009).

8. One significant text that Heidegger complained of difficulty in publishing was the 1942 essay "Platon's Lehre von der Wahrheit" ("Plato's Doctrine of Truth"), subsequently published in *Wegmarken*, *Gesamtausgabe* 9, ed. Friedrich-Wilhelm von Herrmann, 203–238 (Frankfurt: Klostermann, [1967] 1976).

9. See Martin Heidegger, *Seminare: Hegel—Schelling*, *Gesamtausgabe* 86, ed. Peter Trawny (Frankfurt: Klostermann, 2011), 174. For "Carl Schmitt denkt liberal," see Philippe Lacoue-Labarthe, *Heidegger, Art, and Politics: The Fiction of the Political*, trans. Chris Turner (Oxford: Blackwell, 1990), 95.

10. See Martin Heidegger, *Sein und Zeit*, *Gesamtausgabe* 2, ed. Friedrich-Wilhelm von Herrmann (Frankfurt: Klostermann, [1927] 1975), 508.

11. "Das Volk zu sich selbst zurückzubringen … daß das Volk nur 'ist' auf dem Grunde des Da-seins" (Martin Heidegger, *Überlegungen II–VI, Gesamtausgabe* 94, p. 223).

12. Although there is no publicly available digital version of Heidegger's *Collected Works*, much of Heidegger's work has been digitized, irrespective of copyright, and can be found without too much difficulty.

13. See especially Martin Heidegger, "Der Weg zur Sprache," in *Vom Wesen der Sprache*, *Gesamtausgabe* 12, ed. Friedrich-Wilhelm von Herrmann, 229–262 (Frankfurt: Klostermann, [1959] 1985) (especially 252ff.).

14. François Jaran and Christophe Perrin, eds., *The Heidegger Concordance*, 3 vols. (London: Bloomsbury, 2013), vol. 1, xiv.

15. Compare, for instance, Hermann Bonitz's 1870 *Index Aristotelicus* (Darmstadt: Wissenschaftliche Buchgesellschaft, [1870] 1960), which appeared only toward the end of a lifetime's study of Plato and Aristotle.

16. See Martin Heidegger, *The Beginning of Western Philosophy: Interpretation of Anaximander and Parmenides*, trans. Richard Rojewicz (Bloomington: Indiana University Press, 2015).

17. Martin Heidegger, "On the Occasion of Edmund Husserl's 70th Birthday (1929)," in *Reden und andere Zeugnisse eines Lebensweges, Gesamtausgabe* 16, ed. Hermann Heidegger (Frankfurt: Klostermann, 2000), 59.

18. Martin Heidegger, *Einleitung in die Philosophie*, *Gesamtausgabe* 27, ed. Otto Saame and Ina Saame Speidel (Frankfurt: Klostermann, 2001), 227.

19. "Der λόγος als Methode der Untersuchung" (Martin Heidegger, *Platon: Sophistes*, *Gesamtausgabe* 19, ed. Ingeborg Schüßler [Frankfurt: Klostermann, 1992], 250).

20. "Doch damit ist alles das, was in *Sein und Zeit* als neue Position gewonnen wurde, verlorengegangen" (Martin Heidegger, *Seminare*, *Gesamtausgabe* 15, ed. Curd Ochwadt (Frankfurt: Klostermann, [1977] 2005), 204f.).

21. "Er kommt über 'Sein und Zeit' nicht hinaus. Allerdings und zum Glück" (Martin Heidegger, *Überlegungen VII–XI (Schwarze Hefte 1938/39)*, *Gesamtausgabe* 95, ed. Peter Trawny [Frankfurt: Klostermann, 2014], 169).

22. Like Löwith, Marcuse was a student of Heidegger's and an exile from the Nazi racial laws. Marcuse, who had seen in Heidegger the possibility of a new philosophical thinking, remained a Marxist of a kind all of his life. Marcuse remained in the United States; Löwith returned to Germany in 1952, the year of his death.

23. "Hier kehrt das Ganze um" (Martin Heidegger, "Brief über den 'Humanismus,'" in *Wegmarken*, *Gesamtausgabe* 9, ed. Friedrich-Wilhelm von Herrmann [Frankfurt: Klostermann, 1976], 328).

24. "Der fragliche Abschnitt wurde zurückgehalten, weil das Denken im zureichenden Sagen dieser Kehre versagte und so mit Hilfe der Sprache der Metaphysik nicht durchkam" (Martin Heidegger, "Brief über den 'Humanismus,'" in *Wegmarken*, *Gesamtausgabe* 9, p. 328).

25. "Der Brief spricht immer noch in der Sprache der Metaphysik, und zwar wissentlich" (Martin Heidegger, "Brief über den 'Humanismus,'" in *Wegmarken*, *Gesamtausgabe* 9, p. 313, note a, appended to the title).

26. Jean-Paul Sartre, *Existentialism Is a Humanism*, trans. Carol Macomber (New Haven: Yale University Press, 2007).

27. Martin Heidegger, preface to William J. Richardson, *Heidegger: Through Phenomenology to Thought* (New York: Fordham University Press, [1963] 2003), xvi. I have translated what Heidegger says somewhat differently from Richardson. The German says "daß ich bei der zu denkenden Sache 'Sein und Zeit' geblieben bin"; Richardson's translation renders this as "from the fact that I stayed with the matter-for-thought (of) 'Being and Time.'"

28. Martin Heidegger, *Grundfragen der Philosophie: Ausgewählte "Probleme" der Logik*, *Gesamtausgabe* 45, ed. Friedrich-Wilhelm von Herrmann (Frankfurt: Klostermann, [1984] 1992), 193.

29. Martin Heidegger, *Grundfragen der Philosophie*, *Gesamtausgabe* 45, pp. 217ff. The passage in full reads "Das Seyn aber ist Jenes, was den Menschen braucht als den Gründer und Wahrer seiner Wahrheit: den Menschen *als* den und den—nicht einfach nur so den Menschen, sondern ihn, der der Wahrheit Grund und Stätte bereitet, die Offenheit für das Sichverbergen aussteht, das Da *ist*" (Heidegger's emphases). Significantly the English translators of this passage, Richard Rojcewicz and André Schuwer, render the final *das* ("das Da *ist*") as "who," making the human being the "here," to which be-ing, *das Seyn*, is appropriated (see *Basic Questions of Philosophy: Selected "Problems" of "Logic,"* trans. Richard Rojcewicz and André Schuwer (Bloomington: Indiana University Press, 1994)). But the *das* in question must refer primarily to the "that" of be-ing and not the one who, in be-ing, is appropriated to the "here" in bringing this "here" to pass: the kernel of the sentence is "Das Seyn ist Jenes, das Da *ist*.

30. "Die andere Sprache bleibt im Hintergrund" (Martin Heidegger, "Brief über den 'Humanismus,'" in *Wegmarken*, *Gesamtausgabe* 9, p. 313, note a).

31. Martin Heidegger, *Überlegungen II–VI*, *Gesamtausgabe* 94, pp. 168ff.

32. See Martin Heidegger, *Hölderlins Hymnen "Germanien" und "Der Rhein,"* *Gesamtausgabe* 39, ed. Susanne Ziegler (Frankfurt: Klostermann, [1980] 1989).

33. "Der Dichter ist jener, der im voraus das Seyn stiftet—vorausprägend gründet und im ersten Nennen und Sagen das Seiende ins Seyn hebt" (Martin Heidegger, "Letter to Elisabeth Blochmann of 21st December 1934," in Martin Heidegger, *Reden und andere Zeugnisse eines Lebensweges*, *Gesamtausgabe* 16, ed. Hermann Heidegger, p. 335).

34. "Hölderlin als der 'Übergang'" (Martin Heidegger, *Überlegungen II–VI*, *Gesamtausgabe* 94, p. 248).

35. "Die Gründung seines Ortes (Da-sein)" (Martin Heidegger, *Überlegungen II–VI*, *Gesamtausgabe* 94, p. 248).

36. "Dichtung—das Wesung der Kunst—ist *Stiftung des Seyns*. Also nicht Hervorbringung des Seienden" (Martin Heidegger, *Vom Ursprung des Kunstwerks (Erste Ausarbeitung)*, in *Heidegger Lesebuch*, ed. Günter Figal

[Frankfurt: Klostermann, 2007], 165 [first published in *Heidegger Studies* 5 (1989)]).

37. "Der Mensch—nicht als Einzelner, auch nicht als Gemeinschaft. … Diese Weise, das Da zu sein, nennen wir die Geschichte. Indem der Mensch das Da ist, d.h. geschichtlich ist, wird er ein Volk" (Martin Heidegger, *Vom Ursprung des Kunstwerks (Erste Ausarbeitung)*, 166).

38. "[Das] geschichtlichen Dasein[] eines Volkes" (Martin Heidegger, "Der Ursprung des Kunstwerkes," in *Holzwege, Gesamtausgabe* 5, ed. Friedrich-Wilhelm von Herrmann [Frankfurt: Klostermann, (1950) 2003], 66).

9

The *Black Notebooks* and Heidegger's Writings on the Event (1936–1942)

Daniela Vallega-Neu

1   Introduction

Contributions to Philosophy (1936–1938), *Mindfulness* (*Besinnung*, 1938), *Die Geschichte des Seyns* (1938–1940), *Über den Anfang* (1941), *The Event* (*Das Ereignis*, 1941–1942), and the yet-to-be-published *Stege des Anfangs* (1944) are volumes in which Heidegger develops his "beyng-historical" (*seynsgeschichtlich*) thinking of the truth of beyng as event.[1] This development is far from systematic, because Heidegger's intent is to speak not *about* the event, about being, or about the history of beyng but rather to let historical beyng come to the fore performatively in a thoughtful saying. This is why I also like to call these volumes Heidegger's *poietic writings* (in reference to the Greek word *poiesis*, coming forth). In Heidegger's understanding, the thoughtful saying of the event responds to the call of beyng that emerges in the acknowledgment of a distress, the distress of the abandonment of beings by being in our epoch. Beings *are* not, if we take being (the "are") in its fullest sense where being means something like "truly being." Things and events take place but there is no truth in them; they are somehow deeply deprived. The specific way beings "are" not truly in our epoch, Heidegger calls machination. In the *Black Notebooks* Heidegger interprets almost everything happening around him as forms of machination: the university, political events, and all possible -isms like socialism, communism, Judaism, Bolshevism, as well as (and indeed more often) Christianity, the Catholic Church, and all kinds of political and cultural institutions. Heidegger interprets social and political events and institutions "beyng-historically." And yet, in my view, most of what Heidegger writes in the *Notebooks* does not reach the core of his thinking of the event. Although the *Notebooks* are not entirely extrinsic to his thinking of the historicality of beyng, they should be clearly distinguished from his poietic writings.

Something Heidegger wrote in a *Notebook*, probably in 1939, might indicate something else, though. In his own understanding the deliberations in the *Notebooks* are "inconspicuous outposts—and rearguarding positions in the totality of an attempt at a meditation that as yet is unsayable on the way to conquering a *way* for an anew inceptual thinking that is called—in distinction to metaphysical thinking—*beyng-historical* thinking."[2]

Outposts (*Vorposten*) and rearguard (*Nachhut*) connote positions of troops in order to secure the army in relation to enemies or conquests lying ahead or in the back. With respect to Heidegger's thinking, this might mean something like demarcating and defending certain limits of beyng-historical thinking. One might conjecture that Heidegger's many polemics against religious and cultural institutions and political organizations, for instance, help to secure the space for a more "inceptive" thinking by marking off that which clearly is not inceptive but lacks beyng.[3]

In an earlier *Notebook*, Heidegger writes that the issue in the *Notebooks* is not to criticize the state of affairs or to see everything negatively, but to point to what is most proximate in order to "*think ahead* into beyng itself and its simple and basic movement."[4] Pointing to what is most proximate follows the preliminary task of clearing the way for a more originary thinking that would open ways of being that remain closed off in the domination of machination and unsayable in the language of metaphysics. Whether a "thinking ahead into beyng itself" happens in the *Notebooks*, is another question. There are some but not many passages in the *Notebooks* where Heidegger speaks about basic relations of the event (*Dasein*, gods, humans, earth and world) that are more fully developed in the poietic writings. The latter and the *Notebooks* are, then, intimately connected, an intimacy that is troubling especially when it comes to Heidegger's nationalistic and anti-Semitic pronouncements in the *Notebooks*, albeit the former are very rare and the latter completely absent from the writings of the event.[5] Investigations of the relation between Heidegger's writings on the event and the *Notebooks* must also address the question of why this is the case—that is, why Heidegger did not emphasize the task of the Germans or mention Judaism in his poietic writings. Doesn't this indicate that he sensed that the question of the Germans or the Jews did not belong to the core of the question of beyng he was exploring?

To get a fuller sense of the difference between, for instance, *Contributions* and the *Notebooks* and thus to be able to address the question of whether or how Heidegger's nationalism and other political views "infected" his core philosophical activity, one has to engage *Contributions* philosophically—that is, one must be willing to follow Heidegger's thinking of the event. I begin, then, by saying more about what is at stake in Heidegger's writings of the event. I first look at the earlier *Notebooks* (1932, 1934–1936, but not 1933) because they give us some insight into how Heidegger began searching for a new thinking and saying that finally begins to take shape in *Contributions*. Then I return to *Contributions* and the volumes following it. As I will show, Heidegger's stance toward an engagement with machination shifts during the years 1936–1942. This shift is also reflected in how he thinks of power (*Macht*) and will (*Wille*),[6] and I will make the case that with this shift, the relation between the poietic writings and the *Notebooks* changes as well. At the end of this chapter I address some questions that pertain to my own *Auseinandersetzung*: my confrontation with Heidegger's thinking in light of the *Notebooks*. One question has to do with errancy (*Irre*) that Heidegger emphasizes in the *Notebooks* of 1938 and in *Besinnung*. Another question has to do with the role of attunement or disposition (*Stimmung*) in Heidegger's thinking.

These questions implicitly address one of the most fundamental and difficult differentia-tions in Heidegger's thinking, which is the differentiation between beyng and beings or, put very crudely: the relation between, on the one hand, thinking and experiencing be-ing in some fundamental way (such that being cannot be objectified but only undergone), and on the other hand, thinking about and experiencing things and events we relate to and can objectify. At stake here is also the relation between philosophy and life, between the thinker and the human being. But I would like to note right here that I believe that the dif-ficult questions a true engagement with Heidegger opens up for us will come to fruition only once we find the courage to put our own thinking and judgments in question.

2   Contributions to Philosophy

Contributions to Philosophy (1936–1938) is the book in which Heidegger first lays out the different dimensions of his beyng-historical thinking. In a short text from 1937–1938 titled "A Look Back on My Work" he indicates that the plan for *Contributions* had already emerged in the spring of 1932.[7] In the *Black Notebooks*, we find this telling entry: "Today [March 1932] I am in a clear place from which the whole previous writings (Being and Time; What Is Metaphysics?; Kant book, and On the Essence of Ground I and II) have become foreign to me. Foreign like a path that has been set still and that overgrows with grass and shrubs—a path, however, that leads into Da-sein as temporality."[8]

   Indeed this early *Notebook* is distinguished by short entries that often are like directives Heidegger seems to give to himself: "through being to beings"[9] is one of them. At stake is finding a way of thinking that does not question being on the basis of beings (objects of thought) but rather the other way around, that requires thinking in a nonobjectifying way. Heidegger speaks of a new and originary beginning[10] as well as of poetizing being: "the poetizing of being prior to all beings."[11] We can see, then, how important poetry is for the development of Heidegger's thinking of being. The Germans are in the picture right away: "The German alone can poetize and say originarily and anew being—he alone will conquer anew the essence of *theoria* and finally create *the logic*."[12] In these early years, Heidegger clearly had a sense of historical renewal. He repeats how "the world is in reconstruction"[13] and often writes of the "empowerment of being" (*Seinsermächtigung*),[14] an empowerment that requires an originary "effecting" (*erwirken*).[15]

   There are many motifs that Heidegger will carry through all his nonpublic writings. One is a disregard for what people address as "the situation."[16] Another is the necessity of reti-cence or silence[17] and a third is the solitary path or alone-ness of *Dasein*.[18] There begins, then, a division between public lectures and nonpublic writings. The latter have the task to find in disposed reticence a way of speaking and saying being such that being is brought forth performatively in that saying. This is a struggle (*Kampf*), a word that abounds in all of Heidegger's *Notebooks* and there are clear indications that for him this struggle is akin to the Heraclitean *polemos*.[19] The passion Heidegger felt for this project that required a casting free (*Loswurf*)[20] into groundless *Dasein*, becomes apparent for instance when he writes of the lived body (*Leib*) that "in the throw [*Wurf*] gains a completely new and transformed expansion of power [*Machtentfaltung*]."[21] Heidegger's notes sound very much akin to the stark pathos of the late Nietzsche—for instance, when Heidegger speaks of the disciplining (*Zucht*) of the youth[22] and emphasizes hardness.[23] We know where this pathos took Heidegger in 1933. Indeed, there is not much of interest for beyng-historical think-ing in *Notebook III*, which spans 1932–1934. But in *Notebook IV* from 1934 to 1936 we can see how after his disillusionment with the National Socialist movement, Heidegger retreated into thinking and preparing his new work. He focuses less than in the previous and in subsequent *Notebooks* on "critiques" of political events and the university and says more concerning the event.

In 1934 Heidegger thinks of the event in terms of the "worlding" of the world[24] that would empower the "there" (the "Da") and mark a "second" beginning.[25] He begins to write *Seyn* with a *y* to indicate this fuller sense of historical beyng. The task is "to bring the world to occur as world …: to venture once more the gods."[26] But for now we have no world and thus no gods.[27] The second beginning can only be prepared and such preparation requires that one go back into the first beginning, the Greek beginning.[28]

We can see how the major trajectories and relations of beyng-historical thinking are already there in 1932, but in the *Notebooks* they are not much developed. This will be the task of *Contributions to Philosophy*. And still, this first of the poietic writings is only an *attempt* at saying the truth of beyng as event in an originary way.[29] In such a saying— although thinking *responds* to the call of beyng—beyng only comes to language in the saying of the thinker. Beyng is no-thing in itself; indeed, for Heidegger it is first experi-enced as a lack or withdrawal that compels his thinking. And yet, in casting free from any hold in representational/objectifying thinking of beings, thinking finds itself to be appro-priated, *ereignet*, by the appropriating event (*Er-eignis*) such that a thoughtful saying of beyng can take place.

I believe that the experience Heidegger bespeaks here is akin to any form of genuine creative activity. Let's take for instance creative writing in poetry or thought. The exercise here is to let images, concepts, or words arise. And yet, these do not come all on their own but require an attentiveness, an attuned time-space where they can emerge (if they emerge). There is no guarantee of success, no ground to such creative time-space. This is akin to what Heidegger calls Da-sein (now written with a hyphen); literally "there-being" in an abyssal opening. Da-sein, this time-space, is what first needs to be appropriated, what needs to be "grounded." This is the major task of *Contributions to Philosophy*. Heidegger's thinking attempts to move and articulate the spacing of the not-yet-present, the not-yet-said whose coming to presence is not in our power. This is analogous to a sense of lack we carry with us, that we attend to and cannot find words for, a lack that we intimate, may turn into a gifting. For Heidegger the lack he experiences is epochal and what is to be gifted is nothing less than another beginning of Western history. He saw himself in the company of the other great German philosophers who articulated the completion of Western history (Hegel, Nietzsche; Schelling is likewise important for Heidegger).[30] But thanks to what he found in Hölderlin, Heidegger (as he saw it) could think further than all previous philosophers; he had a presentiment of another beginning.

What Heidegger attempts to think and say in *Contributions*, then, is nothing other than how (his) thinking experiences beyng in its historicality in the transition from the first to the other beginning. In thinking ahead into the originary and inceptive (*anfänglich*) dimension of beyng, Heidegger's thinking enters an untimely situation. He calls this transitional thinking inceptive though it cannot initiate the other beginning of history for a people. Transitional inceptive thinking hovers in-between a time-space of decision that cannot be decided: the (perhaps never-ending) end of the first beginning or the other beginning. It is by staying disposed by basic dispositions (*Grundstimmungen*) that this space can be kept open and Heidegger's repetitive rethinking of the event arises from the repetitive exercise of thinking out of such basic disposition. The disposition he most often appeals to in *Contributions* is restraint (*Verhaltenheit*), which includes the shock of the abandonment of beings by beyng and the diffident turn toward the most intimate and concealed dimension of the truth of beyng, a dimension that necessitates reticence or stillness: the dimension of the holy and the gods in the undecidability of their flight *and* arrival.

Although Heidegger's pathos in *Contributions* has lost some of the harshness it has in his earlier *Notebooks*, what I would call a language of resistance is still strong: he appeals to withstanding (*Ausstehen*) and steadfastness (*Inständigkeit*); thinking needs to withstand the withdrawal of beyng and be steadfast in the abyssal opening of truth. Heidegger believes that the only way to a more originary experience of truth is *through* the acknowledgment of the abandonment of beings by being, through the shock in the face of an utter refusal, through the experience of the nothingness belonging to being.[31] The enemy is the lack of a sense of plight (*Not der Notlosigkeit*), the satisfaction people have with lived experiences (*Erlebnisse*), which does not let arise any need to question being. A sense of plight first needs to be awakened and sustained and this requires that it be understood as a result of machination.

Machination determines the relation to beings in our epoch. Symptoms of machination are calculation, organization, speed, gearing everything toward the masses, the divestment and vulgarization of dispositions, the disempowerment of the word, and what is gigantic.[32] Heidegger sees the roots of machination already in classical Greece although it will come to the fore only with Christianity and the idea of a maker God. It will be fully deployed only once subjectivity becomes the center for discovering beings as what can be organized, calculated, enjoyed, and so on (modernity).

What to contemporary readers of Heidegger's *Black Notebooks* looks like hefty polemics against everything, in Heidegger's own interpretation belongs to the necessity of acknowledging the abandonment of beings by beyng and the reigning of machination.

The language of resistance one can find in *Contributions* is tied to the difference between beyng and beings. While machination reigns we only know beings and representational thinking prevails. Thinking thus must be unsettled from its customary relations to beings. It must be dislodged into the groundless experience of beyng. The shock arising from the realization of the abandonment and forgottenness of beyng occurs precisely as such an unsettlement. At the same time, thinking needs to hold at bay and ward off machinational being. To prepare Da-sein as the site of decision over another beginning of history, a beginning that requires the sheltering of the truth of beyng in beings (words, deeds, things), thinking needs to turn away from beings. The relation to beings (things, words, deeds) is thus twofold, and one might say that it is in strife. When Heidegger speaks of the grounding of Da-sein he speaks of the *simultaneity* of beyng and beings: *beyng* occurs historically only *through beings*. But paradoxically, preparing Da-sein requires a *turn away from beings*, a "no-saying," a warding off. Sometimes Heidegger reflects on the danger this implies. As long as we are in a stance of resistance, we remain tied to what we resist. See for instance what he writes in *Notebook V* from the same period he was working on *Contributions*:

You must endure the end if you want to prepare the other beginning. But in the end there is much refusal, extinction, disorder—yet at the same time the appearance of what is contrary [*des Gegenteiligen*]. And thus remaining with the end must accomplish much negation, such that it could appear as if everything dissipated in fruitless "critique." And yet, that no and every uncovering of insufficiencies arises from the *opposition against* [*Widerstreben gegen*] the mere ending of the era and arises *already* from the preparation of the beginning which alone it serves.[33]

I wonder if these and similar pronouncements in other *Notebooks*[34] should be taken, as well, as reminders that Heidegger gives himself. He would certainly like to have all he writes understood as a preparation for the other beginning and not simply as remaining in the shackles of "common" critiques. But especially when it comes to the *Notebooks*, the language Heidegger uses in "uncovering insufficiencies" often is quite blatantly polemical. He writes for instance of the "pitiful bawlers who see 'nihilism' in all genuine *questioning*."[35] Or: "What does it mean that those who overflow with 'Christian humility' elevate beyond bounds self-righteousness?"[36] Or: "What misery and, above all, what low but well-attired business lies in that summum ens."[37] One of the most striking polemical remarks I found in a later *Notebook* features Heidegger's criticism of how "intellectuals" act "as if they were the last saviors and guardians of peasantry." He writes: "My dog—'Spitz'—has more 'peasantry' in the snout than those bloated, bottomless counterfeiters that are avid for professorships."[38]

In the *Notebooks* there are innumerable criticisms of cultural politics (especially Christian cultural politics), of historians, of romanticism, and of all kinds of attitudes that are "low" and "small" and "pitiful." Such language betrays a polemical attitude even if Heidegger wants us to think otherwise. No doubt he gave himself much more freedom to engage in polemical escapades in the *Notebooks* than in the writings of the event.

3   *Besinnung* and *Die Geschichte des Seyns* (1938–1941)

In the years during which Heidegger writes *Besinnung* (1938) and *Die Geschichte des Seyns* (1938–1940) he meditates on beyng as is occurs in the end of metaphysics. He reflects extensively on the history of being, on machination, and on power. The years 1938–1939 are also the years Heidegger makes the most entries in his *Notebooks*. The sections in *Notebooks* VII–XI are often longer reflections on different concepts, especially on history (*Geschichte* for Heidegger means history in a more originary sense of the happening of the truth of beyng), historiology (*Historie* for Heidegger means the representational approach to "history" as a series of facts), and philosophy. There are more similarities between the writings of the event and the *Notebooks* in these years devoted to a *Besinnung*, a mindfulness of historical being especially in the current context and with Nietzsche's impact strongly present. Indeed, in 1939 Heidegger's stance toward Nietzsche sharpens more and more as he sees in Nietzsche the consummation of the end of metaphysics. Heidegger's description of Nietzsche's will to power as the will to will blends with his description of machination: "As the essence of beings, as the way beings as such *are* through and through, machination compels the complete unleashing of all forces capable of power and of transforming power into the self-overpowering of power."[39]

It is striking that as his stance toward Nietzsche becomes harsher, Heidegger begins to think differently of power. We saw how he often speaks "positively" of the empowerment of being in 1932–1934. In *Contributions* that notion is present as well, but rarely.[40] In *Besinnung* the notion of "what is without power" (in the sense of being neither powerful nor powerless) begins to appear. Since it appears only later in the volume, I suspect that it emerged in 1939 (the year World War II began).

The first occurrence of the notion of what is without power (*das Machtlose*) occurs in section 49: "As the event of refusal, beyng guards its singularity in the uniqueness of its clearing through which what is essentially *without power* becomes alienating with respect to all beings (what is effective [*Wirkendes*]) that are 'as usual' and yet disseminates beings in its hidden groundlessness and makes room for the gods and the time-space of their nearness and remoteness."[41] When beyng's refusal opens up, it becomes manifest in its lack of power and strangeness with respect to beings. Heidegger will contrast "what is without power" with beings as they are commonly understood. What is without power (beyng) becomes alienating or estranging with respect to things and events, and this creates a temporal spacing—that is, a time-space for a realm that seems removed from what happens with beings. Heidegger will continue this thought when he writes that the "unusualness of beyng ... has the whole of beings against it."[42] The notion of what is without power is, then, tied to the differencing of beings and beyng and with this to a removal of the thinking of the event from "concrete things."

In section 51, what is without power appears in a slightly different context, namely, in the context of human steadfastness in the truth of beyng. Heidegger writes: "Beyng-historically, this steadfastness [*Inständigkeit*] then is the mastery [*Beherrschung*] over machination without power; the power of machination only collapses when it reaches the empowerment of its overpowering such that it can no longer eschew what uniquely withholds itself from its violence: the groundlessness of the truth *of* being, that itself is machinationally."[43] Here lack of power is attributed to human indwelling in the truth of beyng, a lack of power that does not succumb to machination but "has mastery over" it, in the sense that it is not touched by it. Indeed, we find the following sentence later in *Besinnung*: "What is without power cannot be disempowered,"[44] and this is a consequence of its "nobility" (*Adel*). At the same time Heidegger thinks steadfastness in the truth of beyng without power, he thinks a most extreme development of machination. He thinks of the latter as escalating into the empowerment of its overpowering to such a point that the groundlessness of being becomes manifest.

I believe that one of the topics that make visible the extremity into which Heidegger thinks the "overpowering power," is the culmination of subjectivity in the form of the human animal. Heidegger here is influenced not only by Nietzsche's notion of the last human as the "not yet fixed animal" but also by Oswald Spengler's notion of the predator (*Raubtier*) and by Jünger's notion of the worker.[45] Thus "The human of the consummated modernity is the historical animal, to whom beings as a whole appear as 'life' and who out of his drivenness has elevated his own trafficking to what is desirable as 'lived experience.'"[46]

That Heidegger's reflections on the historical animal (he has begun equating history with technology[47]) were also strongly influenced by the thought of war becomes clear for instance through the following remark from *Besinnung* (that could have come just as well from one of the *Notebooks* of that time):[48] "World War thinking [*das weltkriegerische Denken*] that occurs out of the highest predatory will to power and out of the unconditional character of armament is in each instance the sign of the completion of the metaphysical era."[49]

It all came together as Heidegger thought the epoch of the consummation of metaphysics to the extreme: his stance toward Nietzsche, reading Spengler and Jünger, his critique of National Socialism and of thinking in terms of race, blood and soil, and the war.[50] As all this reaches an extreme in Heidegger's thinking there occurs a shift in the basic attunement in his writings of the event.

4   *Über den Anfang* and *The Event* (1941–1942)

The shift in Heidegger's thinking occurs some time in 1941. With *Über den Anfang* but more clearly with *The Event*, his stance toward history changes. The language of resistance and withstanding in relation to the machinational deployment of beings gives way to another basic disposition that will eventually lead to Heidegger's thinking of *Gelassenheit* (releasement). The relation to the end of metaphysics is no longer one of withstanding but one of letting pass by, of *Vorbeigang*:

The demise [of metaphysics] and the transition [to the other beginning] pass each other by; according to the law of the releasing of being into its extreme distorted essence (into the will to willing), beyng lets the distorted essence go on. Beyng overcomes the dominance of the distorted essence not by "engaging" with it and overpowering it but, rather, by releasing the distorted essence into its demise. The abyssal sort of overcoming is the releasing of that which is to be overcome into the fanaticism of its distorted essence, wherein it is engulfed. This releasing is to be experienced in knowledge of the fissure of the passing by, in which the will to willing [machination] and the event do not and cannot turn to each other.[51]

Strikingly, it is in the middle of World War II that Heidegger achieves a stance in his thinking where he can let machination pass by and dedicate himself to rethinking the event as inception. Heidegger's thinking "twists free" (*verwindet*) from metaphysics and "goes under" into the most concealed dimension of inception in the attempt at an imageless saying of the event. I don't have space here to give a detailed interpretation of Heidegger's thinking in *Über den Anfang* and *The Event*.[52] Let me point out, though, that here Heidegger stays furthest away from representational thinking. He begins to think the appropriating event (*Er-eignis*) as occurring originarily as ex-propriation (*Ent-eignis*). Heidegger's thinking ventures even beyond beyng in the attempt to articulate nothing but this unrepresentable originary or inceptive moment at which even the distinction between first and other beginning is suspended. Responding to the silent word of beyng, Heidegger's thinking becomes a thanking, dwelling in the "poverty" and "dignity" of beyng.[53]

With this renewed approach to the event the relation between Heidegger's writings of the event and the *Black Notebooks* changes. Whereas *Besinnung* and *Die Geschichte des Seyns* are close to the *Black Notebooks* insofar as Heidegger meditates on machination and contemporary occurrences in both, Heidegger's entries in the *Black Notebooks* of 1941 have little to do with what he is after in *Über den Anfang* and *The Event*. Here (as on so many other occasions) I would have liked to have a clearer dating of Heidegger's *Notebooks*. According to the editor, the last two *Black Notebooks* (*Überlegungen* XIV and XV) have entries in 1941 (we already find the date 1941 in *Überlegungen* XIV, *Gesamtausgabe* 96, p. 241).[54] What Heidegger writes at the very beginning of the last *Black Notebook*, in my view, confirms the clearer separation that now happens between the thinking of the event and his reflections on his times. Heidegger writes: "All references to what can be grasped historiologically [*historisch*, i.e., representationally], to incidents, and to what is contemporary, mean this only in a leaving-behind that passes over all that lacks history [*das Geschichtslose*]. Still at times this raveling out of the fluttering semblance of concealed history must be mentioned only in order to have a clue in relation to what a letting-behind can be carried out."[55]

For Heidegger, what one would commonly call historical events, events one can represent and date, are historiological (*historische*) occurrences and not history (*Geschichte*) in the beyng-historical sense. History is, rather, the concealed happening of the expropriating/appropriating event. Consequently, what Heidegger writes in his *Notebooks* with reference to representable historical events or "incidents," and "what is contemporary," does not properly address the history of beyng. It seems, then, that in his own terms, these last *Notebooks* became sites to reflect on contemporary events and were not constitutive of his "real" or more proper thinking that happened somewhere else. Consequently Heidegger's pronouncements on Americanism, Bolshevism, socialism, and World Jewry (as condemnable as these remain for us today) should not be taken as instances of originary thinking. This applies even more blatantly to, for example, the following proclamation by Heidegger regarding history: "At the earliest in 2300 there may still be history. Then Americanism will have exhausted itself in its satiated emptiness."[56]

Still, there are some few passages in *Über den Anfang* and *The Event* where Heidegger makes references to what his thinking otherwise "lets pass by."

In *Über den Anfang* he introduces the notions of "planetarism" and "idiotism."[57] In section 16 he defines planetarism as "the essential ground of what spreads as the equality of peoples (*order* of the masses in service to the worldpower ...)" and idiotism as "the determination of the historical condition according to which everybody always recognizes and either willfully or ignorantly pursues their *idion*—that is, what is proper to them as that which is the same with what is proper to all others."[58] He mentions the notions of planetarism and idiotism briefly at a later point in the volume (inserting a cross-reference to *Überlegungen XV*)[59] and then once more when he calls "'Americanism' the proper form of planetarism."[60]

Almost all references to historiological instances in *The Event* occur in sections 131–136 when Heidegger reflects on the more proper meaning of *Abendland* (literally, the "land of evening" and commonly translated as the "West") in distinction to Europe: "The beyng-historical concept of the Abendland has nothing to do with the modern concept of 'Europe.' What is European is a preliminary form of the planetary. ... What is European and planetary is the ending and completion. The Abendland is the beginning."[61] Heidegger then writes that Europe is the completion of both the Western Hemisphere (*Amerika*) and "the East of Russian Bolshevism."[62] He thus extrapolates the notion of *Abendland* from any geographic connotation and tries to think it beyng-historically.

If "Europe" is a "historiological-technological (i.e., planetary) concept," as Heidegger writes,[63] then shouldn't this apply as well to everything he writes in his last *Notebooks* about Americans,[64] Italians,[65] the English,[66] and also World Jewry[67]? This does not preclude that one (and I count myself among the "one" here) might also see what Heidegger says about the *Abendland* or about the Germans[68] as not entirely different from the notion of Europe because he is dealing here with concepts laden with representations and preconceptions. In my view, his "political pronouncements" need to be distinguished from poietic thinking/saying.

But if, following Heidegger's own indications, we say that the *Notebooks* from 1941 are essentially different from his writings of the event, should we not say (perhaps retrospectively) the same of all the *Notebooks*? How should we understand the greater proximity between *Contributions*, *Besinnung*, and the *Notebooks* of that same time? Is it not telling that—in contrast to *Über den Anfang* (where there is one cross-reference) and *The Event* (where there are no cross-references), Heidegger includes several cross-references to the *Notebooks* in these earlier beyng-historical writings?[69] We could say that these earlier writings are more transitional, more "contaminated" by what they intend to leave behind when they "leap ahead" into the more inceptive realm of the event. This changes in 1941.

5 Errancy

The question for us remains: What shall we do with these generalizing nationalistic, political, and often blatantly polemical remarks in the *Notebooks*? What should we do with Heidegger's anti-Semitism? Perhaps we should simply say that he was erring. Indeed, is it not Heidegger who since his essay "On the Essence of Truth" (1930) has always thought of errancy (*Irre*) as being constitutive of truth? Over the years, however, Heidegger's reflections on errancy shift a little. In 1930, he thinks of errancy as a turning away from the mystery (i.e., from the originary concealment belonging to truth) and toward what is readily available (i.e., beings). This errancy belongs to the inner constitution of Da-sein: "Errancy is the free space for that turning in which insistent ek-sistence adroitly forgets and mistakes itself constantly anew."[70]

   Around 1938 Heidegger appears to begin to differentiate a more originary sense of errancy—that is, an errancy that remains alert to the originary concealment of truth—from an errancy that turns away from and forgets the originary concealment (this latter sense is the meaning of errancy in 1930).[71] Heidegger will also continue to think errancy in the more originary sense in the 1940s.[72] In *Besinnung*, there are three sections (7, 38, and 72) in which he emphasizes how errancy needs to be sharply distinguished from falsity and how it belongs to truth of beyng: "Truth (clearing) of beyng is the beyng of errancy."[73] Such errancy also needs to be distinguished from distortion (*Verkehrung*) that is rooted in errancy and that addresses a falling for beings and their exclusive predominance. This suggests that although beyng-historical thinking is prone to be turned toward beings, it can hold at bay their prevailing power. Such power manifests itself in a reckoning with causes such as "drives, inclinations, pleasures, and delectations." Against such powers one can prevail, Heidegger suggests:

What is true occurs [*ereignet sich*] only in the truth: that we belong to its essential occurrence, that we know the danger of distortion as being rooted in it and that we do not allow entrance to what is distorted in its unfettered power and don't fear it, steadfast in the venture of beyng, belonging to the unique service of the not-yet-appeared but announced god."[74]

This passage suggests that beyng-historical thinking experiences errancy, the turn toward beings, their ambiguity between standing in the clearing and concealing the clearing,[75] but that—insofar as it knows about errancy and remains alert to it—thinking can keep distortion at bay. The clearing of the truth of beyng as a clearing of errancy thus occurs as a space of decision that decides between truth (with its errancy) and distortion through beings. In relation to the human being, this requires that beyng-historical thinking holds at bay a reckoning with things according to drives, inclinations, pleasures, and delectations.

But would it not be "human all too human" for Heidegger to sometimes err from the proper path? We indeed find reflections by Heidegger himself that show his awareness that even inceptive thinking remains prone to errancy: "In all that is inceptual, … it easily may occur that, who has to think and poetize in its area goes astray with respect to that which has already been assigned and consigned to him, and yet is still unkept property. … Thus it is rare that thinking ahead into inception is constantly (i.e., always unusually) inceptive."[76] This leads me to the question of passions, feelings, and attunement. Besides the passages in *Besinnung* I just discussed, I am not aware of places where Heidegger thinks errancy in relation to passions or to attunements (*Stimmungen*). We know that since *Being and Time* Heidegger's thinking is always an attuned thinking, that it seeks to move in the time-space provided by basic attunements. Basic attunements are, for Heidegger, nonsubjective but overcome us. They disclose abyssal truth and historical beyng. But what about the relation between attunements and errancy, and what about what happens when we begin to speak? What about the truth and errancy of those beings we call words?

Most importantly, how can we distinguish fundamental attunements that reveal a moment of truth from "attunements" that lead us astray (Heidegger may call them drives and inclinations), "attunements" that are more like infectious moods that make us follow a crowd or "attunements" that arise from resistances that keep us blind? Heidegger's anti-Semitism and all his other "anti-" pronouncements clearly belong to the latter category. Perhaps he had a sense of this when he kept certain remarks limited to the *Notebooks*. But in the *Notebooks* themselves, it seems to me that there are many moments when the limits between revealing and blinding dispositions get blurred.

The question of revealing dispositions and misleading "dispositions" is one we need to address for ourselves as well. Is any of us willing to call into question a "gut feeling" or a moment of truth when speaking with a friend? What about our gut reactions against Heidegger's anti-Semitic remarks in the *Notebooks*?

Sustaining such questions means knowing of errancy. It is difficult. Reading Heidegger seriously requires that one sustain this space of errancy and questioning.

6   Conclusion

In the *Notebooks* Heidegger writes that he sees these in the context of his other nonpublic writings on the event. I pointed out how the earlier *Notebooks* (1932–1936) actually show how in the *Notebooks* Heidegger began to develop his beyng-historical thinking that finds its first fuller articulation in *Contributions to Philosophy*. The *Notebooks* from 1938–1939 stand in close proximity to *Besinnung* (*Gesamtausgabe* 66) and *Geschichte des Seyns*

(*Gesamtausgabe* 69) and are marked by criticism of political, religious, and cultural institutions and events that Heidegger interprets as forms of machination. He would like to see his many polemics in the *Notebooks* not as polemics but as reflections on manifestations of machination. They are supposed to ward off what needs to be overcome in inceptive beyng-historical thinking. I have made the point that, measured with what Heidegger calls inceptive thinking (thinking of the event) in his writings of the event, the *Black Notebooks* cannot be called instances of inceptive thinking. This becomes even more obvious in 1941–1942, when Heidegger's thinking in the writings of the event (*Über den Anfang* [*Gesamtausgabe* 70]; *Das Ereignis* [*Gesamtausgabe* 71]) transforms. Here he abandons resistance against machination that marked earlier writings and "goes under" into the most concealed dimension of being in the attempt to respond to nothing but the silent call of beyng. Here, in the "poverty" and "dignity" of beyng, thinking becomes a thanking. A gap opens between what and how Heidegger writes in the *Notebooks* of that time and his beyng-historical writings. This still leaves us with a question: How are we, as readers and interpreters of Heidegger's texts, to reconcile the apparent humility and responsiveness of his thinking in *The Event* with the hard polemical critiques in the concurrent *Notebooks*? But perhaps this question and the unease it creates need to be sustained for those who wish to think seriously with and beyond Heidegger.

Notes

1. Heidegger writes beyng (*Seyn*) with a *y* in order to indicate that being is not thought metaphysically but rather out of its historical occurrence.

2. *Überlegungen VII–XI (Schwarze Hefte 1938/39), Gesamtausgabe* 95, ed. Peter Trawny (Frankfurt: Klostermann, 2014), 274.

3. This is how Heidegger likes to see it: "What therefore at first looks like a rejection and 'critique' of the era, is indeed only the takeoff for a meditation on that which is older than the covered up and yet still essentially occurring ground" (*Überlegungen VII–XI, Gesamtausgabe* 95, p. 221).

4. *Überlegungen VII–XI, Gesamtausgabe* 95, p. 24.

5. In *Contributions*, Heidegger speaks once of the German people (*Beiträge zur Philosophie (Vom Ereignis)*, *Gesamtausgabe* 65, ed. Friedrich-Wilhelm von Herrmann [Frankfurt: Klostermann, 1989], 42). In *Besinnung*, he speaks of Germany only once when he mentions the future ones who will save the Germans in the plight of their essence (*Besinnung, Gesamtausgabe* 66, ed. Friedrich-Wilhelm von Herrmann (Frankfurt: Klostermann, 1997), 61). *Die Geschichte des Seyns, Gesamtausgabe* 69, ed. Peter Trawny (Frankfurt: Klostermann, 1998), has more pronouncements that could have come from the *Notebooks*. Heidegger mentions the Germans three times (*Die Geschichte des Seyns, Gesamtausgabe* 69, pp. 86, 108, 119) and in one instance writes "The history of the world is allotted to the mindfulness of the Germans" (*Die Geschichte des Seyns, Gesamtausgabe* 69, p. 108). In *Das Ereignis, Gesamtausgabe* 71, ed. Friedrich-Wilhelm von Herrmann (Frankfurt: Klostermann, 2009), Heidegger mentions the Germans twice, once when speaking of how it is dangerous for the West that the Germans are succumbing to the modern spirit (see *The Event,* trans. Richard Rojcewicz (Bloomington: Indiana University Press, 2012), 78) and another time when he says that inceptual thinking is grounded by Germans (*The Event*, 251).

6. For how Heidegger's thinking about and stance toward the will change throughout his works, see the in-depth study by Bret Davis, *Heidegger and the Will: On the Way to Gelassenheit* (Evanston, IL: Northwestern University Press, 2007).

7. *Besinnung, Gesamtausgabe* 66, p. 424.

8. *Überlegungen II–VI (Schwarze Hefte 1931–1938), Gesamtausgabe* 94, ed. Peter Trawny (Frankfurt: Klostermann, 2014), 19.

9. *Überlegungen II–VI, Gesamtausgabe* 94, p. 25.

10. *Überlegungen II–VI, Gesamtausgabe* 94, pp. 17, 19.

11. *Überlegungen VII–XI, Gesamtausgabe* 95, p. 15.

12. *Überlegungen II–VI, Gesamtausgabe* 94, p. 27.

13. "Die Welt ist im Umbau" (*Überlegungen II–VI, Gesamtausgabe* 94, pp. 26, 31, 38).

14. "Überlegungen II," *Überlegungen II–VI, Gesamtausgabe* 94, pp. 39, 43, 45, 55f., 62, 98.

15. *"Empowerment of* being—not to subsequently catch and harness in concepts what we anyway already have, but first effect that which is not yet occurring. Therefore philosophy essentially has no object" (*Überlegungen II–VI, Gesamtausgabe* 94, p. 39).

16. *Überlegungen II–VI, Gesamtausgabe* 94, pp. 1, 7f. Heidegger does not elaborate on what he means by "the situation" but I assume that he means a current political situation in the way it would be ordinarily addressed, analyzed, and discussed.

17. The German words are *Schweigen, Erschweigen,* and *Verschweigen.* See *Überlegungen II–VI, Gesamtausgabe* 94, pp. 10, 16, 28, 38, 43, 47, 51, 52, 68, 74, 78.

18. *Überlegungen II–VI, Gesamtausgabe* 94, pp. 7, 20f., 40, 56, 71.

19. *Überlegungen II–VI, Gesamtausgabe* 94, pp. 113, 217.

20. *Überlegungen II–VI, Gesamtausgabe* 94, pp. 78–80.

21. *Überlegungen II–VI, Gesamtausgabe* 94, p. 84.

22. *Überlegungen II–VI, Gesamtausgabe* 94, p. 61.

23. *Überlegungen II–VI, Gesamtausgabe* 94, pp. 10, 23, 36, 61, 82, 97.

24. *"The world worlds in order for beyng to hold sway, such that beyngs be* (Event)" (*Überlegungen VII–XI, Gesamtausgabe* 95, p. 211).

25. Eventually Heidegger will think the second beginning in terms of "the other beginning" that is "the inauguration for the time of *the last god*" (*Überlegungen II–VI, Gesamtausgabe* 94, p. 262).

26. *Überlegungen II–VI, Gesamtausgabe* 94, p. 209.

27. *Überlegungen II–VI, Gesamtausgabe* 94, pp. 210, 218.

28. *Überlegungen II–VI, Gesamtausgabe* 94, p. 234.

29. See the first section of *Beiträge zur Philosophie, Gesamtausgabe* 65.

30. See *Überlegungen II–VI, Gesamtausgabe* 94, p. 523, where Heidegger places his own birth year at the end of a series of dates referring to Hölderlin and Nietzsche. The dates are preceded by the following words: *"Play and uncanniness of historiographical numbers that reckon time [and this play] on the foreground of the abyssal German history."*

31. Being-there (Da-sein) is first and foremost being-away (Weg-sein) both in the sense of beings closed off from the truth of being in our relation to beings (machination) and in the sense of the nothingness belonging to being that is mirrored in death.

32. See sections 59 and 70 of *Beiträge zur Philosophie, Gesamtausgabe* 65. If one follows Heidegger's analysis and critique of machination it is clear that the calculated mass extermination of the Jewish people is a prime manifestation of machination.

33. *Überlegungen II–VI, Gesamtausgabe* 94, pp. 384f.

34. *Überlegungen II–VI, Gesamtausgabe* 94, p. 352; *Überlegungen VII–XI, Gesamtausgabe* 95, pp. 37, 221.

35. *Überlegungen II–VI, Gesamtausgabe* 94, p. 327.

36. *Überlegungen II–VI, Gesamtausgabe* 94, p. 329.

37. *Überlegungen II–VI, Gesamtausgabe* 94, p. 394.

38. *Überlegungen XII–XV (Schwarze Hefte 1939–1941), Gesamtausgabe* 96, ed. Peter Trawny (Frankfurt: Klostermann, 2014), 91.

39. *Besinnung, Gesamtausgabe* 66, pp. 17f.

40. *Beiträge zur Philosophie, Gesamtausgabe* 65, pp. 338, 430.

41. *Besinnung, Gesamtausgabe* 66, p. 130.

42. *Besinnung, Gesamtausgabe* 66, p. 130.

43. *Besinnung, Gesamtausgabe* 66, p. 135.

44. *Besinnung, Gesamtausgabe* 66, p. 191.

45. *Besinnung, Gesamtausgabe* 66, p. 27.

46. *Besinnung, Gesamtausgabe* 66, p. 27. All translations from *Besinnung* are my own.

47. *Überlegungen VII–XI, Gesamtausgabe* 95, pp. 235f. Heidegger cross-references this passage in *Besinnung, Gesamtausgabe* 66, p. 183.

48. Heidegger speaks of the historical animal—for instance, in *Überlegungen VII–XI, Gesamtausgabe* 95, pp. 182f., 196f., 224f., 287, 289, 293, 320.

49. *Besinnung, Gesamtausgabe* 66, p. 28.

50. *Überlegungen VII–XI, Gesamtausgabe* 95, pp. 40f.

51. *Das Ereignis, Gesamtausgabe* 71, p. 84; *The Event*, 70f. See also sections 116 and 117 of *The Event*.

52. See Daniela Vallega-Neu, "At the Limit of Word and Thought: Reading Heidegger's *Das Ereignis*." In *Internationales Jahrbuch für Hermeneutik*, 77–91 (Tübingen: Mohr Siebeck, 2013), and "Heidegger's Reticence: From *Contributions* to *Das Ereignis* and Toward Gelassenheit," *Research in Phenomenology* 44, no. 1 (2015): 1–32.

53. See, for instance, *The Event* (*Das Ereignis, Gesamtausgabe* 71), sections 259, 306.

54. We already find the date 1941 in "Überlegungen XIV," *Überlegungen XII–XV, Gesamtausgabe* 96, p. 241.

55. *Überlegungen XII–XV, Gesamtausgabe* 96, p. 250.

56. *Überlegungen XII–XV, Gesamtausgabe* 96, p. 225. Also compare an earlier reference to a similar date. Heidegger asks when it will be time to have his name reemerge and then writes: "Perhaps in the year 2327? Or is this an error as well, nourished by historiography and its reckoning? That may well be" (*Überlegungen XII–XV, Gesamtausgabe* 96, p. 196).

57. *Über den Anfang, Gesamtausgabe* 70, sections 15, 16.

58. *Über den Anfang, Gesamtausgabe* 70, pp. 34f.

59. *Über den Anfang, Gesamtausgabe* 70, p. 100.

60. *Über den Anfang, Gesamtausgabe* 70, p. 107.

61. *Das Ereignis, Gesamtausgabe* 71, p. 95; *The Event*, 80.

62. *Das Ereignis, Gesamtausgabe* 71, p. 95; *The Event*, 80.

63. *Das Ereignis, Gesamtausgabe* 71, p. 97; *The Event*, 80.

64. *Überlegungen XII–XV, Gesamtausgabe* 96, pp. 253, 257–260, 266, 268f.

65. *Überlegungen XII–XV, Gesamtausgabe* 96, p. 257.

66. *Überlegungen XII–XV, Gesamtausgabe* 96, pp. 258, 263.

67. *Überlegungen XII–XV, Gesamtausgabe* 96, p. 262. (This is one of the Heidegger's worst passages on World Jewry, and I'm hesitant to simply list it together with his polemical remarks concerning the English, Italians, and Russians. Here Heidegger writes that emigrants—who are part of World Jewry—did not need to participate in war acts, whereas the Germans had to sacrifice the best blood of the best of their people.)

68. See note 3 above.

69. There are eight references to the *Notebooks* (*Überlegungen*) in *Contributions* and five in *Besinnung*.

70. *Wegmarken, Gesamtausgabe* 9, ed. Friedrich-Wilhelm von Herrmann (Frankfurt: Klostermann, [1967] 1976), 196f.; Martin Heidegger, *Basic Writings*, ed. David Farrell Krell (New York: HarperCollins, 1993), 133.

71. *Überlegungen VII–XI, Gesamtausgabe* 95, pp. 8, 14, 16, 27, 34.

72. See *Über den Anfang, Gesamtausgabe* 70, p. 62, where Heidegger also rethinks his earlier understanding of truth (1930) as remaining stuck in a first leading indication.

73. *Besinnung, Gesamtausgabe* 66, p. 11.

74. *Besinnung, Gesamtausgabe* 66, p. 12.

75. *Besinnung, Gesamtausgabe* 66, p. 259.

76. *Über den Anfang, Gesamtausgabe* 70, p. 155. Certainly such reflections are not quite openly self-criticism. The lack of—let me call it a "more human"—self-criticism is one of the things David Krell finds missing in the *Black Notebooks* as well (see David Farrell Krell, *Heidegger, Ecstasy, Tragedy: From* Being and Time *to the* Black Notebooks [Albany: SUNY Press, 2015], chap. 6).

III METAPHYSICS, ANTI-SEMITISM, AND CHRISTIANITY

10

"Heidegger" and the Jews

Michael Fagenblat

When the opponent is immediately turned into the enemy but the enemy has previously been turned into the "devil" then all opposition loses not only creativity but even all room for struggle.
—*Black Notebooks, Gesamtausgabe* 95, p. 56

1   Balaam's Ass

I begin with Heidegger's anti-Semitism, but only so as to begin again. For the beginning, as inception (*Anfang*), is precisely what is at stake. Heidegger's radicalization during the 1930s involves the thought of "another inception" (*andere Anfang*), which, refracted through the *Black Notebooks*, casts the shadow of anti-Semitism across the history of beyng (*Seyn*). Heidegger's dogma is well known: "What had its inception there [with the Greeks] has remained unfulfilled to this day" and "did not disappear nor is it disappearing … and it persists as a distant enjoining that reaches far out beyond our Western fate and links the German destiny to it."[1] The *Black Notebooks* show, however, that the *Seynsgeschichte* consists not only of the forgetting of beyng and the quest for its traces but also of an enframing of ontological evil under the all-too-ontic sign of "World Jewry" (among others). The other inception of the Greeks that Heidegger cultivated, that of German destiny, is at the same time a history of the manifest concealment of evil. As such it is the history of beyng's own evil, of the evil *of* the *Seynsgeschichte* concealed from the thinker of beyng himself, for Heidegger almost failed to register the evil of beyng and decisively failed to respond to it. "He got the wrong people, earth, and blood," as Deleuze and Guattari put it, for he failed to see that "the race summoned forth by art or philosophy is not the one that claims to be pure but rather an oppressed, bastard, lower, anarchical, nomadic, and irremediably minor race."[2] The thought of another inception of philosophy demands its deterritorialization from the German destiny where Heidegger located it. This does not mean that we should be rid of the Greco-German history of beyng but that this history must be itself abandoned to, and entwined with, another destiny, and indeed several.[3] The promise of a new inception for philosophy therefore demands not only another sounding of the Greco-German origin but a stealing of its birthright. Only a divine wink or a quintessentially biblical ruse will make another inception manifest. It will be a case of switching—neither arbitrarily nor exclusively—Heidegger's Greco-Germans for the Jews, proper ones, as it were, rather than "the jews" that Jean-François Lyotard set against him; and thereby of risking to switch the promise of a philosophical reinception that remained "unthought" by Heidegger, as Màrlene Zarader demonstrated.[4] In this other inception of the history of beyng, the voice is the voice of Jacob but the hands are the hands of "Heidegger"; Jacob—whose name, it is sometimes forgotten, means "trace" and "trick."

The approach I adopt to Heidegger's ontological anti-Semitism differs from that of Richard Wolin and Emmanuel Faye, for whom this feature of his work makes him the enemy of the Enlightenment project with which philosophy is still entrusted. My approach is closer but for that reason also more resolutely opposed to the Christian Heideggerianism of Gianni Vattimo. In a cynical invocation of "deconstruction" and "hermeneutic ontology" (for they are deployed extraneously, against rather than within the discourse of Zionism, as Derrida would never have done), Vattimo decries the political reinception of the Jews as "only so much putrid, hot air from which one must free oneself in order to avoid spilling blood."[5] But in seeking to purify himself from the violence of the Old Testament, *redivivus* in "Zionism" (as he sees it), Vattimo aims at nothing less than the destruction—and precisely not the deconstruction—of the state of Israel, the "Middle-Eastern policeman." But since I am not one of those "who think of liquidating him [Heidegger] because he sided with Hitler," as Vattimo tactfully puts it, I feel obliged at least to note my goal and guiding principle, which I take to be consonant with whatever deconstruction and weak thought still promise: "Where the danger is, grows / the saving power also."[6]

But drawing near the danger is not enough. If Heidegger lost his way it is not, as Deleuze and Guattari suggest, simply because he sought to reterritorialize the errancy of thought but because even his *de*territorialized thinking is grounded in the relation between people and language.[7] All the more reason, then, to consider that other inception, that of the Jews. For as Gershom Scholem reflected in 1926 in a letter to Franz Rosenzweig, "a necessary consequence of the Zionist undertaking" is the "threat" resulting from the "actualization [*Aktualisierung*]" of the Hebrew language. "Is not the holy language, which we have planted among our children, an abyss that must open up?"[8] The condition diagnosed by Scholem is embraced by Heidegger, namely, a heritage erupting through the power of a holy language releasing the originary subterranean forces sedementized over generations. Like Scholem's volcanic preacher of old-new Hebrew, the German poet brings "the flaming light of the holy" to earth, catching sight of the divine wink that signals the relation between people and place in the hour at hand: "The poet's saying is the intercepting of these hints (*Winke*) in order to beckon [*zu winken*] his people."[9] German poets, like Hebrew preachers, are little volcanoes, "consumed by fire … They are the *signs* which, as signifying, reveal and conceal at the same time … having become ripe to their being … They are *prophetic*."[10]

If Heidegger lost his way, if he got the wrong people, earth and blood, this errancy at the same time betrays his proximity to the very Jews he anathematized. Like Balaam's ass, he "strayed from the way and went into the field" (Num. 22:23) when the Angel of Yhwh confronted him on the road—the Angel of Yhwh, which Heidegger could even be forgiven for having mistaken for *die Schicken des Seyns*.[11] And if he "strayed from the way" and was "thrashed thrice" for his trouble, we now find ourselves, like Balaam, sitting on the donkey's back in "a narrow place, where there was no way to turn either to the right or to the left" (Num. 22:26). The prophetic ass once spoke, and good readers always laughed; this one kept his silence but for some notebooks. Decent folk think it is no laughing matter—not the silence, not the notebooks, and not the narrow place in which we, who are also straying, find ourselves. *Der mentsh trakht un got lakht.*

2   The "Absolutely Unbound": On "the Role of World Jewry" in "Uprooting All Beings from Beyng"

There are two ways Heidegger's anti-Semitism is expressed in the *Black Notebooks*. These confirm, for what it's worth, the distinction he relied on in December 1945 to justify his Rector's Address of 1933, namely, the gap between his "private" National Socialism and that of the party.[12] Just as Heidegger thought he could distinguish between his "private" National Socialism and the popular one, so too does he invoke a distinction between his private, philosophical anti-Semitism and the vulgar common one. The distinction goes back at least to 1929 when he worried that Germany's indigenous spiritual life was being eroded by a process of "Jewification [*Verjudung*]," "in the broad and narrow sense," at once introducing the distinction and allowing for unhindered passage from "private," "broad," and "spiritual" anti-Semitism to vulgar, narrow, inauthentic racism.[13] The *Black Notebooks* show how Heidegger conceives the distinction at a philosophical level even as he himself crosses from metaphysical to vulgar anti-Semitism according to the opportunism of the moment.

It must be supposed that Heidegger's vulgar anti-Semitism precedes and makes possible his attempt to legitimate it philosophically. This conforms to the schema of *Being and Time* according to which *Dasein* makes sense of its world by first immersing itself in inauthentic idle talk (*Gerede*). Heidegger's anti-Semitism is in the first instance an expression of his own inauthentic adoption of the anti-Semitic idle talk with which *das Man* understood Jews in everyday German existence of the 1930s.[14] The *Black Notebooks* confirm the type of folkish anti-Semitism Heidegger expressed to Karl Jaspers on June 30, 1933, when he referred to "a dangerous international alliance of Jews" that gave *The Protocols of the Elders of Zion* a ring of truth despite his admission that it was a forgery.[15] For example:

World Jewry, spurred further by emigrants that Germany let go, is ungraspable everywhere and even though its power is widespread it does not need to participate in military action, whereas we are left to sacrifice the best blood of the best of our people.[16]

Here too Heidegger adopts the "deposited" (*hinterlegte*) stereotypes[17] that *das Man* propagates, thereby *falling* into, or falling prey to (*verfällt*), vulgar anti-Semitism.

The more notable development, however, involves the emergence of a philosophical rationale for this vulgar anti-Semitism. Given Heidegger's philosophical objection to biologism, it was to be expected that vulgar racialized anti-Semitism would be subject to critique in the name of a more philosophical anti-Semitism. And indeed Heidegger's "private" National Socialism finds its correlate in a private anti-Semitism that is more authentic than garden-variety racism but for that reason also *more radical*, more "primordial" or "originary" than biologistic anti-Semitism:

The question of the role of World Jewry [*des Weltjudentums*] is not racial; it is rather the metaphysical question of the nature of a type of humanity [*Menschentümlichkeit*], the *absolutely unbound* [*schlechthin ungebunden*], that can assume the world-historical "task" of uprooting [*Entwurzelung*] all beings from beyng.[18]

This philosophical dimension of Heidegger's anti-Semitism is already subtly glimpsed in *Being and Time*, where the calculative rationalism of Kantian morality is denounced as a type of "Pharisaism" and the corrupt, traditional concept of truth as *adaequatio intellectus et rei* is traced to Isaac Israeli (d. 955) who, it is implied, mislead Avicenna and in turn Aquinas.[19] But it is in the *Black Notebooks* that Heidegger develops and deploys the idea of a "metaphysical" anti-Semitism. It licenses him at once to distance himself from crude biological racism and at the same time to hold the Jews responsible for the *Machenschaft* and associated catastrophes besieging beyng in the modern age. The Jews, he supposes, participate in, and indeed intensify the calculative rationality of modern metaphysics *not* because they are racially or biologically disposed to calculative thinking but because they, more than any other people, are alienated from their concrete historical existence. The "worldlessness of Judaism" is "grounded" on the "forms of the *gigantic*, tenacious skillfulness in calculating, hustling and intermingling,"[20] but it does not ground them. Accordingly, the Jews are not the cause, or even *a* cause, of the deracinated rationalism they promote. The relation between "World Jewry" and modern Western rationalism is typological, not historical, causal, or biological. The root causes of the overwhelming of *Seyn* in modernity are Platonism (theory, abstraction), Cartesianism (subjectivism, certitude), Neo-Kantianism (individualism, idealism), and scientism (reductionism, *Machenschaft*, technology). World Jewry propagates the cardinal sins of "empty rationality and calculative efficiency" even if it did not initiate them.[21]

If Platonism and, later, Christian rationalism set the metaphysics of uprootedness in motion, the *Black Notebooks* confirm that Heidegger thinks "World Jewry" plays the decisive role in internationalizing it. Having become an absolutely unbound type of humanity, World Jewry can only feign to participate in "spirit" (*"Geist"*); concretely it is unable to access the decision regions (*Entscheidungsbezirke*) belonging to "the grounding of the truth of beyng."[22] The Jews have adopted this faux-Geist for themselves and play a crucial,

though not exclusive, role in globalizing it. The history of beyng thereby reveals the falsity
of biologistic anti-Semitism and at the same time grounds its metaphysical legitimacy.
Thus Heidegger regards the biologistic ideology of National Socialism as a "lording [*Ver-
herrlichung*] of 'blood'" that is "just surface and pretense" that intensifies "the unconditional lordship [*Herrschaft*] of the machination of destruction," even as he seeks the
significance of German poetry for the destiny of the world.[23] The nadir of this repeatedly
undertaken passage from the vulgarity of ideology to its "spiritual" truth, which is the
philosopher's way of taking responsibility for what he believes by involving himself truth-
fully and authentically in politics, consists of Heidegger's blaming the Jews for the racial
anti-Semitism that besets them. The breeding programs, eugenics, and killings waged on
account of modern racism result not from the biological constitution of peoples like the
Jews but from *Machenschaft*, which, as it happens, is the metaphysical vocation of Jews:

> The Jews, with *their emphatic talent for calculation*, have already been "living" for the longest
> time according to the principle of race, which is why they also take a stand as vigorously as they
> can against its unrestricted application. The establishment of racial breeding does not stem from
> "life" itself, but from the overpowering of life by machination. What machination is up to with
> such planning is the complete deracialization of peoples, by binding them to the equally assembled,
> equally divided arrangement of all beings. Deracialization goes hand in hand with a self-alienation
> of peoples—the loss of history—that is, of the decision regions of beyng [*Entscheidungsbezirke
> zum Seyn*].[24]

The Jewish "talent for calculation" is, for Heidegger, complicit in the root cause of the
racial anti-Semitism assailing them. The Jews promote *Machenschaft*, in which the concept of "life" is manipulated into "what one can breed [*Züchtbarkeit*], which is a type of
calculation," and therefore the Jews themselves are responsible for the racialized thinking
they hypocritically denounce.[25] The image of Jewish existence that Heidegger elliptically
outlines in the *Black Notebooks* is thus of a vicious but also tragic circle: disconnected
from the decision regions grounded in beyng's specific modes of appearing, the Jews have
become *symbolic* exponents of the empty rationality and calculative thinking that global-
ize alienation in the modern age, including racialized ways of determining humanity. The
Jews advance a type of thinking that determines the anti-Semitism they themselves suffer.

One final example of this passage from inauthentic to authentic anti-Semitism will
suffice. Peter Trawny has pointed to a shocking remark from the 1938–1940 manuscript
of *Die Geschichte des Seyns* that was censored by Fritz Heidegger when he published the
text. In discussing "the greatest planetary criminals of the most recent modern times,"[26]
the manuscript records Heidegger suggesting that one should ask how "the peculiar prede-
termination of Jewry [*Judenschaft*] for planetary criminality is grounded."[27] Trawny sen-
sibly links this to Heidegger's oblique endorsement, expressed to Jaspers, of slander of
the *Protocols of the Elders of Zion*. Even so, as Richard Polt notes, Heidegger thinks of
criminality in light of the history of beyng rather than in a "juridical-moral way."[28] Criminality refers to the "invisible devastation" of beyng under the sway of machination, not the

"visible destructions" of "the catastrophes of war."[29] Here too, then, the charge of "planetary criminality" is not simply aimed at the supposed machinations of scheming Jews but at *Machenschaft* as such, in which Jews are, he thinks, especially caught up. What we find in the *Black Notebooks* is not simply vulgar, racial anti-Semitism but its nonbiological reinscription into the apocalyptic history of beyng.

In sum, for Heidegger World Jewry stands for the metaphysical movement at work in the uprooting of the modern world. This ontological rather than ontic construal of the Jews makes them not merely an uprooted people but the vanguard and symbol of the uprooting of the world that characterizes the modern epoch. Uprooted from their proper land and language, World Jewry is "everywhere" that formal and abstract calculative thinking works to homogenize beyng. It represents, or allies itself with, everything that converts beyng into the global currencies of capitalism (which abstracts to a homogeneous exchange value) and technology (in which specificity is substituted for mass production and replication). But it also allies itself with forms of political existence that disfigure humanity according to uniform standards, thus with both liberalism and communism. That is why in the blink of an eye it can be conflated with historical processes that far exceed its visible influence such as those taking place within "imperialist England" or "Americanism and Bolshevism," which in Heidegger's schema of an uprooting *type* of humanity means "at the same time World Jewry."[30]

The philosophical grounds of Heidegger's "metaphysical" anti-Semitism can be traced to *Being and Time*, where Heidegger argues that *Dasein*'s spatiality is not a mathematicized extended field but involves "an ontological connection with the world" that arises through its ready-to-hand relations with the "aroundness of the environment [*Umwelt*]."[31] In the 1930s this primordial spatiality assumes a political profile. The concept of space is given an "essential" interpretation that attempts to excavate the sense of spatiality that precedes and enables the natural sciences. Space is philosophically grounded in an ontological rather than a naturalistic sense. Place gives rise to a conception of space. Whereas the mathematicized geometric conception of space involves its homogenization, the ontological conception of place on which it is grounded is intelligible by virtue of those beings emplaced there relationally. And since the Jews, for one reason or another, are afflicted with uprootedness, they are constitutively unable to access this primordial sense of place that precedes the naturalistic, mathematicized notion of space. His 1933–1934 seminar "On the Essence and Concept of Nature, History, and State" spells this out:

From the specific knowledge of a people about the nature of its space, we first experience how nature is revealed to this people. For a Slavic people, the nature of our German space would definitely be revealed differently from the way it is revealed to us; to Semitic nomads, it will perhaps never be revealed at all. This way of being embedded in a people cannot be taught; at most, it can be awakened from its slumber.[32]

On Heidegger's view, spatiality takes on different meanings in accordance with a people's specific modes of emplacement. This is why some people, like "Semitic nomads," may never gain access to the specific sense of place manifest by way of another people's sense of being-rooted, since they themselves relate to place by virtue of being-uprooted. Heidegger clearly seems to have inferred that this "worldlessness of Jewry,"[33] its lacking a land and language of its own, determined the Jews as the vanguard of the globalizing *Machenschaft*, abstract calculativity, and capitalism that displace beings from beyng.

3   The Evil of Being

There is little comfort in the thought that "World Jewry" is a placeholder in the *Seynsge-schichte* that others can fill with greater philosophical authority (Platonism, Cartesianism, Neo-Kantianism) or greater historical efficacy (Bolshevism, Americanism), or that the Jews are not the cause of the forgetting of beyng but merely its most aggravated symptom. Anti-Semitism remains, for Heidegger, a proper *ontological* disposition, one intrinsic to the history of beyng, like a shadow accompanying it in the measure of the forgetting of beyng. Lyotard was right to argue that Heidegger's anti-Semitism is *more* problematic on account of it applying not only to Jews but to "jews." In this he followed Levinas, who understood that "the same hatred of the other man, the same anti-semitism"[34] is not an inci-dental accretion to Heidegger's account of the history of beyng but its dark side, for beyng shines only on the enrooted.[35]

   In this respect Heidegger's anti-Semitism gives us to think the history of beyng *critically*, not only as a critique of the forgetting of being by modern rationalism and scientism but as the installing/enframing of the evil of Beyng itself, as the Israeli philosopher Adi Ophir has compellingly argued.[36] For the most part, Heidegger accounts for the entire experience of ethics as an epiphenomenal effect of the epochs and epistemes of being, as articulations of the enframing of beyng into particular formations of knowledge, norms, and praxes in which beyng manifests its reserves of intelligibility. If there is an ethics *of* being, it is gen-erally a matter of the attunement or proper relation to the truth of being, be that under the exigency of authenticity, of having-a-conscience, or of releasement. What this approach neglects, however, is that regimes of signification, the activity enabling *being-intelligible as such*, involves not only a concern for being but *always also possibilities* for *being-with-others* and *being-for-others*. This specific concern for being-with and being-for others sig-nifies not only in the epiphenomenal register of "values," "principles," "rights," "duties," "judgments," or even "virtues"; it is an irreducible condition of the making sense of being itself, one that can neither be exhausted by any determined regime of signification nor reduced to a mere epiphenomenon of being. Heidegger's attempt to deny the difference between ethics (as inhering in being) and morality (as enframing being) turns a blind eye to being's *own* way of putting itself in question by manifesting *itself* as Evil. Evil is not merely the moral enframing of beyng; it is beyng's own excess manifest as "superfluous excess that should never have come into being."[37]

   Evil is the excess of beyng itself, the manifestation and production of superfluous suffering and the presencing of loss that escapes every historical enframing of morality. Evil is neither a lack nor, as Heidegger usually proposed, a mere *Gestell*, an enframing of beyng in opposition to morality. Rather, evil is being's own excess, the excess of being that should not have taken place. Heidegger's attempt to account for the sources of normativity—of our beholdenness to a being *as* such or thus—in purely ontological terms (authentication, attunement, releasement) misses something essential in being itself, for being manifests not merely as it is but as it is for us and others. Essential to being itself is its manifesting as it ought not be, namely as evil, as the excess of suffering that should not have been. Beyond the question of intention or motive, cause and effect, evil is being in the mode of "should not have been," the surging of superfluous suffering, unwanted loss, and gratuitous indignity.

On one occasion Heidegger broaches this idea, which harks back to his reading of Schelling: "The essence of evil is the rage of insurgency, which never entirely breaks out, and which, when it does break out, still disguises itself, and in its hidden threatening is often as if it were not." An ontological account of evil is intimated here, as "the insurgency and the turmoil that we presage on all sides, where we encounter a dissolution that seems to be unstoppable" and that can neither be abolished nor even mitigated by universal moral condemnation because it involves "the devastation" internal to being itself.[38]

Heidegger never developed the thought of evil as the forgetting of beyng's own excess, as that which opens sense by virtue of the meaninglessness of what manifestly should not have been. The voice of spilled blood cries out from the ground, however, even when it disappears from view. Neither ethics nor ontology is "first philosophy," neither is "primordial" or "fundamental," for as the appropriation *and* forgetting of the being-with and being-for-others through which it opens to meaning, beyng itself always already signifies as that which should not have been. Ethics is beyng's own excess. Heidegger's anti-Semitism thus marks a forgetting, a decisive and willful forgetting, of the evil excess of beyng manifest in history.

The evil of beyng which Heidegger's philosophical anti-Semitism betrays thus gives rise to the task of thinking with and against Heidegger in order to attend to the devastating excesses by which beyng conceals aspects of itself (as being-with, being-for, etc.). This task calls for us to stop, rather than continue, interpreting Heidegger's anti-Semitism so that the question of the self-transcendence of beyng as evil can be taken up on new ground. Only in this way can the evil of beyng be deterritorialized, rather than simply reterritorialized, and its concealments of modes of being-with and being-for brought to light.

4   "A Philosophical Position That Is Precisely Our Position"

From the outset Heidegger was surrounded by a brilliant cadre of young, secular Jewish thinkers.[39] But it was Franz Rosenzweig who was the first to note the elective affinity between Heidegger's thought and Jewish *theology*. In one of his last writings before his premature death in 1929, Rosenzweig remarked on the "irony of intellectual history" in which Heidegger was emerging as the most passionate and articulate exponent of "a philosophical position [that is] precisely our position."[40]

Following Rosenzweig, other Jewish theologians built on the common ground between Heidegger's philosophy and a phenomenological account of Jewish existence. A point Heidegger emphasized better than anyone before him was that selfhood, and therefore "identity," is a matter of dynamic social, historical, and pragmatic relations that can neither be formalized nor universalized and that afford access to the experience of objectivity and indeed of intelligibility as such. Beneath the values of Enlightenment humanism, with its idea that people are equal by virtue of a rationality or universal nature that transcends their worldly formations, Heidegger showed how our experience of the world and our capacity to understand ourselves is based on passive, opaque, but insurmountable conditions. For numerous Jewish thinkers, here, finally, was an "ontology" that made sense of *being Jewish*.

In the course of his captivity as a French POW, Emmanuel Levinas began to adapt Heidegger's insight by wondering if one should think of ontological passivity "starting from Dasein or from J[udaism]."[41] This enabled Levinas to distinguish the passivity of thrownness (*Geworfenheit*) from that of creatureliness, election, and filiation. With Levinas, then, the affinity between Heidegger's account of passivity as *Geworfenheit* and Jewish passivity becomes the place of reckoning and distinction.[42] But this *adaptation* is based on a fundamental *adoption* of Heidegger's ontological prioritization of "we" over "me," his antiliberal, anti-individualistic account of the fundamental experience of being oneself.

Alexander Altmann (1906–1987), a pioneering Orthodox rabbi and phenomenologist who was to become one of the foremost American scholars of Jewish intellectual history, read Heidegger avidly in Berlin before being forced to flee in 1938. In an essay called "What Is Jewish Theology?," published in 1933, Altmann attempts to sketch "the meaning structure of a Jewish theology that is to be fleshed out concretely."[43] Like Levinas, Altmann understood how Heidegger's transcendental account of the "existence structure" of being, which "comes *before* any psychology or anthropology, and certainly before any biology,"[44] made a comparable account of the conditions of Jewish theology possible. Whereas Levinas concentrated on the passivity of the Jewish subject (created, elected), Altmann argues that "two phenomena, revelation and peoplehood," provide the irreducible elements of every Jewish theology. This argument was pitched against the characterization of Jewish faith promoted by his contemporary, Hans-Joachim Schoeps, who dismissed the Law on the grounds that no individual Jew could find the law in his or her ownmost relation to God.[45] Sympathetic to the project—inspired by the dialectical theology of Barth—of retrieving a theology of revelation from the clutches of historicism and legalism, Altmann nevertheless faulted Schoeps for being too individualistic, for too hastily dismissing the law in his (too Protestant) quest for unmediated access to revelation. The theological legitimacy of revealed Law, he argues, derives not directly from Scripture, or from formal, exegetical procedures, or from a sacred institution such as the Church, or from the purely local concerns of the community or synagogue. It is, rather, the fundamental element of peoplehood—"the whole people"—that authorizes the law by being itself the site of divine revelation: "The people, as the immediate correlational link to God, are the subject of [Jewish] theology."[46]

Having ground religious authority in the revelatory life of the people, Altmann explicitly invokes Heidegger's notions of "heritage" (*Erbe*) and "destiny" (*Schicksal*) as "decisive for an understanding of Jewish existence" for, unlike liberal Jewish dialectical theology, they legitimate "what is Jewishly particular in the spiritual situation of the Jews."[47] Like Levinas, Altmann does not simply adopt Heidegger's concepts but adapts them to his critique of liberal Jewish dialectical theology. For the Jew, *heritage is revelation* (Torah) given to the people as a whole, and *destiny is providence*, manifest historically in the life of the people. But the Heideggerian breakthrough remains decisive: only through the specificities of Jewish heritage and destiny can one adduce the "tragic singularity" of Jewish existence.[48] Within a few months of Altmann's Jewish deployment of the concepts of destiny and heritage from *Being and Time*, Heidegger himself marshaled his view in support of Nazism: "The destiny of the nation in the midst of all the other peoples," he proclaimed in the *Rektoratsrede*, actualizes "the historical spiritual mission of the German people as a people that knows itself in its state."[49]

Altmann, a Jewish humanist, favored the prospect of the destiny of the Jewish people actualizing itself in its state.[50] At a time when Zionism was still marginal in most Modern Orthodox circles, Altmann lamented, in a clear phenomenological tone, how the condition of exile (*Golah*) renders Jewish theology "invisible" and thereby prevents it from attaining its "full reality in the world."[51] Only the return to Zion could be adequate to the "confrontation" between tradition and modernity, since it alone would allow the "organic reality of peoplehood in Palestine" to unfold.[52] Altmann specifies three features of this organic reality: the Hebrew language, the biblical landscape, and the fluidity of Jewish life that "cannot be mastered through dialectics." In calling for a relation between life and law that exceeds the reflective work of Talmudic and halakhic (juridical) dialectics Altmann laid emphasis on "the *halakhah [law] of collective decisions*."[53] This position argues against formalistic methods of adjudicating Jewish law on the basis of exegetical principles and their procedural application by expert rabbis in favor of granting jurisprudential priority to the collective historical existence of the people as a collectivity that concretely animates and shapes the law.

Recall that Heidegger's critique of the uprootedness of World Jewry was based on the idea that cosmopolitanism alienated the Jews from the "decision regions of beyng [*Entscheidungsbezirke zum Seyn*],"[54] which, by virtue of beyng's concrete emplacement, are primordially related to its "grounding of the truth of beyng."[55] Attuned to the possibility of the alienation of the individual Jew from the concrete grounding of Jewish existence in its *Miteinanderjüdischsein*, Altmann specifies that the ontological priority of peoplehood generates the very capacity that Heidegger found so utterly lacking in Judaism, namely, *access to the decision regions* (*Entscheidungsbezirke*) from whence the truth of its being manifests. No doubt Altmann's sense of the fragmentation of Jewish peoplehood in an emancipated age bolstered his sympathy for a state, a land, and a language of its own where this people might reach into the decision regions of its existence "as a whole."

Moreover, as Altmann notes, the ontological priority of the people, as the revelatory power that produces authority and decides on the law, is also what makes revelation itself "essentially an 'open system,'" to which the open-endedness of the Talmud corresponds as its proper "form and conception."[56] Altmann thus understands the halakhic-Talmudic life of the Jewish people in complete contrast to the "Pharisaic" picture that German scholars, including Heidegger, imagine. Talmudic life is not a formalism from which rules are derived or otherwise externally imposed but reflects the open-ended way that the people as a whole live with God's word (revelation), precisely enabling the people to access its decision regions.[57] Since revelation *dwells amid* them (Exod. 25:8), their being-together affords access to the revelatory ground of their existence, which, from a sideways-on point of view, seems to stand over and against them.[58] It is "authority-founding peoplehood" that exercises "an actualistic-decisional function" among Jews, and not formalistic ("Pharisaic") exegesis, dogma, mediating institutions like Churches or Synagogues, or even individual experts.[59] Such external authorities are "meaningful only on the basis of halakhically thinking and authority-founding peoplehood. The halakhic atmosphere of this peoplehood produces the authority, and it receives, in return, the decision of authority, to which it bows as belonging to its essence."[60] At the very time that Heidegger was reflecting on the uprootedness of World Jewry from the decision regions of its existence, Altmann, inspired by Heidegger's concrete hermeneutical ontology, was arguing that by virtue of being rooted together in a shared heritage and destiny the Jews reached into the decision regions of their specific modes of existence where its nonuniversal (theological) truth manifests. But if Altmann would have therefore rejected Heidegger's depiction of the Jews as uprooted from the decision regions that manifest the specific truth of their being, he nevertheless agrees that the absence of a land and language renders this truth "invisible." For this reason Altmann was sympathetic to Zionism, which he saw as the means of rendering the revelatory life of the Jews visible, of creating "a reality in which ultimately language and spirit would coincide."[61] In the end, then, despite a fundamentally different understanding of Jewish life, Altmann agrees with Heidegger in the essentials.

As a young Orthodox rabbi enrolled at the University of Berlin, Altmann befriended another young rabbi, Joseph Soloveitchik, scion to an extraordinary dynasty of virtuoso Lithuanian rabbis, who would soon emigrate to the United States and become "the Rav" of Modern Orthodoxy, spearheading its remarkable renaissance in the second half of the twentieth century. Altmann and Soloveitchik were intimate companions, studying philosophy and discussing its relation to traditional Judaism on an almost daily basis. Soloveitchik, consistent with the "Brisker" method of Talmudic study developed by his forebears, regards the halakhah as a system conducive to "objectification" and takes a critical stand against antirationalist interpretations of Jewish spirituality. In a footnote to *Halakhic Man*, his classic exposition of the role of halakhic consciousness in shaping Jewish self-understanding, written in Hebrew in 1944, Soloveitchik denounces "the self-evident falsity" of "the entire Romantic aspiration to escape from the domain of knowledge, the rebellion against the authority of objective, scientific cognition which has found its expression in ... the phenomenological, existential, and antiscientific school of Heidegger and his coterie, and from the midst of which there arose in various forms the sanctification of vitality and intuition," which "have brought complete chaos and human depravity to the world. And let the events of the present era be proof!"[62]

Soloveitchik's halakhic objectivism and his caution with respect to all things Romantic did not, however, inhibit his existential-theological desire for the *manifest* destiny of the Jewish people *in history*. Breaking from his esteemed family's theological antipathy to political Zionism, Soloveitchik sided with the *Mizrachi* movement, which accorded religious significance to the establishment of the State of Israel and became a leading, influential advocate of religious Zionism. Less explicitly but more conspicuously than Altmann, Soloveitchik's account of the religious significance of Zionism recalls Heidegger's discussion of the authentic cohistoricizing of the people. In an address delivered on Israel's Independence Day in 1956, Soloveitchik parsed the erotic language of the Song of Songs in terms of the Jewish people's longing for its land and a state of its own. The salient distinction Soloveitchik develops is that between "a covenant of fate" that binds "the people" and "the covenant of destiny" that unites "the nation."[63] Whereas fate, represented by the Holocaust and secular Zionism, was foisted on the people of Israel, destiny is a religious undertaking to appropriate the return to Zion by becoming "a holy nation" in its own land. This is patently analogous to (and quite possibly directly derived from) Heidegger's distinction between the "inauthentic historicality" of a people determined by disparate events that befall them and the "destiny" of a people able to gather itself by appropriating its spiritual heritage in order to manifest new possibilities for existing historically.[64] Though seemingly averse to some of Heidegger's signature concepts, with respect to Soloveitchik's understanding of "religious Zionism" as the spiritual-historical destiny of the Jewish people, we find a clear Heideggerian tone.[65]

Such a tone can be readily amplified if one sounds out a wider range of characteristic features of Heidegger's thought that a phenomenology of Judaism would have to include. A much larger and more complex project would be required to do this adequately. Here an intimation of the resonances will have to suffice. Leo Strauss, who studied with Heidegger in Germany, already identified "the Biblical elements in Heidegger's earlier thought" as the source of Heidegger's dissatisfaction with "the limitations of western rationalism" and admired how he deployed such biblical elements while rejecting dogmatic Christian accounts of eternal truths and divine morality.[66] There are indeed many biblical elements in Heidegger's thought, and not only in his earlier works. For example, Heidegger argued that time is not a homogeneous sequence of nows or a moving image of eternity but a concrete eruption of the future within the present that unsettles the past and thereby throws up unforeseeable possibilities. Judith Wolfe calls this Heidegger's "de-theologized eschatology," an "eschatology without eschaton."[67] As is now known, Heidegger developed this account of temporality by way of a phenomenological interpretation of Pauline eschatology. The deformalization of time demanded by the turn toward "the How of grasping reality" was first exposed in Paul's witnessing of the first Christians dying-together and their waiting-together for the *parousia*. But, as Heidegger noted, "The basic direction of eschatology is already late Judaic, the Christian consciousness [being] a peculiar transformation thereof," which, moreover, "was covered up in [later] Christianity."[68] This "kairological" time became, in the course of the 1920s, the model for Heidegger's thinking of the concrete temporalization of being.

Leora Batnitzky notes that Heidegger's notion that "Being *reveals* itself in language" is one that "Jewish philosophers would define as fundamentally 'Jewish.'"[69] She suggests that modern Jewish thinkers such as Rosenzweig, Buber, Heschel, Levinas, and Derrida develop philosophies of language that share distinctive features with Heidegger's position and at the same time distinguish these thinkers from the traditional philosophical account of language as a way of representing the world. For Heidegger, words are not instrumental signs that transparently designate things but are themselves things (as in the biblical *devarim*), presences that reveal being. One begins to understand why Elliot Wolfson has made extensive use of Heidegger in his research into Kabbalistic language.[70] Heidegger's subordination of the correspondence theory of truth to the "unveiling" of an event that reveals Being in its concealment is a complex and even obscure notion, but its echoing of biblical and Kabbalistic notions, perhaps through the mediation of Schelling, is clear enough. Likewise Heidegger maintained, as does traditional Jewish thought, that thinking is saturated with interpretation and therefore conceived philosophy as an endless series of commentaries that forget, restore, and unfold an original truth, as does the Jewish tradition of commentary. In his later works he proposed that thinking is not foremost logic and representation but thanking and memory, as Jewish prayer emphasizes. Heidegger also described poetry's capacity to disclose the call of being in a way that clearly recalls prophetic testimonies to the word of God, similar to the way Rashi, one of the greatest and perhaps the most normative of Jewish exegetical authorities, describes prophecy as "God speaking with Godself" while the prophet "listens" (Num. 7:89). Mention should also be made of the metaphilosophical imperative of a new thinking that is neither Western nor Eastern but something at once originary and yet still unthought. A similar effort to perpetually distinguish itself from the Occident as much as from the Orient determines much modern Jewish thought, which it likewise discharges by returning to the revelation (Torah) that remains to be revealed. This is not meant to suggest Jewish influence as much as to call attention to a meaningful confluence between Heidegger's philosophy and some of the "existence structures" of Jewish thought, which, as we have seen, Jewish theologians and scholars have noted in desultory ways.[71] As Zarader has compellingly argued, at almost every point that Heidegger turns away from Western metaphysics and epistemology he pivots on the Hebraic heritage, even as he himself never thought this through. Perhaps this makes it slightly less astonishing to find Strauss's appeal to "Biblical elements in Heidegger's *earlier* thought" extended by Emil Fackenheim, the most famous Jewish post-

Holocaust philosopher, who found "the later Heidegger to be engaged in no less startling an enterprise than the Judaization of the entire history of Western philosophy."[72]

The numerous ways briefly enumerated above show how the vectors of Heidegger's thought can be traced to cardinal points in Jewish theology. The source of this inversion is the foremost biblical element of Heidegger's thought, the way being "calls," "addresses," and demands a "response." John Caputo summarizes the point:

The task of thought [for Heidegger] is to answer and respond to being's address, to hear the call and be responsive and responsible, to let being be, to let it come to words in language. This language is not our own but being's own *Sprache,* even as history is not precisely human history, but being's own history, for being would be our own even as we would be being's own people. ... This discourse is borrowed from the biblical tradition of a salvation history, from the religions of the Book, which are set in motion by the Shema, the sacred command or call—"Hear, O Israel, the Lord Thy God is One" (Deut. 6:4)—a command that defines and identifies a sacred people: one God, one people, one place. Heidegger uses the structure of this call-and-response to frame his reading of the texts of Greek philosophers who have not the slightest idea of a history of salvation.[73]

Following Zarader, Caputo notices the "unthought debt" in Heidegger's thinking that led some of the most important modern Jewish thinkers—Rosenzweig, Levinas, Altmann, Soloveitchik, Wyschogrod, Fackenheim, and others—to find Jewish theology reflected, in a clear if distorted way, in the mirror of his texts and concepts. The task today, however, is to trace the surface of this Klein bottle in other directions, tracking not only the "Hebraic" elements in Heidegger's thought but the becoming-Heideggerian of prominent strands of modern Jewish thought. "The irony is," Caputo notes, that when Heidegger performs his comprehensive refashioning of biblical salvation history in terms of the history of beyng, "he seems to land, alas (for him), back in the holy land, back on Hebrew soil, maybe somewhere on the West Bank, reproducing the dynamics of the Shema, of calling and responding, around which the Jewish history of salvation is structured."[74]

5   "Heidegger's" Zionism

In the 1930s, while penning the *Black Notebooks* and bemoaning the effects of World Jewry's metaphysical uprootedness, Heidegger lectured extensively on the "Heimat" or homeland of being. It is important to note how and why Heidegger distinguished his position from that of the National Socialists, for whom the homeland is the native geographic place of the Aryan race, even as he sympathized with them in crucial respects. For Heidegger, the National Socialists are too "ontic" or "thingy" in their conception of place; they mistake the homeland for a spatial region on the globe where the nation is located. But the homeland is not a spatial location on the globe. It is a place where the nearness to being happens. Just as the National Socialist conception of race is too ontic and essentializing in its biological determination of the people, so too does it misconceive the homeland as a spatial thing. In Heidegger's view, National Socialism has the right objects of criticism in mind, namely, liberal conceptions of a people as the sum of juxtaposed individuals and scientistic conceptions of place as reducible to a geometric calculus, for in both cases the concrete, specific ways of being of the phenomenon are mistaken for homogenized abstractions. And yet, he argues, in both cases National Socialism falls into a type of ontological idolatry by mistaking the phenomena of people and place for particular entities—the Aryan race or the Fatherland—rather than ways of dwelling in the uncanny nearness of being itself.[75]

Heidegger was, then, both critical and supportive of National Socialism. He was critical of it because he regarded Nazi ideology as a type of ontological idolatry that confuses the with-world of the *Volk* and our being emplaced with ontic things. And despite this ideo-logical vulgarity he was supportive of Nazism because he sympathized with its attempt to replace the abstractions of liberalism, humanism, and scientism with specific concrete, historical phenomena by virtue of which the intelligibility of being itself is grounded. To extend the analogy to idolatry: it is as if Heidegger thought Nazism amounted to worship-ing *the right God*—a concrete experience of Beyng—*in the wrong way*, whereas liberals, humanists, cosmopolitans, Bolsheviks, and above all "uprooted World Jewry" have, to use Jeremiah's terminology, exchanged Beyng for vain emptiness and its glory for futility (Jer. 2:11). Their notion of place amounts to a homogeneous conception of space; their notion of being-together amounts to the sum of individuals regarded in their abstract universality. As such they do not even concern themselves with beyng in its concrete ways of being; they have accordingly exchanged the fundamental attunements to and releasements of beyng for futile calculations. If the Nazis were idolatrous in their ontic way, in Heidegger's view they were at least failing with respect to the truth of beyng. Hence his consistent depiction of himself as (mis)taking "National Socialism for the possibility of a transition to another inception."[76]

As a philosophical critic of National Socialism, Heidegger argued that the homeland is a place where one can draw near to the unrepresentability of beyng but never attain it. For Heidegger, the homeland is always a promised land in which one can dwell in the near-ness to beyng, it is not a land that can be acquired or occupied. It is for similar reasons that Rosenzweig rejected Zionism, while Levinas was ambivalent about it.[77] In 1961, following the launch of the first human into space, Levinas wrote a short essay called "Heidegger, Gagarin and Us," published in *Difficult Freedom*, in which he reflected on the significance of humanity's breaking with its absolute attachment to the earth. Whereas Heidegger saw the modern world as being devoured and disoriented by technology, a world where entities were torn from their contexts and subjected to *Machenschaft*, in Levinas's view Gagarin's hour in space exposed another, human face to technology, namely, the distinctly human capacity to free oneself from all attachment to place. The attachment to place "is the very splitting of humanity into natives and strangers" and as such is "the source of all cruelty." For this reason, Levinas continued, "technology is less dangerous than the spirits of Place," for it "does away with the privileges of this enrootedness."[78] Sarah Hammerschlag calls this Levinas's "ethics of uprootedness," which goes some way toward explaining the slow and initially hostile reception of Levinas in Israel.[79] Contra Heidegger, and contra theologies of Jewish enrootedness in the land, Levinas affirmed the genius of Jewish Diasporism. "Judaism has always been free with regard to place," he said; "The Bible knows only a Holy Land, a fabulous land that spews forth the unjust, a land in which one does not put down roots without certain conditions."[80] Hence Levinas's deep ambivalence with respect to Zionism, at times identifying it with the "ethical destiny" of the Jewish people and at other times deeply suspicious of its territorialization of this spiritual destiny—and *both* for Heidegger-inspired reasons.

But other, no-less-influential strands of modern Jewish thought have taken the opposite route. In the course of their "reterritorialization" in the Holy Land, they display further signs of the becoming-Heideggerian of major trends in Jewish thought. This has especially been the case since the mid-1970s, when a distinction emerged between *religious Zionism* and the *theology of Zionism*.[81] The former, as we saw in the case of Altmann and Soloveitchik, emphasizes the religious significance of settling the land within a theological program that seeks to actualize the objectivity of halakhic reality as a whole, a task in which settling the land plays only a partial and inessential role.[82] By contrast, for *theologies of Zionism*, as exemplified by the Gush Emunim (Faithful Bloc) movement that arose in the mid-1970s and drew inspiration from the teachings of Rav Abraham Isaac Kook (1865–1935), dwelling on the sacred land attains a status as elementary as that of revelation (Torah) and peoplehood, becoming a constitutive part of the very "existence structure" of being Jewish and thus determinative of all other doctrines and values. For these theologies of Zionism, the uprootedness of Diasporic Jewish life distorts the fundamental categories of Jewish existence such as revelation and peoplehood, consigning it to artificial institutions like the synagogue or community, fostering reliance on top-down formal exegetical rulings, and sustaining the illusions of individualism.

Consider Rav Zvi Yisrael Tau (b. Vienna 1936), one of the leading proponents of the theology of Zion, an influential interpreter of the work of Rav Abraham Isaac Kook and a disciple of his son, Rav Tzvi Yehuda Kook. His eleven-volume work, *Le'emunat 'iteinu* (*For our time's faith*), embraces all the "Jewish existentialia" adduced too quickly in section 4 above while "correcting" the fundamental mistake of neglecting the theological significance of place in accounting for the historiality of Jewish theology.[83] The primary relation, on the view of Rav Tau and other "Kookist" theologians of the Gush Emunim (Faithful Bloc) movement, is between the People of Israel (as a whole irreducible to its parts), the Torah of Israel (the inceptive revelation that remains to be fulfilled), and the Land of Israel (the place where the people dwell by virtue of the Torah in *nearness* to Y[hwh]). In Tau's words, "Only superficial understanding stemming from spiritual and intellectual laziness grasps the concept of the 'whole' (*klal*) as a collection of many individuals juxtaposed together."[84] But it is only when the people sanctify the land that their being-whole enters into the nearness of being-holy. Likewise Tau adopts a view similar to Rosenzweig's and Altmann's account of the revelatory authority of the people as a whole, rather than formalistic exegetical procedures or other external authorities: "The life of holiness is one with the natural, vigorous, and holistic life. ... The manifestation of the Name in the world, is not revealed like a memo fallen from the sky on which one finds instructions and commandments. ... The more Israel-as-a-whole (*klal yisrael*), the more holy."[85] Just as for Altmann and Rosenzweig, here too the Talmud is in no way abandoned but Talmudic formalism gives way to the life of the people that is capable of reaching into the decision regions of Jewish-existence.[86] But for Tau, unlike Rosenzweig and Altmann, this life can be properly revealed and lived *only* on the land: "The actualization of our life as a people in the land is being-holy (*havaya shel kodesh*)."[87] In a strikingly Heideggerian tone, Tau suggests that whereas "the spirit (*nishmatan*) of the nations of the world" is "of heaven," which means that the nations share in the universality of spirit, "the spirit of Israel is of the earth, for we sanctify the Name of heaven on earth."[88] As Heidegger might have put it: "In its origin and destiny [*Bestimmung*] this people is singular, corresponding to the singularity of beyng itself, whose truth this people must ground but once, in a unique site, in a unique moment."[89]

Like Heidegger, Tau thinks that the specific contribution of the national spirit goes to remedying the homelessness of the modern age at large. In the "Letter on 'Humanism'" (1946), Heidegger proposes that the singular German spirit, manifest in its unique place and through its unique language, does not have the purpose of conveying some "German essence" that would exemplify the concrete universality of humanity but that "from a destinal belongingness to other peoples they might become world-historical along with them [the Germans]."[90] In other words, by becoming singularly historical in their being, the Germans, through their poets' specific relation to their heritage, people, place, and destiny, will show other peoples the way back to beyng—back to the specificity of beyng's inceptive relationality by virtue of which it is concretely meaningful, a homecoming to being, to the "mystery" (*Geheimnis*) of "nearness to an origin":

What is most characteristic of the homeland, what is best in it, consists solely in its being this nearness to the origin—and nothing else besides this. That is why in this homeland, too, faithfulness to the origin is inborn. That is why anyone who has to, is loath to leave this place of nearness. But now, if the homeland's being a place of nearness to the most joyful is what is most unique about it, what, then, is homecoming? Homecoming is the return to the nearness to the origin.[91]

In much the same way as Heidegger, theologies of Zion view Jewish uprootedness as symptomatic of the malaise of the epoch and its overcoming as the way of restoring access to the Place, to use a traditional rabbinic name for God. The homecoming is not just a political expediency but a matter of the emplacement of Beyng/Yhwh, of the becoming historical of *the Place of revelation*. A call issued in the sacred language through its new inception—"not a new Torah, heaven forbid," Rav Tau insists, "but *existence renewed* in our return to Zion, to 'renew our days as of the Inception [*kedem*] (Lam. 5: 21).'"[92] A singular people, a singular call, a singular place, whereby dwelling in nearness to the origin is made possible.[93] It is not surprising that both Heidegger and the Kookists, at various times, conflate the tight relation between people and place with that of the relation between people and state. In a famous address just weeks before the fateful war of June 1967, Rav Zvi Yehuda Kook proclaimed this new inception of Israel as "the state envisaged by the prophets."[94] He and his followers would agree that a "people and state are not two realities that we might observe isolated, as it were, from one another. The state is the preeminent Being of the people."[95]

Rosenzweig and Levinas express in a Jewish key some of the distinctive contributions that Heidegger brings to modern philosophy while rejecting the notion that the meaning of being must be grounded in the specificity of place. Altmann and Soloveitchik were more sympathetic to the idea, and both for Heidegger-inspired reasons. But thinkers like Tau and Kook, who did not read Heidegger, articulate, by virtue of a Kabbalistic theology of history that is not foreign to "Heidegger," an account of the "existence structure" of being Jewish in which the element of place becomes indispensable. Accordingly, if for Rosenzweig and Levinas the "absolutely unbound" nature of Jewish existence marks its genius, for Tau and Kook, as for Heidegger, it is symptomatic of the fundamental malaise of modernity. Needless to say, theologies of Zion are not to be conflated with Zionism as a historical ideology and movement. But since they play an increasingly prominent role in contemporary affairs, perhaps only "Heidegger" can save the Jews from the danger of the new inception of Israel: "Perhaps even my *errors* still have a power to provoke in an age overburdened with correctnesses that have long lacked truth."[96]

But where this danger is, there grows the saving power. Could beyng's errancy come good? Riding his prophetic ass (the man Heidegger), Balaam ("Heidegger") comes to curse the people of Israel. Standing on the mountain ridge "that overlooks the desert," he pauses—*mit eigentlicher Entschlossenheit*—to curse Israel's disparate tribes that he beholds communicating and struggling with one another. "Setting his face towards the wilderness, Balaam lifted his eyes and saw Israel dwelling (*shoken*) tribe by tribe. And the Spirit of God (*ru'ah elohim*) came upon him, and he bore his *figura* (*vayisah mshalo*) and said … "How good are your tents, O Jacob, / your dwellings O Israel" (Num. 24).

Notes

This is a significantly revised and expanded version of "The Thing That Scares Me Most: Heidegger's Anti-Semitism and the Return to Zion," *Journal for Cultural and Religious Theory* 14 (2014): 8–24. Translations from the *Schwarze Hefte* are mostly based on, often slightly modifying, those of Richard Polt. I would like to thank him for making his translations available and for sharing with me his nuanced forthcoming paper, "Inception, Downfall, and the Broken World: Heidegger above the Sea of Fog," from which I have greatly profited.

1. *Being and Truth*, trans. Gregory Fried and Richard Polt (Bloomington: Indiana University Press, 2010), 5–6. If Heidegger changed his mind about this, it was not by giving up on the Greeks or the Germans as custodians of alethic truth but so as to hold fast to them *in their erring* and their *concealment* of truth.

2. Gilles Deleuze and Félix Guattari, *What Is Philosophy?*, trans. Graham Burchell and Hugh Tomlinson (London: Verso, 1994); subsequent citations from 108–109.

3. In a note to these reflections, Deleuze and Guattari remark that "today, by freeing themselves from Hegelian or Heideggerian stereotypes, certain authors are taking up the specifically philosophical question on new foun-

dations," and then enumerate various examples of the "new foundations" to philosophy. The first in their list is "Jewish philosophy," followed by Islamic, Hindu, Chinese, and Japanese philosophy (see *What Is Philosophy?*, 223n5).

4. Jean-François Lyotard, *Heidegger and "the jews,"* trans. Andreas Michel and Mark Roberts (Minneapolis: University of Minnesota Press, 1990); Màrlene Zarader, *The Unthought Debt: Heidegger and the Hebraic Heritage*, trans. Bettina Bergo (Stanford, CA: Stanford University Press, 2006).

5. Gianni Vattimo, "How to Become an Anti-Zionist," *Deconstructing Zionism: A Critique of Political Metaphysics*, ed. Gianni Vattimo and Michael Marder, 20–21 (London: Bloomsbury, 2014); subsequent citations are also from these pages. For an astute critique of this "theoretical quenelle" of a volume, see Gabriel Brahm, "The Philosophy behind 'BDS': A Review of 'Deconstructing Zionism: A Critique of Political Metaphysics,'" 2014, http://fathomjournal.org/the-philosophy-behind-8bds-a-review-of-deconstructing-zionism-a-critique-of -political-metaphysics/.

6. For a similar anti-Judaic reflex in Vattimo's "weak thought" that on the one hand claims to secularize Catholic theology and yet on the other hand harks back to pre–Vatican II anti-Judaism and indeed to Marcionism, see his *Belief*, trans. Luca D'Isanto and David Webb (Stanford, CA: Stanford University Press, 1999), 83–84.

7. An interpretation along these lines is advanced by Philippe Lacoue-Labarthe in *Heidegger, Art, and Politics: The Fiction of the Political*, trans. Chris Turner (Oxford: Blackwell, 1990), as well as in his *Heidegger and the Politics of Poetry*, trans. Jeff Fort (Champaign: University of Illinois Press, 2007).

8. Gershom Scholem, *On the Possibility of a Jewish Mysticism in Our Time and Other Essays*, ed. Avraham Shapira, trans. Jonathan Chipman (Philadelphia: Jewish Publication Society, 1997), 27.

9. *Gesamtausgabe* 4, 46; Martin Heidegger, *Elucidations of Hölderlin's Poetry*, trans. Keith Hoeller (Amherst, NY: Humanity Books, 2000), 63; translation modified.

10. *Gesamtausgabe* 4, 115; Heidegger, *Elucidations of Hölderlin's Poetry*, 138. Heidegger's emphases follow the text of Hölderlin's "Mnemosyne," on which he is commenting. But the point can be generalized. For an account of how Heidegger thinks of poetry in terms of biblical prophecy and of the German language by analogy with Jewish conceptions of holy language, see Zarader, *The Unthought Debt*, part I, chaps. 2, 4; see also Peter Eli Gordon, *Rosenzweig and Heidegger: Between Judaism and German Philosophy* (Berkeley: University of California Press, 2005), chap. 5.

11. "The word מַלְאָךְ (*mal'akh*—literally 'messenger,' but usually translated 'angel') means a small-scale manifestation of God's own presence, and the distinction between the messenger and God is murky," writes Benjamin D. Sommer, *The Bodies of God and the World of Ancient Israel* (Cambridge: Cambridge University Press, 2009), 40. An "angel," then, is nothing but the messaging or sending (*die Schicken)* of Yhwh, whose Name means Presencing (*Anwesen*).

12. On Heidegger's "private" National Socialism, see Martin Heidegger, "The Rectorate 1933/34: Facts and Thoughts," in *Martin Heidegger and National Socialism: Questions and Answers*, ed. Gunther Neske and Emil Kettering, trans. Lisa Harries (New York: Paragon House, 1990), 22–23, and see James Phillips's discussion in *Heidegger's Volk: Between National Socialism and Poetry* (Stanford, CA: Stanford University Press, 2005), chap. 2, "Ontological Opportunism."

13. Heidegger's warning against *Verjudung* was made in a letter accompanying a grant recommendation for Eduard Baumgarten, dated October 2, 1929. The text is presented by Ulrich Sieg, "'Die Verjudung des deutschen Geistes': Ein unbekannter Brief Heideggers," *Die Zeit*, December 22, 1989, 40, http://www.zeit.de/1989/52/ die-verjudung-des-deutschen-geistes. By 1929, the derogatory term *Verjudung* (Jewify) was well established, as Steven Aschheim showed in "'The Jew Within': The Myth of Judaization in Germany," in *The Jewish Response to German Culture*, ed. Jehuda Reinharz and Walter Schatzberg (Boston: University Press of New England, 1985), 212–224. As early as 1916, Heidegger deems "Jewification" a "frightening" assault on "our culture and universities"; see *"Mein liebes Seelchen!" Briefe Martin Heideggers an seine Frau Elfride, 1915–1970*, ed. Gertrud Heidegger (Munich: Deutsche Verlags-Anstalt, 2005), 51, and for a discussion, Gregory Fried, "A Letter to Emmanuel Faye," *Philosophy Today* 55 (Fall 2011): 219–252 (especially 210–212).

14. *Being and Time*, trans. John Macquarrie and Edward Robinson (New York: Harper & Row, 1962), section 35; the pagination refers to *Sein und Zeit* (Tübingen: Max Niemeyer, 1953), found in the margins of both Macquarrie and Robinson and Stambaugh's English translations and in *Sein und Zeit*, *Gesamtausgabe* 2, ed. Friedrich-Wilhelm von Herrmann (Frankfurt: Klostermann, 1977). This point is addressed by Ingo Farin, chapter 14, this volume.

15. Karl Jaspers, *Philosophische Autobiographie* (Munich: Piper, 1977), 101.

16. *Gesamtausgabe* 96, p. 262.

17. See *Being and Time*, H168.

18. *Gesamtausgabe* 96, p. 243; see p. 121.

19. *Being and Time*, H291, H293, H214. Here too the foil of Pharisaism is typical of the culture of German scholars of the time; Adolf von Harnack's *Das Wesen des Christentums* (Leipzig: Hinrichs, 1900)—translated by T. B. Saunders as *What Is Christianity?* (New York: Harper, 1957)—is an influential example.

20. *Gesamtausgabe* 95, p. 97.

21. *Gesamtausgabe* 96, p. 47.

22. *Gesamtausgabe* 96, pp. 46f.

23. *Gesamtausgabe* 95, p. 381.

24. *Gesamtausgabe* 96, p. 56.

25. *Gesamtausgabe* 96, p. 56.

26. *Gesamtausgabe* 69, p. 78.

27. Peter Trawny, *Heidegger und der Mythos der jüdischen Weltverschwörung* (Frankfurt: Klostermann, 2014), 52.

28. *Gesamtausgabe* 96, p. 266.

29. *Gesamtausgabe* 96, pp. 45, 147. See Polt, "Inception, Downfall, and the Broken World: Heidegger above the Sea of Fog," 6.

30. *Gesamtausgabe* 96, p. 243.

31. Heidegger, *Being and Time*, H101ff.

32. Martin Heidegger, *Nature, History, State: 1933–1934*, ed. and trans. Gregory Fried and Richard Polt (London: Bloomsbury, 2013), 56; see also Peter Eli Gordon's illuminating contribution in the same volume, "Heidegger in Purgatory," 85–108.

33. *Gesamtausgabe* 95, p. 97.

34. The citation from Levinas comes from his *dédicace* to *Otherwise Than Being or Beyond Essence*, trans. Alphonso Lingis (The Hague: Martinus Nijhoff, 1981). The *dédicace* universalizes (by decapitalizing anti-Semitism) the hatred that Levinas regards as inherent in an account that grounds meaning in being and at same time avoids the very charge that such an account levels—namely, that grounding meaning otherwise than being renders meaning abstract, homogenized, deracinated, and so forth—by inscribing the proper names of his family in Hebrew below, as if these proper names "translate" the generic "anti-semitism." The *dédicace* thereby performs *in nuce* a third way of grounding meaning in which abstraction and concretion are not set against each other but *phenomenologically* combined by virtue of there being multiple registers, marked by multiple languages, at work in the activity of making sense.

35. For recent work attentive to this problem, which the previous note touches on, see Peter Eli Gordon, "Displaced: Phenomenology and Belonging in Levinas and Heidegger," and John E. Drabinski, "Elsewhere of Home," both in *Between Levinas and Heidegger*, ed. John E. Drabinksi and Eric S. Nelson (Albany: SUNY Press, 2014), respectively, 209–226 and 245–260.

36. Adi Ophir, "Evil, Evils, and the Question of Ethics," in *Modernity and the Problem of Evil*, ed. Alan D. Schrift (Bloomington: Indiana University Press, 2005), 167–187; for an elaboration of Ophir's view see his important work, *The Order of Evils: Toward an Ontology of Morals*, trans. Rela Mazali and Havi Carel (New York: Zone Books, 2005).

37. Ophir, "Evil, Evils, and the Question of Ethics," 182–183.

38. Martin Heidegger, *Country Path Conversations*, trans. Bret W. Davis (Bloomington: Indiana University Press, 2010), pp. 134–135. My thanks to Richard Polt for this reference. See also the important discussion by Heidegger in *Schelling's Treatise on the Essence of Human Freedom (1936)*, trans. Joan Stambaugh (Athens: Ohio University Press, 1985), which concludes with the thought that evil is "metaphysically necessary" (p. 160). To foreshadow "an irony of intellectual history" that will be made explicit presently, it is likely that Heidegger's thought of beyng's *own* evil, adopted from Schelling, was developed by Schelling on the basis of his understanding of the Kabbalah. For an account of the latter, see Paul W. Franks, "Rabbinic Idealism and Kab-

balistic Realism: Jewish Dimensions of Idealism and Idealist Dimensions of Judaism," in *The Impact of Idealism: The Legacy of Post-Kantian German Thought,* vol. 4: *Religion,* ed. Nicholas Adams, 219–245 (Cambridge: Cambridge University Press, 2013).

39. See Richard Wolin, *Heidegger's Children: Hannah Arendt, Karl Löwith, Hans Jonas, and Herbert Marcuse* (Princeton, NJ: Princeton University Press, 2001), and Samuel Fleischaker, ed., *Heidegger's Jewish Followers: Essays on Hannah Arendt, Leo Strauss, Hans Jonas, and Emmanuel Levinas* (Pittsburgh: Duquesne University Press, 2008).

40. Franz Rosenzweig, "Transposed Fronts," in *Philosophical and Theological Writings*, trans. and ed. Paul W. Franks and Michael Morgan (Indianapolis: Hackett, 2000), 150. For an early discussion of this comparison see Karl Löwith, "M. Heidegger and F. Rosenzweig, or Temporality and Eternity," *Philosophy and Phenomenological Research* 3, no. 1 (1942): 53–77, and for a sustained treatment, see Gordon, *Rosenzweig and Heidegger: Between Judaism and German Philosophy*.

41. Emmanuel Levinas, *Carnets de captivité et autres inédits*, ed. Rodolphe Calin and Catherine Chalier (Paris: Bernard Grasset/IMEC, 2009), 75.

42. See Emmanuel Levinas, "Being Jewish [1947]," trans. Mary Beth Mader, *Continental Philosophy Review* 40 (2006): 205–210.

43. Alexander Altmann, "What Is Jewish Theology? [1933]," in Alexander Altmann, *The Meaning of Jewish Existence: Theological Essays, 1930–1939*, ed. Alfred Ivry, trans. Edith Ehrlich and Leonard H. Ehrlich (Boston: Brandeis University Press, 1991), 42.

44. Heidegger, *Being and Time*, H44–H45.

45. Hans-Joachim Schoeps, *Jüdischer Glaube in dieser Zeit: Prolegomena zur Grundlegung einer systematischen Theologie des Judentums* (Berlin: Jüdischer Verlag, 1932).

46. Altmann, *The Meaning of Jewish Existence*, 47–48. A similar thought became clear to Levinas in the prison camp around January 1944; see his *Carnets de captivité et autres inédits*, 86.

47. Altmann, *The Meaning of Jewish Existence*, 54.

48. Cf. *Being and Time*, section 74.

49. Martin Heidegger, "The Self-Assertion of the German University," in *Martin Heidegger and National Socialism: Questions and Answers*, ed. Gunther Neske and Emil Kettering, trans. Lisa Harries (New York: Paragon House, 1990) (quote on 6).

50. Paul Mendes-Flohr provides a beautiful and informative outline of Altmann's life and character in his "Introduction: Theologian before the Abyss" to Altmann's *The Meaning of Jewish Existence*, xiii–xlvii. On Altmann's Jewish humanism, see Alexander Altmann, "'Homo Imago Dei' in Jewish and Christian Theology," *Journal of Religion* 48, no. 3 (1968): 235–259.

51. Altmann, *The Meaning of Jewish Existence*, 112.

52. Altmann, *The Meaning of Jewish Existence*, 115.

53. Altmann, *The Meaning of Jewish Existence*, 100.

54. *Gesamtausgabe* 96, p. 56.

55. *Gesamtausgabe* 96, pp. 46f.

56. Altmann, *The Meaning of Jewish Existence*, 48.

57. For a rabbinic narrativization of such a thought see Tosefta Pesahim 4:14 and Bavli Pesahim 66a; translated in Jeffrey L. Rubinstein, *Rabbinic Stories* (New York: Paulist Press, 2002), 71–79.

58. Altmann's account of the law is thus close to Rosenzweig's, whom he read avidly, though Altmann came from a more traditional Orthodox Jewish background. Their view differs from the account of divine law as standing over and against the Jews, as philosophers from Spinoza to Kant and Hegel to Heidegger, maintained. The relation between law and life, writ and custom, depicted by modern historians would seem to confirm the view of Altmann and Rosenzweig. On this see Rosenzweig's classic 1923 essay, "The Builders," in *On Jewish Learning*, ed. N. N. Glatzer, 72–92 (New York: Schocken Books, 1965), and for the historical relation between law and life see Haym Soloveitchik, "Rupture and Reconstruction: The Transformation of Contemporary Orthodoxy," *Tradition* 28, no. 4 (Summer 1994): 64–130, as well as Menachem Friedman, "The Lost Kiddush Cup: Changes in *Ashkenazic Haredi* Culture—A Tradition in Crisis," in Jack Wertheimer, ed., *The Uses of Tradition: Jewish Continuity in the Modern Era*, 175–187 (New York: Jewish Theological Seminary of America, 1993).

59. Altmann, *The Meaning of Jewish Existence*, 48.

60. Altmann, *The Meaning of Jewish Existence*, 48.

61. Altmann, *The Meaning of Jewish Existence*, 115.

62. Joseph B. Soloveitchik, *Halakhic Man*, trans. Lawrence Kaplan (Philadelphia: Jewish Publication Society, 1983 [Hebrew original, 1944]), 141.

63. Joseph B. Soloveitchik, *The Rav Speaks: Five Addresses on Israel, History, and the Jewish People* (New York: Judaica Press, 2002).

64. *Being and Time*, sections 74–75.

65. It should be noted that Soloveitchik does not think the spiritual destiny of the Jewish people could *only* manifest itself in the form of a state founded on its ancient land. There is, he notes, "a third halakhic approach" between anti-Zionism and religious Zionism, one "positively inclined toward the State … but would not attach [to it] excessive value" (Joseph B. Soloveitchik, *Community, Covenant, and Commitment: Selected Letters and Communications*, ed. Nathaniel Helfgot (Jersey City, NJ: KTAV, 2005), 163–164). Nevertheless, Soloveitchik argues that certain Jewish laws, most notably the commandment to settle the land, could only be fulfilled in the land of Israel, to which he adds the conviction that such commandments necessitate Jewish sovereignty.The question of a more detailed affinity between Heidegger and Soloveitchik requires further investigation. On the one hand, Soloveitchik retains the halakhic objectivity of his Lithuanian tradition and is critical of Romantic and subjective forms of religiosity; yet on the other hand, he invests halakhic Judaism with phenomenological-existential pathos inseparable from its collectivist-historical destiny. Dov Schwartz, *Religion or Halakhah: The Philosophy of Rabbi Joseph B. Soloveitchik* (Leiden: Brill, 2007), even suggests that "the concept of being in Heidegger's thought, for instance, is truly significant for R. Soloveitchik" (p. 178). Here we can also note that Soloveitchik's student, the important Orthodox Jewish theologian Michael Wyschogrod, wrote "the first book-length study of Heidegger in English," *Kierkegaard and Heidegger: The Ontology of Existence* (New York: Humanities Press, 1954). His mature theological work, *The Body of Faith: God in the People Israel* (Northvale, NJ: Jason Aaronson, 2000), is infused with Heidegger's influence. As late as 2010, following Emmanuel Faye's book, Wyschogrod defended the philosophical value of Heidegger's contribution; see "Heidegger's Tragedy," *First Things*, April 2010, http://www.firstthings.com/article/2010/04/heideggers-tragedy.

66. Leo Strauss, "An Introduction to Heideggerian Existentialism," in *The Rebirth of Classical Political Rationalism: An Introduction to the Thought of Leo Strauss*, ed. Thomas L. Pangle (Chicago: University of Chicago Press, 1989), 27–46, especially 43–44.

67. Judith Wolfe, *Heidegger's Eschatology: Theological Horizons in Martin Heidegger's Early Work* (Oxford: Oxford University Press, 2013), 4.

68. Martin Heidegger, *The Phenomenology of Religious Life*, trans. Matthias Fritsch and Jennifer Anna Gosetti-Ferencei (Bloomington: Indiana University Press, 2004), 73.

69. Leora Batnizky, "Revelation, Language, and Commentary," in *The Cambridge Companion to Modern Jewish Philosophy*, ed. Michael L. Morgan and Peter Eli Gordon (Cambridge: Cambridge University Press, 2007), 300–323 (quote on 302–303).

70. Wolfson, who has pioneered research into the relation between Heidegger and the Kabbalah, is currently working on a book devoted to the topic. For now, see Elliot R. Wolfson, "Scepticism and the Philosopher's Keeping Faith," in *Jewish Philosophy for the Twenty-First Century: Personal Reflections*, ed. Hava Tirosh-Samuelson and Aaron W. Hughes, 481–515 (Leiden: Brill, 2014) (especially 500–509). Also see Elliot R. Wolfson, *Giving beyond the Gift: Apophasis and Overcoming Theomania* (New York: Fordham University Press, 2014), especially chap. 6 but passim; Elliot R. Wolfson, *Language, Eros, Being: Kabbalistic Hermeneutics and Poetic Imagination* (New York: Fordham University Press, 2005); Elliot R. Wolfson, "Revealing and Re/veiling Menahem Mendel Schneerson's Messianic Secret," *Kabbalah: Journal for the Study of Jewish Mystical Texts* 26 (2012): 25–96 (especially 35–45); Elliot R. Wolfson, "Nihilating Nonground and the Temporal Sway of Becoming: Kabbalistically Envisaging Nothing beyond Nothing," *Angelaki: Journal of the Theoretical Humanities* 17, no. 3 (2012): 31–45 (especially 40–41).

71. Heidegger explicitly denied that his thought was influenced by the Jewish tradition and claimed instead that he was inspired by the "unthought" of the pre-Socratic Greek tradition. For an excellent discussion, see Zarader, *The Unthought Debt*. More plausibly, it is the German Romantic tradition, especially Hölderlin and Schelling, that inspired many of his departures from the modern philosophical tradition. The migration of biblical-prophetic and Kabbalistic motifs into Heidegger's thought via Hölderlin and Schelling seems to me a plausible if speculative supposition.

72. Emil L. Fackenheim, *Encounters between Judaism and Modern Philosophy: A Preface to Future Jewish Thought* (New York: Basic Books, 1973), 218.

73. John Caputo, "People of God, People of Being: The Theological Presuppositions of Heidegger's Path of Thought," in *Appropriating Heidegger*, ed. James E. Falconer and Mark A. Wrathall (Cambridge: Cambridge University Press, 2000). As Naor Bar-Zeev, notes, however, in contrast to the biblical tradition, in the rabbinic tradition it is not the call that commands directly but the response that produces authority in relation with-others, to-others, and for-others (personal communication).

74. Caputo, "People of God, People of Being," 94.

75. For an elaboration of these distinctions, see the works cited in note 6 and in particular Phillips, *Heidegger's Volk*, chap. 4, "Toward the Uncanny Homeland."

76. *Gesamatausgabe* 95, p. 408. As Polt notes (see p. 7n1), this is consistent with Heidegger's view in the 1966 *Der Spiegel* interview: "I had the feeling that there is something new, here is a new dawn" ("'Only a God Can Save Us': *Der Spiegel*'s Interview with Martin Heidegger," trans. Maria P. Alter and John D. Caputo, in *The Heidegger Controversy: A Critical Reader*, ed. Richard Wolin [Cambridge, MA: MIT Press, 1993], 97).

77. For Rosenzweig's account of the "holy land" as a land of "longing," see Franz Rosenzweig, *The Star of Redemption*, trans. William W. Hallo (New York: Holt, Rinehart & Winston, 1971), 300.

78. Emmanuel Levinas, *Difficult Freedom: Essays on Judaism*, trans. Seán Hand (Baltimore: Johns Hopkins University Press, 1990), 233. Compare this with Heidegger's remarks to *Der Spiegel* (*The Heidegger Controversy*, 105ff.) about how "technology tears men loose from the earth and uproots them. ... I was frightened when I saw pictures coming from the moon to the earth. We don't need any atom bomb. The uprooting of man has already taken place. The only thing we have left is purely technological relationships."

79. Sarah Hammerschlag, *The Figural Jew: Politics and Identity in Postwar French Thought* (Chicago: University of Chicago Press, 2010).

80. Emmanuel Levinas, *Difficult Freedom*, 233.

81. On this, see Gideon Aran, *Kookism: The Roots of Gush Emunim, Jewish Settler's Sub-Culture, Zionist Theology, Contemporary Messianism* [in Hebrew] (Jerusalem: Carmel, 2013); Gideon Aran, "From Religious Zionism to Zionist Religion: The Roots of Gush Emunim," *Studies in Contemporary Jewry* 2 (1986): 116–143.

82. For example, leading rabbinic representatives of this strand of Modern Orthodoxy such as Rav Lichtenstein, the son-in-law of Rav Soloveitchik, have ruled that Jewish law permits leaving or withdrawing from sacred land under certain circumstances (e.g., in order to conform to legitimate political authority).

83. Modern Jewish mysticism, based on the groundbreaking thought of the Kabbalist Ramhal (Rabbi Moses Hayim Luzzatto, 1707–1746), is marked by the historicization of God's being; on this see Yosef Avivi, *Historia tzorekh gavoha* [History, a supernal desire] [in Hebrew], in *Festschrift for Rabbi Mordechai Breuer*, ed. M. Bar-Asher, 709–771 (Jerusalem: Akademon, 1992), and Jonathan Garb, *Kabbalist in the Heart of the Storm: R. Moshe Hayyim Luzzatto* [in Hebrew] (Tel Aviv: Tel Aviv University Press, 2014).

84. Harav Zvi Yisrael Tau, *Le'emunat 'iteinu* [For our time's faith] [in Hebrew], vol. 3 (Jerusalem: Erez, n.d.), 33.

85. Tau, *Le'emunat 'iteinu*, vol. 3, 35.

86. As one anonymous enthusiast from the formative years in the mid-1970s put it to the sociologist Gideon Aran, "One cannot rest content with studying Talmud; one must go out onto the land. There, especially there, religious consciousness will be revealed, holiness will be unveiled. There, no less than in a *yeshiva*, one finds Jewish truth" (Aran, *Kookism*, 369).

87. Tau, *Le'emunat 'iteinu*, vol. 3, 35.

88. Tau, *Le'emunat 'iteinu*, vol. 3, 35.

89. Heidegger, *Gesamtausgabe* 65, p. 97; *Contributions to Philosophy (From Enowning)*, trans. Parvis Emad and Kenneth Maly (Bloomington: Indiana University Press, 1999), 67.

90. Heidegger, *Pathmarks*, p. 257.

91. *Gesamtausgabe* 4, pp. 23–24 (translation slightly modified); Heidegger, *Elucidations of Hölderlin's Poetry*, 42. For an elucidation of these themes see Jeff Malpas, *Heidegger's Topology: Being, Place, World* (Cambridge, MA: MIT Press, 2006). Malpas concludes: "At its simplest and most direct, one can say that what Heidegger hoped to accomplish in his thinking was 'homecoming'—a turning back toward our own dwelling place. ...

As a homecoming, the mood of Heidegger's thinking is nostalgic—it is characterized by the desire for home or for the return to the nearness of home. Such thinking is, of course, inextricably bound to a thinking that is essentially oriented toward place and our belonging in and to place" (p. 311).

92. Tau, *Le'emunat 'iteinu*, vol. 3, 27 (my emphasis). I am of course translating Lam. 5:21 with Heidegger's *Anfang* in mind, though *kedem* means more than just "old," connoting the primordial time of renewal, of the spirit of creation itself.

93. Think of this as a *re-ex-appropriation* of what Caputo noted in "People of God, People of Being": "The call was issued in a rival sacred language, not Hebrew but Greek, which left behind its sacred texts whose depths can be endlessly plumbed. The call was addressed to a rival chosen people, not the Jews but the Greeks and their spiritual heirs, the Germans, in a rival new Jerusalem, not Israel but the Third Reich, with a rival prophet, not Hosea but—if truth be told and with all due modesty!—Heidegger. One call, one people, one place" (p. 90).

94. Rav Zvi Yehuda Kook is credited with transforming his father's mysticism into a political program; the speech he delivered on Israel's nineteenth day of independence, just weeks before the Six Day War of June 1967, envisages a state that would "revive settlement and independent political rule in the Land," where the divine promise to have "gathered the house of Israel" to "dwell in their own land" (Ezek. 28:25–26) will be actualized. The speech can be heard and read at http://www.yeshiva.org.il/midrash/2022; a partial English translation is available at http://www.israel613.com/books/ERETZ_ANNIVERSARY_KOOK.pdf.

95. Heidegger, *Nature, History, State,* 57. There is of course more diversity among theologians of Zion concerning the question of the relation to the state. For a valuable analysis, see Shlomo Fischer, "Self-Expression and Democracy in Radical Religious Zionist Ideology," doctoral dissertation, Hebrew University of Jerusalem, 2007.

96. *Gesamtausgabe* 94, p. 404.

11

Heidegger and the Shoah

Peter Trawny

The fate of Jews and Germans has a truth of its own that our historical thinking does not reach.
—Martin Heidegger[1]

Heidegger and the Shoah—a difficult but by no means impossible relation. It is difficult, because, generally speaking, it is assumed that Heidegger scarcely and, at any rate, not comprehensively expressed his views on the annihilation of European Jews. Unlike Hannah Arendt or Theodor W. Adorno, he did not see it as a turning point in history, nor did he make it the starting point for moral reflection like Karl Jaspers did. For him the Shoah was also not an occasion to express his grief. As has been noted frequently, Heidegger kept silent. Derrida speaks of a "dreadful silence."[2]

It does not need to be said that the Shoah is of such significance that philosophy too cannot avoid it. For Hannah Arendt it is an event that "has really interrupted the tradition of the continuity of Western history, which had been secure for so long."[3] The Shoah—that is *the* break in the tradition, after which the unquestioned hold of and even the intelligibility of moral concepts and categories was and still is at stake.

However, the aftermath of this break seems to harbor its own dialectics. For although or precisely because the break calls into question the very meaning of what is moral, the event inevitably makes the answer to it ethical.[4] The destruction of ethical normalcy constitutes a caesura, which touches thought as something morally decisive. After the Shoah, Arendt too adopted the view that evil had occurred in it. In the context of the "historians' quarrel" Habermas still spoke of "this traumatic not-going-away of this moral past that is burnt into our national history"—that is, a festering moral wound.[5] It is curious that the most abysmal collapse of morality leaves only one answer, the moral answer.

In Heidegger we do not find anything about this, or hardly anything. The publication of the *Black Notebooks*, especially the notebooks composed between 1938 and 1945, throws new light on this lacuna. Whereas before the publication one could assume that Heidegger had no interest in "the fate of the Jews," this assumption must now be revised. The notebooks just mentioned inscribe this "fate" into the narrative of the "history of being [*Seyn*]." In pursuit of this narrative Heidegger makes use of stereotypes surrounded (*belagert*) by a specific anti-Semitism. Furthermore, when he inscribes Jewry into the "history of being [*Seyn*]," he appears to assign Jewry a narrative role that entirely passes by the facticity of persecution and annihilation. One must ask about the motivation for this omission. It was impossible *not* to know that Jews were deprived of their rights and persecuted in Germany at the time of the Nuremberg Race Laws and the November 1938 pogrom. Wasn't it equally impossible *not* to know or to guess what would happen to those deported to the East?

But it is doubtful whether this is the relevant question. The Shoah took place, evil occurred. And wasn't it Heidegger who, in the summer of 1943, the time of annihilation, in his lecture course on Heraclitus said: "The planet is aflame. The essence of man is out of joint."[6] Undoubtedly, Heidegger thought here of Heraclitus's saying that the Fire will judge and engulf Everything when the time has come for it. Heidegger had in mind the war, which he liked to call the "planetary war." But which role, which part were the Jews to play in this war, which was perhaps a "war between races" (*Rassenkrieg*)[7] from the start? A note from 1941 reads: "World Jewry, spurred on by the emigrants that Germany let out, remains elusive everywhere. Despite its increased display of power [*Machtenfaltung*], it [i.e., World Jewry] never has to take part in the practice of war, whereas we are reduced to sacrificing the best blood of the best of our own people."[8] Heidegger speaks of "World Jewry" quite frequently. "World Jewry" or, as people also said, "International Financial Jewry," has its reference point in the *Protocols of the Elders of Zion*. According to this malicious fiction, Jews strive for world domination by means of a universal world conspiracy. Those who strive for world domination need and foment war, and if they can keep out of the battles they have triggered and in which their enemies are destroyed, they are the smartest warriors. In his last "political will," written just nine days before the unconditional surrender on April 29, 1945, Hitler still denounced "Jewry," these "international monetary and financial conspirators," as the "real culprits in this murderous struggle."[9] That "World Jewry" wished for and encouraged this war, from which it would profit, was an incessant propaganda slogan.

However, especially with regard to this particular note in "Überlegungen XV" quoted above, we must pay attention to its context. The whole note is titled "At the Beginning of the Third Year of the Planetary War." Under this heading Heidegger then lists ten points, of which the remark quoted above is the ninth. Moreover, he introduces the series of remarks with the following words:

If one ... thinks merely historiologically [*historisch*], and not historically [*geschichtlich*], and counts even planetarianism [*Planetarismus*] among the changes of history [*Geschichte*], instead of only and merely using planetarianism as the geographic frame for "historical" events [*"historische" Begebenheiten*], and, furthermore if one accepts only "facts" [*"Tatsachen"*], which are always half true and therefore false, one may well assert the following: ... .[10]

Heidegger apparently wishes to clarify that the "following remarks" are not of a "historical [*geschichtlichen*]" or "ontohistorical [*seinsgeschichtlichen*]," but rather "historiological [*historischen*]" character. "'Historical' events" or "facts" cannot claim the same status as "ontohistorical" assertions. But to infer from this that these "remarks" are altogether false, meaningless, or intended as criticisms is precipitous judgment.

In fact, in this particular note Heidegger insists on arguing that the restriction of the scope to the historiological (*auf Historisches*) is "valid." Indeed, one of the novel and hitherto unknown traits of the *Considerations* is precisely that, on the whole, and, unlike in his "ontohistorical" treatises (*Contributions to Philosophy*, *Mindfulness*, and the *History of Being* [*Geschichte des Seyns*]), the philosopher pays so much attention to the "facts."

For Heidegger reads these "facts" as "signs of being [*des Seyns*]" or "signs of machination [*machenschaftliche Zeichen*]." Like Hegel, who posits the objectification of "spirit" (*Verobjektivierung des "Geistes"*), Heidegger thinks of a kind of objectification of "being" [*Verobjektivierung des Seyns*], and so of a history that would, as it were, run counter to the "ontological difference." However, at bottom this is an impossible construal, because, strictly speaking, "being" could be adequately represented only by "signs" that elude manifestation in "beings [*Seiendem*]." This seems to be the reason, on the one hand, for a tendency in Heidegger's thinking that comes to the fore during the war and is reminiscent of a certain Neoplatonism or Gnosticism. On the other hand, Heidegger also deploys the notion of the "ontological difference" in a way charged with an ideological interpretation. Where being (*Sein*) and beings (*das Seiende*) are contrasted like "enrootedness" versus "uprootedness," philosophical thought turns against itself and becomes ideology.

In his interpretation of the "signs of machination" Heidegger notes on one occasion, in November 1940, that Vyacheslav M. Molotov had come to Berlin for talks with Hitler. A little later he notes: "The Jew Litvinov has turned up again."[11] In May 1939 Stalin had dismissed Maksim Litvinov and replaced him with Molotov. The initiation and signing of the Hitler-Stalin Pact in 1939 required that Stalin could send a non-Jewish foreign secretary to the negotiations. Heidegger seems to have understood this constellation when he remarks that the "Jew Litvinov" had turned up again. Furthermore, when Heidegger quotes from *Izvestia* that Litvinov had "proved that he understood, in Bolshevik fashion, the need to find allies wherever they could be found, even if only temporarily," he could have had in mind the policy Litvinov pursued of forming alliances with the West. Thus, as late as April 1939, the former Russian foreign secretary tried to move Great Britain and France to conclude a mutual defense alliance against any possible attacker. One provision in this alliance was to be a guarantee of protection for Poland, among other countries. Was the "Jew Litvinov" not a member of "World Jewry"?

One should not ignore Heidegger's belief that the assertion that "World Jewry" in its "increased display of power" remains "elusive everywhere" is as much a "fact" as the "war on multiple fronts [*Mehrfrontenkrieg*]," which has come about by "a freely taken decision."[12] Moreover, seen in the context of the "planetary war," the remark about "World Jewry" means that it is not on "our" side that they display their power. Thus, "World Jewry" should be counted among the enemies. However, the argument about "World Jewry's" belligerence (*Feindseligkeit*) or viciousness (*Bösartigkeit*) is one of the claims with which National Socialist propaganda justified persecution and deportation of Jews.

As we have seen, Heidegger had restricted the scope of this assertion about "World Jewry" to the historiological (*das Historische*). He spelled out the "ontohistorical" significance of "World Jewry" in a later part of the *Considerations*. The "question concerning the role of *World Jewry*" was not "a racial, but a metaphysical question about the kind of humanity which, *absolutely unattached* [*schlechthin ungebunden*]," could "take upon itself as a world-historical 'task' the uprooting of all beings from being."[13] Obviously, the import of this characterization goes beyond the assertion of the "fact" of "World Jewry." Given the ideological rendering of the "ontological difference," connecting the "fact" of "World Jewry" with its "metaphysical" and thus "ontohistorical" meaning is unavoidable.

The "metaphysical" (i.e., "ontohistorical") significance of "World Jewry" lies in its ability to carry out, while being "*absolutely unattached*," "the uprooting of all beings from being." The predicate "*absolutely unattached*" is reminiscent of the stereotype of the nonsedentary, cosmopolitan Jews. In fact, this stereotype is intensified here to its extreme by the added qualification "*absolutely*." Yet this absolutizing of unattachment concerns not only the stereotype of a life without a place—which ignores the historical fact of Jewry's assimilation going back generations—but also, in the end, thought itself. If the formulation of the "uprooting of beings from being" is to have any meaning whatsoever, it is on the grounds that the uprooting is pursued by an "*absolutely unattached*" thinking.

But even then it remains obscure how "entities" could be "uprooted" "from out of being," and conversely, how they are "rooted" "in being." The philosophical attraction of the *ontological difference* or *distinction* lies precisely in the fact that the relation of what is different or distinct is such that it does not permit a unilateral grounding or "enrooting" ("*Verwurzelung*"). Accordingly, "being" never was ground or cause of "beings," just as these are never the consequence or effect of the former. Although Heidegger has indeed attempted to think through "being" "without beings,"[14] the most mature elucidations concerning this relation emphasize their groundless and abysmal togetherness. To reduce it to an "origin" would mean to mistake "being [*Sein*]" for "an entity [*einem Seienden*]." However, Heidegger seems to do just that when in his discussion of the relationship between "being" and "entities" he draws on the ideologically fraught metaphor of "en-" and "uprooting." Although one might argue that Heidegger takes the "earth," which corresponds to the metaphor of the "root," in terms of "being [*Sein*]," nevertheless, the simple identification of "being" with "earth" is mistaken.

Thus it appears that in the course of inscribing Jewry into the narrative of the "history of being" Heidegger has betrayed a central idea of his philosophy. Are anti-Semitic stereotypes responsible for putting an ideological slant on the concept of *ontological difference*? Where does the *nonrelation* (*Unverhältnis*) come from in the relation (*Verhältnis*) of thinking, indeed, *the* relation as such?

The nonrelation in the relation of Heidegger's thought gives rise to an "ontohistorical Man-
ichaeism,"[15] a struggle between the realm of "being" and the realm of "beings," between
two topographies, or, better, topologies. At this point Heidegger's "ontohistorical" thought
falls into a crisis, shaking his philosophy as if by an echo of the "facts." War signifies a
"decision," in which everyone becomes "a slave to the history of being [*Seyn*]."[16] However,
the "slave" is not only the one who is forced to work, but rather, seen more clearly, the one
who serves through his work. But how do Jews and Germans serve the "history of being
[*Seyn*]"? What is the meaning of this service?

The nonrelation in the relation as such leaves a trace. The "ontohistorical" meaning of
the war consists of "purifying *being* [*Sein*] of its deepest disfigurement brought about by
the supremacy of beings."[17] For Heidegger, this "supremacy" is a sign of the "greatest completion of technology." This "completion," this "highest stage of technology," is "reached
when what is left for it to consume is nothing more than—itself."[18] Heidegger asks: "In
what form does this self-annihilation take place?" The "purification of *being*"—the "self-
annihilation" of "machination" that happens in the war?

The "self-annihilation" of "machination" in the destructiveness of war is the last chapter
of a narrative played out between the "first beginning" of the Greeks and the "other beginning" of the Germans.[19] Indeed, Heidegger maintained his belief in the "necessity" of an
"other beginning" even after he had advanced from his erstwhile revolutionary hopes for
the "other beginning" of Hitler's "politics" to a kind of reasonable distance from National
Socialism. But since the "other beginning" was not realized by way of the instruments of
revolutionary "politics," it was to be realized by way of the "self-annihilation" of these
very instruments—that is, ontohistorically thought, by means of the "self-annihilation" of
metaphysics in the "fate [*Geschick*]" of "machination."

In this changed narrative, the service for the sake of the "history of being" comes
around to itself: "self-annihilation."[20] "All" protagonists in this narrative—expropriated,
enslaved—are immersed in "self-annihilation": they are placed at the war fronts, show
themselves in "Americanism and 'Bolshevism'" (in the "ontohistorically" understood
"communism"), as "England" and "France," in "Christendom" and "World Jewry."

These figures of the "history of being," agents of "machination"—not humans but
"slaves" of "machination," ordered about but acting nevertheless—all serve the "other
beginning."[21] With regard to this purported turning of Western history, its fatal breakdown, the question concerning the Shoah finds its foothold (in Heidegger's thought). The
"fate of Jews and Germans" is decided at this point, as is their "own truth, which our
historical thinking cannot reach" and that can be grasped only by way of the "history
of being." On one occasion, around 1941–1942, Heidegger writes: "When what in the
metaphysical sense is essentially 'Jewishness' [*das wesenhaft Jüdische*] fights against
Jewishness [*das Jüdische*], self-annihilation has reached its historical apex, provided
that 'Jewishness' has seized power everywhere such that, first and foremost, the fight
against 'Jewishness' becomes subservient to it too."[22] In an ontohistorical sense, the

essential character of "Jewishness" is to stir up (or to excite, to agitate) the no-relation in the relation of the difference between "being" and "beings" and to bring about the "uprooting of all beings from being." According to Heidegger, this "task" was assigned to "World Jewry" by the "history of being." It is "machination" itself that figures in "World Jewry" in this manner (admittedly, not only in it, but, nonetheless, in a distinguished manner, namely, insofar as it is "*absolutely unattached*").

If this "Jewishness" (i.e., "machination") fights "against Jewishness," "self-annihilation has reached its apex in history." What, however, is "Jewishness [*das Jüdische*]"? Is it possible to see in this reference to "Jewishness" anything but the factically existing Jewry? But what does the "fight" look like between "Jewishness" and "Jewishness"? It is "self-annihilation." What if here the Shoah were to be thought of as the "self-annihilation" of Jewry, as this "historical apex of self-annihilation"?

Yet Heidegger seems less concerned about a real event (which is no incidental nuance). Rather, what "self-annihilation" seems to amount to is that "everything" becomes "Jewishness," mere "machination, including even countermovements." "Everything—also Jewishness"? Even Heidegger's thinking itself? The importance of this nuance goes far beyond this question. Can one understand "self-annihilation" without a factical happening, without a "fact"? What does it look like, this "fight" between "Jewishness" and "Jewishness"?

Much could be said concerning the brief duration of the semantic field of "self-annihilation [*Selbstvernichtung*]" [in Heidegger's works, IF]. It is obvious that Heidegger quickly dropped the concept of "self-annihilation" as the "*greatest completion of technology.*" After the war he was confronted with the Shoah itself.

Confronted by posters disseminated by the Psychological Warfare Division of the Supreme Headquarters Allied Powers Europe, he does refer to the Shoah. Under the heading "These Shameful Acts—Your Guilt!" one poster showed pictures of liberated concentration camps. Looking back at the past, he tries to find meaning in this "fate [*Geschick*]."

Heidegger writes that "we" are still "within the unassuming preciousness of the saved treasure."[23] But in order to "let" "us" be there, "first we had to experience what is our own and be freed for *it* [*zu ihm ge-freyt seyn*], and, at the same time, the strangers [*die Fremden*] had to let us be in the sense of an *assistance* [*Hilfe*], which required a no less free and freeing sentiment [*freye-freyende Gesinnung*]." "Ownness" had to be experienced in order to stay within the "saved treasure." Almost unintelligible is the reference to the "strangers," who had to "let" us be as well. How did the "strangers"—often signifying Jews—assist us? Did they let us be, or did they abandon us? Or are the "strangers" here even the "Greeks"? But the Greeks could be characterized as strangers only in the onto-historical context of Heidegger's Hölderlin interpretation, and in that case no historical relevance could be ascribed to them. The philosopher adds to this: "How dark it is above all that is so elemental, and yet, how close is the possibility of the one and own destiny [*des einen eigenen Geschicks*], demanding of us to shape and suffer much [*viel auszutragen verlangt*]." Heidegger continues:

If one thought it through from the perspective of destiny, would not, for instance, the *failure to grasp* this destiny—which would not belong to us, if the *world-willing* [*Weltwollen*] was suppressed [*Niederhalten im Weltwollen*]—would this failure not be much more essentially a "guilt" and "collective guilt," the magnitude of which essentially could not even be measured against the gruesomeness of the "gas chambers" [*Greuelhaften der "Gaskammern"*]; a guilt—uncannier than all "crimes" that can be "inveighed against" publically—which surely no one would forgive in the future. Already today "one" has a foreboding that Germany and the German people are but one concentration camp—the likes of which "the world" has not "seen" indeed, and which "the world" does not *want* to see—*this* not-willing is far more *willing* than our spinelessness [*Willenlosigkeit*] in the face of the brutalization [*Verwilderung*] of National Socialism.[24]

The "failure to grasp" "the destiny" to be allowed to stay inside the "unassuming preciousness of the treasure" is characterized as "world-willing [*Weltwollen*]." The temporal structure of the context links the past to the present. "Ours" is still "the saved treasure," but first we had "to experience" what is "our own." But "world-willing" is apparently something current. It still corresponds to the "destiny" over which we do not have control, precisely because it is "destiny." If "we" were "suppressed" in pursuing this "world-willing"—now, after the war—this "suppression" would be "guilt," the magnitude of which could not even be measured against the gruesomeness of the gas chambers. The "world-willing" of the "Germans" is ontohistorically more important than the "gruesomeness of the gas chambers."

"Not-willing-to-see" that "Germany and the German people" are "but one concentration camp" is even "more *willing* than our *spinelessness*" in the face of the degeneration (*Entartung*) of National Socialism. Thus both statements aim at the victorious forces, the Allied Forces. Their policy to limit German world-willing is more criminal than the mass murder, which "surely no one could forgive in the future."

The train of thought is convoluted. There is no German "destiny" of "world-willing," an experience of what is one's "Own" with the assistance of "strangers." This "destiny" is foregrounded against the "brutalization of *National Socialism*." Therefore, it did not all lead to the "gruesomeness of the gas chambers," which Heidegger attributes to degenerated (*entartetem*) National Socialism. But the crimes of the Allied Forces could even surpass the crimes that Heidegger concedes.

It is clear that Heidegger differentiates between "National Socialism" and the "Germans." This is also the case with the narrative of "self-annihilation." When after the war Heidegger had to abandon the idea of the "self-annihilation" by means of "machination," which was plausible only within the context of a narrative anyway, he transferred this idea to the figure in the "history of being" that had to carry out the "other beginning": the "Germans," who were driven to their "self-annihilation of their essence by the others."[25] The "others"— these were the victorious forces, which admittedly were unable to will anything but "machination." In any case, in the eyes of Heidegger, the "Germans" no longer wanted to be "Germans." Now the Germans turned out to be the ones who, "murdered by invisible killing devices," plunged headlong into the "self-annihilation of their essence."

Thus it was perhaps somewhat premature to think that Heidegger's comment that "the destiny of Jews and Germans has a truth of its own, which our historical thinking does not reach" refers to the Shoah, insofar as we assume that the Shoah is a crime perpetrated by the Germans against the Jews. For Heidegger might well have entertained the idea that Jews as well as Germans had been enmeshed in "self-annihilation," which on either side was bound up with a factical, physical, as well as cultural annihilation. Admittedly, this interpretation requires that the murderers of the Jews were not Germans, but National Socialists.

The "self-annihilation" of "machination," the global conflagration, had not taken place. Or it had happened, but not as Heidegger had envisioned it. Technology remained unscathed. This created a new situation in which the idea of the "other beginning" had to be revised. In his exoteric texts Heidegger stopped attributing knowledge or premonition about the "other beginning" to the "Greeks" or "Germans." The narrative had to be rescripted.

Technology proved to be an absolute and unshakable foundation. This absoluteness had to be considered anew. The Shoah scarcely played a negative or positive role in this, as is well known. Only the following often-quoted statement is on record:

Today agriculture is a motorized food industry, in essence the same as the fabrication of corpses in gas chambers and death camps, the same as the blockade and starvation of countries, the same as the fabrication of hydrogen bombs.[26]

The problematic character of this statement has often been noted.[27] It has less to do with Heidegger's choice of the phrase "the fabrication of corpses," a formulation Hannah Arendt used as well. In fact, it has to be said that the starkness of the formulation can have a disturbing—that is, healing—effect. What is problematic is that Heidegger ignores the moral claim of the Shoah. He thinks that one can erase the unique moral signature of the event by integrating it into the "sameness" of other production processes. Thus he does not realize that the Shoah is an event that in the first instance lets the alleged normalcy of the "same" appear in all its abysmal groundlessness. It was Ernst Jünger who ranked the cruelty of war lower than the Nazi "murder caves," which "will remain in people's memory for the longest time."[28]

But eight years earlier Heidegger had tried to think differently about the event. It was not the "enframing" that required reflection in the face of the universal leveling through production, but rather "Jewishness" in its fight "with Jewishness." Was it "Jewishness" that destroyed itself in the "fabrication of corpses"? Is there a link between the "enframing" and "Jewishness"? What had changed in these eight years? Can one pose these questions? After that there is only silence. Or rather, there is already silence in the remark from the "Bremen Lectures." What had to be talked about is passed over in silence. "Keeping silent"—after *Being and Time* it plays a constant, if changing, role in Heidegger's thought. In the *Überlegungen* (*Considerations*) and *Anmerkungen* (*Remarks*) of the *Black Note-*

books, Heidegger frequently talks about "keeping silent"—of "keeping silent" in speaking, of "reserved silence [*Verschwiegenheit*]," of "taciturnity [*Schweigsamkeit*]"—and emphasizes that one must "keep silent" about silence. In the *Contributions to Philosophy* as well as in other "ontohistorical" manuscripts "keeping silent [*Schweigen*]" is expounded with reference to "*Erschweigen*" (i.e., "what is said and brought about in keeping silent"). Therefore, with some justification one can say that keeping silent about the Shoah could be discussed and assessed with reference to Heidegger's own ideas about silence.

Keeping silent about the Shoah has distinctive implications. I will pass over the question of what Heidegger kept silent or could have ignored in silence—in other words, the things hinted at by his suggestive remarks about "keeping silent." But if the Shoah is an event to which one must respond unreservedly and morally, then it is not just any strange or trivial subject that one could either stay silent or write about. The Shoah deprives us of the right to keep silent. It requires that we speak about it; it requires the word, the response. The silence about the Shoah can be understood only in terms of a refusal to respond.

On the occasion of the "Exhibition: Prisoners of War Talk," Heidegger, in a lecture from the summer of 1952, encouraged his audience "to go to the exhibition in order to hear the silent voices and never to let these voices grow dim in their ears."[29] Without a doubt, fine words, mindful of the suffering of German soldiers. But who heard the "silent voices" of those murdered in the "gas chambers and death camps"? Who was to hear them, who wanted to hear them? Who heard the "silent voices" of the murdered Jews? Who said they had heard them? After the war, Germany was a country of silence.[30]

One could ask whether the refusal to hear the "silent voices" of *these* dead, in order to express what is undoubtedly owed to them—namely grief, perhaps even innocent grief—does not inevitably become a deadly silence, indeed a silencing that kills, a silent killing-once-again, a killing of the dead, and in any case, the avoidance of remembering what "really" happened to the Jews. One could ask whether the refusal to express grief does not become a deadly silence. In that case, keeping silent about the Shoah would be telling enough. If not indicative of tacit consent (i.e., "consenting to the horrible"),[31] it would be, nonetheless, a recalcitrant refusal to acknowledge the unconditional moral meaning of the Shoah.

But one can also keep silent out of a sense of shame. Much could be said about this shame, about the shame of the perpetrators as well as that of the victims.[32] Heidegger has written about this—his shame, that is—in letters to Karl Jaspers in 1950. He confesses that "since 1933"[33] he could not visit Jaspers's house not because a "Jewish woman" lived there, but because he "*simply was ashamed.*" Toward "the end of the 1930s," when "the worst" was set in motion with "the vile persecutions," he had immediately thought of Jaspers's wife. It is at the same time that Heidegger, in "Überlegungen XII," speaks of "the Jews," who "with their decidedly calculative talent" had lived "according to the racial principle for the longest time," "which is why they also most vehemently oppose the unrestricted application of it."[34]

Notes

1. *Hannah Arendt/Martin Heidegger: Briefe 1925 bis 1975 und andere Zeugnisse*, ed. Ursula Ludz (Frankfurt: Klostermann, 2002), 94, letter to Hannah Arendt dated April 12, 1950.

2. Jacques Derrida, "Heideggers Schweigen," in *Antwort: Martin Heidegger im Gespräch*, ed. Günther Neske and Emil Kettering (Pfullingen: Günther Neske, 1988), 160.

3. Hannah Arendt, *Zwischen Vergangenheit und Zukunft: Übungen im politischen Denken I*, ed. Ursula Ludz (Munich: Piper, 1994), 35. See my "Das Trauma des Holocaust als Anfang der Philosophie: Nach Hannah Arendt und Emmanuel Levinas," *Zeitschrift für Genozidforschung* 2 (2007): 118–131.

4. Of course, this does not mean that when faced with the Shoah one can only adopt a moral attitude. There is historical remembrance, in which the only task is to find out what exactly happened, as for instance, research into the French Revolution. But as soon as one articulates the event beyond its mere dates, the concepts inevitably take on a moral cast, even in historiography. However much language pretends to be neutral, it is attracted to the event as if by a magnet—that is, as if it is drawn into its gravitational field. It seems to me that when faced with this event no other response is possible. This is so, not because there is some prior subjective duty calling for it, or because some "visceral sadness [*Betroffenheit*]" can arise, but rather because the Shoah is the event that it "is."

5. Jürgen Habermas, "Vom öffentlichen Gebrauch der Historie: Das offizielle Selbstverständnis der Bundesrepublik bricht auf," in *"Historikerstreit": Die Dokumentation der Kontroverse um die Einzigartigkeit der nationalsozialistischen Judenvernichtung*, ed. Rudolf Augstein et al. (Munich: Piper, 1987), 243–255 (quote on 243). It is my view that every genocide, every ethical event (for instance, the rape of a child), is "unique." It is a different question to what extent such an event can claim universal significance.

6. Martin Heidegger, *Heraklit, Gesamtausgabe* 55, ed. Manfred S. Frings (Frankfurt: Klostermann, 1994), 123. See Hermann Diels and Walter Kranz, eds., *Die Fragmente der Vorsokratiker,* 18th ed., vol 1 (Zurich: Weidmann, 1989), frag. 22 B 66: πάντα γάρ τὸ πῦρ ἐπελθὸν κρινεῖ καὶ καταλήψεται.

7. Götz Aly, *Hitlers Volksstaat: Raub, Rassenkrieg und nationaler Sozialismus* (Frankfurt: Fischer, 2005).

8. Martin Heidegger, "Überlegungen XV," 17, in *Überlegungen XII–XV (Schwarze Hefte 1939–1941), Gesamtausgabe* 96, ed. Peter Trawny (Frankfurt: Klostermann, 2014), 262.

9. Adolf Hitler, "Hitlers politisches Testament," in *Hitlers Briefe und Notizen: Sein Weltbild in handschriftlichen Dokumenten*, ed. Werner Maser (Düsseldorf: Econ, 1973), 3.

10. Heidegger, *Überlegungen XII–XV, Gesamtausgabe* 96, p. 261.

11. *Überlegungen XII–XV, Gesamtausgabe* 96, p. 242.

12. *Überlegungen XII–XV, Gesamtausgabe* 96, p. 261.

13. *Überlegungen XII–XV, Gesamtausgabe* 96, p. 243. The talk of the "world-historical task" is strongly reminiscent of Hegel's philosophy of history. In the winter semester 1939–1940, Heidegger wanted to give a seminar on Hegel's "Metaphysics of History." It seems that nothing came of it.

14. Martin Heidegger, "Nachwort zu: 'Was ist Metaphysik?,'" in *Wegmarken, Gesamtausgabe* 9, ed. Friedrich-Wilhelm von Herrmann (Klostermann: Frankfurt, 1996), 306.

15. See Peter Trawny, *Heidegger und der Mythos der jüdischen Weltverschwörung* (Frankfurt: Klostermann, 2014), 22.

16. *Überlegungen XII–XV, Gesamtausgabe* 96, p. 141.

17. *Überlegungen XII–XV, Gesamtausgabe* 96, p. 238.

18. Martin Heidegger, "Anmerkungen I," 26, in *Anmerkungen I–V (Schwarze Hefte 1942–1948), Gesamtausgabe* 97, ed. Peter Trawny (Frankfurt: Klostermann, 2015).

19. *Überlegungen VII–XI (Schwarze Hefte 1938/39), Gesamtausgabe* 95, ed. Peter Trawny (Frankfurt: Klostermann, 2014), 204.

20. "Service through attendance at and attention to the routines and chores of the equipment of what is [*des Seienden*]. Service from out of solitude through surmounting the hold of beings in the founding of the truth of being [*Seyn*]" (*Überlegungen XII–XV, Gesamtausgabe* 96, p. 190). Both forms of service belong together. The first form carries out the "self-destruction," the second thinks it.

21. See the following line: "The history of being rolls the dice and at times it lets it appear as if human machina-

tion determines how they fall" (Martin Heidegger, *Die Geschichte des Seyns, Gesamtausgabe* 69, ed. Peter Trawny (Frankfurt: Klostermann,1998), 213). This too is reminiscent of the Heraclitus fragment B 52: αἰὼν παῖς ἐστι παίζων, πεσσεύων. παιδὸς ἡ βασιληίη. After the war Heidegger translates this as follows: "Fate of being, child is it, playing, playing the board game; the kingdom is of a child" (Martin Heidegger, *Der Satz vom Grund, Gesamtausgabe* 10, ed. Petra Jaeger (Frankfurt: Klostermann, 1997), 168).

22. "Anmerkungen I," 30, *Anmerkungen I–V, Gesamtausgabe* 97, ed. Peter Trawny (Klostermann: Frankfurt, 2015).

23. "Anmerkungen I," 151, in *Anmerkungen I–V, Gesamtausgabe* 97.

24. "Anmerkungen I," 151, in *Anmerkungen I–V, Gesamtausgabe* 97.

25. "Anmerkungen II," 72, in *Anmerkungen I–V, Gesamtausgabe* 97.

26. Martin Heidegger, *Bremer und Freiburger Vorträge. 1. Einblick in das was ist; 2. Grundsätze des Denkens, Gesamtausgabe* 79, ed. Petra Jaeger (Frankfurt: Klostermann, 2005), 27.

27. For instance, by Emmanuel Levinas: "This stylistic device, this analogy, this structure of composition needs no commentary" ("Das Diabolische gibt zu denken," in *Die Heidegger Kontroverse*, ed. Jürg Altwegg [Frankfurt: Athenäum, 1988], 101–109 [quote on 104]).

28. Ernst Jünger, *Der Friede: Ein Wort an die Jugend Europas und an die Jugend der Welt, Die Argonauten* (Amsterdam: Erasmus, 1946), 15.

29. Martin Heidegger, *Was heißt Denken?*, *Gesamtausgabe* 8, ed. Paola-Ludovika Coriando (Frankfurt: Klostermann, [1954] 2002), 161.

30. See the chapter "Le silence d'une génération" in the important book by Maurice Olender, *Race sans histoire, Points Essais No. 620* (Paris: Seuil, 2009), 249–291. Olender puts Heidegger's silence in context with the silence of Hans Robert Jauss, Karlheinz Stierles, Reinhart Kosellecks, and Günter Grass. Olender speaks of an "authentic silence" or "what is explicitly not said" (*Race sans histoire*, 283) in a way that is not restricted to Koselleck alone. It is precisely in question whether such a silence is to be found in Heidegger—perhaps it is there, but certainly not with regard to the Shoa.

31. "But keeping silent about the gas chambers and death camps after the return of peace—is that not, apart from the bad excuses, testimony to the complete hardening of the soul against all feeling, as if consenting to the horrible?" (Levinas, "Das Diabolische gibt zu denken," in *Die Heidegger Kontroverse*, 104).

32. "Does your shame result from the fact that you live in lieu of someone else? And most of all, in lieu of a human being more generous, more feeling, more understanding, more useful, and more worthy of life than you? You cannot exclude this possibility" (Primo Levi, *Die Untergegangenen und die Geretteten* (Munich: Carl Hanser, 1990), 81).

33. *Martin Heidegger/Karl Jaspers: Briefwechsel 1920–1963*, ed. Walter Biemel and Hans Saner (Frankfurt: Klostermann/Piper, 1990), 196.

34. *Überlegungen XII–XV, Gesamtausgabe* 96, p. 56.

12

Heidegger's Metaphysical Anti-Semitism

Donatella Di Cesare

1   The Jew and the Oblivion of Being

What Heidegger wrote in the *Black Notebooks* about Jews and Judaism can in no way be minimized or trivialized. In a passage from 1941, he clearly warns that the "Jewish question" is a "metaphysical question":

The question of the role of World Jewry [*Weltjudentum*] is not a racial question [*rassisch*], but the metaphysical question [*metaphysisch*] concerning the kind of humanity [*Menschentümlichkeit*], which, free from all attachments, can assume the world-historical 'task' of uprooting all beings [*Seiendes*] from being [*Sein*].[1]

What is the relationship between being and the Jew? What is the link between the *Seinsfrage*, philosophy's question par excellence, and the *Judenfrage*?

Anti-Semitism takes on a new philosophical relevance in the *Black Notebooks*. The Jew is positioned at the heart of Heidegger's thought, and as central to his philosophy. Yet, to the Jew, inscribed in the history of being, is also ascribed the greatest fault, the oblivion of being.

Metaphysical anti-Semitism sheds new light on Heidegger's adherence to Nazism, which can no longer be considered a mere political interlude, but represents, rather, a key philosophical moment in his work. Anti-Semitism is the cornerstone of National Socialism, and not some ideological decoration. The "Heidegger affair" cannot be clarified within the gap between politics and philosophy. Since Heidegger's decision to support Nazism is a philosophical one, the "Heidegger affair" must be discussed first in its philosophical context.

Faced with the *Black Notebooks*, some critics have been quick to accuse Heidegger of being a strange obscurantist, closing the issue of totalitarianism with a totalitarian gesture. Alternatively, others have unthinkingly acquitted him, thus immediately dismissing the question. These two gestures are completely inadequate and deeply antiphilosophical. The seriousness of the issues themselves should prohibit criminalizing condemnation as well as complicit denial, moral indignation, and cynical banalization. Yet hasty judgments and absolute verdicts have multiplied and the discussion surrounding the Heidegger affair has become increasingly agitated. What has developed, especially in France, is a form of "process" that also exhibits some highly problematic traits.

What purpose is served by such a "process"—by putting the philosopher on trial? And who is served by that "process"? The not-too-secret hope of those who prosecute the case, both old and new, is to do away with Heidegger once and for all, thereby also bringing on a confrontation with that mode of philosophy, the "continental," in which Heidegger is a central figure.

Getting rid of Heidegger, however, would mean getting rid of the difficult questions he has raised, and, above all, erasing the question (perhaps the most complex of all) concerning the responsibilities of philosophers toward the Shoah. If one defines Heidegger's reflections as "pathological," then in so doing one also effectively participates in the continued setting of Nazism apart from philosophy—as if Nazism were a "folly" outside reason, outside history. In contrast, the *Black Notebooks* can provide an opportunity to think philosophically about what happened—an opportunity to think not only about the Third Reich, nor only about Auschwitz, but also about the place of the "Jewish question" in the history of the West.

2   Philosophers and the "Jewish Question"—from Kant to Hitler

What, however, is the "Jewish question"? This way of formulating what is at issue, and so the phrase itself, has for too long been assumed uncritically. As Hannah Arendt rightly noted, the "modern Jewish question dates from Enlightenment; it was the Enlightenment—that is, the non-Jewish world—that posed it."[2] Jews were both seen as representing an unknown—because Judaism seemed to escape definition—and as a problem that had to be solved.

When one speaks about the "Jewish question" in its conventional historical context, what is usually taken to be at issue is the historical process by which the Jews of Europe gained social and political equality. Paradoxically, however, the problem of the irreducible strangeness of the Jews is hidden behind this phrase "the Jewish question," even as it appears in this conventional context. How, in fact, should "the Jews" be defined? Is their identity as Jews based on their religion? Is it the identity of a people? Is there a "Jewish nation," and if so, does that "nation" represent a threat—might it even constitute a "state within the state"?[3]

In his metaphysical anti-Semitism, Heidegger is not isolated, but follows a long line of previous philosophers. Kant had accepted Jews as citizens on the sole condition of the "euthanasia of Judaism."[4] Hegel had stopped them at the door to Europe and salvation: from a theological point of view, Judaism had to be overcome by Christianity; from a political point of view, Jews were foreigners without a land and without a state, incapable of possessions and property—in short, as citizens they were "nothing."[5] Nietzsche foreshadowed a disquieting alternative: the Jews "will either become the masters of Europe or lose Europe as once, long time ago, they lost Egypt"[6]—but even at that time the idea was already emerging that the Jews had begun subtly to war against the Germans.

That Jews falsify and lie is an accusation that has been repeated from Luther to Schopenhauer, and right up to Hitler. In *Mein Kampf* the lie becomes the key to deciphering the arcanum of Judaism. As masters of deception, Jews hold themselves out to be Germans. Yet since they are actually *Fremde*, "foreigners," they pretend to be what they are not, thereby camouflaging their nonbeing, their constitutive nothingness.[7] This metaphysical accusation was to have devastating results.

3   The Complicity between Metaphysics and Judaism

The landscape in which the Jew appears in Heidegger's pages is that in which the history of being is also outlined. Therefore Trawny speaks of anti-Semitism as *seinsgeschichtlich*[8]— as belonging to the history of being. Yet it is preferable to qualify it, not as *seinsgeschichtlich,* but rather as *metaphysical*.

What is at issue here is not merely a question of labels. First, *seinsgeschichtlich* has an esoteric tone and mystical aura that soften and mitigate the brutality of the discriminatory act. Second, the use of *seinsgeschichtlich* wrongly tends to isolate Heidegger's position, as if it were unique, and it is misleading for that reason. On the contrary, Heidegger deals with a topic that is not at all new in Western philosophy—that of the relationship between being and the Jew. Moreover, although the Jew appears in Heidegger's history of being, he has no proper place in that history and so is immediately expelled from it. When Heidegger tries to define the Jew, he does not abandon metaphysics, but instead falls back on it.

A short hermeneutical remark on the texts is necessary, however, before outlining this metaphysical anti-Semitism in greater detail.

The terms *Jude, jüdisch, Judentum*, occur precisely fourteen times in the last two volumes of the *Black Notebooks*—that is, in the *Überlegungen* ranging from 1938 to 1941. One might infer that this sporadic occurrence would prove the marginality of the topic. However, there are similarities here with Carl Schmitt's texts, in which anti-Semitic expressions emerge only in 1933 and become more and more frequent during the war years. Heidegger and Schmitt both followed similar strategies: if in the *Black Notebooks* Heidegger limits the number of passages in which he plainly speaks of Jews and Judaism, the indirect references are more frequent. Through easily decipherable insinuations, allusions, and reminders, which are appropriately translated into his philosophical idiom, Heidegger refers to the Jews even when not mentioning them directly. As such, the way Heidegger uses a range of terms supports the conceptual network that surrounds, delimits, and attempts to define the Jew. The terms at issue here include *Verwüstung* (desertification), *Entrassung* (deracination), *Entwurzelung* (rootedness), *Herdenwesen* ("herd's essence"), *Rechenfähigkeit* (calculative ability), *Beschneidung des Wissens* (the "circumcision" of knowledge), and *Gemeinschaft der Auserwählter* (community of the chosen). The passages in the *Black Notebooks* that treat the issue of Judaism are therefore far more numerous than the explicit appearance of terms like *Jude* and its cognates would suggest, and the image that Heidegger provides of the Jew must be read within this wider speculative network.

A key feature of the *Black Notebooks* is the sharpening of the ontological difference and its emergence as an extreme dichotomy, a fatal gap, an irreconcilable conflict. The Second World War is read through the pattern of the ontological difference, and thus it reveals itself as the war of beings against being. The planetary clash has at the same time an ontological, theological, and political meaning. The history of being becomes a narrative with apocalyptic tones, the tale of a final battle, the metaphysical version of the war of Gog and Magog.

If the destiny of being is entrusted to the Germans, the vanguard of the European peoples, the attempt to assert dominion over being is imputed to the Jews. Not only is the Jew hopelessly separated from being, he is also accused of being the one who brings about this separation. His doom is in some way already determined: split from being, the Jew comes dangerously close to nothing, a fate to which Hegel had already sentenced him.

Heidegger denounces the complicity of Judaism in metaphysics. If metaphysics, in its modern results, has paved the way for Judaism, it is because Judaism already favors metaphysics:

The reason why Judaism has temporarily increased its power is that Western metaphysics, at least in its modern development, has offered a starting point for the spread of an otherwise empty rationality and calculating ability, which have, consequently, acquired a shelter [*Unterkunft*] in the "spirit" [*Geist*] without nevertheless being able to grasp, moving from themselves, the hidden ambits-of-decision [*Entscheidungsbezirke*]. The more original and captured-in-their beginning the prospective decisions and questions, the more they remain inaccessible to this "race."[9]

The relationship at issue here is reciprocal. Metaphysics has provided the basis for empty rationality and calculating thought—the latter two, according to Heidegger, being characteristic of Judaism. On the other hand, calculating thought has found *Unterkunft*, shelter, in *Geist*. It has settled inside "spirit," perverting and preventing it from reaching those realms where the authentic decision—the decision *for* being—is possible.

The doom of Judaism is tied to the destiny of metaphysics. Here lies one of the key points in Heidegger's vision: overcoming metaphysics also means getting rid of Judaism, and vice versa. As the final outcome of modernity, Jewish power is the domination of being, which forces the identification of the metaphysical enemy as the Jew. Heidegger repeats the gesture of exclusion in a much more radical way than previously, carrying it out at the very edge of the abyss.

The occurrence of the word *Feind*, "enemy," in the *Black Notebooks* does not give rise to questions about the enemy's location, the method by which he can be attacked, or with what weapons this can be done—the sorts of questions that would ordinarily arise in line with the usual canons of belligerence, which are also those of National Socialism.[10] Instead, the metaphysical conflict directly challenges the philosopher:

Committed to *philosophy*, the thinker stands in opposition to the *enemy* (the insubstantiality of beings, which disown themselves while in existence), and, without ever ceasing hostilities, the thinker establishes himself as *belonging* to that which at bottom must be the thinker's friend (the essence of being).[11]

4   Heidegger's Accusations against the Jews

Proceeding from this nexus of complicity between Judaism and metaphysics, Heidegger levels precise accusations against Jews, which serve to fill out his sketch of the Jews and to delineate their role. Since they are groundless, Jews are said to be agents of the speeding-up of the world: their uprootedness corresponds to the advances in technology enveloping the planet, and they are seen as the main promoters and profiteers of this process. Also traced back to Jews is the devastation of the planet and the "complete deracination of peoples [*vollständige Entrassung*]" (i.e., the attempt to bastardize them).[12] Despite being taken for no race—or even contrary to all race as a *Gegen-Rasse*—Jews are accused of being the first racists: "They have already lived much longer than others according to the principle of race, which is why they are resisting its consistent application with the utmost vehemence."[13]

Here Heidegger condemns Israel's separateness, its election. Infiltrating the host people and hiding there, Jews would bastardize them. For his part Schmitt speaks of the *Dämon der Entartung*, "demon of degeneration."[14] The charge is very serious: the "self-alienation of the peoples" is the political strategy pursued by Jews, in order to realize democracy, parliamentarianism, equality, and thus to attain "world domination."[15] To this end, they do not fight honestly: through deception they erase demarcations and the friend-foe distinction. Therefore, assimilated Jews are the ones most to be dreaded.

Although or because they are worldless, Jews plot to rule the world. Heidegger speaks of "powers" holding in their hands the strings of an unstoppable "machination." Machination, then, is the other charge. In other words, the purported Jewish lack of world is not just a statement of fact, but indeed an accusation.

Precisely their uprootedness—that is, the ontological and political condition whereby Jews, without bonds and ties, have been scattered across the globe (remaining as foreigners among their host peoples and unassimilable)—is what enables them to build and maintain relationships among themselves. But since these relationships transcend national borders, and so are international, this rouses their desire, above all, for an uprising—a desire to rule the world. Being worldless, they are at a distance from the world, which in turn allows them to cast a web around the globe, plotting a planetary conspiracy whose aim is the Jewish domination of the world.

"Judeo-Bolshevism"—really a secularized messianism—is, for Heidegger, nothing other than the manifestation of that occult Jewish power that fights by deception under different guises. In a text from 1941 Heidegger writes: "World Jewry [*Weltjudentum*], instigated by emigrants allowed to leave Germany, is elusive everywhere, and even though its power is increasing, it does not need to participate in military actions, whereas all that remains to us is to sacrifice the best blood of the best of our own people."[16] In his apocalyptic vision, Heidegger sees the Jew as the figure of an *ending*, constantly repeating itself, and preventing the German people from reaching the "other beginning" that is the West's new dawn.[17] Like others around him, Heidegger believes that Germany, called to its own self-defense, can constitute itself by reconnecting, beyond Rome, with the never-realized Greece. But the *Imperium* had always been attacked by Israel. The centuries-old theological-political confrontation becomes a planetary war against the Jews.

5   Germans, Greeks—and the Jews

In the *Black Notebooks,* Heidegger calls many peoples onto the stage of world history. The main protagonists are, however, the Germans and the Greeks. Their place is determined by the axis of being, projected between the "first beginning," inaugurated by the Greeks, and the "other beginning," the mission entrusted to the Germans. The other peoples—the Russians, Americans, Chinese, British, and Italians—all mark a place along the path of the history of being. But the Jews?

For Heidegger, decline, *Untergang*, in the sense used by Spengler, must be reinterpreted as a passage, *Übergang*: "An age of transition. ... Standing in the midst of it, and yet also on the other side."[18] The gloom of night should not be misunderstood, since it is not the darkness of death, but the quenching of last evening's light so that the dawn of morning can shine in the distance.

But who can cross the cold night of being? Who can glimpse the passage through, where everyone sees only an impassable collapse? Who can follow the road to its end, in order to enter the path of the beginning?—only the Germans. The destiny of the West is in their hands: "Endowed with the great legacy of the Greek being-there, we dare, with secure spirit, the leap toward the freely binding opening of the future."[19]

The German *imitatio* is the aspiration to a Greece that does not exist, that has never existed, that can only exist thanks to Germany. It is the mystical and nocturnal, archaic and tragic, purely pagan Greece, sung by Hölderlin, wished by Hegel, longed for by Nietzsche. Greece is the *Heimat*, the land of autochthony, of being-at-home with oneself.

The history of being appears, then, as a way toward that beginning that remains preserved for the future of the West. Only the German people are called to follow it. Only the German people can overcome metaphysics. Only the German people are the custodians of being because in the wake of Hölderlin they can "say and poetize it anew in an original way."[20] Thus we come to the long-anticipated arrival of the German people onto the world stage, where they are destined to fulfill the mission that, with the accelerated character of the world, has become planetary.

The devastating effects of technology, machination, estrangement, and desertification can only be countered by Germany thanks to the iron cohesion of its *Volksgemeinschaft*—its "people's community"—deeply rooted in the soil.

The Greek-German coupling leaves out the Jews; the axis of being excludes them. There is no longer space for them in the topography of the *Abendland*, the Land of Evening. If that land is to reawaken to a new dawn and discover itself as the Land of Morning, it must face up to the question of the metaphysical enemy who, by his very presence, undermines being from within and impedes the access to the other beginning.

Yet, one should ask whether this exclusion, which heralds a new historicity of being and a new geopolitical order, targets other people, not just the Jews. Is it not perhaps a discriminatory gesture that regards others as well?

The unity of the West is a theme that permeates European culture and assumes an exaggerated character in the 1930s. Heidegger is not the only one who launches an appeal for extreme salvation. To the Germans, a "great civilized people," Max Weber opposes "Senegal's Negro."[21] Not even Husserl escapes the Eurocentric prejudice. The universalism of reason does not prevent him from engaging in discrimination. And so, while the "Papuan," as symbol of the primitive, seems for him to be contiguous to animality, the concept of the human inevitably collapses.[22]

Thus, the dichotomy prevails between Western and westernized peoples, on the one hand, and those groups, on the other, that are marginalized by the West.

For Heidegger—and not just for him—things are very different. And this emerges clearly in the *Black Notebooks*. The Jews are not excluded from the West in the sense that, in a sort of geopolitical hierarchy of the globe, where Germany is at the center, surrounded first by the Western and then by the Westernized peoples, Jews could live on the periphery, with the "Negroes," who are always already excluded from human history. Jews are excluded from being. The Greek-German coupling, which discloses a new historicity, cannot, by definition, leave room for the Jew, the opponent, or rather, the metaphysical enemy who, just as he has lied for centuries, letting others believe what he is not, so he conceals the being, occludes it, prevents the passage, bars the German from reaching the other beginning.

This is not just a matter of discriminating, as happens with the gesture that puts the Other outside history; rather it is a matter of facing the enemy in order to decide the history of being. The conflict has planetary dimensions and ontological depth. Is it still possible to say that anti-Semitism is just a form of racism?

6   Metaphysics of the Jew

Why is it necessary to speak of the *metaphysics of the Jew*? Heidegger's reflections are not influenced either by anthropological conceptions or, even less, by biological doctrines. Those reflections are fully embedded in the tradition of German thought, from Kant to Hegel and to Nietzsche, out of which those reflections take up, albeit often implicitly, many themes and topics. Despite his criticism of metaphysics, Heidegger inherits its method of interrogation. His considerations all answer the ancient question: *Ti ésti,* What is it?

Introduced in *Theaetetus* by the Platonic Socrates, *Ti ésti* is set to become the paradigmatic question in Western metaphysics. "What does science seem to you to be?," Socrates asks. Theaetetus responds by listing a range of sciences. Irritated, Socrates replies: "But the question put, Theaetetus, was not about the various subjects of science, or their number. We did not ask with a wish to count them, but to know what [*Ti ésti*] *science itself* is."[23]

In the same years in which Heidegger is writing (1933–1934), it is Ludwig Wittgenstein who lets this question implode in the *Blue Book*. When asked *Ti ésti,* What is it?, "the philosopher is led to reject as irrelevant the concrete cases." This "contemptuous attitude towards the particular case" is linked with the desire to uncover the essence. The question *Ti ésti* suggests that there is a *was,* an identical essence, despite and beyond the differences. This tendency to generalize is the "real source of metaphysics."[24]

Heidegger similarly criticizes both the definition of identity and the concept of essence. Nevertheless, the way he asks about the Jews is metaphysical because it responds, albeit implicitly, to the question *Ti ésti,* What is it? What is the Jew? How should he be defined? What is his identity? What is his essence?

Heidegger seems to take part in the wide enterprise to define the Jew in the period of the Nuremberg Laws, an enterprise that not only engages jurists and scientists, since the racist fantasies are not based on "scientific" criteria. The attempt to define the Jewish "essence" through a metaphysics of blood is in vain. The philosopher is rightly called to respond to that attempt.

Heidegger shares the concern to define and identify the Jew that prevails in those years. This concern is also present in Schmitt, who ends up with the tautology: "the Jew is the Jew."[25] But there is a major difference on the one hand between the "who" of the jurist, who has to promulgate laws, as well as of the politician, who oversees their application, and on the other hand the "what" of the philosopher. *Who* is the Jew? *What* is the Jew? Schmitt is on the border between these two questions and, although his juridical approach places him closer to political practice, he is aware of the relevance of the philosophical question. More important than the "who" is the "what": the definition of identity is an indispensable requirement in establishing the limits of the who—the boundaries of the Jew's identity.

It is the philosophical question that is raised by Heidegger, who, recognizing its significance, situates it within the history of being. In this way he links the tradition that had reflected the relationship of the Jew with being, and its place within the history of the West. Paradoxically, however, when Heidegger asks about the Jew, unlike his questioning of being, he slips into metaphysics, and so looks to the uncovering of an essence.

The character of the question is not, however, the only reason it is necessary to speak of a metaphysics *of* the Jew. The genitive has an objective, but also a subjective value. The claim is even more fundamental (or fundamentalist): it is the will to define the Jew, with a capital *J,* to whose essence the flesh-and-blood Jews are reduced. The *metaphysics of the Jew* gives rise to the *metaphysical Jew*, an abstract figure to which the qualities are abstrusely conferred that should belong to the "idea" of the Jew, to the model, to the ideal Jew, onto whose ghostly substance the past representations are conveyed and the spectral nightmares of the present and hidden visions of the future are projected.

But there is also another reason to speak of metaphysics. The way the Jew is defined, in which the supposed qualities are attributed to or denied him, falls within the centuries-old metaphysical dichotomies that Heidegger contests elsewhere. Therefore, not only is his language metaphysical, but also his use of those binary and hierarchical oppositions that have dominated the Western tradition.

Proceeding from the original to the derivative, the Jew represents the negative pole of every dichotomy: beginning/end, pure/impure, autochthon/foreign, same/other, proper/improper, authentic/inauthentic, truth/lie, nature/civilization, quality/quantity, creative/reproductive, original/imitation, life/death, and being/nothingness. This list could go on and become more detailed: blood/gold, forest/desert, soil/rootedness, sedentary/nomadic, *nómos*/law, country/city, hero/merchant, equality/hierarchy, legality/legitimacy, meditation/calculation, nationalism/cosmopolitanism, and *Reich*/revolution.

The *metaphysics of the Jew* produces a *metaphysical Jew*, the idea of a Jew *metaphysically* defined on the basis of those centuries-old oppositions that reject the Jew in the inauthentic form, relegate him to a soulless abstraction, to spectral invisibility, and so on.

If the dichotomous proceeding could be more understandable for a jurist, it is not so for a philosopher who continually raises the question of metaphysics and tries to deconstruct, to make implode, through etymology, the language that has fossilized over the centuries. But this does not happen on the border between being and the Jew.

The metaphysical dichotomies decide on being and the Jew, since these dichotomies take precedence over all others. Here arises, then, the paradoxical position of the philosopher: if the philosopher is, on the one hand, not directly involved in the practice of the law and of its application, and, unlike the jurist, does not participate in defining and selecting Jews, therefore appearing more distant from any immediate responsibility, the philosopher is, on the other hand, much *more* responsible since he is close to, and his thinking is bound up with, the metaphysical dichotomies in his own response to metaphysics. If the Jew falls outside, if he is condemned to nothing, it is because the philosopher has made this decision to exclude him.

The real Jews, with their countless differences (which become completely indifferent), hand over their place to the Jew, the *Jude*, the Jew in himself, whose essence must be laid bare and known. Aside from the substantive, even still too concrete, the substantivized adjective surfaces, *das Jüdische*, which, according to the linguistic canons of German philosophy, should condense the *quidditas*. Similarly, *Judentum* does not indicate Judaism in its history, in the fascinating, tormented, complex vicissitudes of the Jewish people; this latter is declared *geschichtslos,* without history. *Judentum* represents a further abstraction, where all substantial traits attributed to the Jews merge in a substantivized collective, a substantive which, assuming the features of a subject, behaves and acts, as it were, as a monolithic agent, a disquieting, hostile, threatening *Moloch*, which ends up representing a threat par excellence.

Heidegger's metaphysical anti-Semitism revolves around these three terms, *Jude, Jüdisches, Judentum*. Speaking of metaphysical anti-Semitism means approaching and comparing Heidegger's position to that of others—and not only to the philosophers of the past, who are for him inscribed in Western metaphysics. The discriminating gesture that introduces the concept of "race" is philosophical. Later it is supported and scientifically legitimized through biologization. It is what happened in Nazism, which is completely misunderstood if it is reduced to a mere biologism. Metaphysical anti-Semitism must still be considered in its breadth and depth. Our own qualms and repressions, difficult to overcome, seem to hamper such consideration, but for contemporaries the matter was clear. In his work *Um des Reiches Zukunft*, published in Freiburg in 1932, Gurian writes:

Anti-Semitism, which arises in the new nationalism, has much deeper foundations than those of the 19th century. The Jew is regarded as a metaphysical phenomenon [*eine metaphysische Erscheinung*], and, as such, is rejected from/outside life. Metaphysical anti-Semitism [*der metaphysische Anti-Semitismus*] becomes a mass faith, after having been, despite the popularity of certain *völkisch* authors, especially Chamberlain, only a matter for educated circles.[26]

Moreover, even the fierce hostility of the most violent anti-Semites, such as Blüher, is first of all metaphysical. Blüher was very well known in academic circles, particularly for his 1931 work *Die Erhebung Israels*, and is referred to by Schmitt. Blüher attempts to pass anti-Semitism off as a defensive strategy and to legitimate it on a theological and philosophical basis.[27]

There is thus another argument, one that speaks explicitly of metaphysical anti-Semitism, which constitutes the link between metaphysics and theology—a link that might otherwise be overlooked. The hierarchical oppositions, starting with soul/body, spirit/letter, and internal/external, barely betray their theological provenance. In this sense, metaphysical anti-Semitism brings out the legacy of Christian anti-Judaism—an old heritage of gloomy images, sinister figures, demonizing metaphors—to which the Jews were nailed over centuries. It is a body of despicable reproaches, perverse slander, and heinous charges that culminate in accusations of deicide. This anti-Judaism—which can also be expressed in a pretended secular laicism and that can even operate in a self-forgetful, unconscious, but not innocent, fashion—has permeated the whole Western metaphysics without being disavowed.

It is legitimate, therefore, to ask a question that so far has been evaded. To the Jew is ascribed the oblivion of being, the most unforgivable fault, but in this fault could one not perceive the echo of another, older, and still unmistakable fault, that of deicide? As in theology, the Jew is responsible for the death of God, so, in ontology, he is responsible for the oblivion of being.

7   The "Purification" of Being: Auschwitz

Heidegger compromises, then, with metaphysics. His mistake is not that of a naive politician who joins with Nazism following the general flow; it is not the ordinary and trivial being led astray. It is instead a philosophical error, the error of the philosopher—of the philosopher who had himself put metaphysics in question.

Heidegger compromises in two ways: he accepts the compromise of National Socialism, allowing himself to be involved, because even before he compromises his path, he exposes it to ruin, destines it to failure. This occurs when—along that path on which he has pushed himself alone, having moved from his outpost to peer into what ought to be the soaring future of the German people, in the cold night of being before the dawn light of the other beginning—he runs into the Jew.

But what Jew? Not one of the many—not one of his pupils, not one of his teachers, not one of his friends, not one of his lovers. Not Hannah. Instead, he comes across the shadow of the Jew—the specter, the projection, the figural Jew burdened by a metaphysical weight. This is the *Jude* who must answer for his belonging to *Judentum.*

But how? The Jew seems always to have escaped the attempt to conceptualize his essence. The more philosophers have tried metaphysically to comprehend the Jew as a figure, a phenomenon, whose essence has to be sought behind—or rather beyond (*metà*)— the more the Jew has evaded such attempts at comprehension. This is why he has been rejected, refused—from Kant to Hegel. Hegel sees in the Jew a heart of stone, petrified in his Pharisaic letter, a remnant that will not let itself be overcome, that defies resistance, and that should thus be excluded from the dialectic of world history.

For Heidegger too, the Jew is an obstacle, a barrier in his path through the history of being. The easiest way to remove him, to free up the terrain, is to define him. What other method could be effective against those who, by definition, trespass and exceed the boundaries? So Heidegger tries to grasp their secret and immutable essence, the metaphysical arcanum of Judaism. To define the Jew, he falls back on metaphysics; gives in to the impulse to legitimize the atavistic repugnance for that Other, who is the next; supports the *Kult der Art*, the formative imprint that must remain identical; and shares, without mentioning it, the autopoietic myth of Germanness as that which stands in opposition to the shapeless, unformed people. The point of exception here is that Heidegger also raises the topic of a metaphysics of the Jew—a topic on which he bestows ontological significance, and that he bases on an invention, that of "race." Here metaphysical anti-Semitism makes explicit the absence of a foundation for every anti-Semitism.

He does not reshape the question; instead, he exacerbates it. He says that there is a "Jewish question," a *Judenfrage,* and binds it to the *Seinsfrage,* the question of being. Never before has the Jew had more importance—he now appears at the heart of being and of philosophy. And never before has he represented so great a threat.

The Jew Heidegger meets up with there, along the history of being, blocks his way, prevents him from reaching the source, purity, *Reinheit*. It is as if the Jew warned him: there is no source and there is no purity. Neither source, nor origin, nor purity, nor authenticity, nor autochthony—these are not for the Jew, but not for the German either.

That warning sounds to Heidegger like a threat—even more, it seems to articulate what the *Ruf des Gewissens*, the "call of conscience," has already been repeating to him for a long time. The Jew tells him that his *Entscheidung*, his decision, or rather, his *Scheidung*, his "cutting off," himself heading toward being, is an interrupted path.

The Jew undermines being. He jeopardizes its safety and purity, he anarchically subverts the *arché*. This is what the *Judenfrage* has to do with the *Seinsfrage*. Jews are uncomfortable witnesses of the noncoincidence of the self, of the immemorial expropriation, of the insuperable otherness, of the impossibility to be by oneself. They hinder every project of appropriation, every foundation and self-foundation, every compulsion to fulfillment. Therefore National Socialism gave them the status of enemies.

In the eyes of those who think that the question of being is the authentic question for the West, the place of the Jews begins to become uncertain, unsteady and vacillating. What place in the history of being could anyone ever have who threatens it so profoundly? The nonplace of the Jews becomes unavoidably concrete.

Judaism is, Heidegger asserts, complicit in metaphysics—each supports the other. To recover from metaphysics, which is the illness of the West, it is necessary, then, to recover from Judaism. But Judaism offers no possibility of remittance. Consequently, the only genuine chance of salvation for the West lies in retracing the path to back its uncontaminated origin, back to the purity that it is in danger is losing forever. The Jew encountered on that path, the Jew who is complicit in metaphysics, is the concretized being-there, the being (*Seiende*) that, split from being (*Sein*), makes its own rootlessness planetary, preventing access to being, whose machinations have already become part of the workings of world history.

In an exaggerated ontological difference, the Jew already appears as the being that, detached from being, has lost any possibility of regaining a reference to being. Accused of having abandoned being, the Jew is condemned to being abandoned by being.

Proceeding up there, alone on the brink of the abyss, Heidegger senses that the Jew he has encountered is not a petrified and obsolete remnant of which the West—which, in its will to be "total," is (as Schmitt claimed) "catholic" by vocation—can rid itself.[28] Heidegger perceives that the Jew is beyond—that indeed he *is* the beyond. The Jew is not the ontological enemy. The limit that the Jew represents is not some wartime "line in the sand," but rather the limit of the beyond that only the Other, in his otherness, can disclose.

Yet Heidegger steps back. More important to him is being and so he lets the Jew fall away. He reiterates a gesture that has often been repeated by philosophers. For the Jew there is no place in the history of being. Heidegger's gesture of exclusion, however, is much more disturbing than anything that has gone before because it is accomplished in a time of poverty, in the night of the world, on the edge of the abyss. Thus, he does not hesitate to speak of a "first purification of being in the face of its profound disfigurement by the domination over being."[29] When he writes in the early 1940s, however, the *Reinigung des Seins*—the purification of being—has already become *Vernichtung*, annihilation.

After the *Black Notebooks,* Auschwitz appears more closely connected with the oblivion of being. As for Heidegger, the questions multiply, at least for those who do not look for hasty answers. Even so, he has provided those concepts that today allow a reflection on the Shoah: from *enframing, Gestell,* to technology, from the banality of evil to the "fabrication of corpses."[30] Before being political, Heidegger's mistake has been philosophical. The mistake lies in the compromise with metaphysics that leads him to a definition of the *essence* of the Jew, rather than to see in this "Other" the passage to a new beyond. If he had recognized the trauma of Auschwitz, he would have let that trauma shatter the history of being.

Notes

1. See Martin Heidegger, *Überlegungen XII–XV (Schwarze Hefte 1939–1941), Gesamtausgabe* 96, ed. Peter Trawny (Frankfurt: Klostermann, 2014), 243.

2. Hannah Arendt, "The Enlightenment and the Jewish Question," in *The Jewish Writings,* ed. Jerome Kohn and Ron H. Feldman, 3–18 (New York: Schocken Books, 2007) (quote on 3).

3. See Jakob Katz, "A State within a State: The History of an Anti-Semitic Slogan," in *Emancipation and Assimilation: Studies in Modern Jewish History,* 47–76 (Farborough: Gregg, 1972).

4. Immanuel Kant, *The Conflict of the Faculties,* trans. Mary J. Gregor (Lincoln: University of Nebraska Press, 1992), 95.

5. Georg Wilhelm Friedrich Hegel, *On Christianity: Early Theological Writings,* trans. T. M. Knox (Chicago: University of Chicago Press, 1948), 198. See Jacques Derrida, *Glas,* trans. J. P. Leavey (Lincoln: University of Nebraska Press, 1986), 52.

6. Friedrich Nietzsche, *The Dawn of Day,* trans. J. M. Kennedy (Dover: Courier Corporation, 2012), section 205, p. 211.

7. Adolf Hitler, *Mein Kampf* (Munich: Zentralverlag des NSDAP, 1942), 329–362.

8. Peter Trawny, *Heidegger und der Mythos der jüdischen Weltverschwörung* (Frankfurt: Klostermann, 2014), 31.

9. *Überlegungen II–VI (Schwarze Hefte 1931–1938), Gesamtausgabe* 94, ed. Peter Trawny (Frankfurt: Klostermann, 2014), 46.

10. See *Überlegungen VII–XI (Schwarze Hefte 1938/39), Gesamtausgabe* 95, ed. Peter Trawny (Frankfurt: Klostermann, 2014), 141, 147.

11. See *Überlegungen II–VI, Gesamtausgabe* 94, p. 474.

12. *Überlegungen XII–XV, Gesamtausgabe* 96, p. 56.

13. *Überlegungen XII–XV, Gesamtausgabe* 96, p. 56.

14. Carl Schmitt, "Die Verfassung der Freiheit," *Deutsche Juristenzeitung* 40 (1935): 1133–1135.

15. *Überlegungen XII–XV, Gesamtausgabe* 96, p. 56.

16. *Überlegungen XII–XV, Gesamtausgabe* 96, p. 262.

17. See *Überlegungen VII–XI, Gesamtausgabe* 95, pp. 48–49.

18. *Überlegungen II–VI, Gesamtausgabe* 94, p. 195.

19. *Überlegungen II–VI, Gesamtausgabe* 94, p. 171.

20. *Überlegungen II–VI, Gesamtausgabe* 94, p. 31.

21. Max Weber, *Gesamtausgabe*, vol. II/9: *Briefe 1915–1917* (Tübingen: Mohr Siebeck, 2008), 66.

22. Edmund Husserl, *The Crisis of European Sciences and Transcendental Phenomenology: An Introduction to Phenomenological Philosophy*, trans. David Carr (Evanston, IL: Northwestern University Press, 1970), 290.

23. Plato, *Theaetetus*, 146c–e.

24. Ludwig Wittgenstein, *The Blue and Brown Books: Preliminary Studies for the Philosophical Investigations* (Oxford: Blackwell, 1964), 18; Ludwig Wittgenstein, *Zettel*, ed. G. E. M. Anscombe and Georg Henrik von Wright, trans. G. E. M. Anscombe (Berkeley: University of California Press, 1967), section 444, p. 118; Ludwig Wittgenstein, *Philosophical Investigations*, trans. G. E. M. Anscombe (New York: Macmillan, 1958), section 92, p. 43.

25. Carl Schmitt, "Die deutsche Rechtswissenschaft im Kampf gegen den jüdischen Geist: Schlußwort auf der Tagung der Reichsgruppe Hochschullehrer des NSRB am 3. und 4. Oktober 1936," *Deutsche Juristen-Zeitung* 41 (1936): 1193–1199.

26. Waldemar Gurian, *Um des Reiches Zukunft* (Freiburg: Herder, 1932), 77.

27. Hans Blüher, "Die Gegengründung des nachchristlichen Judentums," in Hans Blüher, *Die Erhebung Israels gegen die christlichen Güter*, 87–138 (Hamburg: Hanseatischer Verlagsanstalt, 1931).

28. *Überlegungen VII–XI, Gesamtausgabe* 95, pp. 325–326.

29. *Überlegungen XII–XV, Gesamtausgabe* 96, p. 238.

30. Martin Heidegger, *Bremen and Freiburg Lectures: Insight into That Which Is and Basic Principles of Thinking*, trans. A. Mitchell (Bloomington: Indiana University Press, 2012), 53.

13

Metaphysics, Christianity, and the "Death of God" in Heidegger's *Black Notebooks* (1931–1941)

Holger Zaborowski

Heidegger's *Black Notebooks* are incredibly complex texts.[1] More than a few of his notes are quite irritating and shocking as well as highly ambivalent and challenging for any interpretative approach. It does not come as a surprise that the ongoing public discussion of these texts is contentious. However, this very debate—be it in print, in speech, or online—still tends to underplay their intrinsic intricacy. A proper scholarly examination is much needed even though any interpretation has to be preliminary for now, given that not all the *Black Notebooks* have been published yet.[2] For what is currently at stake is the legacy of Heidegger's thought in general. This is why scholars face a great many open questions with a certain level of urgency.

There are general hermeneutical questions that focus not only on the proper method, as it were, of reading and interpreting the *Black Notebooks*, but also on Heidegger's reasons for writing them and, more importantly, for deciding to let them be published as part of his collected works. Other questions concern their relation to *Being and Time*, to his lecture courses and seminars, to his book-length manuscripts such as *Contributions to Philosophy*[3] and *Mindfulness*,[4] and to his postwar publications. And there are, of course, specific questions with respect to the *Black Notebooks* that address Heidegger's relation to National Socialism and the overall political dimensions of his thought,[5] his anti-Semitism, his interpretation of modernity and the course of Western philosophy, and his idea of a history of being.

A question that has so far not yet attracted a great deal of scholarly attention, even though it is crucial for an understanding of these texts, is Heidegger's relation to Christianity in the *Black Notebooks*. This chapter deals with this topic in an initial and somewhat tentative manner. For the reasons mentioned above, this is what is at best possible at this early stage in reading the *Black Notebooks*. The following remarks—observations rather than fully fleshed-out interpretations—focus on (1) the general significance of Christianity in the *Black Notebooks*; (2) the relation between Christianity and Western metaphysics; and (3) the significance of Heidegger's comments on Christianity in the *Black Notebooks*. A concluding paragraph briefly discusses (4) what an examination of Heidegger's comments on Christianity in the *Black Notebooks* teaches us about how to read these texts.

1   The General Significance of Christianity in the *Black Notebooks*

Heidegger frequently emphasized the importance of his religious and theological origins.[6] As a young lecturer at Freiburg University, he transformed the Husserlian understanding of phenomenology and moved toward a formally indicative "hermeneutics of facticity," which eventually led to the fundamental ontology of *Being and Time*. In so doing, he was heavily influenced by his reading of the Christian tradition—that is, of, among others, St. Paul, St. Augustine, medieval mystics such as Meister Eckhart, Martin Luther, Blaise Pascal, and Søren Kierkegaard.

By the late 1920s, however, Heidegger seemed to have lost interest in this tradition, both for personal reasons and because his philosophical interests now had shifted toward Plato, Immanuel Kant, and the German idealists. Even his famous lecture "Phenomenology and Theology" (delivered in 1927 and 1928), which one could interpret as a counterexample, shows that the Christian and, more specifically, the theological tradition no longer played the important role it had once played (without, of course, ever having turned his thinking into religious thought itself).[7] He slowly moved away from his Christian and theological origins and developed an increasingly critical reading of this tradition as a whole (not just of the "system of Catholicism" that he had abandoned as early as 1919[8]). So in the 1930s, he addresses the question of God in a way that largely leaves Christianity behind. Particularly in his lecture courses on Hölderlin and Nietzsche and in the so-called being-historical manuscripts, the "absence" or "death" of God moves onto center stage. Heidegger now tries to imagine some kind of poetic-philosophical religion of the "last God"[9] or the "coming Gods."[10]

In his works of the late 1920s and 1930s, as they were know so far, there are relatively few detailed comments on Christianity. In fact, from a certain standpoint these comments are surprisingly rare. But given Heidegger's understanding of phenomenology, perhaps this should not come as a surprise after all. From the early 1920s, he emphasized the atheistic character of phenomenology,[11] thus not suggesting that there is no God, but that an important distinction ought to be made not only between phenomenology and theology, but also between philosophy and faith and that, therefore, philosophy should refrain from dealing with what he considered distinctly religious questions such as the question of God's existence. "The philosopher," Heidegger famously said, "does not believe" but instead experiences the radical uncertainty and questionability of human life.[12]

Readers well versed both in Christian thought and in Heidegger's philosophy, however, often find resonances of his religious and theological background even in his work of the late 1920s and 1930s. There is no question that there is often an implicit, possibly at times unconscious involvement with Christianity on Heidegger's part, and his later thought cannot be understood without carefully considering its Christian roots. Yet, on the rare occasions when this involvement is made explicit, it tends to be quite superficial, over-generalizing and stereotypical, lacking Heidegger's otherwise well-known hermeneutical sensitivity and betraying his knowledge of the Christian tradition (it would have been fascinating if he had reread Aquinas over against the Neo-Scholastics as he reread Aristotle over against the Aristotelian tradition).

Whoever reads the *Black Notebooks* carefully, then, cannot fail to notice with a certain degree of surprise that Christianity and the Christian tradition indeed play a significant role in these texts. What is perhaps most surprising about Heidegger's numerous comments on Christianity in the *Black Notebooks* is their relatively detailed and multifaceted character. Only in the *Black Notebooks* do students of Heidegger's thought find him dealing with such a broad spectrum of issues related to Christianity. He addresses Christianity in general, but also Protestantism and Catholicism in particular. There are offhand remarks about the Jesuits;[13] comments on the relation of the Catholic Church to the National Socialist state (including a brief comment on the Concordat of 1933);[14] on the "non-German," "Roman," and "total" character of the Catholic;[15] on Blaise Pascal;[16] on "the lack of significance and the confusion of the so-called dialectical theology"[17] (that Heidegger previously thought quite highly of and that he now considers "Protestant Jesuitism of the most evil observance"[18]); on the "cowardly profession of Christianity to consider oneself better";[19] on Mk 12:17 ("And Jesus answering said unto them, Render unto Caesar the things that are Caesar's, and to God the things that are God's");[20] on the Church Fathers as "the end of Greek culture [*Griechentum*]";[21] on "Christian philosophy";[22] or even biographical remarks about his mother, a "pious woman who bore with no bitterness and with suspecting foresight the way of her son, who only seemingly turned away from God."[23]

In a famous letter to Karl Jaspers written on July 1, 1935, Heidegger speaks of two "thorns" in the flesh (thus alluding to St. Paul in 2 Cor 12:7), the "confrontation with the faith of my origins and the failure of the rectorate."[24] It would be wrong to read this as a merely autobiographical remark. There is no question that Heidegger's philosophy after 1934, particularly his increasing focus on the nihilism of modernity and his shift, roughly speaking, from a philosophy of will and power to one of letting-be and mindfulness, can only (but of course not exclusively) be understood against the background of the failure of his rectorate (and of the general political situation, which, in Heidegger's eyes, was extremely closely related to the problems associated with his rectorate). The same can be said with respect to his relation to Christianity. It also provides an important backdrop against which his thought of the 1930s and 1940s must be read. Being-historical thinking is, as will be shown further below, thinking vis-à-vis the death of God and, therefore, a confrontation with the Christian tradition and with Heidegger's previous Christian faith. That is, he leaves the sharp distinction between philosophy and theology or religious faith behind. The kind of thinking about the event or destiny of being that Heidegger now pursues cannot limit itself in the way he suggested in the early 1920s. It must address and try to understand the phenomenon of Christianity. In other and already well-known texts by Heidegger from this period, this confrontation with Christianity is by and large implicit or limited to brief and suggestive remarks; in the *Black Notebooks* it has become quite explicit. Christianity now plays a rather important role—as belonging to the history of Western metaphysics.

2   The Completion of Western Metaphysics and the Death of God

Particularly in the 1930s, Heidegger deals intensively with Nietzsche's thought and his dictum that "God is dead." He not only interprets Nietzsche's philosophy as a metaphysics and as an inversion of Platonism; he also holds that Western metaphysics has been fulfilled in Nietzsche's nihilism and its message of God's death. As the *Black Notebooks* show, Heidegger is well aware of the controversial character of his own claims regarding the interpretation of Nietzsche's philosophy.[25] In the *Black Notebooks*, however, he not only argues that Nietzsche is a metaphysician. He also points out that he "speaks Christianly" when he says that "God is dead"[26] and that Nietzsche's idea of an "eternal recurrence" "is only a Christian escape [*Ausweg*]."[27] Western metaphysics and Christianity are, therefore, closely intertwined. Just as Nietzsche could not leave metaphysics behind, he could, in Heidegger's eyes, also not leave Christianity behind. The anti-Christian presupposes and continues Christianity in the same way the anti-Platonic cannot but continue the history of Platonism. From this perspective, the end and completion of metaphysics is at the same time the end and completion of Christianity.

But it is not just Nietzsche who is important for Heidegger's view of Christianity in the *Black Notebooks*. Even more important is Hölderlin's poetic insight into the "absence" (*Fehl*) of God. When Heidegger writes that "we have already lived for a long time and will continue to live for a long time in the age of the departing God,"[28] he is clearly alluding to Hölderlin, whom he singles out for particular attention again and again. For the Hölderlin-ian absence or "refuge of the Gods," he finds considerable evidence in the people "who turn 'their' faith into a movement," in the movement of the "German Christians," and in tendencies to found a position on "godlessness" or even on indifference.[29] According to Heidegger, contemporary culture in general (including modern forms of Christianity and religion[30]) is oriented against God or the Gods as they were once understood and makes them disappear. He argues that those who claim to "make history"—that is, those who express a subjectivist and, ultimately, technological understanding of their relation to history—work toward the "last withdrawal of the great Gods."[31]

For Heidegger, not only has God departed or died. It is—consequently and in spite of any signs that could be interpreted as a revitalization of it—Christianity itself that has also died. Heidegger is well aware of an understanding of religion as "an institution that is useful for one's purposes"[32] and argues that "for the many," "*religions*" are always neces-sary (while for the individual person "there is only *the God*").[33] He clearly acknowledges a move, or even escape, to Christianity and the tendency to develop a "Christian culture" as a countermovement to the contemporary age.[34] Yet, he cannot take the general need for, nor the instrumental approach to, religion in general or any kind of "rechristianization," as it were, philosophically seriously. For the move toward Christianity (as well as any instrumental understanding of "religion"), he argues, is characterized by an "indifferent misunderstanding of being" such that being in general cannot "beset us."[35] To him, these contemporary tendencies do not show any kind of real power or significance on the part of Christianity any longer. At best, they concern the surface of culture. This is why Heidegger speaks in almost sociological terms of a "progressive secularization"[36] and of the "increasing powerlessness of the Christian faith."[37]

He interprets the death of Christianity, together with the godlessness of Bolshevism, as a sign that "we have really and knowingly entered the age of the abandonment of being."[38] It is against this background that Heidegger can write (presumably as an imperative to himself): "To present a history of philosophy as the history of a great becoming lonely."[39] Loneliness grew not simply because there is no God any longer and because "we are too 'worldly' and, therefore, godless."[40] This would be all too easy and all too superficial an explanation. For Heidegger, a merely historical, sociological, or psychological analysis cannot help really to understand what happened to Christianity and to the idea, or belief, that there is indeed a God. For the loneliness grew because of the forgetfulness and withdrawal of being, to which only the "lonely" poet Hölderlin can provide a response.[41] This loneliness, however, not only concerns religion. It has momentous implications. For it is not only true that "God is away," as Heidegger points out. He also states—against the background of both Nietzsche's and Hölderlin's analyses of modernity—that "things are exploited; knowledge has fallen into ruin; action has gone blind."[42] For if there is no God, no orientation at all is possible. Everything is in ruins. This means that the crisis or, to be more precise, the dying of Christianity needs to be conceived of being-historically—just as the end of metaphysics, too, needs to be understood. Christianity has, therefore, not only contributed to the forgetfulness of being; it has itself become subject to the abandonment of being.

What is, therefore, perhaps most important and surprising about the *Black Notebooks* is the emphasis Heidegger puts on the close connection between Christianity and Western metaphysics. He explicitly argues that "we still stand entirely outside of the new area of the great decision of the mind: 1. the confrontation with [*Auseinandersetzung*], and clear stance toward, *Christianity* and all of *Western philosophy*."[43] In so arguing (and, second, in mentioning the "confrontation with Nietzsche" immediately afterward), he implies that Christianity and Western philosophy are so closely intertwined that they can be considered almost one. They both have been completed and stand under the verdict of the death of God. This verdict, however, does not leave Heidegger entirely pessimistic. For he raises the question of God in a new way: "Where is God? Before and actually asking the question: Do we have a 'where'? And do we stand in it such that we can ask for the God?"[44] Heidegger thus remains open to the "furthest vicinity of the last God."[45] This "last God" is, according to him, "totally other over against the past ones, particularly the Christian one."[46] This is no longer the God of Christianity or of Western metaphysics. It is the God of Heidegger's own thought that he conceives of with Hölderlin's poetry at his side.

3   The Significance of Heidegger's Comments on Christianity in the *Black Notebooks*

Heidegger's critical confrontation with Christianity in the *Black Notebooks* has three dimensions. There is, first, a *philosophical* or, more specifically, a *being-historical* dimension—that is, it is a confrontation from within the framework of Heidegger's reading of the history of Western metaphysics as the history of the first beginning and of the forgetfulness of being. This means that the task of really understanding the meaning of Christianity is no longer left to theologians and religious people. Only being-historical thinking is, according to Heidegger, able to make sense of Christianity and particularly of what he considers its crisis and death. There is no doubt that there is also, second, an *autobiographical* and *personal* dimension to it. In the *Black Notebooks*, Heidegger is still—or, perhaps, again and more forcefully than ever—dealing with his own religious origins and his personal loss of faith in Christianity. He is now explaining it with respect to the general crisis, or "completion," of Christianity due to the forgetfulness and the withdrawal of being and against the background of his somewhat Gnostic talk of the "last" or "coming" God. There is, third, a *historical* and *cultural-critical* dimension, because when Heidegger talks about Christianity or Christian issues, he incorporates many references not only to concrete movements and tendencies within Christianity, but also to events and phenomena in the wider culture that he characterizes as the "age of utter questionlessness" and that he very closely relates to Christianity.[47] For the crisis of Christianity and the death of God both have presuppositions and implications that reach far beyond the realm of religion, strictly speaking.

Not only are these three dimensions provocative in themselves, but the often-puzzling relations between them raise particularly important questions and invite both comments and criticism. It is often not sufficiently clear from which perspective Heidegger writes about Christianity. The three different perspectives, or dimensions, are often intermingled such as to be almost indistinguishable. This essentially means confusing the being-historical and ontic perspectives in a way that Heidegger himself would otherwise have considered impossible.[48] Furthermore, his critique of Christianity—particularly in its simplistic tendencies—is often anything but fair and persuasive. It is rather based on dubious assumptions and reflective of the kind of highly ideological Weltanschauung that Heidegger criticizes throughout his career.[49] For example, he only focuses on Western Christianity—that is, on the Catholic and Protestant traditions. He shows no particular interest in the details even of these traditions that could contradict, or modify, his apodictic statements. What can critically be said about his reading of the Western philosophical tradition—that it is highly eclectic and perspectival and that it often does not do full justice to the complexities of the thinkers he has chosen to discuss—can also be said with respect to Heidegger's often crude comments on Christianity. Ironically, his own position is now characterized by what he accuses the Western tradition of: a forgetfulness of being. For the modern tendency toward a closed Weltanschauung that no longer leaves anything open and thus evades the basic questionability of human existence, he holds, shows the nihilism of the completion of metaphysics in modernity. There is no question that, however insightful some of Heidegger's comments are, in many of his notes about Christianity he falls below his own intellectual standards (the ones about Nietzsche's Christianity, for example).

It needs to be asked, now, without psychologizing or trivializing anything, how the problematic nature of many of his notes about Christianity and the puzzling intermingling of a philosophical, an autobiographical, and a historical and cultural perspective can properly be understood. I would like to suggest that the problematic and irritating character of Heidegger's comments on Christianity in the *Black Notebooks* betrays a crisis that itself has three closely related dimensions. It is primarily a philosophical crisis. After the publication of *Being and Time*—that is, after what he conceives of as the failure of the project of *Being and Time*—Heidegger looks for new ways to understand and practice philosophy. What may appear retrospectively as a relatively consistent intellectual path is by no means smooth and without internal tensions and ruptures. Particularly the 1930s and 1940s are characterized by these intellectual tensions, triggered not only by the failure of his own previous philosophical position, but also, and more importantly, by what Heidegger considers the completion of Western metaphysics in Nietzsche's nihilism. He now also realizes that this completion is closely related to his personal situation—that is, the "thorn" of his having lost his Christian faith. And he realizes that it is intimately intertwined, too, with the cultural and historical turmoil of the times, of which the failure of the rectorate is an important example. In his lectures, seminars, and manuscripts, he is dealing with this threefold crisis in different but clearly related ways. The *Black Notebooks*, too, are documents reflecting this crisis and need to be read as such.

4   Conclusion, or How to Read the *Black Notebooks*

This interpretation of Heidegger's comments on Christianity allows some concluding remarks about a necessary hermeneutics of the *Black Notebooks*. Heidegger's multidimensional crisis in the 1930s and 1940s may not fully explain everything he wrote in the *Black Notebooks*. There is no single key to reading and interpreting them. But considering this interpretation can help to contextualize the *Black Notebooks* and shed light on them, not only on their tentative and also repetitive character, but particularly on some of their most problematic, shocking, and objectionable passages—beyond the undesirable alternatives of exaggerating or of playing down their significance.

It goes without saying, but needs to be emphasized in the context of the current debate, that great philosophers are great because of their many great thoughts. This, however, does not prevent them from being constrained by social, political, psychological, and historical circumstances and by what later readers would rightly consider moral and intellectual failures. In the 1930s and 1940s, Heidegger was a very lonely thinker, partly because he chose to be lonely. He felt misunderstood by his contemporaries, disrespected what they could have offered him, and limited himself to a reading of a small number of key figures in Western metaphysics and to thoughts about the possibility of a new relation between human beings and Being and the transition toward another beginning of thought. There is no doubt that this loneliness oscillated between hubris and despair and, among other factors, led to the errors and significant problems that Heidegger research now has to acknowledge, to try to understand, and to deal with.

It was not until the mid-1940s that Heidegger found a new tranquillity of thinking and moved toward his mature thought about language, poetry, technology and science, release-ment, or letting-be (*Gelassenheit*), and mindfulness. Now, the history of being no longer plays the kind of role that he attributed to it in the 1930s. His late thinking is also considerably less polemical than that of the 1930s and 1940s. It is almost as if Heidegger, without ever "reconverting," finds a new relation to Christianity such that he eventually will ask the priest, theologian, and philosopher Bernhard Welte, also from Messkirch, to speak at this funeral.[50]

There is, however, also no doubt that his later philosophy can only be understood against the background of the crisis of the 1930s and 1940s. Heidegger knew this very well. It may also explain why he wanted the *Black Notebooks* published. The most likely interpreta-tion, therefore, is not at all that he considered them the esoteric heart of his philosophy such that they should finally shed the definitive interpretative light on his collected works. Heidegger, on the contrary, most likely considered them important because they show the unfolding and crisis of this thought in the 1930s and 1940s. He never wrote "works"—at least as he thought of them—the completion of which would make the path that led toward them negligible. Even errors and detours off the beaten track seemed to him important in order to facilitate an understanding of his thinking—which was never a result, but always a process, an event, something that happened to him.

Scholars of Heidegger's thought have to take this crisis seriously; it provides many chal-lenges and leaves many unanswered questions. They should, however, not fall prey to the temptation, so common in the current debate, to make the extraordinary the key to understanding the ordinary. Heidegger does not need apologetics. Any blind, naive, or even tendentious defense of Heidegger would betray his own philosophy. What he needs is something different (and the contributions to this book can be read as attempts to provide precisely this): a hermeneutics not of hate and prejudice, but of turning toward the texts themselves—in order to read carefully what he writes, to put it into wider philosophical, biographical, and historical contexts, to identify difficulties and problems, to interpret and judge it soberly, and to criticize it fairly.

Notes

1. So far, the following volumes have been published: *Überlegungen II–VI* (*Schwarze Hefte 1931–1938*), *Gesamtausgabe* 94, ed. Peter Trawny (Frankfurt: Klostermann, 2014); *Überlegungen VII–XI* (*Schwarze Hefte 1938/39), Gesamtausgabe 95*, ed. Peter Trawny (Frankfurt: Klostermann, 2014); *Überlegungen XII–XV (Schwarze Hefte 1939–1941), Gesamtausgabe 96*, ed. Peter Trawny (Frankfurt: Klostermann, 2014); *Anmerkun-gen I–V (Schwarze Hefte 1942–1948), Gesamtausgabe 97*, ed. Peter Trawny (Frankfurt: Klostermann, 2015).

2. It also remains open at this point exactly what differences there are between the *Überlegungen* (*Consid-erations*, vols. 94–96 of Heidegger's *Gesamtausgabe*) and *Anmerkungen* (*Remarks*, vols. 97 and 98 of the *Gesamtausgabe*) (and the other *Black Notebooks*, to be published in vols. 99–102) and how these differences

are to be interpreted. This chapter limits itself to a discussion of Heidegger's *Überlegungen* (1931–1941), with a special focus on the first volume of the *Notebooks* (*Gesamtausgabe* 94), since the topic of Christianity is most prominent in these texts. Heidegger's confrontation with both Christianity and Judaism plays an important role in *Anmerkungen I–V* (*Gesamtausgabe* 97), too. Because this volume was not published until the spring of 2015, it could not be considered for the purposes of this chapter. For helpful comments on an earlier draft of the chapter I wish to thank the editors of the present volume, as well as Dr. Chris Bremmers, Dr. Antonio Cimino, Professor Françoise Dastur, Dr. Alfred Denker, Professor Gert-Jan van der Heiden, Dr. Bogdan Minca, and Professor Ben Vedder. I also would like to thank Professor van der Heiden for the opportunity to present the chapter at a conference at Radboud Universiteit Nijmegen on April 2, 2015.

3. Martin Heidegger, *Beiträge zur Philosophie (Vom Ereignis), Gesamtausgabe* 65, ed. Friedrich-Wilhelm von Herrmann (Frankfurt: Klostermann, 1989); for the (new) English translation see Martin Heidegger, *Contributions to Philosophy (of the Event)*, trans. Richard Rojcewicz and Daniela Vallega-Neu (Bloomington: Indiana University Press, 2012).

4. Martin Heidegger, *Besinnung, Gesamtausgabe* 66, ed. Friedrich-Wilhelm von Herrmann (Frankfurt: Klostermann, 1997); translated into English by Parvis Emad and Thomas Kalary as *Mindfulness* (London: Continuum, 2006).

5. For a detailed discussion of Heidegger's relation to National Socialism see Alfred Denker and Holger Zaborowski, eds., *Heidegger und der Nationalsozialismus, Heidegger-Jahrbuch*, vols. 4 and 5 (Freiburg: Karl Alber, 2010), and my *"Eine Frage von Irre und Schuld?" Martin Heidegger und der Nationalsozialismus* (Frankfurt: Fischer, 2010).

6. For Heidegger's religious origins see Alfred Denker, Hans-Helmuth Gander, and Holger Zaborowski, eds., *Heidegger und die Anfänge seines Denkens, Heidegger-Jahrbuch* 1 (Freiburg: Karl Alber, 2004); see also my "A 'Genuinely Religiously Orientated Personality': Martin Heidegger and the Religious and Theological Origins of His Philosophy," in *The Companion to Heidegger's Philosophy of Religion*, ed. Andrew Wiercinsky and Sean McGrath, 3–19 (Amsterdam: Rodopi, 2010).

7. Martin Heidegger, "Phänomenologie und Theologie," in *Wegmarken, Gesamtausgabe* 9, ed. Friedrich-Wilhelm von Herrmann (Frankfurt: Klostermann, [1967] 1976).

8. See Heidegger's letter to Engelbert Krebs of January 9, 1919, in *Heidegger und die Anfänge seines Denkens, Heidegger-Jahrbuch* 1, ed. Alfred Denker, Hans-Helmuth Gander, and Holger Zaborowski, 67–68 (Freiburg: Karl Alber, 2004).

9. See Heidegger, *Beiträge zur Philosophie*, 403–417.

10. For the "coming Gods" see, for example, Heidegger, *Überlegungen XII–XV*, pp. 136f.

11. For his understanding of philosophy as atheistic see Martin Heidegger, *Phänomenologische Interpretationen zu Aristoteles: Ausarbeitung für die Marburger und die Göttinger Philosophische Fakultät (1922)*, ed. Günther Neumann (Stuttgart: Reclam, 2002), 28.

12. Martin Heidegger, "Der Begriff der Zeit (Vortrag 1924)," in Martin Heidegger, *Der Begriff der Zeit, Gesamtausgabe* 64, ed. Friedrich-Wilhelm von Herrmann, 105–125 (Frankfurt: Klostermann, 2004) (quote on 105).

13. Heidegger, *Überlegungen II–VI*, p. 180; see also Heidegger, *Überlegungen VII–XI*, p. 326.

14. "Die katholische Kirche—sie allein 'ist' Christentum—wie jederzeit bemüht, ihre Gegner zu haben—um sich an ihnen zu messen, wach und stark zu bleiben" (Heidegger, *Überlegungen II–VI*, p. 182). See p. 184 for a reference to the concordat, the treaty between Germany and the Vatican.

15. Heidegger, *Überlegungen VII–XI*, p. 325f. For the "total" character of "'Catholic' thought" see also Heidegger, *Überlegungen VII–XI*, p. 429.

16. Heidegger, *Überlegungen VII–XI*, pp. 342–346.

17. Heidegger, *Überlegungen II–VI*, p. 51.

18. Heidegger, *Überlegungen II–VI*, p. 91.

19. Heidegger, *Überlegungen II–VI*, p. 351.

20. King James Version. See Martin Heidegger, *Überlegungen II–VI*, pp. 439ff.

21. Heidegger, *Überlegungen VII–XI*, p. 47.

22. Heidegger, *Überlegungen XII–XV*, pp. 214f.

23. "Die Mutter—meine einfache Erinnerung an diese fromme Frau, die ohne Bitterkeit den Weg des scheinbar gottabgekehrten Sohnes im ahnenden Vorblick ertrug" (Heidegger, *Überlegungen II–VI*, p. 320).

24. *Martin Heidegger/Karl Jaspers: Briefwechsel 1920–1963*, ed. Walter Biemel and Hans Saner (Frankfurt: Klostermann/Munich: Piper, 1990), 157.

25. "Nur Einen zu nennen—Nietzsche! Er wird ausgeäubert willkürlich und zufällig—aber keine Anstrengung, sein innerstes Wollen auf Grund und zu Werk und zu Weg zu bringen" (Heidegger, *Überlegungen II–VI*, p. 39).

26. "Nietzsche sagte: 'Gott ist tot'—aber gerade dieses ist christlich gesprochen, eben weil un-christlich" (Heidegger, *Überlegungen II–VI*, p. 76).

27. Heidegger, *Überlegungen II–VI*, p. 76.

28. "Jetzt kommt es an den Tag, dass wir seit langem schon und für lange noch im Weltalter der scheidenden Götter leben" (Heidegger, *Überlegungen II–VI*, p. 167).

29. Heidegger, *Überlegungen II–VI*, p. 185. See also Heidegger, *Überlegungen II–VI*, p. 223, and Heidegger, *Überlegungen VII–XI*, pp. 25, 37, 51, 66f., 144f., 194, for the "refuge of the Gods."

30. See Heidegger, *Überlegungen II–VI*, pp. 522f., for the godless character of modern Christianity; Heidegger, *Überlegungen VII–XI*, p. 110, and Heidegger, *Überlegungen XII–XV*, p. 148, for the godless character of the (modern) "religious people."

31. "Vergnüglich zerrend an den Stricken ihrer Machenschaften und Berechnungen meinen sie, Geschichte zu machen und betreiben nur die letzte Entwöhnung von den großen Göttern. Wie soll hier ein Wort vom Seyn das gehörige Wort finden?" (Heidegger, *Überlegungen II–VI*, p. 372).

32. See Heidegger, *Überlegungen II–VI*, p. 331.

33. "Und deshalb müssen für die Vielen stetes 'Religionen' sein—für die Einzelnen aber ist der Gott" (Heidegger, *Überlegungen II–VI*, p. 398).

34. Heidegger, *Überlegungen II–VI*, p. 40. See p. 92 for Heidegger's reference to the "terrible project of a Christian culture." For the "escape into Christianity" see also Heidegger, *Überlegungen VII–XI*, p. 349.

35. Heidegger, *Überlegungen II–VI*, p. 41.

36. Heidegger, *Überlegungen II–VI*, p. 90.

37. Heidegger, *Überlegungen II–VI*, p. 388; in this context, also see Heidegger, *Überlegungen VII–XI*, pp. 184ff.

38. "… d. h. Gott-losigkeit des Bolschewismus ebenso wie die Abgestorbenheit des Christentums als die großen Zeichen zu nehmen, daß wir in das Zeitalter der Seinsverlassenheit wirklich und wissend eingetreten sind" (Heidegger, *Überlegungen II–VI*, p. 351).

39. "Eine Geschichte der Philosophie darstellen als Geschichte der großen Vereinsamung" (Heidegger, *Überlegungen II–VI*, p. 218).

40. "Das Zeitalter ist nicht deshalb ohne Götter, weil wir zu 'weltlich' und deshalb gottlos geworden sind, sondern weil wir keine Welt haben und nur eine Wirrnis des Seyns" (Heidegger, *Überlegungen II–VI*, p. 218).

41. See Heidegger, *Überlegungen II–VI*, p. 340.

42. "Der Gott ist fort; die Dinge sind vernutzt; das Wissen zerfallen; das Handeln erblindet" (Heidegger, *Überlegungen II–VI*, p. 231).

43. Heidegger, *Überlegungen II–VI*, p. 178. See also the following observation: "Wir müssen einen tiefen und scharfen Verdacht bereithalten, solange alles sich um die Auseinandersetzung mit dem Christentum drückt" (Martin Heidegger, *Überlegungen II–VI*, p. 120).

44. "Wo ist Gott? Zuvor und eigentlich fragen: haben wir ein Wo? Und stehen wir in ihm, daß wir nach dem Gott fragen können?" (Heidegger, *Überlegungen II–VI*, p. 240).

45. See Heidegger, *Überlegungen II–VI*, p. 304: "… die fernste Nähe des letzten Gottes."

46. Heidegger, *Beiträge zur Philosophie*, 403.

47. Heidegger, *Überlegungen II–VI*, p. 440: "Das Zeitalter der völligen Fraglosigkeit bricht an." See also Martin Heidegger, *Überlegungen II–VI*, p. 331; for the relation between Christianity and culture in modernity see Heidegger, *Überlegungen VII–XI*, pp. 70f.

48. Heidegger, *Beiträge zur Philosophie (Vom Ereignis)*, 32ff. and passim.

49. For Heidegger's critique of Weltanschauungen see also Heidegger, *Überlegungen VII–XI*, pp. 18f.

50. See *Martin Heidegger/Bernhard Welte: Briefe und Begegnungen*, ed. Alfred Denker and Holger Zaborowski (Stuttgart: Klett-Cotta, 2003), 124.

IV PHILOSOPHY, POLITICS, AND TECHNOLOGY

14

Nostalgia, Spite, and the Truth of Being

Karsten Harries

While it is not surprising that a rather small number of comments about Jews, made by Martin Heidegger in the *Schwarze Hefte (Black Notebooks)*, should have received so much attention, the danger is that we will miss the forest for the trees, and by isolating a few trees misunderstand both forest and trees. To be sure, Heidegger's is not a welcoming forest. I wonder how many careful readers the often agonizingly tangled and repetitive volumes 94, 95, and 96 of the *Gesamtausgabe*, totaling some 1,200 pages, will really find. Much here, however, is of interest to those concerned with following the twists and turns of Heidegger's *Denkweg*, his path of thinking. Most significant perhaps is that more than any of his other writings the *Schwarze Hefte* reveal Heidegger's ever-darker, ever-more-despairing and spiteful *Grundstimmung* of these years, the darkening in keeping with what was a rapidly darkening age. Heidegger presents himself here as a prophet in a spiritual wilderness, whose often sibylline sayings go unheard or are misunderstood. But I cannot say that I found anything in these many pages that changed my understanding of Heidegger in any essential way. Indeed, despite all that has appeared since, including the many volumes of the *Gesamtausgabe*, also including the books by Farías, Ott, and Faye, what I wrote back in 1976 in "Heidegger as a Political Thinker" still seems to me to have been pretty much on target: "The formal character of *Being and Time*," I wrote, "makes it like a vessel that demands to be filled. This demand does not come to fundamental ontology from without, but is generated by the ontological analysis itself."[1] The *Schwarze Hefte* make clear once again that *Being and Time* and the question of Being it raised remained the foundation of Heidegger's thought; they also make clear that by then Heidegger was convinced that with that book philosophy as traditionally understood, and that also means as he had still understood it when he embarked on *Being and Time*, had come to some sort of end: on *this* path there could be no further progress. And in this Heidegger seems to me to have been right. The philosophically interesting question is whether Heidegger's *Denkweg* is one we philosophers can and should dismiss as just another *Irrweg*, a path that leads us astray, as it did him, or whether there is not only a sense in which philosophy, and not just Heidegger's, has come to some sort of end here, as the *Schwarze Hefte* proclaim over and over, but also a need to engage in another sort of thinking if we are not to lose our humanity. How we answer that question will decide whether we think it important to keep exploring the forest of Heidegger's thought.

But what does that question have to do with Heidegger's embrace of National Socialism? There is indeed such a relationship, a relationship that demands serious attention because unfortunately National Socialism cannot simply be relegated to a barbarian past that today lies happily behind us. The example of Heidegger can help us better understand its roots in the spiritual situation of the age. The *Schwarze Hefte* provide rich material for such a discussion. But serious consideration of that relationship is impeded when the discussion centers on just nine or ten brief passages, mentioning the Jews, torn out of context.

An example of this is provided by an announcement I received for a lecture by Richard Wolin, scheduled for April 23, 2014. Let me quote it in its entirety:

Heidegger intended the *Black Notebooks*, which were recently published in Germany, as the culminating achievement of his 102-volume *Collected Works* edition. They represent among other things, a stark reaffirmation of his philosophical commitment to National Socialism—and as such a point of no return for Heidegger scholarship. But what the *Black Notebooks* also disturbingly reveal is Heidegger's obsession with "World Jewry" in the most negative and cliché-ridden terms: as a pivotal source of cultural and social dissolution that must be eliminated in order to realize National Socialism's "inner truth and greatness" as Heidegger himself put it in 1935. How, then, should one go about resolving the conundrum of a great thinker who remained entirely convinced that the Nazi regime, with its unbridled racism and exterminationist militarism, represented an adequate solution to the "decline of the West"?

Much here is questionable or misleading. First of all: I find it impossible to call the *Schwarze Hefte* the culminating achievement of the 102-volume *Gesamtausgabe*. To be sure, Heidegger wanted them to be published only after all the other volumes had appeared, a wish the executor of his unpublished texts finally chose not quite to honor. But did Heidegger want to conclude the *Gesamtausgabe* with these rambling and repetitious observations and musings, a kind of philosophical monologue, because he considered them his culminating achievement? I very much doubt it. As I suggested, there is little here that will surprise someone familiar with Heidegger's development. Thus they support in tiring detail what a careful reading of *Being and Time* should already have made clear, that the incompleteness of that work was due to the impossible goal Heidegger had set himself there. As he was to remark in the "Letter on 'Humanism,'" a remark anticipated by many of the entries in the *Schwarze Hefte*: "It is everywhere supposed that the attempt in *Being and Time* ended in a blind alley [*Sackgasse*]."[2] Heidegger does not disagree; he leaves the supposition standing: "The thinking that hazards a few steps in *Being and Time* has even today not advanced beyond that publication. But perhaps in the meantime it has in one respect come further into its own matter."[3] The 536 pages that make up volume 94 of the *Gesamtausgabe* support that claim. This further movement led Heidegger to re-describe the path of his thinking, not as a *Sackgasse*, but as a *Holzweg*.[4] And so he gave the most important collection of essays he published the title *Holzwege*. What is the difference? Both suggest a path that comes to a dead end. But the German *Holzweg* has a quite specific meaning: it suggests a path cut by foresters to allow some trees that have been cut down to be brought out of the forest. A *Holzweg* therefore often ends in a clearing or *Lichtung*, one of Heidegger's favorite metaphors to describe *Dasein*. In a sense such a path is a dead end. For a hiker to be on a *Holzweg* means that he has lost his way. But is such a loss of way—what the Greeks called *aporia*—not the beginning of authentic thinking, and thus of philosophy? Heidegger wanted thinking to return to this beginning; to do so, he came to insist, it has to question or destroy—today we can say deconstruct—philosophy as it has come to be established (i.e., it must dig beneath metaphysics, returning to its ground or beginning in order to prepare for a new beginning). And if such a forest clearing often leaves us stumbling in brambles, looking perhaps for some edible berries, that well describes us readers of the *Schwarze Hefte*.

Do the *Schwarze Hefte* support the claim that we find here a "stark reaffirmation of Heidegger's philosophical commitment to National Socialism"? It did not take Heidegger long to realize that the reality did not correspond to what he had hoped for. Only fleetingly, in 1933 and 1934 do we sense genuine enthusiasm, although from the very beginning there are frequent and profound misgivings. Consider the entry that reflects on his assumption of the rectorate: "Pressured to assume the rectorate I act for the first time *against* my inner voices. In this position I will at best be able to *prevent* perhaps this or that. For constructive work—supposing that that is even still possible—the necessary human beings are lacking."[5] The *Schwarze Hefte* support the charge raised by Otto Wacker, at the time secretary of education in the state of Baden, when, having heard Heidegger's rectorial address, he accused him of holding "a kind of 'private National Socialism' that circumvented the perspectives of the party program," that accepted neither the fundamental importance National Socialism attributed to the concept of race, nor the politicization of science on which it insisted.[6] This raises the question of how Heidegger came to understand the real National Socialism and its betrayal of what he had thought its promise. And that other question: How did he understand what in the *Introduction to Metaphysics* he called its inner truth and greatness? To claim that the *Schwarze Hefte* represent a stark reaffirmation of his philosophical commitment to National Socialism is at best misleading. The opposite is more easily defended.

Do the *Schwarze Hefte* show Heidegger to have been obsessed with World Jewry? In the 536 pages of the first of the three recently published volumes, Jews are not even mentioned. I find this silence disturbing, given what took place in the years 1932 to 1938, years covered in this volume, just as I find Heidegger's subsequent almost total silence about the Holocaust disturbing. Such indifference to human suffering is, however, quite in keeping with Heidegger's obsession, not with World Jewry, but with the question of Being, with *Seinsvergessenheit* and S*einsverlassenheit*, the forgetfulness of and abandonment by being, an obsession linked to what Kierkegaard called a teleological suspension of the ethical, of the claims that the world makes on us, a suspension called for by the understanding of authenticity developed in *Being and Time*. Did Heidegger think that the Nazi regime "with its unbridled racism and exterminationist militarism" represented an adequate solution to the "decline of the West," as Wolin suggests? That Heidegger had hoped that National Socialism would stem the "decline of the West" is clear enough, but what he hoped for cannot be linked to "unbridled racism and exterminationist militarism." Quite the opposite! And soon he came to think of National Socialism as just another expression of the modern understanding of reality, which he had come to associate with Nietzsche's last man. With Nietzsche he mournfully wondered whether this last man might not live the longest, where Heidegger was thinking in terms of hundreds of years, a thought he found profoundly depressing. This last man[7] is too unquestioningly sure of his understanding of reality and the pursuit of happiness to fear the "decline of the West."[8]

There are a number of brief passages in volumes 95 and 96 of the *Schwarze Hefte*, which bring us up to 1941, that do mention the Jews; I counted nine or ten, adding up to perhaps two pages. Many of these passages support a charge of anti-Semitism, but not all. Consider for example the following:

Every dogmatism, be it church-political or state-political, necessarily considers as its enemy everything that in its thinking and doing appears to or really does deviate from it, be it the heathens and the godless or the Jews and the communists. In this way of thinking lies a peculiar strength—not of thinking—but in achieving what has been proclaimed.[9]

Or:

One should not express outrage all too noisily about the psychoanalysis of the Jew "Freud" when and as long as one is totally incapable of thinking about everything in any other way than by tracing it as an "expression" of "life" back to "instincts" or the weakening of instinct. This "manner" of thinking, which from the very beginning admits no "being," is pure nihilism.[10]

The majority of these passages do, however, describe the Jews in, as Wolin puts it, "negative and cliché-ridden terms." Consider the first mention of Jews in the *Schwarze Hefte*: "One of the most hidden forms of the gigantic and perhaps the oldest is the unyielding mastery of calculating [*Rechnen*] and questionable trading [*Schieben*] and mixing, which is the foundation of the worldlessnes of Jewry."[11] In another passage Heidegger links this facility with numbers with an empty rationality, which he again associates with Jewry and for which he criticizes Husserl,[12] although more fundamentally he associates it with Descartes.[13]

But if such passages justify a charge of anti-Semitism, we should note that with equal or greater justice the *Schwarze Hefte* reveal Heidegger's anti-Bolshevism, anti–National Socialism, anti-Anglicism, and anti-Americanism, all expressions of a profound anti-modernism based on his understanding of the history of Being. And to me, most surprisingly and tellingly, there are even some passages that could be used to support a charge of anti-Alemannism. What makes them surprising is that repeatedly, in pieces like "Warum bleiben wir in der Provinz?,"[14] and the Schlageter speech,[15] and much later in "Hebel der Hausfreund"[16] and "Sprache und Heimat,"[17] Heidegger had celebrated what had come to be his Alemannic home, its landscape and its language.[18] In the *Schwarze Hefte* such celebration gives way to critique. Here is one of these anti-Alemannic passages:

The longer I do my work here, in my chosen home, as necessary, the more I realize that I do *not* belong and cannot belong to that forced and fruitless fuss made about being Alemannic. My home, the village and the farm of my mother, received its air and water totally from the sources of Hölderlin, has decidedly the forming power and abysmal quality of the Hegelian concept, and is enlivened by that far-venturing spirit of Schelling—it has nothing in common with that deceitful and all too noisy display of power that is so present here. It is therefore quite in order that the "Alemannen" here consider themselves the genuine "Alemannen" and want to have nothing to do with the Swabians.[19]

And here is another passage written a few years later:

And it is well that the land east of the Black Forest severs itself from the noisy "Alemannentum" that, barren in spirit, inflates itself with those who do not belong to it. Now it has also become clear to me that they are unable to even suspect who Hölderlin is and who Hegel and Schelling were. They may now trumpet their noise between the Black Forest and Vosges Mountains into the void and think it was plenitude.[20]

And "Palatines, half-Hessians, quarter-Franconians as 'Alemannen'—and these 'Alemannen' self-important and noisy and deceitful."[21]

What makes these passages revealing is not so much Heidegger's disdain for those self-proclaimed *Alemannen*, but that they suggest that even in provincial Freiburg, surrounded by family and friends, Heidegger did not really feel at home. Home remained the places of his childhood: Messkirch and the nearby Kreenheinstetten. But he had left that home behind, as he had left his faith behind—left behind but not forgotten. In the modern world in which he had made his mark Heidegger could not feel at home. Thus these passages, and more generally the anger at the modern world, at the Enlightenment, the spite that pervades the *Schwarze Hefte*, allow a first characterization of the *Grundstimmung*, the fundamental mood, that presides over Heidegger's thinking from beginning to end: it is a sense of homelessness. This is in keeping with his insistence in *Being and Time* that anxiety reveals the *Unheimlichkeit*, the fundamental homelessness of *Dasein*.[22] The Heidegger student Hans Jonas had good reason to find an affinity between Gnosticism and Heidegger's analytic of *Dasein*, which is a presupposition of his raising the question of Being.[23] This Gnostic willingness to suspend the world finds expression, as war is raging, in this extreme, despairing passage: "The last act of technology will be that the earth blows itself up and humanity disappears. This is no catastrophe, but the first purification of being from its disfiguration by the primacy of entities."[24] Heidegger notes that these demoralizing thoughts came to him on the way to his hut, a fragile oasis in the wasteland of the devastated earth.

But to characterize the *Grundstimmung* of Heidegger's thought as a sense of homelessness is to fail to do full justice to the anger he directed against the *modern* world. He knew that since *Dasein* is essentially a being-in-the-world and with-others, a leave-taking from the world could not have the last word. Just as Kierkegaard's Abraham, having suspended the ethical, had to return home from Mount Moriah, so in *Being and Time* authentic *Dasein*, having suspended the world for the sake of the silent call of conscience, has to return and take its place in it. But what form might this return take? Heidegger never could forget the home he left behind and projected its promise into an uncertain future. The *Grundstimmung* that presides over Heidegger's thinking from beginning to end is thus better described as nostalgia, as a longing for home that the modern world fails to satisfy. Consider the following passage from the *Schwarze Hefte*:

Hölderlin's poem "In lieblicher Bläue blühet …" contains in its first 17 verses my childhood around the church tower of my Swabian home: the bells and the stairs to the cage of the bells, the clockwork with its uncanny weights, of which each had its own character when between them, in the tower's half-darkness, the measured, unstoppable pendulum swung; the broad view—daily—from the tower over the open land and its forests, the day and night mood of each bell—the first great gathering of my little world unto the height and essential being of an abysmal presiding power [*Walten*]—the old towers of the nearby castle and the mighty lindens of its spacious garden—protected an early thinking that did not know where it was heading, but knew of the decisiveness for decisions and of the inescapable elevation unto the restlessness of the abysmal, which slowly gathered itself into an abiding single question, which had to search out what is most questionable: the truth of being [*Seyn*].[25]

In this passage, Heidegger places the tower of St. Martin in Messkirch at the origin of his *Denkweg*, his quest for the truth of Being. Here that quest is said to have its source. The spell of this origin Heidegger projects uncertainly into the future. Much later, in "Das Geheimnis des Glockenturms" (1954), he was to expand on this earlier recollection. Every day, he remarks there, the ringing bells marked the passing seasons, the hours of each day, permeating young hearts, dreams, prayers, and games. Heidegger sought to hold on to the magical secret, which, as he puts it, "always different and unrepeatable, the tower grants until the final ringing into the mountain range of being [*Gebirg des Seins*],"[26] a metaphor that will call for further consideration and, recalling Hölderlin's *Patmos*, figures importantly in the *Schwarze Hefte*.[27] But the world in which Heidegger found himself had no place and felt no need for the magic of the tower, for that truth of being Heidegger thought buried within it. And so he lashed spitefully out against that world and its different manifestations, railed against the Enlightenment and all that it inaugurated.

Nostalgia presides over Heidegger's *Seinsgeschichte*, his history of Being, which, as Peter Trawny points out, is succinctly summarized by Heidegger as follows: "first beginning: rise, (idea), *Machenschaft* [a difficult-to-translate term meant to characterize the modern face of being, inaugurated by Descartes and presided over by an ever-more-devouring technology that increasingly considers all that is as available material]." This is followed by: "other beginning: *Ereignis* [also a difficult-to-translate term, naming the event of Being (*Seyn*), another name for the truth of Being that promises something like a homecoming]." A bracket gathers the whole together under the label "Being": *das Seyn*.[28] Heidegger's history of Being is the story of a progressive forgetfulness of or abandonment by Being, to be followed by a hoped-for new beginning that would leave all *Machenschaft* behind and again allow human beings to call this world home. Like his anti-Americanism, anti-Bolshevism, and anti–National Socialism, Heidegger's anti-Semitism, too, has it foundation in this history. Trawny thus has good reason to accuse Heidegger of what he calls a *seinsgeschichtlicher Antisemitismus*, an anti-Semitism that has its foundation in Heidegger's history of Being.[29] Trawny follows the charge of anti-Semitism with the question: Does Heidegger's anti-Semitism contaminate his philosophy as a whole? And that raises a further question: Should we still read Heidegger?

Trawny suggests that following the publication of the *Schwarze Hefte* every attempt to isolate Heidegger's thinking from his anti-Semitism invites objection: "The contamination begins not just in the thinking of the thirties and also is not limited to them."[30] But even if we must grant that Heidegger's history of Being is a presupposition of the anti-Semitic remarks in the *Schwarze Hefte*, this history was well developed long before the first of these remarks and in no way depends on what is said there. The claim that Heidegger's history of being entails anti-Semitism lacks support, which is not to say that it may not have invited it. But had the anti-Semitic remarks been deleted from the *Schwarze Hefte*, no reader would have noticed. They are not essential.

Philosophically more interesting is the question: What is the connection between Heidegger's *Seinsgeschichte* and *Being and Time*, which figures so importantly in the *Schwarze Hefte*? The *Schwarze Hefte* confirm what a careful reading of *Being and Time* should already have made clear, that there is such a connection. I am not thinking just of that phenomenological destruction of the history of ontology that the promised part 2 of *Being and Time* was to accomplish, allowing us to recover what the history of ontology had obscured and thus to arrive at an adequate conception of Being. Moving back in time from Kant to Descartes to Aristotle and beyond, it was to lay bare the phenomenon of Being. Something like what was to become the later history of Being was to be accomplished by the promised regressive analysis. But Heidegger's *Seinsgeschichte* responds to the failure of *Being and Time* to arrive at that determination of being that it had promised. Consider the following remark:

Sein und Zeit is the first and in its brokenness inescapable attempt to say the essential surpassing of metaphysics (the meta-metaphysics) metaphysically. In that we still speak of *meta*-metaphysics, that which is be leaped over draws us back to its essence.[31]

One question this raises is: Why does Heidegger think it so important to leave metaphysics behind, a thought inseparable from his critique of modernity and also a presupposition of his anti-Semitic remarks? What is at stake?

I return to these questions at the end of the chapter. But first we need to consider why *Being and Time* in its effort "to arrive at the basic concept of 'Being' and to outline the ontological conceptions it requires and the variations it necessarily undergoes,"[32] as an attempt to lay hold of being as the presupposition of all that is, remained within the orbit of metaphysics and as such had to suffer shipwreck on the reef of Being. Not that Heidegger considered this a catastrophe. Quite the opposite: *Bene navigavi, cum naufragium feci*, as Nietzsche said about Wagner. Or, to quote the *Schwarze Hefte*: "If there is something like a catastrophe in the creating of great thinkers, then it does not consist in the fact that they suffered shipwreck, but in that they continued to go 'on,' instead of *remaining* back at the source of their great beginning."[33]

The key to Heidegger's shipwreck is what Heidegger calls the "truth of Being," which leads us into something like an antinomy.[34] Heidegger confronted this antinomy in *Being and Time* in his attempt to think the ontological difference, the difference between beings and being, the latter referring to the way things disclose themselves to *Dasein* (i.e., to human being). When we approach that difference from the perspective of transcendental philosophy we can say: being is constitutive of and therefore transcends beings. As Heidegger points out in *Being and Time,* there is a family resemblance between Kant's forms of intuition, space, and time, and Heidegger's being: beings can present themselves only to a being that is such as we are, embodied and dwelling in language, open to a world in which beings have to take their place and present themselves if they are "to be" at all. Being names the mode of their presencing. The way beings present themselves is always mediated by the body, by language, by history, and founded in the being of *Dasein* as care.

Already in *Being and Time* Heidegger had written "Only as long as *Dasein* is, i.e. the ontic possibility of understanding being, 'is there' [*gibt es*] being."[35] In the "Letter on 'Humanism'" Heidegger repeats the sentence in abbreviated form.[36] Berkeley's *esse est percipi* comes to mind. But Heidegger cannot appeal to a perceiving God, only to *Dasein*. And is *Dasein* not essentially historical? And must the same then not be said of being? Trawny to be sure confidently denies this: "The thought of being itself precludes inscribing into it historical, be they *geschichtliche* or *historische*, attributes and thus reserving it for specific narratives."[37] He supports the claim that the meaning of being cannot be tied to a specific language by pointing out that the sentence "This is a table" as far as the *is* is concerned, can be said in all languages. But does radical translatability provide ontology with an adequate key? Think of the way a person or poem presents itself to us. Trawny presupposes that leveling of being Heidegger associates with metaphysics. That such a leveling is not only possible but potent, Heidegger admits. The evolution of metaphysics that, if we follow Heidegger, presides over our modern world is after all a fact. But he would insist that this fails to do justice to things, fails to do justice even to the way they present themselves to us first of all and most of the time. Presupposed by metaphysics is a reductive ontology that Heidegger's question of Being renders questionable. And a willingness to engage in such questioning is a prerequisite to reading the *Schwarze Hefte* in a way that is responsive to what concerns Heidegger.

Already in *Being and Time* Heidegger recognized that a determination of being that makes it dependent on *Dasein* is insufficient, and he qualifies it when he speaks in section 43 of the dependence of being, but not of beings, of reality, but not of the real, on care—

that is, on the always understanding and caring being of human beings.[38] In the "Letter on 'Humanism'" this qualification becomes: "But the fact that the Da, the lighting as the truth of Being itself, comes to pass is the dispensation of Being itself."[39] There is therefore a sense in which beings and the real must be said to transcend that being (*Sein*) that is said to be relative to *Dasein*. To be sure, beings could not "be" in the first sense without human beings. Only human consciousness provides the open space that allows things to be perceived, understood, and cared for. That space, that clearing is a presupposition of the presencing of things, of their being. But this is not to say that we in any sense create these beings. Our experience of the reality of the real is thus an experience of beings as transcending Being. This demands a distinction between two senses of being, the first transcendental sense relative to *Dasein* and in this sense inescapably historical, the second transcendent sense, gesturing toward the ground of *Dasein*'s historical being and thus also of being, understood transcendentally. Being so understood is also essentially historical. Heidegger's *Seinsgeschichte* traces that history. But any attempt to comprehend that history as Hegel attempted to do inevitably fails by assigning it a place in an inevitably historically conditioned linguistic or logical space. The same goes for any attempt to conceptually lay hold of being. Here our thinking bumps against the limits of language and logic. And yet this ground, Heidegger insists, though metaphysics has no ear for it, calls us, if in silence, opening a window in our modern world, a world shaped by the progress of metaphysics. The deepening of Heidegger's thought since *Being and Time*, which we can also follow in the *Schwarze Hefte*, can thus be described as supplementing the silent call of conscience in *Being and Time* with the silent call of Being in the *Ereignis*, where there is the suggestion that only a response to the latter allows for authentic dwelling. To speak here of a *Kehre*, as Heidegger himself does, for the first time in print in the "Letter on 'Humanism,'"[40] is misleading, in that it suggests a reversal. But, as he points out, "there has been no change of standpoint." The question of Being remains central. The so-called *Kehre* is thus better understood, as Heidegger himself describes it here, not as a philosophical advance, but as a more thoughtful attempt to attend to or better to excavate the matter to be thought.[41] What makes this necessary is the abysmal essence of Being, which denies thinkers a foundation they can capture with their concepts.

Heidegger's *Seinsgeschichte* invites comparison with Hegel's philosophy of history, and after Nietzsche, Hegel, along with Descartes, is the philosopher most often mentioned in the *Schwarze Hefte*. Hegel's account of history as the progress of spirit is in many ways not all that different from the story Heidegger tells of the progress of metaphysics. Both seem to betray a deeply disturbing indifference to the fate of particular human beings, which seem hardly to matter given the sweep of history. Consider Hegel's devaluating *Aufhebung* of the particular, both of the sensuous and the individual, in the name of the "absolute spirit," whose throne's "reality, truth, and certainty" is identified at the end of the *Phenomenology* with its "recollection and Golgatha," with "comprehended history,"[42] or Heidegger's already-cited frightening remark in the *Schwarze Hefte* that the self-destruction of our modern world might be considered a purification of being.

But there is of course this all-important difference: Hegel's confidence in reason is so great that it leaves no room for that other thinking, *das andere Denken*, of which Heidegger speaks. Consider this statement from Hegel's Heidelberger *Antrittsrede*:

Man, since he is spirit, may and should consider himself worthy even of the highest; he cannot think the greatness and power of his spirit great enough; and with this faith nothing will be so stubborn and hard as not to open itself to him. The essence of the universe, hidden and closed at first, has no power that could offer resistance to the courage of knowledge; it must open itself to him and lay its riches and depths before his eyes and open them to his enjoyment.[43]

But where Hegel sees progress, the progressive realization of the Cartesian promise to render man with his method the master and possessor of nature, Heidegger sees a progressive *Seinsvergessenheit* and *Seinsverlassenheit*, a forgetting of and an abandonment by Being. At issue here is the commensurability of reason and reality. Is the principle of sufficient reason constitutive of reality as Leibniz and Spinoza claim? Heidegger offers an analysis of the scope and limits of this principle in *Identität und Differenz*.[44] The truth of Being, as Heidegger understands it, or what I called the antinomy of being, calls this into question. Heidegger considers the Hegelian faith in the power of reason to overpower reality and to lead us to the good life groundless. But that faith has shaped our modern world or what Heidegger calls the "age of the world picture" and thereby demonstrated its potency. The anti-Americanism, anti-Anglicism, anti-Semitism of the *Schwarze Hefte* are all bound up with that critique. If we endorse what is criticized by Heidegger, that critique turns around and England, America, and the Jews become decisive contributors to the formation of our modern world. That is indeed how Heidegger understands them. We have to ask ourselves: Is Heidegger's critique of metaphysics (i.e., of the Enlightenment) altogether without substance? How secure are we in our trust in reason? What is the foundation on which it rests?

When Heidegger links what Hegel understands as progress to an increasing forgetfulness of the "truth of being" in which that progress has its origin, he recalls Nietzsche's understanding of history, and no philosopher is mentioned more often in the *Schwarze Hefte* than Nietzsche. Both Nietzsche and Heidegger would have us return to Greek tragedy and to the pre-Socratic beginning of the history of metaphysics to reestablish contact with its Dionysian ground, covered up by the Socratic, Cartesian, and Hegelian faith in the commensurability of reason and being that presides over the progress of metaphysics and our modern world. Both hoped for a new beginning that would return us to that ground. Both came to realize that such hope had misled them to embrace the wrong hero—Wagner in Nietzsche's case, Hitler in Heidegger's case—where it is interesting to note that in the *Schwarze Hefte* Heidegger too came to think it important to follow Nietzsche and to criticize Wagner, whom he associates with National Socialism. The hoped-for new beginning is now deferred to an indefinite future. The parallels between his and Nietzsche's thought are striking—reason for Heidegger, concerned with his own originality, to attempt to distance himself ever more decisively from Nietzsche, who with his inversion of Plato and his emphasis on earth and the body is said by Heidegger to have remained within metaphysics and with his teaching of the will to power to have invited the National Socialist appropriation of his thought. If Hegel's faith in reason marks the end of metaphysics in one sense, Nietzsche's faith in the body marks it in another. Heidegger rejects such faith, which fails to recognize the radical transcendence of Being.

I said at the beginning of this chapter that I did not find anything in the many pages of the *Schwarze Hefte* that changed my understanding of Heidegger in any essential way. The *Schwarze Hefte* presuppose a reductive picture of the modern world essentially the same as that developed concisely in "The Age of the World Picture."[45] Just what does Heidegger have in mind when he calls the modern age "the age of the world picture"? The word *picture* offers a first answer: we can stand before and look at pictures, but we cannot enter or leave them, cannot live or dwell in them. Pictures are not like buildings. This suggests what is at stake in the phrase "age of the world picture." To the extent that we understand the world as a picture, we stand before it but have lost our place in it. We can no longer be said to dwell in such a world; such a world entails a rootless existence.

Such a displacement is demanded by science, which presupposes a self-elevation that transforms the embodied self into a disembodied thinker, a Cartesian *res cogitans*—and it is significant that after Nietzsche and Hegel, Descartes is the philosopher most often mentioned in the *Schwarze Hefte*. Descartes presides over Heidegger's caricature of the modern world. The transformation of the embodied self into a disembodied thinking substance, into a Cartesian *res cogitans*, harks back to the very origin of metaphysics, and so also to the origin of science. Scientists want to see, want to understand what is as it is, bracketing for the sake of such objectivity themselves and their place in the world. Absentmindedness characterizes the very origin of philosophy and science; it caused Thales to tumble into his well. It is but the other side of that disinterested objectivity that we demand of all who lay claim to the pursuit of truth. A Cartesian *res cogitans* or thinking substance has no need for a house. And to the extent that human beings understand themselves first of all as such thinking subjects, who just happen to find themselves in some particular body, in a particular place and time, male or female, Jewish or German, they will not allow such particularities to circumscribe their freedom, but will consider all of this material to be fashioned into a successful life. In their essence they will be mobile, rootless. Here, in his understanding of the progress of metaphysics, lies the key to Heidegger's caricature of the rootless Jew, as to so much else that he bemoans in the *Schwarze Hefte*. I don't consider Heidegger's characterization of the modern age an adequate description: in everyone's experience there is hopefully much that does not fit what is being claimed here. What Heidegger offers us is no more than a simple model that focuses on certain key aspects of the world we live in but leaves out other important features. Or, we can say, what he offers us is a caricature. But if so, we must add, like any good caricature, it captures something essential and in this case deeply disturbing. What makes this caricature so disturbing is precisely the violence it does to what we consider our humanity, presided over by our highest values. But this caricature would not be found so disturbing, if we did not recognize that it captured something essential and all too familiar about our world.

The pursuit of truth as it presides over our science demands objectivity. And objectivity demands that we not allow our understanding to be clouded by our inevitably personal desires and interests. It wants just the facts. With good reason, Wittgenstein could therefore say in his *Tractatus* that "in the world everything is as it is and happens as it does happen. In it there is no value—and if there were, it would be of no value."[46] It would be just another fact that, like all facts, could be other than it happens to be. If there is something that deserves to be called a value, it will not be found in the world of science. To find it we have to step outside that world. On this Heidegger and the Wittgenstein of the *Tractatus* agree. And the same goes for freedom. Persons as persons have no place in the scientific world picture.

Heidegger makes this elision of meaningful reality a defining feature of our age or of what he calls the "age of the world picture": "When we think of a 'picture' we think first of all of a representation of something. Accordingly the world picture would be, so to speak, a picture of what is in its entirety. But 'world picture' says more. We mean by this term the world itself, what is in its entirety, as it measures and binds us."[47] To the world so understood we, too, belong, for it is said to include all that is. The world picture thus transforms itself into something like a house, a building, in which we, too, have our place. If this world picture is to include all that is, it cannot have an outside. But this means the loss of what Kant calls things in themselves, and every time we experience as person as a person we experience such a thing in itself. There is no experience of persons without at least a trace of respect. In this sense we can agree with Kierkegaard that subjective truth is higher than objective truth, where we must resist the temptation to translate such subjective truth into some version of objective truth, as phenomenology so often has attempted to do. To the extent that the modern world is indeed what Heidegger calls the "age of the world picture," it has become a prison that denies us access to the reality of persons and things. To experience the aura of the real that gives to persons and things their proper weight, we have to escape from that prison by opening a door, or at least a window, in the world building that scientific understanding has created, a door or window to the truth of things, but now "truth" may no longer be understood as objective truth. In the *Schwarze Hefte*, and of course not only here, Heidegger gestures toward such an opening with his invocations of the *Ereignis,* an event where we are seized by a reality that transcends and transforms us, letting us stand differently in the world. Tatjana Tömmel has pointed out in her remarkable *Wille und Passion: Der Liebesbegriff bei Heidegger und Arendt* that Heidegger's ruminations on the *Ereignis*, so prominent also in the *Schwarze Hefte*, are anticipated by what he had written to Hannah Arendt a decade earlier about the meaning of love.[48] Love remains the most convincing illustration of what an *Ereignis* might be, which makes it all the more significant that love is totally absent from the *Schwarze Hefte*. It is as if the world had fallen under the rule of *Machenschaft* to such an extent that it no longer had room for love. If so, an *Ereignis* is needed that would transform our world, not just the individual.

Let me conclude by taking a closer look at the first, already-cited, and particularly objectionable remark Heidegger makes about the Jews in the *Schwarze Hefte*, to which Trawny, too, keeps returning:[49] "One of the most hidden forms of the gigantic and perhaps the oldest is the unyielding mastery of calculating [*Rechnen*] and questionable trading [*Schieben*] and mixing, which is the foundation of the worldlessnes of Jewry."[50]

The characterization of the Jew as *Schieber* is an ugly cliché that the Nazis propagated and that Heidegger appropriates. The *Schieber* is an unscrupulous businessman for whom money is the measure of value: everything has its price. As Trawny points out, the cliché has a historical foundation: "Since the 12th century the collection of interest had been forbidden in the Christian West. By papal decree the Jews were expressly exempted. They were the only group in society allowed to loan money."[51] To be sure, others were to become major players: think of the Medici, of the Fugger, and the Welser of Augsburg. The role money played in the emergence of the modern world has often been noted. Here the Florence of Cosimo de Medici, of Brunelleschi and Alberti, deserves a closer look, as does the "conversion of the human mind from *theoria* to *praxis*," from theory to practice, from the speculative contemplative science of the medievals to a science aiming at domination and mastery. As Descartes later was to oppose his practical philosophy to the speculative philosophy of the Schools, Alberti already teaches a practical science that brackets philosophical questions when these have no bearing on the craft that concerns him, taking from the mathematicians only "those things with which my subject is concerned."[52] In this respect, *On Painting* belongs with a by then well-established tradition:

From the late thirteenth century onward such mathematical skills were recognized as useful in wider contexts and were increasingly taught in abacus schools specially set up for the purpose. These abacus schools did their teaching in the vernacular. ... In Florence, one of the best abacus schools, in the late fourteenth century was that run by the Goldsmiths' Guild.[53]

Brunelleschi belonged to that guild. Descartes's *Discourse on Method*, with its promise of mastery that would render us the masters and possessors of nature, has its precursor in Alberti's *On Painting*.[54] The key to such possession is mastery of calculating.

Descartes, as I noted, is, after Nietzsche and Hegel, the philosopher most often mentioned in the *Schwarze Hefte*. To understand Descartes is to understand the origin of the modern world picture. That mathematics is of key importance here requires no comment, nor is it necessary to point out that the Cartesian mathematization of nature has issued in a progressive homogenization of all that is. By subjecting everything to the measure of what can be counted, emphasis on the quantitative threatens to obscure what was, for Heidegger, the all-important significance of the inescapably unique particular. Here lies the key to his critique of metaphysics and to his understanding of the *Ereignis*. Contrary to Trawny's suggestion,[55] Heidegger's history of metaphysics does not attribute a very significant role to the Jews, although they, like so much else, are placed within it and become its victims.

In conclusion, I would like to suggest that Heidegger's critique of a thinking seduced by the power of numbers cannot simply be dismissed. First two more quotes from the *Schwarze Hefte*:

The now published reports of the Bolshevist killing cellars are supposed to be horrifying.[56]

Trawny notes that Heidegger hesitates to say anything comparable about the Germans. But that he was also thinking of the Germans is suggested by this slightly earlier comment:

Whether the Bolshevists murder a single person without legal judgment and investigation, only because he is of another mind, or hundreds of thousands, counts *the same*. Our age, used to the quantitative, thinks a hundred thousand are "more" than one, but a unique individual is already a maximum to which no number can do justice. In order not to confuse the German position, we may not, and also not here, get drunk with numbers. Otherwise the danger would arise that the killing of a few, compared to that of many thousands, is no longer considered so terrible and subhumanity [*das Untermenschentum*] is thought to begin only with a sufficiently large number.[57]

The following portion of the quotation is crucial: "a unique individual is already a maximum to which no number can do justice." That holds not only for each person, but finally for every thing experienced in its unique particularity. The truth of being is experienced in the mysterious aura of what is unique and cannot be captured by concepts and therefore has no place in the modern world picture. To gesture toward such experiences Heidegger inserted into the *Schwarze Hefte* a number of very brief evocative sentences such as "Silver-thistles glisten unobtrusively in the clear air of the beginning late summer."[58] They point us in the same direction as the rose that "blooms without a why" of Angelus Silesius, which Heidegger opposed in *The Principle of Reason*[59] to Leibniz's principle of sufficient reason: *nihil est sine ratione*, a principle that, if Heidegger is right, rules our science and technology and has shaped our modern world picture.

Should we accept Heidegger's characterization of the modern age as the age of the world picture or of *Machenschaft*? I spoke of a caricature, but one that captures something essential. As if to confirm this, the *New York Times* published a piece by Bruce Feiler titled "Statisticians 10, Poets 0" on May 15, 2014.[60] In humorous detail the article gives many examples of the way the quantitative thinking deplored by Heidegger has come to pervade our lives. There are of course many who, like the social scientist Duncan Watts, quoted in the article, welcome this development: "If you had to choose between a world in which you did everything based on instinct, tradition or some vague received wisdom, or you do something based on evidence, I would say the latter is the way to go." But as the article points out, there are also those who share Heidegger's concerns, such as the statistician Nicolas Taleb: "Once you reduce a human to a metric, you kill them." And the article concludes: "Or, as the greatest numbers person of the 20th century, Albert Einstein warned, 'Not everything that can be counted counts and not everything that counts can be counted.'" Heidegger could only have agreed.

Notes

1. Karsten Harries, "Heidegger as a Political Thinker," *Review of Metaphysics* 29, no. 4 (1976), 644–669, reprinted in *Heidegger and Modern Philosophy: Critical Essays*, ed. Michael Murray (New Haven, CT: Yale University Press, 1978), 304–328 (quote on 309).

2. Martin Heidegger, *Wegmarken, Gesamtausgabe* 9, ed. Friedrich-Wilhelm von Herrmann (Frankfurt: Klostermann, [1967] 1976), 343.

3. *Wegmarken, Gesamtausgabe* 9, p. 343.

4. Martin Heidegger, *Aus der Erfahrung des Denkens, Gesamtausgabe* 13, ed. Hermann Heidegger (Frankfurt: Klostermann, 1983), 91.

5. Martin Heidegger, *Überlegungen II–VI (Schwarze Hefte 1931–1938), Gesamtausgabe* 94, ed. Peter Trawny (Frankfurt: Klostermann, 2014), 110.

6. Martin Heidegger, "Die Selbstbehauptung der deutschen Universität: Rede, gehalten bei der feierlichen Übernahme des Rektorats der Universität Freiburg i. Br. am 27.5. 1933," in *Das Rektorat 1933/34; Tatsachen und Gedanken* (Klostermann: Frankfurt, 1983), 30–31; translated by Karsten Harries as "The Self-Assertion of the German University: Address, Delivered on the Solemn Assumption of the Rectorate of the University of Freiburg. The Rectorate 1933/34: Facts and Thoughts," *Review of Metaphysics* 38 (1985), 467–450 (especially 490).

7. *Überlegungen II–VI, Gesamtausgabe* 94, p. 239.

8. *Überlegungen II–VI, Gesamtausgabe* 94, p. 484.

9. Martin Heidegger, *Überlegungen VII–XI (Schwarze Hefte 1938/39), Gesamtausgabe* 95, ed. Peter Trawny (Frankfurt: Klostermann, 2014), 325.

10. Martin Heidegger, *Überlegungen XII–XV (Schwarze Hefte 1939–1941), Gesamtausgabe* 96, ed. Peter Trawny (Frankfurt: Klostermann, 2014), 218.

11. *Überlegungen VII–XI, Gesamtausgabe* 95, p. 97.

12. *Überlegungen XII–XV, Gesamtausgabe* 96, p. 46.

13. *Überlegungen VII–XI, Gesamtausgabe* 95, pp. 172–174.

14. *Aus der Erfahrung des Denkens, Gesamtausgabe* 13, pp. 9–13—the full title is "Schöpferische Landschaft: Warum bleiben wir in der Provinz?"

15. Martin Heidegger, *Reden und andere Zeugnisse eines Lebensweges, Gesamtausgabe* 16, ed. Hermann Heidegger (Frankfurt: Klostermann, 2000), 760.

16. *Aus der Erfahrung des Denkens, Gesamtausgabe* 13, pp. 133–150.

17. *Aus der Erfahrung des Denkens, Gesamtausgabe* 13, pp. 155–180.

18. See also *Reden und andere Zeugnisse eines Lebensweges, Gesamtausgabe* 16, p. 240.

19. *Überlegungen II–VI, Gesamtausgabe* 94, p. 350.

20. *Überlegungen II–VI, Gesamtausgabe* 94, p. 350.

21. *Überlegungen XII–XV, Gesamtausgabe* 96, p. 200.

22. Martin Heidegger, *Sein und Zeit, Gesamtausgabe* 2, ed. Friedrich-Wilhelm von Herrmann (Frankfurt: Klostermann, 1977), 188–189.

23. Hans Jonas, *The Gnostic Religion: The Message of the Alien God and the Beginnings of Christianity* (Boston: Beacon Press, 2001), 330–336.

24. *Überlegungen XII–XV, Gesamtausgabe* 96, p. 438.

25. *Überlegungen XII–XV, Gesamtausgabe* 96, p. 438.

26. *Aus der Erfahrung des Denkens, Gesamtausgabe* 13, p. 116.

27. *Überlegungen XII–XV, Gesamtausgabe* 96, p. 144; see *Überlegungen VII–XI, Gesamtausgabe* 95, pp. 63, 227, 276.

28. Peter Trawny, *Heidegger und der Mythos der jüdischen Weltverschwörung* (Frankfurt: Klostermann, 2014), 22; Martin Heidegger, *Die Geschichte des Seyns, Gesamtausgabe* 69, ed. Peter Trawny (Frankfurt: Klostermann, 1998), 27.

29. Trawny, *Heidegger und der Mythos der jüdischen Weltverschwörung*, 32–56.

30. Trawny, *Heidegger und der Mythos der jüdischen Weltverschwörung*, 100.

31. *Überlegungen XII–XV, Gesamtausgabe* 96, p. 97.

32. *Sein und Zeit, Gesamtausgabe* 2, pp. 52–53.

33. *Überlegungen II–VI, Gesamtausgabe* 94, p. 264.

34. I developed that antinomy in "The Antinomy of Being: Heidegger's Critique of Humanism," in *The Cambridge Companion to Existentialism*, ed. Steven Crowell (Cambridge: Cambridge University Press, 2012), 178–198, and much more fully in *Wahrheit: Die Architektur der Welt* (Paderborn: Fink, 2012).

35. *Sein und Zeit, Gesamtausgabe* 2, p. 281.

36. *Wegmarken, Gesamtausgabe* 9, p. 336.

37. Trawny, *Heidegger und der Mythos der jüdischen Weltverschwörung*, 76.

38. *Wegmarken, Gesamtausgabe* 9, p. 336.

39. *Wegmarken, Gesamtausgabe* 9, p. 336.

40. *Wegmarken, Gesamtausgabe* 9, p. 328.

41. *Wegmarken, Gesamtausgabe* 9, p. 343.

42. Georg Wilhelm Friedrich Hegel, *Phänomenologie des Geistes* (Hamburg: Meiner, 1952), 564.

43. Georg Wilhelm Friedrich Hegel, *Vorlesungen über die Geschichte der Philosophie I, Jubiläumsausgabe*, ed. H. Glockner, vol. 17 (Stuttgart: Frommann, 1968), 22.

44. Martin Heidegger, *Identität und Differenz, Gesamtausgabe* 10, 2nd ed. ed. F.-W. von Herrmann (Frankfurt: Klostermann, 2006).

45. Martin Heidegger, "The Age of the World Picture," in *The Question Concerning Technology and Other Essays*, trans. William Lovitt, 115–154 (New York: Harper & Row, 1977); Martin Heidegger, *Holzwege, Gesamtausgabe* 5, ed. Friedrich-Wilhelm von Herrmann (Frankfurt: Klostermann, [1950] 2003), 75–113; *Überlegungen VII–XI, Gesamtausgabe* 95, p. 314; *Überlegungen XII–XV, Gesamtausgabe* 96, p. 112.

46. Ludwig Wittgenstein, *Tractatus Logico-Philosophicus*, trans. D. F. Pears and B. F. McGuinness (New York: Humanities Press, 1961), 6.41.

47. Heidegger, "The Age of the World Picture," 49.

48. Tatjana Tömmel, *Wille und Passion: Der Liebesbegriff bei Heidegger und Arendt* (Frankfurt: Suhrkamp, 2013), 103. Tömmel refers to Heidegger's letter to Arendt of February 21, 1925.

49. Trawny, *Heidegger und der Mythos der jüdischen Weltverschwörung*, 33–34, 38, 52, 65.

50. *Überlegungen VII–XI, Gesamtausgabe* 95, p. 97.

51. Trawny, *Heidegger und der Mythos der jüdischen Weltverschwörung*, 35.

52. Leon Battista Alberti, *On Painting*, trans. John R. Spencer (New Haven, CT: Yale University Press, 1966), 43.

53. J. V. Field, *The Invention of Infinity: Mathematics and Art in the Renaissance* (Oxford: Oxford University Press, 1997), 14.

54. Karsten Harries, *Infinity and Perspective* (Cambridge, MA: MIT Press, 2001), 77.

55. Trawny, *Heidegger und der Mythos der jüdischen Weltverschwörung*, 37.

56. Martin Heidegger, *Metaphysische Anfangsgründe der Logik im Ausgang von Leibniz, Gesamtausgabe* 26, ed. Klaus Held (Frankfurt: Klostermann, 1990), 241.

57. *Überlegungen XII–XV, Gesamtausgabe* 96, p. 237.

58. *Überlegungen XII–XV, Gesamtausgabe* 96, p. 107.

59. Martin Heidegger, *Der Satz vom Grund, Gesamtausgabe* 10, ed. Petra Jaeger (Frankfurt: Klostermann, 1997), 192.

60. Bruce Feiler, "Statisticians 10, Poets 0," *New York Times*, May 15, 2014, Sunday Styles, 1, 8.

15

On Relevant Events, Then and Now

Tracy B. Strong

[I am not interested in being] … cultivated. My will … aspires to living in an actual revolutionary situation, … [pursuing] what I feel to be "necessary" without caring to know whether a new "culture" will emerge from it or an acceleration of decline.
—Martin Heidegger[1]

The philosopher's every attempt at directly influencing the tyrant is necessarily ineffectual.
—Alexandre Kojève[2]

Heidegger's National Socialism is not news. In 1962, Guido Schneeberger published a compendium of documents detailing among other things Heidegger's involvement with National Socialist ideas and policies. In 1965, Dagobert Runes published *German Existentialism: Martin Heidegger*, a short collection, taken mainly from Schneeberger, of Heidegger's National Socialist–oriented speeches between 1933 and 1934. And one need not mention Farías, Faye, Wolin, and many others. With each new book, the armory of supposedly smoking guns grew larger. The most recent powder for such guns is, of course, the publication of the *Schwarze Hefte*, the notebooks in which Heidegger recorded his reflections on the questions and concerns of the day between 1931 and 1941.

These volumes, it needs to be emphasized, are *not* the equivalent of Nietzsche's *Nachlass*—the notebooks in which he tried out and rejected ideas and jotted down thoughts and musings ("*Ich habe meinen Regenschirm vergessen*"),[3] nor are they something like Hannah Arendt's *Denktagebuch*, in which she worked out material that she would use in future publications. In contrast to the Nietzsche and Arendt volumes, Heidegger intended for these *Notebooks* to be published and read as the final volumes in his collected works. They are written not just for himself but for a readership and are thus not random musings. If they were intended as the last volumes (the editors have jumped the gun somewhat), in effect they are saying "now that you have seen all that I have put before the world, see this also—me before myself").[4]

One kind of reading that has been made, in particular of the *Black Notebooks*,[5] focuses on the anti-Semitic or derogatory passages about various peoples (in particular about

Weltjudentum) (I am told that there are more in the recently published fourth volume), which, while not extensive, are held to nonetheless infect and devalue everything else. For some, they devalue every word that Heidegger wrote. All that matters for such a judgment is anti-Semitism. (Defenses are of course advanced on the grounds that the passages are slight, that this is not *Being and Time,* and so forth.)

I do not think that these passages devalue everything else, *but I do think that they are not incompatible with everything else, nor indeed irrelevant to it.* It is thus important to note that Heidegger chose to leave those passages in with the rest of his work. This is in contrast to, say, Gottlob Frege, who while (much more) rabidly anti-Semitic, did not, as far as I know, include such thoughts in his work on logic. As Harry Redner says about Frege, anti-Semitism plays an "inconspicuous part" in Frege's thought.[6] One may wonder about the accuracy of Redner's judgment on Frege, but with Heidegger, and in particular in the *Black Notebooks*, such themes are clearly part of the same work. At a recent conference in Paris on "Heidegger et les juifs," it was generally agreed that one must read the *Notebooks* en bloc, as a whole. And yet the question of what that would mean for our understanding of them as a whole was hardly broached.

The *Notebooks* were written during a time of tremendous turmoil and for many in Germany at least initially of great hope. The legislature appeared incapable of resolving problems; violent pitched battles between right-wing and left-wing groups left many dead. *Biedermeier* culture was apparently fading. The *Notebooks* were also written in an international situation of enormous complexity—the presence in the East of the USSR was seen as a threat to traditional European political and social culture. The forceful arrival and continuing presence of the United States changed the dynamics of the international system. Hyperinflation between 1921 and 1924 led the French and Belgians to occupy the Ruhr in order to exact payment in goods. By late 1924, one US dollar was valued at over four billion marks. In 1931, the combination of the Depression and massive deflationary fiscal policy led to more crises and to the invocation in July 1930 by Chancellor Brüning of Article 48 of the Constitution, allowing him to rule with dictatorial powers. (Article 48 was never rescinded.)

If these were the political and social contexts at the time of Heidegger's writing, the *Notebooks* were furthermore written as he was lecturing, writing, and publishing; thus they comment both on world events and on the work Heidegger was making or would make public. All of these factors constitute the context or part of the context for the *Notebooks*, and it is not only impossible but wrong to try to understand them outside of that context. This does not mean, however, that *tout comprendre, c'est tout pardonner*—that because we understand, we forgive. Quite the contrary.

One thing *is* relatively clear here. As Graeme Nicholson has pointed out, Heidegger tries, in the *Rektoratsrede* and elsewhere, to give philosophical significance to several Nazi catchwords—"street language," as Nicholson puts it. Most prominent among these catchwords are *Führer, Kampf,* and *Volk.* Heidegger takes the opportunity, for instance, to call his position that of *Führer*, not *Magnifizenz*, the title that was and remains to this day standard practice in German universities. One could add to this the use of the "*Blut und Boden*" slogan, popularized by the *Reichsbauernführer* Richard Walther Darré. It is true, as Nicholson notes, that Heidegger "exposed his philosophy to the world of power, and he lost,"[7] but his naming himself *Führer* in the context of Germany in the 1930s was actually potentially subversive. (As we know, he would later be accused of having a *Privatnationalsozialismus*.) I think, however, that Nicholson's account of part of Heidegger's attraction to National Socialism is accurate—in particular, his attraction to the possibilities the movement seemed to offer him.

How one understands this is of the utmost importance. In his 2009 book—taken by some to be the now penultimate nail in the Heidegger-Nazi joint venture—Emmanuel Faye has shown the depth and extent of Heidegger's involvement with Nazi or Nazi-like activities before, during, and after his period as rector.[8] From this, Faye argues that Heidegger imported Nazism into philosophy and that, consequently, his work is not really philosophy at all. Indeed, he urges that it be removed from the "Philosophy" shelves in libraries. It is not clear why the importation of Nazism into philosophy should automatically disqualify it as philosophy any more than the importation of free-market economics would; in any case, the argument I am making here—following to some degree the implications of Nicholson's work—is that it is instead the other way around. There is no doubt as to Heidegger's profound involvement with Nazism. However, it was his philosophy that led him to find in his understanding and experience of National Socialism a potential actualization of his philosophical thought. And Heidegger tells Löwith that it does.

The question then becomes whether the fact that an apparently serious philosophical understanding can lead its author to see a possible realization of his thought in something like National Socialism is a reason to reject that thought. For many it has been. One might, however, rather than closing down this path *ab initio*, ask if there are other possible realizations of such thought—ones that Heidegger never saw or discarded. What is clear is that if the position I am advancing is accurate, Heidegger's thought has and must have political or practical implications. It is thus significant that he finds the need to translate the analysis of individual *Dasein* into a *volkish*, German, *Dasein*.[9] What will make the Germans German is that they will their *Dasein*—by a decision and pursuit of that which is theirs.[10]

The willing of a collective (i.e., political) *Dasein*, however, must differ from an individual *Dasein*, for the individual is made in the constant presence of the actuality of individual death. No matter how a community or a nation dies, it does not die like an individual, even if, as Carl Schmitt claimed, it is "only a weak people [that] perishes." Nor can it will like an individual. We are thus led to the need to bring the collective into actuality: this is the gloss that Heidegger attempts for *Führer*. Who and what Heidegger considers to be the *Führer* is complex. Having said in the *Rektoratsrede* that "the leaders shall be led," when he then says that "the *Führer* alone is the present and future reality of Germany and its law,"[11] Heidegger is envisaging an achievement of the German *Dasein* that cannot succeed unless led, from above, by a philosophically informed leader, whose own proper context is the world of *Wissenschaft*—that is, a properly reconstituted university.[12] To make such a willing possible he is also calling on the supposed legitimacy offered by the existing political situation in Germany: a double game, not without its dangers. There is, however, a picture of the political here that has some relation to the "inner truth and greatness" of the movement Heidegger claims to see around him (whatever one makes of that), something that is not (necessarily) the same as what were (becoming) the practices of National Socialism, although National Socialism is highly relevant to it.

I wish then to approach Heidegger's work in the *Black Notebooks* from this vantage point. While the above remarks merely sketch the kind of debate that has raged around the question of Heidegger and politics, especially over the last twenty years, much of this debate fails to deal with the question of what Heidegger actually thought about the political, even if he, inescapably, for a time at least, associated himself with a grandiose and awful political movement. More important is that *he could not perceive a way to dissociate himself from it*, even, and especially, after the fact. When Elizabeth Hirsch (who had studied with Heidegger at Marburg and taken a doctorate there) asked him after the war to apologize or express regret for his allegiance to the NSDAP, he responded, "*Aber wie?*"—"But how?"[13] What to make of this? His is, I take it, a serious question. It is not philosophically adequate to attribute this response, as Thomas Sheehan does, to a lack of "courage."[14] In Heidegger's "A Dialogue on Language" in his *On the Way to Language*, originally published in 1959, speaking about dialogue and language, the "Inquirer" says to the "Japanese," "Above all, [there would be] silence about silence," and then asks, "Who could simply be silent of silence?," to which the "Japanese" responds, "That would be authentic saying."[15]

We may take this to be one-half of Heidegger's response to those questioning his silence. This points us in a direction but does not solve the question: *About what* could he not find the words to express regret? Is this a matter of there not being a way to express authentic regret, or of there being no regret? In Shakespeare's *King Lear*, Lear orders his daughters to express their love for him, in return for which they shall receive a proportionate dowry. The youngest, Cordelia, loves her father but cannot "heave her heart into her throat" to speak the words he orders, for such words cannot honestly be *meant* if a response to an order. After the war, the Allies instituted a "denazification" process. It is not too exaggerated to say that if one said one was sorry and had been desperately wrong, one was forgiven. The four rectors at Freiburg who followed Heidegger were more virulently and conventionally Nazi than he : within a year after the war they all had highly paid positions in academia or research foundations. Heidegger, in contrast, was barred from teaching or participation in any university activities until March 1949 and only resumed teaching as *emeritus* in the winter term of 1950–51.

Heidegger's silence is consequent, I think, neither to weakness, nor to a temporary mistake, nor to accident. It may, however, be consequent to a particular quality of his thought. If Heidegger's thought opens a path to the choices he made (to join the Party, to actively urge support for the regime),[16] what did he understand to be down that path, and what permitted him to think that National Socialism was along that path? Most centrally: How did he understand the role of philosophy in and for human life?

This question must be approached with regard to Heidegger's understanding of the relation of philosophy to the political. While during the period of the *Rektorat* he might have appeared to have subordinated philosophy to political events, he in fact sought pride of place for philosophy: it is to be a time when the "leaders are themselves led"[17] (and might this include the *Reichskanzler* himself?). To be blunt: I am arguing that Heidegger's thought did open *a* path to National Socialism *and that this is a price one must be willing to pay*—for it is not the only path opened. This opening *also* opens several other paths—and in that there is danger, for we become responsible for which path we take or let ourselves take. As Stanley Cavell has importantly noted: Heidegger's attraction to Nazism might be "internal to understanding Heidegger's work. ... The terrible fact, one that the principle of simple separation may wish to deny, is that Nazism has its philosophical as well as political attractions."[18]

There are then two issues here: the nature of his support for the NSDAP and for Hitler, as evidenced in the writing from the early 1930s, and the question of "world-historical Jewry." I will take them in turn.

"From the time of the *Rektorat*" is apparently a title that Heidegger gives to a section of *Gesamtausgabe* 94. (I am assuming the editor did not insert it.) He starts with this: "With each struggle to become more assured and more flexible. That which fails is a lesson; where there is opposition, tighten the belt!"[19] This leads to and forms the context for the next entry: "The great experience and happiness, that the leader has awakened a new reality, that gives to our thinking the correct path [*Bahn*] and impact." He goes on to say that without this, there would only be a "literary existence."

Heidegger thus is someone who remains dedicated to what Badiou calls "the event," that moment of καιρός, the indeterminate moment that explodes on the earth and changes the configuration by which the world is understood.[20] (Paul Tillich, who taught at Marburg in 1924 and 1925 and acknowledges Heidegger's influence, makes it a central concept in his theology.)[21] Heidegger clearly wishes for his thought to make a difference in the world, to the world; without this transformation (this "revolution," as he calls it in the letter to Löwith), it will not be anything other than a literary exercise. What National Socialism has, in his judgment, made possible, though not (yet) realized, is the actualization of the transformative imperative of his thought. Such a transformation, not so incidentally, was what Nietzsche had hoped his first book would achieve.

With this sense of what it takes to make philosophy actual, the chance to become rector had to present itself as an opportunity to do what philosophy should do. Some (Farías, Faye) had argued that Heidegger actively sought the position. An entry in *Gesamtausgabe* 94,[22] apparently from the period just preceding his assumption of the position, indicates rather a reflective ambivalence: "Pushed to take over the *Rektorat*, I acted for the first time *against* the most interior voice. In this position I will at best in any case be able to avoid this or that. As for building something—assuming that it is still even possible—the right people are lacking."[23] Later in the volume he will attribute this lack to general weakness (Responding to Oswald Spengler, he says: "For now, it is not because of being too weak that the West will go under, rather because it is still not strong."[24])

I call attention here to the sense that philosophy is incomplete if it does not accomplish a transformation in the way humans live their lives is not unique to Heidegger. I have already mentioned Nietzsche but one finds, for instance, similar thoughts in Emerson or Thoreau.[25] It is clear though that Heidegger was willing to make the attempt. And this is to be done with "no program, no system, and no theory and even no empty 'organizing.' But create the actual [*Wirkliche*] and the next possibility—not to shirk the actual—that is, *the new courage for destiny [Schicksal] as the basic form [Grundform] of truth.*"[26] Such concerns continue: he will come back to his misgivings about "organizing" in Gesamtausgabe 94.[27]

The goals of philosophy will necessarily be accomplished only in terms of the realization of the destiny of a people: "Ultimately: Joined together in the creative joint responsibility of the truth of the *Dasein* of a people. Basic point [*Grundstimmung*]."[28] Thus Heidegger's understanding of philosophy is necessarily bound up with its realization in a "people."

There are two elements to this claim: the first has to do with this understanding of philosophy—that to be truly itself, philosophy needs to be realized in and transform the world we experience and are shaped by. Marx after all said in the eleventh of his "Theses on Feuerbach" that "all previous philosophers have merely interpreted the world differently. The problem however is to change it."[29] Stanley Cavell has written regarding the understanding of philosophy he finds in Wittgenstein that "belief is not enough. Either the sentiment penetrates past assessment and becomes part of the sensibility from which assessment proceeds, or it is philosophically useless."[30] In this understanding, philosophy must be incarnated—made flesh. Philosophical mistakes derive from how we are shaped by the particular world in which we live, as Wittgenstein remarks: "The sickness of a time is cured by an alteration in the mode of life of human beings, and it was possible for the sickness of philosophical problems to get cured only through a changed mode of thought and mode of life, not through a medicine invented by an individual."[31] Philosophical errors derive from the form of life that we lead and its problems and achievements, from a life poorly lived. Without producing a full argument here, if there is something called "The Art of Living," I think I can say that Heidegger's understanding of what philosophy must accomplish to be what it is is not so idiosyncratic as to be out of court.

There is, however, a second issue: for Heidegger philosophy must realize itself in and as the destiny *of a people*. When this happens, the German people will, according to Heidegger in the *Rektoratsrede*, have attained the "highest freedom," namely, "to give the law to oneself."[32] Giving the law to oneself was, we remember, the Kantian definition of autonomy and freedom. Heidegger opposes this freedom of the German *Dasein* to the "so-called academic freedom," which, he says, is merely "negative"—that is, it creates neither autonomy nor any kind of shared enterprise of *Wissenschaft*.[33] Rather, the collective enterprise of the university should bind students and faculty, first, into the "community of the people"; second, to the "honor and destiny of the nation"; and last, to the "spiritual mission of the German people." In his *Spiegel* interview, Heidegger will relate the special world-historical task that he finds Germany to have to the "special inner relationship between the German language and the Greeks," the Greeks being for Heidegger the origin of that which we call "the West."[34] Heidegger will in fact always differentiate "the West" from "Europe." The first is a metaphysical concept; the second a historical one.

This sounds bad and can be. One should note two things. First, the notion that a particular people have a "historical mission" is not peculiar to Heidegger or to romantic nationalism. Take this well-known passage:

It has been frequently remarked that it seems to have been reserved to the people of this country, by their conduct and example, to decide the important question, whether societies of men are really capable or not of establishing good government from reflection and choice, or whether they are forever destined to depend for their political constitutions on accident and force. If there be any truth in the remark, the crisis at which we are arrived may with propriety be regarded as the era in which that decision is to be made; and a wrong election of the part we shall act may, in this view, deserve to be considered as the general misfortune of mankind.[35]

Here we have Alexander Hamilton in the first of the *Federalist Papers* invoking not only a particular historical mission for the new United States but also, much as Heidegger does in the *Rektoratsrede*, suggesting that what happens in his particular country is tied to (what Heidegger was to call) the "spiritual strength of the West." Note that Hamilton's "the people of this country" is precisely what is meant by *Volk*. And much is at stake: a mistake as to destiny will redound to "the general misfortune of mankind." One already found much the same thing at the end of "A Modell of Christian Charitie," the sermon that John Winthrop preached on board the *Arabella* to the settlers arriving in New England in 1630.[36] Nations, for Heidegger (and indeed Hamilton), come into existence with a destiny (what Heidegger calls *Geschick*) and they are aware of their *Geschick* when they acknowledge and instantiate the fate of their nation (what is "reserved to the people of this country").[37] The *Geschick* of the Greeks is summarized in the great choral ode from *Antigone* on which Heidegger spends much time in his *Introduction to Metaphysics*: sailing and navigation, agriculture, hunting, animal husbandry, speech, ruling, the polis, dwelling.[38] The actual working out of these elements becomes their *Geschichte*—their history, lived and told by and to them. For Heidegger, "self-assertion" means that Germany should be free to follow its own destiny—a destiny he conceives of as linked to National Socialism—and hence should resign from the League of Nations. About that choice he writes: "This is not a turning away from the community of peoples, but on the contrary: Our people, with this step, sets itself under the essential law of human Being to which every people must render allegiance if it is to remain a people."[39] Note that "remaining a people" requires "allegiance" to the "essential law of … Being."

Heidegger is quite clear in 1933–1934 that National Socialism has "not fallen as an accomplished eternal truth from the sky—to take it as such would be an error and a stupidity."[40] Several pages of GA 94 are filled with questioning—for example, "*Ist das der rechte Weg?*"… "*Soll unser Volk...?*"[41] Heidegger actually manifests more questioning about what might count as the "success" of National Socialism than did many others at the time (see, e.g., GA 94, pp. 190, 196). For instance, David Lloyd George, the first British prime minister of working class origins, sent a signed picture of himself to Hitler in December 1933 inscribed "To Chancellor Hitler with admiration for his brilliant gift of courage," and in a September 1935 article in the *Daily Express* wrote that Hitler was the "greatest living German" and the "George Washington of his people." The point is not that Lloyd George was misled by his experiences in Hitler's Germany, but that in the early 1930s a judgment such as his was easily possible. He was to oppose Chamberlain's appeasement policies in 1938.

The question here, however, is not about hopes for and doubts about National Socialism in 1933 but has to do with the status of "*völkisches Dasein.*" Is there such a thing? We do speak with no problem of "French cuisine," the "American Dream" (whether realizable or not), or "German engineering." Hamilton, quoted above, believed a particular destiny had been reserved for the people of the United States (which some will hold responsible for recent foreign adventures and think should be given up). There clearly is something called "American history" or "British history"—can one think of this *Geschichte* as the working out of a *Geschick*?

Whether or not one can, Heidegger is clear that the working out of a destiny is not something that happens on its own: "The tuning [*stimmende*] and modeling [*bildschaffende*] power of the concept [*Entwurf*] is decisive—the matter cannot be estimated. Attunement and model—but one must deal with the closed-off structure of the will of the *Volk.*"[42] As noted above, Heidegger thus sees the need for an education or rather educations to fulfill this destiny. The elements of the destiny of a people are given in the choral ode of the *Antigone* discussed above. The particular way a given group instantiates these elements makes it a particular people, or what Hamilton calls "the people of this country." There is thus in each people categories of what is of the people and what is not. Too much anxiety over what "is of the people" can lead to dangerous consequences—in the United States there was even a congressional committee charged with the investigation of "Un-American Activities" (originally created in 1938 to investigate those with Nazi ties but after World War II focused solely on potential and actual Communist sympathizers). But people of all political persuasions may speak of a country having "lost its way" and may call upon folk to "take back" their country. The fact that a concept can be pushed too far does not mean that it has no meaning. Heidegger will say in a lecture course given at this time that "the people and the state have a space that belongs to them. But it has not been decided whether the space of the people corresponds to the space of the state. [The] state … is essentially related to space and formed by space."[43]

Heidegger is clear that the realization of a destiny requires shaping education. In a long entry around the time of the *Rektorat* speech he sets out his goals and how to achieve them. The most authentic but most distant goal is the "historical greatness of the people in the 'working out and configuration [*Erwirkung und Gestaltung*]' of the powers of Being [*Seinsmächte*]." A more proximate goal is the "coming-to-itself of the people." A still nearer goal is the "provisional or preliminary creation of the community of the *Volk*." This is to be done through the most immediate goal, the fostering of the delight in *Arbeit* (a central theme of the *Rektoratsrede*).[44] All this is to be done by leadership. This "means: educating to independence and self-responsibility; and *spiritual* [*geistig*] leading implies: to awaken the creative forces and build them up to leadership."[45] However, "leading and following are in particular not to be understood as related to over and under," that is, they do not correspond to relations of domination and subordination (one might think of a healthy teacher–student relation). And he goes on to condemn the "irredeemable flatness of the *Geistigen*," citing as an ironic negative example Ernst Krieck, a pedagogue who believed in "German physics" and was the first Nazi to become a university rector (of the University of Frankfurt).[46] Whether or not one thinks Heidegger's program possible and/ or desirable, it is extraordinarily ambitious and is dedicated solely to the goal of restoring human *Dasein* to its pre-Socratic position—the *Erwirkung* of *Seinsmächte*.

It is clear from the material in GA 94 and elsewhere that Heidegger thought National Socialism might be the vehicle for bringing the *Volk* to its destiny *and* that he also had serious questions as to whether it would accomplish that ("We today can already speak of a 'vulgar National Socialism'"[47]). Significantly, he had real doubts as to the ability of the Germans to realize their *Volk*. "The *folk*! This is the decisive matter—all must be put to its service." Then a paragraph break in the same entry and: "The folk—good—but whither the folk? And *why* the folk: Is it only a giant jellyfish …?"[48]

For these reasons, Heidegger finds the task he sets for himself arduous and dangerous. In *The Essence of Truth: On Plato's Cave Allegory and* Theaetetus,[49] first given as lectures in 1932, thus at the time of some of these *Notebook* volumes, Heidegger will write of "The φιλόσοφος as Liberator of Prisoners. His Act of Violence, His Endangerment, His Death." Liberating will necessarily involve violence, a violence to which the *philósophos* is entitled from having beheld the *agáthon*. This violence, however, is what it takes to effectuate the *periagoge* in the Cave—the point is that people will not in and of themselves come to see the world differently. In *Introduction to Metaphysics*, Heidegger insists on the violent character of the δεινόν that is the central quality of the great choral ode from *Antigone*. *Deinón* (which carries the senses of *fearful, terrible, dread, dire, wondrous, powerful*) is violent because it is in the nature of human *Dasein* to constantly reach beyond itself.[50]

Somewhat later in that book, Heidegger notes the following:

Plato maintains as his first principle that the guardians of the state must be those who philosophize. He does not mean that philosophy professors are to become chancellors of the state [*Reichskanzler*] but that philosophers are to become φυλακες—guardians. Control and organization of the state is to be undertaken by philosophers, who set standards and rules in accordance with the deepest freely inquiring knowledge, thus determining the general course which society should follow.[51]

In 1932, the question of who would be *Reichskanzler* and what course he might follow pressed heavily on Germany. It is not going too far to say that 1932–1933 seemed to Heidegger to present the possibility that he could become a guardian to the new regime, the leader of the leader. Hence, as rector, his taking the designation of *Führer* (and, as noted, not *Magnifizenz*) is not an aping of Nazi usage but an assertion of superiority, even if it seeks to draw energy from the more popular use of that word in Germany at the time. Heidegger did seek to take over and give the "street vocabulary" of the Nazis a philosophical meaning and did so in order to use the energy of that movement to his advantage. While being a "guardian" was a logical development of his thought, it also betrays an arrogance and naïveté about his potential role, given the developing actuality of events in Germany.[52]

Reflecting on the Cave allegory, Heidegger argued that liberation did not consist simply in the ascent from the cave to the sun: "Rather genuine freedom means *to be a* liberator from the dark: True freedom is realized in the descent back into the cave and the freeing of those who are there."[53] Heidegger is also clear that this return to the cave exposes the philosopher to death—not necessarily an actual death but rather the death of being unable to overcome "prevailing self-evidences," such that he will be rendered "harmless and unthreatening." (Socrates was put to death and thought the man returning to the cave would also be—I detect a certain jealousy.) Only "by laying ahold of [the cave dwellers] violently and dragging them away" is there any hope for success.[54] Indeed, the philosopher does not "despair," but "remains firm," and "will even go over on the attack and will lay ahold of one of them to try to make him see the light in the cave."[55] It is not clear exactly how far Heidegger might extend what he means here by violence, although the use of the term is in line with his discussion of *pólemos*. It is likely, though, that he thought the violence associated with the installation of a new regime was not unrelated to what the philosopher had to do. In the Germany of the time, this might have appeared necessary. Hitler impressed many as behaving like a true statesman in exceptional times: legally elected but capable of making the hard, extralegal decisions that seemed necessary. When, in the midst of increasingly public conflict between various factions of the Party, Hitler and Goering ordered, between June 30 and July 2, 1934, the arrest and execution of the entire leadership of the *Sturmabteilung* (the SA), within two days almost all the press was congratulating them on having saved the country from civil war. Hindenburg sent (or was led to send) a telegram of thanks to the new chancellor.[56] On August 1, 1934, the jurist Carl Schmitt published a newspaper article titled "*Der Führer schützt das Recht*—The Führer protects the legal order," defending Hitler's actions. Thus it is the reality of taking power and manifesting sovereignty in the use of power that attracted Schmitt—and Heidegger—it was never simply a matter of succumbing to sorcery, though that certainly helped.

The above discussion establishes that (1) Heidegger sought the realization of his thought in the achievement by a people of that which was definingly their own (call it their destiny); (2) it was possible and likely that a people would not attain this on its own (much as Lenin thought that the working class could not by itself rise above trade-union consciousness); (3) to move toward this destiny a philosophically motivated and led political movement was necessary; and (4) such a process might potentially be to some degree violent as well as potentially dangerous to the philosophical "guardian," although it would more likely render him unheard. This understanding holds that under all political pluralism there must be a commonality—a *Volk* in its own space—that can define and make possible its own realization as to what it means to be itself—American or English or German and so forth. The position is clearly not that of liberal democratic individualism but does not strike me as incoherent.

There are, however, consequences and since the context of this book and this essay is that of the *Schwarze Hefte*, I need to turn to them. I noted at the beginning that I thought the anti-Semitic (or rather anti-Judaic) passages were an integral part of these volumes and that these volumes were, while different in style and form, of a broad piece with the rest of his writing. I also asserted that this was not a reason to reject his thought—the question was if that thought opened roads that Heidegger did not take but made available, perhaps without full cognizance.

So: what about "world-historical Judaism"? An important preliminary remark is that it is explicitly not for Heidegger a biological concept. The matter is more complex and more, can one say, philosophical. He writes: "The question of the role of World Jewry is not racial, but rather the metaphysical question as to the kind of humanity that quite unattached can assume as a world historical 'task' the uprooting of all beings from Being."[57] If I read this correctly Heidegger is making a much deeper accusation than run-of-the-mill anti-Semitism. He is not making an accusation against any individual Jew—and we know that Heidegger had many Jewish students who did not feel mistreated by him as Jews. He is asserting about "World Jewry" that it hinders or seeks to make the idea and achievement of a German *Volk* impossible. In the lecture course of 1933–1934, he will close one session by saying that "our German space would definitely be revealed differently [for a Slavic people] from the way that it is revealed to us; to Semitic nomads, it will perhaps never be revealed at all. This way of being embedded in a people, situated in a people, this original participation in the knowledge of a people, cannot be taught; at most, it can be awakened from its slumber."[58] There is some caution here ("differently," "perhaps"), even if that caution could also express darker consequences, but the direction of thought is clear.

The ice is thin here but there is no other way to another shore. It was the case that as Hitler came to power the official line of the Zionist Federation and of its paper, the *Jüdische Rundschau*, was to recognize openly the importance of fundamental national differences, in other words to use rising German anti-Semitism as a Zionist resource. Joachim Prinz, a German Zionist who was to emigrate to the United States in 1937 and become the president of the American Jewish Congress, wrote in 1934 in *Wir Juden*: "We want assimilation to be replaced by a new law: the declaration of belonging to the Jewish nation and the Jewish race. A state built upon the principle of the purity of nation and race can only be honored and respected by a Jew who declares his belonging to his own kind. Having so declared himself, he will never be capable of faulty loyalty toward a state. The state cannot want other Jews but such as declare themselves as belonging to their nation."[59] I am aware of the controversies surrounding Prinz's early work and that he is cited by Holocaust deniers: *I share nothing* with that fallacious position. Prinz's statement, however, implies that unless Jews have a state of their own ("a purity of nation and race") they will be "capable of faulty loyalty" toward the state in which they live. The point, however, has to be that in the 1930s it was not meaningless to perceive that there was in the world a movement of something one might name "World Jewry," which had as its aim the foundation of a state by and of and for Jews. (One would point to the foundation of the Zionist movement in the 1890s, the Balfour Declaration after World War I [a letter from Foreign Secretary Balfour to Baron Rothschild for transmission to the Zionist Federation],[60] the fact that two of Woodrow Wilson's closest advisors [Louis Brandeis and Felix Frankfurter] were strong Zionists, the 1920 Mandate of Palestine establishing a "Land of Israel," and the several Aliyahs ["ascent"—the immigration of diaspora Jews to Eretz Israel] from 1882 until 1948 and continuing to this day.) These are facts that can be approved of, regretted, condemned, or applauded. These facts also do not mean that someone holding this opinion should think that every Jew was a fervent proponent (any more than one should think—as some do or did—that every "real" American is white or every "real" German was a Nazi Party member), but it does mean that one could find credible that there was a broad political movement aiming at the establishment of a Jewish state.

Where Heidegger seems to me wrong is not, then, on the notion of "world-historical Jewry" but in the more-or-less tacit assumption that any Jew (unknown to him presumably) was likely to find himself or herself with at most divided loyalties in relation to the progress of this movement. He certainly had from his students, however, some sense that not all Jews were subject to Zionist appeals. Hannah Arendt, for instance, remarks in her Lessing lecture that she came to think of herself as Jewish because "they told me that that was what I was."[61]

This understanding takes me now to issues that I cannot approach, if only because I do not have the knowledge. I have asserted that it was not irrational for Heidegger to find that there existed a broad movement he names "world-historical Jewry" and that there was confirmation of this both in Zionist writings and in the response of Western countries (in particular, England and the United States) to Zionist urgings. (England actually proposed establishing a Jewish homeland in Angola.) I have also noted that while Heidegger seems tacitly to assume that all, or most, or a significant number of important Jews are subject to this "uprooting" pull, he must have known Jews who clearly were not pulled to an essentialist Zionism. His brush is very big. The question that remains is as to what vague interpretation of "world-historical Jewry" average middle-class, non-Jewish, probably non-left-wing Germans might have shared of those they perceived as "Jews"—and why. There is more to anti-Semitism than the fact that Jews "killed Christ." What exactly? Such concerns suggest work that might be done.

Should Heidegger not have applauded Zionism?[62] After all, it urged the creation of a *Staat* for a *Volk*. We do not—I do not—know what Heidegger thought about Zionism per se were it to succeed. (He did supervise Hans Jonas's 1928 doctoral dissertation on *Der Begriff des Gnosis* at a time that Jonas was an active Zionist.) It does seem to me clear, however, that in the 1930s, with no State of Israel, he could generally only perceive Zionism as undermining the possibility of the realization of a German *Geschick* in that it called that *Geschick* into question. (Not for nothing will Arendt say that *she* has her origins in "German philosophy."[63])

These volumes leave me, then, with questions that need exploration: (1) What are the uses and abuses of the idea of a "people"? (2) Is the conception of a people essentialist? If so, what does one make of that? (3) Is Heidegger's conception of *Geschick* essentialist? If so, what do we make of it? If not, what is it? (4) What is the proper relation of philosophical thought to its actualization? The *Black Notebooks*, contrary to what many have said, leave me with more to do, as they should for us all. And for that they should be read. The questions they raise for us are salient in multiple parts of our world.

Notes

1. Heidegger to Karl Löwith, cited in Karl Löwith, *My Life in Germany before and after 1933: A Report* (Champaign: University of Illinois Press, 1994), 29.

2. Alexandre Kojève, "Tyranny and Wisdom," in Leo Strauss, *"On Tyranny," Including the Strauss-Kojève Debate*, ed. Victor Gourevitch and Michael Roth (New York: Free Press, 1991), 165–166.

3. Babette Babich has argued that the *Beiträge* were structured by Heidegger precisely to prevent from happening to him what he had observed happening to Nietzsche's *Nachlass* (which becomes various versions of "The Will to Power"). See her "Heideggers *Wille zur Macht*: Die *Beiträge* lesen im Ruckblick auf Nietzsche, Wissenschaft und Technik," trans. Harald Seubert and the author, in *Heidegger und Nietzsche*, ed. Babette Babich, Alfred Denker, and Holger Zaborowski (Amsterdam: Rodopi, 2012), 283–321.

4. That said, they are certainly not what Richard Wolin calls the "culmination" of the work—see Karsten Harries, chapter 14, this volume.

5. As it has been about other texts, most recently Heidegger's *Nature, History, State: 1933–1934*, ed. and trans. Gregory Fried and Richard Polt (London: Bloomsbury, 2013), especially 51–64.

6. Harry Redner, "Philosophers and AntiSemitism," *Modern Judaism* 22, no. 2 (May 2002): 115–141.

7. Graeme Nicholson, "The Politics of Heidegger's Rectoral Address," *Man and World* 10, no. 3 (1987): 171–187. One can profit here by reading Kenneth Burke, "The Rhetoric of Hitler's 'Battle,'" in Kenneth Burke, *The Philosophy of Literary Form: Studies in Symbolic Action* (New York: Vintage, 1941; reprint, Berkeley: University of California Press, 1974, 191–220).

8. Emmanuel Faye, *Heidegger: The Introduction of Nazism into Philosophy in Light of the Unpublished Seminars of 1933–1935* (New Haven, CT: Yale University Press, 2009); see the excellent comments by Pierre Joris at http://pierrejoris.com/blog/?p=2377 and the review by Taylor Carman, *Times Literary Supplement*, September 10, 2010. For an extensive and detailed critique of Faye, see Thomas Sheehan, "Emmanuel Faye: The Introduction of Fraud into Philosophy," *Philosophy Today* 59, no. 3 (summer 2015): 367–400.

9. See Karl Löwith, *My Life in Germany before and after 1933: A Report*, 32–33. Also see similar considerations in R. Philip Buckley, *Husserl, Heidegger and the Crisis of Philosophical Responsibility* (Dordrecht:

Kluwer, 1992), 214–218, to which I owe some prompting in this section. Max Weber sees a similar destiny for any Machtstaat.

10. Careful here: we might have to go after Robert Frost for proclaiming in his poem "The Gift Outright" that "The land was ours before we were the land's."

11. "German Students," in *The Heidegger Controversy: A Critical Reader*, ed. Richard Wolin (Cambridge, MA: MIT Press, 1993), 46.

12. It is worth recalling here that in "Wissenschaft als Beruf" Weber had also thought the German university no longer manifested, if it ever did, the Humboldtian idea of "frei lehren und frei lernen" and needed to be reconstituted along different lines.

13. As reported in Elizabeth F. Hirsch, letter to the editor, *New York Times*, March 2, 1988, A22.

14. Thomas Sheehan, "'Everyone Has to Tell the Truth': Heidegger and the Jews," *Continuum* 1, no. 1 (1990): 30–44.

15. Martin Heidegger, *On the Way to Language* (New York: Harper & Row, 1971), 52–53.

16. There were other paths. If you were not Jewish, not particularly ambitious, not openly on the Left, and kept your cards relatively close to your vest, as did a scholar like Bruno Snell, you might very well remain in your post. This is what Arendt, in her response to Gershom Scholem over the *Eichmann in Jerusalem* controversy, refers to as the option of "doing nothing" ("A Daughter of Our People: A Response to Gershom Scholem," in Hannah Arendt, *The Portable Hannah Arendt* [New York: Penguin, 2000], 392).

17. Martin Heidegger, "The Self-Assertion of the German University: Address, Delivered on the Solemn Assumption of the Rectorate of the University of Freiburg. The Rectorate 1933/34: Facts and Thoughts," trans. Karsten Harries, *Review of Metaphysics* 38 (March 1985): 467–502 (quote on 470).

18. Stanley Cavell, *Little Did I Know* (Stanford, CA: Stanford University Press, 2010), 502.

19. *Überlegungen II–VI, Gesamtausgabe* 94, p. 111.

20. See Felix Ó Murchadha, *The Time of Revolution: Kairos and Chronos in Heidegger* (London: Bloomsbury, 2013).

21. See Thomas F. O'Meara, "Tillich and Heidegger: A Structural Relationship," *Harvard Theological Review* 61, no. 2 (April 1968): 249–261. Tillich remarks on Heidegger's influence on him in his *Autobiographical Reflections* (New York: Macmillan, 1952), 14, and in *The Interpretation of History* (New York: Scribner, 1936), 39–40.

22. *Überlegungen II–VI, Gesamtausgabe* 94, p. 110.

23. I say "assuming," because we do not know when that passage was written or if it was reinserted later—all we have here is what the editor has given us.

24. *Überlegungen II–VI, Gesamtausgabe* 94, p. 484.

25. In "The American Scholar," in *Essays and Lectures*, ed. Joel Porte (New York: Library of America, 1985), 60, Ralph Waldo Emerson writes: "Action is with the scholar subordinate, but it is essential. Without it, he is not yet man. Without it, thought can never ripen into truth. Whilst the world hangs before the eye as a cloud of beauty, we cannot even see its beauty. Inaction is cowardice, but there can be no scholar without the heroic mind. The preamble of thought, the transition through which it passes from the unconscious to the conscious, is action. Only so much do I know, as I have lived. Instantly we know whose words are loaded with life, and whose not." Similar understandings of philosophy (with different content, of course) are found in Lenin, Mao Zedong, Rousseau, and Wittgenstein.

26. *Überlegungen II–VI, Gesamtausgabe* 94, p. 111.

27. *Überlegungen II–VI, Gesamtausgabe* 94, p. 125.

28. *Überlegungen II–VI, Gesamtausgabe* 94, p. 112.

29. See "Thesen über Feuerbach [1845]," in Karl Marx and Friedrich Engels, *Werke*, vol. 3 (Berlin: Dietz, 1969), 7.

30. Stanley Cavell, *Must We Mean What We Say?* (New York, Scribner, 1969), 75.

31. Ludwig Wittgenstein, *Remarks on the Foundation of Mathematics* (Cambridge, MA: MIT Press, 1967), 57.

32. Heidegger, "The Self-Assertion of the German University," 3. Arnold Davidson, in "Questions Concerning Heidegger: Opening the Debate," *Critical Inquiry* 15 (1989): 407–426 (especially 413ff.), correctly and insightfully links this to an engagement with and a critique of Kant, especially the latter's "What Is Enlightenment?"

33. One of the meanings of *university*, dating from the sixteenth century, is the "experience of life taken as a means and form of instruction" (OED Online, http://www.oed.com/view/Entry/214804?rskey=YGNOzs&result =1&isAdvanced=false [accessed August 06, 2015]).

34. "'Only a God Can Save Us': *Der Spiegel*'s Interview with Martin Heidegger," trans. Maria P. Alter and John D. Caputo, in *The Heidegger Controversy: A Critical Reader*, ed. Richard Wolin, 113–115 (Cambridge, MA: MIT Press, 1993). Note that a non-Nazi like Bruno Snell can write in his *The Discovery of Mind: The Greek Origins of European Thought* (Cambridge, MA: Harvard University Press, [1946] 1953), 7, 205: "If we are to be Europeans, we must ask 'what were the Greeks?'"

35. Publius (Alexander Hamilton), *The Federalist Papers* (CreateSpace Independent Publishing Platform, 2015), 3.

36. John Winthrop, "A Modell of Christiane Charitie," https://history.hanover.edu/texts/winthmod.html.

37. See similar remarks by Graeme Nicholson, "Justifying Your Nation," in Graeme Nicholson, *Justifying Our Existence: An Essay in Applied Phenomenology* (Toronto: University of Toronto Press, 2009).

38. Martin Heidegger, *Introduction to Metaphysics*, trans. Gregory Fried and Richard Polt (New Haven, CT: Yale University Press, 2000), 156–157. Nicholson makes the same link.

39. Cited from Guido Schneeberger, *Nachlese zu Heidegger: Dokumente zu seinem Leben und Denken* (Bern: Suhr, 1962), 149.

40. *Überlegungen II–VI, Gesamtausgabe* 94, pp. 114–115.

41. *Überlegungen II–VI, Gesamtausgabe* 94, pp. 121–122.

42. *Überlegungen II–VI, Gesamtausgabe* 94, p. 135.

43. Heidegger, *Nature, History, State: 1933–1934*, 55.

44. *Überlegungen II–VI, Gesamtausgabe* 94, p. 136.

45. *Überlegungen II–VI, Gesamtausgabe* 94, p. 138.

46. *Überlegungen II–VI, Gesamtausgabe* 94, p. 138.

47. *Überlegungen II–VI, Gesamtausgabe* 94, p. 142.

48. *Überlegungen II–VI, Gesamtausgabe* 94, p. 195.

49. Martin Heidegger, *The Essence of Truth: On Plato's Cave Allegory and* Theaetetus, trans. Ted Sadler (New York: Continuum, 2002), 58.

50. Heidegger, *Introduction to Metaphysics*, 160.

51. Heidegger, *The Essence of Truth*, 73.

52. See Otto Pöggeler's essay, "Den Führer führen; Heidegger und kein Ende," *Philosophische Rundschau* 32 (1985): 26ff.

53. Heidegger, *The Essence of Truth: On Plato's Cave Allegory and* Theaetetus, 66. I am informed and assisted in this paragraph by the excellent discussion in Mary-Jane Rubenstein, *Strange Wonder: The Closure of Metaphysics and the Opening of Awe* (New York: Columbia University Press, 2008), 51–54.

54. Heidegger, *The Essence of Truth: On Plato's Cave Allegory and* Theaetetus, 61, 62.

55. Heidegger, *The Essence of Truth: On Plato's Cave Allegory and* Theaetetus, 65.

56. See the discussion of the event in Ian Kershaw, *The "Hitler Myth"* (Oxford: Oxford University Press, 2001), 84–95.

57. *Überlegungen XII–XV, Gesamtausgabe* 96, p. 245. "Die Frage nach der Rolle des *Weltjudentums* ist keine rassische, sondern die metaphysische Frage nach der Art von Menschentümlichkeit, die *schlechthin ungebunden* die Entwurzelung alles Seienden aus dem Sein als weltgeschichtliche 'Aufgabe' übernehmen kann."

58. Heidegger, *Nature, History, State: 1933–1934*, 56. The same idea occurs at the end of Ernst Kantorowicz, *Kaiser Friedrich der Zweite* (Berlin: Georg Bondi, 1927): *rex quondam, sic futurus*.

59. Joachim Prinz, *Wir Juden* (Stuttgart: Reclam, [1934] 1993), 155.

60. "His Majesty's government view with favour the establishment in Palestine of a national home for the Jewish people, and will use their best endeavours to facilitate the achievement of this object," http://www.mfa.gov .il/mfa/foreignpolicy/peace/guide/pages/the%20balfour%20declaration.aspx. Balfour and Lloyd George were also responding favorably to urgings from Chaim Weizmann, a British Zionist chemist who had developed a way to synthesize acetone, then desperately needed for munitions.

61. See in particular her unfinished essay "Antisemitism" in Hannah Arendt, *The Jewish Writings* (New York: Scribner, 2007), and the excellent review by Gabriel Piterberg, "Zion's Rebellious Daughter: Hannah Arendt on Palestine and Jewish Politics," *New Left Review* 48 (November–December 2007), http://newleftreview.org/ II/48/gabriel-piterberg-zion-s-rebel-daughter.

62. Eyal Chowers, *The Political Philosophy of Zionism: Trading Jewish Words for an Hebraic Land* (Cambridge: Cambridge University Press, 2012), 124–126, finds only a slight similarity. The most complex study is Peter Eli Gordon, *Rosenzweig and Heidegger: Between Judaism and German Philosophy* (Berkeley: University of California Press, 2005).

63. Letter to Gershom Scholem, July 24, 1963, in Hannah Arendt, *The Jewish Writings*, 466.

16

Heidegger and National Socialism: Great Hopes, Despair, and Resilience

Thomas Rohkrämer

In recent decades, researchers have discovered an increasing amount of evidence for the fatal attraction of National Socialism among the German population in general, and among German academics in particular.[1] A large majority easily fell in line because they were attracted to Nazism or viewed it from a pragmatic career perspective. They made use of the new regime to gain support for their research and to overcome any hindrance to their own professional goals. Philosophers proved no exception: while twenty professors were forced out of their positions, about thirty joined the Nazi Party in 1933, and almost half had become party members by 1940. Not only did "life philosophers" or radical Nietzscheans support the regime; the rival schools of Neo-Kantians or value philosophers also had adherents who made the same political decision for very different reasons.[2] But Martin Heidegger's case is obviously of particular interest, partly because he pushed the Nazi line with fanatical conviction as rector of Freiburg University in 1933–1934, and partly because he has become a key figure in continental philosophy.

The general story is clear: Jürgen Habermas's exclamation from 1988—"Martin Heidegger? A Nazi, of course a Nazi"[3]—has been confirmed by later research. Up to the publication of *Being and Time* (1927), Heidegger did not engage directly with politics, though his *Kulturkritik,* especially about *das Man* ("the they"), his emphasis on rootedness in a particular world, as well as the importance he attached to a specific ethnic historicity, the possible fate of a people, and the need to consciously accept that fate,[4] would suggest—at least within the discourse of the Weimar Republic—that he had an affinity for conservatism, the conservative revolution, and *völkisch* ideologies. Heidegger had never limited himself to purely academic questions but had sought to address existential issues, and in the early 1930s a crisis in his writing came together with the belief that the Occident faced an apocalyptic crisis that would either lead to a terrible future or be overcome by a new beginning.[5] From 1930 to 1934 he believed that Nazism promised to be the movement that would bring about a new beginning;[6] then a certain disillusionment set in, although the speed and extent of his separation remain controversial, are difficult to determine, and will be the topic of this chapter. In any case, even in the long run he never participated in the turn toward the West of the majority of conservatives under Adenauer's chancellorship, but continued to voice his skepticism toward industrial modernization and democracy as well as positively emphasizing the allegedly particular German affinity for philosophy and deep thought. The problems he had dealing openly with his own past were again typical of elites in postwar Germany.[7] He admitted that he had taken on the rectorate because he had seen "in the movement that had come to power the possibility of an inner self-collecting and of a renewal of the people, and a path toward the discovery of its historical-occidental purpose,"[8] but he played down his Nazi sympathies before 1933 and exaggerated the break with Nazism after 1934. As so many did after 1945, he, and later those publishing his collected works, tried to sanitize his past by holding back the publication of incriminating texts, by making and accepting later changes to texts without pointing out these alterations, and by trying to limit access to archival material—which showed, for example, that Heidegger had used Nazi buzzwords unscrupulously in university politics when opposing appointments and promoting his own candidates.[9]

As always, the endeavor to cover up the past did not curb the debate, but fueled and polarized it. Within this context, the publication of the *Black Notebooks* thus marks a belated but important step toward more transparency, and they are certainly an aid in understanding Heidegger's position within the German Right in the Weimar Republic, his reasons for joining the Nazi movement, and his gradually growing disillusionment—a disillusionment, however, that did not lead to a clear break with Nazism at least within the timeframe of the notebooks published so far.

In line with the philosopher's self-understanding, his followers have long seen Heidegger as an essentially "unpolitical" thinker who slipped up only once, for a brief period, by wholly misunderstanding the character of National Socialism in 1933–1934. And it is true, of course, that his philosophical work mainly engages with Greek philosophy and a few great names of the occidental tradition. However, the term *unpolitical*—in the wake of Thomas Mann's famous First World War book with that title—merely meant a positioning of oneself beyond party politics,[10] and it did not preclude a strong nationalist, militarist, or authoritarian orientation. Not unlike Richard Wagner, Stefan George, or Ludwig Klages, Heidegger attracted dedicated followers throughout the Weimar years, and he exerted fascination as a teacher addressing existential concerns before he confirmed his reputation with the publication of *Being and Time*. The often-noted fascination with his lectures indicates that from early in his career, he was more than just a philosopher, but spoke to the heart of more general concerns of the times. Heidegger had a tendency to interpret his own personal development in more general historical terms, and he found resonance with this— among students and within wider debates about the situation of the times.

This sense of a correspondence between personal and general historical developments seems to have started with his break with the faith in which he had grown up and that he had initially accepted as his vocation: Catholicism. To him, this break was not just a personal step. Rather, he came to think that the horrors of the First World War showed that the Christian God had "lost his effective force in history."[11] In the wake of Nietzsche, the many faithful Christians he knew did not alter his conviction that the Christian God was dead and nihilism reigned because this faith was no longer strong enough to influence the course of history.

What does it mean to say that a god is dead because this god no longer shapes history, and why does humanity need a new beginning and a new god in this situation, if it is to be saved from catastrophe or a shallow life devoid of any meaning and purpose? This viewpoint rejects the modern notion of religion as a private matter, claiming instead the need for a single communal faith that unites an ethnic community and directs public affairs.

The desire for a single communal faith has had a long tradition in German history, reaching back from Romanticism and the desire for a new mythology to the belief in a nationalist faith uniting the whole community in one purpose.[12] The existence of divisions between ethnic groups, between religious convictions and social classes, between opposing political parties and interest groups, and between a plurality of artistic schools and lifestyles, all this was seen as a sign of crisis and decadence.

Heidegger was not just a philosopher, but more generally a *Kulturkritiker*, a critic of current culture as a whole, who reflected on the dangers of the modern condition.[13] As is typical of the long tradition of cultural criticism, he made alarmist proclamations about the state of contemporary society, often by comparing it to allegedly better times in the past, but he was a modern *Kulturkritiker* in the sense that he was equally critical of existing traditions and hoped for a "new beginning." His mobilization of the past was not conservative in that he was not concerned with trying to stop change, nor reactionary in that he did not try to return to a recent period of the past, but his was a revolutionary conservatism that used allegedly great moments of the past to inspire and direct the way to a new and better future. While the conventional everyday existence of the *man* was seen in negative terms, Heidegger's appeal was for decisiveness and commitment in finding one's own authentic existence. And the individual was called for and called on to be decisive, because it was not the masses but a spiritual elite that was to create and promote a new single communal faith.

Cultural critics always have a tendency toward alarmism, but this was intensified by the apocalyptic thinking prevalent in the Weimar Republic.[14] War and what was perceived as a humiliating defeat, bitter revolutionary clashes and irresolvable political conflicts between Left and Right, and above all the "imposition" of an "un-German new political system," all this added up to a situation in which the extreme Right moved toward desperado strategies. The present seemed so intolerable that one could throw caution to the winds: because it was inconceivable to the extremists that things could get worse, there was a tendency toward reckless measures in the effort to turn things around. Since the present seemed utterly dismal, *any* measure seemed justified when working for dramatic change for the better.

In particular, among the political Right there was a call for "heroic realism," a term coined by the Nazi Werner Best and popularized by the soldierly nationalist Ernst Jünger. The harsh reality of the First World War seemed to show that all morality was a deceptive illusion when confronted with the power of a machine gun, and that Romanticism was a futile attempt to escape a sober reality. One needed, it was argued in a wide variety of forms, to "learn ways to behave in a cold world,"[15] and a cold ruthlessness was required when trying to realize one's political goals.[16]

While Heidegger displayed conservative traits—such as an emphasis on rootedness in one's history and *Heimat* or an emphasis on hierarchy and a structured society against a chaotic "mass society"—he only became political in a narrower sense of the word with the economic crisis and the different assaults on democracy toward the end of the Weimar Republic. In particular, he came to be impressed by Ernst Jünger's *Worker* as an accurate description of the contemporary world and by Carl Schmitt's political theories. His support for National Socialism set in before Hitler became chancellor,[17] but he cautiously delayed becoming a party member until their rule seemed secure.

What persuaded Heidegger first to vote for the National Socialists and then to become a party member and a university rector in outspoken support of the regime? The main difficulty in answering this question lies in the fact that National Socialism was many things to many people. Unlike communism, there was no attempt to arrive at one party line. Even among leading Nazis there was a wide range of opinion—for example, between the backward-oriented Rosenberg and Goebbels, who was fascinated by modern technology, in particular film and radio; between Röhm's call for a social revolution and Göring's emphasis on an alliance with the elites; or between Himmler's obscure mysticism and Heydrich's cool, task-oriented fanaticism. In the Nazi propaganda of the early 1930s, the message was left deliberately vague. It included a rejection of Marxism, Jews, and the Weimar system, a turn toward a more authoritarian regime, the restoration of German strength in economic terms and in international relations by revising the Versailles Treaty, and the ideal of *Volksgemeinschaft* or a community of the people as a fairer but not egalitarian society. Promises were made to farmers, the old middle class, and other groups threatened by the forces of change, but assurances were also given to the new middle class of a continued emphasis on technological progress and to big industry that the new primacy of politics would not threaten their entrepreneurial freedom. National Socialism was never a precise doctrine, but a "*Glaubensraum*" (Ernst Bloch),[18] an ideological space with enough common elements to speak of a worldview with a common structure and orientation, but with many different individual variants. Because the views of individuals changed over time and according to circumstances, the best image might even be that of a kaleidoscope in which elements could be arranged and emphasized in a wide variety of ways. The centrality of the *Führer* cult meant that personal loyalty and faith were crucial, whereas purity of dogma was not.[19]

Although Heidegger was a man of letters, his writing does not show any engagement with Hitler's *Mein Kampf* or with other texts on party ideology or the party program; despite this he rhapsodizes about "the great experience and joy that the *Führer* has founded a new reality that will give our thinking the right direction and momentum."[20] While Hitler constantly emphasized his unalterable core convictions and his firm determination to realize them against all odds, Heidegger emphasized the spiritual openness of the new political force: "*National Socialism* has not fallen from the sky as a completed eternal truth—seen like this it becomes a confusion and foolishness. As it has come into existence, it must continue to develop while shaping the future."[21]

One of the main reasons many people shifted their support from conservatism to National Socialism was not ideological, but motivated by the belief that the old forces did not have the power and determination to establish a new and better order. A stronger emphasis on social justice was one of the features that distinguished conservatism from National Socialism, the other the belief that the latter was more decisive and dynamic in breaking with the Weimar Republic and starting a new era. As a Nazi election slogan from 1932 proclaimed: "Those who want everything to stay as it is vote for Hindenburg. Those who want everything to change vote for Hitler."[22] This emphasis on being daring in moving into an unknown future, guided only by the endeavor to gain a new sense of Being, was Heidegger's key ideal. He projected it onto National Socialism, but it had little correspondence with the real Nazism, which was above all a political force trying to consolidate its power and strengthen Germany by creating a superior Aryan race and preparing for war and conquest.

Heidegger was attracted both by the idea of creating a more just community of the people—he joined the party, after all, on the symbolically charged National Labor Day— and by the promise of a forceful policy aimed at a new beginning. In his teaching, he addressed this concept of a new beginning from the winter of 1931–1932 onward, and all the way through the *Black Notebooks*, he is constantly pondering the possibility of a new beginning in Germany: "A new faith is spreading through the young country"; "Only the German can find new expression for a primordial Being in word and poetry."[23] Hermann Mörchen, a student close to Heidegger, remembered that Heidegger even accepted the need for Boxheimer tactics[24]—that is, the plans from 1931 for a violent Nazi takeover of power in response to a communist uprising that would include the death sentence for everyone resisting the coup, even if the resistance only took the form of a strike or other peaceful means. After the "seizure of power" Heidegger spoke about National Socialism as a "barbaric principle. This is essential about it and its potential greatness. The danger is not National Socialism as such—but that it is rendered harmless in sermons about the true, good, and beautiful."[25] It thus seems that it was not the details of the ideology that were decisive for him, but its power to establish a new reality that would then be the foundation of reflections for a new beginning. The belief in an apocalyptic situation with the prospect of disaster and the hope for a new beginning, the conviction that ruthless actions were necessary in this decisive moment, and the hope that the new beginning would lead to a nation united in a single communal faith thus came together to make Heidegger support the most radical political force on the political Right. His radical *Kulturkritik*—leading him to a complete rejection of present conditions—combined with the belief that an apocalyptic situation was approaching that would result in either complete disaster or salvation presumably made him believe in the need for the Nazis' brutal measures. The fact that Nazism used terror against its opponents from the very beginning does not feature at all in the *Black Notebooks*. In the grand perspective Heidegger adopted, the criminal policies of the Nazis clearly seemed of little or no concern.

Nietzsche wrote that "only as aesthetic phenomenon does existence and the world appear justified";[26] Oswald Spengler eagerly anticipated spectacular times;[27] and Ernst Jünger fantasized about "the unity of one rule …, in which the sacrifice finds fulfillment and legitimation, allegories of the eternal in the harmonic rule of the space and in monuments, which will stand the passage of time."[28] In a similar vein, Heidegger rejected the use of moral standards,[29] using instead impressive times of the past—in particular classical Greece "as the memory of past greatness of humans during a new beginning"[30]—as patterns for anticipating an ideal future. He rejected the term *aesthetics*, but he emphasized the desire for a "style … in which the rule of the last god opens and shapes being."[31] For him even the end of a whole ethnic culture was better than a shallow existence—as long as this end occurred in a great, dramatic style.[32]

In the first year of Nazi rule, Heidegger was intoxicated with enthusiasm and hope. According to his reading of the past, nihilism was to be overcome by "great politics,"[33] and in 1933 he believed he was living and participating in such a great historic moment. The *Führer* would establish a new reality, and he would provide the philosophical dimension to it. Philosophy and art were to manifest themselves and explore Being within this new historical framework as freely and openly as possible without political control, but this did not mean a commitment to the pluralism of the Weimar Republic. On the contrary, Heidegger undoubtedly believed that only he and possibly a very small number of thinkers with strong affinities for his philosophical approach should work toward shaping the new communal perspective on existence and Being.[34] All philosophy before him since the early Greek thinkers had been tied up with the rise of nihilism; Catholicism allegedly merely veiled the nihilism of the times and thus hindered an awareness of the need for a new beginning, and dialectical theology was seen as a "Protestant Jesuitism of the worst kind."[35] In the artistic sphere, music was unessential, Wagner only provided shallow Romanticism, and only one person (i.e., Hölderlin) was *the* poet who provided the ultimate diagnosis of the times and gave the decisive indication of a new beginning.

Although the new beginning was supposed to build on the German ethnic tradition and connect with the German soil, it was not the voice of the people that was meant to lead the way forward, but a highly limited number of individuals with the genius to sense Being within the specific ethnic tradition and give expression to it. In accordance with this hierarchical thinking, Heidegger as rector saw the need for camps for university faculty and particularly suitable students where the participants were to be instructed in his way of thinking. The goal was to create a new spiritual elite that would live and promote an individual and collective existence in correspondence with Heidegger's attitude toward existence and Being. More widely, this was also the task he envisaged for the future university: it should not limit itself to producing specialized knowledge or to training students for specific tasks, but should primarily be a philosophical "think tank" to guide Germany in its new beginning. According to Heidegger, the masses had a tendency to slip into a shallow existence focused solely on security and comfort; an elite thus had to lead them to a greatness emerging from a daring exposure to Being. Such a way of thinking—which showed affinities with Goebbels's claim that the true politician is like an artist "forming the solid and complete image of the people from the original brute mass"[36]—tended to disregard the everyday concerns of the masses in favor of grand philosophical visions.[37] Even in wartime, Heidegger remained focused on the nihilism of the times and the chances of a new beginning, while concerns about human suffering play at most a marginal role throughout the *Black Notebooks*.

Heidegger thus had high hopes in 1933. He saw the immediate goal as the provision of work for all "national comrades" to sustain their existence, the further goal as the creation of "a community of the people" that would find itself "in its rootedness and by taking on its mission within the state," and the ultimate decisive goal as "the historic greatness of the *Volk* in effecting and shaping the power of Being."[38] All this was to be achieved under the spiritual guidance of Heidegger (and possibly at most a handful of exceptional people with him) and a spiritual elite supporting him within the framework of the university that would see its primary task in reflecting on the essence of the new Being and the mission of the German people. Obviously, these far-fetched fantasies had to clash with reality: Hitler and the Nazis had their own vision of the future. They liked having a prestigious philosopher on board, but had no inclination to listen to him. The intention of strengthening philosophy within the university at the expense of more practical matters clashed with the Nazi emphasis on strengthening Germany; other Nazi intellectuals competed with Heidegger for the acquisition of power in the new Reich; and the vast majority of students had no idea what Heidegger's philosophy was all about, and little interest in finding out.

Heidegger was first disappointed in the students, then—as early as December 1933—in the university as a whole.[39] He concluded that the university did not have the power to reform itself and called his time as rector "a failed year." At this time, however, he still saw National Socialism on the whole as being on a positive path and moving swiftly to a new beginning.[40]

Over the next few years, his criticism of the Third Reich grew steadily. He came to regard the so-called organic thinking a confused "dark brew,"[41] and he criticized racism as too materialistic. A new beginning, he believed, could not be produced in a Darwinist fashion by racial breeding, but only in the spiritual sphere.[42] He attacked history as a technical discipline merely devoted to telling how the past "really was" (Leopold von Ranke) instead of trying to find relevant patterns—that is, key dangers one needed to reflect on, as well as inspiring examples for the present.[43] He came to reject Nazism's emphasis on the *Volk* since it allegedly glorified the people as they were, instead of trying to promote a greater existence in line with their heritage.[44] The proclaimed attachment to nature was, he claimed, in reality an instrumentalization of it, and the national mobilization occurred, he feared, at the expense of the countryside, with "urbanization and the destruction of villages and farms" proceeding at an unprecedented pace.[45] Finally, the emphasis on "authentic experience," as glorified since the beginnings of the *Lebensreform* ("Life reform") and *Lebensphilosophie* ("Life philosophy") movements (if not since Romanticism), was criticized as a self-centered indulgence of one's own feelings.[46]

Heidegger saw one unified force behind all this, and that was *Machenschaft* or machination. Technology was the most obvious example of this machination, but technology could not have come into existence without a corresponding human mentality. Instrumental reason and technology, the emphasis on security, comfort, and economic growth, the wish to control nature and perfect its exploitation, the will to power and domination, and an ever-growing individualism that realizes its alleged interests at the expense of the rest of the world—all this comes together in the rule of machination, a term anticipating the later analysis of technology as *Gestell* or "enframing." The human that sees himself or herself as a subject separate from its surroundings seeks control over the world instead of aiming to be the shepherd of Being. In the latter half of the 1930s, National Socialism was no longer seen as a turning away from a machination dominant in Western Europe and Bolshevist Russia, but as a variant of machination, and actually together with Bolshevism as its most extreme form. National Socialism had turned, Heidegger feared, into a "Rational Socialism" based purely on calculation and a plan to increase its power.[47] There are still passages expressing hope for a new beginning, but Heidegger had started to think in terms of a much longer timeframe and even considered the possibility that there would never be another new beginning.

Because Heidegger always showed disregard for material questions, his *Kulturkritik* was possibly most concerned about the decline in the cultural sphere. He clearly saw that cultural production in the 1930s did not explore human existence and Being, but merely served to control the masses. Current culture, he claimed, was merely an "add-on to technology," and primarily functioned to make humans conformist and to achieve a "systematic stupefaction." Culture had become an "entertainment industry," propaganda the "art of lying." [48]

In contrast to Nazi glorification of militarism, the war only confirmed Heidegger's pessimism. While he frequently glorified the deeds of soldiers, his opinion of war in general was negative: it not only brought terrible suffering, but failed to bring any positive gains. No change for the better had come from the First World War and nothing good would come from a subsequent world war. Even if Germany succeeded in expanding its territory, such imperialism would only increase the danger that Germans would lose their identity.[49]

Does all this insightful and damning critique of the Third Reich—culminating in the judgment that "the new politics is an essential consequence of technology"[50]—mean that Heidegger had turned against Nazi Germany by the beginning of the war? No. While his initial enthusiastic hope and support had disappeared, he now saw the rise of National

Socialism as a "necessary" development in the history of Being. Thus it would be wrong to oppose it from traditional viewpoints. Instead, one had to follow along with the development in a constructive manner and seek out the opportunities for a new beginning within it.[51] In speculating on the course of history, Heidegger even wondered whether a further intensification of machination might be necessary to avoid "a premature new beginning that would ebb away quickly."[52] In 1938–1939, he explained this position of disillusionment combined with continued support with the words:

Thinking purely "metaphysically" (i.e., according to the history of Being), in the years 1930–1934 I regarded National Socialism as the possibility for a new beginning, and I gave it this interpretation. In this way, this "movement" was misunderstood and underestimated as to its true powers and its inner possibilities as well as its kind of greatness and its delivery of greatness. Here begins in fact in a much deeper—that is, wider and more thorough fashion than in Fascism—the complete realization of the modern era. ... This complete realization requires the decisiveness of ... complete "mobilization."[53]

Heidegger thus recognized that he had been wrong in seeing National Socialism as a "new beginning." His love for the new regime had led to disappointment, but now he saw National Socialism as necessary for the most extreme realization of the modern technological frenzy, a point that might then also be the historic tipping point where a completely different new beginning might set in. To put it differently: his perspective on National Socialism could change completely from being the "new beginning" to being the high point of *Seinsverlassenheit* or dereliction of Being, but Heidegger still accepted the regime as inevitable and necessary. His "blind support" had been replaced, he wrote, by an "essential affirmation."[54] For Heidegger, it seems, there was nothing that Nazism could do that would put it in the wrong.

Any possible opposition to National Socialism in Heidegger is not only undermined by a belief in its necessity beyond any possible moral condemnation, but also by his firm belief that Germany was *the* nation in which a new beginning might take place. Heidegger scrutinized and deconstructed many ideas and concepts in an enlightening fashion, but his crude belief in ethnic stereotypes reached new heights when the war began. He had always believed that Germans had a special ability and mission to contemplate Being and to bring about a new beginning, but now ethnic stereotypes reigned freely. Through the provocation of increasing international tensions and war, the Nazis had created a situation in which their polarized racist worldview gained plausibility. Heidegger might still have rejected a racism that saw differences in something as material as blood, but even if for him the ethnic differences emerged from different historical developments, the end result was crude national and racial stereotypes. A cultural racism allowed for making individual exceptions—such as his close relationship with some Jewish students in the Weimar Republic or his relationship with the Jewish Hannah Arendt, which resumed as friendship after 1945—but from 1938 on, ethnic prejudices were expressed with growing frequency and intensity. Even if it is interesting that such statements are much more common and extreme in these private notes than in his lectures and publications (and this although public statements of this kind would have only promoted his career prospects in the Third Reich; was there still an inkling in Heidegger that those thoughts were not quite "proper" within philosophy?), they do show that Heidegger associated different attitudes toward existence and Being with different groups of people.

Heidegger's anti-Semitic statements have attracted the most attention and provoked the deepest shock, even among those who value Heidegger's philosophy highly.[55] Heidegger did not think twice about using Nazi terms such as "international Jewry" or "World Jewry"; independent of their very different backgrounds in different countries, Jews are allegedly all characterized by an "empty rationality and an affinity for calculation [*Rechenhaftig-keit*]."[56] While Heidegger believed that he did not think in racial categories, he did ask the allegedly "metaphysical question" about what kind of humanity "World Jewry" embodied so that they as a "people of no ties [*ungebunden*]" had the ability to take on the "task in world history" of "uprooting all human existence from Being."[57] He added: "World Jewry, goaded on by Jewish emigrants who had been allowed to leave Germany, is everywhere unfathomable. It exerts power without ever participating in battle, while we cannot avoid sacrificing the best blood of the best of our own nation."[58]

Heidegger's crude anti-Semitism is shocking, but his opinion of the Anglo-Saxon world was hardly less extreme. Britain and the United States were characterized by the same affinity for calculation and rationality, although there was an attempt to disguise this by the pretense of morality. They were seen to be more dangerous than Bolshevism, because their "sweeping and ruthless suffocation of all creative historical existence" was worse than the high number of repressed and executed people in the Soviet Union.[59] Thus "the bourgeois-Christian form of English 'Bolshevism' is the most dangerous. Without its annihilation, the modern era will be preserved. The final annihilation can, however, only take the form of essential self-annihilation, which is furthered most strongly by the overcharging of the pretense that it is the savior of morality."[60] The Anglo-Saxon world was not seen as part of the occidental tradition, but—in contrast to the rest of Europe—as rootless and devoid of any reason to exist.[61]

While Jewry, England, and America were thus wholly condemned (and Bolshevism was seen as an outgrowth of this Western tradition), the Russian and German people were seen in a much more positive light. While the Nazis despised the Russians as "subhuman Slavs," Heidegger—like the prominent conservative revolutionary Moeller van den Bruck and others—glorified them as a profound and rooted people, and he even speculated whether a combination of an alleged Russian depth of experience and a German thoroughness in searching for the truth might combine to bring about a new beginning.[62]

In such sweeping associations between nations and metaphysical positions, and between these metaphysical positions and the chances for a "new beginning," the real war and questions of responsibility were completely ignored. Human suffering was as peripheral in Heidegger's history of Being as were more profane questions such as: Who unleashed the war, who committed crimes against humanity, and who was responsible for all the suffering? No matter what the German side did, Heidegger identified with his nation because he believed that only this nation could possibly bring about a new beginning. Or one could also turn the logic around: Heidegger was so nationalistic that he could never withdraw his support from Germany in the war, and the justification that trumped the responsibility for human suffering was that only the Germans could bring about the all-important "new beginning." During the war, he thus still saw the essential alternative as Germany being pulverized between England and the Soviet Union or that "we can become a new beginning of the Occident."[63]

While Heidegger thus became increasingly disillusioned with Nazism in the latter half of the 1930s—recognizing the shallowness of its ideology, its manipulative strategies, and its destruction of German traditions—his support for the regime did not disappear. Love was replaced by a belief in the inevitable necessity of a National Socialist Germany, but he was unwavering in his belief that a German victory would be best for what he took to be all-important: a new beginning.

Notes

1. For a general discussion see Thomas Rohkrämer, *Die fatale Attraktion des Nationalsozialismus: Über die Popularität eines Unrechtregimes* (Paderborn: Schöningh, 2013).

2. Hans Sluga, *Heidegger's Crisis: Philosophy and Politics in Nazi Germany* (New York: Cambridge University Press, 1993), 8–9.

3. Jürgen Habermas, "Ein Gespräch mit Jürgen Habermas: 'Martin Heidegger? Nazi, sicher ein Nazi!,'" Interview by Mark Hunyadi, in *Die Heidegger Kontroverse*, ed. Jürg Altwegg (Frankfurt: Athenäum, 1988), 172–175.

4. Martin Heidegger, *Sein und Zeit, Gesamtausgabe 2*, ed. Friedrich-Wilhelm von Herrmann (Frankfurt: Klostermann, 1977), 508–516.

5. For a concise summary see Peter Trawny, *Heidegger und der Mythos der jüdischen Weltverschwörung* (Frankfurt: Klostermann, 2014), 17ff.

6. Martin Heidegger, *Überlegungen VII–XI (Schwarze Hefte 1938/39), Gesamtausgabe 95*, ed. Peter Trawny (Frankfurt: Klostermann, 2014), 408.

7. For Heidegger within this wider context see for example Daniel Morat, *Von der Tat zur Gelassenheit: Konservatives Denken bei Martin Heidegger, Ernst Jünger und Friedrich Georg Jünger 1920–1960* (Göttingen: Wallstein, 2007).

8. Martin Heidegger, "Das Rektorat 1933/34," in *Reden und andere Zeugnisse eines Lebensweges, Gesamtausgabe 16*, ed. Hermann Heidegger (Frankfurt: Klostermann, 2000), 374.

9. See above all the works of Hugo Ott, Victor Farías, Emmanuel Faye, Rainer Marten, Marion Heinz, and Sidonie Kellerer.

10. Thomas Mann, *Betrachtungen eines Unpolitischen* (Frankfurt: Fischer, [1919] 2001).

11. Heidegger, "Das Rektorat 1933/34," 376. Similar thoughts are found frequently in the *Black Notebooks*—for example, see *Überlegungen VII–XI, Gesamtausgabe 95*, p. 81.

12. Thomas Rohkrämer, *A Single Communal Faith? The German Right from Conservatism to National Socialism* (Oxford: Berghahn Press, 2007).

13. For a general discussion of *Kulturkritik* see Georg Bollenbeck, *Eine Geschichte der Kulturkritik: Von Rousseau bis Günther Anders* (Munich: Beck, 2007) (for his definition and characterization of "*Kulturkritik* as a particular mode of reflection in modernity," see pp. 10–12); Ralf Konersmann, *Kulturkritik* (Frankfurt: Suhrkamp, 2008); and the different contributions on this topic in Ralf Konersmann, John Michael Krois, and

Dirk Westerkamp, eds., *Kulturkritik: Zeitschrift für Kulturphilosophie* 2007/2 (Hamburg: Felix Meiner, 2008).

14. Jürgen Brokoff, *Die Apokalypse in der Weimarer Republik* (Munich: Fink, 2001); Klaus Vondung, *Die Apokalypse in Deutschland* (Munich: dtv, 1988).

15. Helmut Lethen, *Cool Conduct: The Culture of Distance in Weimar Germany* (Berkeley: University of California Press, 2002). The quotation is the literal translation of the less elegant but more precise German title: *Verhaltenslehre der Kälte: Lebensversuche zwischen den Kriegen* (1994).

16. Ulrich Herbert, *Best: Biographische Studie über Radikalismus, Weltanschauung und Vernunft, 1903–1989* (Bonn: Dietz, 1996); Michael Wildt, *Generation des Unbedingten: Das Führungskorps des Reichssicherheits-hauptamtes* (Hamburg: Hamburger Edition, 2002); Thomas Rohkrämer, "Kult der Gewalt und Sehnsucht nach Ordnung—der soldatische Nationalismus in der Weimarer Republik," in *Sociologicus* 51 (2001): 28–48.

17. Emmanuel Faye, *Heidegger: The Introduction of Nazism into Philosophy in Light of the Unpublished Seminars of 1933–1935* (New Haven, CT: Yale University Press, 2009), 30f.

18. Ernst Bloch, *Das Prinzip Hoffnung* (Frankfurt: Suhrkamp, 1976), 178, 64; Ernst Bloch, *Erbschaft dieser Zeit* (Frankfurt: Suhrkamp, 1962), 58.

19. Rohkrämer, *Die fatale Attraktion des Nationalsozialismus*, 11–13.

20. Martin Heidegger, *Überlegungen II–VI* (*Schwarze Hefte 1931–1938*), *Gesamtausgabe* 94, ed. Peter Trawny (Frankfurt: Klostermann, 2014), 111.

21. *Überlegungen II–VI*, *Gesamtausgabe* 94, pp. 114f.

22. Reprinted in Jeremy Noakes and Geoffrey Pridham, eds., *Nazism 1919–1945: A Documentary Reader,* vol. 1 (Exeter: Exeter University Press, 1983), 73.

23. *Überlegungen II–VI*, *Gesamtausgabe* 94, p. 27.

24. Faye, *Heidegger*, 30.

25. Heidegger, *Überlegungen II–VI*, *Gesamtausgabe* 94, p. 194.

26. Friedrich Nietzsche, *The Birth of Tragedy,* trans. Walter Kaufmann (New York: Vintage, 1966), 24.

27. See for example Oswald Spengler, *Jahre der Entscheidung* (Munich: dtv, 1980), 71, 212.

28. Ernst Jünger, *Der Arbeiter: Herrschaft und Gestalt* (Hamburg: Hanseatische Verlagsanstalt, 1932), 217ff.

29. *Überlegungen VII–XI*, *Gesamtausgabe* 95, pp. 394f.

30. *Überlegungen VII–XI*, *Gesamtausgabe* 95, p. 79.

31. *Überlegungen VII–XI*, *Gesamtausgabe* 95, p. 274.

32. *Überlegungen II–VI*, *Gesamtausgabe* 94, p. 485; *Überlegungen VII–XI*, *Gesamtausgabe* 95, p. 427.

33. Martin Heidegger, *Nietzsche: Der Wille zur Macht als Kunst*, *Gesamtausgabe* 43, ed. B. Heimbüchel (Frankfurt: Klostermann, 1985), 284.

34. *Überlegungen II–VI*, *Gesamtausgabe* 94, p. 190.

35. *Überlegungen II–VI*, *Gesamtausgabe* 94, p. 51.

36. Reprinted in Hildegard Brenner, *Die Kunstpolitik des Nationalsozialismus* (Reinbek: Rowohlt, 1963), 178f. For the importance of leading Nazis regarding themselves as artists see Eric Michaud, *The Cult of Art in Nazi Germany* (Stanford, CA: Stanford University Press, 2004), chaps. 1–2; Rohkrämer, *Die fatale Attraktion des Nationalsozialismus,* 158–165.

37. *Überlegungen II–VI*, *Gesamtausgabe* 94, p. 338.

38. *Überlegungen II–VI*, *Gesamtausgabe* 94, p. 136.

39. *Überlegungen II–VI*, *Gesamtausgabe* 94, pp. 116, 128, 150f., 154f.

40. *Überlegungen II–VI*, *Gesamtausgabe* 94, p. 160.

41. *Überlegungen II–VI*, *Gesamtausgabe* 94, p. 223.

42. *Überlegungen II–VI*, *Gesamtausgabe* 94, p. 142f.

43. *Überlegungen II–VI*, *Gesamtausgabe* 94, pp. 407, 432.

44. *Überlegungen VII–XI*, *Gesamtausgabe* 95, pp. 299f.

45. *Überlegungen VII–XI*, *Gesamtausgabe* 95, p. 361.

46. *Überlegungen VII–XI*, *Gesamtausgabe* 95, pp. 109, 148–155.

47. Martin Heidegger, *Überlegungen XII–XV* (*Schwarze Hefte 1939–1941*), *Gesamtausgabe* 96, ed. Peter Trawny (Frankfurt: Klostermann, 2014), 195. For earlier explorations of machination see for example *Überlegungen II–VI*, *Gesamtausgabe* 94, pp. 363, 420, 427; *Überlegungen VII–XI*, *Gesamtausgabe* 95, p. 392.

48. *Überlegungen II–VI*, *Gesamtausgabe* 94, p. 365 (first quotation) and p. 381; *Überlegungen XII–XV*, *Gesamtausgabe* 96, p. 192 (second quotation) and p. 229 (third quotation).

49. *Überlegungen VII–XI*, *Gesamtausgabe* 95, pp. 188f.; *Überlegungen XII–XV*, *Gesamtausgabe* 96, pp. 50f., 113, 131, 141f.

50. *Überlegungen VII–XI*, *Gesamtausgabe* 95, p. 473.

51. *Überlegungen VII–XI*, *Gesamtausgabe* 95, p. 472.

52. *Überlegungen VII–XI*, *Gesamtausgabe* 95, p. 211.

53. *Überlegungen VII–XI*, *Gesamtausgabe* 95, p. 408.

54. *Überlegungen VII–XI*, *Gesamtausgabe* 95, p. 408.

55. See for example Trawny, *Heidegger und der Mythos der jüdischen Weltverschwörung*.

56. *Überlegungen XII–XV*, *Gesamtausgabe* 96, pp. 133, 243, 46.

57. *Überlegungen XII–XV*, *Gesamtausgabe* 96, p. 243.

58. *Überlegungen XII–XV*, *Gesamtausgabe* 96, p. 262.

59. *Überlegungen XII–XV*, *Gesamtausgabe* 96, p. 114.

60. *Überlegungen XII–XV*, *Gesamtausgabe* 96, p. 154.

61. *Überlegungen XII–XV*, *Gesamtausgabe* 96, pp. 243, 257f., 269.

62. *Überlegungen VII–XI*, *Gesamtausgabe* 95, p. 402 (here the speculation about a cross between the German race "with the Slavs (the Russian—on whom Bolshevism was only superimposed without being rooted)"). In another moment he feared, however, that the "inexhaustibility of the Russian soil" combined with the "irresistible force of German planning" could lead to unprecedented heights of machination (*Überlegungen VII–XI*, *Gesamtausgabe* 95, p. 403).

63. *Überlegungen XII–XV*, *Gesamtausgabe* 96, p. 174.

17

Philosophy, Science, and Politics in the *Black Notebooks*

Andrew Bowie

"Heidegger's Philosophy"

It is perhaps best to begin by making it clear that I think that Heidegger was one of the greatest philosophers of the twentieth century. My—albeit already quite critical—positive view of Heidegger has, though, been sorely tested by reading the volumes of the *Black Notebooks* published so far. At times this has been reminiscent of reading those passages in Thomas Mann's *Magic Mountain* or *Doktor Faustus* where Mann parodies intellectuals who respond to historical crises with a desperate desire to reveal the deeper philosophical roots of the crisis, while actually just spouting hot air, or worse. One too often finds oneself saying "What is he talking about?," as the prose piles up, and reference to concrete historical, cultural, and social phenomena that would make things clearer remains sparse or obscure. When Heidegger does discuss such phenomena, the impression is too often of a peeved cultural critic, of the kind that were two a penny in Germany before and after the First World War. Global consequences are inferred from local phenomena, like the contentions of some German church or other, or some aspect of the culture industry, from boxing to cinema, which cannot bear the weight being attached to them, and that have now anyway been consigned to the dustbin of history. My old teacher and namesake, the late, lamented Malcolm Bowie, once advised me to avoid "local skirmishes" with others' positions in my work, because they make one appear insecure and aggressive, and Heidegger could have done with Malcolm's advice. Things are, of course, compounded when anti-Semitism and racist nationalism poison too many passages of the *Notebooks*. The overall impression they give is somehow cold and inhuman: in a period of intense human suffering there is little sense of sympathy or fellow feeling. If ever there was a case where one feels the need to invoke the distinction between the empirical and the intelligible character of an author, this is it.

At this point one needs to make a decision that often occurs with respect to Heidegger's work: Is one to paraphrase its philosophical content in terms that locate that content as constituting "Heidegger's philosophy," or does one seek what Robert Pippin terms a "philosophical engagement"[1] with it, by bringing out the potential contribution of the *Notebooks* to our understanding of Heidegger's significance for contemporary thought? Given the ongoing revelations about Heidegger's anti-Semitism, focusing the discussion on questions about how his philosophy related to Nazism is vital, but might also obscure important dimensions of what he says. What Heidegger says *is* inherently suspect because of his involvement with the Nazis and his anti-Semitism. However, the claim that, because his anti-Semitism can be connected to his philosophy as a whole, it invalidates "his philosophy," assumes that his philosophy is indeed to be construed as forming a whole, and that this whole is inseparably connected to the racist views of its author. The reason this move is problematic is that key ideas in Heidegger are paralleled in so many thinkers, like Wittgenstein,[2] Adorno,[3] and others, that they cannot be invalidated just by the fact that they are also linked to his deeply objectionable political stances. I take it as a given that the *Notebooks* underline in even more disturbing fashion than heretofore the already well-established and depressing fact that Heidegger was a Nazi and an anti-Semite, but this does not exhaust what they show with respect to Heidegger's understanding of modernity. It is not at all the case, as we will see, that this understanding is defensible, but the problems I want to suggest with respect to this understanding do have ramifications for how philosophers approach issues of politics, economics, and culture.

The Roots of Historical Crisis

The *Notebooks* published so far—the postwar ones do not seem to render the charge of anti-Semitism any less serious[4]—fall in the period of the declining Weimar Republic, the rise of Nazism, and the beginning of the Second World War. The reflections in the *Notebooks* are a response to a historical crisis and present themselves as part of an attempt to make a new beginning, which entails a radical rejection of Western metaphysics. A. W. Moore rightly suggests that, if one sees metaphysics as "maximal making sense" and "making sense of making sense," there is no reason not to see Heidegger as a metaphysician.[5] Heidegger, though, gives a specific meaning to "metaphysics," which will become clear in what follows. He had already, in *Being and Time*, made a serious contribution to the reinterpretation of a world that had been shaken by the failure to anticipate the appalling industrialized brutality of World War I. *Being and Time*'s redirection of philosophical attention to basic questions of how the world is intelligible at all, given the radical finitude of human existence, has resonated ever since in discussions of the pathologies of modernity. Unlike *Being and Time*, which largely eschewed direct examination of political phenomena, the *Notebooks* do see themselves as responding to a specific historical and political crisis, to which Heidegger sees Nazism, for a time at least, as a possible response. It is therefore important to reflect on Heidegger's diagnosis of this crisis, before interrogating his wider reflections on philosophy, science, and politics.

The disintegration of the Weimar Republic and the rise of the Third Reich would not have occurred but for the massive dysfunction of the world economic system stemming from before World War I, which is arguably being echoed by the contemporary world economic crisis that came out into the open in 2007. The present disintegration of an economic system based on neo-liberal principles of reliance on inadequately regulated markets and the privatization of public resources is leading to social, political, and cultural consequences that look all too familiar. Increases in forms of intolerance, indifference to the suffering of the poor in the name of sustaining the failed economic model by demanding impossible debt repayments, the growing destruction of the social solidarity that was the positive response to the horrors of World War II—all are evidently products of the crisis of the form in which capital functioned in the wake of the oil crisis in the 1970s, and of the ensuing change of relationship between finance capital and the state associated with Reagan and Thatcher.

The question is whether there are "deeper" sources of such crises that necessarily require philosophical reflection to render them apparent. Is the German political crisis after World War I, which so obviously had essentially economic roots in the issues suggested below, and in the fear of déclassement on the part of the German lower middle class, illuminated by Heidegger's claims concerning the forgetfulness of being? Does the history of philosophy really trump the kind of economic and historical analysis offered, to take an outstanding example, by Karl Polanyi in *The Great Transformation*, written around the same time as some of the *Notebooks* and first published in 1944, whose continuing relevance to contemporary political economy is now being widely recognized? For Polanyi the "proximate cause" of the crisis that led to the world wars was the failure of the attempt to sustain the gold standard:

Nineteenth-century civilization rested on four institutions. The first was the balance-of-power system which for a century prevented the occurrence of any long and devastating war between the Great Powers. The second was the international gold standard which symbolized a unique organization of world economy. The third was the self-regulating market which produced an unheard-of material welfare. The fourth was the liberal state.[6]

Such an account might seem very far from the concerns of Heidegger, but Polanyi is nothing like the one-dimensional economists who helped to get us into the contemporary mess.

The following passage begins to suggest how the connection to Heidegger can be made:

Our thesis is that the idea of a self-adjusting market implied a stark utopia. Such an institution could not exist for any length of time without annihilating the human and natural substance of society; it would have physically destroyed man and transformed his surroundings into a wilderness. Inevitably, society took measures to protect itself: but whatever measures it took impaired the self-regulation of the market, disorganized industrial life, and thus endangered society in yet another way.[7]

Polanyi admits that

to trace the institutional mechanism of the downfall of a civilization may well appear as a hopeless endeavor. Yet it is this we are undertaking. In doing so, we are consciously adjusting our aim to the extreme singularity of the subject matter. For the civilization of the nineteenth century was unique precisely in that it centered on a definite institutional mechanism. ... If the breakdown of our civilization was timed by the failure of world economy, it was certainly not caused by it. Its origins lay more than a hundred years back in that social and technological upheaval from which the idea of a self-regulating market system sprang in Western Europe.[8]

The upheaval is the rise of modern industrial capitalism and the concomitant commodification of labor and natural resources that forms the core of the aim of the self-regulating market: "All transactions are turned into money transactions, and these in turn require that a medium of exchange be introduced into every articulation of industrial life."[9] Polanyi maintains that "the dislocation caused by such devices must disjoint man's relationships and threaten his natural habitat with annihilation."[10]

Heidegger's attachment to the supposed integrity of rural life and his ecological concerns relate to the threats suggested here, though he seems more concerned in the *Notebooks* with things like the effect of the radio on rural culture than with its destruction by the depredations of capital. This strange focus is already indicative of the failings of his approach. The decisive factor in producing the politico-economic situation to which Heidegger is responding in the *Notebooks* is seen by Polanyi as the breakdown of the gold standard, which was supposed to ground the value of national currencies, and the effects of this on a Western civilization based on the social and technological changes associated with modern capitalism. The very fact that a civilization could rest on such "precarious foundations"[11] escaped those in charge of the economic and political fate of Europe, with consequences that are still being felt today.

Reification

The kind of systemic blindness at issue here is a key concern of the era. Lukács's *History and Class Consciousness*,[12] written between 1919 and 1923, with which Heidegger seems to have been familiar, was in many respects a response to the blindness of politicians and others to the nature of the technological and economic developments that occasioned the catastrophe of World War I. The idea that, rather than technological, industrial, and economic command of more and more aspects of the world inevitably leading to more just, tolerable, and creative forms of human existence, it could also produce disaster, suggests that such command involves a constitutive blindness. This realization demands a different route for philosophical reflection than the one manifest in taking the natural sciences as its essential point of orientation, which was characteristic of much of Neo-Kantianism in Heidegger's time, and is now characteristic of most analytical philosophy. The possibilities that the best work of Heidegger opens up have to do with his articulation of different points of orientation for philosophy, which enable questions to be asked about the meaning of science and that take history into account in new ways.

So how exactly does one connect these kinds of responses to historical crises caused by systemic blindness to the reality of what is being produced by modern social and economic forms to Heidegger's ideas about the meaning of being? The obsessive recurring theme of the *Notebooks* is the domination of "entities [*Seiendes*]," "machination [*Machenschaft*]" (which we will consider in more detail later), and "administration," over the "truth of being." The themes are familiar from such essays as "The Age of the World Picture": natural science is oriented toward "rightness [*Richtigkeit*]" and frames the world in mathematical terms, so making it increasingly the object of human manipulation, and obscuring other kinds of relationships to nature. Lukács, Adorno, and others refer to what is at issue here as "reification." Axel Honneth maintains that what links Heidegger, Lukács, Adorno, (and Dewey) is a search for an alternative to the model of philosophy based on the search for scientific objectivity, a model that privileges the "ruling idea, according to which an epistemic subject stands opposite the world in a neutral manner."[13] The question is how this model relates to the specific political and cultural conclusions that Heidegger draws from it, given that his response leads in such disastrous political directions.

It is precisely Heidegger's failure to countenance the kind of issues suggested above by Polanyi that opens the way for a perspective on why Heidegger gets things so wrong. Reference to economic factors is sparse in the *Notebooks*: indeed, Thomas Sheehan points out the striking fact that the term *Kapitalismus* only appears twice in ninety-six volumes of Heidegger's writings.[14] *Kommunismus* is seen in the *Notebooks* as the "metaphysical condition in which modern humanity finds itself" during the "final culmination of modernity,"[15] not as a different economic and political model. Indeed, he insists that the danger of communism does not lie "in its economic and social consequences," but in its "spiritual essence."[16] Elsewhere he talks of the essence of modern humankind "for whom the *self-certainty* of itself, in whatever way this may be determined as *Subjektum*, is the first—and only truth."[17] We will return to this conception later.

Politics, Economics, and Ontological Difference

Let us first, though, take two extreme passages from the *Notebooks* (there are a lot more like this), which reveal how far Heidegger can go, and just how objectionable he can be. Awful as these are, they do help to make clear various symptoms in Heidegger's thought that distinguish his diagnoses from related ones in Adorno and others. The first passage goes as follows: "The question of the role of *World Jewry* is not a racial question, but rather the metaphysical question about the kind of humanity [*Menschentümlichkeit*] which, *absolutely unattached* [*schlechthin ungebunden*], can undertake the deracination of all entities from being as a world-historical 'task.'"[18] The second involves the claim that imperialism "is driven toward a *final culmination* [*höchste Vollendung*] of technology. Its last act will be that the earth blows itself up and present humankind disappears. Which is not a misfortune

[*Unglück*], but the first purification *of being* from its deepest disfigurement [*Verunstaltung*] by the supremacy of entities."[19] Deep breath. If you thought ontological difference was about how the primary modes of intelligibility of the world are obscured by the objectify-ing stance of the modern sciences, you might be a bit surprised to see that its overcoming now makes the end of humankind no misfortune, and that its source as a "world-historical 'task'" is "World Jewry." A recent joke meme on the Internet has a photo of Heidegger that is headed by his revelatory dictum that "language is the clearing-concealing event of being itself." At the bottom of the photo it says: "BTW Nazis R Cool LOL."[20] Sadly, this juxtaposition seems about right in the case of the passages quoted.

Heidegger's pernicious nonsense here could easily be dismissed if it came from someone less important, but the question as to whether his philosophy is, as Adorno once said, "fascist to its innermost cells" can't really be evaded in the face of his own bringing together of ontological difference with such politico-historical issues. (He does something similar with the notion of *Dasein*, to which he sometimes gives a racist and nationalist aspect absent in *Being and Time*.) In the first passage the anti-Semitic trope of the rootless Jew is linked to the forgetting of being, but rather than this forgetting happening in a way that is not adequately understood in terms of agency, "World Jewry" has it as a "task." The anti-Semitic trope is based on the historical role of Jews, first as moneylenders and then as agents of capitalism, which has no respect for communities, nations, and so on, in its making "all that's solid melt into air."

Absent the racism and there is actually some kind of historical substance to this, but one has to be very specific about just what it is. Polanyi suggests the central role of *"haute finance"* in the late nineteenth and early twentieth centuries via the Rothschild family, who

were subject to no *one* government: as a family they embodied the abstract principle of interna-tionalism; their loyalty was to a firm, the credit of which had become the only supranational link between political government and industrial effort in a swiftly growing world economy. In the last resort, their independence sprang from the needs of the time which demanded a sovereign agent commanding the confidence of national statesmen and of the international investor alike; it was to this need that the metaphysical extraterritoriality of a Jewish bankers' dynasty domiciled in the capitals of Europe provided an almost perfect solution.[21]

In this version of the story the "deracination of entities from being" is also seen in terms of "metaphysics": what enables the constitution of things as marketable commodities is a world system that is not tied to the specific local meanings of the things in the lifeworld and that relies on blotting out particularity in the name of limitless exchangeability. Polanyi cites Aristotle's awareness that the "principle of production for gain," which is unique to market economies, would lead to the "divorce of the economic motive from all concrete social relationships which would by their very nature set a limit to that motive."[22] The fact that by the nineteenth century Jewish bankers ended up in the situation of administering a system that was "divorce[d] ... from all concrete social relationships" has to be understood in terms of the history of anti-Semitism's exclusion of Jews from so many such relationships, which forced some of them into this "metaphysical extraterritoriality." Heidegger doesn't go to the trouble of trying to understand this. Given his obsessive thoroughness with respect to trying to understand ontological difference, a degree of attention to empirical history would have been the least one might expect.

The second passage underlines what is going wrong in another way. Whereas ontological difference can be understood in terms of the hollowing out of the meaningfulness of the human world, and the need to attend anew to how we really make nontheological sense of things in that world, here the world becomes disposable, in the name of a purification of being from the effects of "present humankind." The truth of being can do without humankind, which seems to be being punished for its transgression in unleashing the power of technology. Just how the truth of being in Heidegger's sense is supposed to be an issue in the wake of the end of the human world is beyond any kind of intelligible thought. The suspicion that being sometimes functions in an essentially "negative theological" manner in Heidegger is hard to resist in this case, and this potentially undermines the ways he elsewhere reveals how acceptance of finitude should make us think differently about how we make sense. Heidegger's tendency to turn being into some kind of historical demiurge here reaches its apotheosis, and there is an obvious link to his political failures, because ultimate importance can be attached to something indifferent to human suffering. The *Notebooks* are meant as "thoughts in progress," so one should be careful about their status, but even entertaining such thoughts testifies to a deep-rooted malaise that reifies human issues in a way uncomfortably close to the reifications that helped to enable the Nazi genocide.

"Historie," "Technik," and "Geschichte"

We have seen so far that Heidegger is obviously blind to decisive factors that influence how one should interpret modern history. Why is this so? Throughout the *Notebooks* he insists on the difference between *Historie*, which is what historians write, and *Geschichte*, which is where the truth of being could become manifest. *Historie* is essentially "calculating production and representation of entities as a whole *from out of* and *for* the center of the self-securing of man as *Subjektum*."[23] As such, *Historie* is *Technik*, "technology," as the technology of *Geschichte*; *Historie* and *Technik* are therefore "*metaphysically* the same. ... Man can only see what he has made himself."[24] *Historie* is "explanation,"[25] so is analogous to the natural sciences. The identity of *Historie* and *Technik* is a result of their both being ways in which being is subjected to the control of a frame of understanding that predetermines the kind of results that are possible. Instead of an open questioning of the meaning of things, there is a continuation of a pattern of reducing things to forms that result from the dominance of the subject.

While the status of *Geschichte* remains persistently vague, the distinction between *Technik* and *Geschichte* that Heidegger makes is not without justification, and even the vagueness makes some kind of sense for a form of thinking predicated on questioning rather than on the providing of explanatory answers. Historiography depends on the frames that determine which historical data are regarded as significant. What historical developments mean is, therefore, in a sense that is admittedly hard to characterize, not fully captured by what historiography itself can tell us, as the changing history of historiography makes clear. That changing history could, as such, itself be regarded as belonging to *Geschichte*. Heidegger's response to the issues involved in the notional identity of *Technik* and *Historie* is, though, symptomatic of a crucial difficulty.

His constant reference to Descartes as initiating the essence of modernity as the subjectification of being is the key here. Modernity is characterized by the search for a stable ground in subjectivity, starting from Descartes's rejection of skeptical doubt via the cogito, which, for Heidegger, then goes, via Kant's transcendental subject, to Hegel's absolute knowing, to Marx's paradigm of production, and to Nietzsche's will to power. The search is supposed to lead, as the late (and brilliant) essay "The End of Philosophy and the Task of Thinking" suggests, to the culmination of metaphysics in modern natural science and technology's control of nature. The concomitant need is for new "thinking," which, as the *Notebooks* already show, Heidegger associates in particular with Hölderlin, without ever making at all clear what might actually ensue from this, beyond a sense of the need to be open to things in new ways by responding to the "flight of the Gods."

The big problem, which Sheehan has very effectively underlined,[26] lies in Heidegger's assimilation of history to the history of philosophy, in the sense of the history of being as manifested in the essential thinkers. Sheehan argues that Heidegger's "etiology of *die Technik*" would only deserve taking seriously if "the relation between his ontological history of being and the ontic course of lived history in its concrete material manifestations"[27] were rethought. The *Notebooks* are an extended, and often very tedious and objectionable, demonstration of Heidegger's failure to see that his largely arbitrary choice of empirical examples from the "ontic" political and social world of his time is at odds with the epochal consequences he seeks to draw from ontological difference that go back to the ancient Greeks. That mismatch is part of what opens the door to his affiliation with Nazism. He obviously wants something epochal in the present that will resonate with the philosophical story he tells. How, given the nature of the actual manifestations of Nazism, he could, albeit only briefly, believe the Nazis might initiate a new epoch of the history of being is mysterious, to say the least. In one sense this is just a psychological failing of a flawed, provincial man, with the kind of prejudices that go with a narrow understanding of human diversity, seeking to inflate his own importance. At the same time, the best parts of his own work actually suggest a way of immunizing oneself against such blindness, offering a reminder of the necessary contingency involved in the ways we make sense that results from the essential hiddenness of being. The question is in this respect how we respond to that contingency, and Heidegger's own response is significantly divided between blindness and insight.

Metaphysics and Modernity

So is there nothing to be made of the way Heidegger addresses the crises of his time in the *Notebooks*? We are, after all, still faced with profound problems occasioned by the dominance of technology, involving what Habermas has termed the "colonization of the lifeworld" by bureaucratic and technological systems as well as the growing ecological crisis, which puts in question the very way humankind now inhabits the earth. The vital issue is how the relationship between philosophy, science, and politics is to be understood. As Lukács, Adorno, and others in the Marxist tradition see, the nature of modern capital does involve global systemic changes in the way the world is constituted, which relate to some of the phenomena that concern Heidegger. Faith in "the market" as the means of regulating the human exchange of goods does, for example, involve something like what Heidegger sees in metaphysics as the global reduction of things to quantitative ways of being, and has now, as Polanyi already warned, led to a dangerously unstable world.

Heidegger is, in the—admittedly pretty rare—better moments of the *Notebooks*, concerned with the way a modernity whose direction is dominated by the effects of the natural sciences gives rise to a crisis in how to make sense of things as a whole. He rejects the redemptive alternatives in Christianity and much of Western philosophy, and also seeks to show why philosophy should not be beholden to the sciences. Similar stances with respect to the refusal to see philosophy as either a science or as a means of validating the sciences recur in Wittgenstein and others, so there is nothing inherently problematic here. The problems lie in the connection of this questioning stance to specific political developments, and to the cultural manifestations associated with those developments. The obvious fact that any idea of resolving a crisis that is seen as worldwide—see the remark above about *Kommunismus* as the "metaphysical condition in which modern humanity finds itself"—by attaching oneself to a movement based on the idea of one nation finding a way out for itself is clearly delusory.

Here we reach another low point in texts that are hardly short of them. Part of this way out is supposed to be the Nazi "creation of joy in labor and the new will to *labor*" for the *Volk*, and the ultimate goal is the "historical greatness of the *Volk* in the realization and formation of the powers of being."[28] Reading through the great mass of the *Notebooks*, such gestures toward the future, which are often seen in terms of the "truth of being," are striking for the fact that it is almost wholly unclear what Heidegger thinks this future will concretely involve. Indeed, he often suggests that it would be mistaken to think one could specify this. The specification here, from the early part of the Nazi period, is, to say the least, hardly promising. The perversion of labor under the Nazis is now indelibly ingrained in its despicable history: at the time Heidegger writes this, it would not yet be apparent just what was to come, but the connection of the problems of labor to the economic dysfunction of the times was readily apparent and gets no mention.

Polanyi's diagnosis of the state of the world in this period recognized that the totalizing effects of a profoundly flawed economic system can lead to a devastation of society and the natural world by inflation, mass unemployment, and war. That system is itself not the result of specific human intention and "happens" in a manner that can be seen as an event in the history of being, but this is precisely not how Heidegger sees it, because of his too exclusive association of the history of being with the key philosophers. Is there, then, a way of seeing the history of political economy as grounded in the philosophical story? In the *Notebooks*, what is at issue in this respect depends, once again, on the understanding of the history of "metaphysics."

Let us consider parts of one longer passage that connects to the issues we have been exploring, namely *Reflections* X, no. 39. Here Heidegger claims, in a manner that recurs in his work from this period, that Hegel and Nietzsche are "the same" insofar as "the modern *form of metaphysics* reaches its complete development [*Ausgestaltung*]"[29] in them. (He says elsewhere—really—that Wagner's *Lohengrin*, military tanks, and squadrons of planes are "the same."[30]) In both Hegel and Nietzsche "'life' as the unconditioned (absolute spirit—embodied universal life) becomes the 'origin' for all entities that are constituted in the main forms of culture (religion—art—morality)."[31] Both are "grounded on the subject," which they take as "*absolute* life,"[32] and for them "thought is the guideline for the determination of the 'is,'"[33] as it was for Descartes. The "shared—everyday public conception and evaluation of entities is—without it coming to a knowledge of it—carried by that completion of metaphysics."[34] The "hidden historical [*geschichtliche*] power of their [Hegel and Nietzsche's] subterranean common bond is the metaphysics of Leibniz," in the popularized form given to it by Herder and Goethe, so a "thoroughly German necessity."[35]

The consequence is that

our reality does not consist in the palpability of lorries and planes and not in the organizations of the body of the *Volk*—rather what is nearest and most effective, and for this reason *not* graspable, is the explication [*Auslegung*] of entities in the field of vision of modern metaphysics. This explication completes itself in the dominance [*Herrschaft*] of being, such that it forces itself into oblivion as machination, in favor of entities which are penetrated [*durchherrscht*] by it as the "real" [*des "Wirklichen*," which has the sense of that which is "in effect" in a particular period].[36]

Just how it is that the completion of metaphysics actually "carries" the everyday conception of entities is not clear, given that the everyday conception is seen as having no "knowledge" of that completion. Despite this implausible conjunction, the relationship between manifest social phenomena and their hidden ground is part of what can help explain how mass delusions like Nazism, in which otherwise normal people produce unthinkable brutality, come about. It is precisely the destabilizing of peoples' sense of secure location in the world by inflation and the threat of destitution, thus by systemic economic factors, that, as Heidegger puts it, leads to everyday conceptions that have no "knowledge" of what underlies them.

The problem is that without any reference to the empirical history of the world economy—which precisely functions such that capital is effectively the "field of vision of modern metaphysics"—or to the development of modern science in relation to the history of philosophy, using that history as the ground of understanding modernity is a hopeless task. At the same time, the sense that the dynamic of the development of economics, technology, and science is such that nobody knows where it is taking us, and yet is largely uncontrollable, seems undeniable, and poses serious questions about how effective political responses to that development can be arrived at.

This situation does demand some kind of philosophical response, of the sort Heidegger's best work suggests can be at least initiated by understanding key philosophers as revealing a history of being, even if the actual story going back to the Greeks that he tells is highly questionable. Horkheimer and Adorno's *Dialectic of Enlightenment*[37] essays a related account, based on the idea of reason's inseparable link to self-preservation from the very beginning, which makes it repress aspects of our relationship to external and internal nature. There are reasons for seeing philosophy as a possible means of accessing the hidden tensions involved in "ontic" empirical manifestations of culture, from "lorries and planes," to Wagner's music dramas, but the relationship between the empirical and that which may ground it is not explained just by the stages from Descartes, to Kant, to Nietzsche, or by the revelation that "reason" is inseparable from instrumental control. If we look in a bit more detail at the idea of machination, we can see better where what Heidegger offers does have some potential to generate insight, and where it breaks down, leaving the way open to the dire consequences seen in the *Notebooks*.

Machination, Science, and Politics

Given that they are roughly contemporaneous with the *Notebooks*, and often more illuminating on the same issues, it is also worth drawing on the *Contributions to Philosophy*. In a section on "The Abandonment of Being" Heidegger advances a version of an idea discussed above, which has inspired some of the best recent work on Heidegger,[38] namely, the idea that being is essentially hidden: "*Abandonment of being*: that being [*Seyn*] leaves entities … this means: being conceals itself in the openness [*Offenbarkeit*] of entities. And being itself is determined essentially as this self-withdrawing concealing."[39] In doing so, it becomes the "object of machination."[40] Machination is explained as where "truth becomes correctness of re-presentation,"[41] and "what really is, is that which is constantly present, and so that which con-ditions everything, the un-conditioned, the ab-solute, *ens entium*, God, etc."[42] The course of the Western "metaphysics of presence," from Plato via Christianity to modern philosophy, is, then, determined by thought as true representation, which culminates in "*Erlebnis*," "experience": "Only what is ex-perienced [*das Er-lebte*] and what is ex-periencable [*das Er-lebbare*] which forces itself into the closed circle [*Umkreis*] of ex-perience [*des Er-lebens*], what man can bring to himself and bring before himself can count as 'being' [*als 'seiend'*]."[43] Heidegger's essential idea is that what is thereby forgotten is the "clearing," or, more problematically, the "truth of being,"[44] the way that sense emerges in the world at all, which makes possible what he describes in terms of "machination" and "correctness of representation" in the sciences. The hiddenness of being results from the occlusion of how the meaning of things unfolds temporally, demanding specific kinds of attention and response that are obscured if the focus is on objective explanation.

The underlying sense of machination can be seen in terms of the question of what motivates scientific inquiry. This motivation is not itself scientific: the "science of science" is precisely what German Idealism can be said to have failed to establish via its new ways of conceiving of self-determining subjectivity. Metaphysics in its last, Nietzschean, guise sees what motivates inquiry in terms of the value of truth, which is linked to self-preservation as the core of a subjectivity that is essentially will to power. In the *Notebooks* a general attack on the "philosophical ignorance" of "today's German 'scientists'" refers to the "complete dissolution of 'science' und so of 'knowledge' into the machination of being itself."[45] He elucidates this conception in the *Contributions*, suggesting that medieval "doctrine [*Lehre*]" and Greek "cognition [*Erkenntnis*]" are "fundamentally different" from contemporary "science [*Wissenschaft*]."[46] Science is now the "opening up in the manner of machination of a circumscribed circle [*Umkreis*] of rightnesses [*Richtigkeiten*] within an otherwise hidden area of a truth which is not at all worthy of questioning for the sciences."[47]

In these terms one therefore either has to seek to specify what the appropriate alternative goals of *Wissenschaft* would be, or one looks to a wholesale alternative to *Wissenschaft* as "machination." The latter is what Heidegger is interested in, and this is also, along with his obvious psychological failings, what leads him to his political failure. He maintains that

philosophy is neither against nor for science, but leaves it to its own obsession with its own use in securing, in ever more manageable and rapid ways, ever more usable results, and so linking using and needing ever more indissolubly with dependence on the results in question and their being surpassed.[48]

More concretely, though again without any analysis of the economic aspect of this, he sees the "progresses" of science as bringing "the exploitation and using of the earth, the breeding and training of man into states that are today still unthinkable."[49] The "hidden goal" of this development is the "state of complete boredom";[50] the example that points in this direction is that "the historical humanities [*Geisteswissenschaften*] become the *newspaper* sciences. The natural sciences become *machine* sciences."[51]

The descent here into the bathos of the second-rate cultural critic makes it hard to take this seriously, but the link of machination to boredom is still telling. If one sees the sciences as just machination, and philosophy as essentially other than the sciences, problem-solving science of the kind that has given us antibiotics, modern surgery, modern communication technology, insight into the macro- and microstructure of the universe, and all those aspects of modern technology that most would not wish to be without, becomes "the same" as the science that gives rise to so much money being spent on arms research. The attempt to make science a proper servant of humankind, which includes the realization that nature cannot be endlessly exploited, is essentially a political battle over who controls the economy and how they do so. One aim, which is demonstrably achievable, at least in local contexts, is to use technology to liberate human potential wasted in often meaningless forms of work. This does not, though, accord with a totalizing view of machination, let alone with Heidegger's admittedly only temporary hope for the Nazi galvanizing of the laboring *Volk* as a way beyond machination. At the same time—and this is why aspects of Heidegger continue to nag away at one's political analyses—one can ask why Keynes's prediction in 1930 of a future where people worked less and had more time for creative self-development proved so wrong. What is it precisely about the culture and politics of capitalism that obstructs the liberation of human potential by technology? The answer seems, though, more likely to come from a philosophically informed combination of economic, political, and cultural perspectives, of the kind one gets in Adorno's best analyses of the contradictions generated by capitalism, in such texts as *History and Freedom*,[52] than from Heidegger's philosophical perspective.

The fact that the cumulative effects of technology take on their own often destructive momentum is a justified object of Heidegger's philosophical reflections, including in the *Notebooks*, but his sense that only a wholly transformed understanding of being is the adequate response to this situation lies at the root of his political delusions. Machination can be connected to looming ecological and other devastation, but how does one interpret things like green technologies, which seek to sustain ecological balance while solving problems of human habitation of the earth in these terms? These technologies do benefit from phenomenological attention to how sight is lost of the forms of meaningfulness that make sense of existence, including making sense of scientific exploration. Heidegger's Manichaean vision, however, gets in the way of an appraisal of how to reform our self-understandings in a manner that can have transformative political effects, and leads to his espousal of a form of politics that is actually essentially at odds with his core insights.

Convincing enough people that many modern forms of inhabiting the earth are unsustainable, and ultimately self-destructive, is not going to be simply a matter of winning rational arguments based on the best science. Major historical shifts in understanding and responding to the world come about in a manner that resists fully grounded explanation, sometimes, as Heidegger shows, being most effectively articulated through major works of art. The change in the status of nature from the second half of the eighteenth century onward is, for example, in many ways best grasped through painting, music, and literature. This is why Heidegger's ideas of a history of being and of "unconcealment" still have something to tell us about Western metaphysics as a key to understanding modernity. But without constant empirical and theoretical attention to the changing ways the philosophical, the economic, the political, the social, the cultural, and the technological interact, the danger is that we will rush into the kind of deluded judgment that made Heidegger see the Nazis as an answer to a philosophical crisis, when they were primarily a result of systemic economic and political breakdown. The recurrence of the rise of xenophobic far-Right movements in postwar Europe and elsewhere when economies go into crisis simply does not need a deep philosophical explanation. Economic instability generates the desire for a scapegoat in "the Other," and rather than seeing the systemic causes, which are not empirically manifest, people look to something that is. At a stretch, the xenophobes could be seen as part of machination, which hides the economic reality that gives rise to their xenophobia, but Heidegger himself falls precisely into this trap. We have, then, to make a separation between the Heidegger, who, through the ideas of the clearing and the hiddenness of being, reminds us of the blindness of many forms of philosophy and science to the complexity of how meaning arises in the world, and the Heidegger predominantly evident in the *Notebooks*, who sought a mythical exit from modernity that is more blind to the historical world than the metaphysics he sometimes so penetratingly analyzes. Future scholarly engagement with the latter Heidegger seems certain to become more and more demoralizing, as more material appears confirming the worst suspicions; the task of work on the former should be to realize the potential in Heidegger's texts by extending the increasingly well-established dialogue with other kinds of philosophy that can both reveal Heidegger's failings and learn from his unique insights.

Notes

1. Robert Pippin, *Hegel's Practical Philosophy* (Cambridge: Cambridge University Press, 2008), 33.

2. See, for example, Lee Braver, *Groundless Grounds* (Cambridge, MA: MIT Press, 2012).

3. See, for instance, Andrew Bowie, *Adorno and the Ends of Philosophy* (Cambridge: Polity, 2013).

4. See Donatella di Cesare, "Heidegger—'Jews Self-Destructed,'" 2009, http://www.corriere.it/english/15_febbraio_09/heidegger-jews-self-destructed-47cd3930-b03b-11e4-8615-d0fd07eabd28.shtml; see also *Anmerkungen I–V (Schwarze Hefte 1942–1948)*, *Gesamtausgabe* 97, ed. Peter Trawny (Frankfurt: Klostermann, 2015).

5. A. W. Moore, *The Evolution of Modern Metaphysics: Making Sense of Things* (Cambridge: Cambridge University Press, 2012).

6. Karl Polanyi, *The Great Transformation: The Political and Economic Origins of Our Time* (Boston: Beacon Press, 2001), 3.

7. Polanyi, *The Great Transformation*, 3–4.

8. Polanyi, *The Great Transformation*, 4–5.

9. Polanyi, *The Great Transformation*, 43.

10. Polanyi, *The Great Transformation*, 44.

11. Polanyi, *The Great Transformation*, 21.

12. Georg Lukács, *Geschichte und Klassenbewußtsein: Studien über marxistische Dialektik* (Neuwied: Luchterhand, 1970).

13. Axel Honneth, *Verdinglichung: Eine anerkennungstheoretische Studie* (Frankfurt: Suhrkamp, 2005), 31.

14. Thomas Sheehan, *Making Sense of Heidegger: A Paradigm Shift* (London: Rowman & Littlefield, 2015), Kindle ed.: loc. 6909.

15. Martin Heidegger, *Überlegungen VII–XI (Schwarze Hefte 1938/39)*, *Gesamtausgabe* 95, ed. Peter Trawny (Frankfurt: Klostermann, 2014), 371.

16. *Überlegungen VII–XI (Schwarze Hefte 1938/39)*, *Gesamtausgabe* 95, p. 150.

17. *Überlegungen VII–XI (Schwarze Hefte 1938/39)*, *Gesamtausgabe* 95, p. 371.

18. Martin Heidegger, *Überlegungen XII–XV (Schwarze Hefte 1939–1941)*, *Gesamtausgabe* 96, ed. Peter Trawny (Frankfurt: Klostermann, 2014), 243.

19. *Überlegungen XII–XV (Schwarze Hefte 1939–1941)*, *Gesamtausgabe* 96, p. 238.

20. http://t.qkme.me/35bhow.jpg.

21. Polanyi, *The Great Transformation*, 10–11.

22. Polanyi, *The Great Transformation*, 57.

23. *Überlegungen VII–XI*, *Gesamtausgabe* 95, p. 350.

24. *Überlegungen VII–XI*, *Gesamtausgabe* 95, p. 351.

25. *Überlegungen VII–XI*, *Gesamtausgabe* 95, p. 222.

26. Sheehan, *Making Sense of Heidegger*, loc. 6909.

27. Sheehan, *Making Sense of Heidegger*, loc. 6989.

28. Martin Heidegger, *Überlegungen II–VI (Schwarze Hefte 1931–1938)*, *Gesamtausgabe* 94, ed. Peter Trawny (Frankfurt: Klostermann, 2014), 136.

29. *Überlegungen II–VI (Schwarze Hefte 1931–1938)*, *Gesamtausgabe* 94, p. 310.

30. *Überlegungen VII–XI*, *Gesamtausgabe* 95, p. 133.

31. *Überlegungen VII–XI*, *Gesamtausgabe* 95, p. 133.

32. *Überlegungen VII–XI*, *Gesamtausgabe* 95, p. 133.

33. *Überlegungen VII–XI*, *Gesamtausgabe* 95, p. 311.

34. *Überlegungen VII–XI*, *Gesamtausgabe* 95, p. 312.

35. *Überlegungen VII–XI*, *Gesamtausgabe* 95, p. 312.

36. *Überlegungen VII–XI*, *Gesamtausgabe* 95, p. 312.

37. Max Horkheimer and T. W. Adorno, *Dialektik der Aufklärung* (Frankfurt: Fischer, 1988).

38. See Mark Wrathall, *Heidegger and Unconcealment* (Cambridge: Cambridge University Press, 2011).

39. Heidegger, *Beiträge zur Philosophie (Vom Ereignis)*, *Gesamtausgabe* 65, ed. Friedrich-Wilhelm von Herrmann (Frankfurt, Klostermann, 1989), p. 111.

40. *Beiträge zur Philosophie (Vom Ereignis)*, *Gesamtausgabe* 65, p. 111.

41. *Beiträge zur Philosophie (Vom Ereignis)*, *Gesamtausgabe* 65, p. 115.

42. *Beiträge zur Philosophie (Vom Ereignis)*, *Gesamtausgabe* 65, p. 115.

43. *Beiträge zur Philosophie (Vom Ereignis)*, *Gesamtausgabe* 65, p. 129.

44. See Sheehan, *Making Sense of Heidegger*.

45. *Überlegungen VII–XI*, *Gesamtausgabe* 95, p. 394.

46. Heidegger, *Beiträge zur Philosophie (Vom Ereignis)*, 145. An empirically detailed account of the role of the development of mathematics in this change is offered by Heidegger's pupil, Jacob Klein, in Jacob Klein, *Greek Mathematical Thought and the Origin of Algebra* (New York: Dover, 1992).

47. *Beiträge zur Philosophie (Vom Ereignis)*, 145.

48. *Beiträge zur Philosophie (Vom Ereignis)*, 156.

49. *Beiträge zur Philosophie (Vom Ereignis)*, 156–157.

50. *Beiträge zur Philosophie (Vom Ereignis)*, 157.

51. *Beiträge zur Philosophie (Vom Ereignis)*, 158.

52. T. W. Adorno, *Zur Lehre von der Geschichte und der Freiheit* (Frankfurt: Suhrkamp, 2001).

18

Thinking the Oblivion of Thinking: The Unfolding of *Machenschaft* and *Rechnung* in the Time of the *Black Notebooks*

Nancy A. Weston

Mit dem Ausmaß der einzigartigen politischen Erfolge wächst die Verborgenheit der seynsge-
schichtlichen Not und verschärft sich die Befremdlichkeit der wesentlichen Besinnung.
—Martin Heidegger, 1939[1]

I

The publication, at the conclusion of Martin Heidegger's *Gesamtausgabe*, of the notebooks he kept from 1931 on, has been greeted with shock, dismissal, alarm, and defense. It
has been asserted that the notes not only confirm Heidegger's early hopes for the National
Socialist Party, but reveal a pervasive and continuing anti-Semitism, that his work as a
whole is "contaminated" by it, and that it must, on that account, be called into question,
even banished.[2]

The three volumes published so far contain his notes from 1931 to 1941, a profoundly
fraught era in German and world history. The notes found most inflammatory, those mentioning *Judentum*, number a dozen or fewer on a handful of pages, out of 400,000 notes
on 1,200 pages; far more ink and attention are spent in scathing denunciation of "English"
Bolshevism, "Americanism," and Nazism itself. That Heidegger ever supported the party
remains, however, incomprehensible. Though he resigned in bitterness ten months after
he took up the rectorship at Freiburg in 1933[3]—a repudiation detailed in these notebooks,
which one commentator has called "The Diaries of a Dissident National Socialist"[4]—he
never apologized for his involvement, a matter of grave dismay to many. It is said in condemnation that Heidegger never spoke of the Holocaust, never expressed regret or contri-
tion for it; that, indeed, beyond a single remark widely taken as only further compounding
the offense, he never addressed it at all.

As a result, even the most temperate and thoughtful of these commentators, those who
regard wholesale condemnation as unwarranted and misguided, find themselves confronted with the question that cannot be ducked or denied: How could he have joined up
with, subscribed to, and supported a party of such thoughtless barbarism? As phrased by

Gregory Fried to open a widely noted article: "Why would Martin Heidegger …, one of the most celebrated and influential philosophers of the last century, embrace National Socialism, one of the most infamous regimes of any century?"[5]

The question is all the more acute for those who have worked with his thought and come to see its depth and richness. *How could* someone of Heidegger's penetrating intelligence, capable of ushering in the deconstruction and retrieval of the entire philosophical tradition and of opening twentieth-century philosophy to wholly new avenues of thought, yet be so imperceptive, insensitive, even obtuse as to align himself, no matter how briefly, with that morally monstrous regime? Its companion question is equally insistent, equally unavoidable: How is the philosophy he offers implicated in this adherence? This question is still more disquieting, for what is at stake in it is not merely the possible bias or blind spot of a single individual (dismissed and dismissible as provincial, benighted, or worse), but the entirety of what he saw, and articulated. Not the thinker, but the thought now appears to be thrown into question: What becomes of that thought, if it is capable of being drawn into such morally repellent alliances? Does its thinker's complicity suggest that the thought itself rests upon morally repellent foundations—or, at least, precarious ones, if available to such thrall and capture, offering no reliable bulwark against its danger, and no criterion that would allow its recognition and refusal? The continuing urgency of this question shows why Heidegger's resignation from the Rektorat wasn't enough for his critics, and why the decades of silence thereafter matter: If we can't understand Heidegger as repudiating his early allegiance, we can't excuse or forgive it, and thereby put it behind us. And perhaps it is just such distance that we seek as well from his exclusion.

And so we must ask: What are the *philosophical* grounds and implications of that involvement—and of that silence?

II

To engage seriously with that question, we must engage with the whole of his thought, and attend to the place of the notebooks within it. In what follows, that place comes to appearance in the running notes appended throughout, which bring together accordant thoughts in passages from the notebooks and from the ensuing published works, showing that later thought in its nascency, in the depth of its roots, and in its growing responsiveness to the profound peril of the times.

The notebooks are being published as the last in the nearly one hundred volumes of the *Gesamtausgabe*, which Heidegger expressly presents as offering "ways, not works." That is not for any reason of tentativeness, and is no expression of professional modesty; it arises from requirements lying at the very core of Heidegger's undertaking—and ours, if we would understand what he offers us, not merely of his thought, but of thinking.

By all reports a consummate teacher, Heidegger's teaching ventures to open to us, not a doctrine or theory, but a way of thinking, to be understood as something other than the goal-oriented problem-solving activity to which we commonly give that name. He invites us to take the questions we encounter in earnest, to enter into the puzzlement they present, and to allow their question-worthiness to grow, that it might draw us to follow where those questions lead, rather than where we direct them to from the outset in our haste for their solution and disposal.

To undertake to enter into this experience of thinking—addressed at greatest length in *Was heißt Denken?*, though exemplified everywhere in his writings—we must, as he says there, "unlearn" the very familiarity of our familiar practices of reasoning, suspending our immediate, nearly instinctive resort to them so as to be able to come to contemplate their source and nature. We are to relinquish the customary academic-scholarly sport of forming, subscribing to, and arguing over doctrines and theories, and attend instead to the questions from which the thinking we take as doctrine arises.

Significantly, those are the very questions foreclosed in advance by our usual practices of analysis, whereby we take questions to be but problems, like all else readily subjected to our mastery, our cleverness in devising technical fixes and solutions, to which they are but a marginal irritant and quarry. This way of engaging, which our customary ways of thinking exemplify and further, is one so commonplace as to be invisible, unremarkable in its ubiquity and its "obvious" warrant and necessity. This uncanny availability makes resort to it seem necessary, even strangely compulsory, while it also inveigles us with a promise of ease—one that is accompanied, always, by a relentless insatiability with which it is not at all incompatible, but fully in accord, for the "ease" to which we are thereby delivered is not that of rest, but of efficiency, the extraction of ever more gain to the end of nothing but perpetually feeding its own perpetual demand.

Attending to this accustomed way of comporting ourselves—thinking on it, contemplating its source and hold on us—became its own wonder and puzzlement, a leading and increasingly central concern of Heidegger's work. It is not a separate concern from the well-known central question of his work, the question of being; it *is* that question, understood as asking after what gives us to think, what calls on us to think, what is most "thought-provoking": literally, what *calls forth*, and *calls for*, thinking. Heidegger names this *das Bedenklichste*, with its overtones of disturbing, alarming, ominous: of danger.[6]

What is *most* thought-provoking in this deep and disturbing way Heidegger tells us scores of times in *Was heißt Denken?*, presumably because we need to hear it, because we have not yet heard it: It is *that we are still not thinking.* ... But what, then, are we doing instead?

This.

III

At first and for the most part, we do not understand this, our usual way of proceeding—what we take, without thinking, to be thinking—as *a way* at all, nor as distinctive, still less distinctively ours, but as what thinking is and must be, what it inevitably requires; we do not understand it as anything but normal and "necessary"—that is, as needed in order to achieve whatever goal we summon up: as requisite—and as exclusive.

What is this way of addressing and relating to beings, which we find ever-present and available, even inescapable? It is peculiarly hard to think on: In its constancy, we cannot distinguish it, identify it, or define it; its ubiquity renders it elusively indefinite and indiscernible. It is that which pursues and provides grounds, and yet gives us no hint, beyond "necessity," of what might be its own ground. In its very omnipresence, it vanishes from our explanatory grasp, which, in principle—*its* principle—nothing else can escape. As it is thoroughly routine, it appears as "just the way things are"—and, precisely in this, as no mystery, and nothing calling for thought. At the same time, in its exceptionless rule, it demands that all challenges to it, which is to say not replications of its investigatory assault but thinking that would shake its hold by illuminating it, are turned aside by invoking motivating causes, fortifying its prevailing sway by explaining away any and all thought as explicable on grounds other than its possible sense or truth.

We carry out this demand whenever we take such thinking—as we straightaway do—as necessarily presenting a doctrine or position, seeking reinforcement by gaining assent through the triumph of argumentative force. We then assess that force, evaluating it against the counterforce of the doctrines, theories, and opinions we already hold, to assess its agreement with them and so our willingness to award our agreement in turn; or, to avoid dealing with such thinking at all, we assess instead the personal motivating interest that we take to lie behind the imputed drive to propose and persuade, which, taken as such, we imagine to "need uncovering," taking this interest as the "real," causal ground and dispositive explanation of the thinking in question.

Thus we find ourselves, with strange immediacy, bringing to bear *here, too*, the assault of analysis and its attendant reduction of the question of its nature to a soluble problem, as even thinking that attempts to illuminate or diverge from this prevailing mode is attributed to any of a host of such ready explanantia as ideology, theoretical commitments, personal ties or bias—and all such accounts promise to render the matter neatly explained, bounded and contained by its ready explanatory configuration. In this, again, the prevailing comportment of problem-solving dismissal replicates itself even as it further entrenches its dominance and claim to exclusivity, for this explaining-away by resort to extraneous grounds, aims, and motives is the comportment brought to bear upon everything we encounter, as providing warrant for the existence and activity of whatever is.

But the matter in question here is just this way of engaging. Accordingly, precisely when we proceed so, this very way thereby remains still invisible, still prevailing, still exclusive—and, still, awaiting a thoughtful engagement that does not simply replicate and re-commit it.

This difficulty gives us pause, and rightly so, before attempting to define this way of proceeding, or explain it, or trace its causes, for these "obvious," "necessary," thoroughly familiar procedures, prescribed and sanctioned by logic and rationality, all partake of this single and singular way of proceeding, whereby we do not illuminate it but only instantiate it yet again. And, crucially, when we resort to this explanatory disposition, in any of its myriad forms, we shrink the phenomenon, so as to fit it within the frameworks we enlist to explain it—and thereby miss its sheer scope and all-embracing character: that is to say, its character as metaphysical.

There is, then, a need, perhaps itself only faintly or intermittently sensed, for caution and reserve in coming to address this overwhelmingly present and yet elusive phenomenon, and perhaps a period of groping and false starts as well, while various attempts are made to think on what is too vast, too immediate, and too omnipresent to grasp in ready systematic ways, and whose totality comes, at every turn, to prescribe and conscript those very ways and attempts.

How, then, to come to understand, and to think on, this phenomenon that is more and other than all the phenomena it offers, that exceeds the scope of what appears, as itself the way of appearing of all that we come to engage with? How to think through this singular way of engagement in its endlessly protean constancy, its obviousness and invisibility, its pressing availability? Above all: How to think through, not its instances, but its *hold*?

By experiencing it—in its full scope and enormity, as the event of events.

This is what Heidegger did, and what he invites us to do.

IV

Was heißt Denken? was the first—and last—course of lectures Heidegger gave, after nearly a decade's postwar exile from the academy. Speaking simply and profoundly of thinking, of what is called by that name and what calls for it, he put into that book, as he says there of Nietzsche, "everything he knew."[7] And yet found it strangely neglected,[8] despite its strikingly limpid quality—or perhaps because of it, for what he tells us there so clearly is not flattering, but deeply disturbing and highly demanding, and perhaps as a result difficult to hear. Indeed, that we are not hearing—and so do not hear that, as well as what, we are not hearing—is the same fundamental absence and plight as our not thinking, for what we do not hear, or heed, is the call of thinking; and that we do not is what most calls for just that: "Das Bedenklichste … in unserer bedenklichen Zeit" is *that we are still not thinking*—"not even yet, although the state of the world is becoming constantly more thought-provoking."[9]

Our constantly more thought-provoking time: Then, the bloody, world-shattering twentieth century, only half passed when this was written; now, that century's long dénouement—which seems but continuance: still bloody, still shattered and uprooted. And marked, ever more thoroughly, by something else as well, something so pervasive as to go unremarked, a broad current from which all these newsworthy incidents arise and on whose course they play themselves out. Like Nietzsche before him, Heidegger saw with remarkable acuity the depth, scope, and scale of what was occurring in his time and the time to come, and which has continued to unfold and fulfill itself as he foresaw. And, like Nietzsche, he saw it with a dawning and gradual horror, a concern all the more grave for its clarity, which it took many exploratory efforts and much solitary grappling to try to think through and bring to articulation.

He saw, too, that this is not what the world expected as a response: That this is the most thought-provoking time, in which the world becomes ever more thought-provoking, ever more rife with cruelty and calamity, "seems to demand rather that man should act, without delay, [that] what is lacking is action, not thought. ... And yet—it could be that prevailing man has for centuries now acted too much and thought too little"[10]: that, indeed, it is precisely "the will to action, which here means the will to make and be effective, [that] has overrun and crushed thought."[11]

Heidegger had many years to think =on what he would say in this pensive valediction—cataclysmic years, not merely for him, and not only in Germany, and for the world, but for the history of its course, on which we are borne still. Where that course has brought us, in this cruelest of centuries, he tells us just here, where he speaks of "what is most thought-provoking, in our thought-provoking time": He invokes Nietzsche's terrible pronouncement, "*die Wüste wächst.*" *The wasteland grows*, a wasteland of quiet and thoroughgoing devastation, more profound and disturbing than even the destruction of the world wars, "despite all the unspeakable suffering, all the distress"[12] they undeniably bring.

Indeed, it is from out of this fundamental devastation that "man is driven from one world war into the next"—and *just so, too,* in waging a "peace offensive" aimed at securing through war a peace that is to eliminate war, fixing hostilities in place through the mutual extraction of gain in a *pax* of pacts.[13] For the pursuit of these cold hostilities, too, arises "out of an unearthly fate that forbids modern man to look beyond himself and his type of ideas" such that he "has no other choice but to search [there] for the form of those measures that are to create a world order": "Congresses and conferences, committees and sub-committees," self-sustaining systems of methodical regulation, numbingly banal in the institutional regularity of their routine bureaucratic proceedings—and precisely in that insinuating blandness and normalcy carrying out an insidious danger. And so Heidegger describes them, "blinking organizations of blinking arrangements of distrust and treachery"[14]—a soberingly clear-eyed description of contemporary political institutions; as he notes in his reflections surrounding these events: "Politics no longer has anything to do with the πόλις."[15] These securing and regulating activities do not exist in service to a "world order," but constitute world order*ing*, as the exhaustive content and aim of activity. He concludes: "Any decision in this realm of ideas must by its very nature fall short."[16] And so, he continues to think[17] ...

Far from ignoring the shattering violence and tragedy of the war—or settling for "a sham peace and security"[18] that merely cements power's victories and perpetuates its dynamic—Heidegger is drawn by that very experience to think on its deeper source and significance: ... *And yet,* he wonders—could it be that—this blinking way of forming ideas lies beyond the reach of man's mere whims, even his carelessness … that there prevails [here] … a peculiar relation regarding that which is, a relation that reaches beyond man … [and] is of such a kind that it will not allow man to let Being in its essence be?[19]

V

This is the question to which Heidegger devotes himself, throughout these tumultuous years. Through its pursuit, he comes to see that this single, and singular, way of relating to things and others has the entire world in its thrall, that it is a juggernaut of ever-expanding scope and exclusivity, that it drives all before itself in the relentless promotion of efficiency, as its own endless end

He gives it many names. Indeed, the very identification of this way of "thinking," as it comes to occupy and lay exclusive claim to that name, is itself a question calling for sustained thinking—and so it becomes, through a long inquiry into the question that, in turn, gives that book its name and its arc. As he comes to see, what most calls for thinking is precisely "this way of forming ideas [that] at bottom sets upon everything it sets before itself, in order to depose and decompose it … set[ting] all things up in such a way that it pursues and sets upon them in principle"[20]—each verb here a form of *setzen* and *stellen*, a setting that does not merely set what it encounters back into its place, in an order that prevails already, but *sets up* that order in that setting encounter, summoning, regulating, supplying, and positioning, "giving order" by giving orders. In doing so, this way does not allow the thing in question to appear and be encountered (still less to be in question, nor a thing[21]), but summons it forth in order to deploy it, such that it is thereby consigned in advance to the furtherance of goals and programs extrinsic to it, from which it takes its always-provisional warrant for being.

This setting-upon that marks our relation to ideas, to one another, and to the world—and that sets upon man in turn, or rather from the outset—presents itself as what thinking is; and, in so doing, bars us from precisely the thinking that is most called for, now. This it does not only by usurping the place of that thinking, and the relation it affords to what is, preempting it in the setting-upon that does not let beings be[22]—nor, therefore, man. It does so, further, precisely in giving us over to the ingratiating thought that we are masters of this very way of proceeding, and, through it, of all we encounter,[23] though our conscription into this fundamental comportment is not, and cannot be, itself our doing.[24]

This paradoxical double thrall and embroilment renders it peculiarly difficult to think on this setting-upon, to think through its source, essence, and implications—and peculiarly necessary to do so with extreme care, as, in its very ubiquity, it presents itself as the "obvious" and "necessary" manner of relating to all that we encounter—including itself. And yet this profoundly thought-provoking and thought-evading ubiquity, *experienced* in its compelling claim to exclusivity, offers, finally, the brightest of windows, opening unexpectedly onto a vast and unimagined horizon, as it gives us the way, and obligation, to think—finally—on being, as that which, in its sending as metaphysics, gives us over to encounter the world and its beings in this very way.

Just such thinking-through is the task that Heidegger takes on in "Die Frage nach der Technik," emerging in the time of *Was heißt Denken?* as its necessary complement. There, Heidegger thinks on the source and nature of this distinctive way of relating, which he identifies as the essence of that to which he gives the name *Technik*. In coming to think on the *essence* of its way of encounter, Heidegger speaks of the "setting-upon that challenges forth" as "an expediting"—his word is *Fördern*, a verb that names a wide range of ways of *furthering*, its essential thrust—"and in two ways. It expedites in that it unlocks and exposes. Yet that expediting is always itself directed from the beginning toward furthering something else, that is, toward driving on to the maximum yield at the minimum expense."[25]

This drive goes, now, by the prosaic name of efficiency, and we encounter it at every turn in contemporary life, even in those regions that might be thought immune (such as the university, long a concern of Heidegger's[26]). But nothing is immune to this single and singular drive, whose unending end consists in only its own perpetuation; nothing can be so immune in principle, because it *is* the principle—the ἀρχη, the governing sway itself. It is, accordingly, the ground and measure of beings as such and as a whole: that which, summoning them into being and providing their ground, gives them to be at all, and so gives us over into how we are given to encounter them.

VI

At once the most difficult and most essential task in our times is coming to understand the sheer scope and sweep of this sway. For the difficulty of doing so lies not merely in that it evades all our usual methods of analysis, and all partial accounting and illustration, every instance of which instead reinstantiates that familiar drive and extends that sweep. Much more fundamental than any merely methodological impediment or analytical conundrum is the hold that brings us to just such ways of engaging, as it commands of us the commanding by which, in these myriad ways, we set out to set upon all that we encounter. And yet it is in experiencing that very hold that we can come to understand the unexpected depth and source of this sway, the ungrounded ground from which it springs.

This sway and its character—if not its origin or essence—are vividly revealed in Nietzsche's thought of the Will to Power, and it is to that thought that Heidegger turns in the latter 1930s, entering into a prolonged and intensive engagement with Nietzsche's metaphysics—which is to say, with ours. This encounter with Nietzsche, at just this time, is by no means a merely scholarly pursuit, unconnected to the world's turmoil as it surrounded Heidegger in those years; rather, it was necessary precisely for the attempt to think through that cataclysm whose repercussions were becoming devastatingly manifest, in its fundamental metaphysical ground, sense, and implications. For, as he perceived: "Once we reach [the] heartland [of Nietzsche's metaphysics], we are in the realm from which the word was spoken: 'Die Wüste wächst … .'"[27] As, indeed, we are.[28]

Nietzsche, of course, did not understand his thought as metaphysics, but as the overcoming of metaphysics, accomplished in the overturning of Platonism and the conscious revaluation of all values; in just the same way, we imagine our rational, "realistic" reduction of the world to calculable forces and effects to be non- or "post-" metaphysical, and our thinking to be "past" metaphysics … owing precisely to its ongoing reign.

This makes Nietzsche, with whom Heidegger now entered into his longest sustained engagement with a single thinker, of paramount importance, as Nietzsche both illuminates this metaphysics and illustrates its sway, thereby holding a profound mirror up to our own understanding.[29] Nietzsche's thought accomplishes the consummation of Western metaphysics as a whole,[30] and in two senses: That metaphysics comes to its fulfillment in the understanding of the world as will to power, an understanding now so tamely conventional that it is rendered bland and unthought in its being taken as a matter of common knowledge, at least in sophisticated discourse, that all relations, interactions, institutions, and ideals present, at bottom, "only" matters of power. Its consummation is, further, rendered fully and abidingly complete in its totalizing hold, as is revealed in nothing so much as precisely that blandness, with which we affirm its relentless pressing of its exclusivity upon us as we shrug—or, perhaps, blink?—in agreement, finding it unremarkable that "of course" there is no "real" truth or right, but only the occasions and enactments of power. And so Heidegger concludes in his reading of Nietzsche on the ways of the sway of will to power, under which "'all events, all motions, all becoming, [appear] as a determination of degrees and relations of force, as a *struggle*'": "What loses the struggle is—because it has lost—untrue and in the wrong. What emerges victorious is—because it has won—true and in the right."[31] In this convergent evaporation of truth and right Heidegger sees will to power's conscious ascension into its full metaphysical dominion, whereby the truth of beings becomes a matter of and for the self-justifying justice of *Gerechtigkeit*, "the way in which the essence of truth must be understood at the end of Western metaphysics … as [its] consummation."[32]

This subsumption of truth and right to power—properly and fully said, to *will to* power— appears to us as a matter of course because it is indeed our course, that is, the course of the modern West, of modernity as it fulfills itself in the metaphysics Nietzsche names and Heidegger thinks through in the lectures and book that, accordingly, bear the title *European Nihilism*. The title does not name a limitation (geographic, political, or otherwise) set to nihilism, as though that were possible, but instead notes the historic site of its growth and bloom, just then caught in the throes of its worldwide metastasis.[33] In fact, Heidegger comes to see nihilism's fullest flower in what he calls "Americanism."[34] That, too, is not a limiting specification or an empirical designation of persons—every such reference from Heidegger is mis-taken when it is so construed—but an appellation for a temporal abode, a way-station serving as the site of a way of thinking that, by its nature, has the world as a whole increasingly in its thrall.[35]

This planetary sway is not itself political, economic, technological, scientific, or cultural; it is not even of human origin and invention. It is, rather, what gives us to understand what occurs in all these realms as—ever and only—the strategic play of forces, powers, and interests, commandeering and exhausting the possibilities of our relations and engagements with the world, with the things of the world, and with one another. Its ascendancy and consummation as a way of thinking—as our way of thinking, now—is the deep and quiet horror of our times, rendered innocuous and unremarkable and, precisely in that, wholly insidious and triumphant. And it is just this familiar, quotidian prevailing that brings the other, more infamous horrors to be conceivable, even to follow "as a matter of course," for it is itself the course on which the modern West is borne.

VII

The question of the ground, essence, and peculiar cogency of this distinctive modern way of encountering beings presented a fundamental concern and sustained source of contemplation for Heidegger, one he engaged continuously, making a number of attempts to name it, to understand its source and its hold, and to think through its implications. This sustained engagement surfaces most visibly in *Die Frage nach der Technik*, but it pervades all of his work, as does his commensurate concern with its occluded other, the meditative thinking that surrenders calculation, a concern that emerges in and as the engagement with poetry,[36] as well as, thematically, in *Gelassenheit*[37] and *Was heißt Denken?* But the roots of Heidegger's concern with the question, and his efforts to understand the source, nature, and scope of this modern way of encounter, reach back far earlier.

The depth and duration of those efforts become vividly present in the *Nietzsche* volumes of courses and lectures, which, over four years with an additional decade of reflective essays, undertake to think through the will to power in its myriad manifestations, showing its activity as art,[38] as knowledge,[39] as truth become justice and justification,[40] as "constructive, annihilative, exclusive" in its ceaseless activity of valuation[41]—and as the culmination of Western metaphysics. These efforts reach a climactic point in, and as, European nihilism, not as that which is countered and overcome by will to power, but as will to power's full florescence, the path of the lectures coming to constitute the path, not merely of Nietzsche's thought, or of Heidegger's account of Nietzsche's thought, but the path of Western thought itself, unfolded to its consummation.[42]

Now, with the publication of Heidegger's notebooks from what appears without a doubt to be the most crucial decade of his thinking, we can see the dawning and development of this profound insight, as his thinking emerges from out of the experience of those years. And, as that is also the most crucial—in the strictest sense of the word—decade of his personal life, and of the world history through which he lived, we glimpse as well the place of those notorious events in spurring that thought. And illuminating our own.

The notebooks make absorbing reading, for one can see the thinking slowly unfold from out of those extreme hopes and their corresponding despair; can witness the remarkable patience and discipline necessary, in dark and trying times, to resist any early temptation to end that despair by labeling and disposing of the "problem"; and can follow the think-ing from its nascency, as we encounter, in the decade's early and middle years, numerous short and scattered notes, attempts, and culs-de-sac, intermittent entries that sometimes run on, circle back, or break off into extended silence, notes that are exploratory, oblique, and episodic: a state of reflective indeterminacy lasting through much of the mid-1930s[43]—and then can see that bitter confusion gathering into a resolve to *think*, and witness that think-ing's slowly mounting illumination.

The notes, accordingly, are not served by being plucked from context and "reassembled" into a sustained account, interposing a clarity and continuity they lacked then. (One is put in mind of Elisabeth Förster-Nietzsche's exertion brought to bear upon *The Will to Power*—and Heidegger's contempt for it.[44] Perhaps this already sufficiently illuminates his decision to have the notebooks published last, leaving us, in the end and in the most expres-sive way possible, with "ways, not works.") Rather, the thought those entries evidence is better honored as well as better understood by viewing its emergence over that long time—for it grew from out of the experience of that time, signally marked by just such thoughtless efficiency and the violation of beings' integrity it accomplishes, in what became its most egregious eventuation.

Heidegger came to see the disarmingly colorless routinization and management of all we encounter as the manifestation of something far darker, as that which emerges later as the will to power and as *Technik*.[45] Here, he names what is at work *Machenschaft*, and its close complement *Rechnung*. *Machenschaft* ("the boundless producibility of all beings as the single but unrecognizable truth of Being"[46]) is the understanding of what is, of all that is, as a matter of, and for, contriving: for devising, manipulating, engineering, organizing, strat-egizing, evaluating, assessing, adjusting; an "understanding" that does not, in fact, under-stand or engage with what it encounters as existing in or for itself, but instead looks past it, to a justification for its being to be found elsewhere. Such a regard looks out, always and instead, to what else something can yield, for what it can produce, for its consequences—which are, in turn, to be assessed, the involvement contrived and adjusted accordingly, in the ongoing pursuit of efficient gain that is its own unending end. Such assessment is *Rechnung*—not only calculation in a narrow or numerical sense, but *reckoning*—what, thinking through Nietzsche, Heidegger comes to understand as valuation, the essence of will to power.[47] In seeing the essence and implications of this way of encounter—and so, its ubiquity—Heidegger was astonishingly prescient, writing at barely the nascent edge of the computer age that is now become full-blown, as we experience the exactions of its calculating machination pressing on all sides, its ravening appetite for speed and the production of assessable results, its open celebration of incessant, self-justified growth and disruption, its importuning demands, its insatiable intrusiveness, its relentless drive—all of which spring from its distinctive essence, just as Heidegger saw, and said, three-quarters of a century ago.[48]

Together, *Machenschaft* and *Rechnung* present a single and singular way of approaching everything in the world[49]—a way that is so pervasive and ordinary now as to seem unexceptionable. Under its totalizing sway, all is but grist for the grinding mill of calculation, ever disposed and disposed of in advance toward a result that is in turn of the same conditioned and provisional being, such that what is continually present and decisive is, only and ever, instrumentality alone.[50] This strange absence, in which things come to presence in a way that does not let them *be*, is uncanny.

To attend to it—as we too rarely do, driven as we are in carrying out its execution instead[51]—is to experience both that we are given over into encounter with beings … and that we are peculiarly deprived in that impoverished encounter, as beings are attenuated such that we find ourselves engaged ever and only with the counterforces, reckoning, machination, causation, and drive as which the being of all has been rendered.

Heidegger will come to see in such present absence the withdrawal of being, even as it sends this very way of encounter with beings.[52] This momentous double insight, abyssal in every way, opens profoundly thought-provoking vistas for his later works. And it is in the incubation afforded by the notebooks that Heidegger is first able to begin to fathom and to voice it, as he comes, there, to identify what is at work in our uncanny modern thoughtlessness, and to contemplate its implications. For they are a matter of enormity. In every sense.

VIII

The sheer scope of its totalizing reach, taking up all it encounters and every manner of encounter into its reckoning machination, renders this metaphysics exceedingly difficult to discern, as precisely that insinuating prevalence veils its question-worthiness. At the same time, that all-embracing scope—its prevalence as *prevailing*—is the hint it gives of its essence as a sending of being, for no resort to machination and reckoning can yield machination and reckoning itself as that which beings as such call for by way of encounter and comportment.

Heidegger will later find in Hölderlin the words for this profound insight that experiences the sending of beings in its totality, seemingly exclusive of being, as that very saving absence: "Wo aber Gefahr ist, wächst / Das Rettende auch."[53] In our experiencing metaphysics in its totalizing reach there faintly glimmers the sending-withdrawal of being. Coming thereby to comprehend the felt necessity of its drawing-forth, its "obvious" claim on us—"ob-vious" as that which lies across our path, or *via*—we can come to attend for the first time to that path, and to its metaphysical provenance and destination.

Heidegger conveys the experience and articulation of this double insight, later crystallized in the words of Hölderlin, in reflection on the events of the 1930s and their source and significance. An entry from 1939 looks back to his misplaced hopes at the opening of that decade, concluding that, in taking National Socialism to offer "the possibility of a crossing-over to another beginning," he had been "thinking in purely 'metaphysical' terms," thus underestimating its "essential power and inner necessity": That power and necessity lay in advancing the "dis-humanizing [*Vermenschung*] of mankind in self-certain rationality," whereby it accomplished in a "much deeper, that is, encompassing and enmeshing manner … the consummation of modernity."[54] As that consummation is the fulfillment of metaphysics in its destiny as European nihilism, he could conclude: "Aus der vollen Einsicht in die frühere Täuschung über das Wesen und die geschichtliche Wesenskraft des National-sozialismus ergibt sich erst die Notwendigkeit seiner Bejahung und zwar aus denkerischen Gründen": "Only from full insight into the earlier illusion concerning the essence and historically essential power of National Socialism arises the necessity of its affirmation, and this is so indeed on the basis of thinking." That we may hear and attend to what is said here, as well as to all that Heidegger comes to see and to say regarding the nature of truth and of metaphysics, we must hear *Bejahung*, conventionally translated "affirmation," not as the subjective assent or endorsement of any one or all of us—as though that could be necessary or decisive to its metaphysical standing—but as acknowledgment of the movement's *essential* power and *inner* necessity in carrying out that completion of modernity's metaphysical destiny.[55] *Und zwar aus denkerischen Gründen.*

IX

Enormity is indeed the fittingly odious name for what attains terrible actuality in the mass, methodical slaughter, of unprecedented scale and efficiency, that began in 1941. The word names as well the departure from normativity that marks that horror, but not it alone, as though it were aberrational—hence, like all else, merely to be explained, fixed, and dismissed. Rather, it identifies the loss of normativity as such, as truth and right are transmuted into just another servant and prize of power, the most disturbing and momentous[56] fulfillment of the ascendancy of that metaphysics whose prevailing as the understanding of the world and its beings brings such horrors to be conceivable. For nothing is beyond the pale when there is no longer a pale, the pale itself now become but the provisional goal of a will to power inimical to limits, which it posits only to surpass.

Heidegger saw all this, in its essential unfolding.[57] He ventured through the thinking of it, in the notebooks. And he spent the following years, and beyond, working to understand and to bring us to understand this, the destined eventuation of modernity in its final fruition—to experience not simply discrete incidents occurring in his times and ours, but their spring and significance arising from out of the understanding of beings and their dominance, the withdrawal of being, and the reign of the metaphysics of will to power, now come into the full sweep of its prevailing sway. For the events of his time and ours are born of *the* event,[58] the sending of being by which we are given to encounter—and so engage with, and treat—beings as we do, in the reck-less, exploitative, calculating way that brings just such horrors, as well as the quiet, daily horror we no longer see.

These are the ways of *Technik*, whereby beings are marshaled, organized, and deployed to the solitary end of furthering productivity, and all is as resource, its very being conditioned upon its capacity to feed that relentless demand. The efficiency of machination, now loosed from its first appearance as a matter of subjective intentionality, thereby comes to trump, depose, and obliterate every other consideration and all restraint of principle, as beings are subjected to efficient mass production, management—and disposal. *Even human beings.* This is the sense of Heidegger's notorious observation, widely misunderstood, that "farming is now a motorized food industry, in essence the same as the fabrication of corpses in gas chambers and extermination camps, the same as the blockade and starving of the peasantry, the same as the fabrication of the hydrogen bomb."[59] These profoundly disparate undertakings are not identical, not indistinguishable, but *the same in essence*, for that essence—as the essence of all, now—is just that subjection to the indiscriminately uniform, morally oblivious demands of *Technik*. This is no endorsement (as though that could be germane or decisive to its truth, an expectation born of the very metaphysics in question); it is a seeing and saying of what is, in its essence. If the statement is shocking—as it is—it is a shock offered to help us to see and to *experience* that essence, in its thought-provoking ubiquity.

Coming to do so, to understand its hold on us, experiencing its pull into just this way of encounter *as* pull and not merely our choice and achievement, we can perhaps begin to sense the profound question-worthiness its ubiquity obscures. And in the sweeping destruction of bodies and communities it engenders we can perhaps catch the darkest of hints of its threatened loss of human being as such, in our essential relation to being and hence to beings, to the earth, and to one another—and so, perhaps, of the saving to which that hint faintly beckons.

Heidegger experienced the seductions of power, and not only in a personal capacity: He saw the whole world caught up in its excitation. Reflecting throughout the decade on the source and significance of those events as they unfolded, he came to see how, from out of that inducement and under its sway as, first, *Machenschaft* and *Rechnung*, concerns of power and efficacy commandeer thinking and consign us, unmoored, to the oblivion of being—and how, in that very not-thinking to which we are given over, we are given as well the first hint of the *not* that reveals what this metaphysics *is*, as the sending of being from out of its withdrawal.[60]

Heidegger comes to understand Nazism accordingly, as the historically destined fulfillment of the metaphysics of *Machenschaft*.[61] This recognition is not (as some may be quick to brand it) an effort to whitewash or excuse his succumbing to its inducement, but to *understand* it—and ours. For its thrall is nothing merely idiosyncratic or biographical: *Far more* is at stake.

To see *in* that inducement of power its metaphysical essence and origin is to *think through*—in both senses—the events through which he lived, from out of the event of their eventuation. Far from never addressing the events of these terrible years, he attended to little else: How were they possible?—yet asked not as a matter of causation's explanatory disposition, or of the arbitrariness of isolated willful action, all metaphysically questionable—but from out of sober regard for that eventuation's being-historical significance: What happened here?[62] *Was ist geschehen—und was ist die Geschichte, woraus es geschieht? What held sway in those perilous times—and does so still?* No mere apology—as for a mistake, leaving the dominion of rational will undisturbed—can reach *this* event, as it is nothing our actions could devise, or remorseful re-actions reverse. Supposing otherwise (as we do) is not only a metaphysically founded bit of anthropocentric vanity; the charge and discharge of isolated blame is further misguided (if tempting) because it is too easy, absolving all the "rest" of us—not of blame, but of ongoing involvement: We are *im-plicated* here, folded into the unfolding of this history. It is nothing past, and nothing limited; on the contrary, it is now planetary, ruling in full scope and sway as it manifests itself in our distinctively uprooted and calculating way of dealing with the things and others of the world, to which it gives us over.

An unbearably painful thought hovers here, requiring almost more courage to face than we are capable of: As unfathomably horrific as the Holocaust was, the unthinking that allowed that atrocity had deeper, more pervasive, and still more sobering roots than its chronology-bound moment in historiography would grant, for these roots reach to the way we—all of us, in the modern West—live and encounter the world. *Still.* For we are still not thinking …

Heidegger invites us, and himself, in the notebooks and their contemporaneous essays and essayings, to begin to start to prepare to commence to do so.

Acknowledgments

I thank Charlie Zaharoff for research and translation assistance.

Notes

1. "Überlegungen X" §1, *Überlegungen VII–XI (Schwarze Hefte 1938/39), Gesamtausgabe 95*, ed. Peter Trawny (Frankfurt: Klostermann, 2014), 275.

2. Emmanuel Faye, *Heidegger: L'introduction du nazisme dans la philosophie: Autour des séminaires inédits de 1933–1935* (Paris: Albin Michel, 2005); *Heidegger: The Introduction of Nazism into Philosophy in Light of the Unpublished Seminars of 1933–1935* (New Haven, CT: Yale University Press, 2009); cf. Peter Trawny, Heidegger und der Mythos der jüdischen Weltverschwörung (Frankfurt: Klostermann, 2014), 12 ("… ob wie und inwiefern die Antisemitismus Heideggers philosophie als ganze kontaminiert. Gibt es eine antisemitische Ideologie, die das Denken Heideggers so sehr besetzt, dass wir von einer 'antisemitischen Philosophie' sprechen mußten?"), 87, et passim.

3. See "Überlegungen und Winke III" §112, *Überlegungen II–VI (Schwarze Hefte 1931–1938), Gesamtausgabe* 94, ed. Peter Trawny (Frankfurt: Klostermann, 2014), 160: "Ich stehe am Ende eines *gescheiterten Jahres*."

4. Greg Johnson, "Heidegger's Black Notebooks: The Diaries of a Dissident National Socialist," 2014, http://

www.counter-currents.com/2014/03/heideggers-black-notebooks.

5. Gregory Fried, "The King Is Dead: Heidegger's 'Black Notebooks,'" *Los Angeles Review of Books*, September 13, 2014, https://lareviewofbooks.org/review/king-dead-heideggers-black-notebooks.

6. See *Was heißt Denken?*, *Gesamtausgabe* 8, ed. Paola-Ludovika Coriando (Frankfurt: Klostermann, [1954] 2002), 32: "Das Bedenklichste braucht auch nicht, gerade wenn es das Höchste ist, auszuschließen, daß es zugleich das Gefährlichste bleibt," *What Is Called Thinking?*, trans. J. Glenn Gray (New York: Harper & Row, 1976), 31; cf. "Überlegungen XIII" §73, *Überlegungen XII–XV (Schwarze Hefte 1939–1941)*, *Gesamtausgabe* 96, ed. Peter Trawny (Frankfurt: Klostermann, 2014), 110: "Gefahr waltet dort, wo der Vorbeigang am *noch verborgenen geschichtlichen* Wesen droht, so zwar, daß diese Bedrohung gar nicht als eine solche erkannt wird, ja nicht einmal erkannt werden kann. Die Gefahr ist, daß die Vollendung der Neuzeit, die sich nicht abdrosseln läßt, als der einzige Grund des Fortgangs der 'Geschichte' sich behauptet; die Gefahr ist die Ausschließlichkeit des 'Erfolges' der Machenschaft im metaphysischen Sinne—die nicht wissenkönnende und nichtahnende Untergrabung jeder Möglichkeit eines ganz anderen geschichtlichen Anfangs ..."

7. *Was heißt Denken?*, *Gesamtausgabe* 8, p. 54, *What Is Called Thinking?*, 51

8. "Nur noch ein Gott kann uns retten," interview with *Der Spiegel*, September 23, 1966, reprinted in *Reden und andere Zeugnisse eines Lebensweges*, *Gesamtausgabe* 16, ed. Hermann Heidegger (Frankfurt: Klostermann, 2000), 676.

9. *Was heißt Denken?*, *Gesamtausgabe* 8, p. 6; *What Is Called Thinking?*, 4.

10. *Was heißt Denken?*, *Gesamtausgabe* 8, p. 6; *What Is Called Thinking?*, 4.

11. *Was heißt Denken?*, *Gesamtausgabe* 8, p. 27; *What Is Called Thinking?*, 25.

12. *Was heißt Denken?*, *Gesamtausgabe* 8, p. 89; *What Is Called Thinking?*, 84. Cf. "Überlegungen XIV," *Überlegungen XII–XV*, *Gesamtausgabe* 96, p. 173: "Der jetzige Weltkrieg ist die äußerste Umwälzung alles Seienden in das Unbedingte der Machenschaft"; "Überlegungen XII" §24, *Überlegungen XII–XV*, *Gesamtausgabe* 96, p. 45: "Wo könnte hier noch eine Spur jener Angst erwachen, die erkennt, daß ... das ungreifbar um sich greifende Anwachsen der Bestimmung zu dieser Lage bereits und allein nicht nur Zerstörung, sondern die Verwüstung ist, deren Herrschaft durch Kriegskatastrophen und Katastrophenkriege nicht mehr angetastet, sondern nur noch bezeugt werden kann"; "Überlegungen XIII" §73, *Überlegungen XII–XV*, *Gesamtausgabe* 96, pp. 113–114: "Mag der Grauen noch so fürchterlich, mag die Tapferkeit unerhört, mag das Opfer unvergleichlich sein, durch all das wird nie die Grundbedingung zur Besinnung geschaffen: die innere Freiheit des Menschen zu den wesentlichen (nicht interessehaften) Entscheidungen, die Bereitschaft zur geschichtlichen Fragwürdigkeit des Sein. Überall hat sich schon die Machenschaft aller Möglichkeiten des Seienden bemächtigt und sie mit ihren Auslegungen belegt, so daß der Mensch trotz aller Bedrängnis und Bestürzung nicht mehr in die wesentlich Bezirke einer dem Seyn entstammenden Not vorzudringen vermag."

13. *Was heißt Denken?*, *Gesamtausgabe* 8, p. 88; *What Is Called Thinking?*, 83. Cf. "Überlegungen XIV," *Überlegungen XII–XV*, *Gesamtausgabe* 96, p. 173.

14. *Was heißt Denken?*, *Gesamtausgabe* 8, p. 88; *What Is Called Thinking?*, 84.

15. "Überlegungen XII," *Überlegungen XII–XV*, *Gesamtausgabe* 96, p. 43: "Politik hat nichts mehr mit der πόλις, ebensowenig mit Sittlichkeit und noch weniger mit der 'Volkwerdung' zu tun"; cf. "Überlegungen VI" §87, *Überlegungen II–VI*, *Gesamtausgabe* 94, p. 472: "*Die neue Politik ist eine innere Wesensfolge der Technik ...*"

16. *Was heißt Denken?*, *Gesamtausgabe* 8, p. 88; *What Is Called Thinking?*, 84; cf. "Überlegungen XII," *Überlegungen XII–XV*, *Gesamtausgabe* 96, p. 43: "Die 'Politik' ist die eigentliche Vollstreckerin der Machenschaft des Seienden; sie ist nur metaphysisch zu begreifen—jede andere Bewertung greift zu kurz."

17. Cf. "Überlegungen XII" §48, *Überlegungen XII–XV*, *Gesamtausgabe* 96, p. 66: "Alles Gemächte wird abgetragen bis, auf den bodenlosen Anspruch auf eine ziellose Macht. Allein bleibt das noch verborgene Vermögen des Erdenkens"; "Überlegungen V" §124, *Überlegungen II–VI*, *Gesamtausgabe* 94, p. 390: "Was also ist dann zu tun? Das, was du von jeher schon tun mußtest: Übe unerbittlich das einfache Handwerk der Auslegung der großen Denker, der Gewöhnung an das lange Denken und denke selbst—im Verborgenen—dein Notwendigstes."

18. *Was heißt Denken?*, *Gesamtausgabe* 8, p. 88; *What Is Called Thinking?*, 84.

19. *Was heißt Denken?*, *Gesamtausgabe* 8, p. 89; *What Is Called Thinking?*, 84.

20. *Was heißt Denken?*, *Gesamtausgabe* 8, p. 89; *What Is Called Thinking?*, 84.

21. See "Das Ding" (1951), *Vorträge und Aufsätze, Gesamtausgabe* 7, ed. Friedrich-Wilhelm von Herrmann (Frankfurt: Klostermann, [1954] 2000), 167–187; "The Thing," in *Poetry Language, Thought*, trans. Albert Hofstadter (New York: Harper & Row, 1971).

22. See "Brief über den Humanismus," *Wegmarken, Gesamtausgabe* 9, ed. Friedrich-Wilhelm von Herrmann (Frankfurt: Klostermann, [1967] 1976), 313–364, here 349; "Letter on 'Humanism,'" trans. Frank A. Capuzzi and J. Glenn Gray, in *Basic Writings*, ed. David Farrell Krell (New York: HarperCollins, 1993), 251; cf. "Überlegungen V" §53, *Überlegungen II–VI (Schwarze Hefte 1931–1938), Gesamtausgabe* 94, p. 340: "Warum darf jetzt kein Ding mehr in sich selbst und seinem Wesen ruhen?"

23. Cf. "Überlegungung XIII," *Überlegungen XII–XV, Gesamtausgabe* 96, p. 132: "… die Zuführung der neuzeitlichen Menschheit an die unbedingte Machenschaft … bedient sich eines unwiderstehlichen Lockmittels: sie überläßt dem Vollstreckerwesen der Machenschaft das Bewußtsein, in solchem 'Imperialismus' der Machenschaft (hier im vordergründlichen Sinne der planend-einrichtenden Berechnung) sich zu bedienen, während in Wahrheit, d.h. im Wesen des hier als Geschichte noch Verborgenen die Auslieferung des Imperialismus in die unbedingte Sklaverei der Machenschaft schon entschieden ist."

24. Cf. "Überlegungung XIII," *Überlegungen XII–XV, Gesamtausgabe* 96, p. 111: "Machenschaft ist nie Gemächte des Menschen, sondern dieser ist—gerade dort, wo er sich auf sich selbst stellt—der in die Machsamkeit verstrickte Vollstrecker der Machenschaft."

25. "Die Frage Nach der Technik," *Vorträge und Aufsätze, Gesamtausgabe* 7, p. 16; "The Question Concerning Technology," trans. William Lovitt, in *Basic Writings*, ed. David Farrell Krell (New York: HarperCollins, 1993), 321.

26. Cf. "Überlegungen und Winke III," *Überlegungen II–VI, Gesamtausgabe* 94, p. 193 (*"Die Universität wird Fachschule.—Alles läuft dahin aus"*); "Überlegungen XIV," *Überlegungen XII–XV, Gesamtausgabe* 96, p. 175 ("Die 'Universitäten' sind jetzt als 'lebenswichtige Betriebe' erklärt; diese Festsetzung ist heute unumgänglich; aber diese Festsetzung ist zugleich eine Deutung ihres Wesens, die dem Todesurteil über diese Einrichtung gleichkommt").

27. *Was heißt Denken?*, 98; *What Is Called Thinking?*, 94.

28. Cf. "Überlegungen XV" §4, *Überlegungen II–VI, Gesamtausgabe* 94, p. 316: "Wo stehen wir? Am Rande der äußersten Verzweiflung? Ja—aber hier ist noch und hier allein für den, der diese Stätte für einen Augenblick aussteht, das volle Licht der Leuchte des Seyns, in dem der letzte Gott sich verbirgt."

29. Cf. "Überlegungen XII" §57, *Überlegungen XII–XV, Gesamtausgabe* 96, pp. 69–70: "Nietzsche—spielt das Wesen des Seins hinaus auf einen Kampf von Machtlagen und Machtverhältnissen—dieser 'kämpferische' 'Aspekt' des Seienden im Ganzen deutet auf eine 'heroische' Denkweise. Und dennoch: gerade denkerisch ist dieses Denken die vollständigste Waffenstreckung, die metaphysische Feigheit schlechthin—das Ausweichen vor der einzigen und entscheidenden Frage nach der Wahrheit des Seyns—. Sucht deshalb alle Angst vor dem Begriff ihre Zuflucht bei diesem Denker, der in dieser Waffenstreckung nur die in der Geschichte der Metaphysik zur Herrschaft gekommene Seinsverlassenheit des Seienden vollstrecken muß und als Vollstrecker nun doch ein Denker wird?"

30. "Überlegungen XIII" §31, *Überlegungen XII–XV, Gesamtausgabe* 96, p. 92: "… zum Nach-denken der Nietzscheschen Gedanken … der Grund kommt aus der von Nietzsche geleisteten Vollendung der Metaphysik im Ganzen."

31. *Der europäische Nihilismus* (1940), in *Nietzsche II, Gesamtausgabe* 6 (II), ed. Brigitte Schillbach (Frankfurt: Klostermann, 1997), 109; *European Nihilism*, trans. Frank A. Capuzzi, in *Nietzsche IV: Nihilism* (New York: Harper & Row, 1982), 82. Heidegger is here quoting Nietzsche, *Wille zur Macht* n. 552 (1887). Cf. "Überlegungen XII" §9, *Überlegungen XII–XV, Gesamtausgabe* 96, p. 15: "Recht und Rechtmäßig ist jetzt nur jenes, was in die von der Übermacht gesetzte und d.h. stets wieder veränderliche 'Ordnung' sich einpaßt."

32. *Nietzsches Lehre vom Willen zur Macht als Erkenntnis* (1939), in *Nietzsche I, Gesamtausgabe* 6 (I), ed. Brigitte Schillbach (Frankfurt: Klostermann, 1996), 574; *The Will to Power as Knowledge*, trans. Joan Stambaugh, in *Nietzsche III: The Will to Power as Knowledge and Metaphysics* (New York: Harper & Row, 1987), 141.

33. Cf. *Nietzsches Metaphysik* (1940), in *Nietzsche II, Gesamtausgabe* 6 (II), 299–300; *Nietzsche's Metaphysics*, trans. Frank A. Capuzzi, in *Nietzsche III: The Will to Power as Knowledge and as Metaphysics*, 250–251.

34. See, e.g., "Überlegungung XII" §18, *Überlegungen XII–XV, Gesamtausgabe* 96, p. 39; "Überlegungung XIV," *Überlegungung XII–XV, Gesamtausgabe* 96, p. 225: "Im Amerikanismus erreicht der Nihilismus seine Spitze"; "Überlegungung XV," *Überlegungen XII–XV, Gesamtausgabe* 96, p. 257: "Der Amerikanismus ist die historisch feststellbare Erscheinung der unbedingten Verendung der Neuzeit in die Verwüstung."

35. Indeed, distinctive particularity is effaced by that very metaphysics, which "unifies" the world by subjecting it to a relentless uniformity, reducing the singular being of persons and things to what can be calculated—and so compared, marshaled, deployed, exchanged, and disposed of. We are thereby given to understand each and all as but bits and bytes of resource: as *Bestand*, within the enframing of *das Ge-stell*. We call this enforced homogenization—again, blandly—"globalization," the rendering uniform of the world and all it holds in the service of efficient fabrication and consumption; Heidegger, seeing its destined emergence from the metaphysics then becoming apparent, three-quarters of a century ago, called it *Planetarismus*. See "Überlegungen XV," *Überlegungen XII–XV, Gesamtausgabe* 96, pp. 260–261: "Dieser … ist der *Planetarismus*: der letzte Schritt des machenschaftlichen Wesens der Macht zur Vernichtung des Unzerstörbaren auf dem Wege der Verwüstung … . Der *Planetarismus* ist die historisch gedachte Bestimmung der überall gleichen, die ganze Erde überdeckenden Seinsverlassenheit des Seienden. Die Gleichheit und Einebnung des Menschentums auf die eine Art der Bewerkstelligung der Lebensordnung, trotz der scheinbaren Verschiedenartigkeit der Herkunft und Tragweite der 'Kulturen' und volklichen Bestände (Japan, Amerika, Europa), hat ihren Wesensgrund darin, daß die Macht selbst, sobald sie zur unbedingten Ermächtigung gelangt, in sich das Gleiche und die Eintönigkeit der immer einfacheren Mittel fordert. Jede Macht versucht sich zu erweitern und trifft sich dabei mit jeder anderen in derselben Machenschaft. Diese Wesensselbigkeit ist der Grund der historisch feststellbaren Totalität und Unbedingtheit des Machtwesens."

36. See, e.g., *Erläuterungen zu Hölderlins Dichtung* (1936–68), *Gesamtausgabe* 4, ed. Friedrich-Wilhelm von Herrmann (Frankfurt: Klostermann, 1996); *Elucidations of Hölderlin's Poetry*, trans. Keith Hoeller (Amherst, NY: Humanity Books, 2000); *Hölderlins Hymnen "Germanien" und "Der Rhein,"* *Gesamtausgabe* 39, ed. Susanne Ziegler (Frankfurt: Klostermann, [1980] 1989); *Hölderlin's Hymns "Germania" and "The Rhine,"* trans. William McNeill and Julia Ireland (Bloomington: Indiana University Press, 2014); *Hölderlins Hymne "Andenken,"* *Gesamtausgabe* 52, ed. Curd Ochwadt (Frankfurt: Klostermann, 1992); *Hölderlin's Hymn "Andenken,"* trans. William McNeill and Julia Ireland (Bloomington: Indiana University Press, forthcoming); *Hölderlins Hymne "Der Ister,"* *Gesamtausgabe* 53, ed. Walter Biemel (Frankfurt: Klostermann, 1993); *Hölderlin's Hymn "The Ister,"* trans. William McNeill and Julia Davis (Bloomington: Indiana University Press, 1996).

37. *Feldweg-Gespräche* (1944–1945), *Gesamtausgabe* 77, ed. Ingrid Schüssler (Frankfurt: Klostermann, 2007); *Country Path Conversations*, trans. Bret W. Davis (Bloomington: Indiana University Press, 2010).

38. *Der Wille zur Macht als Kunst* (1936–37), in *Nietzsche I, Gesamtausgabe* 6 (I); *The Will to Power as Art*, trans. David F. Krell, in *Nietzsche I* (New York: Harper & Row, 1979).

39. *Nietzsches Lehre vom Willen zur Macht als Erkenntnis* (1939), in *Nietzsche I, Gesamtausgabe* 6 (I); *The Will to Power as Knowledge*, trans. Joan Stambaugh, in *Nietzsche III: The Will to Power as Knowledge and as Metaphysics* (New York: Harper & Row, 1987).

40. *Nietzsches Lehre vom Willen zur Macht als Erkenntnis* (1939).

41. *Nietzsches Lehre vom Willen zur Macht als Erkenntnis* (1939).

42. See generally, *Der europäische Nihilismus*; *European Nihilism*, supra n. 31.

43. The notebook entries are undated, but the first of the three volumes before us so far, containing *Notebooks II–VI*, comprises notes from the years 1931–1938, a span several times longer than for each of the next two volumes; it appears that the nearly eight years of *Überlegungen II–VI, Gesamtausgabe* 94, were a time in which Heidegger was engaged in substantial rumination, while largely restrained from drawing conclusions despite the apparent urgency of world events, and in little extended writing. The notes of the latter two volumes, together covering 1938–1941, show a marked increase in sustained focus, and convey a sense of renewed clarity and direction, as if gained only after long reflection. Similarly, his generation of major works increases dramatically at the same time, with *Beiträge zur Philosophie* (*Gesamtausgabe* 65), *Besinnung* (*Gesamtausgabe* 66), several significant works on Hölderlin, and the numerous lectures and essays of the four Nietzsche volumes all emerging in a few fruitful years beginning in 1936.

44. See, e.g., *Der europäische Nihilismus*, 33–34, 35, 154; *European Nihilism*, 11, 13, 123.

45. See "Überlegungen XIV," p. 70, *Überlegungen XII–XV, Gesamtausgabe* 96, pp. 211–212: "Die 'Technik' ist nie im 'Technischen' zu finden, sondern west als eine letzte und äußerste Weise der Wahrheit der Seiendheit im Sinne der Machenschaft."

46. "Überlegungen XIII" §4, *Überlegungen XII–XV, Gesamtausgabe* 96, p. 79: "der Machenschaft (der schrankenlosen Machbarkeit alles Seienden als der einzigen aber unerkennbar gewordenen Wahrheit des Seins)."

47. Cf. *Nietzsches Metaphysik*, 244–245, 255–256, 290; *Nietzsche's Metaphysics*, 199, 200, 210, 241; *Der europäische Nihilismus*, 85, 86–87, 94: "Wille zur Macht und Wert-setzung sind *dasselbe* …," *European Nihilism*, 59, 61, 68.

48. Indeed, he anticipated the omnipresence of those very "thinking" machines (which we revealingly call "computers," i.e., *reckoning machines*) themselves: See "Überlegungen XIV," *Überlegungen XII–XV, Gesamtausgabe* 96, p. 195: "Nach der Schreib-, Zähl-, Rechen-, Buchungs-Maschine ist die Herstellung der *Denkmaschine* nur noch eine Frage der 'Zeit'… Denken ist ja bereits zum Rechnen geworden. Und weshalb soll dieses 'Denken' nicht seine Maschine haben? Dem Menschen wird immer mehr abgenommen, sogar das Denken (und schon längst die Besinnung). Die Folge dieses Vorgangs ist, daß der Mensch immer weniger mit sich anzufangen weiß—umso mehr muß er sich mit Apparaturen umgeben." See also "Überlegungen XV," *Überlegungen XII–XV, Gesamtausgabe* 96, p. 265, where he speaks of the radio, "das Sinnbild der Zusammengehörigkeit von Planetarismus und Idiotismus," in terms still more fully apposite to the computer: "Es genügt nicht, daß in jedem Haus und in jedem Stockwerk ein Apparat in Gang ist. Jedes 'Familien' mitglied, die Dienstleute, die Kinder müssen je ihr eigenes Gerät haben, um so jedermann sein zu können, schnell und leicht das zu kennen und zu hören und zu 'sein', was jeder andere ebenso ist."

49. Cf. "Überlegungen XII" §52, *Überlegungen XII–XV, Gesamtausgabe* 96, p. 68: "… was erst zu begreifen uns bevorsteht, vom machenschaftlichen Wesen der Seiendheit, die, voll entfaltet, der Rechenhaftigkeit des historisch-technischen Vorgehens erst die unbedingten Ansatzpunkte darbietet und so den Menschen selbst in die Machenschaft einrollt."

50. See *Überlegungen XIII* §73, *Überlegungen XII–XV, Gesamtausgabe* 96, p. 112: "Wo in Maßnahmen gedacht und gerechnet wird, ist wesensmäßig jede Bindung und Bindbarkeit preisgegeben. Diese Preisgabe bedeutet ein eigenes Grundverhältnis zum Seienden—setzt dessen Seiendheit voraus im Sinne der Machenschaft."

51. Cf. "Überlegungen VII" §13, *Überlegungen VII–XI, Gesamtausgabe* 95, p. 14: "Die *Irre* ist … jenes, was zum Da—des Da-*seins* gehört … . aber wie selten darf einer 'irren', wie oft und wie ausschließlich müssen wir uns damit begnügen, Unrichtiges richtigzustellen und außerhalb der Irre gutgesichert einen Umtrieb zu veranstalten, mit dessen Hilfe wir 'Ergebnisse' hervorbringen."

52. See generally "Die Seinsgeschichtliche Bestimmung des Nihilismus (1944–46)," in *Gesamtausgabe* 6 (II), pp. 301–361; "Nihilism as Determined by the History of Being," trans. Frank A. Capuzzi, in *Nietzsche IV: Nihilism*, 199–250.

53. From "Patmos," in Friedrich Hölderlin, *Die Gedichte* (Frankfurt: Insel, 1999), 350. Quoted in "Die Frage nach der Technik," *Vorträge und Aufsätze, Gesamtausgabe* 7, p. 29; "The Question Concerning Technology," supra n. 25, p. 333.

54. See "Überlegungen XI" §53, *Überlegungen VII–XI, Gesamtausgabe* 95, p. 408:

> Rein "metaphysisch" (d.h. seyn geschichtlich) dankend habe ich in den Jahren 1930–1934 den Nationalsozialismus für die Möglichkeit eines Übergangs in einen anderen Anfang gehalten und ihm diese Deutung gegeben. Damit wurde diese "Bewegung" in ihren eigentlichen Kräften und inneren Notwendigkeiten sowohl als auch in der ihr eigenen Größengebung und Größenart verkannt und unterschätzt. Hier beginnt vielmehr und zwar in einer viel tieferen—d.h. umgreifenden und eingreifenden Weise als im Faschismus die vollendung der Neuzeit—; diese hat zwar im "Romantischen" überhaupt begonnen—hinsichtlich der Vermenschung des Menschen in der selbstgewissen Vernünftigkeit, aber für die Vollendung bedarf es der Entschiedenheit des Historisch-Technischen im Sinne der Vollständigen "Mobilisierung" aller Vermögen des auf sich gestellten Menschentums. … [¶] Aus der vollen Einsicht in die frühere Täuschung über das Wesen und die geschichtliche Wesenskraft des Nationalsozialismus ergibt sich erst die Notwendigkeit seiner Bejahung und zwar aus denkerischen Gründen.

55. See Friedrich Kluge, *An Etymological Dictionary of the German Language*, trans. of the 4th German ed. by John F. Davis (New York: Macmillan, 1891), 158 (noting the root senses of *Ja* embracing "yes, thus," "truly, forsooth," and the Old High German verb *jahan*, "to acknowledge, confess").

56. See "Nietzsches Wort 'Gott ist tot'" (1943), in *Holzwege, Gesamtausgabe* 5, ed. Friedrich-Wilhelm von Herrmann (Frankfurt: Klostermann, [1950] 2003), 209–267; "The Word of Nietzsche: 'God Is Dead,'" in *The Question Concerning Technology and Other Essays*, trans. William Lovitt (New York: Harper & Row, 1977).

57. See "Überlegungen XIII" §67, *Überlegungen XII–XV, Gesamtausgabe* 96, pp. 105–106: "Sobald die Machenschaft die unbeschränkte Vormacht erreicht hat und lediglich das Seiende—das jeweils erwirkte und bewirkbare Wirksame und Wirkliche, die sogenannten 'Tatsachen' und das 'Reale'—jede Rechnung und Einrichtung der gerade 'benötigten' 'Ziele' und 'Ideale' bestimmt, da können diese gleichzeitig hochgepriesen und scheinbar festgehalten, aber auch vergessen und weggeworfen werden zugunsten der 'Tatsachen'. Dieses Preisgegebenwerden 'heiligster' 'Überzeugungen' kann nicht einmal mehr als 'inkonsequent', 'wortbrüchig', 'wurzellos' und 'willkürlich' gebrandmarkt werden, weil mit der Hinfälligkeit aller Ideale vor allem zuvor schon jeglicher Bezirk für 'Idealität' verschwunden ist."

58. See "Überlegungen XII" §41, *Überlegungen XII–XV, Gesamtausgabe* 96, p. 58: "Die Sinnlosigkeit 'welt-geschichtlicher' Vorkommnisse darf jetzt und künftig nicht verwundern, da die Seinsverlassenheit des Seienden zugunsten der unbeschränkten Vormacht des Seienden in seiner Machenschaft entschieden ist."

59. See *Bremer und Freiburger Vorträge, Gesamtausgabe* 79, ed. Petra Jaeger (Frankfurt: Klostermann, 2005), 27: "Ackerbau ist jetzt motorisierte Ernährungsindustrie, im Wesen das Selbe wie die Fabrikation von Leichen in Gaskammern und Vernichtungslagern, das Selbe wie die Blockade und Aushungerung von Ländern, das Selbe wie die Fabrikation von Wasserstoffbomben," *Bremen and Freiburg Lectures*, trans. Andrew J. Mitchell (Bloomington: Indiana University Press, 2012), 27.

60. See "Überlegungen XII" §41, *Überlegungen XII–XV, Gesamtausgabe* 96, p. 59: "Die Sinnlosigkeit hat sich des Seienden bemächtigt; das Seyn west trotzdem; aber seine Wahrheit bleibt tief verborgen und das Geschenk der reinsten Augenblicke"; "Überlegungen VII" §13, p. 18, *Gesamtausgabe* 95, p. 14: "Die *Irre* ist das verbor-genste Geschenk der Wahrheit—denn in ihr verschenkt sich das Wesen der Wahrheit als die Wächterschaft der Verweigerung und als die reinste Verwahrung des Seyns im unkenntlichen Schutz des Immerseienden."

61. See, e.g., "Überlegungen XIV," *Überlegungen XII–XV, Gesamtausgabe* 96, p. 195: "Vom National-sozialis-mus zum *Rational-sozialismus*, d.h. zur unbedingten Durchrechnung und Verrechnung des Zusammenseins der Menschentümer in sich und miteinander ... . Das Wesen des abendländischen Geistes als τέχνη."

62. Cf. "Überlegungen XII" §3, *Überlegungen XII–XV, Gesamtausgabe* 96, p. 79: "*Was geschieht*—(aber auch dies Wort, wie jedes, ist schon vernutzt—'Geschehen' heißt alles). Dennoch ist die Frage in diesem Wort zu behalten! Denn nicht Tatsachen sollen festgestellt und nicht Begebenheiten berichtet werden—sondern das Geschehen muß in die Entscheidung erinnert sein; Geschehen aber heißt hier nur: was die Geschichte im Wesen gründet: die Wahrheit des Seyns und wie das Seyn sich in seine in ihm wesende Wahrheit verschenkt."

19

The *Black Notebooks* in Their Historical and Political Context

Ingo Farin

All the World Interprets, Nobody Thinks.[1]

I   Introduction

The publication of the *Considerations,* the volumes that make up the first series of Heidegger's so-called *Black Notebooks*, spanning the years from 1931 to 1941, has created an enormous sensation. Many commentators have zeroed in on Heidegger's undeniably anti-Semitic remarks and his endorsement of National Socialism, leading to widespread condemnation of the *Considerations* and, by extension, Heidegger's works at large. Some writers have declared that Heidegger's reputation is in tatters and that the very significance of his philosophy has been irredeemably undermined. I do not agree with this assessment, even though I think that his anti-Semitism and his pro-Nazi sentiments cannot be swept under the rug as merely incidental "errors" of a political dilettante. They call for deeper philosophical reflection. In the following I propose a hermeneutical approach to the *Black Notebooks*, which is quite appropriate because Heidegger himself was deeply indebted to the hermeneutical tradition, even though he transformed it.[2]

II   General Remarks about the Hermeneutical Reading of the *Black Notebooks*

With Schleiermacher we should note that an "utterance" or "discourse [*Rede*]" becomes intelligible only "via the knowledge of the whole of the historical life [*geschichtlichen Gesamtlebens*] to which it belongs, or via the history which is relevant for it."[3] Moreover, just as any discourse is related to the historical situation in which it is composed, it is also related to "the totality of language" from which it arises and the "totality of thought" of its "originator" (i.e., the author).[4] Consequently, the *Considerations* must be understood as emergent from Heidegger's historical situation in Germany and from within the whole of his thought.

Considering the first point, it is vital to note that except for the first two individual notebooks of the *Considerations*, all of them were written during the National Socialist regime in Germany. Therefore, if we want to talk about Heidegger's *Considerations* we cannot pass over National Socialism—all the more so because Heidegger himself makes numerous references to it. However, I believe that there are two pitfalls that we must avoid. Our moral repugnance at what occurred in the name of National Socialism must not trump the attempt to understand it, or, in our case, to understand Heidegger's involvement with it. We can learn here from the eminent historian Richard J. Evans, who has given critical testimony against the Holocaust deniers. In his monumental three-volume study of the Third Reich he argues that in studying National Socialism we must avoid the "luxury of moral judgement," since it is "inappropriate for a work of history," because moralizing is "unhistorical," "arrogant and presumptuous."[5] As Evans points out: "I cannot know how I would have behaved if I had lived under the Third Reich, if only because, if I had lived then, I would have been a different person from the one I am now."[6] I think that refraining from a priori moralizing and sermonizing also makes good sense for our attempt to understand Heidegger and his *Notebooks* composed during the Third Reich. Of course, this does not preclude subsequent critical and moral assessment based on our very different, present historical situation. But resting content with protesting one's moral outrage at Heidegger's *Notebooks* is no substitute for proper understanding. Part and parcel of studying Heidegger *sine ira et studio* is to acknowledge that under Nazi rule even a privileged professor of philosophy might fear detection and possible persecution. The *Notebooks* are just another component of the many works written by Heidegger, but they are not private confessions. While a different literary persona comes to light in them, it is entirely unwarranted to conclude that this persona reveals the *true* Martin Heidegger.

A careful reader of the *Notebooks* will realize that soon after 1933–1934, Heidegger came to believe that the Nazi regime or some other form of machination would last for many decades, if not centuries. His bitter lament about the "age of total unquestionableness"[7] is testament to this pessimistic outlook, as is his statement that "history may set in again around 2300 at the very earliest."[8] Thus Heidegger's remarks in the *Considerations* are not aimed at the literary public of his time, which was subject to extreme censorship in any case. Rather, they are the written documents of a desperate thinker writing for a time *after* the catastrophic end of modernity. We miss this dimension if we read the *Notebooks* as mere situational reports for an immediate audience. And we likewise miss the point if we read the *Notebooks* with a narrow moralistic compass in hand, content only with registering whether or not Heidegger defends or gives up moral values we deem important today.

The second pitfall, which is related to the first one of mere moralizing, concerns the ahistorical and distorting tendency to read all events in Nazi Germany as if they assumed their sole significance and meaning by reference to the Holocaust. For, while the Holocaust is arguably the most decisive and most catastrophic rupture in recent history, it is identified as such by hindsight. History is written with hindsight and from the end, but historical life is *lived* forward, without knowledge of the end. To read all texts and actions in Nazi Germany from the perspective of the Holocaust is a case of metaphysical teleology, or a kind of negative theodicy, and as totalizing as ever an ideology was. It is quite outlandish to assume that the end (of the Holocaust) was already inscribed and present in the horizon of the people living, working, and writing in Germany in the 1930s.

It is instructive to read what the historian, eyewitness, and critic Fritz Stern writes about Germany around 1936, at the time of the Olympic Games in Berlin:

> Bread, circuses, and mass mobilization gave most Germans a sense of certainty, of faith in present and future: they perceived the Führer as a divinely inspired commander in chief. If Hitler had died that summer of 1936, or indeed at any time before the outbreak of the war, he would probably still, in today's Germany, be hailed as a hero—a murderer of thousands, yes, but the saviour of millions, an oppressor and demonic genius. For a brief moment that summer and for the politically naïve, Germany was transformed into a bustling Potemkin village, and the armed malevolence was hidden. And this false Germany aroused much sympathy among prosperous conservatives elsewhere.[9]

While I do not believe that Heidegger would have been among those duped by bread and circuses—in fact, much of his criticism of "culture" and "historicism" is informed by his critical look at the incessant propaganda show staged by National Socialism—there is clear evidence that between 1930 and 1933 Heidegger hailed Hitler as a hero who opened up a singular opportunity in history. By 1934, however, Heidegger no longer supported National Socialism. The crucial point I want to make is that Heidegger's pro-Hitler views between 1933 and 1934 cannot be equated with the toleration, endorsement, or outright complicity in the later genocide set in motion between 1941 and 1945. The very monstrosity of Auschwitz can distort our judgment by inviting such a telescopic misreading of historical life.

In fact, this very mistake finds its farcical repetition and amplification in the much-belabored "paradox" that journalists and commentators employ when they write that Martin Heidegger, supposedly the "greatest philosopher in the twentieth century," fell for and endorsed the "most barbaric regime in history." This gothic tale of a white knight of philosophy ending up as the darkest villain in the realm of thought may have some entertainment value, but it wrongly assumes, first, that one could rank philosophers like athletes and, second, conveniently forgets the historical reality, namely, that while Heidegger, regardless of his rank among the great philosophers, did indeed endorse National Socialism until 1933–1934 and did maintain anti-Semitic beliefs until after World War II, he did not argue for or endorse the systematic mass murder of innocent people.

It is all too often simply assumed that National Socialism was a well-defined ideology with clearly laid-out strategies and objectives. But this is quite wrong. To quote Evans one more time:

> Leading Nazis did not spend time disputing the finer points of their ideology like medieval scholastics or Marxist-Leninist philosophers, their modern equivalents. There was no sacred book of Nazism from which people took their texts for the day, like the bureaucrats of Stalin's Russia did from the works of Marx, Engels, and Lenin. Hitler's *My Struggle*, though everyone had to have it on their bookshelf, was too verbose, too rambling, and too autobiographical to lend itself to this kind of use. Nor in the end did Nazism promise any kind of final victory to be followed by a Heaven-like stasis; rather it was a doctrine of perpetual struggle, of conflict without end.[10]

Under these circumstances we can only conclude that the label "National Socialism," understood as an ideological marker, lacks precise contours. Given that Nazi ideology was "too meagre, too crude, too self-contradictory and in the end too irrational" to underwrite a coherent and cohesive worldview in a modern society,[11] it is no wonder that it lent itself to all sorts of disparate projections. The grand designs that intellectuals and artists harbored but could not find room to realize in the Weimar Republic could be seen as somehow suitably aligned with National Socialism. But this does not mean that all these intellectuals or even the (self-) declared Nazis themselves shared a definitive political or cultural outlook, let alone a philosophical one. Without a doubt, Heidegger's Nazism, whether private or public, puts him in very bad company. But it does not absolve us from the task of understanding *how* he conceived and interpreted National Socialism, which from 1934 onward he tended to view with increasingly critical eyes, albeit never as a moralist and by taking his starting point from the suffering of persecuted minorities in Germany. Heidegger's focus was on being, not the suffering of people.[12]

This brings us to the second hermeneutical point—that is, the importance of reading Heidegger's *Considerations* within the context of his overall work. There is no evidence whatsoever that Heidegger saw the *Black Notebooks* as anything but preliminary sketchbooks, in which he recorded ideas, reflections, commentaries, considerations, and observations, ranging from the personal to the political and philosophical. The numbered entries are not ordered according to any thematic thread; they range from pithy, single sentences to short paragraphs, occasionally amounting to two or three pages of running text. The black-oilcloth notebooks are written in Heidegger's own handwriting; they show few correction marks, crossed-out sentences, or later insertions, suggesting that the notebooks are the *clean copy* made from original notes and remarks that probably are no longer extant.

Before his death Heidegger authorized the publication of the *Black Notebooks*, stipulating that they should come out last, after all other volumes had been published in the *Gesamtausgabe*. The notion that the *Black Notebooks* could constitute anything like a key or even a capstone to Heidegger's works is highly questionable, if only because he forgot to alert his readers to such a hidden treasure. In fact, in a reflection from 1937–1938 Heidegger mentions notebooks II, IV, and V of the *Considerations* (*Überlegungen*) as being part of the *preparatory* steps toward what, at that time, he considered his second major work after *Being and Time*—that is, the *Contributions to Philosophy (Of the Event)*[13]—and he does indeed refer to the *Notebooks* in this and other works of the 1930s. Moreover, while Heidegger readily admits in that same note that it may look as if the *Considerations* were just occasional, spur-of-the-moment reflections, he insists that they are part of his constant effort to articulate the "one-and-only question," the question of being.[14] Hence it would be just as false to underrate them as merely incidental and inconsequential breadcrumbs from the high table of Heidegger's otherwise pure theorizing, as it would be false to overrate them as the secret and unsurpassed culmination of his philosophical work.

In fact, when Heidegger describes the notebooks as preparatory sketches toward *Contributions*, he only mentions volumes II, IV, and V, conspicuously leaving out volume I (which no longer exists[15]), *as well as* volume III (which is part of the now-published *Considerations*[16]). In other words, notebook III of *Considerations*, which covers the period from 1932 to 1934 (and thus includes the time when Heidegger was *Rektor* at the University of Freiburg), is no longer endorsed by Heidegger a mere three or four years after it was written. In fact, this is not the only time he tries to distance himself from his earlier writings. For instance, in 1937–1938 he specifically mentions that his lecture course from the summer semester of 1933 is "insufficient" because of his "preoccupation" with his duties as rector of the university.[17] Moreover, in another reflection on the overall development of his thought, written between 1938 and 1940, Heidegger lists, among many other unpublished manuscripts, the *Contributions* and *Besinnung*, but does not mention the *Black Notebooks* at all, which at the very least shows that he did not always think that these *Notebooks* contained essential stepping-stones of his philosophizing.[18]

While there is no blanket endorsement of the *Contributions* as such by Heidegger, let alone a sustained argument for their systematic centrality in his life's work, it is nevertheless true that he wanted them published, presumably as evidence of way stations on his philosophical journey. As such they can be assessed only after his life's work is available, which is why it makes sense to have them published after everything else. To view the *Notebooks* in isolation and outside the entire body of work is untenable.

If we now focus just on the *immediate* context of *Considerations II–XV*, it is clear that they fall in the period of Heidegger's career when he departed from the fundamental-ontological language in *Being and Time* and began to recast the question concerning being in terms of the "history of being [*Seynsgeschichte*]," unencumbered by what he considered the constraints of phenomenology and hermeneutics.

III   The *Considerations* in the Context of Heidegger's History of Being

While in *Being and Time* Heidegger highlights *Dasein*'s inherent historicity or *Geschichtlichkeit*, after *Being and Time* he instead emphasizes the historicity of being or *Seyn*. One decisive consequence of the introduction of history into being or *Seyn* is that Heidegger's earlier ontological categories and existentialia are set in motion; they lose their appearance of ontological invariance. Furthermore, because he now holds that the very "essence of being [*Wesen des Seyns*]" is "historical" or *geschichtlich*, there is no suprahistorical, selfsame, and permanent realm of being.[19] The historicity of being means that being "is" only as *event* or *Ereignis*. Ontohistorically understood, "being," or as Heidegger adds, "historicity [*Geschichtlichkeit*]," is never the same in different ages.[20] In fact, being itself "is" only as the unique event or *Ereignis* in and through which *Dasein* is brought into its own or appropriated by being. It is precisely for this reason that Heidegger also insists on the "singularity of being [*Einzigkeit des Seyns*],"[21] or the "singularity and uniqueness of being [*Einzigkeit und Einmaligkeit*]."[22] Being is in each case its own.[23]

Consequently, Heidegger revises the earlier ontological concept of historicity laid out in *Being and Time*.[24] The ontological distinction between *Dasein*'s authentic or inauthentic being in *Being and Time* is now reinscribed diachronically within the historicity of being. Some historical appropriations of the event of being, epochs if you will, are more authentic than others—that is, they are more authentic in relation to being, or are more authentically appropriated by it. If the task of philosophy is to "put being into words," this cannot be done by way of "putting up and disseminating ontologies."[25] It requires a historical effort as well.

It is clear that by 1931 Heidegger has arrived at this general ontohistorical understanding of philosophy. And it is obvious that he considers the cultural and political crisis of the time as a political and philosophical opportunity to usher in a new epoch in being. Moreover, Heidegger assigns Germans a leading role in this new epoch, for instance when he declares that "the German alone is able to compose and articulate being originally and anew—he alone will conquer the essence of *theoria* and finally create the [new] logic."[26] Notwithstanding the unmistakably ontohistorical impetus, it is evident that in 1933 Heidegger is still thinking in metaphysical terms and in terms of the renewal of metaphysics. For example, he writes: "Meta-physical thinking [*Meta-physisches Denken*] is geared toward thinking up [*Erdenken*]—bringing about through thinking—a change in being [*des Seins*]."[27] In other words, Heidegger still aligns his own incipient ontohistorical project with that of metaphysics and he presents it in metaphysical language, arguing that proper reflection (*Besinnung*) stands in the service "of the metaphysical transformation [of man] into Da-sein."[28] Indeed, even when he begins to turn away from his erstwhile hope that the Nazi movement would bring about an epochal change, he still couches his frustration in metaphysical terms, lamenting the failure to reinstitute metaphysics proper. In the new Germany there is much room for bread and circuses, but not much room for metaphysics:

In an age where a boxer is regarded as a great man and is revered and honored, where the pure masculinity of the male body in its brutality counts for the heroic—where the delirium of the masses counts as community and the latter as the basis for everything else—what room is there for "metaphysics"?[29]

All of this suggests that despite his move toward an ontohistorical conception, Heidegger's initial support for National Socialism is still caught up with finding the new logic or theory of being to be imposed by metaphysics from above, which also discloses the proper political order, which is why he speaks of "metaphysics as metapolitics."[30] That is, Heidegger's attempt to overcome metaphysics begins to take shape only after his disappointment with National Socialism in the years following 1934. Moreover, his concept of the "other beginning," also closely associated with his ontohistorical turn, is not present in the early 1930s. In fact, what the *Überlegungen* clearly show is that Heidegger's groping for the "other beginning" (as opposed to reinstituting metaphysics proper) coincides with his *disaffection* with the Nazi movement—that is, the period after his resignation from his *Rektorat* at Freiburg University in 1934. *Überlegungen IV*, written after his resignation in 1934, introduce for the first time the theme of the "second beginning" as a response to the first beginning in Greek philosophy.[31] Furthermore, it also appears that Heidegger's signature postmetaphysical thinking about the gods,[32] art, and the utter singularity of *Ereignis*, which is not amenable to human willing, are all developed in the aftermath of, and in reaction to, his active support of National Socialism. In another early entry from Considerations *IV*, Heidegger explicitly forgoes all political and metaphysical intervention, as if to account for his break with National Socialism:

One can comprehend world only by means of art as the original *Ereignis*, not by means of knowledge (thought), nor by action (deed).[33]

Like so many other revolutionary spirits, Heidegger overcomes his disillusionment with revolutionary politics by turning toward art, and hence against the authority of metaphysics.

If my reading is correct, we cannot maintain that Heidegger's notion of the "other beginning" precedes his involvement with the Nazi movement and that he tried to inscribe the perceived "national revolution" within the "other beginning."[34] Rather, this narrative emerges out of his later disappointment with the Nazi movement. The "other beginning" is decidedly not one that is meant to propagate anything akin to National Socialism. That is, although it is right to link Heidegger's support of National Socialism with his ontohistorical turn, a more fine-grained analysis shows that the specifically nonmetaphysical and contra-metaphysical interpretation and "hope" for "another beginning" is something that Heidegger works out in the years after 1933–1934. His support for National Socialism is predicated on his attempt to renew and re-install metaphysics at a decisive historical point, as has been argued by Iain Thomson.[35] What the *Black Notebooks* show is that Heidegger's groping for "another beginning" that overcomes metaphysics is the critical response and reaction to his failed political and philosophical engagement in 1933.

While the ontohistorical horizon is without doubt the pertinent reference point for Heidegger's *Considerations*, it is by no means reducible to a fixed and unchanging doctrine. In fact, Heidegger uses the *Considerations* to develop, revise, refine, expand, and apply his ontohistorical thought. In a late note from the 1970s he writes: "At bottom the sketches in the *Black Notebooks* are attempts at simple naming—not assertions or even notes for a planned system."[36] It is therefore no surprise that, for all his ontohistorical endeavors, Heidegger did not somehow abandon his earlier thought. In the *Considerations* he frequently uses an idiom first worked out in his early lecture courses at Freiburg and Marburg. There is even a Kantian echo in the very first entry in the *Considerations*, written in 1931:

What shall we do? Who *are* we? Why ought we to *be*? What is beingness [*das Seiende*]? Why does being [*Sein*] happen? Philosophizing is what arises in unity from these questions.[37]

It is one of the more enigmatic features of the *Considerations* that Heidegger's entries vary from rather peremptory sentences, angry attacks, and diatribes, to more reflective and melancholic musings about the human condition and the bitter absence of truth. Questions figure prominently in the *Notebooks* too. The claim that Heidegger is only fulminating against his various opponents and enemies is quite misleading. A full account of his writing would have to address the different styles in the *Black Notebooks*, as well as the different positions that Heidegger takes over the years. The idea that there is one unchanging core message in the *Black Notebooks* is pure fantasy. This is especially true with regard to National Socialism.

IV Heidegger's Support for National Socialism in *Überlegungen II* and *III*

Heidegger had great hopes and sympathies for National Socialism. This has been amply documented in his political statements from this period,[38] as well as in more recently and posthumously published lecture courses,[39] seminars, and other materials.[40] The *Notebooks* allow us to understand this better. We can see that he greeted the National Socialist regime with great enthusiasm. For instance, he notes his "great cheer and happiness" on the grounds that "the Leader" "has given rise to a new reality, which gives our existence [*Dasein*] the proper projection and vigor."[41] And he sees "a magnificent awakening of the folkish will" shining into "the great world-darkness."[42] Heidegger approvingly notes: "A great faith sweeps through the young country."[43] Moreover, he clearly assigns the German people a world-historical role, mediated or spearheaded by German philosophy, namely his own. Musing about the "incomparability of this hour of the world," Heidegger assigns "German philosophy" the role "of ringing in this new reality [*zum Erklingen bringen*]."[44] German philosophy is to articulate being anew, or more modestly, "'our being'—that is, the being of beings as a whole, which occurs through us and in us [*das durch uns und in uns geschehende Sein des Seienden im Ganzen*]."[45]

Not only is his approach "metaphysical," as we have seen above, but also oddly "technological," if not to say outright demiurgic. For Heidegger defines philosophy as real *poesis*, making and bringing about a new phase of being, "triggering the occurrences of being [*Auslösung der Seinsgeschehnisse*],"[46] and thus effectively working for the "enabling of being [*Seinsermächtigung*]."[47] All of this would fall under Heidegger's own censure of "machination" and "metaphysics" only a little later in 1934.

But there is no question that initially Heidegger is fully determined to yoke together his philosophy and the so-called national revolution in Germany in 1933–1934. He even appropriates the bombastic language of the Nazis, claiming that philosophy has to think, decide, and plan for "millennia"[48] or "centuries"[49] to come:

When the rising German existence [*Dasein*] becomes great, then it bears the burden of millennia to come [*trägt es Jahrtausende vor sich her*]. And it behooves us to think ahead accordingly—that is, to take up the preconception of the emergence of an entirely different being [*eines ganz anderen Seins*] and to begin to sketch out its logic.[50]

However, it is also important to take note of Heidegger's *simultaneously* recorded fierce determination not to elide the essential difference between the autonomy of philosophy and National Socialism. Thus he writes:

We do not want to give the "theoretical" underpinnings of National Socialism, as if to make it by such putative means tenable and secure in the first place. But we want to prepare possible pathways and developments for it.[51]

It is Heidegger's idea that as the intellectual avant-garde, philosophy would not be subordinate to National Socialism. In fact, it would be the ruling principle above National Socialism and not answerable to it.[52] Under the auspices of philosophy, Heidegger thought, National Socialism could help to bring about a new "basic position vis-à-vis being [*Seyn*]."[53] What he calls "spiritual National Socialism"[54] is nothing other than this avant-garde position of philosophy, rendering it independent of the existing National Socialism on the ground, and dedicating it instead to what Heidegger, in Stefan George fashion, calls the "secret spiritual Germany."[55] Heidegger is not willing to renounce the claim of philosophy for the sake of the supposedly new "truth" of National Socialism. In about 1936 he notes that a National Socialist philosophy is an oxymoron: "To say that a philosophy is 'National Socialist' or not means as much as the assertion: a triangle has courage or not, i.e., it behaves in a cowardly way."[56]

Heidegger's insistence that philosophy must be independent from the existing National Socialism is not just the traditional affirmation of the intellectual supremacy of philosophy. It also is based on his early premonition that National Socialism might fall short of the great expectations invested in it. As early as the summer of 1933 Heidegger writes:

National Socialism is a true and rising power only if underneath all its deeds and words it passes something over in silence—and makes a strong, future impact by way of an effective underhandedness [*in die Zukunft wirkenden Hinterhältigkeit wirkt*]. If the current stuff [*das Gegenwärtige*] is already what is to be achieved and what is wished for, then there remains only horror [*Grauen*] in the face of the decline [*Verfall*].[57]

In fact, judging from the *Notebooks* Heidegger's enthusiasm for National Socialism was a very short-lived affair. His decision to take on the *Rektorat* in May 1933 was already marked by ambivalence, as an entry from that period indicates:

Pushed to take on the *Rektorat*, I am acting for the first time against my innermost voices. At best, what I will be able to do in this office is to prevent this or that. For [the task of] building things up from the ground, provided that this is still possible, the right people are missing.[58]

Heidegger's pessimism about National Socialism increased over the following months until he finally despaired, thinking that the movement had no taste for a fundamental "metaphysical" change in people's position vis-à-vis being, and that it was nothing but a continuation of the shallow bourgeois culture and philistinism that he so despised.

Heidegger expresses this growing sense of estrangement when he begins to contrast the avant-garde or spiritual National Socialism with what he calls "vulgar National Socialism" on the ground.[59] He takes exception to the pseudobiologically dressed-up pursuit of material advantages in the name of "the people," which he equates with "ethical materialism" and "murky biologism."[60] Heidegger has no truck with the political hijacking of science and philosophy by means of "folkish dressed-up platitudes," and he loathes those nitwits who deal in "wacky, folkish-racist" slogans.[61] In 1933–1934 he holds that while "race" is part and parcel of *Dasein*'s historical thrownness, it must not be misconstrued as something fixed, determinate, and "absolute."[62]

Heidegger's growing disaffection with the reality of National Socialism results in his resignation from his *Rektorat* on April 28, 1934. In reflections written that day he admits that he "stands at the end of a *failed year.*"[63] As he sees it, the attempt to ensure what he considered the "self-assertion" of the university in Germany had failed, because the university had lost all influence and recognition "in the public life of the people [*Volk*].”[64] But in Heidegger's eyes the universities were partially to blame for this loss of authority. After all, how much trust could one have in universities when they saw to it that "the most important element in the contemporary university is the public-relations office [*Presseamt*], set up with the greatest possible number of staff"?[65]

If one now asks what it actually was that drew Heidegger to support National Socialism in the first place, *Überlegungen II* and *III* show that apart from his obvious belief in the charismatic figure of Hitler and the promise of a radical, albeit entirely undefined transformation of life, there is very little to point to in concrete terms. The restitution of Germany's greatness or the "revenge" for Versailles does not figure much in *Überlegungen II* and *III*,[66] although there is the underlying, but never thematically developed, topic of Germany's spiritual "mission" for the world. This "mission" survives Heidegger's disillusionment with National Socialism.[67] But there is no aggressive advocacy of a new German imperialism, no praise for soldierly virtues, discipline, law and order, or authoritarian regimentation of life. Nowhere does Heidegger record relief at the crackdown on dissidents, the closure of trade unions, the banning of political parties, the persecution of communists and socialists, and so on. Moreover, racial purity is not a goal that Heidegger subscribes to in 1933–1934 or afterward. In fact, there are no anti-Semitic slogans or prejudices at all in *Überlegungen II* and *III*, although they do begin to creep in later. For a card-carrying member of the NSDAP, Heidegger's outlook in the *Considerations* has almost no identifiable overlap with official party platforms or policies. This is certainly insufficient to label Heidegger as "committed" to National Socialism.

However, we cannot conclude that his support for National Socialism was only a strategic alliance to advance his own, very different philosophical agenda. There are real affinities. First of all, Heidegger has some vague sympathy for a more egalitarian and less hierarchical society (i.e., the *Volksgemeinschaft*), although this is coupled with hopes for the organic establishment of natural "rank" and "superiority," and the acknowledgment of the aristocracy of the mind.[68] Second, Heidegger shows a great partiality toward *Bodenständigkeit* (i.e., dwelling on and belonging to the land), and he clearly hopes for a return to a more autochthonous form of life under National Socialism.[69] Moreover, the return to *Bodenständigkeit* is directly related to his rejection of what he calls "progress."[70] For Heidegger, technological progress had become destructive of the earth and the land on which humans dwell.[71] But it is also clear that by 1934 he already realized that none of these particular issues (antimodernism, technology, and autochthony) would be addressed by National Socialism. In other words, the small band of shared concerns on which Heidegger based his support for the Nazis unraveled fast and irreparably in 1933.

A telling list of issues exists that Heidegger thought required urgent and "momentous decisions" in the new Germany:

1. The coming to terms with [*Auseinandersetzung*] and adoption of a clear stance toward *Christendom* as well as *Western philosophy* as a whole.
2. The coming to terms with *Nietzsche*.
3. The creative, not only organizational relation to *technology*.
4. The new *European* world.
5. The *world of the earth* as such.[72]

Nothing on this list is specific to National Socialism. These are points that Heidegger may have thought could not be resolved in the Weimar Republic. But his vague hope that all these goals would be achieved or somehow furthered by National Socialism was as misguided as his hope that the German university could assert its own mission in the new order. In fact, the very last entry of *Considerations III* sums up what Heidegger considered the total (self-) destruction of German universities. Acknowledging his own failure in this regard, he writes:

"The self-assertion of the German university" or—little intermezzo in a great error. *Because* what now wants to come to fruition has been in the making for decades: the natural sciences are rendered entirely technical. The humanities [*Geisteswissenschaften*] become instruments of political worldviews. Juris*prudence* becomes superfluous. Medicine, even as [a] biological [discipline], becomes technique too. Theology becomes meaningless. But what about the university? Not even a bad fig leaf for the nakedness of its disintegration; a sad opportunity for pompous windbags, the Johnny-come-lately types. The university—does not even deserve this reflection.[73]

V   Heidegger's Growing Disaffection with National Socialism after 1934

Heidegger's enthusiasm for National Socialism, perhaps never without a tinge of foreboding, was very short-lived indeed. Almost from the beginning he voiced concerns about the lack of truly radical vision and inadequate commitment to real transformation. Having hoped that "the world was reconfigured" and that "man" was "rising up,"[74] it is easy to understand that Heidegger would soon realize that National Socialism was a failure in this regard. In fact, even before the Nazis came to power he noted:

Neither the immediacy of the "total" state, nor raising the nation from its slumber or the revival of the nation, least of all the salvaging of "culture" as a mere addendum to the people and the state … must be the ultimately and finally determining factors.[75]

It is not surprising, then, that as soon as the Nazis came to power, Heidegger spoke of the looming danger that "the movement" would get stuck in the old "bourgeois" ways of the past.[76] This is the reason he soon began to distance himself from the "vulgar," mindless, sloganeering National Socialism.

But Heidegger also took direct issue with two aspects of National Socialism that have hardly been mentioned in the debates about the *Notebooks*. First, from 1934 onward he is quite vocal in his condemnation of what he considers the "idolatry of the people," "*Vergötzung des Volkes*."[77] In fact, he holds that wherever "a people [*ein Volk*] is postulated as an end in itself [*Selbstzweck*]," the outcome is "egoism writ large," an egoism of "gigantic" proportions.[78] Heidegger does not believe that "a people" is ever an end in itself, nor does he subscribe to the idea that everything has to be measured against its putative gain for "the people."[79] And he condemns such National Socialist attitudes as "'folkish' brutishness [*völkische Vertierung*]."[80] Moreover, Heidegger also considers that the ritualistically invoked "community [*Gemeinschaft*]" is itself nothing but a big lie, hiding its governing "principle of theft," because what counts as community is restricted beforehand to the "clueless" ("*Ahnungslosen*") who would not even understand what they are robbed of.[81] That this kind of "robbery," the spiritual and material exploitation of the people by its new overlords, is an ongoing issue is clearly implied when Heidegger, in real exasperation, asks "for how long this robbery [*Räuberwesen*]" can continue.[82]

Second, he also critiques what he calls the "idolatry of race," "*Vergötzung der Rasse*."[83] While Heidegger accepts that there is something like "race" as part of facticity and as "a condition of historical existence [*Dasein*]," he vehemently and consistently rejects the notion of race as the "unconditional" or absolute factor.[84] Indeed, if race is part of "thrownness," as Heidegger claims, it is neither deterministic nor reducible to biology.[85] Thus, when he looks for an especially illuminating example of a doctrine characteristic of the utter lack of reflection in National Socialism, he selects the "principle of race" as the supposed "basic truth" of "man."[86] That is, Heidegger categorically rejects this view, without any ifs, ands, or buts.

In short, he is not uncritically following the Nazi doctrines of the "community of the people" and the "race principle." On the contrary, his criticism of these political doctrines is quite instrumental in developing and articulating his attack on subjectivism as the characteristic constellation in modernity. Already in *Überlegungen V* Heidegger interprets the National Socialist recourse to "the people" or "race," relative to which objective reality is understood and transformed, as a form of "subjectivism," as the last echo of the "cogito, ergo sum."[87] Thus Heidegger concludes that National Socialism is the continuation of modernity, and not a break with it. And it is this insight that forces him to admit his own mistaken support for National Socialism. By 1938 Heidegger fully acknowledges this. He writes:

During the years 1930 through 1934 I considered, purely from a "metaphysical" (that is, onto-historical) perspective, that National Socialism offered the possibility of a transition to another beginning, and I attributed this meaning to it. I thus misunderstood and underestimated this "movement" with regard to its genuine powers and inner necessities as well as the kind and magnitude of its greatness that belonged to it. For here [with National Socialism] begins the completion of the modern world [*die Vollendung der Neuzeit*]; indeed, it does so in a much deeper, that is, more comprehensive and decisive way, than in [Italian] fascism.[88]

What the *Notebooks* show is that Heidegger did indeed come to this insight gradually. With increasing sarcasm he notes that National Socialism, instead of caring for the land and the purported autochthonous way of life, drives its utter destruction by ruthless modernization:

The villages [*Dörfer*] are no longer peasant settlements [*Bauernsiedlungen*], but towns with agricultural industry, which in turn require their corresponding integration into the general course of life:—the most remote "farmstead" is already destroyed *from the inside out* by radio and newspaper. This destruction, however, is covered up insofar as the "peasants" take over from the "nature-loving" city folks what they designed as old customary ways of "garments," "plays," etc., in accord with which the peasants then run their nature business [*Naturbetrieb*]—and display it—for visitors—, if so ordered.[89]

According to Heidegger, the destruction of peasant life is part of a much bigger "destruction of the earth."[90] And this destruction is directly proportional to the increasingly dominant technological signature with which all things are marked.[91] While Heidegger links technology to breakthroughs by the modern sciences as well as modern philosophy, particularly Descartes, he is also keen on relating technology to what he calls its "twin sister," "organization"[92]—that is, the relentless bureaucratic planning[93] gaining ground in all walks of life, especially to facilitate the war effort. And he clearly notes that the sciences are totally integrated within this technological matrix.[94] For Heidegger, everything becomes doable (through rational planning) and makeable (through technology); everything is reduced to a mere number in the calculation of the powers that direct all efforts toward total mobilization for war. It is this whole political-technological complex of power that Heidegger calls "*Machenschaft*," machination. Machination is his precursor term for *Gestell*,[95] showing that his critique of technology is directly related to and an outgrowth of his critique of National Socialism.

But it needs to be emphasized that *Machenschaft* specifically includes the political arena,[96] which attracts much less attention in Heidegger's writings in the 1950s. In the

1930s he clearly applies *Machenschaft* to the particular political situation in the one-party state of Germany:

Machination holds [its] genuine power all the more securely the more exclusively the political execution of power [*politischer Machtvollzug*] considers itself the first and last [of all things].[97]

In other words, by 1938–1939 Heidegger thinks of the dictatorship in Nazi Germany as machination, certainly a dissident view in Germany at the time. Moreover, the key characteristic of machination is the destruction of the earth.[98] And this destruction stands in direct correlation with the increased power of the military-technological complex.

He further claims that machination or technology or technoscience is not something we can simply switch on or off. It is a way of being in which we are caught up. As in his much later essay "On the Question of Technology," in 1937 Heidegger writes that technology has nothing to do with "machines" or "instruments," as if the problem was one of mastery over or submission to the technological apparatus, because "man" himself is governed and permeated by the same "ground" from which technology "springs forth."[99] In light of this universal entanglement in machination, Heidegger notes:

Is not all humanity [*alles Menschenwesen*] infected, as if by contagion, to view everything with regard to its organized calculability [*Errechenbarkeit*] and feasibility [*Machbarkeit*], and to see in this the prescribed way of all acting, ruling out that any other form of coming into existence would have any force?[100]

According to Heidegger, this one-dimensional cage of technoscience and technothink is apparently hermetically sealed off, almost entirely immune to the possible insight that not everything is orderable, manageable, and producible according to the latest governmental or corporate planning office. No alternative to this is even perceivable, let alone discussable. This apparent lack of any alternative to *Machenschaft* is behind Heidegger's often-repeated claim that the "age of total unquestionability [*Zeitalter der völligen Fraglosigkeit*]"[101] has finally arrived, to wit, in Nazi Germany.[102] And this is not the only critical line Heidegger articulates in the *Notebooks*.

Heidegger also records the human devastation brought about by the sheer brutality with which *Machenschaft* or machination orders everything for its designs. He speaks of the "incomparable brutality" of being under the rule of machination.[103] Whatever one may think of Heidegger's philosophical construct of the forgetfulness of being in the name of machination, what he actually describes under that heading are real, recognizable phenomena, namely, actual deficits, deformations, corruptions, and pathologies in human lives. This is true even though he tends to eschew any overtly moral or ethical language. For instance, in 1939 Heidegger observes what he calls the increased "*Verrohung* [brutalization]" and "*Verwilderung* [brutishness]" of life in Nazi Germany.[104] A little later he returns to this theme, scathingly noting that Germans tend to "justify" the "barbarization of the heart [*Verrohung des Herzens*]" by reference to some so-called necessary "'zippiness' [*des*

'Zackigen']" and "ironclad resolve [*Eisernen*]" in the constant struggle for self-affirma-tion.[105] Heidegger's critical sketch fits the brutal SS officer as much as the heartless block warden or the uncompromising party official. And he concludes this sketch by adding that a person does not escape machination by becoming inured to power and turning himself into a fortress of power, for even though he may feel "all powerful, and knowing, and superior in the realm of all existing things" and may believe himself to "have control over everything," he "nevertheless serves only" the "unleashing" of more and more power, which, in the end, always overpowers its faithful servants.[106]

For Heidegger, brutality is the signature name for the age, next to machination and power. In this context he also reflects on the National Socialist race policies, which he understands as brutal, predatory assertions of the will to power:

That man posits his existence as *factum brutum* and grounds his brutishness [*Tierheit*] in the doc-trine of race, is the effect of the brutality of being—and not its cause.[107]

Although Heidegger eschews the question of ontic responsibility, perhaps out of fear of detection, or because he has lost sight of human agency altogether in his pursuit of being, it is clear that he does not affirm or condone the racial policies of the Nazis, because it is part of the same modern trajectory that is destroying the earth:

Every race doctrine is part of modernity [*Alles Rassedenken ist neuzeitlich*], moving along the tra-jectory according to which man is the subject. The subjectivism of modernity comes to its comple-tion in race doctrine, namely by way of integrating the bodily dimension [*Leiblichkeit*] into the subject and by grasping the subject of the human in terms of the mass of humans.[108]

Throughout *Considerations IV–XV* Heidegger increasingly questions and undermines the claim and hold of brutality, power, and machination over human lives. To the extent that he identifies all of this with what he calls modernity, *Neuzeit*, he is indeed calling into question the legitimacy of modernity and the entire Western tradition, or, as he also calls it, the "metaphysical essence of modernity."[109] In this, he continues what already started with his early reception of Dilthey and Yorck von Wartenburg, in particular Yorck's dic-tum that "'modern man,' that is, man since the Renaissance, is fit for the grave."[110] But it would be quite wrong to assume that this rejection of modernity is automatically indicative of authoritarian politics. The *Black Notebooks* show that from the mid-1930s Heidegger opposes the "unquestionableness" enforced and cultivated by authoritarian or totalitarian forms of government.

This critical side of Heidegger's radical philosophizing about modernity, brutality, and machination has received little or no attention in recent discussions. In fact, he links machi-nation to "crime [*Verbrechen*]" and "criminality [*Verbrechertum*]."[111] According to him, the "crime" of machination is not merely of "breaking" something,[112] but rather the "devas-tation of everything" or, somewhat more loosely translated, the "smashing to smithereens of everything [*die Verwüstung von Allem in das Gebrochene*]."[113] Heidegger clearly thinks that Nazi Germany is part of this "criminal" machination engulfing the globe. In notes to his *Die Geschichte des Seyns*, written about the same time as *Überlegungen XV*, Heidegger minces no words about the main criminals of the twentieth century:

Therefore, the great criminals belong to the age that is characterized by its absolute pursuit of power. They cannot be measured against moral-juridical norms. One may attempt this, but in this way one never reaches their real criminality. There is also no punishment great enough to castigate such criminals. Every punishment remains inappropriate to their criminality. Even hell and suchlike is essentially too small relative to what the absolute criminals smash to pieces. ... The planetary main criminals of the newest modernity, in which alone they become possible and necessary, can be counted with the fingers of one hand.[114]

Even though Heidegger does not refer to them by name, it is clear that he counts Hitler and Stalin among the greatest criminals in the age of absolute unquestionableness, the age of totalitarianism. And this is entirely consistent with Heidegger's aforementioned assertion that from 1934 he viewed National Socialism as a destructive force of modernity. In fact, after 1934 the *Black Notebooks* reveal not a single entry that endorses the senior leadership of the National Socialist Party or any particular measure taken by the National Socialist regime. Contradicting the one-dimensionality of the total "worldview" propagated by the Nazis, Heidegger pleads for "multitrack thought [*vielspuriges Denken*]."[115] Against the common trend of militarizing conflict and pathologizing opposing viewpoints in Nazi Germany, Heidegger defends open engagement:

If the opponent [*Gegner*] is immediately turned into the enemy, and the enemy into the "devil," all opposition [*Gegnerschaft*] is not only deprived of the creative aspect, but the very space for struggle [*Kampf*] is taken away.[116]

Given Heidegger's growing disaffection for and critique of National Socialism, one can hardly maintain that he remained an intellectual supporter of the regime after his initial enthusiasm for the charismatic Führer in 1933. Contrary to the many commentators who can see only incriminating material in the *Notebooks*, I think that the *Notebooks* show also Heidegger's dissidence. But it is also notable that he engages all these issues on an ontological or ontohistorical plane only, with scant regard for the real subjects and the victims on the ground, or with the intention of opposing National Socialism. Untouched by human suffering, Heidegger ontologizes the horror of the world around him and projects it onto the plane of being and its history. But the shock of this horror has its ontic foundation in the experience of the broken and damaged lives under the hegemony of machination.

VI   Heidegger's Accommodation to the Nazi Regime

In the *Black Notebooks* Heidegger has nothing to say about the political atrocities perpetrated by the Nazis, from state-sponsored pogroms and wholesale plunder of Jewish businesses and families to the systematic terrorization of dissidents and minority groups through the secret police and the system of concentration camps. For all his ontological insight into brutality and machination, Heidegger does not register on the 1,300 pages of the *Notebooks* the brutal infringements of rights and the immense suffering inflicted by the German government. What makes reading the *Black Notebooks* so painful is the ghostly absence of almost any sympathy for the humiliated, wronged, and mistreated victims of Nazi violence, the lack of moral or ethical critique of the perpetrators themselves, and the outright contempt with which Heidegger dismisses all moderate or principled voices attempting to hold up traditional standards and values of a Christian or liberal-democratic provenience, all of which he considers hopelessly implicated in the very same modernity that caused the problems in the first place.

Moreover, for all his critical questioning of National Socialism, Heidegger did not look for real allies and an audience to foster a critical attitude, let alone meaningful resistance. Heidegger's deep (self-)isolation is quite palpable in the *Notebooks*. Hand in hand with this growing isolation, we can observe that for him ontic matters receded into the background, as he devoted himself entirely to the thought of being.

In short, the attempt to overcome the "forgetfulness of being" resulted in another forgetfulness, the forgetfulness of the very same lifeworld that Heidegger championed in the early 1920s. In the 1930s he no longer held that philosophy sprang forth from the lifeworld and must return to it. Since the lifeworld itself was corrupted by the project of modernism, philosophy could only restart thinking by leaving the lifeworld behind. Despite his emphasis on belongingness and his great respect for the pastoral, as a thinker Heidegger defined himself outside any particular lifeworld and any special allegiance owed to it. In other words, he did not acknowledge ties of human solidarity. As if to emphasize this point, he insisted that the philosopher was an *Alleingänger*, someone who goes it alone, thinking the singular being alone.[117] For Heidegger, this means a certain epoché, the blocking out of the other. Thus he jots down something of a "rule" for himself:

In philosophizing never think of the "others"—of the "You," but likewise never think of the "I," [but think] only of the origin of being and [think] for [the sake of] being—this holds equally for the subject matter and the path on which it is pursued.[118]

Thus absolving himself from the responsibilities that come with belonging to the with-world or *Mitwelt*, the circle of friends, acquaintances, colleagues, officials, and fellow citizens, Heidegger invokes the higher responsibility that has called him to respond to being alone. Hence the *Notebooks* show only a few entries, some of which I have dealt with above, in which he is humanly engaged with other people, their viewpoints, or the inevitable contradictions and upheavals in their lives in Germany, let alone outside of Germany. For Heidegger, National Socialism is almost exclusively an intellectual-philosophical problem, revolving around the fate of modernity. It is curiously removed from existential questions of guilt, the call of conscience, and the cruelty of fate.

On the other hand, it is true too that all of Heidegger's ontological characteristics of modernity—machination, power, brutality, criminality, devastation, and so on—have concrete, ontic manifestations, which are simply described as abhorrent. He explicitly acknowledges this when he holds that "shock," *das Erschrecken*,[119] or "horror," *das Entsetzen*,[120] is the basic mood in philosophy at a time when "the 'world' is out of joint," and "there is no longer a world."[121] The premonition of a catastrophic end to modern history permeates Heidegger's writings from the mid-1930s. And yet, next to this abyss of being, he writes with great detachment, matter-of-factly thinking through a catastrophe of being without sufficiently analyzing the concrete, ontic phenomena on the ground, and possible ways of averting the worst. The very same metaphysical detachment that Heidegger so convincingly criticized in the early 1920s finally caught up with him, at the exact wrong moment in time. Like the absentminded philosophy professor Hegel, Heidegger had no real regard for the empirical hustle and bustle of the times and the concrete lives of his fellow citizens. Instead, he devoted his time to thinking being, at a safe distance from the messiness of real life.

Heidegger's great distance from the empirical world is reflected in what is really a revival of intellectualism by other means. In *Geschichte des Seyns*, written between 1938 and 1940, he holds that what philosophy *thinks* through and determines is what being actually *is*.[122] The decisive realm is thought, not praxis. And if praxis does not conform to thought, the answer is: "so much the worse for it." Thus in 1939, long after his break with National Socialism, Heidegger writes the following:

In completely recognizing the earlier mistake about the essential reality [*Wesen*] and the historical force of National Socialism, the necessity arises of affirming it, indeed for *reasons of thought* [*denkerischen Gründen*].[123] Having said this, it needs to be added that this "movement" remains independent from its respective contemporary shape and the duration of these visible forms. How is it that this essential affirmation [*wesentliche Bejahung*] counts less or for nothing at all in comparison with the mostly superficial and subsequently clueless and blind assent?[124]

While it cannot be ruled out entirely that Heidegger would write down such a staunch "affirmation" as an insurance policy against possible blackmail and denunciation, it is conceivable that it indicates Heidegger's real view.[125] That is, even after conceding his fundamental error in judging the very essence and historical significance of National Socialism, Heidegger *still* holds fast to his earlier, idealized view of it, namely, as a revolutionary movement to break the spell of modernity. He does this despite his understanding that National Socialism had proved to be the exact opposite in reality![126]

Although Heidegger usually reserves his most scathing criticism for the proponents of "values" and "ideals," here he exploits precisely the gap between the ideal and the real, and it allows him to affirm and denounce National Socialism at the same time—in other words, it allows him to be an "opponent" and "advocate" simultaneously. In practical terms it allows him to accommodate himself to National Socialism (i.e., resisting National Socialism "in thought" only, while going along with it "in reality").

Throughout the 1930s Heidegger found himself (*Befindlichkeit*) in the relatively safe bourgeois milieu of academia (which he himself always liked to castigate for the idolatry of convenience and security), and he ignored or suppressed his ties to specifically targeted and oppressed groups (Jews and Christians alike) (*Entwurf*).Moreover, he nurtured his growing distaste for anything merely "subjective" and turned toward the thought of being alone. Within this framework of understanding (*Verstehen*), there simply were no "subjects" on behalf of which he would have transformed his disaffection and disagreement with National Socialism into a more urgent, concrete confrontation, with all the concomitant risk that he favored in theory but not in practice. In the end, Heidegger found a philosophical niche from which to observe the regime, dedicating himself to a radical ontological critique of it and of modernity at large.

VII Heidegger's Anti-Semitism

Many debates about the *Black Notebooks* have concerned Heidegger's anti-Semitism. Some commentators have claimed that the *Notebooks* reveal Heidegger's deeply ingrained, systematic, even ontohistorically undergirded anti-Semitism. However, a careful reading brings to light a different picture that is actually far less incriminating and much more nuanced than what the many public condemnations make one think.

Indeed, that Heidegger held anti-Semitic prejudices was widely documented before the *Notebooks* came out. In fact, he proclaims himself an anti-Semite in a letter to Hannah Arendt, written some time during the winter of 1932–1933:

In any case, with regards to university matters I am as much an anti-Semite today as I was ten years ago in Marburg, where I even found support for this anti-Semitism in Jacobsthal and Friedländer. This has nothing to do with personal relations to Jews (for example Husserl, Misch, Cassirer, and others). Most of all, this cannot affect the relation with you.[127]

The anti-Semitism that Heidegger avows here, apparently without any sense of impropriety, reflects resentment of the supposed overrepresentation of Jews in universities.[128] In fact, when he resumed teaching after his suspension in the 1950s he again looked askance at the allegedly high number of professorships held by Jews, counting them on the fingers of his hand in front of his students. On the basis of the evidence that we have at the moment, we must assume that Heidegger never gave up this kind of anti-Semitic resentment.

Moreover, before the *Notebooks* were published, it was already known from a conversation with Jaspers in 1933 that Heidegger had come to believe in a worldwide Jewish conspiracy. However, as Jaspers also pointed out, Heidegger apparently held this view "without inner conviction."[129] Given this context, we have to ask what the *Notebooks* add to this.

The *Notebooks* certainly underscore that Heidegger was an anti-Semite. However, contrary to some reports, his remarks about Jewish matters are neither systematically developed nor sustained over time, or even frequently addressed in the *Notebooks*. Of course, that does not mean that we should take any of the anti-Semitic pronouncements lightly. But when added up, the scattered anti-Semitic remarks amount to about five pages, out of a grand total of some 1,300 pages of the first three volumes of the *Black Notebooks*. The fourth volume, *Anmerkungen I–V*, covering notes from 1942 to 1948, shows one anti-Semitic passage (from 1942) of half a page out of 518 pages.[130] It is also quite remarkable that Heidegger does not resort to anti-Semitic innuendos or remarks during that crucial year of 1933–1934 when they would have been most opportune, provided he was indeed set on aiding and abetting the violent anti-Semitism of National Socialism. Heidegger's anti-Semitic remarks in the *Black Notebooks* occur between 1938 and 1942. The view that they permeate all notebooks is false. Moreover, at no point in the *Notebooks* does he endorse the racist policies implemented by the Nazis, which is consistent with his rejection of race doctrines. In fact, the very pursuit of racial purity and "breeding" are prime examples of what Heidegger rejects as the modern obsession with "calculation" and ordering things along the lines of machination, power, and so on.[131] Starting with the earliest entries in the *Notebooks* he consistently and constantly rejects what he considers the "muddied waters of biologism"[132] and any biologically undergirded racism. As we have seen, biological racism falls under what he considers the pathology of modern subjectivism.[133]

However, between 1938 and 1942 Heidegger attributes, albeit often parenthetically, characteristics of what he rejects in modernity to Jewry, *Judentum*. In fact, he claims that the race principle is deeply inscribed in Jewish life itself:

That, in the age of machination, race is taken as the explicitly and especially postulated "principle" of history … is not a whimsical invention of "doctrinaires," but a *consequence* of the power of machination, which must overwhelm all entities in all walks of life by means of methodical and planned calculation. The Jews, with their marked talent for calculation, have "lived" longer than anyone by the principle of race, which is why they are resisting its unrestricted application. The establishment of racial breeding does not stem from "life" itself, but from the overpowering of life through machination.[134]

The last sentence in the above quotation shows Heidegger actually attacking eugenics programs in Germany. At the same time it is just as clear that he thinks Jews are to blame for racist conceptions, and, with unsurpassable malice, he then insinuates that they have no grounds for resistance when these conceptions are applied to them, effectively blaming the persecuted for the harm suffered. No mitigating circumstances could make Heidegger's statement any less awful. The only "good" thing is that, as far as I know, he does not return to this particular thought in other parts of the *Notebooks*.

Next, Heidegger also associates Jewry with another ill of modernity, the ever-growing "groundlessness [*Bodenlosigkeit*]," and he specifically argues that the "tenacious talent for calculating" is what conditions the "lack of world" in Jewry.[135] The particular Jewish "groundlessness" and "talent for calculation" are mentioned in a number of entries but are not further elaborated. However, in one entry Heidegger suggests that the "empty rationality" characteristic of Jewry found a foothold in Western metaphysics, which in turn yielded a "temporary increase in power" on the part of Jewry:

The reason, however, for the Jewry's temporary increase in power is that Western metaphysics, especially in its modern development, provided the foothold for the entrenchment and dissemination of the otherwise empty rationality and calculability, both of which thus took refuge in "spirit," albeit without the capacity to grasp the concealed region of decisive choices on their own. The more originary and primordial the future decisions and questions will be, the more they will remain inaccessible to this "race."[136]

Heidegger even applies this general principle to his teacher Husserl, holding that, notwithstanding Husserl's "lasting" contributions to philosophy, his inability to access the question of being is ultimately the result of his belonging to the Jewish "race."[137] This speaks for itself, a sad document in the long history of human prejudice.

Nevertheless, although the exclusionary gesture in the above anti-Semitic quote is as crude as it is baffling, especially given Heidegger's close personal relationship with Husserl, we should note that Heidegger does *not* claim that the turn in Western metaphysics toward reason and/or calculation is somehow Jewish. In fact, for him, Western metaphysics with all its purported faults is fundamentally determined by Descartes's rationalism and Greek philosophy, without any particular Jewish contribution.[138]

If Heidegger had any real philosophical, intellectual, or other interest in Jewish thought as such, one would assume that he would have referred to Jewish teaching, Jewish philosophers, and Jewish thought. But with the exception of the above-mentioned brief remark about Husserl, who did not consider himself a Jewish philosopher, Heidegger does not name or refer to, let alone engage, Jewish philosophers as such. In short, there is no account of how Jewish thinkers have promoted, refined, or entrenched "calculation" or "groundlessness." Instead, having traced calculation and groundlessness back to modern philosophy, especially Descartes, Heidegger then superadds the entirely gratuitous, very general, and totally unsubstantiated attribution of such tendencies to *Jewry as such*, in effect following the conventional, classic anti-Semitic script of implicating Jews in whatever negative phenomena are under discussion, be that perjury, usury, murder, or, in Heidegger's case, calculation, uprootedness, and even the so-called race principle.

Although Heidegger's anti-Semitism employs rather conventional tropes, it does not follow that it is in any way harmless or trivial. In fact, there is one entry where he clearly suggests that Germans are somehow at war with World Jewry. He writes:

World Jewry, egged on by the emigrants Germany let go, is elusive everywhere. For all its increased leverage of power [*Machtentfaltung*], World Jewry does not have to engage in wars, while all that we can do is to sacrifice the best blood of the best of our people.[139]

Although it is important to note that Heidegger rarely reiterates this theme, the statement reveals some telltale continuity with the incriminating remark reported by Jaspers. It may even suggest that there was more "conviction" in Heidegger's belief than Jaspers thought at the time. Moreover, it is striking that in contrast to his many critical and sometimes highly sarcastic comments about National Socialism, there is not a single line in the *Notebooks* in which Heidegger directly questions, comments on, or rejects anti-Semitic prejudices (except racially tinged anti-Semitism). His anti-Semitism remains unchanged and untouched by hesitation or doubt, although it is quite curious that the *Notebooks* show that for long years he had nothing at all to say on Jewish matters.

If we read these passages in context, it is difficult to see in them anything but plain anti-Semitic prejudices. Passed on by hearsay, Heidegger unthinkingly adopted them; he failed to question them and take the phenomena for what they were. If there is a link to Heidegger's philosophy, I would suggest that it is with his account of what he calls the "dictatorship" of *das Man*, "determining" average everydayness.[140] Whether we like it or not, in the 1920s and 1930s anti-Semitic phrases belonged to everyday existence in Germany, as well as in many other countries. Heidegger's anti-Semitic phrases in the *Notebooks* are a testament to the power and corruption of *das Man*.

Discussing this very issue long before the *Notebooks* came out, Klemens von Klemperer has argued that Heidegger's own implication and enmeshment in "das Man" reveals that he himself failed to live up to the aspirations that underlie *Being and Time* (i.e., to extricate oneself from the conformity enforced by *das Man*): "Heidegger did not stand the test of his own message."[141] I agree with this assessment. But I do not share von Klemperer's conclusion that, therefore, Heidegger's philosophy collapses "like a house of cards."[142] For if von Klemperer's analysis is accurate, it follows that it is not Heidegger's *philosophy* that gets him into trouble, but rather his opportunistic *disregard of his own philosophical insight*, namely, the call to be vigilant at all times when faced with *das Man*. In a brief note in *Anmerkungen II* from 1946 Heidegger concedes just this: "*Errancy*: thinking the essence of 'das Man' and yet at the proper moment not seeing or recognizing it."[143]

Peter Trawny has argued that the *Notebooks* not only demonstrate Heidegger's sundry anti-Semitic views, but also his inveterate attempt to inscribe anti-Semitism within philosophy or the history of being. Trawny claims that Heidegger elevates common anti-Semitism to "ontohistorical anti-Semitism" or "*seinsgeschichtlichen Anti-Semitismus*."[144] I can see no evidence whatsoever for this in the *Considerations* or the *Anmerkungen* and I do not believe that Trawny has marshaled persuasive arguments for his case. First of all, although Trawny concedes that Heidegger's anti-Semitism is "not especially elaborate or cunning,"[145] which prima facie speaks against any philosophical significance, he maintains, nonetheless, that Heidegger superadds an "ontohistorical interpretation" to this common anti-Semitism.[146] Astonishingly, Trawny never tells his readers what he means by this. On one level, one might say that everything that Heidegger addressed during his ontohistorical period is by that very fact "ontohistorical." But that is not really informative at all. If the claim is to have any bite, it must mean that Heidegger's history of being either justifies or entails anti-Semitism, or else that the history of being is motivated by anti-Semitism.

However, it will be difficult to argue that it is motivated by it. First, Heidegger's anti-Semitic remarks in the *Notebooks* do not show up before 1938, at least six years after he started working on his history of being. Second, in his ontohistorical works, including the *Notebooks*, Heidegger does *not* draw on anti-Semitic tropes to establish his conception of being. If there is any such connection, one wonders why Trawny does not provide a single passage that would prove his claim.

But does the history of being justify or entail anti-Semitism? After all, the trope of the cunning and calculating Jew seems a "perfect" fit for Heidegger's history of being, which is crucially centered on (1) the claim of the predominance of calculation and machination, and (2) the explicit demand to overcome calculation and machination, in order to establish a freer relationship to being. However, when Trawny himself directly poses the essential question that is pertinent here—that is, whether, according to Heidegger, calculative rationality as such is a "Jewish invention"—he does not attribute such a view to Heidegger, although, characteristically, he then proceeds as if something like it is implied, for instance, in Heidegger's remark about the "calculative gift" of the Jews.[147] But the truth is that in the *Black Notebooks*, as in other writings, Heidegger traces the mathematical and calculative approach in philosophy to Descartes and to Greek thought in Athens, never to Jewish philosophers, or to Jerusalem, for that matter. Since Heidegger does not single out Jews as the sole or even the main agents of calculative rationality or machination, let alone as the original founders of it, Trawny fails to make good on his claim that Heidegger espouses an ontohistorical anti-Semitism. Not one iota in his history of being would have to be changed if one removed all references to Jewish matters.

On the other hand, it is true that Heidegger, unable to shake off the Zeitgeist, gratuitously resorts to *anti-Semitic language* when he counts Jews among the agents of that calculative rationality responsible for the forgetfulness of being. But it is important to note that he implicates not just Jews, but the entire Western tradition of philosophy and the most advanced or entrenched manifestations of it in the present—for instance, in National Socialism, Americanism, Bolshevism, Christianity, and so on. The enormous range of Heidegger's condemnations is a function of the radical abstraction from entities to being. The more he removes being from all beings and from human subjects in particular, the more encompassing and comprehensive his condemnation becomes of ideological formations and ideas that he thinks are subservient to the forgetfulness of being. While this breathtaking loss of discrimination in ontic matters is highly problematic, it is not sufficient to characterize Heidegger's philosophizing as "ontohistorical anti-Semitism," because he is precisely *not* treating Jewish thought and being as the ontological Other, the foreign element in the Western world. While Heidegger certainly makes room for anti-Semitic content in his *Considerations*, it is not a systematic, essential, or inevitable component of his philosophizing in these writings or his other philosophical works.

To single out Heidegger's charges against Jews and separate them from the identical charges he levels at the entire Western tradition is manifestly one-sided. In fact, Heidegger is far less anti-Semitic than he is a critic of the Western tradition. And just as, for instance, the critique of capitalism is not vitiated by the fact that some tend to blame the ills of capitalism on supposedly innate Jewish character traits, so Heidegger's philosophy is not derailed because he himself, without a modicum of justification, slips anti-Semitic prejudices into his account. One puts the cart before the horse if one argues that the critique of capitalism is meant to justify or is motivated by anti-Semitism, and one commits a similar mistake if one argues that Heidegger's critiques of Western homelessness, rationalism, machination, number frenzy, and so on, are philosophical rationalizations to justify anti-Semitism.

Pace Trawny, Heidegger has no systematic ontohistorical conception of Jews as Jews. This would require a sort of "schematism" of being that showed how and why Jews have a particular destiny relative to other peoples. But this is missing in Heidegger's writings, and therefore, there is no ontohistorical anti-Semitism. What we are left with are anti-Semitic prejudices, relentlessly drummed into people's heads by tradition and state propaganda. Clearly, Heidegger was not immune to these prejudices and he made room for them in his philosophy.[148] But that is quite different from attempting to provide a philosophical or ontohistorical foundation for anti-Semitism. In fact, on one occasion Heidegger addresses the conflict between Jewish and anti-Jewish orientations in outright Christian terminology, apparently suggesting that just as "the Anti-Christ" shares a common ground with "the Christ," so conflicts between Jews and anti-Jewish groups must be grounded in a shared essence.[149] But he immediately distances himself from this line of argumentation when he adds that his project is devoted to thinking through the essence of the beginning of thinking in ancient Greece, insisting that it is situated "outside Judaism and therefore Christianity."[150] Indeed, just as Heidegger has no ontohistorical deduction of "the Anti-Christ" or "the Christ," so he has no ontohistorically undergirded anti-Semitism. For Heidegger, Judaism and Christianity are both outside the confines of the history of being.

VIII Heidegger Today

Heidegger's involvement with National Socialism and his anti-Semitic remarks show that he is not easily compatible with the reigning Western liberal, progressivist agenda that first emerged in the aftermath of World War II and that has gained a dominant and global reach today. However, if we identify and discard those aspects of Heidegger's philosophy attributable to his entanglement with the prejudices of his time, we can still explore whether his philosophy sheds light on the deep undercurrents determining the state of the world today. While a full account would have to engage and comprehensively analyze Heidegger's philosophy of the history of being in the 1930s and 1940s, as well as his writings in the 1950s and 1960s, I would like to highlight some themes in Heidegger's *Notebooks* that provide provocative but helpful commentary concerning the pathologies of our own era.

Throughout the *Notebooks* Heidegger is concerned with the modern dominance of technology, rational planning, and the exploitative mindset that views everything with an eye toward its usefulness, serviceability, manipulability, and so on.[151] For him, this "machination" is the result of a metaphysical subjectivism where the subject is posited as absolute self-certainty vis-à-vis the multitude of objects, which are reduced to mere materials, ready to be broken up, shaped, formed, and worked up into products and commodities according to human whim. Realizing that machination is not limited to Europe, but encompasses the entire planet, Heidegger presciently speaks of "planetarianism."[152] By 1969 he calls it "world civilization," which he characterizes in these words: "Predominance of the natural sciences, predominance and primacy of the economy, politics, and technology. Everything else is not even a superstructure but a ramshackle lean-to."[153]

It is in this context that he notes that "homelessness"[154] is the coming fate of the world because global machination reaches deep into the most distant and secluded dwelling places, where it determines what can be extracted and used, thus organizing, alienating, and expropriating the home grounds for the sake of the ever more exploitative and wasteful production and consumption of goods and commodities worldwide. Local attachment and homegrown traditions are undermined by the relentless drive toward machination and globalization.

While Heidegger's recognition of homelessness took shape in the 1930s, it is still relevant today, when globalism, technological advances, and managerialism are the new truths touted by politicians and business leaders alike. Contrary to the claims of many of its current advocates, it must be noted that globalism does not encourage the exchange of views and ideas—unless they facilitate the goals and targets of machination. Internationalization transforms everything into an office and everyone into an officeholder, strictly planned and regimented by rational rules and responsibilities. Thinking through this new dogmatism, at one point Heidegger has the premonition of "Europe as a single office [*Europa als ein einziges Büro*]."[155] In another comment he notes that what "corresponds" to "planetarianism" or globalism is—"idiotism." Understanding this latter term "ontohistorically"—that is, as derived from the Greek word *idion*, what is private or one's own—Heidegger argues that in a globalized world international magazines, radio, and other media will produce a homogenized body of public opinion that offers a surrogate home where everyone can find what is his or her "own," but that in reality belongs to everyone and thus to no one.[156] In other words, the intellectual reflex of globalization lies in the displacement and exteriorization of the individual mind and its resettlement within the "idiotic" stories of the worldwide media. Thus Heidegger writes: "Idiotism is the essential confinement to the course of the world [*das Weltläufige*], i.e., the planetary. And the latter [planetarianism, IF] can exist only in the form of idiotism."[157] According to Heidegger, "planetary [globalized] man can only be idiotic and the idiotic man must be planetary [globalized]."[158] Heidegger calls this the "barbarism of civilization [*zivilisierte Barbarei*],"[159] echoing Hölderlin's attack on the "barbarians" in his *Hyperion*.[160] To question anew the self-congratulatory story that pits

Western civilization against the non-Western "barbarians" is much in order after the last thirty years of Western market triumphalism. From Husserl to Patočka and Henry, from Adorno, Horkheimer, and Marcuse to Habermas, philosophers in the twentieth and early twenty-first centuries have rejected the apologetic story of the West as deeply flawed.

Heidegger's reflections on the global reach of modern technology and machination are governed at bottom by the threat they pose to the earth. He is deeply alarmed at the very possibility of the "destruction of the earth," not only in terms of technologically advanced, extractive economies that threaten the ecological balance of the planet, but also in terms of the imperialistic warfare waged between states that eventually could blow up the planet. Heidegger holds that imperialistic military armament and technological development feed on each other, making possible the ultimate military-technological "feat," namely, "that the earth blows itself up [*dass sich die Erde selbst in die Luft sprengt*]."[161]

Of course, "prophetic" pronouncements like this are proved right only when it is too late, sadly. But the problem is that nothing in post–World War II history can assure us that this danger has been foreclosed. Precisely this sentiment underlies Heidegger's talk of the "world night" in 1946,[162] as well as his dark, provocative statement that although the war is over, "nothing has changed."[163] While one must find fault with Heidegger for his inability or unwillingness to see the major changes that occurred after World War II on the ontic, empirical, and most of all, human level, namely, through the liberation of Germany by the Allied Forces (something he would never admit in these words), it is also important to register the truth of his dark, provocative statement. For Heidegger's pessimistic point about the ongoing dangers of the military-scientific-technological complex is as true today as it was sixty or seventy years ago.

If one looks at Heidegger's *Notebooks* today one is struck by the fact that so much of his work in the 1950s and 1960s condenses and refines his earlier thought from the 1930s and 1940s. However, we can also see that in these later works, he reappropriates a more phenomenological method by ontologically describing how humans dwell on the land when not in the grip of modern technology, machination, and globalism. This later work is closer to "constructive phenomenology"[164] and a necessary corrective to Heidegger's more historical and deconstructive orientation in the 1930s and 1940s. In fact, one of the most fascinating aspects of Heidegger's *Anmerkungen I–V* containing the notes from 1942–1948 is his progressive abandoning of the history of being. He moves from the "other beginning" in history to the "other of history," which is no longer history (*Historie*) or *Geschichte*.[165] He writes in 1946–1947:

In a lucid moment I suddenly recognized that in getting over being [*Verwindung des Seyns*] I had long ago given up philosophy and history [*Historie*] too. But it still required some effort to grasp that with that "*Geschichte*" had fall to the wayside too.[166]

It must have dawned on Heidegger that history as *Geschichte* is still tied to the philosophy of subjectivity. In any case, he now holds that in the *Ereignis* "the essence of history

[*Geschichte*] is given up," and he considers "talk of the history of being [*Seyngeschichte*]" a mere "pretext" or even "embarrassment [*Verlegenheit*]."[167]

Leaving behind the ontohistorical framework, he concentrates on articulating the topology of being, the place of human dwelling.[168] It is an attempt to retrieve what is overlooked and forgotten more than anything else in the modern world: the place where things, gods, and mortals encounter each other. It is what Heidegger calls the clearing.

Acknowledgments

I would like to thank James Mensch and George Heffernan for critical comments on an earlier version of this essay at the OPO Conference in Perth in December 2014, and Babette Babich, Nancy Weston, and Tracy Strong for their insightful comments on my essay at the Heidegger Conference in Messkirch in May 2014. I would also like to thank Jeff Malpas for extensive discussions of Heidegger's philosophy and its political dimension.

Notes

1. Martin Heidegger, *Überlegungen XII–XV (Schwarze Hefte 1939–1941)*, Gesamtausgabe 96, ed. Peter Trawny (Klostermann: Frankfurt, 2014), 276. All parentheses (…) were originally inserted by the author of the texts translated. Square brackets […] are my insertions to clarify or supply original terms where necessary.

2. See my "Heidegger: Transformation of Hermeneutics," in *The Routledge Companion to Hermeneutics*, ed. Jeff Malpas and Hans-Helmuth Gander, 107–126 (London: Routledge, 2014).

3. Friedrich Schleiermacher, *Hermeneutics and Criticism*, trans. Andrew Bowie (Cambridge: Cambridge University Press, 1998), 8. For the German, see Friedrich Schleiermacher, *Hermeneutik und Kritik*, ed. Manfred Frank (Frankfurt: Suhrkamp, 1977), 77.

4. *Hermeneutics and Criticism*, 8; *Hermeneutik und Kritik*, 77.

5. Richard J. Evans, *The Coming of the Third Reich* (London: Penguin Books, 2004), xx.

6. Evans, *The Coming of the Third Reich*, xx.

7. Martin Heidegger, *Beiträge zur Philosophie (Vom Ereignis)*, Gesamtausgabe 65, 3rd ed., ed. Friedrich-Wilhelm von Herrmann (Klostermann: Frankfurt, 2003), 11.

8. *Überlegungen XII–VX, Gesamtausgabe* 96, p. 225.

9. Fritz Stern, *Five Germanys I Have Known* (New York: Farrar, Straus & Giroux, 2007), 119.

10. Richard J. Evans, *The Third Reich in Power* (London: Penguin Books, 2006), 258–259.

11. Evans, *The Third Reich in Power*, 304.

12. Levinas has made this point with great clarity in his writings, and the *Considerations* vindicate him.

13. Martin Heidegger, *Besinnung, Gesamtausgabe* 66, ed. Friedrich-Wilhelm von Herrmann (Frankfurt: Klostermann, 1997), 420.

14. *Besinnung, Gesamtausgabe* 66, p. 426.

15. See the introduction to this book.

16. *Überlegungen II–VI, Gesamtausgabe* 94, pp. 107–199.

17. *Besinnung, Gesamtausgabe* 66, p. 422.

18. Martin Heidegger, *Die Geschichte des Seyns, Gesamtausgabe* 69, ed. Peter Trawny (Frankfurt: Klostermann, 1998), 172–173.

19. *Beiträge, Gesamtausgabe* 65, p. 32.

20. *Beiträge, Gesamtausgabe* 65, p. 28. In an entry from his later notebooks in 1948, Heidegger writes: "The

claims on thinking are different from one epoch of being to another; different too are the criteria of communication, and different the dimensions of the decisions." Martin Heidegger, *Anmerkungen I–V (Schwarze Hefte 1942–1948), Gesamtausgabe 97*, ed. Peter Trawny (Frankfurt: Klostermann, 2015), 471.

21. *Beiträge, Gesamtausgabe* 65, p. 28.

22. *Beiträge, Gesamtausgabe* 65, p. 228.

23. As if transferring the characteristics of *Dasein* (in *Being and Time*) to being or *Seyn*, Heidegger writes: "The extraordinariness of being [*Seyn*] corresponds to the singularity of death in the founding region of its truth, i.e., in *Dasein*" (*Beiträge, Gesamtausgabe* 65, p. 230). Moreover, while in *Being and Time, Dasein* is characterized by discourse; after *Being and Time* Heidegger transfers linguisticality to being as such: "Being [is] not without language—but precisely because of that not 'logical.' Language [is] not without being [*Sein*]" (*Überlegungen II–VI, Gesamtausgabe* 94, p. 11).

24. "But the historicity of humanity [*Geschichtlichkeit des Menschentums*] is grounded in the event character of being [*Seyn*]. Therefore, the historicity of man (and not just his history) varies in accordance with his belongingness to being (forgetfulness of being or founding the truth of being)" (*Besinnung, Gesamtausgabe* 66, p. 182).

25. *Überlegungen II–VI, Gesamtausgabe* 94, p. 19.

26. *Überlegungen II–VI, Gesamtausgabe* 94, p. 27.

27. *Überlegungen II–VI, Gesamtausgabe* 94, p. 256.

28. *Überlegungen II–VI, Gesamtausgabe* 94, p. 253.

29. *Überlegungen II–VI, Gesamtausgabe* 94, p. 183. The boxer in question is Max Schmeling, as Heidegger himself notes in another entry in *Überlegungen VII–XI, Gesamtausgabe* 95, p. 4. See also Heidegger's use of this idea in *Einführung in die Metaphysik, Gesamtausgabe* 40, ed. Petra Jaeger (Frankfurt: Klostermann, 1983), 41.

30. *Überlegungen II–VI, Gesamtausgabe* 94, p. 116. In this same vein Heidegger also writes: "The metaphysics of *Dasein* must, in accord with its inner structure, be deepened and extended toward a metapolitics of 'the' historical people" (*Überlegungen II–VI, Gesamtausgabe* 94, p. 124).

31. *Überlegungen II–VI, Gesamtausgabe* 94, pp. 209, 213.

32. The first entry in *Überlegungen IV* reads: "To bring the world, as a world, to [its] worlding means: to try it once more with the gods" (*Überlegungen II–VI, Gesamtausgabe* 94, p. 209).

33. *Überlegungen II–VI, Gesamtausgabe* 94, p. 216.

34. I respectfully disagree here with Peter Trawny, who writes: "All that which links Heidegger with National Socialism derives from his narrative of the 'first beginning' with the Greeks and the 'other beginning' with the Germans. This story fashions the ground for Heidegger's approval of and his service for the 'national revolution'" (Peter Trawny, *Heidegger und der Mythos der jüdischen Weltverschwörung* [Frankfurt: Klostermann, 2014], 28). If I am right, Trawny confuses Heidegger's earlier attempts at restarting metaphysics *anew*, where Heidegger did align himself with the so-called revolution of National Socialism, with Heidegger's quite different narrative of a "second beginning," aimed at overcoming metaphysics altogether, which he worked out *after* his disillusionment with National Socialism.

35. See Iain Thomson, "Heidegger and National Socialism," in *A Companion to Heidegger*, ed. Hubert L. Dreyfus and Mark A. Wrathall (Oxford: Blackwell, 2005), 32–48.

36. *Überlegungen II–VI, Gesamtausgabe* 94, p. 1. See also the editor's comment on p. 529.

37. *Überlegungen II–VI, Gesamtausgabe* 94, p. 5.

38. Bernd Martin, ed., *Martin Heidegger und das Dritte Reich* (Darmstadt: Wissenschaftliche Buchgesellschaft, 1989).

39. Martin Heidegger, *Sein und Wahrheit: 1. Die Grundfrage der Philosophie, 2. Vom Wesen der Wahrheit, Sommersemester 1933 und Wintersemester 1934, Gesamtausgabe* 36/37, ed. Hartmut Tietjen (Frankfurt: Klostermann, 2001).

40. Alfred Denker and Holger Zaborowski, eds., *Heidegger und der Nationalsozialismus: Dokumente, Heidegger-Jahrbuch* 4 (Munich: Karl Alber, 2009).

41. *Überlegungen II–VI, Gesamtausgabe* 94, p. 112.

42. *Überlegungen II–VI, Gesamtausgabe* 94, p. 109.

43. *Überlegungen II–VI, Gesamtausgabe* 94, p. 112. This kind of sentiment also permeates Heidegger's lecture course from the summer semester of 1933. He begins the lecture course with these sentences: "The academic youth knows of the greatness of this historical moment of the German people. What is happening? As a whole the German people comes to itself, that is, it finds its leadership. Having found itself, the people creates its state in this leadership" (*Sein und Wahrheit, Gesamtausgabe* 36/37, p. 3).

44. *Überlegungen II–VI, Gesamtausgabe* 94, p. 109.

45. *Überlegungen II–VI, Gesamtausgabe* 94, p. 27.

46. *Überlegungen II–VI, Gesamtausgabe* 94, p. 29.

47. *Überlegungen II–VI, Gesamtausgabe* 94, p. 39.

48. *Überlegungen II–VI, Gesamtausgabe* 94, p. 119.

49. *Überlegungen II–VI, Gesamtausgabe* 94, p. 122.

50. *Überlegungen II–VI, Gesamtausgabe* 94, pp. 119–120.

51. *Überlegungen II–VI, Gesamtausgabe* 94, p. 135.

52. Thus Heidegger writes: "National Socialism can never be the principle of a philosophy, but can only be subordinated under philosophy as the principle" (*Überlegungen II–VI, Gesamtausgabe* 94, p. 190).

53. *Überlegungen II–VI, Gesamtausgabe* 94, p. 190.

54. *Überlegungen II–VI, Gesamtausgabe* 94, p. 135.

55. *Überlegungen II–VI, Gesamtausgabe* 94, p. 155.

56. *Überlegungen II–VI, Gesamtausgabe* 94, p. 348.

57. *Überlegungen II–VI, Gesamtausgabe* 94, p. 114.

58. *Überlegungen II–VI, Gesamtausgabe* 94, p. 110.

59. *Überlegungen II–VI, Gesamtausgabe* 94, p. 142.

60. *Überlegungen II–VI, Gesamtausgabe* 94, pp. 142–143.

61. *Überlegungen II–VI, Gesamtausgabe* 94, p. 191.

62. *Überlegungen II–VI, Gesamtausgabe* 94, p. 189.

63. *Überlegungen II–VI, Gesamtausgabe* 94, p. 160.

64. *Überlegungen II–VI, Gesamtausgabe* 94, pp. 161, 154.

65. *Überlegungen II–VI, Gesamtausgabe* 94, p. 148.

66. On one occasion Heidegger affirms as one of the goals to be achieved in the furthest future "the historical greatness of the people in the forming and shaping of the powers of being [*Seinsmächte*]" (*Überlegungen II–VI, Gesamtausgabe* 94, p. 136). But this is a far cry from an aggressive and/or imperialist, perverted nationalism.

67. In 1938 Heidegger writes: "To be German: to tackle and shoulder the burden of the history of the Western world" (*Überlegungen VII–XI, Gesamtausgabe* 95, p. 2).

68. *Überlegungen II–VI, Gesamtausgabe* 94, pp. 133, 124.

69. *Überlegungen II–VI, Gesamtausgabe* 94, p. 38. *Bodenständigkeit* may be translated as "enrootedness." It means actual enrootedness and belongingness to the land, coupled with a positive, even reverent or pious stance toward the land on which one dwells and from which one's ancestors came, often colored by a certain down-to-earth attitude mindful of the limited horizon in which one lives. Here Heidegger writes: "He can be enrooted who, emerging from the land, is nourished by it and dwells on it. The former is the original [thing], the latter is what reverberates in me and courses through my body and mood—as if I walk on the fields behind a plow, along the solitary country paths between the cornfields, through the winds and mists, sun and snow, which kept the blood of the mother and her ancestors in full swing."

70. In an arresting entry from 1932 Heidegger writes: "The running to and fro [*Das Gerenne*] has come to an end—progress has become a nuisance—we want to come to a standstill. *Stop*! And here is the original limit of history—not the empty, extratemporal eternity—but rather the steadfastness [*Ständigkeit*] of enrootedness [*Verwurzelung*]. *Time becomes space* [*Die Zeit wird zum Raum*]" (*Überlegungen II–VI, Gesamtausgabe* 94, p. 38).

71. "How far removed from nature must natural science be such that the devastation wrought by technology [*Wüten der Technik*], which is founded upon it [i.e., natural science], is counted as success?" (*Überlegungen*

II–VI, Gesamtausgabe 94, p. 72).

72. *Überlegungen II–VI, Gesamtausgabe* 94, pp. 178–179.

73. *Überlegungen II–VI, Gesamtausgabe* 94, pp. 198–199.

74. *Überlegungen II–VI, Gesamtausgabe* 94, p. 63.

75. *Überlegungen II–VI, Gesamtausgabe* 94, p. 92.

76. *Überlegungen II–VI, Gesamtausgabe* 94, pp. 131–132, 136.

77. *Überlegungen II–VI, Gesamtausgabe* 94, p. 223.

78. *Überlegungen II–VI, Gesamtausgabe* 94, p. 233.

79. *Überlegungen II–VI, Gesamtausgabe* 94, p. 221.

80. *Überlegungen II–VI, Gesamtausgabe* 94, p. 223.

81. *Überlegungen II–VI, Gesamtausgabe* 94, p. 436.

82. *Überlegungen II–VI, Gesamtausgabe* 94, p. 221.

83. *Überlegungen II–VI, Gesamtausgabe* 94, p. 261.

84. *Überlegungen II–VI, Gesamtausgabe* 94, p. 189.

85. *Überlegungen II–VI, Gesamtausgabe* 94, p. 189.

86. *Überlegungen VII–XI, Gesamtausgabe* 95, p. 397.

87. *Überlegungen II–VI, Gesamtausgabe* 94, p. 350.

88. *Überlegungen VII–XI, Gesamtausgabe* 95, p. 408.

89. *Überlegungen VII–XI, Gesamtausgabe* 95, p. 80. Stating the same point more poignantly, Heidegger writes a few years later: "The campaign against 'urbanization [*Verstädterung*]' is nonsensical when the country has become 'more urban' than the town" (*Überlegungen XII–XV, Gesamtausgabe* 96, p. 220).

90. *Überlegungen II–VI, Gesamtausgabe* 94, p. 316.

91. "How few know the magnitude which the destruction of the earth has reached and what kind of confusion lurks behind the apparently safely planned achievements of 'technology'" (*Überlegungen II–VI, Gesamtausgabe* 94, p. 340).

92. *Überlegungen II–VI, Gesamtausgabe* 94, p. 364.

93. "Bureaucracy unleashed is the essential consequence and at the same time the stimulus of technology" (*Überlegungen II–VI, Gesamtausgabe* 94, p. 477).

94. "All science staunchly marches into the domain where it belongs: technology." And Heidegger adds: "For the first time and unprecedented within Western history, philosophy stands in the strictest opposition to 'science,' to which all 'worldviews' also belong" (*Überlegungen II–VI, Gesamtausgabe* 94, p. 457).

95. See *Nietzsche II, Gesamtausgabe* 6.1, ed. Brigitte Schillbach (Frankfurt: Klostermann, 1997), 445.

96. "Politics is the genuine enactment [*Vollstreckerin*] of the machination of being" (*Überlegungen XII–XV, Gesamtausgabe* 96, p. 43).

97. *Überlegungen XII–XV, Gesamtausgabe* 96, p. 7.

98. In a typical note, Heidegger would write: "What is happening? The destruction of the earth—nations [*Völker*] mutually lying in wait for each other and businesses wheeling and dealing without meaning and goal" (*Überlegungen II–VI, Gesamtausgabe* 94, p. 316). All this falls under machination as well.

99. *Überlegungen II–VI, Gesamtausgabe* 94, p. 426.

100. *Überlegungen II–VI, Gesamtausgabe* 94, p. 471.

101. *Überlegungen II–VI, Gesamtausgabe* 94, p. 459.

102. This suppression of thought has political implications as well. In fact, in a brief sketch of stupidity in Germany, Heidegger himself draws out the more political dimension in the diagnosis of "the age of unquestionableness." Heidegger writes: "What is stupidity? That condition of a community [*Gemeinschaft*] when individuals [first] talk each other into believing that giving up all attempts at reflection [*Verzicht auf jeden Anlauf zur Besinnung*] is the benefit of an unerring instinct whereby they are spared all burden and danger of the questionable, and [second] confirm each other's achievements and unheard-of accomplishments, and [third]

proclaim the feat of leveling down all essential knowledge as the progress of 'culture.' An individual can never be stupid in this sense" (*Überlegungen VII–XI, Gesamtausgabe* 95, p. 195). Clearly, Heidegger did not entertain any faith in some fiction of a "folk-based" community when the reality showed the meticulously planned production of opinions through Nazi propaganda and its subsequent internalization. On the matter of propaganda, Heidegger sarcastically makes fun of the bombastic reports about Nazi events that regularly elicited nothing other than "thunderous applause" or even "*Jubelorkane* [literally, storm of jubilation or applause]." Heidegger notes: "'Jubelorkane' sind heute noch das schwächste, was an Beifall aufgebracht werden kann ['Hurricane-like' applause is the weakest applause that can be given today]" (*Überlegungen II–VI, Gesamtausgabe* 94, p. 194).

103. *Überlegungen VII–XI, Gesamtausgabe* 95, p. 394.

104. *Überlegungen XII–XV, Gesamtausgabe* 96, pp. 16–17.

105. *Überlegungen XII–XV, Gesamtausgabe* 96, p. 209.

106. *Überlegungen XII–XV, Gesamtausgabe* 96, p. 209.

107. *Überlegungen VII–XI, Gesamtausgabe* 95, p. 396.

108. *Überlegungen XII–XV, Gesamtausgabe* 96, p. 48.

109. *Überlegungen VII–XI, Gesamtausgabe* 95, p. 5.

110. Martin Heidegger, *The Concept of Time*, trans. Ingo Farin (New York: Continuum, 2011), 8.

111. *Überlegungen XII–XV, Gesamtausgabe* 96, p. 266.

112. The German word for "crime" is *Verbrechen*, which literally refers to an act of breaking off or breaking apart: *brechen*.

113. *Überlegungen XII–XV, Gesamtausgabe* 96, p. 266.

114. *Die Geschichte des Seyns, Gesamtausgabe* 69, p. 78.

115. *Die Geschichte des Seyns, Gesamtausgabe* 69, p. 87.

116. *Überlegungen VII–XI, Gesamtausgabe* 95, p. 56.

117. *Überlegungen II–VI, Gesamtausgabe* 94, p. 56. *Alleingänger* can also be translated as "outsider." Since "aloneness" or *Allein-heit* is a defining feature of the philosopher alone in pursuit of thinking being alone, Heidegger also speaks of the "*Allein-heit des Denkens*," which lends itself to a certain Gnostic reading, because the "alone-ness [*Allein-heit*]" of thinking is just one syllable apart from the "all-oneness [*All-einheit*]" in thinking (*Überlegungen II–VI, Gesamtausgabe* 94, p. 20).

118. *Überlegungen II–VI, Gesamtausgabe* 94, p. 28.

119. *Beiträge, Gesamtausgabe* 65, p. 15.

120. *Überlegungen II–VI, Gesamtausgabe* 94, p. 98.

121. *Überlegungen II–VI, Gesamtausgabe* 94, p. 210.

122. "Das Sein aber ist das, was die Philosophie denkt [What philosophy thinks is what being is]" (*Die Geschichte des Seyns, Gesamtausgabe* 69, p. 6).

123. What other reasons would there be?

124. *Überlegungen VII–XI, Gesamtausgabe* 95, pp. 408–409.

125. See also *Einführung in die Metaphysik, Gesamtausgabe* 40, p. 208.

126. The very same account emerges as early as Heidegger's 1935 lecture course *Introduction to Metaphysics*, where he dismissively writes about the "the works of philosophy of National Socialism peddled about nowadays," only in order to add that they have nothing to do with "the inner truth and greatness of this movement (i.e., the encounter of the man of modernity with planetary technology)" (*Einführung in die Metaphysik, Gesamtausgabe* 40, p. 208).

127. *Hannah Arendt/Martin Heidegger: Briefe 1925 bis 1975 und andere Zeugnisse*, ed. Ursula Ludz (Frankfurt: Klostermann, 2002), 69.

128. Jewish emancipation and the high value put on learning within the Jewish tradition, coupled with the Christian neglect of education, meant that more Jewish students did very well at secondary schools and university in Germany toward the end of the nineteenth century. The historian Götz Aly holds that "in 1886–87, Jews accounted for 10 percent of Prussia's university students, although by then Jews made up only 1 percent of the total population" (Götz Aly, *Why the Germans? Why the Jews? Envy, Race Hatred, and the Prehistory of the*

Holocaust, trans. Jefferson Chase [New York: Metropolitan Books, 2014], 24). According to Götz, Jewish success translated into economic success as well: "Freed from external and internal constraint, the Jews of Western and Central Europe gladly embarked on the journey into modernity. Thanks to their qualitative and quantitative educational head start, more and more Jews turned toward well-paying forms of intellectual labor or seized the entrepreneurial initiative. By 1895, half of all working Jews were self-employed, twice the percentage of their Christian peers" (Aly, *Why the Germans? Why the Jews?*, 30). As the beneficiaries of modernization and democracy, Jews became the objects of envy and hatred by those left behind. "In the nineteenth century, the Christian majority may still have used the word *Jewish* pejoratively, but its connotation was different from what it had been before. Now it stood for quickness and eagerness of change. The accusation implicit in this usage reflected the unease with which Christians reacted to the dissolution of their comfortably familiar world order. Retreating into smug provincialism, Germans began to accuse Jews of rootless cosmopolitanism and the desire to destroy venerable tradition" (Aly, *Why the Germans? Why the Jews?*, 32). Heidegger's anti-Semitism must be discussed within this broader cultural anti-Semitic climate in Germany.

129. *The Heidegger–Jaspers Correspondence (1920–1963)*, ed. Walter Biemel and Hans Saner, trans. Gary E. Aylesworth (New York: Humanity Books, 2003), 281.

130. In fact, the extensive quotes I give in this section represent the bulk of Heidegger's anti-Semitic comments, and readers can judge for themselves whether any of this amounts to a systematic or ontohistorically justified anti-Semitism.

131. *Überlegungen VII–XI, Gesamtausgabe* 95, p. 96.

132. *Überlegungen II–VI, Gesamtausgabe* 94, p. 143.

133. "All race doctrines belong to the modern age, having their trajectory in the conception of man as subject" (*Überlegungen XII–XV, Gesamtausgabe* 96, p. 48).

134. *Überlegungen XII–XV, Gesamtausgabe* 96, p. 56.

135. *Überlegungen VII–XI, Gesamtausgabe* 95, p. 97.

136. *Überlegungen XII–XV, Gesamtausgabe* 96, p. 46.

137. *Überlegungen XII–XV, Gesamtausgabe* 96, p. 47.

138. In fact, on one occasion Heidegger writes: "Descartes's rationalism is neither 'French' nor Western [*westlich*]—but rather of the Western World [*abendländisch*], and, if one wants to know, the French consists in having brought into play the capacity for making this interpretation of being knowable [*wissbar*]. The knowable itself [*das Wissbare selbst*] is neither French, nor German, nor Italian, nor English, nor American—but instead the very ground of these nations!" (*Überlegungen VII–XI, Gesamtausgabe* 95, p. 173).

139. *Überlegungen XII–XV, Gesamtausgabe* 96, p. 262.

140. Martin Heidegger, *Sein und Zeit, Gesamtausgabe* 2, ed. Friedrich-Wilhelm von Herrmann (Frankfurt: Klostermann, 1977), 169.

141. Klemens von Klemperer, "Martin Heidegger's Life and Times: A Historian's View, Or: Heidegger and the Hubris of Philosophical Policy," in *Martin Heidegger: Politics, Art, and Technology*, ed. Karsten Harries and Christoph Jamme (New York: Holmes & Meier, 1994), 1–17 (quote on 14).

142. Klemperer, "Martin Heidegger's Life and Times," 14.

143. Heidegger, *Anmerkungen I–V (1942–1948), Gesamtausgabe* 97, p. 198. The German sentence reads: "*Irre*: Zwar das Wesen des 'man' denken und es doch him rechten Augenblick weder sehen noch verstehen."

144. Trawny, *Heidegger und der Mythos der jüdischen Weltverschwörung*, 11.

145. Trawny, *Heidegger und der Mythos der jüdischen Weltverschwörung*, 31.

146. Trawny, *Heidegger und der Mythos der jüdischen Weltverschwörung*, 31.

147. Trawny, *Heidegger und der Mythos der jüdischen Weltverschwörung*, 37.

148. Hume could still confidently write that philosophy was the only sure antidote to superstition and prejudice: "One considerable advantage, that rises from philosophy, consists in the sovereign antidote, which it affords to superstition and false religion. All other remedies against that pestilent distemper are vain, or, at least, uncertain" (David Hume, *Essays: Moral, Political, and Literary*, ed. Eugene F. Miller [Indianapolis: Liberty Fund, 1994], 577). But it seems to me that if philosophy is to become "critical" and also mindful of its inherent finitude, we cannot simply uphold Hume's lofty self-assessment of philosophy. Many commentators of Heidegger seem to presuppose that philosophy is the safe haven from prejudice. But a simple look at the history

of philosophy teaches us differently.

149. Heidegger, *Anmerkungen I–V, Gesamtausgabe* 97, p. 20.

150. Heidegger, *Anmerkungen I–V, Gesamtausgabe* 97, p. 20.

151. Already Hegel realized that the Enlightenment culminated in the dictum that "everything is useful" (Georg Wilhelm Friedrich Hegel, *Phänomenologie des Geistes* [Hamburg: Meiner, 1952], 399).

152. *Überlegungen XI–XV, Gesamtausgabe* 96, p. 266.

153. Martin Heidegger, *Reden und andere Zeugnisse eines Lebensweges, Gesamtausgabe* 16, ed. Hermann Heidegger (Frankfurt: Klostermann, 2000), 711–712.

154. *Reden und andere Zeugnisse*, 711. See also Martin Heidegger, *"Brief über den 'Humanismus,'"* in *Wegmarken, Gesamtausgabe* 9, ed. Friedrich-Wilhelm von Herrmann (Frankfurt: Klostermann, 2004), 339.

155. Heidegger, *Anmerkungen I–V (1942–1948), Gesamtausgabe* 97, p. 8.

156. *Überlegungen XI–XV, Gesamtausgabe* 96, p. 265.

157. *Überlegungen XI–XV, Gesamtausgabe* 96, p. 265.

158. *Überlegungen XI–XV, Gesamtausgabe* 96, p. 265.

159. *Überlegungen XI–XV, Gesamtausgabe* 96, p. 225.

160. Hölderlin, *Hyperion, Sämtliche Werke 3, Grosse Stuttgarter Ausgabe* (Stuttgart: W. Kohlhammer Verlag, 1957), 12, 154.

161. *Überlegungen XI–XV, Gesamtausgabe* 96, p. 238. Immediately following these lines, Heidegger writes that this would obviously entail that contemporary humankind would then "disappear." He rounds this thought out by adding: "Which is no misfortune [*Unglück*], but the first purification of being [*des Seins*] from its profoundest disfigurement through the primacy of entities [*Vormacht des Seienden*]" (*Überlegungen XI–XV, Gesamtausgabe* 96, p. 238). In fact, in April 1945 Heidegger writes down a remarkably similar reflection that addresses the speculative question whether "nature" defends "itself" by allowing its own self-objectification and the subsequent rise of technology, which in turn would lead to the "annihilation of man [*Vernichtung des Menschenwesens*]." By way of clarification Heidegger writes that this "annihilation [*Vernichtung*]" does not mean the "elimination [*Beseitigung*]" of man, but rather the "completion" of man's essence as a willing agent (*Feldweg-Gespräche, Gesamtausgabe* 77, ed. Ingrid Schüssler [Frankfurt: Klostermann, 2007], 157). That is, Heidegger's idea of the "disappearance" or "annihilation" of man is best taken as a metaphor for the transformation whereby man (defined as rational animal) "disappears" and makes room for a new form of humankind. In any case, I think that the entire context of the quote in the body of my text above makes it abundantly clear that Heidegger considers the possible military-technological self-destruction of the earth the catastrophic end station of a long errancy, which he does *not* welcome. Moreover, this passage has no anti-Semitic overtones whatsoever. While one can be anti-Semitic and misanthropic at the same time, not every misanthrope is an anti-Semite.

162. Martin Heidegger, *"Wozu Dichter,"* in *Holzwege, Gesamtausgabe* 5, ed. Friedrich-Wilhelm von Herrmann (Frankfurt: Klostermann, [1950] 2003), 269.

163. *Feldweg-Gespräche, Gesamtausgabe* 77, p. 241.

164. Martin Heidegger, *Die Grundprobleme der Phänomenologie, Gesamtausgabe* 24, ed. Friedrich-Wilhelm von Herrmann (Frankfurt: Klostermann, 1997), 30.

165. Heidegger, *Anmerkungen I–V (1942–1948), Gesamtausgabe* 97, pp. 377, 379.

166. Heidegger, *Anmerkungen I–V (1942–1948), Gesamtausgabe* 97, pp. 222–223.

167. Heidegger, *Anmerkungen I–V (1942–1948), Gesamtausgabe* 97, p. 382.

168. See the pioneering work of Jeff Malpas, *Heidegger's Topology: Being, Place, World* (Cambridge, MA: MIT Press, 2006).

Bibliography

A. Works by Heidegger

"The Age of the World Picture." In *The Question Concerning Technology and Other Essays*, trans. William Lovitt, 115–154. New York: Harper & Row, 1977.

Anmerkungen I–V (Schwarze Hefte 1942–1948). *Gesamtausgabe* 97. Ed. Peter Trawny. Frankfurt: Klostermann, 2015.

"Aufzeichnungen zur Temporalität: Aus den Jahren 1925 bis 1927." *Heidegger Studies* 14 (1998): 11–23.

Aus der Erfahrung des Denkens. *Gesamtausgabe* 13. Ed. Hermann Heidegger. Frankfurt: Klostermann, 1983.

Basic Writings. Ed. David Farrell Krell. New York: HarperCollins, 1993.

The Beginning of Western Philosophy: Interpretation of Anaximander and Parmenides. Trans. Richard Rojewicz. Bloomington: Indiana University Press, 2015.

Beiträge zur Philosophie (Vom Ereignis). *Gesamtausgabe* 65. Ed. Friedrich-Wilhelm von Herrmann. Frankfurt: Klostermann, 1989; 3rd ed., 2003. Translated by Richard Rojcewicz and Daniela Vallega-Neu as *Contributions to Philosophy (of the Event)* (Bloomington: Indiana University Press, 2012); translated by Parvis Emad and Kenneth Maly as *Contributions to Philosophy (From Enowning)* (Bloomington: Indiana University Press, 1999).

Besinnung. *Gesamtausgabe* 66. Ed. Friedrich-Wilhelm von Herrmann. Frankfurt: Klostermann, 1997. Translated by Parvis Emad and Thomas Kalary as *Mindfulness* (London: Continuum, 2006).

Bremer und Freiburger Vorträge. *Gesamtausgabe* 79. Ed. Petra Jaeger. Frankfurt: Klostermann, 2005. Translated by Andrew J. Mitchell as *Bremen and Freiburg Lectures: Insight into That Which Is and Basic Principles of Thinking* (Bloomington: Indiana University Press, 2012).

The Concept of Time. Trans. Ingo Farin. New York: Continuum, 2011.

Das Ereignis. *Gesamtausgabe* 71. Ed. Friedrich-Wilhelm von Herrmann. Frankfurt: Klostermann, 2009. Translated by Richard Rojcewicz as *The Event* (Bloomington: Indiana University Press, 2012).

"Der Begriff der Zeit (Vortrag 1924)." In Martin Heidegger, *Der Begriff der Zeit*, *Gesamtausgabe* 64, ed. Friedrich-Wilhelm von Herrmann, 105–125. Frankfurt: Klostermann, 2004.

Der Satz vom Grund. *Gesamtausgabe* 10. Ed. Petra Jaeger. Frankfurt: Klostermann, 1997.

"Die Frage nach der Technik." In *Vorträge und Aufsätze, Gesamtausgabe* 7, pp. 7–36. Ed. Friedrich-Wilhelm von Herrmann. Frankfurt: Klostermann, 2000.

Die Geschichte des Seyns. *Gesamtausgabe* 69. Ed. Peter Trawny. Frankfurt: Klostermann, 1998.

Die Grundbegriffe der Metaphysik: Welt-Endlichkeit-Einsamkeit. *Gesamtausgabe* 29/30. Ed. Friedrich-Wilhelm von Herrmann. Frankfurt: Klostermann, 1992.

Die Grundprobleme der Phänomenologie. *Gesamtausgabe* 24. Ed. Friedrich-Wilhelm von Herrmann. Frankfurt: Klostermann, 1997.

"Die Selbstbehauptung der deutschen Universität: Rede, gehalten bei der feierlichen Übernahme des Rektorats der Universität Freiburg i. Br. am 27.5.1933." In *Das Rektorat 1933/34: Tatsachen und Gedanken*. Frankfurt: Klostermann, 1983. Translated by Karsten Harries as "The Self-Assertion of the German University: Address, Delivered on the Solemn Assumption of the Rectorate of the University of Freiburg. The Rectorate 1933/34: Facts and Thoughts," *Review of Metaphysics* 38 (March 1985): 467–502.

Die Stege des Anfangs (1944). *Gesamtausgabe* 72. Ed. Friedrich-Wilhelm von Herrmann. Frankfurt: Klostermann, forthcoming.

Einführung in die Metaphysik. *Gesamtausgabe* 40. Ed. Petra Jaeger. Frankfurt: Klostermann, 1983. Translated by Ralph Manheim as *An Introduction to Metaphysics* (New Haven, CT: Yale University Press, 1959); translated by Gregory Fried and Richard Polt as *Introduction to Metaphysics* (New Haven, CT: Yale University Press, 2000; 2nd ed., 2014).

Einleitung in die Philosophie. *Gesamtausgabe* 27. Ed. Otto Saame and Ina Saame Speidel. Frankfurt: Klostermann, 2001.

Erläuterungen zu Hölderlins Dichtung (1936–68). *Gesamtausgabe* 4. Ed. Friedrich-Wilhelm von Herrmann. Frankfurt: Klostermann, 1996. Translated by Keith Hoeller as *Elucidations of Hölderlin's Poetry* (Amherst, NY: Humanity Books, 2000).

The Essence of Truth: On Plato's Cave Allegory and Theaetetus. Trans. Ted Sadler. New York: Continuum, 2002.

Feldweg-Gespräche (1944–1945). *Gesamtausgabe* 77. Ed. Ingrid Schüssler. Frankfurt: Klostermann, 2007. Translated by Bret W. Davis as *Country Path Conversations* (Bloomington: Indiana University Press, 2010).

Grundfragen der Philosophie: Ausgewählte "Probleme" der "Logik." Gesamtausgabe 45. Ed. Friedrich-Wilhelm von Herrmann. Frankfurt: Klostermann, (1984) 1992. Translated by Richard Rojcewicz and André Schuwer as *Basic Questions of Philosophy: Selected "Problems" of "Logic"* (Bloomington: Indiana University Press, 1994).

Hannah Arendt/Martin Heidegger: Briefe 1925 bis 1975 und andere Zeugnisse. Ed. Ursula Ludz. Frankfurt: Klostermann, 2002.

Heidegger Lesebuch. Ed. Günter Figal. Frankfurt: Klostermann, 2007.

Heraklit. Gesamtausgabe 55. Ed. Manfred S. Frings. Frankfurt: Klostermann, 1994.

Hölderlins Hymne "Andenken." Gesamtausgabe 52. Ed. Curd Ochwadt. Frankfurt: Klostermann, 1992. Translated by William McNeill and Julia Ireland as *Hölderlin's Hymn "Andenken"* (Bloomington: Indiana University Press, forthcoming).

Hölderlins Hymne "Der Ister." Gesamtausgabe 53. Ed. Walter Biemel. Frankfurt: Klostermann, 1993. Translated by William McNeill and JuliaIreland as *Hölderlin's Hymn "The Ister"* (Bloomington: Indiana University Press, 1996).

Hölderlins Hymnen "Germanien" und "Der Rhein." Gesamtausgabe 39. Ed. Susanne Ziegler. Frankfurt: Klostermann, (1980) 1989. Translated by William McNeill and Julia Ireland as *Hölderlin's Hymns "Germania" and "The Rhine"* (Bloomington: Indiana University Press, 2014).

Holzwege. Gesamtausgabe 5. Ed. Friedrich-Wilhelm von Herrmann. Frankfurt: Klostermann, (1950) 2003.

Identität und Differenz. Gesamtausgabe 10, 2nd. ed. Ed. Friedrich-Wilhelm von Herrmann. Frankfurt: Klostermann, 2006.

Letter to Baumgarten, October 2, 1929. In Ulrich Sieg, "Die Verjudung des deutschen Geistes," *Die Zeit*, December 22, 1989. http://www.zeit.de/1989/52/die-verjudung-des-deutschen-geistes.

Martin Heidegger/Bernhard Welte: Briefe und Begegnungen. Ed. Alfred Denker and Holger Zaborowski. Stuttgart: Klett-Cotta, 2003.

Martin Heidegger/Karl Jaspers: Briefwechsel 1920–1963. Ed. Walter Biemel and Hans Saner. Frankfurt: Klostermann/Munich: Piper, 1990. Translated by Gary E. Aylesworth as *The Heidegger–Jaspers Correspondence (1920–1963)*, ed. Walter Biemel and Hans Saner (New York: Humanity Books, 2003).

"Mein liebes Seelchen!" Briefe Martin Heideggers an seine Frau Elfriede 1915–1970. Ed. Gertrud Heidegger. Munich: Deutsche Verlags-Anstalt, 2005.

Metaphysik und Nihilismus. Gesamtausgabe 67. Ed. Hans-Joachim Friedrich. Frankfurt: Klostermann, 1999.

Metaphysik, Wissenschaft, Technik. Gesamtausgabe 76. Ed. Claudius Strube. Frankfurt: Klostermann, 2009.

Metaphysische Anfangsgründe der Logik im Ausgang von Leibniz. Gesamtausgabe 26. Ed. Klaus Held. Frankfurt: Klostermann, 1990.

Nature, History, State: 1933–1934. Ed. and trans. Gregory Fried and Richard Polt. London: Bloomsbury, 2013.

Nietzsche I. Gesamtausgabe 6.1. Ed. Brigitta Schillbach. Frankfurt: Klostermann, 1996.

Nietzsche II. Gesamtausgabe 6.2. Ed. Brigitte Schillbach. Frankfurt: Klostermann, 1997.

Nietzsche: Der europäische Nihilismus. Gesamtausgabe 48. Ed. P. Jaeger. Frankfurt: Klostermann, (1961) 1986.

Nietzsche: Der Wille zur Macht als Kunst. Gesamtausgabe 43. Ed. B. Heimbüchel. Frankfurt: Klostermann, 1985.

Nietzsches Lehre vom Willen zur Macht als Erkenntnis. Gesamtausgabe 47. Ed. E. Hanser. Frankfurt: Klostermann, 1989.

"Nur noch ein Gott kann uns retten." *Der Spiegel*, September 23, 1966. Reprinted in *Reden und andere Zeugnisse eines Lebensweges, Gesamtausgabe* 16, pp. 652–683. Translated by Maria P. Alter and John D. Caputo as "'Only a God Can Save Us': *Der Spiegel*'s Interview with Martin Heidegger," in *The Heidegger Controversy: A Critical Reader*, ed. Richard Wolin (Cambridge, MA: MIT Press, 1993).

On the Way to Language. Trans. Peter D. Hertz. New York: Harper & Row, 1971.

On Time and Being. Trans. Joan Stambaugh. New York: Harper & Row, 1972.

"The Origin of the Work of Art." In *Poetry, Language, Thought.* Trans. Albert Hofstadter. New York: Harper & Row, 1971.

Pathmarks. Trans. William McNeill. Cambridge: Cambridge University Press, 1998.

Phänomenologische Interpretationen zu Aristoteles: Ausarbeitung für die Marburger und die Göttinger Philosophische Fakultät (1922). Ed. Günther Neumann. Stuttgart: Reclam, 2002.

The Phenomenology of Religious Life. Trans. Matthias Fritsch and Jennifer Anna Gosetti-Ferencei. Bloomington: Indiana University Press, 2004.

Poetry, Language, Thought. Trans. Albert Hofstadter. New York: Harper & Row, 1971.

"The Question Concerning Technology." In Martin Heidegger, *Basic Writings*, 311–341. Ed. David Farrell Krell. London: Routledge, 1933.

The Question Concerning Technology and Other Essays. Trans. William Lovitt. New York: Harper & Row, 1977.

"The Rectorate 1933/34: Facts and Thoughts." In *Martin Heidegger and National Socialism: Questions and Answers*, ed. Gunther Neske and Emil Kettering, trans. Lisa Harries, 15–32. New York: Paragon House, 1990.

Reden und andere Zeugnisse eines Lebensweges. Gesamtausgabe 16. Ed. Hermann Heidegger. Frankfurt: Klostermann, 2000.

Schelling: Vom Wesen der menschlichen Freiheit (1809). Gesamtausgabe 42. Ed. Ingrid Schüßler. Frankfurt: Klostermann, 1988. Translated by Joan Stambaugh as *Schelling's Treatise on the Essence of Human Freedom (1936)* (Athens: Ohio University Press, 1985).

Sein und Wahrheit. Gesamtausgabe 36/37. Ed. Hartmut Tietjen. Frankfurt: Klostermann, 2001. Translated by Gregory Fried and Richard Polt as *Being and Truth* (Bloomington: Indiana University Press, 2010).

Sein und Zeit. Tübingen: Max Niemeyer, 1953. Reprinted as *Gesamtausgabe* 2, ed. Friedrich-Wilhelm von Herrmann (Frankfurt: Klostermann, 1977). Translated by John Maquarrie and Edward Robinson as *Being and Time* (New York: Harper & Row, 1962).

"The Self-Assertion of the German University." In *Martin Heidegger and National Socialism: Questions and Answers*, ed. Gunther Neske and Emil Kettering, trans. Lisa Harries, 5–13. New York: Paragon House, 1990.

Seminare. Gesamtausgabe 15. Ed. Curd Ochwadt. Frankfurt: Klostermann, (1977) 2005.

Seminare: Hegel—Schelling. Gesamtasgabe 86. Ed. Peter Trawny. Frankfurt: Klostermann, 2011.

Über den Anfang. Gesamtausgabe 70. Ed. Paola-Ludovika Coriando. Frankfurt: Klostermann, 2005.

Überlegungen II–VI (Schwarze Hefte 1931–1938). Gesamtausgabe 94. Ed. Peter Trawny. Frankfurt: Klostermann, 2014.

Überlegungen VII–XI (Schwarze Hefte 1938/39). Gesamtausgabe 95. Ed. Peter Trawny. Frankfurt: Klostermann, 2014.

Überlegungen XII–XV (Schwarze Hefte 1939–1941). Gesamtausgabe 96. Ed. Peter Trawny. Frankfurt: Klostermann, 2014.

"Über Wesen und Begriff von Natur, Geschichte und Staat." In *Heidegger und der Nationalsozialismus, Heidegger-Jahrbuch* 4 (2009): 74.

"Vom Ursprung des Kunstwerks (Erste Ausarbeitung)." *Heidegger Studies* 5 (1989): 5–22.

Vom Wesen der menschlichen Freiheit: Einleitung in die Philosophie. Gesamtausgabe 31. Ed. Hartmut Tietjen. Frankfurt: Klostermann, 1982.

Vom Wesen der Sprache. Gesamtausgabe 12. Ed. Friedrich-Wilhelm von Herrmann. Frankfurt: Klostermann, (1959) 1985.

Vorträge und Aufsätze. Gesamtausgabe 7. Ed. Friedrich-Wilhelm von Herrmann. Frankfurt: Klostermann, (1954) 2000.

Was heißt Denken? Gesamtausgabe 8. Ed. Paola-Ludovika Coriando. Frankfurt: Klostermann, (1954) 2002. Translated by J. Glenn Gray as *What Is Called Thinking?* (New York: Harper & Row, 1976).

Wegmarken. Gesamtausgabe 9. Ed. Friedrich-Wilhelm von Herrmann. Frankfurt: Klostermann, (1967) 1976.

Zu Hölderlin/Griechenlandreisen. Gesamtausgabe 75. Ed. Curd Ochwadt. Frankfurt: Klostermann, 2000.

B.   Secondary Works

Adorno, T. W. *Zur Lehre von der Geschichte und der Freiheit.* Frankfurt: Suhrkamp, 2001.

Akehurst, Thomas. "Bertrand Russell Stalks the Nazis." *Philosophy Now* 97 (2013): 20–22.

Alberti, Leon Battista. *On Painting.* Trans. John R. Spencer. New Haven, CT: Yale University Press, 1966.

Altmann, Alexander. "'Homo Imago Dei' in Jewish and Christian Theology." *Journal of Religion* 48 (1968): 235–259.

Altmann, Alexander. *The Meaning of Jewish Existence: Theological Essays, 1930–1939.* Ed. Alfred L. Ivry, introduction by Paul Mendes-Flohr, trans. Edith Ehrlich and Leonard H. Ehrlich. Boston: Brandeis University Press, 1991.

Aly, Götz. *Hitlers Volksstaat: Raub, Rassenkrieg und nationaler Sozialismus.* Frankfurt: Fischer, 2005.

Aly, Götz. *Why the Germans? Why the Jews? Envy, Race Hatred, and the Prehistory of the Holocaust.* Trans. Jefferson Chase. New York: Metropolitan Books, 2014.

Anders, Günther. *Über Heidegger.* Ed. Gerhard Oberschlick. Munich: Beck, 2001.

Aran, Gideon. "From Religious Zionism to Zionist Religion: The Roots of Gush Emunim." *Studies in Contemporary Jewry* 2 (1986): 116–143.

Aran, Gideon. *Kookism: The Roots of Gush Emunim, Jewish Settler's Sub-Culture, Zionist Theology, Contemporary Messianism* [in Hebrew]. Jerusalem: Carmel, 2013.

Arendt, Hannah. "A Daughter of Our People: A Response to Gershom Scholem." In Hannah Arendt, *The Portable Hannah Arendt*, 392. New York: Penguin, 2000.

Arendt, Hannah. "The Enlightenment and the Jewish Question." In *The Jewish Writings*, ed. Jerome Kohn and Ron H. Feldman, 3–18. New York: Schocken Books, 2007.

Arendt, Hannah. *The Human Condition.* 2nd ed. Chicago: University of Chicago Press, (1958) 1998.

Arendt, Hannah. "Interview mit Günter Gauss." In Hannah Arendt, *Von der Wahrheit und Politik: Originalaufnahmen aus den 50er und 60er Jahren. 5 CDs.* Munich: Der Hörverlag GmbH, (1999) 2006.

Arendt, Hannah. *The Jewish Writings.* New York: Scribner, 2007.

Arendt, Hannah. "Martin Heidegger at Eighty." Trans. Albert Hofstadter. *New York Review of Books,* October 21, 1971. http://www.nybooks.com/articles/archives/1971/oct/21/martin-heidegger-at-eighty/.

Arendt, Hannah. "Organized Guilt and Universal Responsibility." In *Essays in Understanding, 1930–1954,* ed. Jerome Kohn, 121–132. New York: Harcourt, Brace, (1945) 1994.

Arendt, Hannah. *Zwischen Vergangenheit und Zukunft: Übungen im politischen Denken I.* Ed. Ursula Ludz.

Munich: Piper, 1994.

Aschheim, Steven. "'The Jew Within': The Myth of Judaization in Germany." In *The Jewish Response to German Culture*, ed. Jehuda Reinharz and Walter Schatzberg, 212–224. Boston: University Press of New England, 1985.

Aschheim, Steven. *The Nietzsche Legacy in Germany, 1890–1990*. Berkeley: University of California Press, 1994.

Augstein, Rudolf, , eds. *"Historikerstreit": Die Dokumentation der Kontroverse um die Einzigartigkeit der nationalsozialistischen Judenvernichtung*. Munich: Piper, 1987.

Aurelius, Marcus. *Meditations*. Trans. C. R. Haines. Cambridge, MA: Harvard University Press/Loeb, 1916.

Avivi, Yosef. "Historia zorekh gavoha [History, a supernal desire] [in Hebrew]." In *Festschrift for Rabbi Mordechai Breuer*, ed. M. Bar-Asher, 709–771. Jerusalem: Akademon, 1992.

Babich, Babette. "Adorno's Radio Phenomenology: Technical Reproduction, Physiognomy, and Music." *Philosophy and Social Criticism* 40 (2014): 957–996.

Babich, Babette. "'The Answer Is False': Archaeologies of Genocide." In *Adorno and the Concept of Genocide*, ed. Ryan Crawford and Erik M. Vogt. Amsterdam: Brill/Rodopi,forthcoming.

Babich, Babette. "Constellating Technology: Heidegger's *Die Gefahr* / The Danger." In *The Multidimensionality of Hermeneutic Phenomenology*, ed. Babette Babich and Dimitri Ginev, 153–182. Frankfurt: Springer, 2014.

Babich, Babette. "Dichtung, Eros, und Denken in Nietzsche und Heidegger: Heideggers Nietzsche Interpretation aus der Sicht der Nietzsche-Forschung." In *Heidegger und Nietzsche, Heidegger-Jahrbuch 2*, ed. Alfred Denker, Marion Heinz, John Sallis, Ben Vedder, and Holger Zaborowski, 239–264. Freiburg: Karl Alber, 2005.

Babich, Babette. "The Genealogy of Morals and Right Reading: On the Nietzschean Aphorism and the Art of the Polemic." In *Nietzsche's On the Genealogy of Morals*, ed. Christa Davis Acampora, 171–190. Lanham, MD: Rowman & Littlefield, 2006.

Babich, Babette. *The Hallelujah Effect: Philosophical Reflections on Music, Performance Practice and Technology*. Surrey: Ashgate, 2013.

Babich, Babette. "Heidegger against the Editors: Nietzsche, Science, and the *Beiträge* as *Will to Power*." *Philosophy Today* 47 (2003): 327–359.

Babich, Babette. "Heidegger et ses 'Juifs.'" In *Heidegger et les "Juifs."* Ed. Joseph Cohen and Raphael Zagury-Orly. Paris: Grassett, 2015.

Babich, Babette. "Heideggers 'Beiträge' zwischen politischer Kritik und der Frage nach der Technik." Trans. Harald Seubert. In *Eugenik und die Zukunft*, ed. Stefan Sorgner, H. James Birx, and Nikolaus Knoepffler, 43–69. Freiburg: Karl Alber, 2006.

Babich, Babette. "Heideggers *Wille zur Macht*: Nietzsche—Technik—Machenschaft." Trans. Harald Seubert. In *Heidegger und Nietzsche*, ed. Babette Babich, Alfred Denker, and Holger Zaborowski, trans. Heidi Byrnes, Harald Seubert, and Holger Schmid, 283–321. Amsterdam: Rodopi, 2012.

Babich, Babette. "Heidegger's Will to Power." Special issue on Nietzsche, *Journal of the British Society for Phenomenology* 38 (2007): 37–60.

Babich, Babette. "Le sort du *Nachlass*: Le problème de l'œuvre posthume." In *Mélivres/Misbooks: Études sur l'envers et les travers du livre*, ed. Pascale Hummel, 123–140. Paris: Philogicum, 2009.

Babich, Babette. "A Musical Retrieve of Heidegger, Nietzsche, and Technology: Cadence, Concinnity, and Playing Brass." *Man and World* 26 (1993): 239–260.

Babich, Babette. "Nietzsche and the Ubiquity of Hermeneutics." In *The Routledge Companion to Hermeneutics*, ed. Jeff Malpas and Hans-Helmuth Gander, 85–97. Abingdon: Routledge, 2015.

Babich, Babette. "*O, Superman!* or Being towards Transhumanism: Martin Heidegger, Günther Anders, and Media Aesthetics." *Divinatio* 37 (2013): 83–99.

Babich, Babette, ed. *Proceedings of the 35th Annual Meeting of the North American Heidegger Conference: Heidegger on Science and Technology*. New York, Fordham University, 2001.

Babich, Babette. "Truth Untrembling Heart: Heidegger's *Parmenides* and Translation." In *Being Shaken: Ontology and the Event*, ed. Michael Marder and Santiago Zabala, 154–176. London: Palgrave Macmillan, 2014.

Balfour Declaration. http://www.mfa.gov.il/mfa/foreignpolicy/peace/guide/pages/the%20balfour%20declara

tion.aspx.

Batnizky, Leora. "Revelation, Language, and Commentary." In *The Cambridge Companion to Modern Jewish Philosophy*, ed. Michael L. Morgan and Peter Eli Gordon, 302–303. Cambridge: Cambridge University Press, 2007.

Barnes, Jonathan. "Nietzsche and Diogenes Laertius." *Nietzsche-Studien* 15 (1986): 16–40.

Berkowitz, Michael. *Zionist Culture and West European Jewry before the First World War*. Cambridge: Cambridge University Press, 1993.

Berkowitz, Roger. "Being Human in an Inhuman Age." *HA: The Journal of the Hannah Arendt Center for Politics and the Humanities at Bard College* 2 (2012): 112–121.

Blackburn, Simon. "Enquivering." *New Republic*, October 30, 2000, 43–48.

Bloch, Ernst. *Das Prinzip Hoffnung*. Frankfurt: Suhrkamp, 1976.

Bloch, Ernst. *Erbschaft dieser Zeit*. Frankfurt: Suhrkamp, 1962.

Blüher, Hans. "Die Gegengründung des nachchristlichen Judentums." In Hans Blüher, *Die Erhebung Israels gegen die christlichen Güter*, 87–138. Hamburg: Hanseatischer Verlagsanstalt, 1931.

Bollenbeck, Georg. *Eine Geschichte der Kulturkritik: Von Rousseau bis Günther Anders*. Munich: Beck, 2007.

Bonitz, Hermann. *Index Aristotelicus*. Darmstadt: Wissenschaftliche Buchgesellschaft, (1870) 1960.

Böschenstein, Bernhard. "Frucht des Gewitters." In *Zu Hölderlins Dionysos als Gott der Revolution und Paul Celan: Der Meridian; Endfassung—Entwürfe—Materialien*. Frankfurt: Insel, 1989.

Böschenstein, Bernhard. *Leuchttürme: Von Hölderlin zu Celan, Wirkung und Vergleich*. Frankfurt: Insel, (1977) 1982.

Böschenstein, Bernhard, and Heino Schmull, eds. *Paul Celan: Der Meridian; Endfassung—Entwürfe—Materialien*. Frankfurt: Suhrkamp, 1999.

Bowie, Andrew. *Adorno and the Ends of Philosophy*. Cambridge: Polity, 2013.

Bowman, John. *The Samaritan Problem*. New York: Pickwick Press, 1975.

Brahm, Gabriel. "The Philosophy behind 'BDS': A Review of 'Deconstructing Zionism: A Critique of Political Metaphysics.'" 2014. http://fathomjournal.org/the-philosophy-behind-bds-a-review-of-deconstructing-zionism -a-critique-of-political-metaphysics/.

Braver, Lee. *Groundless Grounds*. Cambridge, MA: MIT Press, 2012.

Bremer, John. "Some Arithmetical Patterns in Plato's 'Republic.'" *Hermathena* 169 (2000): 69–97.

Brenner, Hildegard. *Die Kunstpolitik des Nationalsozialismus*. Reinbek: Rowohlt, 1963.

Brobjer, Thomas H. *Nietzsche's Philosophical Context: An Intellectual Biography*. Champaign: University of Illinois Press, 2008.

Brokoff, Jürgen. *Die Apokalypse in der Weimarer Republik*. Munich: Fink, 2001.

Buckley, R. Philip. *Husserl, Heidegger, and the Crisis of Philosophical Responsibility*. Dordrecht: Kluwer, 1992.

Burke, Kenneth. "The Rhetoric of Hitler's 'Battle.'" In Kenneth Burke, *The Philosophy of Literary Form: Studies in Symbolic Action*. New York: Vintage, 1941. Reprint, Berkeley: University of California Press, 1974, 191–220.

Caputo, John. "People of God, People of Being: The Theological Presuppositions of Heidegger's Path of Thought." In *Appropriating Heidegger*, ed. James E. Falconer and Mark A. Wrathall. Cambridge: Cambridge University Press, 2000.

Carman, Taylor. "Review of Emmanuel Faye, *The Introduction of Nazism into Philosophy in light of the Unpublished Seminars of 1933–1935*." *Times Literary Supplement*, September 10, 2010, 26–28.

Carr, Nicholas. *The Shallows: What the Internet Is Doing to Our Brains*. New York: Norton, 2011.

Cavell, Stanley. *Little Did I Know*. Stanford, CA: Stanford University Press, 2010.

Cavell, Stanley. *Must We Mean What We Say?* New York: Scribner, 1969.

Caygill, Howard. *Levinas and the Political*. London: Routledge, 2002.

Chowers, Eyal. *The Political Philosophy of Zionism: Trading Jewish Words for an Hebraic Land.* Cambridge: Cambridge University Press, 2012.

Crowell, Steven. *Husserl, Heidegger, and the Space of Meaning: Paths toward Transcendental Phenomenology.* Evanston, IL: Northwestern University Press, 2001.

Crowell, Steven. *Normativity and Phenomenology in Husserl and Heidegger.* Cambridge: Cambridge University Press, 2013.

Dallmayr, Fred. *Between Freiburg and Frankfurt: Toward a Critical Ontology.* Amherst: University of Massachusetts Press, 1991.

Dante. *Dante's Inferno.* Trans. John D. Sinclair. New York: Oxford University Press, 1970.

Davidson, Arnold. "Questions Concerning Heidegger: Opening the Debate." *Critical Inquiry* 15 (1989): 407–426.

Davis, Bret. *Heidegger and the Will: On the Way to Gelassenheit.* Evanston, IL: Northwestern University Press, 2007.

Dawber, Alistair. "Israel Gave Birth Control to Ethiopian Jews without Their Consent." *Independent*, January 27, 2013.

Del Caro, Adrian. "The Columbus Poems of Hölderlin and Nietzsche." *Colloquia Germanica* 21 (1988): 144–158.

Deleuze, Gilles. *Nietzsche and Philosophy.* Trans. Hugh Tomlinson. London: Athlone, 1983.

Deleuze, Gilles, and Félix Guattari. *What Is Philosophy?* Trans. Graham Burchell and Hugh Tomlinson. London: Verso, 1994.

Denker, Alfred, Hans-Helmuth Gander, and Holger Zaborowski, eds. *Heidegger und die Anfänge seines Denkens. Heidegger-Jahrbuch* 1. Freiburg: Karl Alber, 2004.

Denker, Alfred, and Holger Zaborowski, eds. *Heidegger und der Nationalsozialismus: Dokumente. Heidegger-Jahrbuch 4.* Munich: Karl Alber, 2009.

Derrida, Jacques. *Glas.* Trans. J. P. Leavey. Lincoln: University of Nebraska Press, 1986.

Derrida, Jacques. "Heideggers Schweigen." In *Antwort: Martin Heidegger im Gespräch*, ed. Günther Neske and Emil Kettering. Pfullingen: Günther Neske, 1988.

Derrida, Jacques. *Of Spirit: Heidegger and the Question.* Trans. G. Bennington and R. Bowlby. Chicago: University of Chicago Press, 1991.

Di Cesare, Donatella. "Heidegger—'Jews Self-Destructed.'" 2009. http://www.corriere.it/english/15_febbraio_09/heidegger-jews-self-destructed-47cd3930-b03b-11e4-8615-d0fd07eabd28.shtml.

Di Cesare, Donatella. "Selbstvernichtung der Juden: Exklusiv-Interview mit Donatella Di Cesare." *Hohe Luft: Philosophie-Zeitschrift*, February 10, 2015.

Diels, Hermann, and Walter Kranz. *Die Fragmente der Vorsokratiker*, 18th ed. Zurich: Weidmann, 1989.

Drabinski, John E. "Elsewhere of Home." In *Between Levinas and Heidegger*, ed. John E. Drabinksi and Eric S. Nelson, 245–260. Albany: SUNY Press, 2014.

Dummett, Michael. *Frege: Philosophy of Language.* New York: Harper & Row, 1973.

Elden, Stuart. "Heidegger's Hölderlin and the Importance of Place." *Journal of the British Society for Phenomenology* 30 (1999): 258–274.

Elden, Stuart. *Mapping the Present: Heidegger, Foucault, and the Project of a Spatial History.* London: Continuum, 2001.

Emerson, Ralph Waldo. *Essays and Lectures.* Ed. Joel Porte. New York: Library of America, 1985.

Evans, Richard J. *The Coming of the Third Reich.* London: Penguin Books, 2004.

Evans, Richard J. *The Third Reich in Power.* London: Penguin Books, 2006.

Fackenheim, Emil L. *Encounters between Judaism and Modern Philosophy: A Preface to Future Jewish Thought.* New York: Basic Books, 1973.

Fagenblat, Michael. "The Thing That Scares Me Most: Heidegger's Anti-Semitism and the Return to Zion." *Journal for Cultural and Religious Theory* 14 (2014): 8–24.

Farías, Victor. *Heidegger et le Nazism*. Trans. Mynain Bernarroch and Jean-Baptiste Grasset. Paris: Verdier, 1987. Published in English as *Heidegger and Nazism*, ed. Joseph Margolis and Tom Rockmore, French materials translated by Paul Burrell with Dominic di Bernardi, German materials translated by Gabriel R. Ricci (Philadelphia: Temple University Press, 1989).

Farin, Ingo. "Heidegger: Transformation of Hermeneutics." In *The Routledge Companion to Hermeneutics*, ed. Jeff Malpas and Hans-Helmuth Gander, 107–126. London: Routledge, 2014.

Faye, Emmanuel. *Heidegger: L'introduction du nazisme dans la philosophie: Autour des séminaires inédits de 1933–1935*. Paris: Albin Michel, 2005. Translated as *Heidegger: The Introduction of Nazism into Philosophy in Light of the Unpublished Seminars of 1933–1935* (New Haven, CT: Yale University Press, 2009).

Feiler, Bruce. "Statisticians 10, Poets 0." *New York Times*, May 15, 2014, Sunday Styles, 1, 8.

Feingold, Henry L. *Bearing Witness: How America and Its Jews Responded to the Holocaust*. Syracuse, NY: Syracuse University Press, 1995.

Field, J. V. *The Invention of Infinity: Mathematics and Art in the Renaissance*. Oxford: Oxford University Press, 1997.

Fischer, Shlomo. "Self-Expression and Democracy in Radical Religious Zionist Ideology." Doctoral dissertation, Hebrew University of Jerusalem, 2007.

Fleischaker, Samuel, ed. *Heidegger's Jewish Followers: Essays on Hannah Arendt, Leo Strauss, Hans Jonas, and Emmanuel Levinas*. Pittsburgh: Duquesne University Press, 2008.

Franks, Paul W. "Rabbinic Idealism and Kabbalistic Realism: Jewish Dimensions of Idealism and Idealist Dimensions of Judaism." In *The Impact of Idealism: The Legacy of Post-Kantian German Thought*, vol. 4: *Religion*, ed. Nicholas Adams, 219–245. Cambridge: Cambridge University Press, 2013.

Fried, Gregory. "The King Is Dead: Heidegger's 'Black Notebooks.'" *Los Angeles Review of Books*, September 13, 2014. http://lareviewofbooks.org/review/king-dead-heideggers-black-notebooks.

Fried, Gregory. "A Letter to Emmanuel Faye." *Philosophy Today* 55 (fall 2011): 219–252.

Fried, Gregory. "What Heidegger Was Hiding: Unearthing the Philosopher's Anti-Semitism." *Foreign Affairs* 93 (November–December 2014): 159–166.

Fried, Gregory, and Richard Polt, ed. and trans. *Nature, History, State: 1933–1934*. London: Bloomsbury, 2013.

Friedman, Menachem. "The Lost Kiddush Cup: Changes in *Ashkenazic Haredi* Culture—A Tradition in Crisis." In *The Uses of Tradition: Jewish Continuity in the Modern Era*, ed. Jack Wertheimer, 175–187. New York: Jewish Theological Seminary of America, 1993.

Frost, Robert. *The Poetry of Robert Frost*. Ed. Edward Connery Lathem. New York: Holt, Rinehart & Winston, 1970.

Fuchs, Christian. "Martin Heidegger's Anti-Semitism: Philosophy of Technology and the Media in the Light of the *Black Notebooks*; Implications for the Reception of Heidegger in Media and Communication Studies." *Triple C: Communication, Capitalism & Critique* 13 (2015): 55–78.

Fukuyama, Francis. "The End of History?" *Quadrant* 33 (1989): 15–25.

Gadamer, Hans-Georg. *Heidegger's Ways*. Albany: SUNY Press, 1994.

Gadamer, Hans-Georg. *Truth and Method*. Trans. G. Barden. New York: Continuum, 1975.

Gadamer, Hans-Georg. "The Universality of the Hermeneutic Problem (1966)." In Hans-Georg Gadamer, *Philosophical Hermeneutics*, 3–17. Trans. David E. Linge. Berkeley: University of California Press, 1976.

Garb, Jonathan. *Kabbalist in the Heart of the Storm: R. Moshe Hayyim Luzzatto* [in Hebrew]. Tel Aviv: Tel Aviv University Press, 2014.

Gillis, Justin. "Climate Efforts Falling Short, U.N. Panel Says." *New York Times*, April 13, 2014. http://www.nytimes.com/2014/04/14/science/earth/un-climate-panel-warns-speedier-action-is-needed-to-avert-disaster.html.

Goldschmidt, Hermann Levin. *The Legacy of German Jewry*. New York: Fordham University Press, 2007.

Gordon, Peter Eli. "Displaced: Phenomenology and Belonging in Levinas and Heidegger." In *Between Levinas and Heidegger*, ed. John E. Drabinksi and Eric S. Nelson, 209–226. Albany: SUNY Press, 2014.

Gordon, Peter Eli. "Heidegger in Purgatory." In Martin Heidegger, *Nature, History, State: 1933–1934*, 85–108.

Ed. and trans. Gregory Fried and Richard Polt. London: Bloomsbury, 2013.

Gordon, Peter Eli. *Rosenzweig and Heidegger: Between Judaism and German Philosophy*. Berkeley: University of California Press, 2003.

Greenwood, Phoebe. "Ethiopian Women in Israel 'Given Contraceptive without Consent.'" *Guardian*, February 28, 2013.

Grondin, Jean. *Du sens des choses: L'idée de la métaphysique*. Paris: PUF, 2013.

Grondin, Jean. *Le tournant dans la pensée de Martin Heidegger*. 2nd ed. Paris: PUF, (1989) 2011.

Gurian, Waldemar. *Um des Reiches Zukunft*. Freiburg: Herder, 1932.

Habermas, Jürgen. *Der Philosophische Diskurs der Moderne: Zwölf Vorlesungen*. Frankfurt: Suhrkamp, 1985. Translated by Frederick G. Lawrence as *The Philosophical Discourse of Modernity* (Cambridge, MA: MIT Press, 1987).

Habermas, Jürgen. "Ein Gespräch mit Jürgen Habermas: 'Martin Heidegger? Nazi, sicher ein Nazi!' Interview by Mark Hunyadi." In *Die Heidegger Kontroverse*, ed. Jürg Altwegg, 172–175. Frankfurt: Athenäum, 1988.

Habermas, Jürgen. "Martin Heidegger: On the Publication of the Lectures of 1935." In *The Heidegger Controversy: A Critical Reader*, ed. Richard Wolin, 186–197. Cambridge, MA: MIT Press, 1993.

Habermas, Jürgen. "Martin Heidegger—Werk und Weltanschauung." In Jürgen Habermas, *Texte und Kontexte*. Frankfurt: Suhrkamp, 1991.

Habermas, Jürgen. "Vom öffentlichen Gebrauch der Historie: Das offizielle Selbstverständnis der Bundesrepublik bricht auf." In *"Historikerstreit": Die Dokumentation der Kontroverse um die Einzigartigkeit der nationalsozialistischen Judenvernichtung*, ed. Rudolf Augstein et al., 243–255. Munich: Piper, 1987.

Hachmeister, Lutz. *Heideggers Testament: Der Philosoph, der Spiegel und die SS*. Berlin: Propyläen, 2014.

Hammerschlag, Sarah. *The Figural Jew: Politics and Identity in Postwar French Thought*. Chicago: University of Chicago Press, 2010.

Harnack, Adolf von. *Das Wesen des Christentums*. Leipzig: Hinrichs, 1900. Translated by T. B. Saunders as *What Is Christianity?* (New York: Harper, 1957).

Harries, Karsten. "The Antinomy of Being: Heidegger's Critique of Humanism." In *The Cambridge Companion to Existentialism*, ed. Steven Crowell, 178–198. Cambridge: Cambridge University Press, 2012.

Harries, Karsten. "Heidegger as a Political Thinker." *Review of Metaphysics* 29, no. 4 (1976): 642–669. Reprinted in *Heidegger and Modern Philosophy: Critical Essays*, ed. Michael Murray (New Haven, CT: Yale University Press, 1978), 304–328.

Harries, Karsten. *Infinity and Perspective*. Cambridge, MA: MIT Press, 2001.

Harries, Karsten. *Wahrheit: Die Architektur der Welt*. Paderborn: Fink, 2012.

Harries, Karsten, and Christoph Jamme, eds. *Martin Heidegger: Politics, Art, and Technology*. New York: Holmes & Meier, 1994.

Hegel, Georg Wilhelm Friedrich. *On Christianity: Early Theological Writings*. Trans. T. M. Knox. Chicago: University of Chicago Press, 1948.

Hegel, Georg Wilhelm Friedrich. *Phänomenologie des Geistes*. Hamburg: Meiner, 1952.

Hegel, Georg Wilhelm Friedrich. *Vorlesungen über die Geschichte der Philosophie I, Jubiläumsausgabe*, vol. 17. Ed. H. Glockner. Stuttgart: Fromann, 1968.

Hemming, Laurence. *Heidegger and Marx: A Productive Dialogue over the Language of Humanism*. Evanston, IL: Northwestern University Press, 2013.

Herbert, Ulrich. *Best: Biographische Studien über Radikalismus, Weltanschauung und Vernunft, 1903–1989*. Bonn: Dietz, 1996.

Herf, Jeffrey. *The Jewish Enemy: Nazi Propaganda during World War II and the Holocaust*. Cambridge, MA: Harvard University Press, 2009.

Herf, Jeffrey. *Reactionary Modernism: Technology, Culture, and Politics in Weimar and the Third Reich*. New York: Cambridge University Press, 1986.

Herrmann, Friedrich-Wilhelm von. "Die 'Beiträge zur Philosophie (Vom Ereignis)' als Grundlegung des seinsgeschichtlichen Denkens." In *Heideggers Beiträge zur Philosophie/Les Apports à la philosophie de Heidegger*, ed. E. Mejía and I. Schüssler. Frankfurt: Klostermann, 2009.

Herzl, Theodor. *Der Judenstaat: Versuch einer modernen Lösung der Judenfrage*. Vienna: M. Breitenstein, 1896.

Herzl, Theodor. *The Complete Diaries of Theodor Herzl*. Ed. Raphael Patai, trans. Harry Zohn. New York: Herzl Press and Thomas Yoseloff, 1960.

Hirsch, Elizabeth F. Letter to the editor. *New York Times*, March 2, 1988, A22.

Hitler, Adolf. *Hitlers Briefe und Notizen: Sein Weltbild in handschriftlichen Dokumenten*. Ed. Werner Maser. Düsseldorf: Econ Verlag, 1973.

Hitler, Adolf. *Mein Kampf*. Munich: Zentralverlag des NSDAP, 1942.

Hölderlin, Friedrich. *Die Gedichte*. Frankfurt: Insel, 1999.

Hölderlin, Friedrich. *Hyperion, Sämtliche Werke 3, Grosse Stuttgarter Ausgabe*. Stuttgart: W. Kohlhammer Verlag, 1957.

Honneth, Axel. *Verdinglichung: Eine anerkennungstheoretische Studie*. Frankfurt: Suhrkamp, 2005.

Horkheimer, Max, and T. W. Adorno. *Dialektik der Aufklärung*. Frankfurt: Fischer, 1988.

Hühnerfeld, Paul. *In Sachen Heidegger*. Hamburg: Hoffmann & Campe, 1959.

Hume, David. *Essays: Moral, Political, and Literary*. Ed. Eugene F. Miller. Indianapolis: Liberty Fund, 1994.

Hummel, Pascale, ed. *Mélivres/Misbooks: Études sur l'envers et les travers du livre*. Paris: Philogicum, 2009.

Husserl, Edmund. *The Crisis of European Sciences and Transcendental Phenomenology: An Introduction to Phenomenological Philosophy*. Trans. David Carr. Evanston, IL: Northwestern University Press, 1970.

Idhe, Don. "Can Continental Philosophy Deal with the New Technologies?" *Journal of Speculative Philosophy* 26 (2012): 321–332.

Idhe, Don. *Heidegger's Technologies: Postphenomenological Perspectives*. New York: Fordham University Press, 2010.

Intergovernmental Panel on Climate Change. *Climate Change 2014: Synthesis Report*. Ed. The Core Writing Team, Rajendra K. Pachauri, and Leo Meyer. Geneva: World Meteorological Association, 2014. http://www.ipcc.ch/report/ar5/syr/.

The Israelite Samaritan Version of the Torah: First English Translation Compared with the Masoretic Version. Ed. and trans. Benyamim Tsedaka, ed. Sharon Sullivan. Grand Rapids, MI: Eerdmans, 2013.

Jaeger, Werner. *Paideia: The Ideals of Greek Culture, vol. 2: Archaic Greece: The Mind of Athens*. Trans. Gilbert Highet. 2nd ed. Oxford: Oxford University Press, 1945.

Jaran, François, and Christophe Perrin, eds. *The Heidegger Concordance*. 3 vols. London: Bloomsbury, 2013.

Jaspers, Karl. *Philosophische Autobiographie*. Munich: Piper, 1977.

Johnson, Greg. "Heidegger's Black Notebooks: The Diaries of a Dissident National Socialist." 2014. http://www.counter-currents.com/2014/03/heideggers-black-notebooks.

Jonas, Hans. *The Gnostic Religion: The Message of the Alien God and the Beginnings of Christianity*. Boston: Beacon Press, 2001.

Jonas, Hans. "Wandlungen und Bestand: Vom Grunde der Verstehbarkeit des Geschichtlichen." In *Durchblicke: Martin Heidegger zum 80. Geburtstag*, ed. Vittorio Klostermann, 1–26. Frankfurt: Klostermann, 1970.

Joris, Pierre. "Emmanuel Faye: The Introduction of Nazism into Philosophy in Light of the Unpublished Seminars of 1933–1935." *Nomadics*, November 16, 2009. http://pierrejoris.com/blog/?p=2377.

Jünger, Ernst. *Der Arbeiter: Herrschaft und Gestalt*. Hamburg: Hanseatische Verlagsanstalt, 1932.

Jünger, Ernst. *Der Friede: Ein Wort an die Jugend Europas und an die Jugend der Welt, Die Argonauten*. Amsterdam: Erasmus, 1946.

Kahn, Charles. *Anaximander and the Origins of Greek Cosmology*. New York: Columbia University Press, 1960.

Kant, Immanuel. *The Conflict of the Faculties*. Trans. Mary J. Gregor. Lincoln: University of Nebraska Press, 1992.

Kant, Immanuel. *Kritik der reinen Vernunft*. Ed. Raymund Schmidt. Hamburg: Felix Meiner, (1787) 1993.

Kantorowicz, Ernst. *Kaiser Friedrich der Zweite*. Berlin: Georg Bondi, 1927.

Kaplan, Lawrence. "Kashrut and Kugel: Franz Rosenzweig's 'The Builders.'" *Jewish Review of Books* (winter 2014): 41–43.

Katz, Jakob. "A State within a State: The History of an Anti-Semitic Slogan." In *Emancipation and Assimilation: Studies in Modern Jewish History*, 47–76. Farborough: Gregg, 1972.

Kaube, Jürgen. "Die Endschlacht der planetarischen Verbrecherbanden." *Frankfurter Allgemeine Zeitung*, December 3, 2014.

Keiling, Tobias. *Seinsgeschichte und phänomenologischer Realismus: Eine Interpretation und Kritik der Spätphilosophie Heideggers*. Forthcoming.

Kennedy, Jay. "Plato's Forms, Pythagorean Mathematics, and Stichometry." *Apeiron: A Journal for Ancient Philosophy and Science* 43 (2010): 1–32.

Kershaw, Ian. *The "Hitler Myth."* Oxford: Oxford University Press, 2001.

Kimmerling, Baruch. *The Invention and Decline of Israeliness: State, Society, and the Military*. Berkeley: University of California Press, 2005.

Kisiel, Theodore. "The Demise of *Being and Time*: 1927–1930." In *Heidegger's Being and Time: Critical Essays*, ed. Richard Polt, 189–214. Lanham, MD: Rowman & Littlefield, 2005.

Klemperer, Klemens von. "Martin Heidegger's Life and Times: A Historian's View, Or: Heidegger and the Hubris of Philosophical Policy." In *Martin Heidegger: Politics, Art, and Technology*, ed. Karsten Harries and Christoph Jamme, 1–17. New York: Holmes & Meier, 1994.

Kluge, Friedrich. *An Etymological Dictionary of the German Language*. Translation of the 4th German ed. by John F. Davis. New York: Macmillan, 1891.

Kojève, Alexandre. "Tyranny and Wisdom." In Leo Strauss, *"On Tyranny," Including the Strauss-Kojève Debate*, ed. Victor Gourevitch and Michael Roth, 165–166. New York: Free Press, 1991.

Konersmann, Ralf. *Kulturkritik*. Frankfurt: Suhrkamp, 2008.

Konersmann, Ralf, John Michael Krois, and Dirk Westerkamp, eds. *Kulturkritik: Zeitschrift für Kulturphilosophie* 2007/2. Hamburg: Felix Meiner, 2008.

Kook, Rav Zvi Yehuda. "On the 19th Anniversary of Israel's Independence Weeks before the Unification of Yerushalaim." http://www.yeshiva.org.il/midrash/2022; partial English trans. available at http://www.israel613 .com/books/ERETZ_ANNIVERSARY_KOOK.pdf.

Krell, David. *Ecstacy, Catastrophe: Heidegger, From* Being and Time *to the* Black Notebooks. Albany: SUNY Press, 2015.

Lachterman, David. *"Die ewige Wiederkehr des Griechen*: Nietzsche and the Homeric Tradition." In *Nietzsche und die antike Philosophie*, ed. Daniel Conway and Rudolf Rehn, 13–37. Trier: Wissenschaftlicher Verlag, 1992.

Lacoue-Labarthe, Philippe. *Heidegger, Art, and Politics: The Fiction of the Political*. Trans. Chris Turner. Oxford: Blackwell, 1990.

Lacoue-Labarthe, Philippe. *Heidegger and the Politics of Poetry*. Trans. Jeff Fort. Champaign: University of Illinois Press, 2007.

Lescourret, M.-A., ed. *La dette et la distance: De quelques élèves et lecteurs juifs de Heidegger*. Paris: Éditions de l'Éclat, 2014.

Lethen, Helmut. *Cool Conduct: The Culture of Distance in Weimar Germany*. Berkeley: University of California Press, 2002. Originally published as *Verhaltenslehre der Kälte: Lebensversuche zwischen den Kriegen* (Frankfurt: Suhrkamp, 1994).

Levi, Primo. *Die Untergegangenen und die Geretteten*. Munich: Carl Hanser, 1990.

Levinas, Emmanuel. "Being Jewish [1947]." Trans. Mary Beth Mader. *Continental Philosophy Review* 40 (2006): 205–210.

Levinas, Emmanuel. *Carnets de captivité et autres inédits*. Ed. Rodolphe Calin and Catherine Chalier. Paris: Bernard Grasset/IMEC, 2009.

Levinas, Emmanuel. "Das Diabolische gibt zu denken." In *Die Heidegger Kontroverse*, ed. Jürg Altwegg,

101–109. Frankfurt: Athenäum, 1988.

Levinas, Emmanuel. *Difficult Freedom: Essays on Judaism*. Trans. S. Hand. Baltimore: The Johns Hopkins University Press, 1990.

Levinas, Emmanuel. *Otherwise Than Being or Beyond Essence*. Trans. Alphonso Lingis. The Hague: Martinus Nijhoff, 1981.

Lilla, Mark. *The Reckless Mind: Intellectuals in Politics*. New York: NYREV, 2001.

Löwith, Karl. "Les implications politiques de la philosophie de l'existence chez Heidegger." *Les temps modernes* 2 (1946): 343–360.

Löwith, Karl. "M. Heidegger and F. Rosenzweig, or Temporality and Eternity." *Philosophy and Phenomenological Research* 3, no. 1 (1942): 53–77.

Löwith, Karl. *My Life in Germany before and after 1933: A Report*. Champaign, IL: University of Illinois Press, 1994.

Lütkehaus, Ludger. "In der Mitte sitzt das Dasein: Die Philosophen Günther Anders und Peter Sloterdijk lesen zweierlei Heidegger." *Die Zeit*, May 2002, 42.

Lyotard, Jean-François. *Heidegger and "the jews."* Trans. Andreas Michel and Mark Roberts. Minneapolis: University of Minnesota Press, 1990.

Lyotard, Jean-François. "Heidegger and 'the jews': A Conference in Vienna and Freiburg." In *Political Writings*, trans. Bill Readings with Kevin Paul Geiman. London: University College Press, 1993.

MacIntyre, Alasdair. *After Virtue*. Notre Dame, IN: University of Notre Dame Press, 1981.

MacIntyre, Donald. "The Birth of Modern Israel: A Scrap of Paper That Changed History." *Independent,* May 26, 2005.

Magen, Yitzakh. "The Dating of the First Phase of the Samaritan Temple on Mt Gerizim in Light of Archaeological Evidence." In *Judah and the Judeans in the Fourth Century B.C.E.*, ed. Oded Lipschitz , 157–211. Winona Lake, IN: Eisenbrauns, 2007.

Malpas, Jeff. *Heidegger's Topology: Being, Place, World*. Cambridge, MA: MIT Press, 2006.

Malpas, Jeff. "Putting Space in Place: Relational Geography and Philosophical Topography." *Planning and Environment D: Space and Society* 30 (2012): 226–242.

Malpas, Jeff. "Re-Orienting Thinking: Philosophy in the Midst of the World." In *Commonplace Commitments: Thinking through the Legacy of Joseph P. Fell*, ed. Peter S. Fosl, Michael J. McGandy, and Mark Moorman. Lewisburg, PA: Bucknell University Press, forthcoming, 2015.

Mann, Thomas. *Betrachtungen eines Unpolitischen*. Frankfurt: Fischer, (1919) 2001.

Margolis, J., and T. Rockmore, eds. *Heidegger and Nazism*. Philadelphia: Temple University Press, 1989.

Martin, Bernd, ed. *Martin Heidegger und das Dritte Reich*. Darmstadt: Wissenschaftliche Buchgesellschaft, 1989.

Marx, Karl. "Thesen über Feuerbach [1845]." In Karl Marx and Friedrich Engels, *Werke*, vol. 3, pp. 5–7. Berlin: Dietz, 1969.

McClain, Ernest. *The Pythagorean Plato: Prelude to the Song Itself*. York Beach, ME: Nicolas Hays, 1978.

Michaud, Eric. *The Cult of Art in Nazi Germany*. Stanford, CA: Stanford University Press, 2004.

Morat, Daniel. *Von der Tat zur Gelassenheit: Konservatives Denken bei Martin Heidegger, Ernst Jünger und Friedrich Georg Jünger 1920–1960*. Göttingen: Wallstein, 2007.

Murrey, Lucas. *Hölderlin's Dionysiac Poetry: The Terrifying-Exciting Mysteries*. Frankfurt: Springer, 2014.

Nancy, Jean-Luc. "Heidegger's 'Originary Ethics.'" In *Heidegger and Practical Philosophy*, ed. Françoise Raffoul and David Pettigrew. Albany: SUNY Press, 2002.

Nehamas, Alexander. *Life as Literature*. Cambridge, MA: Harvard University Press, 1985.

Nicholson, Graeme. "Justifying Your Nation." *Symposium* 13 (2009): 40–58.

Nicholson, Graeme. "The Politics of Heidegger's Rectoral Address." *Man and World* 10, no. 3 (1987): 171–187.

Nietzsche, Friedrich. *Beyond Good and Evil*. Trans. Walter Kaufmann. New York: Random House, 1989.

Nietzsche, Friedrich. *The Birth of Tragedy*. Trans. Walter Kaufmann. New York: Vintage, 1966.

Nietzsche, Friedrich. *The Dawn of Day*. Trans. J. M. Kennedy. Dover: Courier Corporation, 2012.

Nietzsche, Friedrich. *Frühe Schriften*. 5 vols. Munich: Beck, 1994.

Nietzsche, Friedrich. *Kritische Studienausgabe*. 15 vols. Berlin: De Gruyter, 1980.

Nietzsche, Friedrich. *Morgenröte*. Vorwort 5. In *Sämtliche Werke: Kritische Studienausgabe*. 15 vols, vol. 3. Ed. Giorgio Colli and Mazzino Montinari. Munich: De Gruyter, 1999.

Nittenberg, Joanna, ed. *Wandlungen und Brüche: Von Herzls "Welt" zur Illustrierten Neuen Welt, 1897–1997*. Vienna: INW, 1997.

Noakes, Jeremy, and Geoffrey Pridham, eds. *Nazism 1919–1945: A Documentary Reader*, vol. 1. Exeter: Exeter University Press, 1983.

Olender, Maurice. *Race sans histoire: Points Essais No. 620*. Paris: Seuil, 2009.

O'Meara, Thomas F. "Tillich and Heidegger: A Structural Relationship." *Harvard Theological Review* 61, no. 2 (April 1968): 249–261.

Ó Murchadha, Felix. *The Time of Revolution: Kairos and Chronos in Heidegger*. London: Bloomsbury, 2013.

Ophir, Adi. "Evil, Evils, and the Question of Ethics." In *Modernity and the Problem of Evil*, ed. Alan D. Schrift. Bloomington: Indiana University Press, 2005.

Ophir, Adi. *The Order of Evils: Toward an Ontology of Morals*. Trans. Rela Mazali and Havi Carel. New York: Zone Books, 2005.

Osborne, Catherine. *Rethinking Early Greek Philosophy: Hippolytus of Rome and the Presocratics*. London: Duckworth, 1987.

Ott, Hugo. *Martin Heidegger: Unterwegs zu seiner Biographie*. Frankfurt: Campus, 1988. Translated by Allan Blunden as *Martin Heidegger: A Political Life* (New York: Basic Books, 1993).

Panofsky, Erwin. "Die Perspektive als 'symbolische Form.'" In *Vorträge der Bibliothek Warburg 1924–1925*. Nendeln, Liechtenstein: Kraus Reprint, (1927) 1967.

Panofsky, Erwin. *Gothic Architecture and Scholasticism*. Latrobe: Archabbey, (1951) 1957.

Pedaya, Haviva. "The Divinity as Place and Time and the Holy Place in Jewish Mysticism." In *Sacred Space: Shrine, City, Land: Proceedings from the International Conference in Memory of Joshua Prawer*, ed. Benjamin Z. Kedar and R. J. Zwi Werblowsky, 84–111. New York: Palgrave Macmillan, 1998.

Phillips, James. *Heidegger's Volk: Between National Socialism and Poetry*. Stanford, CA: Stanford University Press, 2005.

Pippin, Robert. *Hegel's Practical Philosophy*. Cambridge: Cambridge University Press, 2008.

Piterberg, Gabriel. "Zion's Rebellious Daughter: Hannah Arendt on Palestine and Jewish Politics." *New Left Review* 48 (November–December 2007). http://newleftreview.org/II/48/gabriel-piterberg-zion-s-rebel-daughter.

Plato. *Theaetetus*.Trans. Robin A. H. Waterfield. London: Penguin Books, 1987.

Podach, Erich F. *Nietzsches Zusammenbruch*. Heidelberg: N. Kampmann, 1930.

Pöggeler, Otto. "Den Führer führen; Heidegger und kein Ende." *Philosophische Rundschau* 32 (1985): 26–67.

Pöggeler, Otto. *Neue Wege mit Heidegger*. Freiburg: Karl Alber, 1992.

Polanyi, Karl. *The Great Transformation: The Political and Economic Origins of Our Time*. Boston: Beacon Press, 2001.

Polt, Richard. "Inception, Downfall, and the Broken World: Heidegger above the Sea of Fog." http://www.youtube.com/watch?v=_ZpWnYGqBPw.

Prinz, Joachim. *Wir Juden*. Stuttgart: Reclam, (1934) 1993.

Publius (Alexander Hamilton). *The Federalist Papers*. CreateSpace Independent Publishing Platform, 2015.

Pummer, Reinhard. *The Samaritans*. Leiden: Brill, 1897.

Redner, Harry. "Philosophers and AntiSemitism." *Modern Judaism* 22, no. 2 (May 2002): 115–141.

Richardson, William J. "Dasein and the Ground of Negativity: A Note on the Fourth Movement in the Beiträge-Symphony." *Heidegger Studies* 9 (1993): 35–52.

Richardson, William J. *Heidegger: Through Phenomenology to Thought*. New York: Fordham University Press,

(1963) 2003.

Riedel, Manfred. *Hören auf die Sprache: Die akroamatische Dimension der Hermeneutik*. Frankfurt: Suhrkamp, 1989.

Rohkrämer, Thomas. *Die fatale Attraktion des Nationalsozialismus: Über die Popularität eines Unrechtregimes*. Paderborn: Schöningh, 2013.

Rohkrämer, Thomas. "Kult der Gewalt und Sehnsucht nach Ordnung—der soldatische Nationalismus in der Weimarer Republik." *Sociologicus* 51, nos. 1–2 (2001): 28–48.

Rohkrämer, Thomas. *A Single Communal Faith? The German Right from Conservatism to National Socialism*. Oxford: Oxford University Press, 2007.

Rorty, Richard. "Heidegger, Contingency, and Pragmatism." In Richard Rorty, *Philosophical Papers*, vol. 2: *Essays on Heidegger and Others*. Cambridge: Cambridge University Press, 1991.

Rorty, Richard. *Philosophy and the Mirror of Nature*. Princeton, NJ: Princeton University Press, 1979.

Rosenzweig, Franz. "The Builders." In Franz Rosenzweig, On Jewish Learning, ed. N. N. Glatzer, 72–92. New York: Schocken Books, 1965.

Rosenzweig, Franz. *Philosophical and Theological Writings*. Trans., ed., notes and commentaries by Paul W. Franks and Michael Morgan. Indianapolis: Hackett, 2000.

Rosenzweig, Franz. *The Star of Redemption*. Trans. William W. Hallo. New York: Holt, Rinehart & Winston, 1971.

Rubenstein, Mary-Jane. *Strange Wonder: The Closure of Metaphysics and the Opening of Awe*. New York: Columbia University Press, 2008.

Rubinstein, Jeffrey L. *Rabbinic Stories*. New York: Paulist Press, 2002.

Runes, Dagobert. *German Existentialism: Martin Heidegger*. New York: Philosophical Library, 1965.

Russell, Bertrand. *History of Western Philosophy*. London: Allen & Unwin, 1946.

Sand, Schlomo. *The Invention of the Jewish People*. Trans. Yael Lotan. London: Verso, 2009.

Sand, Schlomo. *The Invention of the Land of Israel: From Holy Land to Homeland*. Trans. Geremy Forman. London: Verso, 2012.

Sartre, Jean-Paul. *Existentialism Is a Humanism*. Trans. Carol Macomber. New Haven: Yale University Press, 2007.

Schleiermacher, Friedrich. *Hermeneutik und Kritik*. Ed. Manfred Frank. Frankfurt: Suhrkamp, 1977. Translated by Andrew Bowie as *Hermeneutics and Criticism* (Cambridge: Cambridge University Press, 1998).

Schmitt, Carl. "Die deutsche Rechtswissenschaft im Kampf gegen den jüdischen Geist: Schlußwort auf der Tagung der Reichsgruppe Hochschullehrer des NSRB am 3. Und 4. Oktober 1936." *Deutsche Juristen-Zeitung* 41 (1936): 1193–1199.

Schmitt, Carl. "Die Verfassung der Freiheit." *Deutsche Juristenzeitung* 40 (1935): 1133–1135.

Schmitz-Berning, Cornelia. *Vokabular des Nationalsozialismus*. Berlin: de Gruyter, 2007.

Schneeberger, Guido. *Nachlese zu Heidegger: Dokumente zu seinem Leben und Denken*. Bern: Suhr, 1962.

Schoeps, Hans-Joachim. *Jüdischer Glaube in dieser Zeit: Prolegomena zur Grundlegung einer systematischen Theologie des Judentums*. Berlin: Jüdischer Verlag, 1932.

Scholem, Gershom. "Offener Brief an den Verfasser der Schrift *Jüdischer Glaube in dieser Zeit*." *Bayerische Israelitische Gemeindezeitung*, August 15, 1932, 241–244. Reprinted in Gershom Scholem, *Briefe I, 1914–1947*, ed. Itta Shedletzky (Munich: C. H. Beck, 2000).

Scholem, Gershom. *On the Possibility of a Jewish Mysticism in Our Time and Other Essays*. Ed. Avraham Shapira, trans. Jonathan Chipman. Philadelphia: Jewish Publication Society, 1997.

Schuessler, Jennifer. "Heidegger's Notebooks Renew Focus on Anti-Semitism." *New York Times*, March 30, 2014. http://www.nytimes.com/2014/03/31/books/heideggers-notebooks-renew-focus-on-anti-semitism.html.

Schwartz, Dov. *Religion or Halakhah: The Philosophy of Rabbi Joseph B. Soloveitchik*. Leiden: Brill, 2007.

Sheehan, Thomas. "*Caveat Lector:* The New Heidegger." *New York Review of Books* 28, no.19 (December 4, 1980): 39–41.

Sheehan, Thomas. "Heidegger and the Nazis." *New York Review of Books* 35, no. 10 (June 16, 1988): 38–47.

Sheehan, Thomas. "'Everyone Has to Tell the Truth': Heidegger and the Jews." *Continuum* 1, no. 1 (1990): 30–44.

Sheehan, Thomas. *Making Sense of Heidegger: A Paradigm Shift*. Lanham, MD: Rowman & Littlefield, 2015.

Sheehan, Thomas. "A Paradigm Shift in Heidegger Research." *Continental Philosophy Review* 34 (2001): 183–202.

Sieg, Ulrich. "'Die Verjudung des deutschen Geistes': Ein unbekannter Brief Heideggers." *Die Zeit*, December 22, 1989, 40. http://www.zeit.de/1989/52/die-verjudung-des-deutschen-geistes.

Sluga, Hans. *Heidegger's Crisis: Philosophy and Politics in Nazi Germany*. New York: Cambridge University Press, 1993.

Snell, Bruno. *The Discovery of Mind: The Greek Origins of European Thought*. Cambridge, MA: Harvard University Press, (1946) 1953.

Soloveitchik, Haym. "Rupture and Reconstruction: The Transformation of Contemporary Orthodoxy." *Tradition* 28, no. 4 (Summer 1994): 64–130.

Soloveitchik, Joseph B. *Community, Covenant, and Commitment: Selected Letters and Communications*. Ed. Nathaniel Helfgot. Jersey City, NJ: KTAV, 2005.

Soloveitchik, Joseph B. *Halakhic Man*. Trans. Lawrence Kaplan. Philadelphia: Jewish Publication Society, 1983. Originally published in Hebrew, 1944.

Soloveitchik, Joseph B. *The Rav Speaks: Five Addresses on Israel, History, and the Jewish People*. New York: Judaica Press, 2002.

Sommer, Benjamin D. *The Bodies of God and the World of Ancient Israel*. Cambridge: Cambridge University Press, 2009.

Spengler, Oswald. *Jahre der Entscheidung*. Munich: dtv, 1980.

Spinoza, Benedict de. *Theological-Political Treatise*. Ed. Jonathan Israel, trans. Michael Silverthorne and Jonathan Israel. Cambridge: Cambridge University Press, 2007.

Stern, Fritz. *Five Germanys I Have Known*. New York: Farrar, Straus & Giroux, 2007.

Strauss, Leo. "An Introduction to Heideggerian Existentialism." In Leo Strauss, *The Rebirth of Classical Political Rationalism: An Introduction to the Thought of Leo Strauss*, ed. Thomas L. Pangle, 27–46. Chicago: University of Chicago Press, 1989.

Tau, Harav Zzi Yisrael. *Le 'emunat 'iteinu* [For our time's faith] [in Hebrew]. Vol. 3. Jerusalem: Erez, n.d.

Thomson, Iain. "Heidegger and National Socialism." In *A Companion to Heidegger*, ed. Hubert L. Dreyfus and Mark A. Wrathall, 32–48. Oxford: Blackwell, 2005.

Tillich, Paul. *Autobiographical Reflections*. New York: Macmillan, 1952.

Tillich, Paul. *The Interpretation of History*. New York: Scribner, 1936.

Tömmel, Tatjana. *Wille und Passion: Der Liebesbegriff bei Heidegger und Arendt*. Frankfurt: Suhrkamp, 2013.

Trawny, Peter. *Adyton: Heideggers esoterische Philosophie*. Berlin: Matthes & Seitz, 2010.

Trawny, Peter. "Das Trauma des Holocaust als Anfang der Philosophie: Nach Hannah Arendt und Emmanuel-Levinas ." *Zeitschrift für Genozidforschung* 2 (2007): 118–131.

Trawny, Peter. "Heidegger et les *Cahiers noirs*." *Esprit* 407 (August–September 2014): 133–148.

Trawny, Peter. *Heidegger und der Mythos der jüdischen Weltverschwörung*. Frankfurt: Klostermann, 2014.

Trawny, Peter. *Martin Heideggers Phänomenologie der Welt*. Freiburg: Karl Alber, 1997.

Vallega-Neu, Daniela. "Heidegger's Reticence: From *Contributions* to *Das Ereignis* and Toward Gelassenheit." *Research in Phenomenology* 45, no. 1 (2015): 1–32.

Vallega-Neu, Daniela. "At the Limit of Word and Thought: Reading Heidegger's *Das Ereignis*." In *Internationales Jahrbuch für Hermeneutik*, vol. 12, ed. Günter Figal, 77–91. Tübingen: Mohr Siebeck, 2013.

Vattimo, Gianni. *Belief*. Trans. Luca D'Isanto and David Webb. Stanford, CA: Stanford University Press, 1999.

Vattimo, Gianni. "How to Become an Anti-Zionist." In *Deconstructing Zionism: A Critique of Political Metaphysics*, ed. Gianni Vattimo and Michael Marder, 20–21. London: Bloomsbury, 2014.

Vietta, Silvio. *"Etwas rast um den Erdball..." Martin Heidegger: Ambivalente Existenz und Globalisierungskritik*. Munich: Fink, 2015.

Vietta, Silvio. *Heideggers Kritik am Nationalsozialismus und an der Technik*. Tübingen: Niemeyer, 1989.

Volpi, Franco. *Aportes a la filosofía de Martin Heidegger*. Madrid: Maia ediciones, 2010.

Volpi, Franco. *La selvaggia chiarezza*. Milan: Adelphi, 2011.

Vondung, Klaus. *Die Apokalypse in Deutschland*. Munich: dtv, 1988.

von Herrmann, Friedrich-Wilhelm. "Die 'Beiträge zur Philosophie (Vom Ereignis)' als Grundlegung des seinsgeschichtlichen Denkens." In *Heideggers Beiträge zur Philosophie/Les Apports à la philosophie de Heidegger*, ed. E. Mejía and I. Schüssler. Frankfurt: Klostermann, 2009.

Weber, Max. *Gesamtausgabe*, vol. II/9: *Briefe 1915–1917*. Tübingen: Mohr Siebeck, 2008.

Wildt, Michael. *Generation des Unbedingten: Das Führungskorps des Reichssicherheitshauptamtes*. Hamburg: Hamburger Edition, 2002.

Winthrop, John. "A Modell of Christiane Charitie." https://history.hanover.edu/texts/winthmod.html.

Wittgenstein, Ludwig. *The Blue and Brown Books: Preliminary Studies for the Philosophical Investigations*. Oxford: Blackwell, 1964.

Wittgenstein, Ludwig. *Philosophical Investigations*. Trans. G. E. M. Anscombe. New York: Macmillan, 1958.

Wittgenstein, Ludwig. *Remarks on the Foundation of Mathematics*. Cambridge, MA: MIT Press, 1967.

Wittgenstein, Ludwig. *Tractatus Logico-Philosophicus*. Trans. D. F. Pears and B. F. McGuinness. New York: Humanities Press, 1961.

Wittgenstein, Ludwig. *Zettel*. Ed. G. E. M. Anscombe and Georg Henrik von Wright, trans. G. E. M. Anscombe. Berkeley: University of California Press, 1967.

Woessner, Martin. *Heidegger in America*. Cambridge: Cambridge University Press, 2011.

Wolfe, Judith. *Heidegger's Eschatology: Theological Horizons in Martin Heidegger's Early Work*. Oxford: Oxford University Press, 2013.

Wolfson, Elliot R. *Giving beyond the Gift: Apophasis and Overcoming Theomania*. New York: Fordham University Press, 2014.

Wolfson, Elliot R. *Language, Eros, Being: Kabbalistic Hermeneutics and Poetic Imagination*. New York: Fordham University Press, 2005.

Wolfson, Elliot R. "Nihilating Nonground and the Temporal Sway of Becoming: Kabbalistically Envisaging Nothing beyond Nothing." *Angelaki: Journal of the Theoretical Humanities* 17, no. 3 (2012): 31–45.

Wolfson, Elliot R. "Revealing and Re/veiling Menahem Mendel Schneerson's Messianic Secret." *Kabbalah: Journal for the Study of Jewish Mystical Texts* 26 (2012): 25–96.

Wolfson, Elliot R. "Scepticism and the Philosopher's Keeping Faith." In *Jewish Philosophy for the Twenty-First Century: Personal Reflections*, ed. Hava Tirosh-Samuelson and Aaron W. Hughes, 481–515. Leiden: Brill, 2014.

Wolin, Richard. *Heidegger's Children: Hannah Arendt, Karl Löwith, Hans Jonas, and Herbert Marcuse*. Princeton, NJ: Princeton University Press, 2001.

Wolin, Richard, ed. *The Heidegger Controversy: A Critical Reader*. Cambridge, MA: MIT Press, 1993.

Wolin, Richard. "National Socialism, World Jewry, and the History of Being: Heidegger's *Black Notebooks*." *Jewish Review of Books* (summer 2014). http://jewishreviewofbooks.com/articles/993/national-socialism-world-jewry-and-the-history-of-being-heideggers-black-notebooks/.

Wrathall, Mark. *Heidegger and Unconcealment*. Cambridge: Cambridge University Press, 2011.

Wright, Georg Henrik von. "Dante between Ulysses and Faust." In *Knowledge and the Sciences in Medieval Philosophy (Acta Philosophica Fennica 48)*, ed. Monika Asztalos, John E. Murdoch, and Ilkka Niiniluoto, 1–9. Helsinki: Yliopistopaino, 1990.

Wyman, David S. *The Abandonment of the Jews: America and the Holocaust*. New York: Pantheon Books, 1984.

Wyschogrod, Michael. *The Body of Faith: God in the People Israel*. Northvale, NJ: Jason Aaronson, 2000.

Wyschogrod, Michael. "Heidegger's Tragedy." *First Things,* April 2010. http://www.firstthings.com/article/2010/04/heideggers-tragedy.

Wyschogrod, Michael. *Kierkegaard and Heidegger: The Ontology of Existence.* New York: Humanities Press, 1954.

Yapp, Malcolm. *The Making of the Modern Near East, 1792–1923.* London: Routledge, 1988.

Zaborowski, Holger. *"Eine Frage von Irre und Schuld?":* Martin Heidegger und der Nationalsozialismus. Frankfurt: Fischer, 2010.

Zaborowski, Holger. "A 'Genuinely Religiously Orientated Personality': Martin Heidegger and the Religious and Theological Origins of His Philosophy." In *The Companion to Heidegger's Philosophy of Religion,* ed. Andrew Wiercinsky and Sean McGrath, 3–19. Amsterdam: Rodopi, 2010.

Zarader, Màrlene. "The Mirror with the Triple Reflection." In *Martin Heidegger: Critical Assessments,* 4 vols., vol. 2, ed. Christopher Macann, 35–36. London: Routledge, 1992.

Zarader, Màrlene. *The Unthought Debt: Heidegger and the Hebraic Heritage.* Trans. Bettina Bergo. Stanford, CA: Stanford University Press, 2006.

Zimmermann, Michael E. *Heidegger's Confrontation with Modernity: Technology, Politics, and Art.* Bloomington: Indiana University Press, 1990.

Zuckert, Catherine H., and Michael Zuckert. "Strauss: Hermeneutics or Esotericism." In *The Routledge Companion to Hermeneutics,* ed. Jeff Malpas and Hans-Helmuth Gander, 127–136. Abingdon: Routledge, 2014.

Zweig, Stefan. *The Struggle with the Daemon: Hölderlin, Kleist, Nietzsche.* Trans. Eden Paul and Cedar Paul. London: Pushkin Press, (1925) 2012.

Contributors

Babette Babich is Professor of Philosophy at Fordham University in New York and executive editor of *New Nietzsche Studies*. She is author of *The Hallelujah Effect: Philosophical Reflections on Music, Performance Practice and Technology* (Avebury, 2013) and *La fin de la pensée? Philosophie analytique contre philosophie continentale* (Paris, 2012). Her book on *Nietzsche's Philosophy of Science* (1994), also available in Italian (1996), appears in a revised edition in *German* as *Nietzsches Wissenschaftsphilosophie* (Oxford/Bern, 2010).

Andrew Bowie is Professor of Philosophy and German at Royal Holloway, University of London. He has published ten books on modern philosophy, including *Music, Philosophy, and Modernity*, as well as many articles; he is also a jazz saxophonist. His *Adorno and the Ends of Philosophy* was published by Polity Press in 2013.

Steven Crowell is Joseph and Joanna Nazro Mullen Professor of Humanities and chair of the Department of Philosophy at Rice University (Houston, Texas). He is the author of *Husserl, Heidegger, and the Space of Meaning: Paths toward Transcendental Phenomenology* (Evanston, IL: Northwestern University Press, 2001) and *Normativity and Phenomenology in Husserl and Heidegger* (Cambridge: Cambridge University Press, 2013).

Fred Dallmayr is Packey J. Dee Professor Emeritus in philosophy and political science at the University of Notre Dame. He is past president of the Society for Asian and Comparative Philosophy (SACP). He has worked in recent European philosophy, comparative philosophy, and cross-cultural political thought. He is the author of *Dialogue among Civilizations* (2002), *In Search of the Good Life* (2007), *The Promise of Democracy* (2010), and *Being in the World: Dialogue and Cosmopolis* (2013).

Donatella Di Cesare is Professor of Philosophy at the Sapienza University of Rome. She is the author of *Utopia of Understanding: Between Babel and Auschwitz* (Albany: SUNY Press, 2012) and *Gadamer: A Philosophical Portrait* (Bloomington: Indiana University Press, 2013), and has published extensively on topics ranging across political philosophy, hermeneutics, and Jewish philosophy.

Michael Fagenblat is Senior Lecturer at Shalem College, Jerusalem, and Adjunct Senior Lecturer at Monash University. He is the author of *A Covenant of Creatures: Levinas's Philosophy of Judaism* (Stanford, CA: Stanford University Press, 2010), as well as articles on European and Jewish philosophy.

Ingo Farin teaches philosophy at the University of Tasmania, Hobart, Tasmania. He is the coeditor of *Hermeneutic Heidegger* (Evanston, IL: Northwestern University Press, forthcoming, 2016), the translator of Heidegger's *The Concept of Time* (London: Continuum, 2011), the cotranslator of *The Basic Problems of Phenomenology* (Dordrecht: Springer, 2006), and the author of articles on Heidegger and phenomenology.

Gregory Fried is Professor of Philosophy at Suffolk University, Boston. He is the author of *Heidegger's Polemos: From Being to Politics* (New Haven, CT: Yale University Press, 2000) and, with Richard Polt, translator of Martin Heidegger's *Introduction to Metaphysics* (New Haven, CT: Yale University Press, 2014) and other works. With his father, Charles Fried, he is the author of *Because It Is Wrong: Torture, Privacy, and Presidential Power in the Age of Terror* (New York: Norton, 2010), and he is director of *The Mirror of Race Project* (mirrorofrace.org).

Jean Grondin is Professor of Philosophy at the Université de Montréal. His research interests are in hermeneutics, metaphysics, and German philosophy. His publications include *Introduction to Philosophical Hermeneutics* (New Haven, CT: Yale University Press, 1994), *Hans-Georg Gadamer: A Biography* (New Haven, CT: Yale University Press, 2003), and *Introduction to Metaphysics* (New York: Columbia University Press, 2012). He is a Killam Prize winner and Officer of the Order of Canada.

Karsten Harries is the Howard H. Newman Professor of Philosophy at Yale University. He is the author of *The Meaning of Modern Art* (1968), *The Bavarian Rococo Church: Between Faith and Aestheticism* (1983), *The Broken Frame* (1990), *The Ethical Function of Architecture* (1997), *Infinity and Perspective* (2001), *Art Matters: A Critical Commentary on Martin Heidegger's The Origin of the Work of Art* (2009), *Die bayerische Rokokokirche: Das Irrationale und das Sakrale* (2009), *Between Nihilism and Faith: A Commentary on Either/Or* (2010), and *Wahrheit: Die Architektur der Welt* (2012).

Laurence Paul Hemming is a research professor jointly in Lancaster University's Philosophy, Politics and Religion Department, and the Lancaster University Management School, UK. He was formerly Dean of Research for one of the colleges of the University of London. Among his published works are *Heidegger's Atheism* (Notre Dame Press, 2002), *Postmodernity's Transcending* (Notre Dame, IN: University of Notre Dame Press, 2005), and *Heidegger and Marx: A Productive Dialogue over the Language of Humanism* (Evanston, IL: Northwestern University Press, 2013). With Bogdan Costea, he is currently working on a translation of Ernst Jünger's 1932 text *Der Arbeiter*.

Jeff Malpas is Distinguished Professor at the University of Tasmania, Hobart, Tasmania, and Visiting Distinguished Professor at Latrobe University in Melbourne, Victoria. He is the author of *Place and Experience* (Cambridge: Cambridge University Press, 1999) and *Heidegger's Topology: Being, Place, World* (Cambridge, MA: MIT Press, 2006), and has published extensively on topics ranging across art, architecture, film, geography, and philosophy.

Thomas Rohkrämer is Reader in Modern European History at Lancaster University, UK. His research focuses on nineteenth- and twentieth-century Germany with particular emphasis on cultural and intellectual history. He is the author of *Der Militarismus der "kleinen Leute": Die Kriegervereine im Deutschen Kaiserreich* (1990), *Eine andere Moderne? Zivilisationskritik, Natur und Technik in Deutschland 1880–1933* (1999), *A Single Communal Faith? The German Right from Conservatism to National Socialism* (2007), *Die fatale Attraktion des Nationalsozialismus: Über die Popularität eines Unrechtregimes* (2013).

Tracy B. Strong is Professor of Political Theory and Philosophy at the University of Southampton (UK) and UCSD Distinguished Professor, emeritus. He is the author of many books and articles, most recently *Politics without Vision: Thinking without a Banister in the Twentieth Century* (Chicago: University of Chicago Press, 2012). His most recent work is on Hobbes, Heidegger, Nietzsche, Rousseau, and American literature.

Peter Trawny teaches at the Bergische Universität Wuppertal, where he is the director of the Martin-Heidegger-Institut. Specializing in political philosophy and aesthetics, he is the author of *Adyton: Heideggers esoterische Philosophie* (Berlin: Matthes & Seitz, 2010), *Medium und Revolution* (Berlin: Matthes & Seitz, 2011), *Ins Wasser geschrieben: Philosophische Versuche über die Intimität* (Berlin: Matthes & Seitz, 2013), and *Heidegger und der Mythos der jüdischen Weltverschwörung* (Frankfurt: Klostermann, 2014). He is also the editor of several volumes of Heidegger's *Gesamtausgabe*.

Daniela Vallega-Neu is Associate Professor at the University of Oregon. Among her authored books are *Heidegger's Contributions to Philosophy: An Introduction* (Bloomington: Indiana University Press, 2003) and *The Bodily Dimension in Thinking* (Albany: SUNY Press, 2005). She is cotranslator of Heidegger's *Contributions to Philosophy: Of the Event* (Bloomington: Indiana University Press, 2011).

Friedrich-Wilhelm von Herrmann is Emeritus Professor of Philosophy at the University of Freiburg. Completing his doctorate in 1961 and his habilitation in 1970, he was scientific assistant to Eugen Fink and private assistant to Martin Heidegger. His research has focused on metaphysics, ontology, and the phenomenology of Husserl and Heidegger. He has published monographs on Augustine, Descartes, Leibniz, Husserl, and Heidegger, and has also had a close editorial involvement with Heidegger's *Gesamtausgabe*.

Nancy A. Weston teaches continental philosophy, the history of philosophy, and the philosophy of law in the Department of Rhetoric at the University of California at Berkeley. Her publications and papers address the philosophical origins and implications of the course taken by modern moral, political, legal, and social thought, tracing in particular the history of Western understandings of truth and of right, their metaphysical source and grounds, and the world-historical implications of their conjoint course.

Holger Zaborowski is Professor of the History of Philosophy and Philosophical Ethics at the Catholic University Vallendar, Germany. He is coeditor of the *Heidegger-Jahrbuch* and of the *Martin-Heidegger-Briefausgabe* and author of, among many other publications in the area of modern German thought, *"Eine Frage von Irre und Schuld?": Heidegger und der Nationalsozialismus* (Frankfurt: Fischer, 2010).

Index